An
HISTORICAL and DESCRIPTIVE ACCOUNT
of the
COAST OF SUSSEX

Brighton

EASTBOURN	WORTHING
HASTINGS	ARUNDEL
St LEONARDS	GOODWOOD
RYE	CHICHESTER
&c. &c. &c.	&c. &c. &c.

BATTLE, HURSTMONCEAUX, LEWES & TONBRIDGE WELLS.

Forming also a Guide to all the Watering Places.

By J. D. PARRY, M.A.

Dedicated by Permission to the King & Queen.

'Nothing extenuate or set down ought in malice.'
'Modo te Thebis, modo ponit Athenis.'

1970
E & W BOOKS (Publishers) LTD

© *E & W Books (Publishers) Ltd 1970*
A facsimile of the 1833 edition

Published by
E & W BOOKS (Publishers) LTD
and distributed by
Robert Hale & Company
63 Old Brompton Road,
London, S.W.7.

SBN 85104 010 1

REPRODUCED AND PRINTED IN GREAT BRITAIN BY
REDWOOD PRESS LIMITED
TROWBRIDGE AND LONDON

TO

𝕿𝖍𝖊𝖎𝖗 𝕸𝖔𝖘𝖙 𝕲𝖗𝖆𝖈𝖎𝖔𝖚𝖘 𝕸𝖆𝖏𝖊𝖘𝖙𝖎𝖊𝖘,

WILLIAM IV., KING,

AND

A D E L A I D E , Q U E E N

OF THE

BRITISH DOMINIONS,

THIS VOLUME

IS INSCRIBED,

WITH THE HIGHEST RESPECT AND DEFERENCE,

BY

THE AUTHOR.

January, 1833.

PREFACE.

THIS volume was begun, completed, and published within the space of six months, although it had been meditated for about the same number of preceding ones, which, with one or two brief previous exceptions, forms the whole of the author's acquaintance with the County of Sussex.

It has been conducted under every possible discouragement and want of support; the particulars, however, it will be superfluous and unavailing to detail; it will be sufficient to describe it negatively, and say that every instance of courteousness which the author *has* met with, either from those in the higher or middle ranks, is carefully acknowledged and acted upon in the following pages. Such disappointment was almost sufficient to have induced an abandonment of the work, but that he had the consciousness of its not being merited: he considered, also, that it might live to see an improvement of spirit, that it would come under the notice of an extensive cycle of Visitors, embracing many individuals of liberal minds, and, though last mentioned, first in importance, that it had received the honour of the sanction of their Majesties.

After their distinguished names, then, he has only to acknowledge the following obligations :—to their Royal Highnesses the Princess Augusta and the Duchess of Gloucester; the gallant and courteous Earl of Munster, famous " both with sword and pen," whose appointment to the custody of a still more re- nowned palace than that of Brighton was witnessed with sincere pleasure; Sir Herbert Taylor, to whose patient civility he owes a debt of much gratitude; the Dukes of Richmond (of whose courtesy he cannot say too much), Devonshire, and Bedford, and the Bishop of Chichester.

———

It is, perhaps, scarcely necessary to inform the reader, that this volume has been executed in the most unshrinking style of expense, and has actually cost a considerable sum ; the only portion of which he re- grets, is that which was applied to making its design extensively known, as it was entirely sacrificed. Pub- lication is always a dangerous thing in these times, but, perhaps, when the Rubicon is passed, it may be, upon the whole, as politic to apply the advice of Polonius

——— Being in,
Bear it that the opposer may beware thee.

———

The author has to express his sense of the ability and conscientious exertions of the artists employed in its embellishments, as well as the skill and patience of the excellent printers. The sole failure was the *vignette* of the Pavilion, which he sincerely regretted, especially as it was absolutely too late to cancel or improve it.

Every place here described has been carefully visited, at an expense, arising from local circumstances, by no means inconsiderable. The very few exceptions are either specifically alluded to, or indicated by the following mark *⁎*.

———

It is *not* easy in practice, however it be recommended in theory, to speak with perfect impartiality and good temper, where that courtesy is not obtained which a person feels he has a right to claim. The author can respectfully, but boldly, assert, that he has not merely earnestly attempted this, but knows that he has succeeded ; and verily believes that he could not have spoken more impartially, if he had been upon oath. May he venture, on this score, to expect, if the reader concurs with him, a share of his approbation ?

———

He has fortunately met with some facilities for obtaining valuable information; especially the almost unequalled MSS. collections of Sir William Burrell, deposited in the British Museum. He has also obtained

a great number, though not all, of the works he desired
to see, from the University Library of Cambridge.
There is *one* MS. in this volume of very high importance to the curious in the general History of
England.

On examining and collating the works already
published, relating to the Topography of Sussex, the
following appeared to be the only important standard
ones : — " Dallaway's History of the City and Rape
of Chichester," 4to. 5*l.* 5*s.*, very scarce ; " Ditto of
the Rape of Arundel, republished by Cartwright,"
5*l.* 5*s.* ; " Cartwright's History of the Rape of
Bramber," 5*l.* 5*s.* ; " Horsefield's History of Lewes
and its Vicinity," 4*l.* 4*s.* ; " Moss's History of Hastings,"
12*s.*

These are not only very expensive publications, but,
with scanty exceptions, leave the whole of the eastern,
and by far the more interesting half of the county
undescribed. The following places, which have been
principally enlarged upon in this volume, were almost
untrodden ground : — NEWHAVEN, SEAFORD, EAST-
BOURNE, PEVENSEY, ST. LEONARD'S, WINCHELSEA,
RYE, BATTLE, and HURSTMONCEUX. Whilst, for the
very same reasons, the account of the western division
has been rendered very concise, with the exception of
Worthing and Goodwood; the former from its in-

creased interest, and the latter from real respect for
the noble possessor.

———

The extent and responsibility of this undertaking,
compared with the limited time in which it was
desirable it should be produced, were found so unexpectedly weighty, that the spirit and ability, and
latterly, the health of the author nearly sunk beneath
it. Although it is published by the highly respectable
booksellers at Brighton, with perfect mutual good
understanding, he alone is responsible for any sentiments it may contain. Whilst the materials were
collected with industry, a considerable part of the
volume was written with the greatest haste; he is well
aware it cannot stand the test of CALLIGRAPHY, perhaps
in some instances scarcely of ORTHOGRAPHY. Such
as it is, however, it is now before the world, and they
must deal with it and its author as they please. For
his own part, he can only say, that he takes his leave
of them with all charitable and good wishes.

London, January, 1833.

CONTENTS.

Historical and Descriptive

ACCOUNT

OF

THE COAST OF SUSSEX.

BRIGHTON

ANCIENT HISTORY.

VERY little can be said, with any positive certainty, to be known of the history of Brighton until about a century before the Norman conquest. Now that it has attained a degree of consequence, in size and population, of a most unprecedentedly rapid increase, the inquirers into its origin are willing to persuade themselves and others of its always having possessed some claims to notice. On the same principle, we suppose, as actuates the admirers of a great man, risen from obscurity, who would, if possible, make out his claim to some quartering, ten times removed, to be sought out in the archives of the Heralds' College. But, as it our purpose, in every instance, to speak impartially, without fear or favour, we will simply put the reader in possession of such actual facts as we have been enabled to discover, and add little more :—we may possibly amuse him with a few theories, like gleams of Romance scintillating through the dull and murky atmosphere of a commonplace generation, but we shall give to them no further weight than we humbly conceive them to merit.

We shall not, therefore, go back to " Brute or King Lud," or seriously disprove the nonsensical tale of Julius Cæsar having landed at Brighton. Nor shall we occupy ourselves with the Druids, some of whose altars, or sacred stones, have been supposed to be found on the hills above Brighton. We know little of these gentry, though that is nearly as much as any one else does with positive accuracy, and we have quite as little liking for them. Had a Boadicea been connected with this vicinity, we should perhaps have been tempted to pause for an instant over the fate of a not uninteresting British heroine *.

* The conclusion of a Cambridge prize poem—subject "*Boadicea,*" by W. Whewell, 1814, has always appeared to us very beautiful.

" Yes, Roman ! proudly shake thy crested brow,
    'Tis thine to conquer, thine to triumph now ;
  For thee, lo ! Victory, lifts her gory hand,
  And calls the fiends of Terror on the land,
  And flaps, as tiptoe on thy helm she springs,
  Dipping with British blood her eagle wings.

" Yet think not, think not, long to thee 'tis given
  To laugh at justice and to mock at Heaven ;
  Soon shall thy head, with blood-stain'd laurels crown'd,
  Stoop, at the feet of Vengeance, to the ground.
  I see, amid the gloom of future days,
  Thy turrets totter and thy temples blaze ;
  I see upon thy shrinking Latium hurl'd
  The countless millions of the northern world ;
  I see, like vultures gathering to their prey,
  The shades of states that fell beneath thy sway ;
  They leave their fallen palaces and fanes,
  Their grass-grown streets, and ruin-scatter'd plains,
  Where lonely long they viewless loved to dwell,
  And mourn the scenes that once they loved so well :
  Triumphant, lo ! on all the winds they come,
  And clap the exulting hand o'er fallen Rome,
  And hovering o'er thy domes that blazing glow,
  Their waving pennons fan the flame below ;
  They view rejoiced the conflagration's gleams
  Shoot their long glare o'er Tiber's reddening streams ;
  And snuff the carnage-tainted smokes that rise,
  An incense sweet, a grateful sacrifice.

" Sad Tiber's banks with broken columns spread ;
  Fall'n every fane that rear'd to heav'n its head !
  Poor heap of ashes ! Grandeur's mouldering tomb !
  Art thou the place was once Eternal Rome ?

" Yes, Roman ! snatch thy triumph whilst thou may,
  Weak is thy rage, and brief thy little day :
  Vanished and past the momentary storm,
  Albion ! my Albion, brighter shows her form,
  Far o'er the rolling years of gloom I spy
  Her oak-crown'd forehead lifted to the sky,

Those, however, who wish to see further conjectures respecting the Druids, may find them in the small volume published by Dr. Relhan.

This learned antiquary has also been willing to believe that Brighton was actually a Roman station, but has not succeeded in obtaining consent to his theory, as his arguments merely prove that it would have been an eligible locality for one, and are not borne out by external testimony. It has been observed by others, that if Brighton possessed any Roman influence, it must have been derived from the closely-adjoining settlement of Aldrington, or *Portus Adurni**.

" The Præpositus of the Exploratores, whose office was to discover the state and motions of the enemy, and who was certainly in this part of Sussex, could be nowhere more advantageously placed than in the elevated situations of the strong camps at Hollingsbury and White-Hawke, commanding a most extensive view of the whole coast from Beachy-Head to

---

Above the low-hung mists unclouded seen,
Amid the wreck of nations still serene;
She bursts the chains, when hands like thine would bind
The groaning world, and lord it o'er mankind.
Amid yon glittering flood of liquid light
Float regal forms before my dazzled sight;
Like stars along the milky zone that blaze
Their scepter'd hands and gold-bound fronts they raise.
My sons!—my daughters!—faint, alas! and dim,
Before these fading eyes your glories swim,
Mix'd with the mists of death—'Tis yours to throw
Your radiance round, while happier ages flow;
I smile at storms of earthly woe, and rise,
Shades of my Sires! to your serener skies."

---

* Did the reader ever hear the tale of " Cæsar's Stile?"—that of Agricola's Long Ladle, he may probably have read in the " Antiquary." Dr. Stukely, or some other antiquarian, was travelling through England, when he heard, that on a certain hill there was a stile called " Cæsar's Stile." " Ay," said the doctor, " such a road, mentioned in Antoninus, passed near here; and the traditional name of this stile confirms the probability of a Roman camp on this spot." Whilst he was surveying the prospect, a peasant came up, whom the doctor addressed:—" They call this Cæsar's Stile, my friend, do they not?" " Ees, zur," said the man, " they calls it so a'rter poor old *Bob Cæsar*, the carpenter (rest his soul!); I holped him to make it, when I was a boy."

A Brighton Guide, after conjecturing that this place " was in some repute in the time of the Romans," says,—" In fact, there is every reason to think Brighton was a town or village *long antecedent to the coming of the Romans*, and that it owed its rise to the *Saxons*." " O Dii, homines, et columnæ!" here is a new historical theory of the invasions of Britain!

the Isle of Wight. The form of this town is almost a perfect square; the streets are built at right angles to each other, and its situation is to the south-east, the favourite one among the Romans. To these may be added, that an urn has been some time ago dug up in this neighbourhood, containing a thousand silver denarii marked from Antoninus Pius to Philip, during which tract of time Britain was probably a Roman province. And, lastly, the vestiges of a true Roman via running from Shoreham towards Lewes, at a small distance above this town, have been lately discovered by an ingenious gentleman truly conversant in matters of this nature.

"The light sometimes obtained in these dark matters from a similitude of sounds in the ancient and modern names of places, is not to be had in assisting the present conjecture. Its ancient one, as far as I can learn, is no way discoverable: and its modern one may be owing either to this town's belonging formerly to, or being countenanced in a particular manner by, a Bishop Brighthelm, who, during the former government of the island, lived in this neighbourhood: or perhaps may be deduced from the ships of this town having their helms better ornamented than those of their neighbouring ones*."—*Dr. Relhan.*

The following observations, on Roman camps and on the etymology of Brighton, are extracted from the *Burrell MSS.*:

CAMPS.

"There are three Roman castra, lying in a line over-thwart the Downs from Brighthelmstone to Ditchelling, from south to north. The first, a

---

* This, for an intrinsically learned man, as we fully know Dr. Relhan to have been, is certainly the most ludicrously absurd vagary that was ever indulged in. It would be very amusing to go round the coast etymologising at this rate. "*Worth*-ing" must always have been a place of merit, whilst "*Lanc*-ing" sounds both military and chirurgical, and "*Bog*-nor" was a northern bog. "*Little-ham*-pton" Dulcineas must have been famous, like her of Toboso, in Cid Hamete Berengeli's famous history, for the curing of (small) pork; whilst, if they gave their principal attention to this, they probably obtained their milk and butter from "*Cowes*," in the Isle of Wight. Their peas, of course, came from "*Hastings*," to which they might send their hams in return; and the same vessels might bring them "*Rye*" bread, a palatable and nutritious though brown-looking article; but it is to be hoped they had not to send for their eggs as far as "*Eg*-ham," in Surrey, as the expense would be so great, they would hardly "save their bacon." "*Good*-wood," we are inclined to believe, was always a good sort of place; but, surely, the inhabitants of "*Sel*-sea" had not the arrogance to vend any part of that common element either by public or private auction; this would have been their neighbour Selden's *Mare Clausum* with a vengeance. Proceeding westward, we shall find the Isle of "*Pur*-beck," famous for the tameness and docility of its cats, who were wont to *purr*, when any one *beck*oned to them. "*Il-fra-comb*" must have been derived from some lady paramount, whose beautiful or ugly head, as the case might be, was wounded by the tortoise shell, ivory, or gold article stuck in it. The *mouth* of the arm of the sea, at "*Wey*-mouth," must have looked like *whey*, or else the inhabitants had a particular *taste* for that composition. But we have not time to pursue Dr. Relhan's rules of etymology any further.

large one, called the Castle, about a mile from Brighton eastward, and a mile from the sea, on the summit of a lofty hill commanding the sea-coast; the next a smaller, called Hollingbury Castle, nearly about the middle of the Downs, also commanding from a lofty hill, by Stanmer, the whole western sea-coast of Sussex: and the third, a large one, called Ditchelling Castle, containing between twelve and fourteen acres, is the highest point of the Downs thereabouts, and commands part of the sea-coast and all the northern edge of the Downs, with the wild underneath it. These are not above three or four miles distant from each other, and form an easy military line of communication with each other, so that nothing of consequence could escape their power when well manned with Roman forces, and a Roman navy attendant, if occasion for necessaries. These seem the work of Vespasian, who reduced the Regni, the Belgæ, and the Isle of Wight, whilst he commanded the second legion here under Claudius, and his general Aulus Plautius.

" There are two other Roman camps of considerable magnitude in the parish of Tetscomb, near Newhaven, whither, it is probable, Vespasian had driven the Regni, as the estuary and final boundary of the district of that tribe, who held the space between Shoreham and Lewes rivers. Here probably they made their last stand, and then submitted. The whole margin of this estuary, from Newhaven to Lewes, seems to have been very populous, and had many towns and vills. The hundred is called Holmestren in Domesday, or Homestren. *Tren* is the British word for towns; *holme* is of Saxon original, and means an isle or fenny place, and this derivation agrees with the situation of the vills along the margin of this estuary. It was usual for the Saxons to compound their names half British and half Saxon, and to put prepositions and adjectives to the names of places before named by the Britons. The pass over this estuary must have been at Lewes, where it was narrowest, by the close approach of the opposite Downs, so as just to leave a narrow pass for the river and land floods; above and below it was impassable. Thus, the Romans must of necessity be well acquainted with this pass over the estuary here, or they could never get from *Portus Adurni*, or *Shoreham* Harbour, to *Anderida*, or *Eastbourn*, unless by sea, which would not answer to the necessity of their military marches and convoys from station to station, to keep the Britons under in cases of rebellions and insurrections.

ETYMOLOGY.

" Various are the opinions touching the etymology of this town; if of British denomination, *brit, brist, briz,* signify divided or separated, as in former ages it most probably was, by a *mere* flowing along the bottom from *Stanemere* and *Falemere,* into the sea, at this town, by the side of the Stane. If of Saxon etymon, the word *beorht, briht, berht,* and *byrht,* signifying *bright;* and *heal* a pharos, or watch-tower, also angulus, a corner or point of a wedge; and hall; and *healme,* the genitive of which word is *healmes;* may all enter their claim as component parts of the name. Camden, in his Latin edition, 1607, says, our Saxon ancestors called it Brighthealmestun, but the mistake of a Saxon �“p” for a p is easily made in printing or reading it; yet if Camden be right, then *Brighthealmestun,* taking *heal* to be a *pharos,* is " the sea-town by the bright or burning watch-tower," to give directions to sailors by night. If *heal* is to be rendered "angulus," *a wedge*, point, or corner, then Dr. Tabor (*Philos. Trans.* No. 356) explains the meaning. "That you may more clearly understand the ancient state of this country, look into the best map; at the west end you will find West Harting and Stanstead, distant from each other six or seven miles. Imagine a straight line to be drawn from Harting to Bourne, near Pevensey, and another from a point a little south of Stanstead to Brighthelmston; what lies north of these lines is the *weald* or low lands, formerly the *Sylva Anderida;* that which is comprehended between these lines, bounded by the sea, from Brighthelmston, is Bourne and the Downs; the part south of these lines is a flat champaign ground, ending like a wedge at Brighthelmston." Here the flat shore ends in a point at the *stane*, instantly rises to bold ground next the sea, and in this sense amounts to the "bright sea town," at a point or corner of the flat shore. If by *heal* is meant a hall, we find, by Domesday, it had a hall, and might from thence give name to the town. If *healme* be the origin of hawme or thatch, then *healme-es* is the genitive case, which makes it the bright-thatched town. Again, *Brighthelme* was no unusual name amongst the Anglo-Saxons, and the town might have had a Saxon owner of that name, whence it might be so called, which, on mature consideration, I conceive to be the true etymology, as Domesday expresses it to be an allodial tenure, and that the Saxon thane who had his hall here gave it his own name."— *J. Elliot.—Burrell MSS.*

It is doubtful who *the* Brighthelm was, from whom this place derived its appellation, as there are three individuals of that name who have some claim to the distinction. One a bishop of Fontenoy in France, canonised about the middle of the tenth century, whose claim is favoured by Skinner, but opposed by Mr. Lee, on the ground that the church would have been dedicated to him, whereas its patron saint was St. Nicholas prior to the Norman Conquest; the second is thus designated in the *Burrell MSS.*:—

" A. D. 958.—Elfin, archbishop of Canterbury, dyeing on his way to Rome, Brighthelm, bishop of Welles, was translated to the archbishoprick; he was a pious, good man. Though a friend to the monks, would not join in violent measures to establish them upon the ruins of the secular clergy; being therefore charged with the want of a proper spirit, he was ejected, and Dunstan put in possession of the church of Canterbury."

A third is thus alluded to in the " Family Topographer," 1832:—

" 693, Brightelm was slain on the down immediately above Brightelmstone, to which place he gave name."

From what chronicle or authority the information is derived, we are left to guess. On consulting Ingram's Saxon chronicle at

that year, we find that he was also called Drythelm, and that
the original has only the following allusion, simply implying
that he died : —

"Anꝺ Bꞃiꞇhelm þæꞃ oꝼ lȳꝼe ᵹelæꝺ."

We are referred, however, in a note by the editor, for sóme
additional particulars to Bede, or Matthew of Westminster; and
in the latter, we find that he was a father of a family (pater-
familias) in Northumberland, and afterwards took the tonsure
in the monastery of Mailros. (Melrose? not founded then, we
believe.) It seems, therefore, very unlikely that he should
have any connexion with Brighthelmstone, especially as he has
another *alias* in the margin of the chronicle, viz., *Dritheline.*
The interest of his story detained our attention; but it is too
long, and otherwise unsuitable for insertion. He is said to have
had a remarkable vision during a trance, when he was supposed
to be dead, in consequence of which he adopted the monastic life,
having first assembled his family, and divided his fortune
into three parts; one of which he gave to his wife, one to his
children, and one to the poor. His vision, which related to
future states of beatitude and purgatorial punishments, though
mixed up with superstitious details, is really beautifully related,
in a pure, though flowery Latin style; in some parts strongly
resembling that of the " Somnium Scipionis," and scarcely inferior to it.

As Brightelm is, however, said to have been by no means
an uncommon name amongst the Saxons, there may be other
claimants of great probability; but to determine the exact individual seems, at the present time, impossible.

We may take occasion to speak of Alfred, of his connexion
with Sussex, and of other particulars of Anglo-Saxon rule
hereafter; but we return now to the authentically recorded
history of Brighthelmstone, which, at the conclusion of the tenth
century, we find to have belonged to Wulnoth, father of Godwin, who was appointed by Ethelred, the King, captain of the
Sussex quota of ships towards the famous armament of A. D.
1009, to oppose Canute. On this occasion every proprietor of
310 hides (about 31,000 acres) was required to provide one

galley or skiff, and of 8 hides (about 800) a helmet and breast-plate.

" This year were the ships ready, that we before spoke about; and there were so many of them as never were in England before, in any king's days, as books tell us. And they were all transported together to Sandwich; that they should lie there, and defend this land against any outforce. But we have not yet had the prosperity and the honour, that the naval armament should be useful to this land, any more than it often before was. It was at this same time, or a little earlier, that Brihtric brother of Alderman Edric, bewrayed Wulnoth, the South-Saxon knight, father of Earl Godwin, to the king; and he went into exile, and enticed the navy, till he had with him twenty ships; with which he plundered everywhere by the south coast, and wrought every kind of mischief. When it was told the navy that they might easily seize him, if they would look about them, then took Brihtric with him about eighty ships; and thought that he should acquire for himself much reputation, by getting Wulnoth into his hands alive or dead. But, whilst they were proceeding thitherward, there came such a wind against them, as no man remembered before; which beat and tossed the ships, and drove them aground; whereupon Wulnoth soon came and burned them. When this was known to the remaining ships, where the king was, how the others fared, it was then as if all were lost. The king went home, with the aldermen and the nobility; and thus lightly did they forsake the ships; whilst the men that were in them rowed them back to London. Thus lightly did they suffer the labour of all the people to be in vain; nor was the terror lessened, as all England hoped. When this naval expedition was thus ended, then came, soon after Lammas, the formidable army of the enemy, called Thurkill's army, to Sandwich; and soon they bent their march to Canterbury; which city they would quickly have stormed, had they not rather desired peace; and all the men of East-Kent made peace with the army, and gave them three thousand pounds for security. The army soon after that went about till they came to the Isle of Wight; and everywhere in Sussex, and in Hampshire, and also in Berkshire, they plundered and burned, AS THEIR CUSTOM IS *. Then ordered the king to summon out all the population, that men might hold firm against them on every side; but nevertheless they marched as they pleased. On one occasion the king had begun his march before them, as they proceeded to their ships, and all the people were ready to fall upon them; but the plan was then frustrated through Alderman Edric, AS IT EVER IS STILL. Then after Martinmas they went back again to Kent, and chose their winter-quarters on the Thames; obtaining their provisions from Essex, and from the shires that were next, on both sides of the Thames. And oft they fought against the city of London; but glory be to God, that it yet standeth firm: and they ever there met with ill fare."—*Saxon Chronicle.—Ingram.*

---

* " These expressions in the present tense afford a strong proof that the original records of these transactions are nearly coeval with the transactions themselves. Later MSS. use the past tense."—*Ingram.*

Wulnoth, it should seem, was very ill used in the first instance, having been scandalously misrepresented by the treacherous Brihtric, whose brother also, " the Alderman" (or Earl), Edric Streon, Duke of Mercia, was a very false character. Brihtric, conscious of his own ill intentions towards the weak Ethelred, his father-in-law, whom he afterwards betrayed to Canute, receiving a villain's recompense, viz. the unexpected loss of his head, dreaded the probity and influence of Wulnoth, and consequently did his best to drive him from the court, and Wulnoth, aware that he should not have justice, did not repair thither to answer the accusation against him. The ships which revolted to him consisted entirely of the Sussex quota, by which it seems probable that he was there well thought of. Nothing further is reported of him, but it is supposed that he returned under Canute, and enjoyed his confidence, as we find his son, Godwin, in early favour with that monarch. In 1019 the latter accompanied Canute in his expedition to Denmark, to repel the invading Vandals, and in the course of the warfare performed an act of romantic bravery. Perceiving a favourable opportunity on the evening previous to an intended engagement, he left his post, which was the nearest to the enemy, attacked and routed them: so that when the king reached the hostile camp next morning, having been abandoned, as he supposed, by Godwin, he found the camp strewed with the enemies' bodies, and the latter, whom he afterwards met, in the quality of a conqueror. For this and other services he was created Earl of Kent, Sussex, and Surrey; married first Thyra, sister to Ulphon, brother-in-law to Canute, and after her death the Lady Girth, sister to Swayn, King of Denmark, and continued to extend his numerous possessions.

Of the lives of Godwin and Harold we cannot, however, now speak further; we have merely alluded to them as being lords of Brighton, together with about forty other places in Sussex. On the hasty approach of Harold towards that part of the southern coast, where the Norman invader had encamped, the neighbourhood of Pevensey, he increased his forces by some levies quickly raised in Brighthelmstone and some neighbouring places, whose inhabitants flew with alacrity to the succour of the popular and unfortunate monarch. His lamented catastrophe need not be now related.

Among the various incursions of the sea, by which it has been supposed the Sussex coast has been ravaged, we have not seen the following alluded to, mentioned in the Saxon Chronicle, A. D. 1014.

" This year, on the eve of St. Michael's day, came *the great sea-flood*, which spread wide over the land, and ran so far up as it never did before, overwhelming many towns and an innumerable multitude of people."

Harold succeeded his father in two of the manors of Brighthelmstone; the third was given to a man named Brictric, for his life only, an established term of possession, under the title of *Thaneland* *.

DOOMSDAY BOOK.—1086.

BRIGHTHELMSTON.   THREE MANORS.

" Radulfus ten. de Will'o, Bristelmestune. Brictric tenuit de dono Godwini. T. R. E. et m⁰, se def'd p. 5 hid' et dimid'. Tra' e' 3 car. In d'nio e' dimid' car. et 18 vill'i et 9 bord' cu' 3 car. et uno servo. De Gablo 4 mill' aletium †. T. R. E. val't 8 lib. et 12 sol. et post c. sol. modo 12 lib.

" In ead' villa, ten^t Widardus de Will'o 6 hid' et una v^a. et p' tanto se defd'.

" Tres aloarii tenuer' de Rege E., et potuer' ire quolibet. Un^s ex eis habuit aula': et vill'i tenuer' partes alior' duor. T'ra e' 5 car. et est in uno M. In d'nio un' car. et dim', et xiii vill'i, et xxi bord', cu' 3 car. et dimid': ibi vii ac' p'ti et silua porc. In Lewes 4 hagæ. T. R. E. val't x lib., et post viii lib., modo xii lib.

" Ibide' ten' Wills. de Watevile Bristelmestune de Willo. Uluuard tenuit de Rege E. T'c et modo se defd' p. 5 hid' et dim'. T'ra e 4 car. In d'nio e' 1 car', et 13 vill'i, et ii Bord' cu' una car'. Ibi Œccl'a.

" T. R. E. val't x lib. et post 8 lib', modo 12 lib'."

TRANSLATION.

" Ralph holds of William (de Warren) Bristelmestune. Brictric held it from the gift of Earl Godwin. In the time of King Edward and now,

---

it defends itself for 5 hides and a half. The land (arable) is 3 carucates. In demesne is half a carucate and 18 villeins and 9 bordars, with 3 ploughs and one servant. Of the gabel (customary payment) 4 thousand of herrings. In the time of King Edward it was worth 8 pounds and 12 shillings, and afterwards 100 shillings. Now 12 pounds.

" In the same vill, Widard holds of William 6 hides and one virgate, and for so much it defends itself. Three aloarii (customary tenants) held it of King Edward, and could go where they pleased. One of them had a hall, and the villeins held the portions of the other two. The land is 5 carucates, and is in one manor. In demesne one caracute and a half and 14 villeins and 21 bordars with 3 carucates and a half: there are 8 acres of meadow and a wood for hogs. In Lewes 4 Hagæ (not exactly known, by some thought to be *shops*.) In the time of King Edward it was worth 10 pounds, and afterwards 8 pounds: now 12 pounds.

" In the same place William de Wateville holds Bristelmestune of William. Ulward held it of King Edward. Then and now it defends itself for 5 hides and a half. The land is 4 carucates. In demesne is 1 carucate, and 13 villeins and 2 bordars with one plough. There is a church.

" In the time of King Edward it was worth 10 pounds, and afterwards 8 pounds, now 12 pounds."

The first of these is the manor called " Brighthelmstone-Lewes," the second "*Michel-ham*," and the third " *Atlyng-worth*." William de Warren, Earl of Surrey, was son-in-law to the Conqueror, who bestowed on him, in addition to many possessions in other counties, the whole Rape of Lewes, forming about a sixth part of the county of Sussex. We subjoin the various possessors, the succession, and a few incidental particulars of these manors from the Norman conquest till the commencement of the present century: an inquiry which many of our readers may consider of a dry and generally uninteresting nature; and we confess that we heartily agree with them; but custom and inexorable criticism require it, and will launch their fulminations at our head if we omit it; we therefore enter upon it, with no indisposition to find ourselves at the end—" 'Tis a very excellent piece of work, madam lady; —would 't were done !"

BRIGHTHELMSTON-LEWES.

Burrell MSS :—partly abridged.

" Hen. I. or Stephen. Radulfus de Caisneto or Ralph de Cheney was seised of a manor or lands here.

" 29 Hen. III. Walter de Grey, abp. of York, granted all his lands at

Brightelmston to Walter de Grey, son of his brother Robert de Grey, which he had from Joane.

" 6 Ed. I. John Earl Warren.

" 6 Ed. II. John de Warren, Comes, Surr:—Brightelmston, *Mercat'*: *Fer'* :

" 9 Ed. II. Prior of Lewes seised. Qy. *Ib.* John E. Warren released this manor to the king and his heirs.

16 Ed. II.		4 Aug., 1317, John E. Warren.
19 Ed. II.		—— John Earl Warren.
21 R. II.	same as "*Worth*"	—— Richard E. of Arundel.
22 R II.		6 Octr. same year, granted to Thomas D. of Norfolk.
1 Hen. IV.		This manor (inter alia) parcel of possessions of D. of Norfolk to John D. of Exeter.
		Earl of Arundel restored to his estate.

" 21 E. III. John de Warren, Earl of Surrey: and the Earl of Arundel is his heir.

" 1 Hen. IV. Thos. E. of Arundell being restored in blood, and the judgement against his father reversed in parliament, this manor became vested in him (inter alia) of which he died seised. 3 Hen. V., Oct. 13, 1415, was succeeded by his cozen, hr. male, Sir J. Fitzalan at Arundell, who dyed 29 April, 9 Hen. V.

" 3 Hen. V. Thos. Earl of Arundel died seised of this manor, being restored in blood by act of parliament, 1 Hen. IV., and his father's judgement reversed: he married, 6 Hen. IV. Beatrix, an illegitimate daughter of the King of Portugal, and d. 3 Hen. V., 13th Oct. S. P. this manor, by virtue of an entail of Rd. E. of Arundell, passed to his cousin and next male heir, Sir John Fitzalan E. of Arundel.

" 4 Hen. V. Thos. Earl of Arundel.

" 7 Hen. V. Philip St. Clere.

" 1 Hen. VI. Margaret, wife of Philip Seynt Clere and John her son.

" 4 Hen. VI. On the partition in Chancery. John D. of Norfolk had this manor with its appendages, estimated at 18*l.* 16*s.* 7*d.*

" 17 Hen. VI. Thos. Seynt Clere holds the manor of Brighton with lands and messuages in the same.

" 18 Hen. VI. Beatrix, Countess of Arundel, held Brighton manor.

" 3 Henry VII. Wm. Marqs. of Berkeley was seised of $\frac{1}{4}$th of this manor, which he devised to Hen. VII. in default of issue male of his owh body, to the disinheritance of his brother Maurice, who recovered this $\frac{1}{4}$th part in 19 Hen. VII.

" In 4 Hen. VIII. One moiety of this manor, with several other possessions in Sussex, was recovered by petition by Thomas Earl of Surrey, they having been devised by the Marquis of Berkeley to Hen. VII., and an act passed in the 7th of that king, whilst the petitioner was absent on the king's business in the north, and ignorant of it till the said parliament was ended. The answer is ' *Soit fait come i lest desirée.*' The petition, which is complex, is contained in the Burrell MSS. 5685. Fol. 36, 37.

" 32 Hen. VIII. The king granted this manor and advowson to Ann of Cleves ; with a great many others in Sussex.

" 2 Mary. ' The queen on the 27th day of Nov. let to farm to William May, valet of the kitchen, the manor of Brightelston with all its appurtenances for 21 years, from the feast of St. Michael last past, for the annual rent of 6*l.* 13*s.* 4*d.*' (Translation.)

" 8 Eliz. Richard Sacvile held it at 6*l.* 13*s.* 4*d.* who died Apl. 21 in that year.

" 28 Eliz. 17 Oct. Sir Philip Sidney died, and Eliz., wife of Roger, E. of Rutland, was, on inquisition, found his daughter and heir, and so seised of one moiety of this manor, value 10*l.* 13*s.* 4*d.*

" 39 Eliz. E. of Arundel and E. of Dorset held it between them.

" 1 James, 1603, Tho. Lord Buckhurst held one moiety.

" 1612 to 1621, Richard E. of Dorset held it.

" Richard E. of Dorset was seized of the manor of Brighton, which descended to his 2 daughters. 1. Margaret, m. John E. of Thanet, 21 April, 1629. 2. Isabella, married James E. of Northampton; she died 14 Oct. 1661.

" E. of Thanet sold his moiety to Mr. Thos. Friend, which descended to his nephew, Mr. Thos. Kempe.

" The other moiety passed by the heirs female of the aforesaid James Earl of Northampton to the family of Shirley, and thence to Mrs. Sparrow of Anglesey, whoso son sold that moiety to Mr. Charles Scrase, attorney at law of Brighton.

" 26 Jan. 1735, E. of Thanet, John Sparrow, Esq.

" 21 March, 1743, John Sparrow, Eliz., his wife, and Thos. Friend, gent., as also 16 Sept. 1747.

" 2 May, 1750, Eliz. Sparrow, widow, and Thos. Friend, gent., as also 23 Sept. 1760.

" 25 May, 1762, Thos. Friend, gent., as to his part, 19 Oct. 1762; Eliz. Sparrow, widow, as to her part allowed by chancery.

" 25 May, 1766, a general court held by order of chancery, in pursuance of a certificate from the commissioners appointed by the court in a cause of Eliz. Sparrow, widow, and Bodychen Sparrow, Esq., complainants, v. Thos. Friend, respondent, to whom one part was allotted by chancery.

" 15 Oct. 1767, Eliz. Sparrow and John Kempe, gent.; 1 April, 1768, Eliz. Sparrow, as to her part; 12 Dec., 1768, Hen. Sparrow, Esq.

" 4 March, 1771, John Kempe, Hen. Sparrow, lords of certain portions. 7 Oct., 1771, Charles Scrase, Esq., bought Sparrow's moiety.

" 5 Jan. 1773, Charles Scrase, Esq., John Kempe, lords of the undivided part of this manor.

" 25 May, 1774, ditto. ditto.

" 15th February, 1775, Chas. Scrase, Esq., and Thos. Kempe, Esq., as also 1770, 1786, 1790.

" N.B. This manor being the joint property of Sparrow and Friend, Mr. Sparrow sold his moiety to Charles Scrase, Esq.; and a dispute arose about Mr. Friend's purchase of perishable houses, and lands, and copyhold, he refusing to be admitted to them, because he was a joint lord, which defeated Mr. Sparrow of the right belonging to his moiety."

BRIGHTELMSTON-MICHELHAM.

Burrell MSS.

" Hugo Baudefor donationem per cartam suam fecit Priori et conventui de Michelham de tota terra sua cum pertinentiis quam habuit in Brithel-mustune quam de Johanne de Berners emit."—*Dugdale, Burrell MSS.*

" 15 R. II. Willm. Bateford et al, p. Priore de Michelham, Bright-elmestone, 1 Mess. 60 acr. terr."—*Tower Records, No.* 168.

" 9 Eliz., April. Sir Thomas Sackville, Lord Buckhurst.

" Ib. Customary rents, 6s. 2d.

" 1603. Thomas Lord Buckhurst.

" 26 March, 1624. Rd. E. of Dorset one moiety, holden of the king *in capite* by knight's service, valued at 10l. per annum.

" 1728. Lionel Cranfield, Duke of Dorset.

	£.	s.	d.
Rents of assize . .	0	6	10 per ann.
Site and demesnes .	34	0	0 ditto.

" 15 Geo. III. John Frederick, Duke of Dorset."

ATLINGWORTH.

Burrell MSS. (in full.)

ADELINGWORTH.   ABLINGWORTH.

" This manor lies in the parishes of Brighthelmston and Lewes; it is the paramount manor, and extends over the Hoddown (Lord Pelham's estate), formerly a warren.

" 7 Ed. I. John E. Warren, by inheritance from his father, Wm. Warren, appears seized of Adelingworth."—*Placit. Assis. Sussex, rot.* 53. *Peck's Stamford, b.* 9, *p.* 8.

" This manor belonged to the Priory of Lewes, and at the dissolution, 29 Hen. VIII., was granted to Sir Thomas Lord Crumwell, as also the rectory, with the advowson of the vicarage.

—" Radulphus de Clera, fil. et heres Radulphi de Clera salutem. Sciatis quod concedo monachis S'ti Pancracii terram de Hakelingsford, quam Radulphus pater meus et Rogerus patricus meus iisdem monachis ante donaverant. Ego Radulphus eandem terram obtuli percultellum meum super majus altare S'ti Pancratij eodem die quo R'ds. de Plaiz. pater meus in lege receptus fuit ibi ad sepeliendum. Test. Rob'to. de Petraponte. Hugone de Plaiz., Anchero de Frescanville, Osberto Giffard, Ricardo de Cumba, Will'mo. de Bellamonte."—

—" Radulphus de Clera frater et heres Rogeri de Clera omnibus salt'm. Sciatis quod ego dono et concedo monachis S'ti Pancratii totam terram de Athelingworda quam Rogerus frater meus eisdem monachis in elemosynam ante donaverat. Et hanc donationem ego feci pro salute dn'i nostri Hen-

---

* Register of Lewes Priory in Bodley Library, Oxon. MS.

rici, Regis Angliæ, et meâ, et Radulphi de Glanvilla, et prænominati Rogeri de Clara fratris mei et D'næ Bertæ uxoris prædicti Radulphi de Glanvilla; corpus etiam meum eidem loco S'ci Pancracii et patribus meis, monachis de Lewes ibidem sepeliendum. Test. Rado. de Plaiz, Rado. fil, ejus., Will'mo de Garen, Rob'to de Petraponte, Bartho'meo de Caineto, Rad'o de Clera."—

—" Carta qualiter Rogerus de Clere filij Rogeri de Clere dedit monachis de Lewes totam terram de Athelingworth. Test, &c. " Hawisia de Gurnaico salutem" Sciatis me concessisse monachis de Lewis totam terram de Athelingworth quam in dotem accepi ex donatione Rogeri de Clare mariti mei, sicut Roger de Clera et Radulphus frater et heres ipsius dederunt. "—

" 25 E. 1. Ric'us, fil. Johannis, Addlingworth."—*Tower Records, No.* 50.

" 6 H. 6. De quarta parte feod. milit. in Athelyngworth in Hundr. de Fyshergate dicunt quod sit in manu Prioris de Lewes et est dec."— *Inq. capt. ap. Lewes,* 6 *Hen.* 6.

" 11 H. 4." As *Clayton.*

" 38 Eliz.* Mem. at this c⁺ there was much question betw. Mr. Snelling, now lord of this manor, and divers customary tenants of yᵉ said manor, whose fynes and heriots were stinted by Sir Jn. Caryll during yᵉ time he was lord of yᵉ manor, whether yᵉ sᵈ fynes and heriots shd continue and remain stinted accg to Sʳ Jn. C.'s grant (which yᵉ tenants laboured to uphold) or be arbitrable at yᵉ lord's will (which Mr. Snelling urged), for that all or most part of yᵉ sᵈ copyholds so granted were formerly parcel of yarde landes (ut dicitur), all which are arbitrable; and therefore maintained, that yᵉ former lord coᵈ not stinte them to yᵉ prejudice of yᵉ succeeding purchaser. And this was the reason that so many were put in proclamation at this court.

20 Eliz. Julii 3. Cur. 1ma Johis Caryll, *arm.*	.	Court Rolls
28 Eliz. Oct. 18. Ditto p. Robt. Kyllam		
31 Eliz. Jan. 10, and 32 Eliz. Jan. 2. Ditto p. Tho.		
Churchar. . . .	Ditto	

Stewards.

38 Eliz. March 29. Richd. Snellinge, *gent.* Ct. Rolls	John Rowe	
41 Eliz. Jan. 5. No name		
43 Eliz. Aug. 7. No name		
March 21, 1603 . . .	Rd. Killycke	
5 Jac. June 4. Curia prima, Geo. Snellinge, *mil.*		
8 Jac. Aug. 28. Ditto, Abr. Edwards, *sen.*		
and Abr. Edwards, jun. 11 Jac. Ditto Apr. 9		
12 Jac. June 17. Curia prima, Lancelot Fawkenor, *gen.*		
15 Jac. Jan. 15. Ditto, Abr. Edwards, gen. *consang.*		
Abr. Edwards, *defuncti*		
17 Jac. Aug. 21. Ditto, Abr. Edwards, *gen.*		
Apr. 4, 1632. Abr. Edwards, *sen. gen.*		
6 Car. Abr. Edwards, *sen. gen.* 22 Dec.	John Rowe	

* Transcribed from the Court Rolls, Oct. 1783, in Mr. Atree's, of Brighton, possession.—W. B.

17 & 18 Car. Jan. 15, 1639; 17 Car. Sept. 14. Do.
    and 18 Car. Mch. 23. Ditto   .   .   Thos. Houghton
19 Car. Oct. 14. Curia prima, Abr. Edwards, gen.
    fil and her. Abr. Edwards, *sen. gen. def.*
22 Car. Mch. 29, 1670. Ditto   .   .   Chas. Goodwin
    Feb. 9, 1696. No name   .   .   W. Westbrook, *Ar.*
    Jan. 5, 1699. No name   .   .   Jn. Foreman
3 Wm. 3. July 24, 1701. June 8, 1702. Wm. West-
    brooke, esq, last ct.   .   .   Jn. Foreman
3 Anne. Oct. 13, 1704. Elizabeth Westbrook, spinster   John Taylor
    July 3, 1706. Ditto   .   .   Jn. Whitpain
    Dec. 8, 1706. Ditto.   9 Oct. 1716. Her last
    ct. as a spinster   .   .   Jn. Wakeford
4 Geo. 1. Oct 30, 1717. Thos. Andrew, esq. and Eli-
    zabeth his wife
4 Geo. 2. Apr. 17, 1731. Ditto, ditto. N.B. Their dr.
    m. Thos. Foley   .   .   Joseph Richardson
    Oct 8, 1734. No name   .   .   Wm. Michell
9 Geo. 2. Oct. 17, 1735. Thomas Foley, jun. esq.   .   Ditto
    Nov. 10, 1743, and Oct. 30, 1746. Thos.
    Foley, esq. 9 Nov. 1749. Ditto   .   Ditto
25 Geo. 2. Oct. 31, 1751. Wm. Watson, esq. (whose
    dr. and h. m. Davies, of Rye   .   .   Ditto
    Jan. 9, 1754. Ditto, last ct.   .   .   Ditto
4 Geo. 3. Jan. 5, 1765. Wm. Davies, esq.   .   Ditto
    March 12, 1772. Ditto   .   .   Jas. Michel
    Aug. 24, 1773. Ditto. 11 Mch. 1780. Ditto.
    N.B. He died about Sept., 1783, leaving
    his dr. and sole heire,   , wife of
    Thos. Lamb, esq. of Rye   .   .   Ditto."

" 4 Jac. Sir Edw. Bellingham held freely to himself and his heirs lands and tenements in Aldrington, as of the manor of Allingworth."—*Rowe's* MS. p. 156.

" 9 Jac. 3 Jan. The homage presented that the north part of the Block-house in Brighton stands on the demesne lands of this manor.   The customs of this manor (as also of all other the manors belonging to yᵉ late dissolved priory of Lewes), are the same with the customs of the manor of yᵉ barony of Lewes.

" 21 Jan. 5 Car. The younger brother is heir.

" 8, 9, 15 Jac. and 5 Car. The younger daughter is heir.

" The yearly quit rents of yᵉ manor, 6*l.* 18*s.* 7*d.*, there being about 60 tenants, whereof 8 pay each of them a yard land, and some two yards, and pay fine at the ld's will, on death and alienation, and the best beast for a heriot; and most of yᵉ rest of yᵉ tenants being for houses, pay 6*d.* fine, and 6*d.* heriot at every death and alienation; and some pay fines at will, and their best beast for a heriot.

" 1790. Thos. Philips Lamb, esq.

" It was lately the property of Thos. Foley, esq., and now belongs to Mr. Jn. Davis, of Rye. 1774.

E R L E E S.

Burrell MSS.

" This small manor lies in the parish of Brighton.
" 1782. Thos. Kempe, Esq. 1790. Ditto.

HARE COURT.

Ibidem.

" This manor lies in Brighton p'sh.
" 19 Sep. 1690, Jn. Friend. 26 Sep. 1709, Jn. Friend, gen., ⎫
   27 Oct. 1725, ditto.   ⎬ Ct.
" 3 Nov. 1744. Jn. Friend, gen.   ⎭ Rolls.
" 28 Aug. 1760. Mary Friend, widow.
" 1782. Thos. Kempe, Esq."

Mr. Lee offers a conjecture that from the surnames of some of the oldest families, and also the phrases and pronunciation of some of the inhabitants in 1795, and some peculiar customs still extant, it is not improbable that a colony of *Flemings* had been once established here; and he extends his ideas to a very remote period, viz. soon after the Conquest, when he thinks that facilities might have been afforded from the circumstance of the Queen Matilda, daughter of Baldwin, Earl of Flanders, being their country-woman, and her being able to influence a grant of lands, &c. from her son-in-law, William Earl de Warren. An inundation of the Low Countries had occurred about that time, and he thinks Brighton would have been a desirable residence, as they would have had a good market for their cured herrings, &c. at some of the continental ports. The conjecture, however, is rather far-fetched; and it is equally probable that the emigration, if it ever took place, occurred at a much later period.

In the " Pleas of Quo Warranto," taken before John de Rygate and his fellows, justices itinerant at Chichester in the 7th year of Edward (the first), son of Henry, Brighton is included with a great number of other places in Sussex, valued in the whole at 1000 pounds per annum, and forming the Honor and Rape of Lewes, in the claim of John de Warren, Earl of Surrey, who succeeded in establishing his right.

In the year 1313, John de Warren obtained a charter for a *market* at Brighton every Thursday.

In Pope Nicholas' taxation, 1291*, these entries occur.

" ' Eccl'ia de Brighelmeston' (a various reading is given in a note ' *Brist-alnerston.*')   £ s. d. 20 0 0 h'b't breve P'or Lewens.
" Vicar' ejusdem 5 0 0

The antiquity of the name of *Russell* in this county (which ought to be revered as that of the founder of Brighton's prosperity) is shown in the same record. The entry occurs after *Holewyk*, a name of which we know nothing, but some of our readers may, " Quod p'cpt Lucia Russell ad t'm vite sue de tannaria sua, £4 0 0."—" What Lucy Russell has assigned for the term of her life, out of her tannery, £4 0 0."

In the " Nonarum Inquisitiones" is the following amply descriptive valuation of Brighton.

" BRIGHTELMESTONE.

" Hæc indentura testatur q^d capta fuit inq'si'co coram Henr' Husse et sociis suis collectorib's et assessor' ix^e garb. veller. et agn' ac xv^e d'no regi concess' in com' Sussex assig't' apud Lewes die d'nica in medio xl^o anno regni regis Edwardi t'cii a 9 questu xv^o sup' vero valore ix garbar. ix vell. et ix agn' p' commissione dni' regis p'fato Henr' et sociis suis directis p' sacr'm John de Erlee, Hugon Russell, John Dac, et Rad'i Grabbe, p'ochiani de Brighthelmeston, qui dicunt q'd extenta ecc'lie ibidem taxat' ad xxv^{li} cu$_e$ vicaria. Et dicunt q'd ix p's garb' valet p' annu ibidem ix^{li} viii^s x^d de coitate ville. It' ix p's veller' ibid' valet xxvi^s vi^d et ix p's agn' ibid' valt vi^s viii^d. It' dicunt ix p's garb' et vell prior de Lewes ibid'm valet vii^s viii^d. It' ix p's garb' et vell' prior de Michelm' valet xxx^s iiii^d. Et sic est s'm totius none garb' vell' et agn. hoc a^o xiii^{li}. It dicunt q'd ix p's p'dica no' respondet' n^c attinge' potest ad taxam eccl'ie p'dicæ p' eo q'd xl acr' t're submer's sunt p' mare imppetuu' quæ valuer' p' annu' xl^s. Et etiam clx acr' t're in co'i campo que deficier hoc a^o ibid' in blad seiat p't x^{li}. Et q. lane no' possunt vendi sic' solebant p'c xiii^s iiii^d indefectu. Et agni deficiet' ibid' in mora hoc a^o p' defectu p'c vi^s viii^d. Et vicarius h't ibid' p'ficuu' de uno columbar. p'c ii^s. It id'm h't ibid' in oblat' minut' decimis vid't auc' porcell' mell' lact' cas' vitul' et ovor. et aliis minutis decimis que valent p' annu' lxx^s. It' dicunt q'd nulli sunt ibid' m'cator' set tr'e tenent qui triis p'priis et magn' labor' suis viv'ut t'mmodo. In cuj^t rei testimonia' p'dici jur' huic indente' sigilla sua apposuer'."

---

* The tenths of all the monasteries and churches in England were granted to the king for seven years by Nicholas IV., to encourage a crusade, on the event of the recent capture of Acre by the Soldan of Babylon.

" BRIGHTHELMSTONE.

" This indenture testifies that an inquisition was taken before Henry Husse and his fellows, collectors, and assessors of the ixth of garbel fleeces and lambs, and of the xvth granted to our lord the king, in the county of Sussex, assigned at Lewes on a Sunday in the middle of the 40th year of the reign of King Edward the Third, from the nonal inquest, and the quindecimal concerning the true value of the ninth of garbel, ninth of fleeces, and ninth of lambs, by commission of our lord the king directed to the aforesaid Henry and his fellows, by the oath of John de Erlee, Hugh Russell, John Dac', and Ralph Grabbe, parishioners of Brighthelmston— who say, that the extent of the church there is taxed at 25 pounds with the vicarage. And they say that the ninth part of garbel (corn) is worth, this year, there, 9 pounds 8 shillings and 10 pence from the community of the town. Also the ninth part of fleeces there is worth 26 shillings and 6 pence, and the ninth part of lambs there is worth 6 shillings and 8 pence. Also they say, that the ninth part of garbel (corn) and fleeces of the prior of Lewes there is worth 7 shillings and 8 pence. Also the ninth part of garbel (corn) and fleeces of the prior of Michelham is worth 30 shillings and 4 pence. And so is the sum of the whole ninth of garbel, fleeces, and lambs, this year, 13 pounds. Also they say, that the ninth part aforesaid cannot answer nor attain to the taxation of the church aforesaid, for that 40 acres of land are drowned by the sea for ever, which were worth per annum 40 shillings. And also 160 acres of land in the common plain which have been deficient there this year in corn sown, to the value of 10 pounds. And because the wool cannot be sold as it was wont, the value of 13 shillings and 4 pence is deficient. And also the lambs there will be deficient in the pasture* this year by defect of value, 6 shillings and 8 pence. And the vicar has there the first-fruits of one dovehouse, value 2 shillings. And the same has there in offerings, small tithes of geese, sucking pigs, honey, milk, cheese, calves, and eggs, and other small tithes which are worth yearly 70 shillings. Also they say, that there are here no merchants, but tenants of land who live by their own lands, and their great labours only. In testimony of which thing, the aforesaid sworn men have affixed their seals to this indenture."—*Editor*.

Those of the inhabitants who gained their living by husbandry and fishing are supposed, in this case, to have become prosperous under the Norman rule, which led to the establishment of their market. The landsmen dwelt on the cliff; the mariners under it : in process of time the latter increased so as to form two-thirds of the population. The lower town, beneath the cliffs, becoming, in the fourteenth century, too

---

* " *Mora :*" of about twenty renderings in Facciolatus, not one was at all applicable to the context here. In " Blount's Legal Tenures" we found it interpreted " a marsh, meadow, or heath."— Qy. *Moor ?*

small for the mariners, they built " East-street" and " West-street." The landsmen also built some intermediate streets, and the proprietors of the North Lanes formed, for their convenience, at that end of the town, the " North-street."—*From Lee.*

In 1377, immediately after the death of Edward III., and in the nonage of his son, Richard I., the French, in retaliation of the bold and ambitious projects of the former (the " lion being dead"), embarked an armament and sailed, with vindictive and predatory intentions, for the southern coast of England. Their purpose was to a certain degree successful; but their course seems to have been extremely vague and eccentric. They first burnt Rye, then made a jump westward to the Isle of Wight, where the inhabitants, after some part of their island had suffered ravages, were compelled to purchase their absence by a bribe of 1000 marks of silver. Thence they advanced and pillaged Portsmouth, Plymouth, and Dartmouth; returned to Southampton, where they were repelled by Sir John Arundel, the governor; made an excursion to Hastings, which they pillaged and burnt, but were foiled at Winchelsea, and at length effected a landing at Rottingdean. Here they were met by an intrepid Prior of Lewes, *John de Carileco,* Sir Thos. Cheney, Constable of Dover castle, Sir John Falseleg, John Brocas, Esquire, and others, with their tenants and vassals, aided by the peasantry of the neighbourhood in general, who came to render their assistance with right good will. The numbers and experience on the side of the English were unable to compete with the Gallic invaders: the peasants were compelled to retreat with the loss of one hundred men, whilst the Prior, Sir Thomas Cheney, and Sir John Falseleg, were made prisoners, and carried to France. They accomplished however one most beneficial end, their gallant struggle checked the further attempts of the invaders, who retired to their ships and sought again their native land.

No accounts have been transmitted to us of depredations committed at Brighton by these ravagers, but there can be little doubt this was the case, if there was any thing valuable and worthy of being carried away, as the town possessed no means of effectual defence.

The coast " Watch and Ward," called in the King's writs " *Vigiliæ minutæ*," are said to have been of great service at this juncture. Their duties were nocturnal, and they were only called upon in great emergencies. They consisted of men at arms and light cavalry mounted on fleet horses, termed " Hobilers," from a certain jacket they wore, which was called a " Hobil."

In 1513, when Henry VIII. had, without much reason, declared war against Louis XII., Brighton was attacked, pillaged, and partly burnt by a French fleet, commanded by a Monsieur Pregent. After the defeat of Sir Edward Howard off Brest, the French sailed to the coast of Sussex, landed some men at Brighthelmston in the night, who plundered it of every thing valuable which was removeable, set many houses on fire, and wantonly slew some inhabitants. They fled and alarmed the neighbours; but the French re-embarked the next morning, before the country could be assembled in any force. On this occasion the free chapel of St. Bartholomew, in the centre of the town, was so far destroyed that it never afterwards recovered its accustomed use and influence.

The next year, Brighton was also annoyed by a nocturnal visit from some French ships, commanded by Prior Jehan, the high admiral : " but when the people began to gather, by firing the beacons, Prior Jehan sounded his trumpet to call his men aboard, and by that time it was day. Then certain archers that kept the watch followed Prior Jehan to the sea, and shot so fast that they beat the galley men from the shore, and wounded many in the fleet : to which Prior Jehan was constrained to wade, and was shot in the face with an arrow, so that he lost one of his eyes, and was like to have died of the hurt, and therefore he offered his image of wax before our lady at Bullogne, with the English arrow in the face, for a miracle*."—*Holinshed.*

* Or were these two invasions only one and the same ? The reader must excuse us if we make a mistake, we find them differently related.—*Ed.*

In the year 1535, a few years before the dissolution of the monasteries, a general ecclesiastical valuation was made by order of the King, whose avarice was whetted towards the seizure of their spoils. The following particulars are included respecting Brighton.

DECANATUS LEWENS'. PRIORATUS LEWENS'.

BRIGHTELMYSTON.

" Firma rectorie ibidem cum o'mibus proficuis et com'odit et di^r, Ric'o Nicolle p' termino annorum, et red' inde per annu' xvi^{li}."

DECANATUS LEWENS'.

" Leonardus Savell cl'icus vicarius ib'm : valet clare per annu' cum omib's p'ficuis et comoditatibus, ultra ii^s ii^d ob, annuati' sol' epo' Cicestren' pro procuracœ' annua : vi^s viii^d sol archno Cicestren' pro procuracœ' annua : xviii^d sol eidem arohno pro sinodal' ; vii^s vi^d annuatim sol' vicario eccli'e de Hova pro pensione annua xx^{li} ii^s i^d ob.

" Inde x^a xl^s ii ^{l} ob'q'."

PRIORATUS DE MICHELHAM, UNDE

BRIGHTHELYMYSTON.

" Firma certarum terr' et tenementorum ib'm in tenurai Johannis Smyth al' Waterman : reddend' inde per annu' C^s."

DEANERY OF LEWES; PRIORY OF LEWES.

BRIGHTHELMYSTON.

" Farm of the rectory there, with all first-fruits and advantages and various things, let to Richard Nicolle for a term of years, and the rent thence by the year 16l."

DEANERY OF LEWES.

" Leonard Savell, clerk, vicar there; it is worth, clear, by the year, with all first-fruits and advantages, beyond 2s. 2$\frac{1}{2}d$. annually paid to the Bishop of Chichester for annual procuration; 6s. 8d. paid to the Archdeacon of Chichester for annual procuration ; 18d. paid to the same Archdeacon for synodals ; 7s. 6d. paid to the Vicar of the church of Hove, for annual pension ;

	20l. 2s. 1$\frac{1}{2}d$.	
" Thence the tenth	40s. 2$\frac{3}{4}d$.	

PRIORY OF MICHELHAM,

WHENCE,

BRIGHTHELYMYSTON.

" Farm of certains land and tenements there in the occupation of John Smyth, otherwise, Waterman, returning thence by the year, 100s."

In the year 1545, the French again invaded this often unlucky town. Hollinshed gives a very full account of their proceedings.

" In 37 Hen. 8th, 1545, July the 18th, the admiral of France, Mons, Donebatte, hoised up sailes, and with his whole navy (which consisted of 200 ships and twenty-six gallies) came forth into the seas, and arrived on the coast of Sussex, before Bright Hampstead, and set certain of his soldiers on land to burn and spoil the country : but the beacons were fired and the inhabitants thereabouts came down so thick, that the Frenchmen were driven to their ships with loss of diverse of their numbers, so that they did little hurt there. Immediately hereupon they made to the Isle of Wight, when about two thousand of their men landed, and one of their chief captains, named Chevalier Daux, a Provencois, being slain with many other, the residue, with loss and shame, were driven back again to their gallies. And having knowledge by certain fishermen whom they took, that the king was present on the coast*, and a huge power ready to resist them, they disanctioned †, and drew along the coast of Sussex, and a small number landed again in Sussex, of whom few returned to their ships; for divers gentlemen of the country, as Sir Nicholas Pelham and others, with such power as was raised upon the sudden, took them up by the way and quickly distressed them. When they had searched every where by the coast, and saw men still ready to receive them with battle, they turned stern, and so got them home again without any act achieved worthy to be mentioned. The number of the Frenchmen was great, so that diverse of them who were taken prisoners in the Isle of Wight and in Sussex, did report they were three score thousand."

A curious *Pictorial Map* of this attack is engraved in the 24th vol. of the *Archæologia* for 1832, communicated by Mr. Ellis from the Cottonian Library. We have now in our possession a coloured copy of the original, and will give the best account of it we can. The map is dated " 1545, Julye, 37 Hen. VIII.," and appears to have been taken with the double design of affording a representation of the attack, and also a plan of the coast, with a view to fortifications being

---

* The king was then at Portsmouth.—*Mr. Ellis.*

† Disanchored.—*Mr. Ellis, from Grafton.*

established against future incursions. First then as to the ships, their number rather exceeds twenty: the largest has four masts, several three, some two, and the remainder are long row-galleys with one mast and a single long and large Latine sail (though not so immense as that of Mr. Bruce's Abyssinian Raïs, which was 200 feet in length). We should not suppose, from its appearance, that the largest exceeded 600 or 700 tons, and it does not seem as if it carried more than about twelve *large guns* *. The decks are raised at the prows and sterns in three or four stages, like the towered barks of the Romans. Each ship is adorned with eight or ten pennons or streamers; some have a large gold fleur-de-lys on blue, others a red cross on white. On the sea, towards the west side, is inscribed—" Shypes may ride all somer tem in a myle the towne in V fathome water." On the west side— " Thesse grete shyppes rydeng hard abode shore by shoting into the hill and wallies on the towne, so sore oppresse the towne that the countrey dare not aduenture to resscue it."

---

* There are smaller apertures, which may be port-holes, above, but only four large ones on each side. This is much inferior to the armament of the brave Sir Andrew Barton, in the year 1511, as described in the fine old ballad in Dr. Percy's collection.

    * * * *

He is brass within, and steel without,
 With beams in his top-castle strong,
And eighteen pieces of ordinance
 He carries on each side along—
And he hath a pinnace deerly dight,
 St. Andrew's cross, that is his guide,
His pinnace beareth ninescore men,
 And fifteen cannons on each side.

Were ye twenty ships, and he but one,
 I swear by kirk and bower and hall,
He would overcome them every one,
 If once his beams they do down fall.
    * * * *

 Dr. Percy thinks that the mode of defence here alluded to, was the relic of an ancient invention of the Romans, called *Dolphins*, which were heavy weights of lead or iron, or, in the present instance, beams, suspended by ropes to the main-top-mast. On an enemy's ship being brought close alongside, the ropes were cut, and the beams falling on the deck of the hostile ship with great force, either sunk or materially damaged it.

Next, as to the shore and town. There are no houses here under the cliff, which puzzles us as to the meaning of that expression. The town lies west of the present opening to the Steyne, and consists of two or three streets and lanes, the outer line of the whole forming a square, " a felde" is in the middle of the town. The valley coming from Lewes is designated, as also that from " Ponynge," between " Brithampston" and Hove. At the bottom, next the sea, is inscribed—" Upon this west pte may lond c m p'sones (100,000 persons) unletted by any p'vision there." The church is badly drawn, some persons near it appear as if in an attitude of supplication: above are two " wynde mylles," and still higher " the bekon of the towne," a blazing saucer-shaped receptacle on a pole. Hoove church is, judging from the ruins, very incorrectly drawn; the village consists of a few houses near the sea. Further westward is inscribed—" The west parte of Brethampston, lowe all daungerous and wout cleves (without cliffs)." At the present opening of the Steyne is inscribed—" Here landed the galeys." Many houses in the town are on fire. The soldiers represented on the shore we suppose to be meant for the French : they are dressed in red, with the red cross banner on a white ground ; others just landing are in blue, with the banner of blue and fleur-de-lys, whom we conjecture to be the sailors. About the spot where Tuppen's library now stands is " the towne fire cage,"—a large blazing grate, very similar to those now suspended in an evening at the yard-arms of colliers— hanging by a massive chain from a cross beam, on the see-saw principle, raised on an upright, probably from thirty to forty feet high : this must have been an effective beacon, but it is surprising that it was not placed on higher ground. On the east cliff is inscribed—" The east pte of Brithampston riseng onelye on cleves high:" but there are no houses in this direction.

There is in this map a reckless and intrepid abandonment of what is now termed perspective. It appears by it, that the roads to the church, also to Poynings and Lewes, were exactly perpendicular ; and the inhabitants must have perpetually been under the unpleasant necessity of going on all fours, and even then would often need a little friendly assistance, *à priori*, or otherwise. Some of the galleys on landing at the beach are making a summerset, and tumbling backwards. The relative dimensions of the men and their houses must also have been then on a very different plan to what they are now, the former being larger than the latter: but these are trifles.

In 1558, 1 Eliz., was erected the Block-House, a circular building, fifty feet in diameter, eight feet thick, and eighteen feet high; in the walls were arched apartments for powder, &c.; and in front the " Gun Garden," containing a battery of four pieces of iron ordnance. A further description of these works will be found a few pages beyond.

Court Rolls.

" 1 Eliz. At a Court Baron, holden for this manor, 27th Sept., there was granted to the inhabitants of Brighton town by the lords, one parcel of land, containing in length 30 feet, in breadth 16 feet, to build thereon a store-house to keep armes, &c., now called the Block-house. Also at the Court, holden for Atlingworth manor, 3 Jac. 9 Jan. the homage presented that the north part of the block-house aforesaid is built on part of the demesnes of that manor."—*Rowe's MSS. apud Burrell.*

A record, dated 1579, states that, " there are in the said town of Brighthelmston of fishing-boats four score in number, and of able mariners four hundred in number, with ten thousand fishing-nets, besides many other necessaries belonging to their mystery."—*Relhan.*

A false alarm, in 1586, of the approach of the Spanish armada, gave the inhabitants of the coast an opportunity of evincing their promptitude and zeal. Fifty ships appeared in the offing, apparently waiting for a suitable time for landing. An express was sent to Lord Buckhurst, lord lieutenant of the county, and one of the lords of the manor of Brighton, who assembled all the armed men he could muster, and took post between Brighton and Rottingdean. In the night his forces were increased to 1600 men, with the additional encouragement of the announced approach of a body of Kentish men to render their aid. The fleet still showing no demonstrations of hostile intention, in the morning a few boats ventured out to reconnoitre, and found them to be Dutch vessels laden with Spanish wine, and waiting for a favourable wind to proceed up the Channel. —*Lee.*

At the actual approach of the Spanish armada the inhabitants exerted themselves with diligence; they had then in the town, belonging to government, six pieces of great iron ordnance and ten " *qualivers*," a kind of small cannon.—*Ib.*

The shores of Sussex were lined by people when this armada passed by, pursued by the light and expert navy of England, with a determination of obstinate resistance.—*Ib.*

In 1584, Willm. Midwinter, sailor, sold the scite of St. Bartholomew to Thos. Friend and others, in trust for the town, for the sum of 44*l.*—*Ib.*

In 1648, Henry Hilton, commonly called Baron Hilton, of Hilton, Co. Palatine of Durham, left to the town of Brighton 24*l.* per ann. for 99 years.—*Lee.*

Court Rolls.

" 1 April, 1645. Homage present Willm. Gallan, jun., for not paying to Rd. Cook, lord's reeve, for his lady net's fishing, according to ye ancient custom 4*d.*, give him time to pay it to the said R. C., at or before St. Jn. Baptist next, on payn of 5*s.*"—*Burrell MSS.*

" 25 Aug. 1648. We present Nichs. Payne for building his new house and shop under the cliffs, upon the bank of the cliff, to the hurt and annoyance of the whole towne, if we shd. have any occasion to use the ordnance, or that there shd. be any invasion by a foreign enemy."—*Ib.*

" 25 Aug. 1654. We present Nics. Payne for encroaching on the lord's waste, and building of his walls 14 feet, or thereabout, more than he is admitted to, to ye cliffe side, before ye place where ye great guns path doth stand to ye annoyance and great hindrance of ye whole towne and country, and we fine him for it."—*Ib.*

About the middle of the 17th century, the mariners of Brighton were not prosperous; frequent captures had injured their trade. The sea began to encroach on the coast of Sussex, by one of those unaccountable revolutions of nature, deserting

some places and invading others. Previous to 1665 it had destroyed 22 copyhold tenements under the cliff, in the manor of
Brighton Lewes, among which were 12 shops, with 4 *stake-
places* and 4 *capstan-places* attached to them, and 3 cottages
and 3 parcels of land adjoining. There remained under the
cliff 113 tenements, shops, capstan-places, stake-places, and
cottages, which were finally demolished by terrible storms in
1703 and 1705.—*From Lee.*

———

The next and most remarkable event in the history of
Brighton, is the escape of Charles II.: and here we are
enabled to lay before the reader a VERY curious and *recherché*
article INDEED, to which we beg strongly to challenge his
attention ; as to those who have an avidity for curious pieces
of antiquity, it will be actually worth more than the cost of
the volume. The MS. has only recently come into the
possession of the British Museum, and was not previously
generally known to be in existence. It has, of course, never
been published, nor even publicly read throughout; but on a
part of it being read, Nov. 21, 1832, before the Royal Society
of Literature, they pronounced it to be a work of great
curiosity, as supplying a gap (connected with the escape of
Charles II.) in the general history of England, never before
filled up. The MS. was copied for our express use, and is
now published by special permission (limited to us), obtained
with some little difficulty from the trustees of the British
Museum.

Information of the existence of this manuscript came to us at
a very late period, and we had not even time to read it through
previous to its being transcribed; but we can rely with the
fullest confidence on its fidelity ; and of the original we may
say, as Hamlet did of the Ghost,—" We would take its word
for a thousand pound."

It may not be inappropriate to add, in this captious age,
that we insert this ancient record as a curious article of history,
which may now be read with the interest of a romance, and

that we do not desire to be identified with all the sentiments it contains. Still less, however, do we wish to venture out on the tempestuous sea of politics. May fair morning yet betide us after a stormy night; and may our best and most worthy landmarks, after being long darkened by boiling and contending surges, lift up their snowy heads again in calm and sunshine! Still we fearlessly hasten to acknowledge, even in this age, that we entertain a respect for the motives and principles of many of the Royalists; as undeniably possessing one intrinsically noble quality, not always practically experienced in modern times—faithful disinterestedness. Really believing in the divine right and sacredness of person in the existing monarch, they were willing to risk their whole substance and their life in defending it. Granting it might be a delusion, was it not a happy one, as supplying a highly interesting motive of action, where virtue was associated with the most cherished sympathies? And where, in any party of the present day, shall we easily find love and friendship equal to loyalty in the seventeenth century!

———

" *The last act, in the miraculous Storie of his Mties escape; being a true and perfect relation of his conveyance, through many dangers, to a safe harbour; out of the reach of his tyranicall enemies; by Colonell Gounter; of Rackton in Sussex; who had the happines to bee instrumentall in the busines, (as it was taken from his mouth by a person of worth a little before his death).*"

" The king was now att Heale, within three miles of Salisbury, where we begin our storie:—My Lord Willmot, his faithful and watchful attendant, att Salisburie; there Dr. Hinchman, now the right reverend Bp. of Salisbury (inspired by God himself, as may well be thought by the successe), gave him counsell; first, to try att Lawrence Hyde's, Esq., living at Hinton Dambray in Hamshire, neere the sea side, what could be done for a passage; then, if that did not succeed, to repaire to Coll. George Gounter at Rackton, fower miles from Chichester in Sussex, being verie confident of his fidelitie, and that he would contribute to the uttmost of his power to bring this great and weightie business, as for the difficulties they must encounter, soe for the consequence, if conclusive, to a good end. Here, before I proceed with, hope the reader will give mee leave to put in mind, that wee wryte not an ordinarie storie, where the reader, engaged by noe other interest than curiositie, may soone bee cloyed with circumstances, which signify no more unto him, but that the author was all good leisure, and was very confident of his readers patience. In the relation of miracles every petty circumstance is materiall, and may affoard to the judicious reader matter of good speculation; of such a miracle, especiallie where the restauration of noe less than three kingdomes, and his owne particular libertie and safetie (if a good and faithful subject) was att the stake; I may not, therefore, omitt to lett him knowe howe things stood with the Colonell at that tyme. Not above fourteene dayes before the said Colonell Gounter was confined, upon paine of imprisonment, not to stirre five miles from home. In the very nick of tyme, when hee was first thought upon for soe great a worke, comes a messenger with a warrant from the Commissioners of Haberdashers Hall, London, to summon him to appeare before them within ten dayes to pay twoe hundred pounds for his fifth and twentieth part which they had sett him, upon peyne of sequestration upon default. He first refused, and told the messenger that he was confined, and could not goe five miles from home; but he left with him the order, and told him it should be att his perill if he did not obey it. The Coll. the next day repaired to Chichester, fower miles from him, to the commissioners there, to shew them his order; they peremptorily replyed he must goe, and his order would bear him out. Hee went accordingly and compounded with them, and gott off a 100*l.* of the twoe hundred he was sett att; but his credit being shaken, the current running then soe hard against the king, the royal party, and all good men, that he could not borrowe the money in all London; hee was forced,

with all speede, to repaire into the countrey, and went privatly
to his usurer, who had the security of his whole estates; he
shewed him his danger, and requested to borrowe [the money]
upon his bond and his former securitie, who readily con-
descended, and told him out the money ; the next day he was
to call for it and seale the bond. Hee had noe sooner ended
this busines, beeing stayed by some friends longer than hee intended, butt that very night hee came home (being 7 October,
1651) hee found some att his house whoe were come about
their designe. I think it will easily bee graunted by any that
reades and considers, that this was not without a providence,
since that it is apparent, that if his friends had come before
hee had beene licensed to goe abroad, hee must needes have
been excused; and if they had come much after, it was possible
a new restraint might have come betweene ; or his libertie in
goeing soe freely up and downe after his busines ended more
suspected. But now to the storie and entertainement of his
guests : — betwixt eight and nine of the clock att night, the
Coll. came home ; entering in at his doore the Coll.'s ladye
mett him, and told him there was in the parlour a Deavonshire
gentleman, sent by Mr. Hyde, aforesaid, about a reference,
which none besydes yourself can decide: at the Coll.'s comming
in, he found his Deavonshire gentleman sitting att one end of
the chimney, Captain Thomas Gounter att the other, and his
lady (which was gone in before) in the middle. The gentleman
rose and saluted him : the Coll. presently knewe him to be the
Ld. Wilmot ; which the noble Lord perceiving, took the Colln
asyde to the windowe : I see you know me (said he) doe not
owne mee. Captaine Thomas Gounter, the Colls. kinsman, for
all he had a long tyme beene in the Army and under his command, knew him not, wch was strange, the noble Lord beeing
but meanly disguised. After a bottle of sack, a short collation
which was made readie as soon as it could. My Lords man
Swan coming in to waite whispered his maister in the eare;
and told him, my Lord Wentworths boy Lonie was without,
and wished him to bee carefull for feare the boy should knowe
him : being taken by Captaine Thomas Gounter in distress att

Chelsey, and cloathed by him to wayte upon him. Supper
ended, there was whispering betweene the Colls kinsman and
his lady, and shee told him shee was confident of a disguise,
and that it was the Mr. by his hand. Hee beat her off of
it as much as he could, suspecting noe such matter himselfe.
Within halfe an hower after supper the Coll. offered the
                    noble lord
[my Lord Wilmot] then by name Mr. Barlowe, it being late,
and as the greatest courtesie hee could then shewe him, to
waite upon him to his chamber, and to bedd ; which hee readily
                    tooke up the candle the noble lord following him
accepted. The Coll [accordingly waited onn him   ], his
Lady and kinsman attending. When he came into the chamber, it beeing late, the Coll. desired his Lady and kinsman to
goe to bedd and leave him ; for he was bound to waite upon
this Gentleman awhyle. They tooke leave, and bidd him
                    The noble
good night. [My   ] Lord, and yᵉ Coll. being alone, hee
broke the business unto the Coll. with these words, sighing :
The King of England my maister, your maister, and the
maister of all good Englishmen, is neere you and in great
distresse ; can you help us to a boate ? The Coll. looking very
saddly, after some pause, said, Is hee well : Is hee safe : He
said yeas : The Coll. replyed God be blessed, and gave him a
reason for his question ; if he should not bee secure, he
doubted not but he could secure him, till a boate could bee
gotten. The noble Lᵈ. not knowing what had beene done,
                    beene
and what course had [Mrs. Hide] taken for securing of his
Maᵗⁱᵉ. at Heale, since he came away, answered the Col. He
hoped hee was out of daunger at present, but intended to bee
at his house with him, on the Wensday. Soe he said and soe
it seemes it was resolved : but second thoughts, and unexpected accommodations elsewhere, had altered the designe.
However upon the hearing of this the Coll'ˢ. thoughts were
much raised, in expectation of such a guest ; untill he was
better informed as hee was soone after, to his great content
and satisfaction, knowing the house well, and the conveniencies
thereof, and the worth, and fidelitie of the persons. Now to
the maine busines of procuring a boate : The Col. told the

Lord seriously, and nothing but the trueth, that for all he
lived soe neere the sea; yet there was noe man living, soe
little acquainted with these kind of men: However as hee
thought himselfe bound by all obligations sacred and civill, to
doe his utmost to preserve his King: soe he [did] faithfully
promise with all possible care and alacritie, yea expedition
(which he accounted to bee the life of such a busines;) to
acquitt himselfe of his dutie. The noble Lord, my Hon^{ed}
friend (ô that God had beene pleased to have spared him life :)
was abundantly satisfyed with this answer, hugging him in his
armes, and kist his cheeke againe and againe. For that tyme
the Coll. bid him good night, desiring him to rest secure, for
that he would watch, whylest he slept, and that he doubted
not, but in good tyme all would bee well. Comming into his
chamber, he found his wyfe had stayed up for him, and was
very earnest to knowe whoe this was, and what was his busines.
The Coll. desired her to excuse him, assuring her it was
nothing concerning her, or, that would any wayes damnifye
her. Shee was confident there was more in it than soe, and
enough shee doubted, to ruine him, and all his family; and
in that, said shee, I am concerned; breaking out into a very
great passion of weeping. Which the Coll. seeing, tooke a
candle pretending to goe into the next roome, but privatly to
my Lord Willmot, and acquainted him how it was; asking
his advice, whether, as the case stood, it were any way amisse,
to acquaint her with it. That he durst passe his word, for
the loyaltie and integritie of his wife: however without his
allowance shee should knowe nothing. [My] Lord replyed; No, no, by all meanes acquaint her with it. He humbly
thancked him, and badd him good night againe. The Col.
comming into his chamber unfolded the busines, wyped the
teares of his ladyes eyes, whoe smiling, said, Goe on, and
prosper. Yet I feare you will hardly doe it; However said
the Coll. I must endeavour, and will doe my best, leaving the
successe to God Almightie: his lady deporting herselfe, during
the whole carriage of the busines with soe much discretion,

courage, and fidelitie, that (without vanity bee it spoken) shee seemed (her danger considered) to outgoe her sexe. Neyther will the reader thinck this an impertinent circumstance, since the succ11esse of the busines did not a little depend of her concurrance.

" The Coll. contenting himselfe with very little sleepe that night, rose very early the next morning, being Wednesday the 8th of Octobre; as he had promised the Lord Wilmot; and rode to Elmsworth, a place twoe miles from him, and by the sea syde, passing through Boorne. He tooke an old servant of his formerly, John Day, a trustie man and very loyall subject whoe was related to seamen of very good accoumpt; whoe with their Barkes used to lye there: But they being out of the way, could doe noe good there : although fower yeares after, the Col. did att the same place, att his owne charges, hire a barke for the Lord Wilmot, whoe came over att his Mat^{ie} command, and loosing his designe, was forced to come from allmost the furthest North to the South, before hee could gett a passage. Soe few friends had then his Sacred Matie. in his distresses, now soe numerous in expectation of rewards. The Col. hasted all he could home to give my Lord accoumpt, who had promised not to stirre, till the Colonell came; but being impatient of any delay, had left the Col's. house, soe that the Col. mett him within halfe a mile of it ; and gave him an accoumpt of his mornings worke that nothing could be done where he had beene. The noble Lord and the Coll. rid on, and went to Langstone, a place by the sea, and where boates use. As he was riding along hee put his hand in his pocket, and missed his money, for comming away in hast from the Coll's. house he had left it behindé him in his bedd. Immediatly he sent his man Swan for it. The Coll's. Ladye hearing my Lord was gone, which shee much wonderd att, had beene in his chamber and found the bedd open; and in the middle a black purse full of gold, which shee had secured, and gave it the man when he came for it. When [they] came to Langston [they] attempted all [they] could ; but in vaine. The noble Lord and the Coll. eate oisters there,

and then they parted; the Lord, to Mr. Hydes house aforesaid, there to expect the accoumpt of the Colls. proceedings;
the Coll. came home; and immediately imployed his kinsman,
Captaine Thomas Gounter, (whoe by this, was made acquainted;) to inquire of severall other places, and to meet the
Coll. next day att Chichester, to give him an accoumpt: all
which the Coll. imparted that night to my Lord Willmot, att
Mr. Hydes house att Hinton Daubney aforesaid. After supper,
the Coll. tooke his leave of the Lord, it being a very dismall
night for winde and raine: which made the Lord very much
to importune the Coll. to stay; but he refused, replying that
delayes were dangerous, and lett the weather be what it would
he had a sure guide.

" The Coll. touched att his owne house by the way, betwixt
one and twoe of the clock that night; and layd downe upon
his bedd, and after twoe houres rest, rose from bedd and went
immediately to Chichester, to meete his kinsman, Thomas
Gounter (9th of October), according to appointment. From
whome hee received this accoumpt, that both he and his
kinsman, Mr. William Rishton, a loyall gentleman, and one
engaged all along in the warre, under the Colls. command,
had endeavoured all they could, but without successe. Then
the Coll. bethought himself, and conceived the next and best
expedient, would be to treat with a French merchant, one that
usually traded into France; and went to one Mr. Francis
Mancell, a stranger then to the Coll. and only known unto
him by face, as casually he had mett him with severall other
companies, pretending to give him a visitt, and to bee better
acquainted with him. He received him courteously, and
entertained him with a bottle or twoe of his French wine, and
Spanish tobacco. After a whyle the Coll. broke the busines
to him, saying, I doe not only come to visitt you, but must
request one favour of you. He replyed; Any thing in his
power. Then the Coll. asked him, if hee could fraught a
barke; for, said he, I have twoe speciall friends of mine, that
have beene engaged in a duell, and there is mischief done,
and I am obliged to gett them of if I can. Hee doubted not

butt he could att such a place, att Brighthemston in Sussex.
The Coll. prest him then to goe with him immedeatly, and if
he could effect the busines, hee would give him fifty pounds
for his peynes; but it being Stowe faire day there and his
partner out of the way, hee could not possibly untill the next
day, and then he promised him faithfully hee would goe with
him, and doe his best.   Soe accordingly [they] agreed. ^wee

" Then the Coll. whoe had promised to the noble Lord Willmot, an accoumpt att Mr. Hydes house aforesaid, once in twelve
or 24 houres at furthest repayred thyther accordingly and told
him all that was done.   The noble Lord approved, and liked
[the way wondrous] well.   It being very late, and very darke, ^his proceedings
and boistrous weather, the Coll. tooke his leave.   His horse
being allmost spent, he borrowed a horse of his kinsman Mr.
Hide whoe lent him his faulkners horse beeing as it seemes
the best he then had which served to carrie him home; and
the next morning to Chichester.   The Coll. tooke his owne
house in the way, and rested upon a bedd for a whyle, and
went unto Chichester, the 10th of October being Fryday according to former appointment.   The merchant being destitute
of a horse, the Coll. horst him upon the horse borrowed of
Mr. Hyde, and borrowed one for himselfe of his kinsman
Captaine Thomas Gounter, and went away accordingly, desiring his kinsman to repaire to my Lord Willmot, and to give
him the accoumpt of his departure from Chichester, in further
prosecution of the busines, and to remaine with him in order
to his commands during his absense.   The marchant went
immedeatly to inquire; but the seaman he chiefly depended
upon, was gone for Chichester, whoe had bargained for a
fraught there; but as Providence would have it, he touched
att Shoram, fower myles from Brightemston.   I perswaded
the marchant, to send to him immediatly, to come to him upon
earnest busines; and [he] doubted not but he would come, ^I
which tooke effect accordingly.   The Coll. had agreed with
the marchant, to treat with the boatman, beeing his affaire and
trade; he to sett by as newter, promising the marchant, to

make good, and to pay him, whatere he should agree for; but withall desired, to gett it as lowe as he could. They stayed there that night, and by Saturday the 11th of October, by twoe of the clock, made a perfect agreement; which was, that he was to have 60ll. paid him in hand, before he tooke them into the boate. For he would know what he should carrie, or he would not treat; soe that the marchant was forced to tell him, himselfe knowing noe more than what the Coll. had said to him, of twoe friends, &c. Hee was to bee in readines upon an howers warning; and the marchant to stay there, under pretence of fraughting his barke; to see all things in readines against the Coll. and his twoe friends arrival. For the Coll. knew not when he should come, but privatly promised the merchant to defray all his charges and to give him fifty pounds, as aforesaid for his paines, which was afterwards accordingly done. But this 50ll. and the 60ll. paid to the boateman, the king himselfe, before he went away, tooke order for and his order was executed. All things agreed upon, the Coll. tooke leave of the marchant, about 3 of the clock, to give my Lord Willmot this account, and came to Mr. Hydes house aforesaid, betwixt eight and nine in the night; but my Lord, and the Colls. kinsman Captaine Gounter, were remooved, to a tenants [his] of my cozin Hydes one Mrs. Browne and one that had married [his] my my cousin Gounters sister. But the Coll. comming into [his] Cozin Hydes house as aforesaid, found there his cousin Hyde, and Coll. Robert Philipps in his chamber goeing to bedd, whoe was very inquisitive to know how things stood. He gave in short, that all things were well and in a readines. Upon which Col. Philips replyed, Thou shalt be a saint in my Almanack for ever. Mr. Hyde was very earnest to have had the Coll. stay all night, and to goe, and give an account, the morrow morning; butt he desired to be excused, for that he knew he was expected, and could not in honour but give his account without delay. Whereupon Coll. Phil'pps would me And we my cousin goe with [him]. [Soe they] tooke leave of [Mr.] Hyde

for that night; and [went to] ^{came where} my Lord Willmot was and had
earnestly expected [him]. ^{me I} After [he] had saluted him, and
given him a full account of all proceedings, the noble Lord
was infinitly pleased and satisfyed, and presently had in consultation, whoe should goe for the King; and it was agreed
that Coll. Philipps should, by reason that Coll. Gounter was
much tyred out, and would neede rest for further employement.

" Soe Coll. Philipps upon Sunday the 12th of October, went
to give the King an accoumpt, and to conduct him to the
Lord Willmot, and to the said Coll. Gounter. In the interim, whylest they expected, upon Munday the 13th of
October, the Lord Willmot, Coll. Gounter, and Captaine
Thomas Gounter beeing altogether att dinner agreed to ride
out upon the Downes. The Coll. for a blinde went to Hambledon, hard by, to give his sister a visitt, and there borrowed
a brace of greyhounds, for that his Cozin Gounter, and other
gentlemen were upon the Downes, and had a minde to have a
course att a haire, and 'twas possible, if they did not beat to
farre and should stay out late, they might all come and bee
merry with her that night; however, shee should be sure of
her doggs. If you do, you shall be heartely wellcome, was her
answer. The Coll. brought the greyhounds, and beat with my
Lord and his Cozin, untill his tyme served, and then left
them, resolving to ride on, till he mett the King. And just
as he came to Warneford townes end from old Winchester,
hee mett Coll. Phelipps conducting the King. Being neere
the houses, the Coll ridd by them, and tooke noe notice; went
to an Inne in the towne, called for some beare, and tooke a
pipe, and stayed soe long, that they were a topp old Winchester before he overtooke them. When he had overtaken
them and done his dutie to his Matie he directed them the
safest way, and he would ride before, to find out my L^d.
Wilmot. Which beeing done [they] ^{wee} all came together. The
King and my Lord had some private discourse together.
When [they] ^{we} came to Brawde Halfe-penny, a little above

Hambledon, there the King spake to the Coll. Canst thou
gett mee a lodging heereabouts. The Coll. told him, that his
Cozin Hydes house aforesaid was taken up for him, and was
very convenient, beeing neere and in the way ; But whether
his Matie thought it to publick a place, or for what other reason, I knowe not, Hee said, knowe you noe other ? Yeas may
it please your Matie I know divers where for a night wee may
be wellcome, and heere is one who married my sister whose
house stands privatly, and out of the way. Lett us goe thither,
said the King. Whylest wee were consulting this affaire,
Captaine Thomas Gounter the Coll^s kinsman, and Swan, my
Lord Willmots man, ridd scouting about Broade-halfe-penny
aforesaid, the Coll. conducting the King, my Lord Willmot,
and Coll. Robert Philipps, to his sisters house, a private way,
and the backside of Hambledon, it beeing but halfe a myle
from the place aforesaid. Alighting att the doore, the Coll.
lead them in, the Lord Willmot following, the King putting
Collonel Robert Phillipps before him, Thou lookest the most
like a gentleman now. Comming in the Coll^s sister mett him ;
[They] all saluted her. She brought [them] into a little
parlour, where was a good fire. This was about candle lighting. Wine, ale, and bisketts, were presently sett before
[them], with a very cheerfull countenance, as though the
Kings presence had had some secret influence upon her,
whoe suspected nothing lesse than that a King was present.
In an howers space [they] went to supper, beeing all sett
promiscuously att a round table : and having halfe supt,
in comes the Colls. sisters husband, Mr. Thom. Symones,
whoe, as it plainly appeared, had beene in company that
day. This is brave, said he ; A man can noe sooner be out
of the way, but his house must be taken up with I knowe
not whome ; and looking in the Colls. face, Is it you (said he)
you are welcome ; and as your friends, soe they are all.
Passing round the table, and viewing all the company, he said,
These are all Hyds now ; but peeping in the king's face, said
of him, Heer's a Roundhead ; and addressing his speech to

the Coll. said, I never knewe you keepe Roundheads company before. To which the Coll. replyed, Tis noe matter,
he is my friend, and I will assure you, noe dangerous man.
Att which words, he clapt himselfe downe in a chaire downe
next the king, and saying, Brother Roundhead, for his sake
thou art wellcome; all the whyle beleeving the King to be so
indeede, and making himselfe (whether for feare or in courtesie)
to bee one too, as he could act it, the King all the whyle com-
plying with him to all [their] admirations. Now and then
he would sweare, before he was aware; for which the King
reprooved him, O deare brother, that is a scape ; swear not, I
beseech you. Nevertheles in that humor hee was hee plyed
[them] hard with strong waters and beare, the King not
knowing well how to avoid it; but as some body or other
when hee lookt asyde, would take it out of his hand.

"Supper being ended, it beeing tenn of the clock, the Coll. be-
ganne to bethinck himself*, that the King had ridd neere fourty
miles that day, and was to undergoe a very hard journey the next,
and how to gett the King out of his company and to bedd he
could hardly devise. Yet the Coll. whispered his kinsman in
the eare, saying*, I wonder how thou shouldst judge soe
right ; hee is a roundhead indeede, and if we could gett him
to bedd, the house were your owne, and we could be merry.
Hee readily submitted, and the Coll. presently (leaving the
Lord Wilmot behinde) conducted the King and Col. Rob.
Philips (who lay in the King's chamber) to bedd.

"The King slept well all night; and by breake of day, the
Coll. putting up twoe neats tongues in his pocketts, which he
thought they might neede by the way, they sett out, and began
their journey. They were noe sooner come to Arundell hill,
as they rode close by the castle, but the governour, Captaine
Morley, mett them full butt, hunting. The Coll., the better

* Interlined in a different hand. " Therefore thought it convenient to con-
trive a way for him softly leaving the company that soe he might betake himself to his lodging, w'ch he effected after this manner. Whispering his
Bro' Mr. Symonds said"——

to avoid them, presently alighted; and his company, " It beeing
a steepe hill
(as was agreed before) did as he did.   And soe hap- they were
to goe
pily they escaped them.   The King beeing told who downe."
it was, replyed merrily, I did not like his starched mouchates.
            we   we
Soe [they] came to Howton where on horseback [they] made a
stopp, att an alehouse, for some bread and drinck ; and there
     our   us
[their] neats tongues stood [them] in very good stead, and
were heartily eaten.   From thence being come to Bramber
   we
[they] found the streetes full of soldiers, on both sides the
                                            yᵉ Coll.
houses ; whoe unluckily and unknowne to [mee] were come
thither the night before to guard ; but luckily (or rather
by a very speciall Providence) were just then come from
their guarde at Bramber-bridge, into the towne * for re-
               We
freshment. [They] came upon them unawares and were seene,
     we
before they suspected any thing.   My Lord Wilmot was
                           [the Coll]
ready to turne back, when   I   stept in and said : If we doe,
wee are undone.   Lett us goe on boldly, and wee shall not be
                                   [The Coll]   the King
suspected.   He saith well, saith the king.   I went before, hee
followed, and soe passed through, without any hinderance.
It was then betweene three and fower of the clock in the after-
     We
noone.   They went on ; but had not gone farre, but a new
          us   us
terror pursued them ; the same soldiers riding after [them]
                                               The Coll
as fast as they could.   Whereupon the king gave me a hem,
 I   my   me
he slacked [his] pase, till they were come upp to [him] and
by that tyme, the soldiers were come, whoe rudely passed by
 us   we
them (beeing in a narrow lane) soe that [they] could hardly
      our
keepe their saddles for them ; but passed by without any
further hurt ; being some 30 or 40 in number.
          we   ye Coll
  " When they were come to Beeding, a little village where I
had provided a treatment for the king (one Mr. Bagshall's house,)
He was earnest, that his Maᵗⁱᵉ should stay there a whyle, till He

  * Probably *Steyning* is here meant.—*Ed.*

had viewed the coast: But my Lord Willmot would by noe meanes
for feare of those soldiers, but carried the king out of the road
 ⟨I⟩   ⟨we⟩
he knew not whither, Soe they parted; they where they
                               ⟨we⟩
thought safest, I to Brightemston; being agreed, they should
send to me, when fixed any where, and ready.
                                              ⟨I⟩
" Being come to the said Brightemston, he found all clear
there; and the Inne (the George) free from all strangers, att that
tyme.   Having taken the best roome in the house and bespoken
 ⟨my⟩   ⟨I⟩   ⟨myselfe⟩
[his] supper; as [he] was entertaining [hisselfe] with a glass
of wine; the king not finding accommodation elsewhere to
his mind was come to the Inne; then upp comes mine
hoast (one Smith by name)   More guests saith he, He
                                         ⟨I⟩
brought them into another roome ye Coll taking noe notice.
                                                         ⟨I⟩
It was not long but drawing towards the kings roome, He
heard the kings voice, saying aloud to my Lord Wilmot;
Here Mr. Barlow, I drinck to you.   I knowe that name said
 ⟨I⟩   ⟨my⟩   ⟨mee⟩
he to his hoast then by him.   I pray enquire and whether he
were not a Major in the Kings Army.   Which done he was
found to bee the man whome I expected; and presently invited as was likely to the fellowship of a glass of wine.   From
 ⟨I⟩
that He proceeded and made a motion to joyne companee, and
       ⟨my⟩
because his chamber was largest that they would make use of
                                    ⟨we⟩
it.   Which was accepted, and so they became one companie
againe.

" At supper, the king was cheereful, not shewing the least
signe of feare, or apprehension of any daunger; neyther then,
nor att any tyme during the whole course of this busines.
Which is noe small wonder, considering, that the very thought
of his ennemies, soe great, and soe many; soe diligent, and soe
much interested in his ruine; was enough, as long as he was
within their reach, and as it were, in the very middest of them
to have daunted the stoutest courage in the world.   As if God
had opened his eyes, as he did Elisha's servant at his Masters
request, and he had seene an heavenly hoast, round about him

us
to guard him : which to [them] was invisible ; whoe therefore
though much encouraged by his undauntedness, and the as
surance of soe good and glorious a cause ; yet were not without
them
secret terrours within ourselves and thought every minute a
day, a month till they should see his sacred person out of their
reach. Supper ended the king stood his back against the fyer,
leaning over a chaire. Up comes mine hoast (upon some
jealousie, I guess not any certain knowledge ;) but up comes
him whoe called himselfe Gaius runs to the king catcheth
his hand and kissing it, said. It shall not be said but I have
kissed the best mans hand in England. He had waited at
us
table at Supper, where the boateman alsoe sate with them and
were then present. Whether he had feare, or heard any thing
that could give him any occasion of suspicion, I knowe not.
In very deede, the king had a hard taske, soe to carrie himself in all things, that he might be in nothing like himselfe :
Majestie being soe naturall unto him, that even when hee said
nothing, did nothing, his very lookes, (if a man observed)
were enough to betray him. It was admirable to see the king
(as though he had not been concerned in these words, which
might have sounded in the eares of another man as the sentance
of death) turned about in silence, without any alteration of
countenance or taking notice of what had been said. About
a quarter of an hour after the king went to his chamber, where
I
[the Coll] followed him and craved his pardon with earnest
I
protestation that he was innocent, soe altogether ignorant of
the cause ; how this had hapned. Peace peace Colonell, said
the king, the fellow knowes mee, and I him. Hee was one
(whether soe or not, I know not but soe the king thought att
that tyme) that belonged to the back staires to my Father ; I
hope he is an honest fellow.
I
" After this the Coll began to treat with the boateman
(Tettersfield by name) asking him in what readines he
was. He answered he could not of that night, because
for more securitie he had brought his vessel into a breake,

and the tyde had forsaken it; soe that it was on ground.
It is observable that all the whyle this busines had beene
in agitation to this very tyme the wind had been con-
trarie. The king then opening the wenddowe tooke notice,
that the wind was turned and told the master of the Shipp.
                                                              I
Whereupon because of the wind and a cleere night, the coll
offered 10ll more to the man to gett off that night. But that
                          we
could not bee. However they agreed, he should take in his
                                                          we
company that night. But it was a great business that they
                                      us
had in hand : and God would have them to knowe soe, both
by the difficulties that offerd themselves, and by his help, he
                              we   we
afforded to remoove them. When they thought they had
                                                          I
agreed the boateman starts back and saith noe except the Coll
would ensure the barke. Argue it they did with him, how
unreasonable it was beeing so well paid, &c. but to no purpose
soe that the Coll yeelded att last and 200ll was his valuation
which was agreed upon. But then as though he had beene
resolved to frustrate all by unreasonable demands, he required
  my   I
[his] bond. Att which mooved with much indignation [the Coll]
began to be as resolut as he ; saying among other things,
There were more boates to bee had, besydes his; if he would
                                                  I
not another should and made as though [he] would go to
another. In this contest the king happily interposed. Hee
saith right (said his Matie) a Gentlemans word especially
before wittnesses, is as good as his bond. At last, the mans
stomach came downe, and carrie them he would, whatever
became of it ; and before he would bee taken, hee would run
his boat under the water. Soe it was agreed that about tooe in
the morning they should be aboard. The boateman in the
                                          and I
meane tyme, went to provide for necessaries, [soe he] perswaded the king to take some rest ; He did in his cloaths, and
my Ld Willmot with him, till towards twoe of the morning.
          I
Then [the coll] called them up shewing them how the tyme

went by [his]^{my} watch. Horses being ledd by the back way
towards the beach, [They]^{we} came to the boate, and found
all readie. Soe [the Coll]^I tooke [his]^{my} leave craving his Maties
pardon if any thing had happened through error, not want of
will or loyaltie. How willingly I would have waited further
but for [his]^{my} family (being many) which would want [him]^{mee}
and [he]^I hoped his M^{tie} would not, not doubting but in a very
little tyme he should bee where he would. [His]^{my} only request
to his Matie was that he would conceal his instruments ; wherein
their preservation, was soe much concerned. His Matie promised noebody should knowe. [The Coll]^I abided there keeping the horses in a readiness in case any thing unexpected had
happened.

"At 8 of the clock I saw them on sayle and it was the afternoone
before they were out of sight. The wind (O Providence) held very
good till the next morning, to ten of the clock brought them to a
place of Normandie called Fackham* some three miles from
Havre de Grace. 15 Oct. Wenseday. They were no sooner landed
but the wind turned and a violent storme did arise in soe much that
the boateman was forced to cutt his cable, lost his anchor to save
his boate for which he required of mee 8^d and had it. The boate
was back againe at Chichester by Friday to take his fraught."

"I was not gone out of the towne of Brighthemston twoe houres
but soldiers came thither to search for a tall black man 6 foot
and 4 inches high."

"*Unto thee O God doe wee give thancks ; unto thee O God do we give
thancks ; for thy name is neere, thy wondrous workes declare.*"
"*Great deliverance giveth he to his king, and showeth mercy to his
annointed.*"

NOTE BY TRANSCRIBER.

The above narrative has clearly been written originally in the first person ;
the words in brackets, thus [ ], being interpolations in another hand, substi-
tuting the third person, viz. " he " or " the Coll." for " I."

---

* So the worthy Colonel is pleased to spell *Fiscqmp* or *Féchamp.*

In Mr. Lee's History of Brighton, it is stated that the last house, in which the king stayed a short time before he came to the inn at Brighton, was that of a Mr. Mansell of Oving-dean, about three miles from Brighton, to the left of Rotting-dean, a very small village, situated in a valley, and scarcely ever visited. It is to be observed that the colonel leaves them at this point, whilst he goes to Brighton to make preparations. The embarkation is said to have been at Shoreham, but was doubtless somewhere between that place and Brighton. A few trifling particulars of Tattersall and his wife are also related, which are rather creditable to them : and some little anecdotes of the sailors during Charles the Second's voyage *.

He also sums up his account with the following paragraph, which has been copied by several others :—" Yet, whoever candidly investigates the subsequent conduct of that vicious prince (Charles II.), will make no very high estimate of the obligations of posterity to Captain Tattersall."—Certainly *not*, — IF—all the consequences of the measure depended on the per-sonal character of the immediate successor, for his vexatious and disappointing selfishness and shameless profligacy are totally indefensible. But,—if to have then been relieved from a state of anarchy, under opposing leaders and demagogues, so harassing, that it was said on the restoration " the whole population was running about wild with joy, and the only wonder was, where those persons were who had done all the mischief;"—if to have lived from that period to our own day, under a government confessedly the best adapted for England, if not for every other country (the change from James II. to William III. was only an episode) a *limited* Monarchy, in which a king is armed with sufficient power for the govern-ment and protection of all his subjects, yet strongly restrained from abusing it,—constituting in himself a steady bulwark against the encroachments of any faction, as well of aristocracy as of democracy ;—if to be now living under the reign of a mild and temperate monarch, with a quiet line of succession,

* As, of one approaching rather intrusively and smoking his pipe in the monarch's face, and, being reproved by some one, answering—" *A cat may look at a king*," without the slightest idea of its applicability.

instead of suffering from some one of the hundred throes and convulsions of the terrible " beast with many heads ;"—if all this be allowed to be an advantage,—and they are comparatively few, and their opinions such as we have little value for, who will deny it,—then posterity was under actual and substantial obligations to Tattersall *.

We do not mean of course to attribute any extraordinary degree of merit to the man himself, as interest had doubtless a share in *his* willingness to assist ; yet we believe him to have been an honest character. Mr. Horsefield has, in his History of Lewes, brought forward (we really think in this *one* instance, on several accounts, with bad taste), a long account of the persecutions of the non-conformists, in which Tattersall is blamed for having, to a certain degree, acted officially as constable of Brighton, in 1670. We can only say we dislike all persecution quite as much as Messrs. Horsefield or Lee, and have no inclination to defend it, or even palliate it. Still there is one circumstance generally overlooked in the consideration of this period, viz. that the predominant party had been for a series of years quite as ill-treated by those they were then opposing :—(Vide *Evelyn's Memoirs, &c.*)—This, we repeat, is no excuse, but it is a reason.

Tattersall finding the restored king as culpably forgetful of him as of most other of his old friends, sailed in the identical

* " Without doubt, liberty, the source of so many virtues, the mother of so many arts, the spring of public and private happiness, of the glory and the greatness of nations, is and ever will be the idol of liberal and manly minds, and that system which is most favourable to its development must necessarily obtain their approbation. But, fortunately, they need not have recourse to fine-spun theories for the principles, or to look to past ages or to distant countries for the practice of a free, and what may justly be called a republican government. The constitution of England naturally comprises the excellencies of all the ancient commonwealths, together with the advantages of the best forms of monarchy: though liable, as all human institutions are, to abuse and decay; yet, like the works of Providence, it contains in itself the means of correction and the seeds of renovation. Such a system was considered as one of unattainable perfection by Cicero, and was pronounced by Tacitus, a vision, fair, but transient. A scheme of policy that enchanted the sages of antiquity may surely content the patriot and the philosopher of modern days; and the only wish of both must be, that in spite of royal encroachment and of popular frenzy, it may last for ever."—*Introduction to Eustace's Classical Tour in Italy.*

bark up the Thames, and moored it off Whitehall. This public hint was not to be resisted: the brig was taken into the royal navy as a fifth-rate, under the title of the *Royal Escape*, and himself appointed as captain, with an additional pension of 100*l.* per annum ; then, of course, equal to four times that sum in the present day. This pension was for a long time paid to his descendants, but is now said to be disused.

In 1683 a certificate from the parish officers of Brighton to Francis Beard, gent. for the cure of the king's evil (scrofula), is thought by Mr. Lee to argue that the utility of *sea bathing* in some complaints was even then begun to be acknowledged. At the conclusion of this century, Edward Joy, fisherman, left to the poor of Brighton 4*l.* per ann., Thos. Humphrey 40*s.* do. and some one else a tenement in East-street.

1690. It was ordered by Justices at Lewes that, in consequence of the increase of poor-rates, by inroads of the sea, &c. &c. the following parishes in the neighbourhood " *which had no poor of their own*," should contribute to the relief of Brighton, yearly :—

	£	s.	d.
Pacham	17	16	7
Haughton	4	16	4
East Aldrington	6	1	1½
Blackington	4	2	6
Ovingdean	6	0	10½
	38	17	5.—*Lee.*

Having now brought down the history of Brighton to the 18th century, we have to offer the reader a few general and curious particulars relating either to the entire coast, or county of Sussex, which, though not principally applicable to Brighton, may as well come under this head as any other.

HENRY III.

" The Sheriff of Sussex was commanded to buy Brawn and other Provisions for the King's Table.—

—" Rex vice Comiti Sussex', salutem. Præcipimus tibi quod emi facias in balliva tua, contra instans festum Natalis Domini, x braones, ʟ cuniculos, c perdices et ɒ gallinas et omnia prædicta mitti facias usq' Westmon: ita quod sint ibi die lunæ proximâ ante natale Domini. T. R. apud Reading, xi die Decembris."—26 H. 3.—*Madox. MSS. Burrell.*

"The king to the sheriff of Sussex, Health. We order you that you cause to be bought in your bailiwick against the instant Feast of the Nativity of our Lord, 10 brawns, with the heads, 10 peacocks, 50 rabbits, 100 partridges, and 500 hens; and that you cause all the aforesaid to be sent as far as Westminster; so that they may be there on the next Monday before the Nativity of our Lord.—The king holding his court *(tenente rege)* at Reading, the 11th day of December."—*Ed.*

"Rex baronibus. Allocate eidem Nicolao (de Wauney) vice comiti Surr', Sussex, in exitibus eorundem comitatuum, vi¹ xii⁵ quos posuit postpræceptum nostrum, in braonibus, ovis, ducis, gallinis, pullis, et cuniculis emptis adopus nostrum in ballivâ suâ, nobis missis contra festum S. Eduardi."—35 H. III.—*Madox. MSS. Burrell.*

"The king to his barons. Allot ye to the same Nicholas (de Wauney) sheriff of Surrey and Sussex, in the outgoings of the same counties, 6 pounds 12 shillings, which he has laid out according to our command, in brawns, eggs, *ducks* *, hens, pullets, and rabbits, for our use, in his bailwick, sent. to us against the feast of St. Edward."—*Ed.*

23 SEP, 1582. ELIZ.

"It was agreed upon, that in every rape there be two hundred appointed to serve under the captains appointed by the Co. and that either of them said captains appointed by the Co. have 20 pyks, 25 bowes, 25 currets, 25 bills, but more archers and pyks if it may be."—*Burrell MSS.*

In 1584, orders were issued for better training the men to the exercise of shooting, when the quota of Sussex is specified at 2000. Shott 700, bows 800, corslets furnished 500. *Two pounds* of powder, it is said, would suffice with better management for four days training.—*Burrell MSS.*

In 1589, strict orders were given for maintaining beacons in all accustomed places, with orders to the watchmen, that if the number of invading ships did not exceed two, they were not to fire the beacons, but ' to cause larums to be rung from church to church as far as the skirts of the hill reached from the sea shore, and no further;' and to send a post to the nearest justices:—but if the ships exceeded two, they were to fire both their beacons, which were to be duly answered by the corresponding ones, and thus rouse the ' force of the shire.' Five discreet householders in the neighbourhood were assigned to each beacon, one to keep watch constantly. In 1590, the beacon watches were ordered to be discharged till further orders.—*Burrell MSS.*

In 1593, directions were given to the gentlemen appointed to assist the vice admiral and officers of the ports for the strict observance of all who landed or embarked, with orders not to allow any to be landed at creeks without examination at the ports, except in case of tempest.—*Burrell MSS.*

---

* So we suppose, but it should have been "*ducibus*" in this dog-latin:—we need scarcely add, it ought to have been "*anatibus.*"

In Dec. 1595, orders were given for victualling the navy; the articles to be paid for by government at proper prices. The quota of Sussex was 350 quarters of wheat, 400 of malt, 400 "porkes," 500 flitches of bacon.—*Burrell MSS.*

19th June, 1602, an order was issued for impressing 70 men in the port towns of Sussex for the use of the fleet.—*Burrell MSS.*

13th of May, 1605, we find that 400 loads of coals were charged on the county of Sussex by his majesty's purveyor for his highness's expenses; this service, however, it appears, consisted only in the carriage, his majesty paying a fair price, viz. 11*d*. a quarter, for the coals themselves *.—*Burrell MSS.*

31st March, 1609, for the carriage of 500 loads of timber and "try-nails" from his majesty's manors of *Marlpost* and *Colstaple* and disparked parks of *Bewbush* and *Shelley* to the water-side for embarkation for Deptford and Woolwich, for ship-builders: same service to be equally borne by the county. These directions were repeated for wood and coals several times, and occasional complaints made of deficiency.—*Burrell MSS.*

1619 and 21, directions were issued respecting establishing magazines for storing up corn in times of plenty, as an occasional supply in future scarcity; and also, as it appears, by withdrawing a part, to moderate the excessive *cheapness*, which tended to the ruin of the farmers.—*Burrell MSS.* 5702. fol. 262.

In 1614, a "*benevolence*" was requested by the king.—*Burrell MSS.*

Two lists of the "armoury" of the canons of Chichester and the parochial clergy are contained in the MSS.:—who were respectively and relatively required to furnish a horse, man, pike, or musket.—*Burrell MSS.*—The above are only the substance of long articles.

The following has no local application, but we doubt not there are many to whom it will prove both new and interesting.

SHIPS IN THE ROYAL NAVY OF ENGLAND AT THE BEGINNING OF THE REIGN OF JAMES I.

" *The names of His Majesties Shipps with the nomber of Men and Furniture requisite for the settinge forth of them.*"

Extract from an original MS. of that date in the Library of Soc. of Antiquaries.— (*Archæologia*, vol. xv.)

" 1. The *Triumphe*, burthen 1000 tuns,   450 mariners, 50 gunners, 250 souldiers ; *furniture*, 250 calivers, 50 bowes, 100 arrow-sheffes, 200 pyks, 200 bills, 150 corslets, 200 murians.

2. The *Elizabeth*, Burthen 900 tuns,   350 mariners, 50 gunners, 200 souldiers ; *furniture*, 220 calivers, 50 bowes, 100 arrow-sheffes, 280 pyks, 170 bills, 100 corslets, 200 murians.

---

* We at first imagined this to be pit-coal brought in ships from the north, but find it elsewhere stated to be "*char*"-*coal* (Etym. to "*chark*," O. W. "to burn to a black cinder."—JOHNSON.) made in the forests of Sussex."

3. The *White Beare*,   ut ante.

4. The *Marie Rose*, burthen 800 tuns,   200 mariners, 40 gunners, 160 souldiers; *furniture*, 200 calivers, 40 bowes, 80 arrowsheffes, 100 pyks, 180 bills, 80 corslets, 160 murians.

5. The *Victorie*, burthen 820 tuns,   200 mariners, 40 gunners, 100 souldiers; *furniture*, 200 calivers, 40 bowes, 60 arrowsheffes, 100 pyks, 180 bills, 80 corslets, 160 murians.

6. The *Hoope*,   ut ante.

7. The *Bonaventure*,
8. The *Philip and Marie*, } ut ante.
9. The *Lyon*,

10. The *Swallowe*, burthen 400 tuns,   120 mariners, 20 gunners, 80 souldiers; *furniture*, 15 calivers, 15 bowes, 50 arrowsheffes, 60 pyks, 60 bills, 80 corslets, 70 mariners.

11. The *Dreadnought*, burthen 500 tuns,   140 mariners, 40 gunners, 200 souldiers; *furniture*, 80 calivers, 20 bowes, 50 arrowsheffes, 50 pyks, 40 corslets, 80 mariners.

12. The *Swiftsure*,   ut ante.

13. The *Antelopp*, burthen 200 tuns,   120 mariners, 20 gunners, 80 souldiers; articles of *furniture* as above, to which no numbers are affixed.

14. The *Jennett*,   the same.
15. The *Aide*,   the same.

16. The *Bull*, burthen 400 tuns,   70 mariners, 10 gunners, 80 souldiers; *furniture*, 75 calivers, 25 bowes, 50 arrowsheffes, 60 pyks, 60 bills, 30 corslets, 70 murians.

17. The *Foresight*,   ut ante.
18. The *Tyger*,   ut ante.

19. The *Falcon*, burthen 160 tuns,   60 mariners, 10 gunners, 50 souldiers; *furniture*, 24 calivers, 10 bowes, 20 arrowsheffes, 10 pyks, 20 bills, 15 corslets, 15 murians.

20. The *Acates*,
21. The *Handmaide*,
22. The *Arkeraile*, } ut ante.
23. The *Bonavogelie* *,

24. The *Barke of Bullen*, 160 tuns,   30 mariners, 10 gunners, 40 souldiers; *furniture*, 15 calivers, 15 bowes, 25 arrowsheffes, 15 pyks, 20 bills, 10 corslets, 20 murians.

25. The *George*,   ut ante.

" Skinner describes 'caliver,' à Fr. *calibre*, as being 'tormentum bellicum majus.' " See *Skinner* in verbo.

" The 'corslets' mentioned above, are well known to have been a species of ancient armour; and ' the murians' to have been *casques* or *helmets*."

---

* " Good-wish."—Italian.

" MUSTER OF SUSSEX AT THE BEGINNING OF THE REIGN OF JAMES I.

(Archæologia, vol. xv.)

Able men.	*Armed men.*	*Pyoners.*	*Demillances* *.	*High-horses."*
6200	2500	150	16	280

The number of *able men* thoughout England was 295,000. The number of *armed men* is stated in the " Archæologia" to be 1,400,000, which must be some very absurd mistake. The regular army, in the reign of Elizabeth, we have seen elsewhere stated at 111,000, including 40,000 Trained-bands.—*Ed.*

In 1621, it appearing that the harvest the preceding year had been unfavourable, inspection of the storehouses in Sussex is required, to ascertain what could be spared for other parts of the kingdom.

	£.	s.	d.
" 18 Oct. 1644, an ordinance for a weekly assessment for the relief of Ireland, Sussex . . .	104	3	4
" 14 Feb. do., monthly assessment to discharge expense of new modelling the armies . .	3927	15	6
" Do. do. for support of the Scots army . .	912	11	8

Burrell MSS.

OLIVER CROMWELL'S ASSESSMENT FOR SUSSEX.

	£	s.	d.
" From 25 Dec. 1647, to 25 March, 1648	7,134	15	5
25 March, 1648, to 29 Sep. 1648	13,952	13	0
Next half year . .	13,952	13	0

27,905 6 0

25 March, 1649, to 29 Sep. 1649	18,771	4	6
Next half year . .	14,207	14	6

18,771   4   6
18,771   4   6 } equal to about 2*s.* 6*d.* in the pound land tax.

37,542   9   0

" N. B. This is the account of William Alcock, receiver general of the monthly assessments for the county of Sussex, these sums came to his hands; it is possible there might be some deficiencies, and he observes that the salaries of the high collectors were deducted, and never came to his hands. So probably part of the year 1649 was equal almost to three shillings in the pound."—*Burrell MSS.* Sir W. B. has overlooked the monthly assessment specified above, which is at a much higher rate, nearly 60,000*l.* per annum.—*Ed.*

---

* *Demi-lance,* an officer so called. High-horses, it may be presumed, were the heavy cavalry who used Flemish horses. To " ride the great horse" was a term for merely learning to ride.—See *Memoirs of Lord Herbert of Cherbury.* —*Ed.*

VOLUNTEERS.

Extract from the Lewes Journal, 1779.

" Proceedings of a Meeting of the county of Sussex, held at the Town Hall, in Lewes, on Thursday, the 26th of August, 1779, in pursuance of an advertisement from the High Sheriff.

" It was then moved, and unanimously agreed to, ' that an offer be made to the King, to raise 24 companies in the county of Sussex, on the following plan, viz: that the number of companies, so to be formed, be not less than twenty-four ; each company to consist of one captain, one lieutenant, and one ensign, commissioned by his Majesty (having the same qualifications as are required for the militia), and of three sergeants, three corporals, two drummers, and sixty private men, at the least.

SUBSCRIBERS.

	£		£
Richmond	500	James Peachey	100
Egremont	100	H. Fetherston	100
Gage	100	George Medley	50
Abergavenny	100	G. L. Newnham	50
Pelham	100	I. Bridger	50
Geo. Hen. Lennox	50		

And a list of others at 20*l.* or 10*l.*

SUBSCRIBERS SINCE THE MEETING.

	£		£
Ashburnham	200	John Pelham	50
George Germain	100	Godfrey Webster	50
W. G. Hamilton	100		

And others at 20*l.* or 10*l.—Burrell MSS.*

We have seen that at the beginning of the 17th century the state of Brighton was flourishing, and its population considerable ; the latter is stated to have included 600 families, which at the usual estimate of five persons to each, gives 3000 inhabitants : we have also found that towards the middle and conclusion of this century it had suffered considerable reverses, from disturbance given to its trade, and from attacks of the sea ; and we conclude that at the epoch of 1700 the population was much diminished. Still greater misfortunes are now to be related. On Sunday, 27th Dec. 1703, a terrible tempest commenced at midnight and lasted during eight hours. Some houses were totally destroyed, many others unroofed, and the church leads blown up ; the town, it is said, looked like a place

bombarded by the enemy.   Great anxiety was felt by the inhabitants for their relations and friends, who were on the sea,
with much of their property.   Many ketches were lost, with
all or the majority of their crews, and several mariners belonging to the town perished in the Queen's ships.   One
man, from a vessel wrecked between the Downs and North
Yarmouth, supported himself for three days on a mast, and
was at length rescued.—*The Storm*, published by G. Saw-
bridge, Lond. 1704.

In 1705, occurred a second storm not less awful in its
effects; beginning at 1 o'clock in the morning, and manifest-
ing its greatest fury from 3 till 8.   Many houses were again
destroyed, and the church was unroofed.   Several vessels belonging to the town were stranded near Portsmouth, and others on
the coast of Newcastle.   The extent of the storm is proved by
the latter circumstance.   The remaining houses, under the
cliff, were now swept away, and " the Block-house, which
once stood in the middle of the town" (Dr. Relhan denies this),
" now formed its southern extremity."—*Lee*.   The Gates and
Gun Garden were daily, gradually, washed away.

The neighbouring parishes, which had been taxed for the
relief of Brighton, were found in the year 1708 to have evaded
the assessment, by making paupers of their own.   The justices
adopted the expedient of taxing the whole of the three Eastern
Rapes of the county three half-pence in the pound, to be applied
in aid of this impoverished place; but much opposition and
outcry was raised against it, and the magistrates, finding their
policy, or humanity, had exceeded their legal powers, were
obliged to abandon the scheme.—*Lee*.

The sea continued to encroach with alarming rapidity on
the cliff itself, having damaged all beneath it.   The necessity
of erecting groins was now felt to be indespensable to the
existence of the town.   A brief was accordingly obtained, to
help out their means, in 1727, and produced 1700*l*., rather a
large sum for that mode and time, and in its effect showing
the valuable utility of seasonable charity, for without this help
in time of need, the town might never have emerged from its

ruins. In the same year 10 guineas were expended in finishing the "public well." In 1733 "the almshouses" were sold for 17*l.* and a work-house built on the site.—*Ib.*

In 1736 the poor's rates were *eight pence* in the pound on the rack rent, which was then considered "an intolerable burthen."—*Ib.*

About the year 1700, small sums were collected at the Church on the three following occasions:—"The relief of poor captives in Turkey;" for "The distressed inhabitants of the Principality of Orange;" and for "The sufferers by fire in Inniskillen."—*Ib.*

The Author of a Tour through Great Britain, 1724, gives us a very melancholy picture of the reverses under which Brighton was then languishing.

" From this town, [Lewes] following still the range of the South Downs, west, we ride in view of the sea, on a fine carpet ground, for about twelve miles, to Bright Helmston, commonly called Bredhemston, a poor fishing town, old built, and on the very edge of the sea. Here, again, as I mentioned at Folkstone and Dover, the fishermen having large barks, go away to Yarmouth, on the coast of Norfolk, to the fishing fair there, and hire themselves for the season to catch herrings for the merchants; and they tell us, that these make a very good business of it. The sea is very unkind to this town, and has, by its continued encroachments, so gained upon them, that in a little time more they might reasonably expect it would eat up the whole town, above one hundred houses having been devoured by the water in a few years past; they are now obliged to get a brief granted them, to beg money all over England, to raise banks against the water; the expense of which, the brief expressly says, will be *Eight Thousand Pounds;* which, if one were to look on the town, would seem to be more than all the houses in it are worth."

A letter from the Rev. W. Clarke, rector of Buxted (who was grandfather to the celebrated and eloquent traveller), to Mr. Bowyer, dated July 22, 1736, is without these dark tidings, and seems to imply that the place had emerged from a state of extreme poverty, and was approaching one of tranquil mediocrity. The letter was published in the Gentleman's Magazine, 1810.

" We are now sunning ourselves upon the beach at Brighthelmstone, and observing what a tempting figure this island must have made in the eyes of those gentlemen who were pleased to civilize and subdue us. The place is really pleasant; I have seen nothing in its way outdoes it; such a tract of sea; such regions of corn, and such an extent of fine carpet, that give your eye the command of it all. But then the mischief is, that we have little conversation beside the *clamor nauticus,* which is here a sort of treble to the plashing of the waves against the cliffs. My morning business is bathing in the sea, and then buying fish; the evening in riding out for air, viewing the remains of old Saxon camps, and counting the ships in the road, and the boats that are trawling. Sometimes we give the imagination leave to expatiate a little:—fancy that you are coming down, and that we intend, next week. to dine one day at Dieppe, in Normandy; the price is already fixed, and the wine and lodging there tolerably good. But, though we build these castles in the air, I assure you we live here under ground almost. I fancy the architects here actually take the altitude of the inhabitants, and lose not an inch between the head and the ceiling, and then dropping a step or two below the surface, the second story is finished, something under 12 feet. I suppose this was a necessary precaution against storms, that a man should not be blown out of his bed into New England, Barbary, or God knows where. But as the lodgings are low, they are cheap: we have two parlours, two bed chambers, pantry, &c. for 5s. per week: and if you really will come down, you need not fear a bed of proper dimensions; and then the coast is safe, the cannons all covered with rust and grass: the ships moored—no enemy apprehended—

————— ' Nec tela timeres
Gallica, nec Pictam tremeres, nec littore toto
Prospiceres dubiis venturum Saxona ventis.' "

Our final extract, descriptive of this town in the first half of the last century, is derived from the " Magna Britannia," published, we believe, for we have not the date at hand to refer to, about the year 1740.

" It is an indifferent large and populous town, chiefly inhabited by fishermen, and having a good market weekly on Thursday, and fair yearly on . . . . . The situation is pleasant and generally accounted healthfull; for though bounded on the north with the Brittish Channell, yet it is encompassed on the other parts with large corn fields and fruitfull hills, which feed great flocks of sheep, bearing plenty of wool, which is thought by some the best in England. The state of the fortifications and town is this: there is a tradition that Queen Elizabeth thought this town worthy of her regard, and built four strong gates of free stone, three of which were arched twelve or thirteen feet high; but the East gate was the most notable, to which she joyned a wall fourteen or sixteen feet high, extending itself about four hundred feet to the westward. There is also another wall, three feet thick, facing the sea, and in it are many port-holes for cannon. About two hundred and fifty feet to the west end of this wall stands the Town Hall, on the east side of which is the market-house: it is a very strong edifice, in the form of a circumference, built with stone, seven or eight feet thick, and about eighteen feet high, and fifty in the diameter. The Hall is about thirty feet broad, and under it is a dungeon;

it faces the sea, and in its walls are several arched rooms, where the magazines are kept Before it, next the sea, is the Gun Garden, capacious enough for four cannon. This Hall stands in the middle front of the town, and on the roof is a turret and clock. The town contains seven streets, and as many lanes, but the most spacious is devoured by the ocean.

" About ninety years ago this town was a very considerable place for fishing, and one of the principal towns of the county, containing near six hundred families; but since the civil warrs it hath decayed much, for want of a free fishery, and by their ships being often taken by the enemy. The breaking in of the sea has, within these forty years, laid waste above one hundred and thirty tenements, which loss is computed about Forty Thousand Pounds; and if speedy care is not taken to stop the encroach-ments, the town will probably in a few years be utterly depopulated, the inhabitants being already diminished one-third, and many of those who remain are very poor, so that the rates for their relief are at the rack-rent of eight pence in the pound, there being few charities for their support. One of Mr. Barnard Hilton of 16*l.* per ann. with other small Benefactions, which make it amount to 20*l.*

" The church is a vicarage, but meanly endowed. The vicar claims the old episcopal custom of a penny per head, (commonly called smoak money, or a garden penny) as also he requires, as his due, a quarter of a share out of all fishing vessels.

" The parsonage tythes are about 100*l.* per annum, but are in the hands of an impropriator, who allows the vicar no benefit from them, by which means his maintenance is very small; and therefore the neighbouring gentlemen have augmented by a subscription of 50*l.* per annum, on condi-tion he shall instruct fifty poor boys of the town in reading and writing*. The church stands about forty rods from the town, at a little distance from the sea. There was formerly another church, near the middle of the town, which is said to have been burnt by the French."

———

" Jan. 1748–9. By reason of extraordinary high tides, the sea broke in at Brighthelmstone, washed away part of the Block House, and the farm lands called Salts, and did con-siderable damage to the lands adjacent."—*Burrell MSS.*

About the year 1750, visitants began annually to frequent this spot, but lodging-houses had not yet been put in re-quisition, the only accommodation was a few indifferent inns; their diversions were principally hunting, horse-racing occa-sionally only, and water excursions. The Wick spring was then first enclosed by Dr. Russell.—*Lee.*

In 1761, a battery of twelve 24-pounders, with an arched

* This vicarage is now, including the fees of the enormous population, currently estimated at 1200*l.* per annum.

room under it for ammunition, was erected, on the site of the " east gate," on the 17th of Nov. 1786. This battery, not duly protected by a groin, was undermined by the sea, and fell; 17 barrels of powder were in the lower room, and it was considered as a wonderful and providential escape that they did not explode from the concussion.—*Lee.*

The town, which, in 1766, is said to have become a very considerable one, still consisted of six streets only, all of which were situated westward of the Steyne.

The population does not appear to have increased rapidly. The number of settled residents in 1780 was only 3600; 1800 were then *inoculated*, of whom only 34 died. In 1794, the population was 5669; 1900 were at this time inoculated from the town, and 213 from the neighbourhood, and the deaths were only 50.—*Lee.*

A Dr. Awsita, in the year 1768, erected the first set of baths, at the pool between the Steyne and the sea.—*Ib.*

We close our *Ancient History* of Brighton, about the year 1770, with a brief allusion to the celebrated Dr. RUSSELL. Through his fortunate and philanthropic advocacy and confirmation of the grand practice of SEA BATHING, not only is Brighton indebted for all its unexampled prosperity, which it is hoped it will both preserve and merit,—or secure the former *contingency* by a public-spirited and generous attention to the latter *quality*,—but the whole land of Britain is under obligations public and private, which will not cease with the revolutions and generations of succeeding time. To his honour the following distich was composed, which ought to have been engraved in " enduring brass " in the most conspicuous situation in Brighton, nor less to live in the grateful recollections of all its inhabitants.

CLARA, PER OMNE ÆVUM, RUSSELLI FAMA MANEBIT,
DUM RETINET VIRES UNDA MARINA SUAS.

" Bright through all ages Russell's fame shall tower,
Whilst the sea-wave retains its healing power."

MODERN HISTORY.

Chance has thrown in our way, without any trouble, but with some expense, and as we conceive, not without some good fortune, a curious and probably *unique* collection of *Newspaper Extracts*, relative to Brighton, and Sussex in general, but more particularly the former, from the year 1770 to 1810, regularly arranged, in two thick quarto volumes. At the first named period, the *Lewes Journal* had been established, but the articles in question with a very few exceptions, are not derived from this source, but from a regular series of diffuse correspondence in the *London* papers, much of which was addressed to the *Morning Herald.* The perusal is exceedingly amusing; it introduces us, in the mind's eye, to the domestic and local details of a past, and differently circumstanced generation: and amongst other topics of great interest, developes the progressive increase and improvement of Brighton, Worthing, Eastbourne, and some other places, and unfolds the spirit-stirring details of important military preparations, and domestic anxieties, patriotism, and generous hospitality, during the long war with the then sanguinarily revolutionary powers of France. Several great characters are also brought on the scene; and we doubt not that many visitors of Brighton (to say nothing of the highest of all) may be not unpleasantly detained for a short time by our limited extracts, not exceeding a fiftieth part, from this copious repository. On their reception now, will depend their re-insertion in a future edition; that is, if the public are disposed to look with more favour on this little work after its publication than they have previously done. Should any reader be disposed to complain of their length, we beg him to observe, that no other subject has been unduly abridged to make way for them.

We are not called upon to institute any comparison between the manners and customs of that age and the present; and we have endeavoured to include such varied and miscellaneous articles as may suit the taste or curiosity of all parties; every thing inconsistent with decorum we have suppressed. If we may be allowed to express our opinion of the state of Brighton at that time, we think, that, whilst it was much inferior in size and magnificence, it was more social and happy than at present. The visitors appear to have associated with much freedom, and without any exclusiveness; and we read of no internal discords among the inhabitants—such as now (we earnestly beg not to be deemed uncharitable) threaten, if not checked by good sense and charity, to seriously affect its best interests.

" Discordiâ res *maximæ* dilabuntur."

On the other hand, there was more external dissipation, perhaps vice. Whether, upon the whole, the age has materially gained in intrinsic worth is another question; but it is *no* question that it has a Court, in which virtue and goodness are encouraged and fostered. One observation more, only, forces itself upon us. There were at least then no " Crockfords," or similar dens of gilded iniquity, not unfitly called by an infernal name, as being the causes and harbingers of misery, ruin, and untimely death; destructive to domestic happiness, health, and prosperity—to body and soul *.

Neither have we taken upon ourselves the office of panegyrists or apologists of the late King, the *second founder* of Brighton, after Dr. Russell, to whom (if for this alone) the inhabitants owe a debt of gratitude, which if they have not expressed they at least ought to have done so. Some characteristic traits, however, will be found here, which gave us much pleasure on the perusal, and we leave them to speak for themselves. We set out with a determination of speaking on all subjects, " without fear or favour," and we really trust the candid reader will not accuse us of having deviated from it.

The first journey of the Prince of Wales to Brighton, on a visit to his uncle, the Duke of Cumberland, then residing at Grove House, on the Cliff near the Steyne, took place in the year 1782. The town and Steyne were illuminated, and fireworks exhibited in front of Grove House, &c. &c.

------

* During the present month, November, 1832, has occurred the suicide of a respectable party in Regent Street, confessedly brought on by ruin at one of these accursed H——'s; and such events are currently reported in London to be by no means infrequent.

BRIGHTON *.

1761.

" *Brighthelmstone, June* 1.—Arrived here, Lord Abergavenny, Lord Bruce, Mr. and Lady Jane Evelyn, Lady Sophia Egerton," (and a long list of names of some rank.)

1771.

Extract of a Letter from Brighthelmstone, dated June 3.—" From the number of houses already taken, we expect to have a fuller season than was ever known here. Provisions are risen; and mutton and veal are at four-pence halfpenny the pound. Beef and lamb at five-pence. Fresh butter is sold at eight-pence the pound. We have likewise plenty of mackarel at two-pence apiece. Garden stuff is to be had tolerably reasonable. Our balls begin next week. A fishing boat was overset lately in a squall of wind, and of the two hands on board, one was saved, and the other lost, who left a widow and two children, she big with the third ; the company has generously opened a subscription for this helpless family."

1775.

Extract of a Letter from Lewes, Feb. 6.—" On Tuesday last (the wind blowing hard at south) was a prodigious high tide along our coast, whereby damages, to the amount of some thousand pounds, are sustained. At Newhaven, Mr. Martin had several stacks of corn five and six feet under water. At Brighthelmstone, part of the battery is washed away, and the water was so high there, that we hear it run in at the top of a chimney of a house that stood near the battery. At Shoreham, and further westward, many fields sown with grain are under water ; in short, the damage done is inconceivable."

Brighton, June 25.—" Arrived here the Duke and Duchess of Richmond, Duke and Duchess of Marlborough, Caroline and Eliza Spencer," &c. &c. (a very long list of names.) It will be observed, that it is here written *Brighton*.

1782.

Extract of a Letter from Brighthelmstone, Aug. 12.—" About seven o'clock yesterday morning, I was awaked by the firing of guns, which made me rise sooner than I should otherwise have done, and upon going to the beach, was informed that a French privateer, of sixteen or eighteen guns, and about one hundred and thirty men, had just taken a collier close to the shore. After having turned the collier's men in their own boat on shore (they only wanting the vessel) the Frenchmen put on board the collier from the above privateer, ten stout fellows, and then sailed away with their prize. This being observed from the ramparts, signal was given to a cutter, which happened luckily to be near, who directly made sail after the collier, and in about an hour and a half, retook her, and sent the Frenchmen on shore."

---

* Extracts relating to other places will be found under their respective heads.

Extract of a Letter from Brighthelmstone, dated Friday noon.—" We are all alive here, anxiously waiting the arrival of the Duke and Duchess of Cumberland, who are expected here this evening, four houses being taken for them and their suite. The Steine is to be lighted. We are very full; no lodgings to be had for love or money. Lord and Lady Stowell, the Duke and Duchess of Manchester, Lord and Lady Parker, Lady Dartrey, Lady Trafford and daughter, and the Baron and Baroness Nolken, are here. The bells were set a ringing for the arrival of Lord and Lady Fitzwilliam, who came in last night. Our master of the ceremonies' ball is fixed for Friday next, which is expected to be uncommonly crowded."

1784.

Equestrian Feat.—" Lewes, August 2.—At seven o'clock on Monday morning last, the Prince of Wales mounted his horse at Brighthelmstone, and rode to and from London that day. His Royal Highness went by the way of Cuckfield, and was only ten hours on the road, being four and a half going, and five and a half returning."

1785.

Extract of a Letter from Lewes, Sept. 12.—" The violence of the wind on Tuesday last occasioned the highest tide that has been known on this coast for a great number of years. At Brighthelmstone, the fishermen were put to the greatest difficulty in saving their boats, to effect which, many were under the necessity of hauling them up into the town, and others of lashing them to the railing on the bank; some few, however, that could not be secured, were dashed to pieces: had the storm happened in the night-time, the whole must have shared the same fate."

Extract of a Letter from Brighthelmstone, dated September 26.—" A gentleman a few days ago was bathing a little below the machines, and being very calm, he imprudently ventured further into the sea than what is customary. He had not been long diverting himself in the water, before he heard a noise, and discovered the fins of a fish above the surface of the water, which he soon perceived approach him very fast. Alarmed at this, he hastened out of the water, and had scarcely reached the shore, when a large tiger shark plunged after him with that violence, that it forced itself entirely out of the water on dry land. The shark, thus out of its element, had no power of retreating; and the geutleman who providentially escaped, recovering from his fright, collected a number of people, who with hatchets attacked this ferocious creature and killed it. On opening its stomach, the entire head of a man was found in it, no otherwise altered than being very soft and pappy, and the flesh and scalp entirely separating from the bone on touching it. The stomach was half an inch thick, and the shark was twelve feet in length from its head to its tail*."

Brighthelmstone, Sept. 3.—" At a general meeting of the subscribers to the rooms, held at the Castle this day, agreeably to the public notice, it was then unanimously resolved, that all persons who have their admission into

---

* N.B. To prevent unnecessary alarm, we may as well specify, that nothing of the kind has been heard of since.

the rooms during the season, that every non-subscriber do pay as under: —Monday and Wednesday, the ladies 3s. 6d., the gentlemen 4s. 6d. each. Tuesday, Wednesday, Friday, and Saturday, one shilling for every non-subscriber. N.B. Children under twelve years of age are not understood to be included in this last regulation. By order of the subscribers of the rooms—WILLIAM WADE, Master of the Ceremonies."

1786.

" The design of erecting a new theatre at Brighton is dropped; and if the manager of the present theatre endeavours to be a little more of the *fox*, and not so much of the *bear*, he may find it hereafter to his advantage."

1788.

Brighton Theatre.—" The bill for licensing anew the theatre there was read a third time, committed, and ordered to be carried up to the Lords."

Lewes, Dec. 22.—" Last Monday, we are told, the sand at Brighthelmstone, at neap-tide, was covered with a most beautiful sheet of ice, and such as would have afforded excellent diversion to skaiters, had there been any there to have enjoyed it; otherwise, we think, they would have embraced the opportunity of exhibiting in a scene so pleasing and novel as must have appeared, that of skaiting on the skirts of the ocean."

1789.

The Prince's Birth-day.—" The ball and supper were given at the Castle tavern by the Dukes of York and Clarence, and the cards of invitation extending to Lewes, as well as the immediate neighbourhood, the assembly was numerous and highly genteel.

" A very military and striking procession was presented by the javelin men, headed by Sir Ferdinando Poole, the sheriff. This order, which smacks so truly of feudal times, consists of the chief tradesmen of Lewes, from whence they proceeded to pay their respects to the prince. Their uniform is a superfine blue coat, buff waistcoat, and buckskin breeches, with other appendages, the effect of which was striking. Their swords were sustained by blue belts over the shoulder with crested plates. Their horses had blue and buff girths and breast-plates, and the head-dresses of the horses were also of corresponding decoration. The trumpeters, which preceded the procession, were dressed at the expense of Sir F. Poole; their coats were buff, with blue collars and cuffs, and blue waistcoats: they had silk banners to their trumpets, with heraldic bearings. The ordering of this procession depended in a considerable degree on Colonel Pelham; and it was observable that blue and buff cockades were assumed by all the country. Upwards of 500 people dined at the Castle; and an ox was roasted and distributed to the populace with plenteous supplies of strong beer. A very brilliant firework was played off, and a general illumination exhibited.—Brighton never was so joyous or gay before."

" Last Thursday night, a large portion of what is called the bank, between the sea and the Gun Inn, Brighton, suddenly gave way, and fell on the beach, which has occasioned the road there to be fenced off, to prevent accidents, until it can be repaired."—*Date lost.*

1792.

September 13.—" We are still occupied here, as no doubt every where else, with the developement of French affairs. The influx of emigrants begins to lessen, partly because the majority of the clergy are already come over, and because at Dieppe they have put a stop to our packets receiving them, they themselves fitting out their own vessels for the purpose. The subscription for the relief of the priests filled very fast, and was disposed of, by the committee appointed for that purpose, in relieving their present necessities and providing them the means of pursuing their way up to the capital."

September 20.—" This morning one of the packets landed five persons of distinction, one of whom was the Archbishop of Aix; the others were persons of condition, but cannot learn their names. They hired the packet for themselves only.

" This day another packet brought in twenty-six emigrants; and, at ten o'clock this morning, came over, in an open boat, Count Bridges, who was one of the household to the King of France, and in confinement with him, but found means to escape; after which he was concealed, till an opportunity offered to convey him to this place, for which he paid a large sum.

" By order of the Duke of York, an ox is this day roasted whole ;—while I write, it is distributing among the populace, together with ten barrels of strong beer, which will probably cause some broken pates ere night."

Monday.—" This morning, about twelve o'clock, the Duchess of York set out for town. At her departure, great crowds collected before the Pavilion, collected by curiosity to behold; and her highness's behaviour was such as impressed them strongly with the sense of her affability and condescension. Notwithstanding the unfavourable state of the weather, the royal trio rode out every day, attended by several of the nobility and gentry."

August 29.—" The Marchioness de Beaule is arrived at this place, in an open boat, for which she paid two hundred guineas at Dieppe. What adds to the distressing situation of this lady, she was under the necessity of appearing in the uniform of a sailor, and as such assisted the men on board during the whole passage, not only to disguise herself, but in order to bring with her undiscovered a favourite female, whom it is confidently said, she conveyed on board in a trunk, in which holes were bored to give her air.

" The marchioness was received, on coming on shore, by his highness the Prince of Wales, with Mrs. Fitzherbert and Miss Isabella Pigot. The prince, with his usual affability, escorted the fair fugitive to Earl Clermont's, where tea was provided for the prince and twenty of his friends."

*   *   *   *   *

" During the whole time, she was obliged to appear in male and mean attire. She once offered herself to a collier to work her passage as a sailor, but was refused; at length, however, urged by despair, and disclosing her real situation to the captain of one of the packets, he, with much humanity, contrived to bring her off, by concealing her under a coil of cable upon the deck (where she was, incredible as it may seem, obliged to lie for fourteen hours), and was landed safe here yesterday, exhausted with the fatigue and terrors she had undergone*.

" The prince, with that humanity and gallantry that so invariably distinguish him, has paid every attention to this amiable stranger. She this day rode out with Mrs. Fitzherbert.

" Another lady, whose name we have not learned, arrived also yesterday in an open boat, choosing rather to risk almost certain destruction by the sea (for it blew a hurricane all day) than to be exposed to the insults and cruelties of the worse than savages she has left behind."

1792.

" The emigrants still continue flocking over as fast as they can get away ; but great apprehensions are entertained by them for numbers left behind; who unable, though willing to escape from their enemies, and the time limited by the assembly for their departure being expired, it is expected they will fall victims to the savage and unrelenting fury of their persecutors."

" *Aug.* 25.—This morning their Royal Highnesses the Duke and Duchess of York took an airing on foot, and spent the greater part of the day in viewing the *new buildings* and the *cricket ground*. In the evening, their royal highnesses honoured the theatre with their presence."

" *Lewes, Oct.* 22.—Last Wednesday morning were landed at Black Rock near Shoreham, from the Prince of Wales Packet, Captain Burton, thirty-seven nuns. They were all from one convent, and most of them elderly ladies. None younger than forty. They were habited as nuns, and are all going to Brussels, where a convent is prepared for them.

" The packet lay some time off Brighton with a view to land them there, but the roughness of the sea prevented it; and it was no sooner known that they were to land at or near Shoreham, than almost every carriage in Brighton repaired thither to be present at their debarkation, and to assist in conveying them to Brighton, where every accommodation and every attention was shown to them. They had plenty of money. Their passage was not favourable, having been two days at sea."

1793.

" *Brighthelmstone Camp.*—The Duke of Clarence, it is said, wishes much to have the royal Surrey regiment of militia. His royal highness is so partial to them, that he has made them a present of a regimental colours, that is to cost 120 guineas—it is now embroidering."

We insert the following, both because it exhibits much good sense and feeling, and also to express our congratulation on the approaching extinction, great mitigation, or commutation,—with the concurrence, we feel assured, of our benevolent monarch,—of the terrible and too Draconic code of military and naval punishment, which has no antiquity to plead in its

---

* We rather think this refers to another lady, but something is here lost.—Ed.

behalf, and has been often, as we both read and know, almost
as painful to the feelings of the officers to inflict, as the men to
suffer.   This is an unmixed question, on which two opinions
can scarcely exist ; it is, indeed, a blessed " reform."

" *Camp, near Brighton, Oct.* 4.—Late last night orders were issued by the
Duke of Richmond, that the sentence of the court-martial should not be
executed on the soldier of the North Devon, till nine this morning ; this
delay was owing to the desire of the duke, to deliberate on a petition presented to him at the request of the soldiers, on behalf of their unfortunate
comrade ; it was signed by the officers and non-commissioned officers of
the corps.   The petition was laid before the duke by their major, Sir
Thomas Ackland, who was indefatigable in his endeavours to give it effect.

" At nine this morning the piquets of the whole line, and the North
Devon regiment, formed a square six deep.   The Duke of Richmond was
present ; and after the court-martial had been read, his grace addressed
the soldiers, and read to them the petition which he had received from
their major.   He then said, that the answer he meant to give to the petition,
he would read to them.   He began by making several judicious reflections
on the bad effects of want of subordination in soldiers ; reprobated, in
strong terms, the summary manner in which, in many instances, the soldiers
in camp had inflicted punishments on those who they thought had offended
them.   'But,' added his grace, 'if it were possible to aggravate such
unmilitary proceedings, it must be in the present instance, where an unfortunate—unprotected female was the object of vengeance.   It was disgraceful both to their characters as soldiers, and as men.   It had been
alleged, that this wretched woman was a prostitute ; but recollect, soldiers,
whether the crime for which you punished her, you had not been the means
of leading her into.'   Having insisted on this, in a style that affected the feeling
of the soldiers in a very sensible manner, and after paying the regiment some
handsome compliments on their good behaviour last war, &c. he added,
' that though the prisoner was no more guilty that day, than several
soldiers of every other regiment in the line, yet it was not to be understood
that for that reason, he was to escape punishment, &c.'   After having
shown this in a strong point of view, and informed the soldiers of their
duty to their officers, he then came to the subject of the petition itself,
which, he said, ' did honour to the sensibility of the men who felt so
severely for the credit of the regiment, in having one of their comrades
tried by a line court-martial, and in their promises of avoiding every cause
of censure from hence forward.   He was happy in saying, that a petition
drawn up in so soldier-like, manly, and modest a style, met his warmest
approbation, and gave him an opportunity of indulging his own feelings, ever
averse to punishment, by remitting the whole sentence of the court-martial.'

" The duke's speech made a sensible impression not only on the minds of
those to whom it was immediately addressed, but on the mixed crowd of
soldiers of the other regiments who were present.

" As soon as the piquets were ordered away, Sir Thomas Ackland seized
the moment of paying the duke an elegant compliment, by requesting his
permission to have his grace's speech printed, at the expense of the North

G. Scott, delin.

C.J. Smith, sculp.

BRIGHTON EAST.

For the History & Description of the Sussex Coast 1833.

Devon regiment. The duke seemed highly sensible of the compliment, said, that it should to-morrow be copied into the different orderly books, but that he did not wish it to be printed."

"*Brighton Camp, Aug.* 15.—On Monday, at three in the morning, we struck our tents on Ashdown Forest, marched at five, and at half past eleven reached Chely Common. Tuesday morning struck our tents at three, marched at four, and arrived on the hills over Brighton at twelve; the line of baggage, part of the heavy artillery, and corps of artificers, marched by Lewes, sixteen miles; the army took another route over the South Downs, two miles shorter.

"The novelty of seeing near 7000 men, with their park of artillery, battalion guns, &c. in one line of march, drew out the whole town of Brighton. Innumerable carriages of every description, and crowds of people of the first fashion covered all the hills, while the deep azure of the sea, on whose bosom rode a number of ships in full sail, the glittering of the arms on shore, and the beauty of the morning, added to the splendour of the scene, and filled the mind of every spectator with delight. As the columns moved down the hill, the Prince of Wales met them; the troops marched by in open ranks, the officers saluting—and, though the men were loaded with their tent-poles, camp-kettles, knapsacks, &c. and were kept marching one hour, in slow time, they showed the utmost steadiness, notwithstanding their fatigue. By two o'clock the camp was almost completely formed; the left is close to the town of Brighton, and stretches in a direct line along the coast. This has a fine appearance to the eye, and to preserve this effect the comfort of two regiments is destroyed, as the North Devon and East Middlesex are encamped on a newly ploughed field, full of sharp flint stones. Should any wet come, they will be in a deplorable situation; yet almost immediately behind these two regiments they might have pitched their tents on the finest turf in England; but this would not please the eye so well. The sea is close in front of the quarter-guard tents. The prince inserts in orders that no compliment is to be paid to him but as a colonel in the army."

SHAM FIGHT.

"The whole plan (if plan it may be called) was, an enemy attacking Brighton and the camp. The enemy consisted of eight regiments of infantry, with their battalion guns, under General Sir Wm. Howe; the others were four battalions of infantry, the light horse, and mounted artillery, who defended the country. The last general field-day, Brighton was denominated Dunkirk, and of course taken by the British, but names are nothing; yesterday it was not known which were the French. In this action none were killed or wounded; but one officer of the East Middlesex was made a prisoner, after a stout resistance, by his own major, his chief offence sitting on a drum, during the inactivity that generally prevails for hours in the field; the officer was put under arrest, but was, it is said, this day liberated. As the soldiers generally behaved well yesterday, this day was a holiday."

1794.

"*Brighton, Aug.* 17.—The public breakfast on Wednesday was attended by near 200 of the fashionable company of the preceding evening, and the fineness of the morning, together with the increase of music, for Col. Cart-wright had politely ordered the Prince of Wales's band to play alternately with the Dorset band, which had a most enchanting effect, and really makes this delightful shade the most desirable mid-day lounge about Brighton."

" The Prince of Wales's birth-day was celebrated in a style entirely new at this place; the *Promenade Grove*, which has the honour of being under his royal highness's immediate protection, was brilliantly illuminated, and elegantly decorated with transparencies, in allusion to the day. and opened in the manner of Vauxhall. So happy were the visitors and inhabitants of this very fashionable watering-place and its vicinity to join in the general mirth, that about nine o'clock upwards of 1200 people had assembled at these charming gardens, a number far exceeding any thing ever seen here; the coloured lamps were tastefully arranged around the saloon and other buildings. The principal transparencies were, the initials of G. P. W. wrote in coloured flowers, crowned with a wreath of laurel, and encircled with the British oak; the motto, 'Brighton's Support.' The band of music consisted of a choice selection from the different bands at the camps. In the course of the evening Mr. J. Mahon sung two songs with great execution and taste; the scene was entirely new, and though the company was so numerous, nothing could exceed the perfect good humour and good order that the whole concluded with."

" *Brighton, July* 22.—It is reported that the six regiments encamped here will remove for a few days to Seaford. When the harvest is got in, eight more regiments are expected to join them, which, added to the park of artillery, and the Prince of Wales's regiment, will form an encampment of 15,000 men, nearly double the number that were here last summer."

"Crawford exhibited a very beautiful illumination, yesterday evening, over the portico of his library, in consequence of the arrival of his Royal Highness the Duke of Clarence."

" The Prince of Wales and his brother are expected this evening at the theatre, to see the performances of Quick in the *Commissary* and *Miser*. As this will be the first time his Royal Highness has had an opportunity of visiting this place of amusement, there is no doubt but what the exertions of Quick, united with those of Townshend, Rock, Powell, and the Edwins, will cause a frequent repetition of his visit."

1796.

" *Brighton, Aug.* 10.—The Duke and Duchess of Marlborough, with their household, leave this place on the 17th inst. Six weeks is generally the allotted time for their graces residence here, but this summer they have overstopped their stay. The Duke of Marlborough's liberality affords a good and generous lesson to the other nobility who occasionally reside here; for the victuals and milk (the latter of which is a very scarce article in this town), that is left among the household, is distributed every morning, in parcels, to the poor of the place; a good day's provision for several of the fishermen's wives and children."

The late Duke of Marlborough, with his family, was, during many years, a regular, and also a munificent, visitor of Brighton, attended by his chaplain, Mr. Hoyle, a gentleman whose elegant and sterling poetical attainments are still at the service of the public. As regards the particular mode of charity specified, might it not be worthy the attention of many of the nobility who now visit Brighton? and in London it is still more needed. Without any mean restriction or *surveillance* of domestics, great things might be done in the aggregate by this judicious and benevolent foresight; and if any poor family can be supplied with a good meal from even the superfluity of the more abounding, the practice must excite pleasurable feelings, or the neglect self-condemnation. Perhaps, if inconvenient to individuals, there are associations in the town who would manage such a distribution, and a general depository might be established for the reception of the articles to be sent. Do not smile, reader: or, if you do, we have seen too many cases of misery to regard it. We have merely done what is very easy, thrown out the hint; if worthy of notice, it may be considered and improved by others.—*Ed.*

" Mr. Wade's benefit ball, on Friday last, they say, netted him a clear 500*l.*—a convincing proof that we must teem with fashion, taste, and spirit."

" Hollingbury Hill (or what the people here denominate Hollingbury Castle) is finely adapted for a grand review; here are evident remains of an ancient encampment; its figure also still remains complete, being a very extensive circle, which contains a number of tumuli, one of which has been opened to a considerable depth *."

" The Duke of Clarence's birthday was announced here by ringing of bells, &c. At ten o'clock, the Lanark and Dumbarton fencibles, with the flying artillery and the Monmouth regiment of militia, marched to the hill near Falmer, where they were joined by the Northampton regiment of militia, stationed at Lewes. The following new manœuvres were introduced under the command of Major-General Graham. The regiments marched in line, and retreated by battalions through each other. The front battalion retreated from the right or left of companies by files, and the rear battalion opened two or three files, opposite the heads of the columns, to let them through. After marching about one hundred yards, the retreating battalion formed: the front battalion then retreated the same way, never going off with unloaded arms. The battalion next changed their front by companies, firing twice as they came up. They then practised

---

* This description must be our excuse for not having seen this place, or the more famed " Devil's Dyke."—*Ed.*

charging in line after a volley, till they did it, a hundred yards at least, rapid and exact."

" The prince, after Lewes races, returns to town from Brighton, to be present at his name day, which is to be celebrated with much splendor at Windsor; after which he will resume his military duties with his regiment at Canterbury barracks, near which his royal highness has taken a small, but commodious residence."

" The raffling goes on merrily at Gregory's library, who has such a persuasive way with him of circulating the raffle papers about, that none can well refuse their names. The subscribers on his book amount to little short of 1000 names. The lowest subscription is five shillings, many half guineas, and guineas—a net profit, therefore, of about 300*l.* in less than three months."

" By a Gentleman leaving Brighthelmstone, on his observing a gilt Shark placed as a Weathercock on the top of the Church.

" Say, why on Brighton's church we see
A golden shark display'd,
But that 't was aptly meant to be
An emblem of its trade?

" Nor could the thing so well be told
In any other way;
The town's a Shark, that lives on gold,
The Company its prey."

1797.

" Amongst the variety of amusements which divert the crowded company of Brighton is that of the *Fantoccini* exhibition. The Duke and Duchess of Marlborough, Lord Charles Spencer, the Marquis and Marchioness of Worcester, Lord Abergavenny, Sir Harry Englefield, Sir Godfrey Webster, and every person of rank, letters, and distinction, at Brighton, have made this elegant amusement the favourite lounge of their evening recreation. The *Grove*, in which this exhibition is brought forward, has become the Vauxhall of Brighton, and in miniature surpasses it in taste, in brilliancy, and in elegant variety. The dramatic entertainments are enlivened and improved by the addition of a favourite and popular actor, Mr. Quick, who has performed successive nights to crowded audiences; and lest Brighton should be wanting in the mental and more refined amusements of literary conversations, the taste and genius of Monsieur le Texier are employed in giving the greatest satisfaction to the French cognoscenti, who embellish by their politeness these summer retreats."

HAIL STORM.

" *July* 30.—At about half after five this morning there was the greatest storm ever remembered by the oldest of our inhabitants. The firmament was streaked very thick with black clouds at a quarter before five, when soon after, came on such a violent and tempestuous shock of thunder, lightning, and hail, as alarmed the whole town, and roused them from their beds. The hailstones were *three inches circular,* and descended in such rapid torrents as to break every skylight in the place, and several windows. The cucumber-frames in Hicks's gardens, with his hot-houses, were entirely smashed, and the damages therein are estimated at above 40*l.* This relation may almost appear improbable, but we can vouch for its authenticity."

1798.

" *Brighton, August* 7.—The races concluded here on Friday, after three days excellent sport in the finest weather imaginable. The Downs, which give you delightful prospects of the sea, as well as the most complete views of the whole course, were crowded with company, and most of the first families of the neighbouring counties, to pay their respects to the prince, whose graceful attention and manners were highly gratifying to his visitors. The change of society and manners which has taken place at the Pavilion gives the most heartfelt satisfaction to every lover of his country; it is now every way worthy of the heir apparent of the British Empire. We had a most violent thunder storm in the evening, at the close of the races, which continued, almost without intermission, from nine on Friday night till six on Saturday morning. At one particular time, while some beautiful fire-works and rockets were displayed at the gardens, dark and heavy clouds, with tremendous thunder and lightning, spread over the sea, whilst the clearest sky and moon canopied the hills."

" *Brighton, July* 8.—This fashionable place is uncommonly thin for this period of the season. The imports of barbers and milliners are un-usually redundant; but the *haut ton* creep in very slowly. The Marchiones of Abercorn and her lovely daughter are the only ladies of particular dis-tinction as yet arrived."

" The West Essex regiment of militia had a grand field-day on Monday, but the rainy weather prevented many persons from being present on the occasion."

" It is not yet ascertained when the Prince of Wales will arrive this season, as there are no preparations going on at the Pavilion."

" The ladies are forming a subscription for the West Essex band, who contribute so much to their amusement in their evening promenades on the Steyne, by their musical excellence. A new library is established on the Cliff, and, in point of view and accommodation, bids fair to prove a formidable rival to those on the Steyne."

Tuppen's, we presume.

1800.

" *September.*—A fire broke out at a baker's opposite the Duke of Marlborough's, at Brighton, on Saturday night, and the Prince of Wales, with his usual humanity, received the unfortunate family, and exerted himself in protecting their goods, which were brought into the Pavilion."

" *Extract of a Letter from Brighton, dated Oct.* 25.—You will have seen in the papers an account of the sudden death of Captain Finnucane, of the Gloucestershire militia, now quartered at this place. The event itself, and still more the circumstances in which his family were left (a widow and five children being very scantily provided for), excited general compassion; but general compassion is too often satisfied with feeling for distress, and doing nothing to relieve it. This case has fortunately found not only pity, but protection."

" As soon as the Prince of Wales heard of it he desired the officer highest in rank here to wait on Mrs. Finnucane, in order to obtain a more exact knowledge of her situation, and to inform her that he meant to take two of the boys under his own immediate care. This he has done, and the children are to be sent to school, and completely provided for at his Royal Highness's particular charge. Of such an act it is unnecessary to say any thing; but that it was spontaneous and unsolicited, the fact speaks for itself, as would many others of the same sort, if they were more known."

1801.

" *Rejoicings for Peace. Oct.* 14.—On Monday, the joyful tidings of Peace were celebrated here; the bells rang from six in the morning till twelve at night; never was the satisfaction of the people more fully displayed. Young and old wore ribbons emblamatic on the occasion—*Peace* and *Plenty!* The sea fencibles fired a *feu-de-joie,* marched from thence to the Prince's house, and gave him three loud huzzas: with that liberality which has ever marked our royal guest, he ordered them two hogsheads of beer. Brilliant illuminations took place in the evening; the whole town appeared in a blaze. The most distinguished were those of his Royal Highness the Prince of Wales, flambeaux burning round his house, and every window lighted. This happy day closed with a ball and supper at the Castle, attended by near five hundred fashionable visitors; at one o'clock the room was opened with the most sumptuous entertainment; every delicacy that could be procured."

1802.

" The charitable donations and willing assistance which Mrs. Fitzherbert has, and continues to bestow on the unfortunate individuals of this place, have justly endeared her to the inhabitants of every description."

" Last month, a youth of Brighton was rescued from the watery grave, and restored to his father, &c. An application has therefore been made to the managers of the Humane Society of London, to extend its benefits and rewards to that place. On the 29th of July, it was resolved to establish a Brighton Humane Society, and Dr. Tierney has been appointed treasurer and medical assistant; Mr. Barret, with the other professional characters, were likewise elected medical assistants. It has long been the ardent wish of the faculty, and other philanthropists, that a Life-saving Institution should be set on foot at Brighton; it is now happily accomplished; so that the rewards to the common people, and the resuscitative process immediately employed, will be productive of numbers being restored alive to their parents and friends*."

AUCTIONS.

" The auctions at Brighton are now the rage in place of the raffles, which have been demolished by the left handed stroke of an act of parliament. At Fisher's, on the Steyne, which is the fashionable resort, a gold watch was put up a few nights since, and the auditors seemed to demur as to its value. ' Does the watch *go?*' exclaimed one of the company. ' It does,' replied the auctioneer, with a modest bow, ' but I am sorry to say, rather *slowly* at present!' "

———

" A considerable quantity of hams have been sent down to Brighton, and

———

* Is this still in existence?

this is an article of great consumption with the *Jews*, when *from home!* they are, in consequence, early at the market, calling for ' *de mutton* with *de thick rind!*' "

" *Brighton, April* 21.—A copy of the celebrated *Noli me tangere,* by Mengs, at the college of All Souls, Oxford, has been taken by Mr. Buckler, and fixed in the Chapel Royal here. The painting is extremely well executed, and reflects great honour on the talents of the artist."

" *Sept.* 18. – From a moderate computation of the buildings at present here in an unfinished state, and which will shortly be completed, the town, next season, will have the additional accommodations of upwards of *eight hundred* beds."

" The last gala at the Grove this season, with the grand spectacle of Mount Vesuvius, is announced for to-morrow night."

" *Brighton, June* 23.—The Prince of Wales's visit here, to examine the state of the Pavilion, is postponed, in consequence of Ascot Races, which his Royal Highness honours with his presence. The principal alterations and improvements in the Pavilion, which are now nearly completed, are an additional wing to the north, and another to the south of the east front, each containing an apartment forty-six feet in length, twenty-four feet six inches broad, and nineteen feet high. The room to the north commands an uninterrupted view of the Steyne and ocean ; that to the south, a delightful prospect of the extensive flat, and surrounding Downs. Apartments more tastefully contrived and executed can scarcely be imagined. In the western part of the structure is a new entrance hall, a magnificent staircase, and another of an inferior description ; a billiard-room, with an Italian stove, &c , forming, on the whole, an unparalleled display of modern elegance, neatness, grandeur, and simplicity, most happily combined."

" *Sept.* 18.—The Archbishop of Canterbury, Judge Graham, and many others of the first rank and consequence, attended divine service at the Chapel Royal, on Sunday ; at which place the Bishop of St. Asaph preaches a charity sermon on Sunday next, for the benefit of the School of Industry."

" A piece of ground for building, nearly opposite the west front of Marlborough House, was purchased by a lady of this place, a few days ago, at sixteen guineas a foot. It is considered here as remarkably cheap ; and should the lady repent of her bargain, it is supposed that there are many who would gladly take it off her hands at an advanced price."

" *Oct.* 10.—The Archbishop of Canterbury preached a sermon this morning at the Chapel Royal, from the sixth and seventh verses of the fourth Psalm :—' There be many that say, who will show us any good? Lord, lift thou up the light of thy countenance upon us. Thou hast put gladness in my heart, more than in the time that their corn and their wine increased.' The chapel was extremely crowded. The Bishop of St. Asaph, Judge Graham, and many of the most distinguished of the nobility, attended divine service. Captain Bloomfield was in the Prince's pew."

1803.

" At noon, yesterday, the corps of Sea Fencibles were drawn up on the battery to discharge sixteen rounds of forty-two pound shots, at a small boat, moored about half a league from the shore, with the French jack at the mast head. The first shot was apparently within a yard of the object; the second was somewhat closer; the third raked it fore and aft, carrying away its upper streak, and bringing its broadside to face the battery, when the fourth shot literally cut it asunder, and sent the disjointed bark to the bottom. Such is the singular proficiency of this corps in their discipline, and such will be the fate of the Corsican's flat bottoms, should they have the temerity to appear within gun-shot in this quarter. Sir Edmund Nagle, Captain Sproule, and several military officers, were on the fort, while groups of British belles were drawn up as spectators on the cliff, who loudly applauded the successful practice of the day, which (their object of attack having so satisfactorily disappeared) terminated on the fourth round, excepting that one gun was afterwards discharged, properly elevated, to ascertain how far, in case of necessity, it would throw a shot, and which, moderately speaking, struck not the water within the distance of a league."

"In consequence of the prediction of the French prophet, now something more than two centuries ago, but which, within this last week, has been the current topic of tea-table conversation, that the tide in the British channel would rise at least thirty feet perpendicularly above the level it ever reached before, on the twenty-fourth or twenty-fifth of February, 1803, several antiquated spinsters, and superannuated old bachelors, with a numerous retinue of lap-dogs and grimalkin companions, have actually removed from this place to Cuckfield, lest the prognostic should be verified, and the dreadful phenomenon overwhelm the town. They are expected to return to this place to-morrow, unless a recollection of the alteration which has been made in the style, since the prophecy was uttered, should recur to them, when, in all probability, they may deem it necessary to avoid the coast at least eleven days longer than they had first calculated as necessary."

ORIGIN OF BRIGHTON.

"About sixty years ago, Brighton consisted of a few thatched fishermen's huts, a considerable number of which were in ruins. A Sussex farmer, now living, who at that time had never seen the sea, remembers his journey thither; when his breakfast only came to three pence; an excellent dinner of beef-steaks for six pence; and the remainder of the shilling went to pay for his horse, and the ostler: to use his own expression, *they were so unaccustomed to the sight of a stranger, that they made, Sir, as great a to-do with me, as if I had been the King's son.* The Old Ship was then newly opened by Hicks; wheat was only four pounds ten shillings a load, and butter sold for four pence a pound. Lewes Races had been established about eleven years. The first patron of Brighton was Dr. Russell, who then resided at Malling, near Lewes; and one of the first patients whom he sent to bathe, was the wife of the late Rev. Wm. Clarke, Residentiary of Chichester, and Rector of Buxted. Mr. Clarke had the best house in Brighton, at the rate of five shillings per week!"

"The situation of Brighton admits of what Brown termed great *Capability:* trees with little trouble might be planted, and would certainly thrive, when sheltered by the adjoining buildings, from the sea winds. The improvements which his Royal Highness has made, and is still projecting, and the elegant house which Mr. Porden, an architect of uncommon merit, is raising for Mrs. Fitzherbert, will, I trust, check the listless torpor and selfish apathy which has too long prevailed at Brighton, will reflect a certain portion of taste and liberality on the sordid *Natives* of this *lawless waste,* and make them more worthy of the illustrious Patron, who, from a paltry village of fishermen, has formed one of the most delightful and fashionable Bathing Places that our coast presents, and which in time, we trust, will vie, as far as the difference of climate may admit, with the celebrated *Baiæ* of the Romans."

BRIGHTON GUN-BOATS.

" *Dec.* 14.—The Brighton fleet, consisting of forty strong boats, each mounting an eighteen pound carronade, are in a very forward state, and in a few days will be fully equipped to face the enemy, should he shew himself in this quarter. Loyal unanimity is every where the order of the day ; and the most brilliant success, should their courage ever be put to the proof, will, no doubt, attend the united efforts of the hardy volunteers of the coast."

ALARUM.

" *Oct.* 2.—The Prince of Wales, at the conclusion of the Concert at the Pavilion, some time after midnight, on Thursday last, addressing himself to Colonel Leigh, expressed an anxious desire to know in how short a time his regiment of dragoons could be under arms, and ready to face the enemy, should necessity require their exertions in the night. The Colonel immediately proposed, as the best method of satisfying his Royal Highness, instantly to ride to, and order an alarm to be sounded at the barracks, and afterwards return and give his Royal Highness a correct account of the conduct of his troops. This measure being approved by the Prince, the Colonel's horse was soon brought to the door, and he set off with all possible speed to see it carried into effect. On reaching the advanced guard at the entrance of the barracks, the Colonel commanded a black trumpeter on duty to sound to arms. The man, in obedience to the mandate, raised the trumpet to his lips ; but the surprise of the moment so greatly overpowered him, that he wanted breath to put it in execution. An English trumpeter, who overheard the order as he lay in bed, in an instant arose, dashed open the window of his room, and without waiting for further advice, put the bugle to his mouth, gave the proper signal, and the troops in every part were in an instant in motion. The greater part of the soldiers had been in bed many hours, the whole of them were properly accoutred, and on their horses, together with the flying artillery, in readiness to depart, in time sufficient to have reached Brighton within 15 minutes after the bugle gave the alarm. The barracks are situated something better than a mile and a half to the north of the town."

" *April* 24.—The example which the Nobility set here to the lower order of people, by attending divine worship on a Sunday, is productive of the most salutary effect; the respective churches and chapels, morning and afternoon, are literally crowded, and the most decorous solemnity prevails throughout the town."

" A letter from Brighton contains the following advice to Epicures:

' We have *John Dories, turbots, soles, mullets*, and *red gurnets*, jumping alive out of the sea; but as price is the true test of flavour, the Gourmands are assured that they are much dearer here than at Billingsgate. The *South Down mutton* is here in perfection, and floats about the dish in its own gravy upon the first cut. How it contrives to have either flesh or gravy is not for such a *sheepish* understanding as mine to develope, for the Downs on which it feeds are as bald as an old billiard cloth !' "

" A twenty-four pounder is shortly to be placed on the summit of the White-hawk hill, close to the signal house, to report, should it be necessary, a general summons to arms."

THE OFFICER AND POOR PUSS.

" *Aug.* 23.—The *Race-stand*, it appears, was set on fire through the carelessness of the family who had been permitted to occupy it. The conflagration, notwithstanding it happened about mid-day, was distinctly observable at a distance of upwards of thirty miles. Many people from various parts of the county, some on horseback, some on foot, entered the town during the succeeding night and day, to make enquiries respecting it, as apprehensions prevailed that the enemy had made a descent on that part of the coast, and was evincing his love to the natives by setting fire to their property.—It is somewhat singular, that as an officer of the Prince's regiment, attracted to the spot by the volumes of flame and smoke which ascended to the clouds, was reviewing the terrific encroachments of the devouring element, a cat, dreadfully singed and terrified, sprung through the blaze, and alighted on his shoulders. The officer, somewhat surprised, at first endeavoured to shake her off; but poor puss, firmly fixing her claws in his jacket, was not so easily to be got rid of. The officer, perceiving her reluctance to quit him, at length humanely determined, that as she had, in the moment of danger and affright, flown to him for protection, she should accompany him to the barracks. They accordingly descended the Downs together, and puss, well taken care of by her new master, affords much merriment to his friends, as he relates the particulars of the circumstances which first introduced them to each other."

" One of the largest fishing boats here, with nine passengers, the regular packets being either laid up for the winter, or on the other side of the water, sailed for Dieppe at 3 o'clock P. M. to-day."

" One of the fishing-boats, the first of this place which has been converted into a gun-boat, was furnished this morning with an eighteen-pound carronade by the Charlotte armed schooner, lying to off the town, and eight rounds, with shot, were presently after discharged, to ascertain if the boat could bear the shock of the explosion, which was doubted by many. The boat, we are happy to state, fully answers the purpose for which it is designed ; the shock of the explosion affected it not in the most trifling degree ; and it is now the general opinion that a forty-two pound carronade, in lieu of an eighteen, might be used in one of them with the greatest advantage and success. Sir Edmund Nagle, Capt. Sproule, Lieutenant Harvey, and a Lady, whose name we could not learn, &c. &c. were in the boat; the first gun from which was fired within a quarter of a league of the shore, having been previously levelled at one of the buoys, which was floating about a mile to the west, the wind blowing briskly from the east, when the ball dropped apparently within a few yards of the object. The following seven rounds were discharged at a greater distance in the offing. The Cliff parades were thronged with spectators; and the courage of the fair lady, who so bravely trusted herself in the boat, was the general theme of admiration. Fifty boats of this place, it is said, have been found fully competent for the uses of government, the greater part of which, in a short time, will have undergone the necessary alteration, which is simple and effective, and will present no trifling additional force for the protection and defence of the coast."

This lady was really a heroine. She would have made a suitable bride for " Sir Huon of Bourdeaux," or any noble-minded crusader or paladin of the olden time.

> " Over the dark blue waters,
>   Over the wide, wide sea,
> Fairest of Araby's daughters,
>   Say, wilt thou sail with me ?

> " Were there no bounds to the water,
>   No shore to the wide, wide sea,
> Still fearless would Araby's daughter,
>   Sail on through life with thee ! "

1804.

" The Nobility and Gentry of the county of Sussex have set a noble example, worthy the imitation of every other county in the three kingdoms, by the establishment of the Royal Sussex Jennerian Society, for the exter-mination of the Small Pox, under the immediate patronage of the Prince of Wales. Seventeen stations are already appointed at the principal towns in the county. In our opinion, nothing short of such institutions becoming general, will be able to effect that grand object, the extermination of the Small Pox."

A TOLERABLE PUN.

" *Oct.* 25.—As a gentleman yesterday was walking carelessly on the beach on the west side of one of the groins, his foot slipped, and he unfortunately fell over, a depth of some feet, into the sea. Happily, how-ever, the water, which was not very deep, prevented his receiving any injury from the hard stones at the bottom ; sensible of which, he remarked, on releasing himself from the briny element, that the *pickle* had certainly *preserved* him."

" Many of the fashionables from this place attended the last subscription concert of the season, under the patronage of his Grace of Richmond, at Chichester, on Thursday last. These concerts have a celebrity ratified by the test of years ; and we have no scruple in saying, that they are much superior to any regular establishment of a similar nature out of London ; and are more numerously and elegantly frequented. Lady Louisa Lennox, Miss Le Clerc, Colonel Lynn, and upwards of four hundred persons, were present."

" *June* 4.—This being the birth-day of our sovereign, the whole of the military of this district, regulars as well as militia, have been assembled on Newmarket-hill, in honour of the occasion, consisting of about 14,000 men; where, after firing a *feu de joie*, they were reviewed by General Sir William Pulteney. A royal salute, at mid-day, was also fired from the fort; and a ball for this evening is announced for the Castle. The Downs which overtop this place, during the whole of the day have presented a pleasing picture of bustle and hilarity, such as is seldom witnessed here, excepting at the time of the races; coaches, chariots, landaus, landaulets, sociables, curricles, buggies, whiskies, &c. and pedestrians and equestrians beyond all calculation, have been actively employed since eight o'clock this morning till the present time, six o'clock P. M.—The Steyne last night displayed an assemblage of pedestrians, numerous, elegant, and select. The Sussex band for some hours enlivened the cheerful throng by a skilful performance of some of their most favourite pieces. Generals Lennox and Dalrymple, and, of recent arrival, General Churchill, were on the parade. Many fascinating groups of beautiful belles also graced the walk. Towards sun-set a sight novel, and not uninteresting, attracted the fashionables collectively from the Steyne to the margin of the cliff and the water's edge. Several immense Porpoises, the largest of that kind we ever beheld, were observed occasionally to float on the surface of the water, within about a stone's cast of the shore. The sea was perfectly calm; and the variegated rays occasioned by the expiring lamp of day gave a sparkling and crimson hue to the sombre skins of these gigantic inhabitants of the deep, as they severally appeared apparently sportively engaged in the briny element."

" The royal munificence and splendour displayed at the Pavilion, on Friday evening, is here still the prime topic of conversation. His royal highness thus having contributed to the happiness of the higher order of society, on the following day also gave cheerfulness to the spirits of the poor, by commanding that his usual annual bounty, to the amount of fifty guineas, in bread and beef, for their relief, should be doubled; and the above articles, to the amount of one hundred guineas, on Saturday were accordingly distributed among them."

To " tell truth and shame the devil," as we have generally done in this little work, we should have supposed, from the liberal character elsewhere ascribed to the prince regent, that the regular annual bounty would have been four or six times the amount. In a Brighton paper of last winter, we remember to have seen it stated, that the *private* benefactions of the present king and queen, though not publicly announced, were very considerable indeed; and that more than one person was charged to report to them every case of distress, which was promptly relieved.

" The following extract of a letter received here, from a gentleman who lately passed through Holland, &c. on his route to Dusseldorff, may not be unacceptable :—

" The Dutch daily become more dissatisfied with their friends, the French, requisitions upon requisitions being unceasingly made to distress them. One hundred millions of guilders have been recently demanded, of which seventy millions are already paid, and a time specified for the advancement of the remainder. Every man capable of bearing arms, between the ages of sixteen and forty, is also required to assist in the invasion of England, which appears to have given the Dutch the most sincere affliction, though they dare only express their real sentiments in private. The Dutch, in fact, wish all possible success to the British, and rightly conjecture that their future welfare must entirely depend on the prosperity of England. The French themselves do not hesitate openly to declare their fears that inevitable destruction awaits them, should they even succeed unmolested in crossing the *Herring Pond,* the moment they place their feet on the *terra firma* of Albion."

1805.

" *August* 13.—The splendour of rank, the elegance of fashion, and interesting display of female charms, which distinguished the Castle rooms last night, are still here the grateful theme of public animadversion. The supper rooms could not half accommodate the company present: the tables, consequently, on the removal of the first party that surrounded them, were presently occupied by a second, and so on to the third and fourth. The prince was dressed as a field marshal, and looked remarkably well. The Duke of Clarence wore a plain blue coat; the Duke of Kent the uniform of his own regiment, scarlet faced with green. We did not observe the Duke of Sussex in the ball-room. The illuminations, generally speaking, in the town, were in no wise adapted to the occasion. The Theatre, however, was very splendid ; variegated lamps, a blazing star, surmounted with the feathers, and the initials P. W. in front of the building, had a very brilliant and appropriate effect. Mr. Burfield's variegated lamps were very tastefully displayed. Mr. Pearson's variegated lamps ,the feathers, and P. W. ; Donaldson's Library, variegated lamps, with G. P. W. ; Wilkes's Library, the feathers, and P. W. in variegated lamps ; the Coach Offices of Gourd, Crossweller, and Bradford, were all very brilliant; Mr. Cooke, a transparency over his door, with the inscription, ' Long live the Prince.' A few others, whose names we cannot immediately recollect, paid also the requisite attention to the evening."

PAVILION.

" On Friday and Saturday the prince, attended by Colonel Leigh and Colonel Hanger, rode for several hours. Soon after six o'clock, on the former evening, his royal highness, in his carriage, left the Pavilion, to dine with the Marchioness of Downshire, at Westfield Lodge. Among the *elegantes* present on this occasion were, Lord and Lady Harrington, the beautiful and accomplished Lady Ann Maria Stanhope, Mrs. Fitzherbert, Baron Eben, Colonel Hanger, Colonel Leigh, &c. forming, on the whole, a select and sociable party of fourteen. The dinner was of the most brilliant and inviting description ; and the dessert consisted of all the rarities which art or the season could produce. About nine o'clock the prince, the marchioness, and the whole of her guests, from Westfield Lodge, removed to the Pavilion, where a most splendid entertainment, consisting of a ball and supper, &c. was given by the prince, and of which the greater part of the most distinguished persons here at present partook, in number somewhat exceeding one hundred and sixty. Though the whole suite of apartments were not lighted up on this evening, yet, as we have previously promised a description of them, we conceive the present opportunity a favourable one for the performance of the task. To give an accurate relation of the whole of these superb apartments, as they are enriched and beautified, would extend far beyond the limits of a newspaper: we shall, however, endeavour to impress our readers with a faint idea of this superb and enchanting place. From the west, or back front of the structure, you arrive at the grand entrance hall, the colour of which is of a warm clay, with blue and red mouldings. It is thirty-five feet square, and twenty feet high, and is tastefully embellished in the Chinese style. A light Chinese gallery, with an awning, very tastefully designed, crosses it; beneath which are placed Chinese figures, as large as life, habited in the costume of the country, each holding a lantern, glazed with coloured glass, on which are represented flowers, &c. peculiar to the eastern world, very neatly executed, and very beautiful in effect. From this hall you pass to the anteroom, which is decorated with nine very fine Chinese paintings (done in China), representing the manners of the people. The frames of the pictures are novel and striking; the tops are ornamented with trophies of war and military weapons of the Chinese. The ground of this room is scarlet, and it displays the paintings to the utmost advantage. From this you remove to a small drawing-room, the ground of which is bright yellow. On the walls are six Chinese paintings, of the same description as the former; the frames, however, being different, and the tops of them are ornamented with Chinese embellishments, articles of dress, musical instruments, incense pots, &c. &c. The communication of this apartment to the next is, perhaps, the most strikingly beautiful of all that the most exquisite art and refined taste have hitherto invented, of a similar description, to fascinate the eye in this country. It is entirely formed of stained glass, exhibiting the peculiar insects, fruits, flowers, &c. &c. of the Chinese country; and when you are within it, it has the appearance of, and literally is, a magnificent painted Chinese lantern, twelve feet long, and eight feet wide, brilliantly illuminated on the exterior, which shows its transparency, and produces an effect too exquisite to be described. From this you enter the last apartment to the south of the building, called the conservatory, though it is more often distinguished as the music-room. It is fifty feet long, thirty feet wide, and twenty feet high. The roof is painted in imitation of the tea and rose wood, and is supported by twenty columns of a scarlet colour, with the five clawed dragons twining round them. The sides are covered with a Chinese historical paper, superb in appearance, and brilliant in effect. Returning to the ante-room, on the left, you pass to the spacious rotunda, or saloon. This room forms an oblong of fifty-five feet. The ceiling is the best contrived and executed we ever saw, and represents a clouded sky, from which are suspended by flying dragons, not chandeliers, as formerly, three immense Chinese lanterns, on which are seen the *faum*, or bird of royalty, in all its rich and variegated plumage, and such as in China, we believe, is only permitted to ornament the palace of the emperor. The cornice and frieze of this magnificent apartment are scarlet, blue, and yellow, before which hangs a yellow silk net, with tassels and bells, splendid in effect, and is perfectly *unique*. The cornice is supported by four columns and eight pilasters, with dragons twisting round them, &c. A light corridor or charmingly painted gallery passes round the dome, from the open work of which eight dragons appear in the act of flying through, each suspending, by an elegant chain, a painted Chinese lantern, though of much smaller dimensions than the three former. In these lanterns are upwards of thirty Argand burners, which diffuse a brilliance almost equal to the blaze of the finest day, and exhibit the panelled sides of the room, and a beautiful Chinese paper of a blue ground, the ornaments of which are white etched with silver, interspersed with birds of the richest plumage, and which literally appear animated, and fascinate the beholder. You next proceed to the long gallery. This room is fifty-six feet in length, and twenty in width; the walls are covered with an expensive and very beautiful Chinese historical paper. The room adjoining to this is the last to the north, and is generally distinguished as the banqueting-room. This apartment is of the same dimensions as the conservatory or music-room, at the extremity to the south, but the ceiling is clouded.

" The furniture of this superb palace corresponds with the magnificence of the rooms. Mirrors of the largest dimensions, and most elegant description, are seen in all parts, reflecting the indescribable beauties of the place, and producing an effect such as must be seen to be understood, for without which no person can form an adequate idea of its transcendent splendour. The wood-work throughout the structure, the doors, shutters, &c. &c. are painted in imitation of the woods in China. The corridors and staircases are of the same colour as the hall, but ornamented in the peculiar style of the Chinese covered ways. The wood-work and painting are very highly varnished. The whole suite of apartments are illuminated with Chinese lanterns. The furniture is all in the Chinese style, and is of the most rich and rare description. Sofas, chairs, tables, candelabras, &c. correspond in elegance, and splendour of effect. China jars, Mandarine figures, dragons, and every rare specimen of ornamental china, together with cabinets, japanned screens, &c. are in the richest profusion. The rooms illuminated on Friday evening were, the banqueting-room, the long gallery, the grand saloon, the ante-room, and the entrance hall. In the long gallery the company danced. The ball was opened about half-past nine o'clock, by Colonel Fuller, and, we believe, Lady Ann Maria Stanhope. Nearly thirty couple followed, to the agreeable air of Lady Down. The prince looked in extreme good health, and was in most excellent spirits, making happy, by his condescensive affability and polished manners, the elegant crowd by which he was surrounded. In the course of the evening his royal highness danced a waltz with the accomplished Princess de Gerebtzoff. The dresses of the ladies were splendid to a degree. The prevalent dress was white; the hair out of powder, and ornamented with a profusion of diamonds. Marchioness Downshire was habited in white satin, tastefully embellished with diamonds to an immense amount. Many of the most beautiful women we ever saw were present; and never did they appear more interesting and lovely. About one o'clock dancing ceased, and the company removed to the supper-rooms, the tables of which were covered with every delicacy; nor could the taste and elegance of their arrangement be surpassed. About two o'clock the *elegantes* were once more engaged in the ball-room; and about three hours subsequently they, highly gratified with the princely entertainment they had received, began generally to retire. Mr. Sheridan, who arrived here the day before, was of the royal party. On the night following (Saturday) it being the natal day of the little interesting *protege* of Mrs. Fitzherbert, Miss Seymour, this young lady gave a ball and supper to a party of juvenile nobility, at the Pavilion. On Thursday next, according to annual custom, the servants on the royal establishment will be treated with a ball and supper at their royal master's expense. The prince was on the Steyne for a short time before dinner to-day."

" *Oct.* 1.—The town, since the departure of the prince, has been, comparatively speaking, very dull. The rides and walks, however, both yesterday and to-day, have displayed much elegant company. The prince is expected to dine at the Pavilion this evening. The Duke of Clarence returns to this place with the prince. The Duke of Cambridge, we hear, leaves his royal brothers after the review to-day, near Beachy Head, to return to Eastbourne; and from thence to London. Last night there was a dress ball at the Castle, at which, in consequence of the absence of the prince, the company were much more numerous than fashionable. The merry dance commenced, about a quarter before ten o'clock, with the lively air of Lady Caroline Lee's reel, and finished, at about half past one o'clock in the morning, with *Molly put the Kettle on* *."

" The Cygnet weighed anchor, and stood out to sea last night. Scarcely a ship of war has been perceptible from this place the whole of the day."

" One shilling per man was given by the commander-in-chief, after the review on Saturday last, to the privates of the respective regiments on that day engaged, to drink his majesty's health, and to cheer their spirits after the severity of the practice. There were upwards of four thousand men in the field that were entitled to partake of his royal highness's bounty, which consequently amounts to something better than two hundred pounds."

" The Duke of Clarence's three sons were actively employed with their muskets, in receiving the instructions of a serjeant of the South Gloucester Militia, on the Pavilion lawn."

MORNING AIR.

"A few pedestrians of rank here seek health by visiting the steeps at an early hour in the morning, from whence they return refreshed, and with keen appetites, to the breakfast-table. The apothecaries say, that such customs ' are more honoured in the breach than the observance;' for if such practices were general, but few nervous patients would be found, and physic become a *mere drug*."

---

* *Tempora mutantur!*

" *Dec.* 5. This being the day appointed for the general thanksgiving for the late brilliant success of our arms, the same solemnity and decorum has distinguished this town as is usual on a Sunday. The prince attended divine service at the Chapel Royal, where an excellently appropriate and very impressive discourse was delivered by the Rev. Mr. Portis from the 103d Psalm, the 1st and 2d verses:—' Bless the Lord, O my soul! and all that is within me, bless his holy name—Bless the Lord, O my soul! and forget not all his benefits.' In the pew with his royal highness were Colonel Leigh and Mr. Day. After the service, a very handsome collection was made for the Patriotic Fund, the particulars of which have not yet transpired. At the parish church an excellent sermon was preached by the Rev. Mr. Carr. No collection for the Patriotic Fund was there made, as we hear the worthy minister intends personally to visit the individuals of his parish for their donations for so truly praise-worthy a purpose. Both the church and the chapel royal were immensely crowded.—At three o'clock this afternoon, the South Gloucester Militia were drawn up, without arms, on Marlborough Steyne ; when, in consequence of the whole of the privates of the regiment, two only excepted, having signified to their officers their desire of contributing one day's pay to the Patriotic Fund, Lieutenant-Colonel Wall, in a true soldier-like speech, addressed them on the subject. Their conduct, the colonel observed, was highly honourable to themselves both as soldiers and as men, and was such as had afforded their officers great satisfaction. ' It is their intention,' the colonel continued, ' that the request you have made shall be granted. The amount of one day's pay, *in your name*, is to be sent to the Patriotic Fund ; but your officers, in testimony of their esteem of your handsome and feeling behaviour, beg that the whole amount may be paid by them. The act is yours, though the expense will cheerfully be submitted to by them, and to you only will the full credit arising from it attach.' The colonel then dismissed them, remarking that he did not wish them to consider the day altogether as a day of humiliation and self-denial, but as a day of prudent mirth and rejoicing ; wherefore, he should exempt them from their military duties, and dispense with their attending the parade practice that evening. The liberal conduct of the South Gloucester officers on this occasion is, at present, the grateful topic of Brightonian conversation."

It is hard to say whether this was more creditable to the officers or soldiers.

———

" *Dec.* 11.—It was at one time understood that there was not to have been a collection made at the church-doors on the day of thanksgiving, but that the minister, Mr. Carr, would wait on the individuals resident in the town for their respective voluntary contributions in support of the Patriotic Fund. It appears, however, that a collection of between fifty and sixty pounds was made at the church on that occasion. At the Chapel Royal, the collection amounted to nearly ninety pounds. Collections were also made at the Huntingdonian Chapel and the Presbyterian Meeting-house ; at the former place it amounted to twenty-five pounds, and twenty-three pounds at the latter. A contribution of ten pounds was likewise sent from the Jewish Synagogue."

1806.

" Another fall of the cliff to the east took place here a day or two ago. When too late to secure the property in that quarter, in all probability the householders will submit to the expense of erecting groins "

STRIKING WIT.

" An attorney, in presenting a copy of a writ to an auctioneer at Brighton not long since, apologised for his unfriendly visit, and concluded with hoping that the other would not be offended, as he was but merely performing an unpleasant duty of his profession. ' Certainly not,' said the auctioneer; ' you must attend to the duties of your profession, and so must I to mine.' This said, he instantly *knocked him down*."

" *March* 21.—The plan of the intended harbour has drawn crowds of people, of all ranks and description, to the Old Ship for some days past; Admiral Southerby, and a few other high naval characters, were of the assemblage there on Wednesday last. The inspection of the plan, however, operates differently on different individuals, and the opinions regarding it are multifarious and unsettled."

" The inhabitants of this place are at present in some little degree of commotion, in consequence of the bill brought forward by one of the county members, Mr. Fuller, and passed once in the House of Commons, for a jutty or jutties to be erected on this part of the coast, and immediately in front of this town. The inhabitants here are generally of opinion that such a measure, if ever it were to be carried into effect, would prove very destructive to their interests, and, as such, they feel themselves perfectly justified in exerting their united efforts to prevent it."

" On Wednesday there is to be a meeting at the Old Ship of the householders of this place, regarding the establishment, long talked of here, of a regular police, and at which great contrariety of opinions, much noise, discord, and confusion is anticipated."

" *July* 3.—Yesterday there was a general meeting at the Old Ship, respecting the communication which had been made from the Prince of Wales to Mr. Ryecroft, for the incorporating of the town of Brighton, and the establishment of a regular police. The meeting was more numerously and respectably attended than any which on that subject had preceded it, and at which all necessary matters were very ably and dispassionately discussed. After a debate of several hours, the incorporation by charter was unanimously negatived, and an address of thanks was as unanimously voted to his Royal Highness, for the condescensive and kind interest which he, at all times, took in the welfare of the inhabitants of the town. The Rev. Mr. Carr was in the chair. During the above debate, it was made known that the Prince had no particular desire that the incorporation by charter should be adopted, unless the inhabitants of the town should conceive that such a measure would promote their interests; and that any other mode which they might better approve of, for the impartial administration of justice in the place, should be honoured with his royal sanction."

STURGEON.

" A sturgeon, weighing between seventy and eighty pounds, was brought on shore here on Friday last by a fisherman. A sturgeon is a very rare fish in this market, so rare, in fact, that the fish buyers are ignorant of its value. Half a guinea, and subsequently two pounds, were offered for the fish in question; but the fisherman was advised not to part with it at so moderate a price. As the only method of getting it off his hands, with a prospect of fair advantage to himself, he therefore carefully packed it up, and sent it off by one of the coaches for the market at Billingsgate, where it ultimately produced a sum within a few shillings of eight guineas."

BENEVOLENCE.

" A Cyprian here, a day or two ago, from pecuniary embarrassment, being wrought to a pitch of desperation, determined on an act of suicide, and actually threw herself into the sea. Happily she was observed by a Mr. Colwort, who, though there was a heavy swell in the Channel at the time, plunged into the briny element after her, and preserved her life. By this worthy gentleman a subscription was soon after opened at Raggett's, and thirty guineas were presently collected for the poor girl's relief."

We may be allowed to say, that this was very creditable to all parties concerned, as, no person in distress, however unhappy or criminal, should be thought beneath the notice of the best—the best, did we say?—by them they assuredly will not. Few situations are more pitiable than those of persons similarly circumstanced to the unfortunate individual here mentioned. Not always wilfully and perseveringly guilty; often the deserted victims of baseness and heartlessness! who having passed the Rubicon, find no friendly hand extended to invite them back, and restore them to their friends, with some hope and chance of comparative happiness again dawning upon them : not always either deserted by all their better tastes and feelings, any more than superior manners, instances of which have not unfrequently been seen and noticed by many *. If, therefore, any occasion should occur where desperate affliction like the above should be indicated or even expected, we may say, not on insufficient, but on the best and most beneficent authority, " go and do likewise." Is it to be supposed, that any superiority of conduct, if ever so brightly robed in virtue,

* Reference may be made to the *Morning Herald* of Dec. 3, 1832, or any periodical of that date, relating an incident which occurred Nov. 26. We cannot admire the conduct of the official gentleman there concerned.

ought to render any others the objects of contempt alone and not pity? That will be the very Pharisaical antipodes to the spirit of Him whom they perhaps profess to follow as their Lord and benefactor. And if the diamond shield of mercy be extended before any unfortunate person, who is qualified to throw the first dirty pebble at it? "Give every one his deserts, and who shall escape whipping?"

LIBERAL ENTERTAINMENTS.

" *Aug.* 12.—At the Pavilion dinner yesterday, the Prince entertained five of his royal brothers, the Dukes of York, Clarence, Kent, Sussex, and Cumberland. Of the splendid party were also the Duke of Orleans, M. Beaujolois, the Marquis of Winchester, Count Stahremberg, Mr. Sheridan, Colonels Turner and Lee, &c. This being the natal day of the heir apparent, the morning was ushered in by the ringing of bells, and the flag was hoisted on the tower of the church. Two oxen, *pro bono publico*, are roasting whole on the Level. Such an agreeable bustle as this town at present exhibits, was never witnessed here before. Business is totally given up, and pleasure is the standing order of the day. At ten o'clock A.M. the Otter sloop of war, decorated with the colours of all nations, hoisted the royal standard at the main, and announced the event by a discharge of her guns. The Gallant armed brig, the Calypso armed brig, and Earl Craven's yacht, were also dressed out with colours. About this time the Carabineers from Shoreham, and the Fourth Dragoons, passed to the north and south of the town for the Downs. The Artillery, the King's Dragoons, and the Nottingham and South Gloucester Militias were under arms as early as four o'clock in the morning. At half-past twelve o'clock the Prince of Wales, habited as a field-marshal, a star at his breast, accompanied by his royal brothers and a numerous suite of Noblemen, &c. and mounted on a gray charger, splendidly caparisoned, left the Pavilion for the Downs, where the following regiments were drawn up in line in the same order as they are named, beginning at the right wing:—the Royal Horse Artillery, the 1st regiment of King's Dragoon Guards, the 4th Dragoons, the Royal Cheshire, the South Hants, the Nottingham and the South Gloucester Militias, the Carabineers, and the Foot Artillery from Lewes. The royal brothers were all in regimentals, with stars at their breasts. The Duke of Sussex wore his Highland uniform. The Earl of Moira, General White, Count Beaujolois, Lord E. Somerset, the Earl of Barrymore, &c. were in the Prince's suite. Lady Haggerstone and Miss Seymour, the Lord Chancellor, Lord Headfort, Mr. Sheridan, and Mr. Smith were in the Prince's landau. Mrs. Fitzherbert was detained at home by indisposition. As soon as the royal cavalcade was distinguished by the military on the Downs, signal guns were discharged, and every necessary adjustment was in an instant made for its reception. The royal party now advanced, and passed down the centre of the line, each regiment saluting, and the bands alternately playing God Save the King. Having reached the extremity of the line, the cavalcade turned back, and the commander-in-chief and staff, Earl Moira,

Lieutenant-general Lennox, Major-general Huguenin, Earl Craven, &c.
took their stations in the centre of the line, the Prince and the other Royal
Dukes facing them. The whole line now saluted the Prince. This ended,
the line passed the Prince in review order, to slow time, as follows: first,
Captain Downman and the Royal Artillery, the Commander-in-chief and
Staff, Earl Moira and Staff, Lieutenant-general Lennox and Staff, Major-
general Huguenin and Staff, Earl Craven and Staff, the King's Dragoons,
the 4th Dragoons, the Cheshire, South Hants, Nottingham, and South
Gloucester Militias, the Carabineers, and the Foot Artillery; the bands of
each regiment wheeling off, and playing until the regiment to which they
were attached had gone by. The regiments again passed to quick time,
the Duke of York, &c. having stationed themselves with the Prince of
Wales. The line was again formed, when a *feu de joie* was fired in a very
capital style. Huzzas and God Save the King concluded the proceedings
this day on the hill, when a signal was hoisted at the telegraph for the
shipping to salute, which was instantly obeyed; and every house in the
town was shaken by the explosion. In this splendid review the Royal
Cheshire Regiment of Militia particularly distinguished itself. The best
military judges were of opinion that it could not be surpassed by any regiment either in Great Britain or on the continent. The princes returned
to the Pavilion about half-past three o'clock. At six all the splendor and
fashion of Brighton were assembled to dine at the Pavilion."

" *Tuesday Evening.*—The crowd on the Level in number are many
thousands; and his royal highness's butcher, Russell, habited in a white
jacket, the sleeves ornamented with buff and blue ribbons, with a blue sash
containing the words ' Long Live the Royal Brothers,' with a white apron
and steel, and a fanciful cap to correspond, has just given the signal for the
grand carver to do his duty. The acclamations of the multitude are deafening, and all now is confusion, expectation, and joy. The Nottingham
Militia, whose encampment adjoins the public kitchens, are busy actors in
this scene. They distinguish themselves manfully, and many a heavy
joint, after severe struggles for victory, is borne by them triumphantly to
their tents. Amongst the splendid party at the Pavilion are, the six royal
brothers, the Lord Chancellor, Earl Moira, Count Beaujolois, Mr. Sheridan,
Mr. Tierney, with a numerous assemblage of persons, the most distinguished for their rank and talents. Two bands of music, the Prince's own
and the South Gloucester, play alternately on the lawn. The Steyne is
crowded with pedestrians. The town is generally illuminated: Pollard's
and Donaldson's libraries have both a very brilliant appearance. The
Theatre, Fisher's Lounge, Mr. Russell's the Old Ship, the New Inn, the
Coach Offices, Blaker's, Alexander's, and the greater part of the houses
about the bottom of North-street, are also lighted up in a very radiant
style. At ten o'clock the princes and the whole of the royal dinner-party
left the Pavilion for the ball at the Castle. The rooms had a good show of
company as early as half-past eight o'clock, but towards nine they began to
arrive in crowds. Carriages with four and six horses rattled through the
town from Worthing, Rottingdean, Lewes, and Eastbourne. Before
ten o'clock not less than four hundred persons were present; and before
eleven the assemblage had received an addition of two hundred at least.
The crowd occasioned heat, and many ladies nearly fainted, though every

possible precaution was taken to prevent it. When the royal brothers entered the ball-room, the band (the Prince's) struck up God Save the King, all the company standing until they had passed down the room. All the rank, elegance, fashion, and beauty in Sussex were present. A few minutes subsequent to the arrival of the princes dancing commenced with the Honey Moon. About fifty couple stood up; who led off it was impossible correctly to ascertain. This dance was succeeded by Lord Macdonald's reel; at the end of which, about half an hour after midnight, the Prince and his royal brothers removed to the supper-rooms; tables were laid in three separate rooms, but the company was so numerous, that many could not be accommodated with seats, and, consequently, *sans* refreshments, they were compelled to remain in the ball-room. The tables were decorated with every delicacy of the season. The ladies were dressed in an unusual style of elegance; such a rich display of diamonds we never saw at a public entertainment before, and such a fascinating display of beautiful women, perhaps, in one house, was not to be found in any other part of the world. The Princes were all in regimentals, and all appeared in high health and spirits. The attention paid by those illustrious personages to the company was highly flattering. They entered into conversation with all they knew; and the ladies were highly gratified with the marked attention which was so peculiarly bestowed on them; and all ultimately retired, highly gratified with the entertainment they had received."

1807.

" The hundred beds of the Old Ship have been fully occupied for more than the last six weeks. This inn, as it is one of the largest, so, in point of convenience and genteel accommodation, it is one of the best in England."

" On Saturday, some fishermen brought on shore to the fish-market, Brighton, a shark, which measured upwards of eight feet in length. This despot of the deep had pursued a shoal of mackerel into a fleet of nets, and after doing a great deal of damage to them, got so entangled, that he could not extricate himself."

" *June* 27.—The new theatre opened on Saturday, with the tragedy of Hamlet, Mr. and Mrs. C. Kemble represented the Danish Prince and Ophelia. The theatre is very splendid indeed, yet its decorations are at once tasteful and simple. There is nothing to dazzle at the first glance, but every thing on which the eye can rest with pleasure. The proprietor, Mr. Cobb, has done all in his power to render it worthy of royal patronage, and it speaks much for his liberality and the taste of the artists whom he has employed. The management rests with Mr. Brunton, the lessee."

VISIT OF THE PRINCESS CHARLOTTE.

" *July* 27.—About eight o'clock yesterday evening, an open barouche, with four horses, halted for a few minutes nearly opposite to the Pavilion, and shortly after it was ascertained that the carriage contained the Princess Charlotte of Wales. The carriage at length moved for the Buff and Blue Houses, and afterwards down the North and South Parades, followed by an immense confluence of people, anxious to obtain a view of the interesting blossom of royalty. As if to gratify the populace, the carriage moved but slowly, and on the North Parade it again halted for a few minutes. Her royal highness was habited in a very plain and simple style, white frock and slouch straw hat. She appeared in charming health, and much pleased with the respectful notice that she obtained. Her extreme likeness to her royal parent was loudly spoken of, and on that subject there could be but one opinion. Her royal highness, prior to her arrival here yesterday, had paid a visit to Lewes. She returned from hence to Worthing."

VISIT OF THE PRINCESS CHARLOTTE ON HER FATHER'S BIRTH-DAY.

" *Aug.* 12.—His royal highness the Prince of Wales's birthday was announced this morning by the ringing of bells, and every demonstration of joy; colours were hoisted on the church. The gun-brig, the Strenuous, and Earl Craven's boat, were dressed in national colours, and placed in a situation to be seen from the Pavilion. By eight o'clock the whole town was in motion, the Marine Parade was lined with company, the balconies were full of beauty and fashion, and all the telescopes were in use. At ten o'clock the gun-brig fired a royal salute, which was answered by Earl Craven's boat. His royal highness the Prince of Wales's band, in full uniform, played on the lawn in the front of the Pavilion; and on the outside of the railing, the carriages formed a complete line, the ladies sitting on the boxes, surrounded by a vast number of gentlemen on horseback, viewing the lawn in the front of the Pavilion, where all the royal dukes were walking. At eleven o'clock, her royal highness the Princess Charlotte of Wales arrived at the Pavilion from Worthing, in one of her royal father's carriages, drawn by four beautiful bays. Her royal highness was dressed in white muslin, trimmed with point lace, Vandyked at the edges, and wore a Leghorn gipsy hat, with wreaths of small roses round the edge of the leaf, and a second row round the crown. Her royal highness looked most charmingly, and was received at the grand entrance by her royal father and uncles, who conducted her to the Chinese apartment, with which she appeared greatly delighted. The Pavilion was surrounded on all sides by a most numerous concourse of spectators, who waited anxiously to see the royal party proceed to the ground, where the grand review was to take place. At twelve o'clock a royal salute was fired from the batteries; and immediately after two of the royal carriages came out, the first drawn by four bays, with two postilions dressed in blue-striped jackets, and brown beaver hats; in this carriage were Viscount and Viscountess Melbourne, Lord Erskine, and Mr. Dalmy; in the second, her royal highness the Princess Charlotte of Wales, attended by the Dowager Lady De Clifford and another lady; the carriage was drawn by six fine bay horses; after which followed his royal highness the Prince of Wales, mounted on a beautiful iron gray charger. His royal highness was most superbly dressed in the hussar uniform, and wore a diamond belt, with a diamond crown on his breast; the feather in his royal highness's cap was most superb, encircled with diamonds round the bottom, and fixed in a diamond loop; never did we witness his royal highness in better health and spirits. The accoutrements of his charger were most superb. They proceeded slowly to the ground, where the troops were formed in a line, which was on the beautiful hills at the four-mile course, which command a grand view of the sea. At within half a mile from the ground, his royal highness the Duke of York galloped up to the line, which extended upwards of a mile, and passed them without any form. They were placed in the following order: on the right the horse artillery; next, the First Dragoon Guards; then the third, or King's Own; the Cheshire infantry; the Berkshire; the Second Somerset; the South Hants; the South Gloucester; and fourth troop of the fourteenth, or Duchess of York's Light Dragoons; and the foot artillery, which composed the line. At half-past twelve the whole of the royal party arrived on the ground, and took their station in the centre of the line; her royal highness the Princess Charlotte of Wales's carriage stood just behind her royal father. As soon as the royal party had taken their station, a royal salute of twenty-one guns was fired from the horse artillery; the ranks formed into open order, when the royal party went down the front of the line, returned by the rear, and retook their station in the centre, when the whole of the line passed in ordinary and quick time, the different bands playing ' God save the King;' after which they formed the line and fired a *feu-de-joie*, which was followed by three cheers, the bands playing ' God save the King.' Some ships passing at the time, received signals from the telegraph; they immediately fired a royal salute, and hoisted the royal standard. There was also a sham fight on the sea with small boats, which had a very pretty effect. The day was uncommonly fine, and not one accident occurred to damp the joy manifested on this happy occasion. A good deal of mirth was occasioned by the firing; several of the horses that had been taken from the carriages having broken loose, and run in all directions, leaving many of the company fixed in their carriages until the horses were caught. At half-past three the royal party returned to the Pavilion, where his royal highness the Prince of Wales's band was playing to receive them. Her royal highness the Princess Charlotte of Wales, after partaking of some refreshments, walked on the lawn with her royal uncles, who seemed to vie with each other in attention to her. His royal highness the Duke of Cambridge danced with her on the lawn, and at six o'clock she returned to Worthing. At eight o'clock the royal party, the Duke of St. Alban's, the Marquis of Headfort, Earls Berkeley, Craven, Dursley, Bathurst, and Barrymore; Viscount Melbourne; Lords Petersham, Erskine, and Charles, Edward, and Arthur Somerset, and several military officers, sat down to dinner. The Pavilion was most brilliantly lighted, and the South Gloucester band played on the Steyne. The illuminations were splendid. The prince attended the ball at the Castle in the evening, which was crowded with fashion and beauty, but none of the royal party joined in the dance. The supper was of the first description, but would have been better enjoyed had the company been less numerous. The prince retired at an early hour."

STORMS.

" *Nov.* 22.—A more turbulent week in regard to the weather, than the last has proved, in this part of the world, can scarcely be recollected. On Thursday evening, a tremendous gale from the south-west came on, and which raged with the utmost fury during the whole of that night and following day. Several houses here were nearly unroofed, and one or two in an unfinished state were literally blown down. The destruction of glass has been beyond all precedent great. Several houses in St. James's-street had each from twenty to thirty panes demolished, and similar injuries were received in various parts of the town. The most distressing accident, however, on Thursday evening, was with a boat, belonging to a person of the name of Short, who, with a fisherman, an inhabitant of Worthing, had just returned from Hastings with a cargo of herrings, having on board forty thousand.—The boat passed this town about nine o'clock in the evening, with the intention of running into Shoreham Harbour. At the harbour's entrance, melancholy to relate, within a stone's cast of being in a place of safety, the boat upset, and both of the men were drowned. The body of the Worthing man was washed on shore here yesterday, and was conveyed to the workhouse. The body of Short has not yet been picked up. Upwards of ten thousand of the herrings which the boat contained were yesterday washed ashore at Rottingdean, and taken up by the inhabitants there, being a distance of nearly eight miles from the place where the fatal accident occurred. The weather yesterday was boisterous, but comparatively fine to what it had been for several preceding days. In the evening another unfavourable alteration took place, and the whole night proved to be excessively stormy.—At this time it blows a complete hurricane at due south, accompanied with the most soaking rains we ever experienced. Happily not a sail of any description is distinguishable in this part of the Channel; from the highness of the tide, the most serious apprehensions are entertained for the fate of the eastern cliffs."

" The Duke and Duchess of Montrose were here on Saturday, from Worthing, to which place their graces returned towards the evening."

" The gaiety of this place now daily increases; the rides and walks, consequently, until dinner time, have gay appearances. The Steyne, and the libraries, are also crowded of an evening. The donkies, alias *Jerusalem* ponies, are getting rather into disuse, a phalanx of sprightly cropped-eared ponies taking their stand at the south end of the Steyne, where donkies were formerly exhibited. The former are in high favour with the belles. Upwards of fourteen, in one group, we observed, scampering over the Downs with their fair burthens this morning; a few donkies were ambling their snail's pace at the same time, the ponies snorting as they passed, as though they had felt it disgraceful to be seen in such sluggish company."

" It is rumoured here, but with how much truth we know not, that the Princess of Wales will spend the greater part of the summer at Worthing."

Puns.—" Many of our lovely belles took *ducks* for breakfast this morning, purchased of their cateress, Martha Gunn, who boasts that from the fair profits she gains by the sale of her *ducks*, she is often enabled to purchase a goose for dinner.—The hostile *shots* that have lately been exchanged between the Ship and the Castle here, appear likely to end in sociable *balls* at the former place, for the remainder of the season."

1809.

" Some recent alterations, it appears, will shortly take place in the Prince of Wales's establishment, both here and in London, as Mr. Becht, his Royal Highness's house-steward, has resigned his situation; but who is to be his successor, we have not yet heard. Mr. B., than whom we know no person more worthy, was ever honoured with the confidence, so far as related to his department, of his royal master, and who now, in token of his respect for the uprightness of his character, has presented him with a house and farm, the property of his Royal Highness, to the north of this town about half a mile, on the Cuckfield road, which will be Mr. Becht's residence in future, with free permission to visit Carleton-house, or the Pavilion, whenever, and for whatever length of time he pleases."

This was a princely act.

JUBILEE ON THE OCCASION OF THE FIFTIETH YEAR OF THE REIGN OF GEORGE III.

" *Oct.* 25.—The weather yesterday was as favourable as could have been desired. The heavens might be figuratively represented as smiling on creation, in approval of those laudable and loyal rejoicings that, in every quarter, predominated. The morn was ushered in by the ringing of bells, &c., and the shops, as on a Sunday, were all shut, and during the preceding part of the day, the solemnity of Sunday pervaded the town, which was deemed the best mode of celebrating the day, by paying the earliest attention to the rites of religion, and the practice of the moral duties*. At one o'clock a royal salute was fired from the fort, which was repeated by a gun-brig, the only ship of war lying within sight of the town. At half-past one o'clock the doors of the Royal Riding House, in Church-street, were thrown open for the admission of the benevolent Mr. *Mighell's* party, in number about two thousand three hundred, exclusive of the hundred stewards, who were very active on the occasion. Never was any entertainment regulated with more order than was this; every body was happy, and not a single unpleasant accident occurred to impede the harmony of the proceedings. About fifteen hundred poor persons were also dined at the same time in the farm-yard of Mr. *Scrase*, about three hundred yards from the former place, at the expense of a party of gentlemen, who opened a subscription for such a benevolent purpose, and where similar order and harmony prevailed. The breaking up of both parties was attended with the same decorum and regularity as had happily marked their meeting. The grateful poor had retired, generally uttering expressions of loyalty, and invoking blessings on Mr. Mighell and their liberal friends, to their several residences, by five o'clock. There was no illumination in the evening,

---

* We were going to say " *this is all very well*," but on second thoughts it is *not* very well in any sense. They turned the day into a *fast*, and that not of the most legitimate character : " To deal thy bread to the hungry," &c. &c. An inevitable suspicion is excited of *meanness* having thrust itself into the motives of conduct, more especially as we find no objection recorded to the generous bounty of *individuals*. We can remember how that interesting day was observed elsewhere, and we have found a gratifying account which we shall give under the head of *Hastings*.

excepting at the house of Prince Castelcicala, the Neapolitan Ambassador, which exhibited a star, &c. in variegated lamps. The Prince, it is understood, as it had been decided on that no general illumination should take place, had been solicited to desist from such a measure, lest it should excite the people to demand an exhibition of lights in other places; but the reply of the prince, it seems, evinced the full propriety of his intention. As an ambassador to this country, his highness is stated to have expressed himself, he felt it his duty to give some public mark of his participating in the joy of such an occasion, and even his own court might condemn him in the event of his neglecting such an opportunity. The ball and supper at the Castle Rooms in the evening were very elegantly attended, about four hundred fashionables being there."

" An erroneous paragraph, calculated to depreciate the value of the property to the east of this town, has appeared in various London papers, stating, that the erection of a wall at the base of the cliff, to prevent the farther encroachments of Lord Neptune in that quarter, would cost the immense sum of 24,000*l.* Now the case is, that a wall is actually begun, under the direction of John Smith, Esq., after a plan laid down by Major Reynolds, and which the said J. Smith, Esq., has offered to complete for the sum of 3,000*l.* only, to indemnify the parties who subscribe to it, and to keep the said wall in effectual repair, at five per cent. on the cost price, and which has met with general encouragement. Twenty men have been employed for some days past in reducing the summit of the cliff to a gradual declivity, to let off the waters that have lodged, and may fall on the road, and in making other improvements on the Marine Parade, that are already visible on that agreeable and wholesome walk. It was at first proposed to build the wall with Portland stone, but that proposal is now rejected, materials for it being found on the spot, that promise to answer every purpose."

" Yesterday the weather was bright, and the public dejeuné at *Preston Grove* attracted about one hundred individuals of ton to that quarter, of which number was the amiable Duchess of Marlborough."

" There was a great catch of mackarel during the night of Tuesday. One boat brought to shore two thousand, three quarters of a hundred, and eighteen, of these delicacies of the deep, long tale, which allows six score and twelve to the hundred. These altogether were sold at 6*d.* each, or 3*l.* 6*s.* the hundred, which brought the fishermen a sum of upwards of 68*l.* The poor fellows exultingly acknowledged that they had a good *sever,* meaning their cargo, which word, probably, is a corruption of sea-*fare.*"

1810.

" *Dec.* 3.—Several of the enemy's privateers infested this part of the Channel on Friday, and made several captures. Towards seven o'clock in the evening, the flashes from two contending vessels were distinctly seen from the cliffs here. The darkness hid the objects from observation, and they were at too great a distance for the explosions to be often heard. It is feared, however, that the enemy was successful, as no circumstantial particulars of the engagement, nor scarcely any thing relative to it, have since reached us. At Newhaven, a distance of only nine miles from hence, the conduct of the privateers was the most audacious. They are stated to have ran in close enough to fire at the people on the shore, and to have made a capture or two in despite of any and every species of force which could be brought to bear against them."

" On Monday, the Easter holiday folks, in all the brilliance of Sunday finery, assembled in great numbers at the Bear public-house, about a mile north of the town, on the grounds contiguous to which they were subsequently entertained with the polished diversions of cock fighting, and a baiting of a badger. Yesterday, to give interesting variety to their sports, a bull was tied to the stake and baited at Hove, which afforded some amusement, and at which the whole of the Bear assemblage of the preceding day was present. In the latter instance some danger was threatened, as the compact phalanx of gazers was broken through, and put to the rout by the rottenness of the rope, which unexpectedly gave the bull his freedom. The scene of confusion which ensued would be difficult to describe, but happily no serious injuries marred the refined pleasures of the day."

" *July* 3.—Yesterday the weather was bright and sultry during the morning; indeed the solar rays were too oppressive for lengthened exposures to them, and the parched earth literally smoked with the intenseness of their heat. Towards six o'clock in the evening, however, dark clouds began to obscure the sky, menacing an approaching storm, and which came on with uncommon violence about seven. The thunder was awfully tremendous, and nearly every house in the town was shaken to the base, and the lightning was suitably strong and vivid. This storm continued for something better than an hour, during which we were gratified by the fall of two or three very copious showers of rain—a visitation that we had long, very long been in want of. From eight to half-past nine the evening was tolerably fine, but at ten the storm returned with all its former violence, and which raged with more or less fury throughout the night, with the grateful accompaniment of moisture, which the thirsty earth greedily drank as it fell. A delightful day succeeded the inclemencies of the night; vegetation appears completely renovated. The alteration has not been more sudden than great, and all the fashion and beauty of the place this morning in their various exercises enjoyed, as it were, the smiles of the new world, for every thing denoted health, and renewed energies and powers about them. A refreshing breeze from the sea still revivingly predominates."

But few events in the history of Brighton occurred for about fourteen years after. In the summer of 1814, on the occasion of the downfall of Buonaparte, when universal rejoicings prevailed throughout the British empire, the inhabitants of Brighton for once opened their purses as well as hearts in a public celebration of a most liberal and faultless character. Upwards of *seven thousand* persons, men, women, and children, on the Prince Regent's birth-day, August 12, received an excellent dinner of roast-beef, plum-pudding, and ale, in the cricketing-ground, accompanied by flags, military bands, salutes of artillery, &c. &c., and an immense number of gratified spectators on foot, and nearly 300 carriages. The Rev. Dr. Carr presided, and delivered two remarkably appropriate graces. In the evening dancing took place, with excellent order and decorum. Several instances of private liberality occurred. Mr. Trotter, the manager of the theatre, exhibited it in his way by opening the greater part of his house gratis, when ' God save the King,' &c. were sung in chorus. The stewards of the tables distributed to the female part of those entertained various trifling gifts for mementos, as snuff-boxes, rings, &c. &c.* *O si sic omnia!*

From about the year 1824 to the present may be dated the wonderfully rapid improvements and enlargements of Brighton, which has now extended itself along the sea-shore for a space of three miles. The various public buildings and churches have also been erected within this period ; the road to the west of the Steyne opened and widened, the bold sea-road and esplanade constructed, and, lastly, the chain pier. In the autumn of 1830, their present Majesties, King William and Queen Adelaide, made their first most welcome entry into Brighton, with a view of establishing here their annual winter residence. On such an auspicious event, the feelings of the inhabitants must have been pleasurably excited, and displayed in some external indications †. Their majesties found, on their

---

* We derive this account from *Sicklemore's Epitome of Brighton*, 1815, a work which has been shamelessly pillaged *verbatim* by succeeding Guides. His account of the Pavilion, as it then was, has been copied twenty times over, with a few alterations not at all for the better, to make it look original. Mr. Brayley is the only one who has acknowledged his having borrowed it. The " Family Topographer," vol. i. 1832, is still more absurd, having inserted an old transcribed account of the Pavilion as it existed about twenty-five years ago, since when it has been almost entirely rebuilt.

† Not having been in Brighton at that time, we derive this from a very long and minute account in " Bruce's Brighton," 1831.

arrival at Preston, a line of several hundred carriages extending to the new church, filled with well-dressed and gratulating spectators. Near the northern entrance of the pavilion, a temporary triumphal arch was constructed of timber, fifty feet high, with an aperture of twenty five feet, covered to the summit with greens and flowers, decorated with many flags, and comprising three or four galleries, in which were ranged charity children and seamen in their holiday dresses. In the evening there was a splendid illumination of the whole town, the pier, and some vessels in the road, with decorations of flowers, music, and fire-works. Two days after, the school children of the town received a public dinner on the Steyne, accompanied by music, banners, &c., and an enormous concourse of spectators. Their Majesties visited the scene, and evinced the most satisfying affability, and the sincerest pleasure. We cannot, for the life of us, help thinking, though we have no desire to offend by mentioning it, that it would have been still more worthy of the magnitude of the place, and of the occasion, if *all* the more indigent population, old as well as young, had been entertained, as was the case on the former occasion.

From this period to the present, no events of interest or pleasure have occurred. Under the Reform Bill, Brighton will return two members to parliament. The first election had not taken place at the time this was written. The present winter is the second in which their Majesties and the court have resided in Brighton. It is due to the inhabitants to add, that they seem generally sensible of the credit and advantage which their town is thus obtaining. Should this work be thought worthy to live, after it *has* appeared, we wish to close this part of it with good wishes towards the inhabitants in general, as well as towards the visitors of Brighton. May it live to see the benign Olive, interspersed with the Rose and Myrtle in their parterres, and the white flag of Peace floating on their Forum and Acropolis ;—to see their discords healed, and the social body more united, more liberal, and charitable,—it is unnecessary to add, more happy !

DESCRIPTION.

It can scarcely be a necessary object of information to any reader to detail to him the exact situation of Brighton, or its distance from London, which, by the direct road through Croydon, Riegate (or by the new side cut, which leaves the latter to the right), and Cuckfield, is fifty-two miles. Its situation on the coast is usually considered as a suitable point for indicating the separation of the county into two great divisions; the lateral extents are, however, unequal, the line to the west, beyond Chichester, not much exceeding thirty miles, whilst the eastern boundary at Rye is upwards of fifty. Prior to entering upon our miscellaneous detail, we are induced to insert the lively sketch of a fanciful but very good-hearted Frenchman; its hues are certainly of the brightest tint, but it is far better for a traveller, if the state of his own feelings and the reception he meets with from the inhabitants will allow him, to be willing to see all things in a strange country *en couleur de rose*, and to consider the manners of the inhabitants with kind and fair allowance, where that is required, than to set out in a spirit of querulous criticism and proud alienation, which can neither cause pleasure or benefit to himself or others.

"*Brighton Road.*—At four in the morning we had cast anchor in the road, for Brighton has no harbour. The custom-house sends off a boat to the vessels, which receives the passengers and their luggage; but it cannot reach the shore, on account of the shallowness of the water. The passengers are obliged to be carried on the robust shoulders of the sailors, who, for this act of complaisance, ask only the trifle of three shillings a-head. We are in England, where the representative sign of the existence of a French family for two or three days represents nothing.

" These first details will no doubt appear trifling, and particularly so, unless the reader will have the kindness to recollect that I am writing my journal, which contains the history of all my impressions. One of the most lively of them all is the aspect of a new country; and after having been absolutely forced to travel from adventure to adventure, through the rest of Europe, I am now for the first time on the soil of England.

" The shore of Brighton is celebrated for its sea-bathing, which attracts every year the first company in the kingdom. It deserves this celebrity by the picturesque elegance of its charming views, to which no expression can do justice; especially, when the ray of the rising sun, glittering by degrees on the face of the waters which are slowly illuminated, strike here and there with their light, long zones of the sea, which detach themselves from its obscure extent like silver isles; or else play among the sails of a little bark, which floats inundated with brightness on a brilliant plane, among innumerable vessels which the light has not yet touched. It is principally on the horizon that the mixture of departing darkness and advancing light is remarkable. All the obscurities descend, all the lights arise. The earth and the firmament seem to have exchanged attributes. In the air, a sombre vapour is precipitated and dissolved; on the earth, a mild reflexion of light spreads, incessantly increasing in transparency and warmth; and the most distant line of the dark ocean rises resplendent on the shades of the sky."

" *Brighton.*—The extreme cleanliness of the towns in England is so well known, that on arriving at Brighton, I was astonished to find myself still forced to be astonished. Imagine to yourself an assemblage of decorations full of grace and lightness, such as the imagination would wish in a magical theatre, and you will have some idea of our first station. Brighton, however, presents no edifice worthy of remark, with the exception of the king's palace, which is constructed in the Oriental style, and probably on the plan of some building in India. There is not much harmony between this eastern style and the surrounding houses, built like pretty Italian pavilions under a northern sky; but it is the mark of a power which stretches its sceptre over a part of the east, and draws from it the principal elements of its prosperity. This incoherence, notwithstanding, has no bad effect in a picture of illusions. Fairy Land is not subject to the rule of the unities.

" I continued my journey along a road without ruts, without jolting, without any embarrassment, in a commodious elegant vehicle, adorned with taste, drawn, or rather carried away by four beautiful horses, all alike, all with the same pace, who devoured the distance, champing bits of the most splendid polish, and starting and snorting under a harness of a rich and noble simplicity. A coachman in livery drove them, and a handsome neat postilion urged them on. Every two leagues, postilions, attentive, civil, neither impertinent nor in liquor, brought out fresh horses just like the first, which we could see striking the ground at a distance, as if eager and impatient for the career they were to go through. Though the distance to London is not great, no delicate attentions which could embellish it were omitted by the enchanters who led me along. Half-way, an officious major-domo introduced me into a magnificent saloon, in which were served all sorts of refreshments—limpid tea, which sparkled in china; frothy porter, which foamed in silver; and, on another table, choice, copious, varied dishes, watered with port. After this I set out again, and the eager coursers—but perhaps it is time to take breath, and to say, in more positive terms, that England is the first country in the world for its horses, public carriages, and inns. The magnificent equipage I have just mentioned was the diligence, and the caravansera of the Arabian Nights, a *café* on the high road. One might easily, in the environs of London, comprehend the mistake of Don Quixote, who took inns for castles.

" In fact, from Brighton to London, it is merely a street of twenty leagues, bordered with parks, gardens, smiling farms, pretty country houses, charming pavilions, covered from top to bottom with hangings of roses, and preceded by courts or terraces shaded with cool bowers, under which dance young girls, whom Raphael might regret not to have seen. Youth is charming every where, but in England it is ravishing. A plain girl under sixteen years of age is almost a rarity."—*Charles Nodier's Promenade from Dieppe to the Mountains of Scotland.* 1821.

CLIMATE, SOIL, AIR, AND WATER.

No observations we could form or compile on this subject would be equal to Dr. Relhan's, which of course apply, with undiminished effect, to the present state of Brighton and its vicinity. His pamphlet has lately been republished, with some clever notes, principally topographical, by a Mr. Michell, a medical gentleman of Brighton ; but we have felt called upon to abstain from borrowing any of the latter.

———

" The soil here, and over all the South Downs, is a chalk rock covered with earth of various kinds and depths in different places.

" The advantages resulting from this kind of soil are many and considerable. Chalky ground has little or no perspiration, and therefore must be extremely healthy. The fertility of it as to grain is indisputable, and is owing to the native bed of chalk, dug up by the farmers in the very field they restore it to the surface of again, for its own and their enrichment. The abundant crops which it produces, aided by this manure, are not so surprising as the ability of its continuing to do so for upwards of twenty years from a single act of manuring *. The grass of this soil is of the finest texture and of the sweetest taste, and, in this particular place, is interspersed, on the summits of the hills, with wild aromatic plants of different sorts, which might be easily increased to the advantage of the proprietors and the public.

" To these, perhaps with justice, may be ascribed the remarkably sweet flavour of the mutton of this place ; and to the culture of these aromatics we certainly might, and I hope soon shall, be indebted for a medicine used with the greatest success in Wales, Scotland, and Ireland, and much wanted in the neighbourhood of London—I mean goat's milk. The effects which arise from the use of this milk converted into whey, inriched with the aperient, saponaceous powers of these aromatic plants, are well known to the experienced practitioner ; and I am persuaded, that if tried as a preparative for sea-bathing, it would be found extremely serviceable.

" The ground of this soil does not crack, nor the grass burn so soon as

———

* Pliny presumes it will last much longer : " Alterum genus albæ cretæ argentaria est. Petitur ex alto in centenos pedes, actis plerumque puteis, &c. Hâc maxime Britannia utitur. Durat annis LXXX." Hist. lib. xvii. cap. 8.—*Relhan.*

in other soils. This is, perhaps, partly owing to the reflecting power of the chalk, partly to the declivity of the hills; and yet in wet weather it sooner grows dry, so that you may immediately ride after heavy rains, without the least inconveniency. Hence it follows, that in this soil there can be no marshy, swampy ground, excepting in such places as border on rivers. Now, as the nearest river to this town is really distant six miles, and as this is a circumstance peculiar to itself, no other maritime town in England being equally remote from one, I may venture to affirm that the soil here is extremely dry, and that the air of this place must be proportionably pure.

" Lastly, in this soil it is remarkable that water for the necessary uses of life is difficult to be acquired, as it lies deep; but, when obtained, it well rewards the laborious searcher, as it is excellent in its kind, and its sources almost inexhaustible.

*   *   *   *   *   *   *   *

" The advantage of exercise may be always enjoyed in fair weather: it is ever cool on the hills, and a shelter may be constantly found in the valleys from excess of wind.

*   *   *   *   *   *   *   *

" In examining the ancient and modern descriptions of the Baiæ in Campania, where the Romans of wealth and quality, during the greatness of that empire, retired for the sake of health and pleasure, when public exigencies did not require their attendance at Rome, and comparing them with those of Brighthelmston, I can perceive a striking resemblance; and I am persuaded, that every literary person who will impartially consider this matter on the spot, will concur with me in opinion, giving, in some measure, the preference to our own Baiæ, as exempt from the inconvenient steams of hot sulphureous baths, and the dangerous vicinity of Mount Vesuvius.

*   *   *   *   *   *   *   *

" To demonstrate that the town and neighbourhood of Brighthelmston are totally free from the vapours of running water, the more impure ones of stagnant, and the perhaps equally unhealthy ones issuing from trees, it is only necessary to observe, that this town lies six miles distant from the nearest river; that there is no stagnant water near it; and that the want of shelter by trees is the general complaint of those who consider this circumstance, as a conveniency for cover and perspective, and not as a matter greatly contributing to health.

*   *   *   *   *   *   *   *

" The practice of sending persons labouring under pulmonic complaints to similar situations is by no means a recent one. For this purpose we find Galen making use of the *stabiæ*, situated between Naples and Surrentum on the sea-shore: defended from easterly and northerly winds; happily exposed to the south, and the healthful influence of sea vapour. And to this situation, and the use of milk saturated with the juice of healing plants which grew abundantly in that soil, and may be made to do so in ours, he attributed his success in the cure of these disorders.

*   *   *   *   *   *   *   *

" In the summer months a sea-breeze prevails, which rises and dies away with the sun, with this observable in it, that the warmer the day is, the more cooling and fresh is the breeze; so that the almost suffocating heats which sometimes happen in the summer in this island, and which are intolerable even to the natives of Jamaica, are never felt here. Of the grateful enjoyment of a cooling sea breeze the ancient poets we find had so pleasing an idea, that they celebrated it as a principal ingredient in the happiness of the blessed in their Elysium *.

" The same temperature prevails in winter, with respect to frost and snow; the former happens sufficiently often to add to the health of the inhabitants; it is sharp while it lasts, but its duration is short. The latter frequently falls during the winter season, but seldom continues on the ground above a day or two; the warmth from the sea, and the south west winds which prevail, soon dissolve it. The effects, therefore, produced here either by heat or cold, are too transitory and too immaterial to be pernicious."

CONTENTS OF THE SEA WATER.

" It appears, that in summer weather tolerably dry, there are, in every pint of sea water here, at least five drachms and fifteen grains of pure defecated salt, about five of bittern, or a decomposed earth attracting humidity from the air, and six grains of a white calcarious earth. That this proportion of clean contents being nearly a twenty-third of the whole, is as great, or perhaps greater, than is to be found in the sea water of any other port in England; and must be owing to its peculiar distance from rivers, it being further from such, I apprehend, than any one sea-port town in England. And that the existence of bitumen, nitre, &c. in sea water, pure and unadulterated, is fairly contradicted by this evaporation and separation.

" Under these inviting circumstances it is necessary only to add, that the bay here is open and exposed to the sea; free from ooze of its own producing, and not subject to any filth brought from neighbouring sands or shores; and that the beach is a clean gravel and sand, with a gradual descent."

We had at first intended to have gratified the reader with a few extracts from the work of Dr. Harwood, on " the Curative Influence of the Southern Coast of England †," which has a more especial reference to the vicinity of Hastings. On further reflection, however, we considered that if we once entered this field of observation, consistency would require an extended and desultory track to be pursued, for which we have neither

---

* Hom. Odyss. iv. 567, 568. Pind. Olym. ii.

† Colburn, 1828.—Price, we believe, 8 or 9 shillings. It is necessary to add, that we have not the remotest knowledge of this gentleman.

ability nor space; we therefore refer all visitors to the work
itself, with our best wishes, and the satisfactory information,
that there is absolutely no disease whatever, however arising,
or protracted, in either sex, in which the Doctor does not
contemplate the possibility of a cure, from the united effects
of sea air, warm or cold bathing, and mineral waters.

POPULATION.

In 1801, the population of Brighton was not quite 8000;
in 1811, it was 13,000; in 1821, it had increased to 24,000;
and in 1831, to 40,000, besides upwards of 1000 included in
the adjoining parish of Hove. The number of houses at the
latter survey was 8000, a proportion to the inhabitants far
greater than in London and other large towns, the obvious
reason for which is that about one-third are constantly occupied
by visitors. The average number of the latter, with slight
fluctuations, from the 1st of May to the 1st of February, is
from 20 to 25,000. The total number of persons who visit
Brighton, for any space of time not less than a week, during
the year, is supposed to be at least 100,000: perhaps if a less
period of stay were admitted this number would be doubled
or nearly trebled; but these two latter calculations rest on less
certain grounds.

GENERAL APPEARANCE.

The sea line of houses in Brighton now extends from the
eastern extremity of Kemp Town, to Adelaide-terrace, beyond
the western esplanade, full three miles; a range of piles of
buildings, we suppose, alone to be equalled at St. Petersburgh.
Nearly in the centre, but rather inclining towards the west, is
the opening of the Steyne, from whence a noble level extends
into the country, flanked about the centre of the Steyne, on
the west side, by the Pavilion, and terminated by the elegant
pinnacled tower of the new church, with a prospect of the
Downs at a short distance behind it. This fine expanse is
equally conducive to health and pleasure. A little before

we reach the Pavilion, the old North-street, which is in fact
the High-street of Brighton, runs up a hill, eventually at-
taining the height of 150 feet, at the summit of which is the
old church; and on the opposite side of the Steyne, St.
James's-street rises with a slighter elevation towards Kemp
Town; this again may be termed the local Bond or Regent-
street. This outline must suffice for the present:—in a few
pages we shall present the reader with a sufficiently minute
description in detached parts.

Churches.

THE OLD CHURCH, ST. NICHOLAS'S,

Which stands on the top of the hill, to which part North-street
gradually rises to the height before mentioned above low water
mark, is an aged and by no means handsome edifice, scarcely
equal to the average, even in the small towns of this vicinity,
and though not unsuitable to the rude beginnings of Brighton,
possessing little affinity to its present state. We are very
happy to be able to add, that some liberal, though by no means
complete, repairs have been effected by the present churchwardens (1832); otherwise, at any time within the preceding
ten years, we should have had a sad account to give of its
unsuitable appearance. The principal improvements are the
insertion of neat square-topped Gothic windows in place of a
kind of sash ones, with shutters: some painting and cleaning,
&c. The ugly tower, and a frightful and indescribably odd
erection of brick, at the north-west angle, still cry out for
alteration. The church has three long and low aisles, a
chancel, and small south chancel, and a tower barely 40 feet
high. In the interior the aisles are separated by five arches on
each side, of the fifteenth century, with octagonal pillars.
Some ancient texts over them have lately been restored in a
happy style with ornamented borders. At the entrance of the
chancel is a handsome wood screen, also of the Tudor æra,
and formerly supporting the rood loft. There are galleries in
every direction, painted white, with benefactions inscribed on

those at the east and west end. The pews of deal are still unpainted, and have a mean effect; the pulpit also is not handsomely fitted up. The chancel is much neater, being pewed with oak, with a pretty though minute altar-piece of the Ionic order, with white and gold fluted columns, the decalogue, &c. The interior has however a much more neat and cheerful appearance than formerly, and the walls have been coloured in an appropriate style. By means of the extensive galleries, it is said to be capable of containing 1400 persons, and is always crowded. The side aisles are very narrow, that on the north side especially, which does not exceed nine feet in width. In various parts are numerous monuments, some of which are interesting, The organ is a very good one.

Of the rude old font in this church we could say nothing which has not been advanced a hundred times before, and therefore do not enlarge on the subject. It is either of Saxon date, or of an age little posterior to the Conquest, and there is a tradition which asserts it to have been brought from Normandy. Around the circular edge are five or six rough but bold groups, representing the Last Supper; also kings, monks, nuns, on land and in boats, &c. all which will speak for themselves to the spectator. The window at the east end is in the *style* of the fourteenth century, but evidently not 100 years old; whether it is a correct restoration or no, we are unable to tell: the general style of the church is of the fifteenth century.

The tower contains eight bells, of very harmonious tone, but inconsiderable size, the tenor, which is in the key of F, only weighing 16 cwt.: this is the only peal which this great town can boast of, and there is here neither clock or chimes *. The bells were cast by a Mr. Rubhall, a native of Brighton, at his foundery in Bristol, in 1777. On the tower is a short spiral obelisk of wood, with a large broad arrow for a vane, which

---

* The latter, either at the church, or Town-hall, as in the Royal Exchange in London, would form a very pleasing addition to the town, delighting grown children as well as young ones, as they do in Flanders.

" Soon yon sweet chimes the appointed hour will tell,
For here, to music, times moves merrily."—SOUTHEY.

when freshly gilt, as has lately been done, has a very smart appearance. Above, the royal standard or the union jack is displayed when the Pavilion is occupied, as is also the case at the New Church.

In the churchyard is part of the shaft of a cross, raised on four or five steps, to which we may, not improbably, assign as early a date as the thirteenth century. The view from this spot, over the expanse of densely crowded houses and the sea, is magnificent: the Town-hall, from hence alone, appears as a pile, handsome and commanding. The churchyard has been once or twice enlarged, and a new one was consecrated on the opposite side of the road, leading out of Church-street, in 1826. Still, the whole appears scanty when the enormous population is taken into account, and the older one might be better disused, except in the case of family burial-places. We have no other motive than a good one in urging any generous individual to interest himself in improving the decency of some of the least conspicuous parts; as it is, they are painful to the spectator, and certainly not creditable to the place.

There are a great variety of inscriptions, some of which may interest the passenger. The history of the celebrated Phœbe Hassell, the daring heroine who lived from 1713 to 1821, and had served in disguise as a soldier, is given at length. She received a pension from the kindness of George IV., who is said to have offered her a guinea a-week, which she declined, saying half that sum was as much as she should want or use. A rare instance of such a feeling. We subjoin Tettersell's epitaph, which has been lately recut on a blue raised slab near the chancel door.

"Captain Nicolas Tettersell, throvgh whose prvdence, valovr, and loyalty, Charles the IId. King of England, after he had escaped the swords of his merciless rebels, and his forces received a fatal overthrow at Worcester, September the 3d, 1651, was faithfully preserved and conveyed to France —departed this life the 26th day of Jvly, 1674."

" Within this marble monvment doth lie
Approved faith, honovr, and loyalty:
In this cold clay he hath now ta'en vp his station,
Who once preserved the chvrch, the crowne, and nation:

When Charles the Great was nothing bvt a breath,
This valiant hero stept 'tween him and death;
Vsvrpers' threats, nor tyrant rebel's frowne,
Covld not affright his dvty to the crowne;
Which gloriovs act of his for chvrch and state,
Eight Princes in one day, did gratvlate—
Professing all to him in debt to bee,
As all the world are to his memory.
Since earth covld not reward the worth him given,
He now receives it from the King of Heaven.
In the same chest one jewel more you have,
The partner of his virtves, bed, and grave."

In another part is a lofty and handsome monument for Mrs. Crouch, an actress, said to have been of " wonderful" beauty, erected by Mr. Michael Kelly; it states, in conclusion, that " this was erected by him whom she esteemed the most faithful of her friends." This had *far* better have been spared, as it is well known their connexion was adulterous. There were extenuating circumstances in her case; she had a brutal husband, and we should look with mercy and charitable hope both on departed and living frailty; still vice should never be publickly acknowledged and blazoned, least of all here *.

Dr. Carr, now Bishop of Worcester, and late of Chichester, was Vicar of Brighton for about thirty years, and very popular for his affability and kind-heartedness. The present vicar is the Rev. H. M. Wagner, M. A.; the curate, the Rev. C. W. Langden, B. A.

---

* Several dramatic reminiscences have been published lately, and those of Michael, or as he terms himself, Mick. Kelly, (best known by the music of the " Forty Thieves,") display by far the least indications of goodness of heart of any. (O'Keefe's or Dibdin's are pleasing contrasts.) One instance may suffice:—Mr. Kelly was studying music at some conservatorio in Italy, when he heard his mother was dying; " he could have wished to have gone to see her, *but* he had formed some engagements for the next few months, and, *of course*, it was therefore impossible." Poor lovely Anna Maria Crouch, if this was her best friend!

A favourable contrast of virtue as well as gracefulness, in a young member of an employment attended with dangers, presents itself in the following epitaph on a youthful actress, a Miss Campion, written by a nobleman, and recorded in Lyson's History of Buckinghamshire, at Chesham, in that county; which we quote with great satisfaction, as exhibiting another side of the picture. To doubt the purity of his feelings would be base and execrable.

" Requiescit hic pars mortalis Mæ Cn. obiit 19 Maii Ao 1706. Ætatis 19. Quod superest ex altera parte quære.

" Formam egregiam et miris illecebris ornatam virtutes animi superârunt:

THE NEW CHURCH, ST. PETER'S,

Erected at the north end of the town, near the junction of the routes from London and Lewes, in the year 1826, is a fine and beautiful gothic structure, and one of the most pleasing modern specimens in England within the last twenty years. The expense was about £20,000, for which an edifice of ample dimensions has been constructed, with a sufficient display of solid and well arranged ornaments, forming in every light from which it can be viewed, an agreeable *coup d'œil.* The architect was Mr. Barry; and the style is that of the conclusion of the fourteenth century, emerging into the style of the succeeding. The church consists of a lofty nave and two side aisles, upwards of one hundred feet in length, the centre projecting in a semi-octagonal sweep, ornamented with three handsome windows, with ramified tracery : there are parapets and good pinnacles and buttresses throughout ; the parapet of the centre aisle is waved and pierced with quatrefoils, and the pinnacles at

plebeium genus, sed honestum nobilitate morum decoravit*. Supra ætatem sagax; supra sortem præsertim egenis benigna; inter scenicos ludos, in quibus aliquamdiu versata est, verecunda et intemerata. Post quatuor mensium languorum, a febri hecticâ correpta, intempestivam mortem forti pectore et Christianâ pietate subivit. Humanitate præditis, si quid mentem mortalia tangunt †, flebilis; amicis heu flebilior : dilectissimis reliquiis sacrum lapidem hunc poni curavit, G.D.D." (Georgius Dux Devoniæ.)

The following will give some idea of the purport, but the beauty of the original language cannot be translated.

" Here rests the mortal part of Mary Campion, who died the 19th of May, in the year 1706, of her age 19 :—

" Her form, beautiful, and ornamented with 'wonderful' attractions, was excelled by the virtues of her mind : her origin was humble, but she adorned it, and rendered it honourable, by the nobility of her manners. Wise beyond her years; remarkably, and beyond her condition, kind to the needy : amidst the scenic representations, in which she was sometime engaged, modest and unspotted. Cut off, after an illness of four months, by a hectic fever, she endured her untimely death with an intrepid mind, and with Christian piety. By those endowed with humanity (if the mind is open to human sympathy) to be lamented; by her friends, alas! still more to be sorrowed for : to her most beloved remains this stone is placed as sacred by George Duke of Devonshire."

---

* So punctuated in the original.

† " Sunt lachrymæ rerum, et mentem mortalia tangunt."—VIR.

either extremity are larger and loftier than the intermediate ones. At the west end is a neat tower, with deep belfrey windows, some fret-work, and four tall pinnacles; also four handsome Clock-faces. On three of its sides is a lofty and grand projecting porch or vestibule, of a novel design, with beautiful ogee arches and clustered pillars, and turret-like spiral pinnacles at the angles. The lower part of this tower forms a convenient vestibule or hall, with a coved ceiling, forty feet high, and a double staircase to the galleries. In the interior, the nave is nearly fifty feet high, and the aisles thirty, separated on each side by five arches, resting on lofty and light columns, the centre moulding piercing the capital, and rising to the spring of the roof, which is vaulted throughout, in imitation of stone, producing a very happy appearance. The whole is very appropriately fitted up; the pews of the colour of oak, and the fronts of the galleries of stone. At the east end is a neat stone altar screen of fret-work, and at the opposite end a handsome gallery, arched, in imitation of stone, above which is a second of oak, containing the organ, an instrument of sufficient power, with a clear and sweet tone, and a fine swell. This church was built to accommodate eighteen hundred persons, but will conveniently hold two thousand, a considerable number of whom, as at the old church, are free; and it is very fully attended. The present clergyman is the Rev. T. Cooke, M. A., a practical and judicious preacher. The military in the town attend this church; if there are two bodies, on alternate Sundays. The tower contains one deep toned bell for the hours, and two small musical ones for the quarters; but the absence of a good ring of bells here is to be regretted. Around the church is a large space, well railed in, laid out as a lawn or shrubbery, and most abundantly scented with the pleasing fragrance of *mignionette* in the summer and autumn.

THE CHAPEL ROYAL,

Erected in Prince's Place in 1793, as the first Chapel of Ease, has the crest of the Prince of Wales, who contributed largely to it, carved on the west side. It is a square building, capable of holding one thousand persons, with a neat interior, surrounding galleries, and a small organ. The lower short supports are ugly; but the upper range of pillars, in imitation of *Sienna* marble, and the Corinthian capitals of *verd antique,* are very good. The altar had formerly a copy of *Mengs'* beautiful picture at All Souls, Oxford, Our Saviour appearing to Mary in the garden, or the *Noli me Tangere* (a subject also well treated by Annibale Caracci), which has been removed to the vestry, to make room for the Decalogue: a pity, methinks, as some means might have been contrived for including both. The present clergyman is the Rev. J. Urquart, M. A.

ST. JAMES'S CHAPEL,

The second established, is a very plain building, containing 850 persons, with a good organ. Clergyman, the Rev. D. Maitland, M. A.

TRINITY CHAPEL,

In Ship-street, has an indifferent Doric portico, and a very heavy turret; but the interior is handsome, with a neat dome on the roof, and a fine organ. It will contain 850 persons.— Clergyman, the Rev. Robert Anderson, B. D.

ST. MARY'S CHAPEL

Has a remarkably grand portico of four fluted columns in the boldest style of Athenian, or almost of Agrigentine Doric, with corresponding antæ and a massive pediment; but the space between the pillars and the wall, viewed laterally, is much too narrow, and the sides are heavy. The interior is handsome, with an organ, and will contain 950 persons. There is no turret or cupola at this chapel, which, it was supposed, would, as an elevation on the roof, have been out of keeping. We would suggest a *detached* tower or *campanile.*—Clergyman, the Rev. H. V. Elliot, M. A.

ST. GEORGE'S CHAPEL,

The most spacious chapel of ease, situated near the Hospital and Kemp town, will contain 1200 persons. We should observe, that all of them have a certain number of free seats, and are well attended. The interior here is remarkably plain; but the arched roof of the centre aisle, supported by Ionic pillars from the galleries, which form a sweep at the west end, has a pleasing appearance. The organ is a good one. The exterior is heavy : its steeple is said to be 100 feet high, but is plain and deteriorated by Tuscan columns, the most inappropriate order for such an erection, where Corinthian richness or Ionic elegance is required.—Clergyman, the Rev. J. S. M. Anderson, M.A.

ST. MARGARET'S CHAPEL,

At the west end of the town, in Cannon-place, is of a square form, with a large flat cupola on the roof. The Ionic portico is rather meagre, though well relieved by its sides. Above is a turret in humble, but not altogether unpleasing imitation of the *Lantern of Demosthenes;* whilst its columns are of that fanciful Corinthian of which Stuart found an example at the *Tower of the Winds,* of simple lotus leaves, without the acanthus. The interior is simple and grand, with a double tier of columns, and galleries on three sides, and a large recess for the pulpit, above the altar, on the fourth. It has an organ, and will contain 1000 persons.—Clergyman, the Rev. J. Roper, M.A.

ST. ANDREW'S CHAPEL,

Near Brunswick-square, and out of the limits of Brighton, in the parish of Hove, has a neat though low turret. The interior is smartly decorated, with a small organ, and will contain 600 persons.—Clergyman, the Rev. Dr. Everard.

Dissenting Chapels.

The oldest is " Union-street"—Independents; it has a long
and solid Doric front, a spacious interior, and an organ. "West-
leyan," Dorset-gardens, a large plain building. " Huntingdonian," North-street, do. " Hanover"—Independent, Church-
street, a moderate sized building, cemented, with a large
general burying ground, most beautifully laid out with flowers
and shrubs. " Bethesda," Independent, in do., has a rich,
but rather heavy Erecthean Ionic front, and an organ. " Providence," in do. " Salem"—Baptists, Bond-street. " Friends,"
Ship-street. " Unitarian," New-road, has a light and elegant
fluted Athenian Doric portico. " Huntingdonian," London-road, a neat building. " Bethel," West-street, with a
reference to fishermen. " Zion," Upper Bedford-street. " Ebe-
nezer," Baptists, Richmond-hill; and two or three very small
or temporary ones. Several of these have schools and charities
connected with them.

The " Roman Catholic Chapel" has hitherto been a very
humble and crowded edifice in High-street; a new one is now
erecting near Kemp Town; the interior will be airy, but
its external appearance is too low, and the Corinthian pilasters
are disproportionately heavy.

The " Jews' Synagogue" is a plain building in Devonshire-
place, New Steyne.

Town Hall.

In speaking of the erection and expense of this building, we
unavoidably trench on a subject with which, as a visitor, we
have personally no business whatever; and in pursuing it, we
are fully aware of the obloquy always incurred by merging, in
the least, even with the most undeniably good intentions, in
the disputes of others: we allude to the public expenditure of
Brighton during the last few years, in which upwards of
100,000*l.* has been laid out in works of a general character,
30,000*l.* of which has been bestowed on the edifice now in
question. The less we say, therefore, the better; whilst we

desire that little to be after the honest herring-bone fashion of the Manks*. It is impossible, too, in the chequered inquiry into human motives, to ascertain how far, and in what instances, the feeling on either side has been conscientious or invidious. The best will be to " *make* the best" of it, and, as most likely neither party will deny that there are both " faults" and " much to be said" on both sides, to try and unite, as far as they may, to settle the matter quietly and for the general good ; for the honour and credit of their town in the eyes of visitors, and for their own greater prosperity and harmony.

We find it very difficult to speak of this building as a whole, because some parts are decidedly handsome and noble, others as certainly bad; but we fear that, on the summary, the balance will decline on the side of condemnation. Its principal fault is its huge and rambling character ; it is at least twice as large as it need have been. The *three* porticoes, though grand, are unquestionably not required ; and the face towards the sea, where a fine colonnade would have formed a striking and beautiful object in the prospect of the town, is left blank and plain. The dimensions of the edifice are said to be 144 feet by 113. On the other hand, the double porticoes, composed of four fluted Doric columns below, and four Ionic above, with proper entablatures and a pediment, appear to us stately and noble; and though we hear that architects have sneered at them, we can see no possible grounds for their hard criticism. Doubtless the lower colonnade has not the projecting breadth of that at the west end of St. Paul's, but then the nature of the front did not require it. The angles of the upper story and of the wings below have triple antæ, with very neat capitals; but the flanking walls between the porticoes are heavy and ugly, sparingly ornamented in the Erecthean style with the honeysuckle, &c., with very bad windows. In spite of a sure condemnation of our opinion, we should be glad to see a dome, or cupola, or any thing, to break the extensive square roof of this large building. There is a bell from the

---

* " Ye shall administer justice between man and man, as evenly as the bone of the herring lies between the two sides."— *Oath prescribed to the Deemsters or Judges in the Isle of Man.*

old Town Hall, which we suppose will be put up, with a clock. Entering at the north side, the staircase is supported by tall antæ, which, if there be any rule for this kind of support, must be outrageously out of proportion—we should think not less than fifteen diameters or diagonals; yet the effect is by no means bad. Above is a corridor, with a fine double range of Corinthian pillars, and a flat cove or dome, like the sections of the roof in St. Paul's Cathedral. Nothing can be said against the general effect of this part. The railing of the staircase is a very poor and meagre design : it should have been of brass or *handsome* iron-work lightly painted and gilt. In the lower story are various offices for the magistrates, commissioners, directors of the poor, &c., and underneath, dungeons for temporary confinement, said to be dreary enough, and, if ever to be used, not particularly appropriate to the present day. The great room below is a market. On the second story is a very capacious room for the petty sessions, large enough for the county assizes, an object partly contemplated when it was erected ; some smaller rooms, for the magistrates' private sittings, handsomely fitted up; and a room for the commissioners beyond, towards the south, with galleries on each side on fluted columns, which, though handsome, is said to be very inconvenient. The third story has in the centre the assembly room, which may be pronounced, on the whole, to be handsome, though the Corinthian pilasters might have been lighter, and their capitals are after a most eccentric fashion, having only their lower parts foliated, which may remind the spectator of a gentleman in full dress,—without his coat. The ceiling is massive and flat, with sunk panels handsomely decorated. From the balcony at the east end is a view of the town and sea in a striking and novel light, which alone will repay the visitor for his ascent.

Royal Pavilion.

EXTERIOR.

As we have the grateful privilege of introducing our readers to the interior beauties of this grand and elegant palace, we shall the less dwell on its exterior, because it is known not only by personal observation to the visitors of Brighton, but by some species of description or delineation to almost all the inhabitants of the kingdom; yet we must apprise them that the generality of views so far come short of a just appreciation, that they may almost be termed, by comparison at least, caricatures. It is a building of great length, and of a depth not clearly discernible except in the inside. The garden-front*, facing the Steyne, consists, in effect, of three pavilions, connected by two ranges of building; the centre has the large bulbous-shaped dome, so much resembling those of the churches in the Kremlin at Moscow, and flanked by minarets, consisting of open cupolas on tall pillars. The external pavilions have large pagoda spires, tapering to a point from a broad base, and very commanding in their appearance; these have also flanking minarets, and there are two smaller domes on each of the connecting wings. The height of the centre dome is 130 feet; in front is a semi-circular colonnade, and a long flat one to each of the farther pavilions. The general aspect of this front is rather Indian or Persian than Chinese; when examined in detail, it will be found very beautiful. The opposite, or western front of the Pavilion, is nearly similar, but has a centre projecting rather more in advance, with a neat square portico, supported by pillars.

* See vignette on title-page.

INTERIOR.

Having been favoured by Sir Herbert Taylor with an express permission to take a full survey of the interior of this magnificent palace, and having received every civility and assistance in her power from the lady in charge of the same, Miss Lovatt, we can only regret that scarcely any degree of time, taste, or opportunity will do justice to the various attractions and ornaments of so unique and beautiful a place; the reader must, therefore, be content with that modicum of information which it is in our power to afford him, whilst we assure him, however, that it has been a work of zeal, and executed *con amore*.

We know, for we have personally met with it as well as read of it, that an idea has been not sparingly disseminated of the Pavilion's being characterized by frivolity or gaudiness— a " Fancy," or a " Folly," in which costliness is more eminent than taste or beauty. We do not dissemble this circumstance; on the contrary, we draw it forward boldly, because we can have the pleasure of offering it the most decided contradiction; and, if the reader will believe us to speak candidly, we assure him, in simple terms, that it is no such thing. The Pavilion is enriched with the most magnificent ornaments and the gayest and most splendid colours; yet all is in keeping, and well relieved. There is positively nothing glaring or gaudy, and the person who would quarrel with its richness might as reasonably do so with the flowers of the parterre—the lively carnation or painted tulip. It is true that the architectural taste of some may be averse to the adoption of the Chinese and Oriental style, yet by us, who have " some little turn that way," it has been deemed on inspection to possess capabilities of beauty not inferior to the graceful Ionic, stately Corinthian, or elaborate florid Gothic. And whilst the King of Saxony has his *Japanese Palace*, the Emperor of Austria his *Favorita*, and he of Russia his fanciful palaces of heterogeneous outline, whilst the Sovereign of England has in addition the noble and regular Gothic pile of Windsor, and the Roman palaces of

London, we do not see why, if only for the sake of variety, he should not have his *Oriental* Marine Pavilion. It also recalls to us one branch of that mighty continental influence which we wield, it may be hoped and trusted for the general happiness and benefit. The King of England is almost " *de facto*" *King of India ;* and, therefore, may we not say without fanciful exaggeration, that an eastern palace, placed on the shores of that element by the ancient and continual sovereignty of which England wields such a powerful sceptre, presents an idea to the mind, full, interesting, and effective.

> " India mittit ebur, molles sua thura Sabæi.
> ——————— tibi serviet ultima Thule ;
> Te que sibi generum Tethys emat omnibus undis."
>
> *Vir.*

We should inform the reader, in the first place, that within the width of the Pavilion there are two complete and separate lines of rooms, running from south to north, about 300 feet. We shall conduct him first through the left or west range, as being the simplest, though sufficiently handsome, reserving the most magnificent apartments to conclude with. Previously we may mention the principal

KITCHEN,

which has very much the appearance of a college one, but is much more neat, and all the furniture is in the most brilliant state of polish. The apartment is square, lighted from the roof, which is supported by four iron columns in the form of palm trees, with a Chinese lantern hanging at each.

Entering the principal series, and passing through the stately and most beautiful dining-room, to which we shall presently return, we come to the

CHINESE GALLERY,
162 *feet long, and* 17 *wide.*

This room, of immense length, must display its various local ornaments to much greater advantage in the evening than by daylight, when it is rather dark, owing to its being principally lighted from the roof, and partially divided into separate compartments; at the former time, it must have a striking and romantic effect. The divisional compartments are five in number, which have opened doors of painted glass, and trellis-work in imitation of bamboo. The walls throughout are of a dark pink or lilac, termed peach-blossom, with foliage and birds, painted in a subdued style of pale blue, which produces a very good combination. At the north and south ends are double staircases of iron; the fronts of the steps are of open work, giving them a very airy appearance, and the railings are painted in imitation of bamboo; the stairs are inlaid, as it were, with gray cloth, and have some brass ornaments: above are three windows, containing whole length Chinese figures, on pedestals, and in the ceilings a painted sky-light, with various Chinese designs, as the dragons, styled "imperial," with five claws, and the royal bird, the " Fum." These staircases lead to a gallery over the other three compartments, with bed-rooms on each side. The centre of the lower gallery has its roof of equal height with those at the ends, formed by opening a square through the upper floor, which is surrounded by rails, but the deception is so well executed that it appears as one room. It is to this alternate recurrence of compartments rather low and dim with lofty and illuminated ones, which imparts to the gallery a picturesque appearance, which must be greatly enhanced in the evening by the light of the painted lanterns.

In the middle ceiling is a square light, 22 feet by 11, which displays the Deity of Thunder of the Chinese Mythology, flying, and surrounded by a circle of " drums ;" in his left hand he appears to hold by a chain the lantern which is sus-pended from the roof, and in his right is a mace or sceptre, wherewith to strike the drums and produce the thunder. His Chinese thundership is a very remarkably ugly demon—poor Vulcan would have been an Adonis in comparison.

The general furniture of the gallery is either really, or an imitation of, oriental. The centre chimney-piece resembles bamboo, whilst the open cabinets on the opposite side are actually of that material, covered with fine yellow marble slabs. There are various painted lanterns, Chinese cabinets, with rare China vases and figures; and the carpet, of English manufacture, is handsome and appropriate. We must not omit to mention a great number of chairs and couches of ivory variegated with black, the history of which we do not know, but they are abundantly curious. At the outset, however, we deem it right to apprise the reader that we have not by any means attempted to give him a fair description of all the multiplied and separate ornaments of the various apartments; in fact, we considered that it would derogate from the detail of their grand and principal embellishments and proportions. Something must be left to his imagination; and should he discover many lesser beauties on which to dwell, unnoticed by us, he must not suppose that we did not see or admire them.

Beyond the gallery, to the north, are several smaller and more domestic apartments, which the visitor is allowed to see; but we do not dwell on them; they are generally characterised by neatness and consistency: among them is the sleeping room of his late Majesty George IV., which is not luxurious; and near it are baths supplied from the sea. Into the centre of the gallery opens the

ENTRANCE HALL,

which leads out of a neat vestibule adjoining the western portico, containing a polished brass stove. The hall is a square apartment, the walls pale green, painted in fresco, in a very subdued style. At the entrance, which slopes into the vestibule with a tented roofed recess, are two oriental columns, and above, a long horizontal sky-light of green and white; the chimney-piece is of white marble, and there are four Chinese lamps. This room seems in some measure designed as a quiet contrast, or introduction, to the more splendid apartments.

THE BREAKFAST ROOM

is a pretty summer apartment of considerable length, its roof supported by two bamboo pillars with trellis work. The walls are crimson japan, ornamented with a number of small Chinese paintings, all tending to a light blue colour. In a recess is a magnificent sideboard of extensive dimensions.

We now return to the principal suite of State Apartments,

and enter a range said to be unparalleled in Europe. The first is that exquisite structure

THE DINING OR BANQUETING ROOM.

60 feet long, 42 wide, and 45 high.

Popular opinion has given the supreme rank to the music room, placing this in the second rank : we cannot agree in the decision ; splendid as we allow the other to be, there is something more than beauty or grandeur in this ; it is transcendantly graceful and even *lovely :* it is not merely oriental, still less barbaric, richness ; it is a quiet and chaste beauty, which is almost intellectual. When we add summarily that the *coup d'œil* of this room is that of walls of mother-of-pearl, with historic groups in rich enamels, varied by candelabra, like blue lapis lazuli, surmounted by white glass lilies*, and immense

---

* We imagine the beautiful forms of lilies in the candelabra and lustres to be the *nelumbium,* a flower which differs from the *lotus,* the latter being a plant or tree. Of these and some other Chinese flowers and shrubs we extract an account from the work of Dr. Clarke Abel, F.L.S., naturalist to Lord Amherst's embassy, a gentleman whom we had once the pleasure of knowing.

" The Chinese appeared to have confined their attempts at ornament to their yards, which contained plants of various species. The elegant Ipomaca quamoclet, trained on small frames of trellis work, was from its frequent culture obviously a favourite. The Begonia Evansiana, larger Straemia Indica, Nerium oblander, Lychnis coronata, and Tradescantia cristata were abundantly cultivated in pots, together with a species of Dianella with purple flowers, of Hibiscus, and of Plumbago; which, I could not determine. But, cultivated and prized above all others, appeared the *Nelumbium speciosum* the *Lien-wha* of the Chinese. This splendid flower, celebrated for its beauty by the Chinese poets, and ranked for its virtues among the plants which, according to Chinese theology, enter into the beverage of immortality, flourished in the greatest vigour in the gardens of Tung-Chow. It was raised in capacious vases of water, containing gold and silver fish, supported on stands a few feet from the ground. These were surrounded by steps of different elevation, supporting other plants mingled with artificial rocks, representing a hilly country, and covered with diminutive houses, pagodas, and gardens. In this situation the Nelumbium was certainly an object of exceeding beauty. Its tuliplike blossoms of many petals tinted with the most delicate pink, hung over its fan-like leaves, floated on the surface of the water, or rising on long footstalks of unequal height, bent them into elegant curves, and shaded with graceful festoons the plant beneath.

" The Nelumbium is used by the Chinese to decorate lakes and other ornamental water, and to give a charm and productiveness to marshes

chandeliers of numerous flowers in silvery glass, we can, perhaps, afford some faint idea of the effect it is calculated to
produce.   It is a palace for Diana, or some lovely and beneficent fairy who is favourable to virtue.

We scarcely know where to begin a more sober description,
but may as well state, in the first instance, that the ceiling has
a spacious and lofty dome, nearly occupied by a painted Plan-
tain tree, from which hangs the principal lustre, which is *thirty
feet* from top to bottom.   The rise of the dome is handsomely
scaled with whitish green and gold, and rests on four elliptical
arches, with golden columns ; beneath is a painted and gilt
cornice, with bells ; the oblong painted windows, each in five
divisions, under the dome, resemble, as we conceive, the
Persian style,—circles in lozenges, blue, with gold centres and
radiated edges, in some degree resembling the convolvulus
flower.   The north and south sides have recesses with tented
roofs, looped up with scarlet and gold.   The corner lustres are
sustained by magnificent birds, with large feathered tails.   The
two white marble chimney-pieces have respectively a thermo-
meter and time-piece, one of which imitates a sun-flower, and
the other has very finely executed groups of figures.   The
side-boards, as appropriate to a dining-room, are of rich rose-
wood, ornamented with or-molu and Chinese emblems.

The walls of the room, which are twenty-three feet high to
the cornice, constitute that exquisite series of ornaments which
we have before alluded to.   They form eleven compartments
of large size, three of them on the east side much more considerable than the rest ; they are all bordered with trellis-
work of scarlet and gold, and this again is surrounded by blue
and silver paper, imitating enamel.   Besides these, there are
several narrow ones, containing single figures, and also Chinese
standards, hung with banners and pennons, and guarded at the

otherwise unsightly and barren.   Near Yuen-Ming-Yuen, and under the
walls of Pekin, I saw it covering with pink and yellow blossoms large
tracts of land, and could sympathise with the enthusiasm of the Chinese
bards, who have sung of the delight of moonlight excursions on rivers
covered with the flowering Lien-wha."—*Abel's Amherst's Embassy to
China.*   1816.

feet by dragons. The ground of all these compartments is the most wonderful imitation of *mother-of-pearl* that can possibly be imagined,—it may be even touched, and the deception scarcely perceived. The substance on which it is executed is canvas, but by what curious process it is effected, we are unable to guess. When the sun shines on it, the appearance is beautiful, and we imagine it must be equally so when the dazzling lamps are lighted. The pictures in these divisions represent different scenes in the domestic manners of the Chinese* :— feasting, receiving guests, playing with children,

* MANNERS AND CUSTOMS OF THE CHINESE.

" *Of the air and physiognomy of the Chinese, their fashions, houses, and furniture.*

" We should make a wrong judgment of the air and physiognomy of the Chinese, if we gave credit to the pictures that we see on their japanned work and china-ware; if they are successful in painting flowers, trees, animals, and landscapes, they are very ignorant in drawing mankind, maiming and disfiguring themselves in such a manner, that they are hardly to be known, and may justly be taken for grotesque figures.

" It is, nevertheless, true that beauty depends upon taste, and that it consists more in imagination than reality; they have a notion of it little different from that of the Europeans, for, generally speaking, that which seems beautiful to us is agreeable to their taste, and that which appears beautiful to them appears likewise equally so to us; that which they chiefly admire, as making a perfect beauty, is a large forehead, short nose, small eyes, a visage large and square, broad and large ears, the mouth middle-sized, and the hair black, for they cannot bear to see it yellow, or red; however, there must be a certain symmetry and proportion between all the parts, to render them agreeable.

" A fine easy shape is not thought to have any charms among them, because their garments are large, and do not sit so close as those of the Europeans; they think a man well-made when he is large and fat, and fills his chair handsomely.

" Their complexion is not what has been usually represented by those who have seen only the southern parts of China; for it must be owned, that the excessive heats which prevail there, especially in Quantong, Fokein, and Yunnan, give the mechanics and peasants an olive or brown complexion; but in the other provinces, they are naturally as white as the Europeans, and, generally speaking, their physiognomy has nothing disagreeable.

" Among the charms of the sex, the smallness of their feet is not the least; when a female infant comes into the world, the nurses are very careful to bind their feet very close, for fear they should grow too large. The Chinese ladies are subject all their lives to this constraint, which they were accustomed to in their infancy, and their gait is slow, unsteady, and disagreeable to foreigners; yet such is the force of custom, that they not

music, gardening, introduction, and love making, &c. &c. And it should be observed, that these are not merely Fresco paintings, such as are often seen in England, but highly finished *pictures*, displaying much interesting character, and pleasing to the feelings: for this reason we have called this room *intel-*

only undergo this inconvenience readily, but they increase it, and endeavour to make their feet as little as possible, thinking it an extraordinary charm, and always affecting to show them as they walk.

" However, they have, generally speaking, the common vanity of the sex, and though they are not to be seen but by their domestics, they spend several hours every morning in dressing and adorning themselves. Their head-dress consists of several curls, interspersed with little tufts of gold and silver flowers.

" There are some who adorn their heads with the figure of a bird called Fong-hoang, a fabulous bird, of which antiquity speaks many mysterious things. This bird is made of copper, or silver gilt, according to the condition of the person; its wings, extended, lie pretty close on the fore-part of their head-dress, and embrace the upper part of their temples; its long spreading tail makes a sort of plume on the middle of the head, the body is directly over the forehead, the neck and beak fall down upon the nose, but the neck is joined to the body of the animal by a hinge which does not appear, to the end that it may easily play and answer to the least motion of the head. The whole bird lies chiefly upon the head, and the claws are fixed in the hair. Women of the first quality have generally an ornament of several of these birds united together, which makes a sort of crown; the workmanship alone of this ornament is extremely dear. Generally the young ladies wear a kind of crown made of paste-board, and covered with fine silk; the fore part of this crown rises in a point above the forehead, and is covered with pearls, diamonds, and other ornaments; the upper part of the head is adorned with flowers, either natural or artificial, mixed with little bodkins, the ends of which shine with jewels. Women advanced in years, especially those of the common sort, are contented with a piece of fine silk, wrapt several times round the head, which they call Pao-teou, that is to say, a wrapper to the head.

" That which sets off the natural charms of the Chinese ladies, is the uncommon modesty which appears in their looks and their dress; their gowns are very long, and cover them from head to foot in such a manner, that nothing appears but their face. Their hands are always concealed under wide long sleeves, that would almost drag on the ground if they were not careful to lift them up. The colour of their garments is various, either red, blue, or green, according to their fancy; none but ladies advanced in years wear violet* or black."—*Du Halde.*

---

* Dark blue and violet, is the mourning of the East.

      " ―――――――――― that dark blue dress
      Bokhara's maidens wear in mournfulness."

Lalla Rookh.

lectual. The Chinese physiognomy and costume, as here represented, is any thing but unpleasing : many of the representations
are very pretty. A lady and a little boy looking at flowers,

ENTERTAINMENTS.

" The streets were narrow, regular, and paved with large stones brought
from some distance. Whatever taste belongs to Chinese architecture seems
chiefly directed to the roofs, the pediments are in general elegant and
highly decorated. Dwelling-houses were of one story, built of solid brick
work. We crossed a bridge, over the river, the surface of which was
scarcely visible from junks.

" In the Hall of Reception itself was little to remark ; indeed it had
altogether the appearance of a temporary erection. We dined at the upper
end, and the lower was occupied by the stage. Chinese dinners with the
succession of dishes served upon trays, one of which is placed before one or
two persons, according to their rank, have been so accurately described,
that I shall not pretend to enter into any detail. The custard, and the
preserved fruits with which the dinner commenced were very palatable ; I
cannot say that I much liked the bird-nest soup, it was too gelatinous and
insipid for my taste ; nor did the various additions of shrimps, eggs, &c.
improve the compound ; the shark fins were not more agreeable. The
Chinese eat as well as drink to each other, and a Mandarin, who stood behind
us, regulated the times of commencement, both in the dishes and cups of
wine. The wine was heated, and had not an unpleasant flavour : it is not
unlike sherry. The dresses of the actors, and the stage decorations, were
very splendid, and there was noise and bustle enough to satiate the eyes
and ears. Even those who understood Chinese were not able to trace any
story in the performance, which seemed to be more of the nature of a melo-
drama than comic or tragic representation. The part of a stag was the best
performed in the piece, and when in front of the stage, from the shelter afforded
by a group of flag bearers, and the consequent concealment of the boy's legs,
illusion was sufficiently perfect. The instrumental music, from its resemblance to the bagpipes, might have been tolerated by Scotchmen, to
others it was detestable. Of the same description was the singing. Our
admiration was justly bestowed on the tumblers, who yield to none I have
ever seen in strength and agility ; their feats were executed with particular
neatness. In splendour of appearance, the Mandarins did not stand any
competition with the actors, who were blazing with gold ; it was suggested
that their costumes were tbe ancient habits of the nation. The dress of
ceremony of the Mandarins, consisting of blue gauze or crape, with some
flowered satin beneath, is plain and not unbecoming ; an embroidered
badge, marking their rank, whether civil or military, is fixed upon their
robe before and behind. The Peacock's feather, or more properly tail of
Peacock's feather, answering to our orders of knighthood, is worn behind ;
two of these decorations are equivalent to the garter."—*Ellis's Amherst's
Embassy to Chin ',* 1816.

TRAVELLING.

" The larger waggons are covered with matting, and are not unlike a
tilt cart ; they are drawn by five mules or horses, in general the latter ; the

and a bird of paradise *, are amongst these, as is also a child, playing with one of the tame or charmed snakes. In the centre great compartment, on the east side, is a Chinese bride being conducted home, carried in a palanquin by bearers richly dressed, with a parasol canopy over her head, and a peacock by her side. Three boys in front are respectively carrying a blue banner, and playing on the pipe and cymbals. The pearl ground is also worked in oriental patterns, and the doors of the room resemble rich mother-of-pearl, with gold emboss-ments in the Japanese style. The carpet is of Axminster manufacture; and on the west side are five handsome windows, with silk and gold draperies. The whole of the windows in this front are very handsome and tasteful; lofty, and termi-nating in the arabesque arch; the large panes of plate glass, set in frames of dark wood, with rich gold beadings, and borders of amber-coloured glass, and the upper parts are painted.

THE GREEN, OR ANTE-DRAWING-ROOM,
50 *feet long and* 20 *wide,*

so called, from the colour of its pale striped draperies, is, like the other drawing-room beyond the saloon, a domestic apartment; though very handsome, possessing all the quiet comfort of a private residence. The walls are white and gold in broad borders, with a suitable cornice, and the chimney-pieces

carts for personal accommodation are much smaller, drawn by single mules, and hold one person without difficulty, but are extremely inconvenient from their being without springs. The mules are particularly fine, and the better sort of horses resemble the smaller sized Turkoman."—*Ellis's China.*

---

* CHINESE BIRDS.

" In the southern provinces there are parrots of all sorts, exactly re-sembling those brought from America. They have the same plumage, and the same aptness for talking, but they are not comparable to the bird called Kniki or Golden Hen: there is no species in Europe anything like it. The liveliness of the red and yellow, the plume on the head, the delicate shadowing of the tail, the variety of colours of the wings, together with a well-shaped body, have doubtless given occasion for the epithet of Golden conferred on this fowl, to show its preference over the most valuable of the feathered kind;—besides, the flesh is more delicate than that of a pheasant, so that on all accounts not one of the eastern birds can be more desirable than this in our European countries."—*Du Halde.*

white marble and gilt bronze, with grates, as in all the other rooms, of polished steel and *or molu*. On the east side are four tall Chinese ewers, considered as very *récherché*: they are of sea-green, embossed with handles, approaching to the Egyptian form, imitating gold cordage.

THE SALOON,

55 *feet long and* 30 *wide*,

forms the grand centre of the eastern suite, and is of circular shape, with coved recesses to the north and south, and a large dome clouded in a light and cheerful manner, painted also with a gorgeous dragon with silver and gold flowered wings, enwreathed by crimson and green serpents. From this depends a spiral lustre, expanding to the base, eighteen feet in height: at the angles are smaller lustres. The elliptical recesses have silver plantains on their ceilings, and pilasters with fancy capitals, somewhat like the Corinthian, enclosing in an upright panel a golden lotus tree. The chimney-piece, a stately one, of white marble and *or molu*, has fine Oriental niches containing figures: around the room are also many splendid cabinets with niches and recesses, lined with mirrors, and containing figures and jars, &c. Over the chimney-piece is an immense mirror, and in front a splendid time-piece of green and gold, with couchant monsters. The doors are in imitation of mother-of-pearl, embossed with gold, and the hangings throughout crimson and gold-flowered satin in compartments, with silver paper edgings: the ottomans, chairs, and window draperies are in accordance, the latter relieved by blue silk and gold. The carpet, of Axminster work, is of a circular pattern to suit the direction of the room*.

* The carpets were rolled up, and the lustres muffled when we saw the rooms, but we were enabled to form an idea of their appearance when displayed. We may here, once for all, mention what is deserving of remembrance, that almost all the ornaments and furniture of the Pavilion, excepting some Oriental rarities, are of English manufacture, which was an object by no means neglected by the late king. This circumstance should be remembered in an extenuating light by those who complain of George the Fourth's profusion. If the fountain of regal munificence burst

THE YELLOW DRAWING-ROOM,
50 *feet by* 20,

is very similar in appearance to the first Drawing-Room, but
rather richer: the draperies, &c., are of striped satin; the
walls panelled in white with handsome gold borders, and the
ceiling supported by two white and gold oriental columns,
wreathed with serpents, and capped by a canopy with bells.
The chimney-piece is of Oriental porphyry, or some substance
much resembling it in appearance.

THE MUSIC ROOM,
62 *feet long,* 42 *wide, and* 41 *high,*

forms the north wing, and is the most splendid apartment in
the palace, dividing the praise of beauty with the Banqueting-
room. This might have been the fitting dwelling of the
magnificent and courteous Fairy *Pari-Banou*, of the Arabian
Nights. Like the former, it has a fine dome, thirty feet in
diameter, with a projecting cornice and painted windows; but
the walls are on a very different plan, being wholly covered
with crimson and gold Japan, representing Chinese scenery,
said to be taken from actual examples in the neighbourhood of
that far-famed but little known metropolis, Pekin *. The

forth with rather too heedless impetuosity, its waters, on reaching the
level, branched out in various meandering and fertilizing streams into the
quiet retirements of labour and industry; and the resources of many a
poor family have been even kindly supplied by the expense bestowed on the
decorations of a palace. Great and severe economy on the part of a
monarch, as well as his superior and more wealthy nobles, would be almost
a crime:—they have freely received, and should freely give.

---

* VICINITY OF PEKIN.

"We left our quarters at five o'clock, and took the same road as on the day
we visited Ho. After having skirted the walls of the city, in many places
out of repair, we came upon the paved granite road leading to Pekin. One
mile from Tong-chou we crossed a large bridge, with a single arch just
large enough to admit a small barge just passing through. The view from
the bridge was exceedingly striking; the pagoda and watch-tower formed
beautiful objects in the distance, while the banks were prettily diversified
with cultivation and clumps of trees. Near sunset we passed a wall of
good masonry, which seemed to inclose a handsome park; small pavilions
near the road, open on all sides, with highly-decorated roofs, arrested our
attention, as characteristic architecture in their best style, and almost good
taste: they are said to be commemorative of individual worthiness. I could

borders of the large compartments are trellis-work of pale blue and bamboo, with large dragon ornaments at the corners, and the coved roofs of the recesses of bamboo tied with ribbons. The cornice under the dome, which forms an octagon, and projects in the style of a running canopy, is of scarlet and gold, and has rich ornaments and bells. Eight elliptical painted windows, so contrived as to be occasionally illuminated from without, decorate the cove; and in their minutely varied hues remind us of that pretty toy of some years back, the " Kaleidoscope." The cornice is supported both by scarlet en-wreathed columns, painted in perspective, and also by slender cord-like ones of gold. The swell of the dome has scale-work in what is termed " green gold," a combination which produces a happy effect. A magnificent foliated ornament at the apex supports the great lustre, displaying the form of a pagoda connected with an immense lotus. There are eight other

not determine all the animals represented by the sculpture; some were certainly lions.

—" Pekin is situated in a plain ; its lofty walls, with their numerous bastions and stupendous towers, certainly give it an imposing appearance,, not unworthy the capital of a great empire. On the side near Hai-teen we crossed a large common, wholly uncultivated ; a remarkable circumstance so near Pekin. There are large tracts of ground covered with the nelum-brium, or water-lily, near the walls, which, from the luxuriant vegetation of this plant, are extremely grateful to the eye. The Tartarean mountains, with their blue and immeasurable summits, are the finest objects in the vicinity of Pekin ; to many of the party the streets of Pekin might be the great points of attraction, but to myself a visit to this stupendous range would be a source of much higher gratification."—*Ellis's Amherst's Embassy,* 1816.

THE GARDENS OF YUEN-MING-YUEN, NEAR PEKIN.

" The morning was fine, and opened to us a scene of novelty and beauty. After travelling, since leaving Takoo, through an uninterrupted flat of two hundred miles, remarkable neither for its productions or cultivation, we beheld unusual charms in the hills, trees, and flowers which surrounded us. Fields of nelumbo, rearing high its glossy leaves and gorgeous flowers, edged by trees with the foliage of the cassia, spread at our feet, whilst the Tartar mountains, approximated by the haze of the morning, rose in the distance. All the descriptions which I had ever heard of the paradisaical delight of Chinese gardens occurred to my imagination, but in imagination only was I allowed to enjoy them. Acts of fraud, tyranny, and violence speedily effaced the first rising of pleasurable emotion."—*Abel's Voyage to China,* 1816.

lustres of much beauty in this room, and a great number of Pagodas of china and glass, manufactured in England, four of which are fifteen feet in height.

The organ built by *Lincoln* in 1818, unquestionably one of the most powerful, yet sweet-toned ones in England, stands on the north side, but its gilded front alone appears, inlaid in the wall; the instrument itself, which is about twenty feet deep, stands in a separate room behind. " Its compass is from C. C. C. with a double diapason throughout." It has three rows of keys, twenty-eight stops, and twenty pedals.

Over the chimney-piece is a very grand mirror, about twelve feet by eight, with a gilded canopy supported by columns: in front is a time-piece of curious and elaborate pattern. The chimney-piece, executed by *Westmacott*, is by far the most stately in the Pavilion, and has a really noble effect: the projecting sweep of cornice is supported on the wings of an expanding dragon, and the massive, though short, oriental columns, with elaborately carved capitals, and still larger bases of inverted lotus, &c. &c. are in the best possible style, reminding the spectator of the grand conceptions of *Martin*. From some remaining examples, and hints derived from recondite sources, this is supposed to have been actually the style which prevailed some thirty centuries ago, in ancient Babylon and Persepolis.

₊ THE PALACE CHAPEL *

is a very spacious and handsome apartment, eighty feet by forty. The royal seat is splendidly adorned with *or molu* ornaments and crimson velvet; the organ is a very fine one, and the communion plate is of gold. The chaplain is the Rev. Dr. Everard.

* That we did not see the chapel and some other adjuncts of the palace was not owing to our own neglect, or to any deficiency in the obliging and condescending order we received, or any want of courteousness on the part of Miss Lovatt. There must, of course, have been minor incivility to impede us, but we shall not particularise it.

C. Scott delin.

C. J. Smith sculp.

NEW ENTRANCE, PAVILION BRIGHTON.

For the History and description of the Sussex Coast.

Printed by Sark & Co

₊ THE STABLES AND RIDING-HOUSE,

at the north-west angle of the palace grounds, form a large and imposing pile. The interior of the stables, whose outward appearance is octagonal, is a magnificent circular area of 250 feet, with a dome in the centre eighty-eight feet in diameter, and, after St. Paul's, one of the largest in England. Into this area the suites of stables, which will accommodate seventy horses, open. There are also other projecting buildings, and a large square court-yard for carriages. The long front towards Church-street, ornamented by large windows and minarets, is now completed by the erection of the east wing. The riding-house and tennis-court are each 200 feet by fifty. The spacious dome is a handsome object in every view of the town. *Moresque* is the term usually conferred on the architecture of this edifice; but we imagine it possesses some features exhibited in the buildings of Hindostan.

ENTRANCES.

The southern entrance was erected in 1831, opening into Castle-square and East-street. It is a very neat erection, but is, at least by comparison, not much admired. Minarets separate it into three divisions: the centre has the archway, which is of handsome and suitable appearance, but the side divisions are rather too much broken by small windows, which gives the whole the appearance of a house.

The northern gate-house, finished in 1832 (represented in our Plate), is a noble and faultless building, exhibiting every characteristic of boldness and stateliness. The crowning dome, in the style of the central one of the Pavilion, the substantial centre minarets, and the light fluted ones at the wings, with the rich fret-work of the arch and turrets, are all excellent of their kind, and leave nothing to be desired.

STEYNE.

Every one to whom the name of Brighton is familiar has heard of " The Steyne," formerly its sole fashionable promenade, and as intimately identified with its gay renown as Bond-street, Ranelagh, or the Pantheon with that of London in the last century. But, like the latter, it has been shorn of its beams, and by new and usurping comets in the horizon reduced to a minor twinkler. Still, though in a great measure thrust from its place by the Marine Parade, it continues to possess the same advantages, and as a thoroughfare is traversed by continual groups of every description, not omitting the most genteel. The closing of Lucomb's library was a sad cloud over its gaiety, especially in summer evenings. The building has been refitted as a bazaar of a splendid character, and doubtless deserving of notice ; but such an establishment has a much less forcible attraction. The oblong space of the Steyne has two inclosures surrounded by iron rails, and a spacious bricked pavement, nearly twenty feet wide. The air is very fine ; and the effect of the spacious level, opening at the sea, and terminating beyond the town, very interesting.

In the inclosure nearest the palace is a bronze statue of George IV., by *Chantrey*, on a pedestal nine feet in height, erected in 1828, by a subscription of 3000*l*.

THE NORTH STEYNE,

In the continuation of the level, is a new oblong enclosure extending to that of the new church ; it is laid out in a style similar to the squares in the metropolis.

Beyond the new church, to the left, is the London road, which for nearly half the distance to Preston, one mile, is bordered by houses ; those on the left side are neatly built, in the cottage or villa style, with small gardens, and are desirable to those by whom cheapness must be studied in the first instance. At the other angle of the Steyne is the road to Lewes ; on the right hand are some handsome villas, and on the left a spacious open track in a wild state, used as a play or cricket-ground by the boys of the town.

THE ROYAL GARDENS,

NOW THE ZOOLOGICAL GARDENS.

Before we had the advantage, or the misfortune (for we do not exactly know which it will turn out), to have visited Brighton, these gardens were, properly speaking, pleasure gardens, like the famed " Dandelion" of Margate, a mimic Vauxhall or Tivoli, though of a more quiet character. They comprised bowling greens, a fives' court, cricket ground, tea-boxes, an aviary, a Merlin's swing, a maze, &c., &c., a large ball-room, and occasional small temporary erections for that purpose; public breakfasts, &c., were also sometimes held. All this has passed away, and we regret it exceedingly; not that Zoological Gardens have been established within the limits of the town, but that they have superseded the former, which were compelled to be abandoned, and that the industrious and deserving author, Mr. Ireland, lost some thousands of pounds by the speculation, and is now in reduced circumstances, after having certainly conferred some benefit on the town. All this is not as it should be: if the very existence of such a thing as liberality be allowed in the present day——but that sleeps, and is likely to do so, either till happier times come (which pitying Heaven soon grant!), or till the minds of the public open themselves to more generous feelings. We would give it a push, or even a slight goad, to rouse it, if we could, but that we fear

" 'Twould do no good, but ' *wice warsa.* ' "

The dull spirit, now like a " lazy lubber fiend," would only growl and snap at us.

Our business now, however, is with the zoological establishment, and no blame attaches to its proprietors for taking up what others had been compelled to leave. It occupies the same beautifully disposed grounds, with many improvements, at present only in their infancy*. The large cricket ground

---

* By comparing the plans, we think it will have a similarity of appearance to the establishment on *Primrose Hill*, but that of Brighton is deficient in a mount.

before the gardens is now taken into the plan, and a new cricket ground elsewhere has been assigned to the late proprietor, Mr. Brown, who still keeps the inn at the south-west angle. A neat but not very handsome gate has been erected facing the level. The large ball room, eighty feet by thirty, at the entrance of the gardens, is to be *orientalised*, to correspond with some other erections of a smaller character, for beasts and birds. The gardens remain nearly in their original state. At the entrance is a sunk, circular bowling-green, beyond which is an aviary of rustic-work, representing a Gothic building with three aisles; from hence commences a beautiful avenue of small trees, terminated by a narrow canal or ditch, and a bridge, leading to a Saxon tower, which, if it had been a little higher, would have had an admirable effect; it has a battery of six small cannon. The maze beyond the tower terminates the gardens; but on either side are other walks and lawns, also a grotto, tent, basin of water, &c. &c. The band of the regiment stationed in Brighton plays on one afternoon in the week for two hours in the bowling-green, when there is a fashionable promenade. Balls for the middle classes were formerly held, with coloured lamps, fireworks, &c.

The collection of animals is at present small, and kept in a temporary place, but is very well managed. It consists of two young tigers, two fine leopards*, a panther, hyæna, a lynx, two Russian bears, foreign goats, deer, lamas, monkeys, &c. &c. The lion † and the elephant are still wanting. A boa con-

---

* It is not generally known, but we have it on the testimony of a person who watched them by passing the night in a tree in India, that several of this tribe, but especially the leopard, or *cheetah*, when at ease in their own haunts, *purr* like the domestic cat.

† Few descriptions of the lion are more beautifully correct and striking than one contained in an eccentric but, in some parts, noble poem, Smart's " Song to David" :—

> " Strong is the lion ! like a coal
> His eyeball ; like a *bastion's mole*
> His breast against his foes."

Having had the honour of a visiting acquaintance with " His Majesty of Mysore," a British-born lion, who, however, on one occasion, was near inflicting capital punishment upon us, by mistake for a less courteous visitor, who had insulted him, we can speak, from actual contact, of the regal proportions.

strictor is the only curiosity of that class. There is a beautiful assortment of birds, paroquets, cockatoos, macaws, &c. &c. &c. Subscription to the Zoological Gardens is one guinea the year, or one shilling the day.

[Immediately after the above was written, we saw that the proprietor of the Zoological Gardens was also a bankrupt ! ! !]

PARK.

" O Proserpina,
For the flowers now that frighted thou let'st fall
From Dis's waggon ! daffodils
That come before the swallow dares, and take
The winds of March with beauty ; violets, dim,
But sweeter than the lids of Juno's eyes,
Or Cytherea's breath."

WINTER'S TALE.

" Siderum sacros imitata vultus,
Quid lates dudum Rosa ? delicatum
Effer e terris caput, O tepentis
Filia Cœli !
Te semper nubes fugiant aquosæ
Quas fugiunt albis Zephyri quadrigis ;
Te semper mulcet Boream jocantis
Aura Favoni."

CASIMIR *.

To the visitor of Brighton, " in populous city pent," at the genial approach of spring, no resort can be more appropriate than this, or so well calculated as a rich and luxuriant refuge from the dulness and sterility of the surrounding country. Here Nature, new robed in fairy charms, smiles on him after her resurrection from her needful sleep, and

" The earth, the common air, the skies,
To him are opening paradise."

In a densely-peopled town, where the extent of garden, to those houses which can in the least claim such an appendage, is of the most limited character, no idea could have been better than that of enclosing a spacious lawn or shrubbery, presenting a variety of aspects, from the inequality of the ground ; in some

* Matthew Casimir Sarbiewski, a Lithuanian palatine, priest, and poet of the seventeenth century, the purest and most happy imitator of Horace. *Editio Bipontina, Argentorati (Strasburgh)* 1803.

places ornamented with spontaneous wild-flowers, and in others trimly and gorgeously fitted out with the refined parterre; and all this open to the visitor on the most moderate terms *.

The Park is situated just where the elevation of the Downs commences, and nearly in a line with the back of the New Steyne, from which it is about a quarter of a mile distant. Its principal entrance is through a neat Roman arch, and the visitor finds a good carriage-road, leading him a course of nearly a mile round its limits, which comprise sixteen acres. This road is edged with flower-beds and a shrubbery, whilst the centre of the park, which inclines to a hollow form, has more the wild appearance of a meadow, and is diversified by plantations of hazel, mountain-ash, &c. : in one part is a good archery-ground with a rustic arbour or hut. We could occupy much space in dwelling on this pretty spot, but have probably said enough to excite a view of it, when, if no high-flown ideas are entertained, there is little danger of disappointment. It is, of course, an equally agreeable retreat in summer, though the primary vernal attraction we have alluded to has then lost its novelty; and its seclusion from the bustle and publicity of the town, and fine view of the sea, are always attractive. For family parties and associations it is eminently qualified; perhaps for others of a more romantic nature; it would make an admirable scene for one of Wordsworth's love-tales.

> " That day, the first of a re-union,
>   That was to teem with blest communion,
>   That day, of balmy April weather,
>   They tarried in the wood together."

At the south-western angle of the Park is the

GERMAN SPA,

a neat building, with an Ionic portico and a separate pleasure-ground. Here are composed the imitative German waters of various kinds and for various purposes; *Carlsbad, Marienbad*

---

* We believe the liberty of walking here and gathering flowers may be obtained for 12*s.* the season; for a separate visit it is twopence, and for the same consideration the visitor may have a nosegay gathered for him, and carry it away. It is a popular resort for servants and children as well as their friends.

Spa, Pyrmont, Ems, Seltzler, &c , the invention of Dr. Struve of Dresden, about twelve years ago; where, and also at Leipsic and Berlin, similar establishments are in existence. This is a subject on which we are not able to speak, but it is said that they have nearly the virtues of the originals, and that those of Carlsbad in particular have effected the most beneficial results.

CHALYBEATE *.

This spring is situated behind the western end of the town, and is a pleasant walk of less than half a mile from Brunswick or Regency Squares; it is also approached from the Western Road, and by a very pleasant footway from above the Old Church, over an intervening hill, which commands a magnificent view, and has a very fine air. Before the front of the building is a small lawn, and on the right hand is a pretty Swiss cottage, occupied by a confectioner. The edifice has a neat Ionic colonnade, and a very handsome and airy reading-room—decidedly one of the best in Brighton. The small well or fountain is a few feet below the floor of the right wing, and has a very neat staircase descending to it. At the back of the building is a small lawn surrounded by a shrubbery, which is at present only in its infancy, but may, by gradual improvements, be made a pretty place. Archery-fétes have occasionally been held here, with prizes in a good style, and the attendance of a military band; private parties also occasionally frequent it. The proprietor has, with a spirit tenfold valuable in Brighton, from its unfortunate rarity †, employed four musicians, who play in a respectable style during some hours of the day. Admittance to the Chalybeate is at 1*l.* 1*s.* a year, or 6*d.* a time.

* We think it scarcely necessary to inform our readers that this word is derived from the Greek and Latin *chalybs,* " steel," because we suppose them to be rather more awake than the learned doctor, whose servants were engaged in drawing off the water of a pond to catch some of the " finny tribe" (as they are termed by all pretty writers), when a friend came breathlessly to inform him that " they had just discovered a chalybeate;" " O, have they," answered the sage, " well—*put it with the other fish.*"

† Or is it want of encouragement to honest pains, on the part of the visitor? It is not easy to distinguish the respective shares of blame; but that there is a sad dearth of all amusement in the town cannot be denied.

On the hill adjoining the ground is a little sprinkling of wild heath and wooded scenery; not very superior, to be sure, but still a *gem* in the borders of Brighton. The view of the ocean, the harbour of Shoreham, and Worthing Point is very pleasing, and the air so excellent, that this alone is worth a walk to the spot.

On the good qualities of this fountain of relief we are also not competent to offer any observations. The visitor will find one or two pamphlets on the subject, but will, perhaps, do well to seek for that of its promulgator, Dr. Relhan. The component parts of the water have some affinity to those of the Tunbridge Wells chalybeate, but are more strongly impregnated with iron, as may easily be discovered by the slightest taste. In an extensive variety of cases, where a powerful tonic is required, it is said, in conjunction with sea air and bathing, to have almost worked miracles.

NORTH-STREET, LAMPS, PAVEMENT.

North-street is the principal thoroughfare of Brighton, but from its irremediable narrowness at the summit of the hill is often most inconveniently crowded. At the entrance opposite the private entrance to the Pavilion, is an open space, called Castle-square; here a spacious street, termed East-street, is a fashionable avenue to the West Cliff. A little further up North-street is the Colonnade, a handsome piazza extending along two sides of the angle formed by the junction of the New-road. Brighton is lighted with gas, but very indifferently; the individual lights are large and handsome, but much too "few and far between;" and in some parts the illumination is confided entirely to the private lights of the shops, consequently when these are shut up, there is almost total darkness. In some localities, as in Regency-square, the inhabitants have voluntarily incurred the expense of a double number of lamps. Some parts of the Sea-range have their foot pavements flagged, but the greater part of the *trottoirs* are paved with *brick*, which has a very novel appearance, but not unprepossessing, especially when it is washed to a deep red by a shower, and contrasts with the narrow curb edging of stone.

BRIGHTON, EAST OF THE STEYNE.

At the opening of the Steyne, the Parade is not much above ten feet from the sea; it rises gently to the Pier, where it is about thirty feet, and subsequently, before reaching Kemp Town, attains the height of ninety. Facing the Steyne is the lodge entrance to the Esplanade, which extends 1250 feet (about a quarter of a mile) to the Pier: it is merely a narrow carriage road and a foot pavement, raised a few feet above the beach and railed in, with a flanking wall above, protecting the Marine Parade.

CHAIN PIER, DIEPPE, &c. &c.

We believe this was the first edifice of the kind in England constructed on *piles*, the efficiency of which at first excited some doubt, but confidence was secured by information obtained, that the batteries erected on piles by the Czar Peter at Cronstadt remained unimpaired to the present day. The inventor and architect was Captain Brown, R. N., to whom much praise and gratitude is due; we sincerely regret to add, for the sake of all concerned, that it has proved a very losing speculation: it is hard that public-spirited individuals should so often, in this vicinity, lose their reward. Some public means, if possible, should be taken to remedy this untoward event.

The length of the Brighton Chain Pier is 1130 feet, exactly six-sevenths of a quarter of a mile*, and width 13 feet. The platform is supported by the chains, which at the south end pass 54 feet into the cliff, and are there strongly bolted, from thence passing, with alternate dips, over the towers, they descend into the sea at the furthest extremity, and are imbedded in the rock. The rods, individually slender, by which the platform is hung on the chains, are 362 in number; and each division of the chain, of which there are four on each side formed by the intervention of the towers, has 117 links, each weighing 112 lbs. The piles are four in number, at the distance of 258 feet: the first three consist of twenty piles

---

* 1320 feet × 6 ÷ 7 = 1131⅗.

each, with some horizontal and diagonal beams; the fourth, which is the Pier Head, is in the form of a T, and is paved with Purbeck stone, to the weight of 200 tons. The piles here are 150, firmly secured by diagonal ties of great strength. The towers of cast iron, each weighing 15 tons, are 25 feet high from the platform, which is itself 13 feet above high-water mark. In the centres are arches, and the sides are occupied by small shops, tenanted by confectioners, fancy-ware sellers, and a profile artist. The sides of the platform have neat iron railings, and the whole of the iron work in this Pier is painted of a bright green, which has a cheerful effect, Norway fir is the wood used in the piles, which are pitched, and in some places plated with metal, but they are frequently corroded by the water, and removed; and there is no doubt that the lower part of the Pier will often verify the fate of the Irishman's knife,—very old,—but which had first a new handle, and then a new blade. Below the Pier Head is a gallery, where in a high sea the breaking of the waves may be seen and heard to great advantage; and merriment is often excited by hasty runs and jumps to avoid showers of spray. On the platform is a flag-staff, on which colours are hoisted on Sundays and holydays, and also signals; that for the arrival of a vessel is white on red, and for its departure white on blue (the "Blue Peter"). Here are also two signal guns, about six pounders, which have a very loud report. The steam packets to Dieppe, the *Talbot* and *Eclipse*, leave this Pier twice a week in the summer season, and are very safe and convenient vessels; their arrivals and departures generally excite a crowd and some interest. The band of the regiment also plays on the Pier once a week. In the intervals of sailing, the packets are moored in the harbour of Shoreham, and when the tide will not allow of their coming up to the Pier Head, they start from that place; also, in a few instances, when they cannot conveniently make Shoreham, they steer for Newhaven or Little Hampton. Dieppe is 27 leagues or 81 miles distant from Brighton, and 126 miles from Paris. The route lies through the noble and celebrated city of Rouen, which is said to be, alone, worth a visit to France; and, in fact, has interesting associations for an Englishman, possessed by few other places on the continent. We had some thoughts of adding, or publishing separately, a survey of the route from Dieppe to Paris, but were prevented by circumstances, one of which was the miserable deficiency of all encouragement, in this time generally, and particularly in the vicinity of Brighton. We have nothing more to say on the subject of the Chain Pier, but that it has commodious baths at its extremity, and a camera obscura at the descent from the Marine Parade; here is also a Saloon and Reading-room, with occasional accessories of amusement, as foreign musicians, &c. Fireworks have been occasionally exhibited on the Pier, by Mr. Jones, a resident pyrotechnist, whose only remuneration (or " guerdon," for that is " eleven-pence farthing better"—*Shakspeare*) is the voluntary contribution of the company. The total expense, including the Esplanade, was 30,000*l.*, defrayed in shares by a company. The admission is 1*l.* 1*s.* per annum, or two-pence each visit: parties landing at or embarking from it pay sixpence.

On the 23d of November, 1824, the Pier was severely tried by a storm, but found fully competent to endure any such convulsions. The waves ran " mountains high," and often completely obscured the Pier from sight: they broke down the wooden railing at its head, washed up some of the planks, and occasionally raised the platform several feet between the towers, but from its elasticity it speedily recovered its proper place, and no part of the chains or piles was broken. Descriptions and plates of this storm have been published, and may be had in Brighton.

THE MARINE PARADE; KEMP TOWN, &c.

extends about a mile and a half along the Cliff to Kemp Town. This portion of the town is decidedly the best adapted for those who require a bracing air, as the west end is for those to whom a mild and sheltered situation is the primary object. The average difference of temperature between the two is stated to be two degrees and a half. Of the fine effect of the air and prospects here, we cannot speak too highly: they are only to be excelled, on the southern coast, at Eastbourne. The Marine Parade has many fine piles of buildings and some good squares and streets, opening into the interior line of houses. Amongst these are the New Steyne, the Crescent, Rock-gardens, Marine-square, and Portland-street; the latter has a large mansion at the end, called Portland House, surmounted by the lion-statant crest of the Duke of Norfolk. In front is a fluted Corinthian portico, which would be extremely noble, if the entablature and pediment were in proportion to the columns. Near this point is a descent by a staircase to the bottom of the cliff, a walk to which will be found very interesting, as also a ramble amongst the rocks, sea-weeds, and shrimp fishers, &c. at low water. The sea-wall, erected at an expense of 5000*l*., to defend the Marine Parade, from the insufficiency of its prominence as a bulwark, fell down—which was, doubtless, a most provoking circumstance. A new one, on a very solid and grand construction, has been begun, but stopped by disagreements in the town; yet it will probably be completed.

The famed " Kemp Town" occupies the farthest point. This pile is certainly imposing from its extent, and in parts is very handsome. The Crescent is upwards of 800 feet in span, 200 feet more than the largest in Bath, out of which issues a spacious square. The architecture has generally the lower story Doric and the upper Ionic, or in some places Corinthian. The worst part of the erection is the farther terrace, called " Albany," the style of which is very mediocre. A lateral perspective view of the crescent and square can only excite a pleasing idea.

Kemp Town is, however, at present a dull place: " the grass grows in the streets." Its principal attraction is the residence of the Duke of Devonshire, which occupies a part of the most desirable locality, the Crescent, as represented in our plate. The great error was in calling it, or wishing it to be thought, a separate " town" from Brighton, to which distinction it has not the slightest claim. It has no earthly concomitant of a town: no steeple, market-house, shops, or inns. Had it been merely called Kemp Place, or Crescent, considered as a suburb to Brighton, and more closely allied to it, it would have been well; and no

BRIGHTON WEST.

For the History & Description of the Sussex Coast. 1833.

one could have disputed its claim to the character of a fine range of buildings. An attempt was also made to gain for Brunswick-square, and one or two adjoining streets, the appellation of a " town;" but good sense prevailed, and the design was abandoned.

In front of Kemp Town, with a slight descent from the Cliff, is a very desirable esplanade, formed by a mound of sand rising from the beach, with a neat cemented tunnel in the centre issuing from the lawn of Kemp Town. The situation is in a certain degree sheltered, and the views are nevertheless fine. On the beach, at a spot called Black Rock, is also a very long tunnel for carts, which we should think might be a *minute* representation of the Grotto of Pausilippo.

The Cliff continues its ascent to the signal-house, where we should suppose it was from 150 to 200 feet high, and a walk to this spot will repay the time and trouble of the visitor.

BRIGHTON, WEST OF THE STEYNE.

The new sea-road and Esplanade at the back of the Albion Hotel, is one of the most beneficial of the new erections, as previous to this the communication between the two ends of the Town was only by a narrow lane issuing out of the Steyne. The range from hence to the western extremity, about a mile and a quarter, is called " King's Road." The esplanade, which is fortified by wooden flanking walls, and piles of very great strength, is at its commencement low; and a walk along this locality has an interesting and romantic effect in a wintry evening, when the roar of the waves is heard near us, whilst their swell is almost unseen, except when the white fringe of a breaker makes itself conspicuous above the " dark profound." These sights and sounds will strike him, who, like Pelops, " comes down in the dark to the white sea*."

The wholesale Fish-market is held on the beach. Here the colliers and other trading vessels unload, and the sailing and row-boats are moored, or ply for fares and parties. The streets opening into the town are narrow and business-like;

* Pindar.

still the fashionable promenade is in full vigour here, and the houses are in great request. The turn of the street leading out of East Street, and also Pool Lane, are occupied by gay shops of fancy dealers of every description, and milliners. Farther west is the Battery of six guns, taken from a French ship, where they were rated as thirty-eight pounders, but the French pound weighing eighteen ounces English, they carry a ball of forty pounds and a half. At the back of the battery on the opposite side of the street, is an artillery guard-house or barrack. A little to the east of the battery is the custom-house, which has a small neat front, and both of these have flag-staffs.

Regency Square, one of the most fashionable situations, is very regularly built, and is neat, without much architectural ornament : immediately beyond it, Preston Street, a wide and handsome one, runs up to the Western Road, which extends from the top of North Street at the back of the whole west end of the town, and is similar, in appearance, to the suburbs of London. It contains some very good conservatories. The range of buildings from Regency to Brunswick square, is handsome ; the latter is the largest square in the town ; the fronts of its houses are generally circular, and ornamented with columns ; but the large opening at the top is to be regretted, as it has a rather cold and naked effect. The square is inferior in beauty to the terraces on either hand of its front, which are among the best erections in Brighton, ornamented with bold and handsome Corinthian pillars, in a very good style*. At the farthest extremity the new " Adelaide Crescent," so called in honour of the Queen, the patroness of Brighton, is now erecting, and promises to be an unusually fine and stately building†. It was stated in the *Brighton Gazette* that this was " the first attempt at regular architecture in Brighton." This is unfair, as there is much respectable Palladian architecture in that town ; but Adelaide Crescent will unquestionably be one of its best ornaments. The front has no columns, but the windows are very handsomely ornamented

* See Plate.
† The only small object which approaches it in the town, is the front of the " Clarence Mansion" boarding-house.

with stone balconies, mouldings, and pediments; and the enriched projecting cornice is supported by bold cantilivers: the terrace in front, which is rusticated in the Burlingtonian style, the railed square, &c. will all possess features of considerable grandeur.

The western esplanades, which are between half and three quarters of a mile in length, are very spacious and convenient. Some time ago, through an extraordinarily stupid management, the walks were absolutely paved with bruised *chalk*, which rendered them inaccessible in sunshiny weather, on pain of blindness: but on strong remonstrances being made in the newspapers, it was removed, and gravel substituted. A band, consisting of ten persons, was established here last summer to play on three evenings in the week, to which also the inhabitants had been urged in the Brighton papers, from the consideration that they did not provide amusements for visitors; but we believe it was abandoned before the end of the season, from the deficiency of subscriptions. Here, however, the visitors must share the blame with the inhabitants, as they were well contented to walk and listen to the music, which, though not of the highest order, was much better than nothing;—yet kept their purses closed. The small town of St. Leonard's, which has not one-thirtieth part of the population of Brighton, supports a parade band with ease. Perhaps another season will find the latter in a more liberal mood.

The esplanade is a very lively scene on summer mornings, with ladies, gentlemen, and children; bathing machines, horses, donkies, pleasure-boats, &c.; and would form a good subject for a landscape; the evening promenades are also very lively*.

---

* Ah, County Guy, the hour is nigh,
   The sun has left the lea,
The orange-flower perfumes the bower,
   The breeze is on the sea.
The lark, his lay that trilled all day,
   Sits hushed, his partner nigh,
Breeze, bird, and flower, they know the hour,
   But where is County Guy?

Our Gallic neighbours (whom we like very well in their own characters*, and only dislike when vexatiously praised by English Gallo-maniacs, to the entire depreciation of their own countrymen) are very partial to Brighton, compared with which their sole *Bains de Mer* at Dieppe must hide their diminished heads. The promenades here are very well suited to their taste, and they delight to " take a little turn of walking," either of an evening or " of good morning," which enables them to " carry themselves well." Sometimes also they undertake that feat, perilous in sound, which they by a most ludicrous perversion of ideas, call " walking on a horse," which, however, we have no wish to see them literally put in practice, as, especially in the case of ladies, it would be very hazardous†.

LIBRARIES.

The *original* Library of Brighton is now occupied by *Mr. Philips*, confectioner, at the south western angle of the Old Steyne, and was successively kept by Mr. Woodgate, Mr. Crawford, and Mr. Bowen. The second was *Lucombe's* on the Steyne, now converted into a Bazaar, a circumstance to be

> The village maid steals through the shade,
>   Her lover's suit to hear;
> To beauty shy, by lattice nigh,
>   Sings high-born cavalier :
> The star of love, all stars above,
>   Now reigns o'er earth and sky;
> And high and low the influence know,
>   Then where is County Guy?
>
> *Quentin Durward.*

---

* Is the tale of " the Violet Girl of the Pont Neuf," in the November No. of the Court Magazine, true? We hope it is.

† All languages, however, have probably some absurd idioms, not excepting the Greek and Latin, and the English have no right to laugh at their neighbours. Our " shall" and " will," must ever be the torment of foreigners, as they were near proving fatal to the poor Frenchman, who in falling from London Bridge, exclaimed " I *will* be drowned—nobody *shall* help me." We speak of a person's being " in liquor," the only actual instance of which on record was Shakspeare's Duke of Clarence, when drowned in the butt of Malmsey :—also of another's being " beside himself," which if graphically represented, would be a very amusing caricature.

regretted by summer visitors, as its musical and other entertainments rendered it the most lively resort in the town. The third established was *Tuppen's*, facing the sea, near the entrance of the Marine Parade: this is still in existence, and is at present the only establishment for loo and music: the usual vocal performer is Miss Corrie, a young lady known and esteemed in the place, whose voice has a very sweet and silvery tone. *Messrs. Wright*, our highly respectable publishers, amongst whose subscribers are the King and Queen, have two establishments; a large and convenient one in the colonnade, North Street; and a smaller but equally convenient library on the Western Esplanade, near Cannon Place, to meet the views of the residents in that vicinity. At both these are also *musical* libraries, in which they have attained much celebrity, and at the colonnade library is a concert-room. *Mr. Loder's*, in North Street, has a very large collection of books, and a convenient reading-room, as has also *Mr. Taylor's*, in the same street, possessing equal advantages; and a similar character may be given to *Mr. Nash's*, from Tunbridge Wells, at the west end, near Mahommed's baths, and *Mr. Brewer's*, and *Mr. Saunder's*, in St. James Street.

The terms of these libraries are nearly similar, viz. £1. 11s. 6d. per annum ; 18s. per six months; 8s. per month; and 5s. per fortnight. Messrs. Taylor's, and Saunder's are, we believe, rather less. There are also four or five other libraries in the town, the grade and terms of which may not be equal to the preceding; but they may nevertheless have their merits, and be found adapted to the wishes of the visitor.

BATHS,

WARM, COLD, AND SHOWER, &c. &c.

The oldest are *Wood's*, at the south western extremity of the Steyne, which are still equal, though not superior, to the later established ones. The others are *Mahommed's*, celebrated for the process of *shampooing* : *Williams's*, and *Lamprell's*, in the same vicinity ; the latter has a very large circular plunging bath; *Hobden's*, further west, near the battery ;

and an establishment on the New Steyne. It would be invidious to institute any comparison between the several parties: each possesses a convenient reading-room, &c. and affords equal attention and civility.

Nor is it within the compass of our purpose, either here, or at any other place, to digress into any observations on the mode or utility of bathing; the reader must be referred to able medical authorities.

BATHING MACHINES

are found at the western part of the town, and are on the same plan as at most other watering places, and on the same terms. This again is a subject on which the visitor will find immediate information attainable on his arrival.

FLYS, HORSES, &c.

Brighton possesses a very large number, we believe between 200 and 300, of carriages of every description, principally four wheeled. They are in general neat, and the horses tolerably good. We may as well subjoin the list of fares, for the convenience of visitors, particularly as we believe those at *Worthing* and *Hastings* are nearly similar, which will save repetition in our accounts of those places.

" FOR TIME.

" For every hour, or any less time—to commence from leaving the stand,

First class *	3s.	6d.
Second class	2s.	6d.
Third class	1s.	6d.

" For half an hour after the first hour, or any less time,

First class . . .	1s.	9d.
Second class	1s.	3d.
Third class . . .	0s.	9d.

* These depend on the size and the number of persons they carry.

" FOR DISTANCE.

" For any distance not exceeding one mile, including the distance from the stand or place from whence the coach, carriage, or fly shall be called, to the place where the fare shall be taken up,

First class	.	.	.	. 1s. 6d.
Second class	.	.	.	. 1s. 0d.
Third class	.	.	.	. 0s. 9d.

" And for every additional half-mile,

First class	.	.	.	. 0s. 9d.
Second class	.	.	.	. 0s. 6d.
Third class	.	.	.	. 0s. 6d."

There are also sedan chairs and hand flies on proper terms. The small carriages for children are drawn by *goats*, an idea first put in practice by a boy of Brighton : they are generally well treated ; and there is said to be no cruelty in using these animals for the purpose, as, from their strong formation, they are not unfitted for draught. In fact, they are actually employed to assist in drawing ploughs in *Savoy*. Whilst it is added that this remark does not apply to Dogs, and that the use made of them is one for which, as they are not fitted, they certainly could never have been intended, and that employing them is, in many respects, absolute cruelty—a remark which deserves consideration. The car of the famed Princess, *in petto*, " Cinderella," was drawn by two goats at the Brighton theatre.

We feel great pleasure in adding, that we were informed, by an honourable lady, whom we have the pleasure to call a friend, as noble in mind as in person, the munificent foundress and patroness of an Association in London, for " Promoting Rational Humanity towards the Animal Creation," that, during a residence of several weeks in Brighton, she perceived fewer indications of cruelty than in any other place she had visited *.

* We know that this noble lady, or any other person who should recommend such a Society or purpose, would be assailed by some, though not all, with the refuge of inhumanity or cold-heartedness—the epithet of " morbid sensibility," which in her case would be about as much heeded as if " dogs had bayed the moon."

The horses kept at the livery stables in Brighton are generally of a superior kind, and sometimes of high breeding: the
terms are rather expensive.

FISHERY.

THE FISHER'S CALL.

BY THOMAS DOUBLEDAY.

THE thorn is in the bud,
  The palm is in the blossom,
The primrose, in the shade,
  Unfolds her dewy bosom ;
Sweet Coquet's purling clear,
  And summer music making;
The trout has left his lair,
  Then waken, fishers, waken.

The lavrock's in the sky,
  And on the heath the plover,
The bee upon the thyme,
  The swallow skimming over ;
The farmer walks the field,
  The seed he's casting steady ;
The breeze is blowing west,
  Be ready, fishers, ready.

The violet's in her prime,
  And April is the weather;
The partridge on the wing,
  The muircock in the heather ;
The sun's upon the pool,
  His mornin' radiance wasting,
It's glittering like the gold,
  Oh! hasten, fishers, hasten.

Anniversary, 1829.

Probably the description of the Brighton fisheries by the
able zoologist Pennant, about fifty years ago, will nearly
serve for the present time ; or where it differs it will have the
effect of novel historical particulars, and the visitor will easily
discover the mode and degree of difference.

" The fish-market, both wholesale and retail, is kept on
the beach, a little beyond the baths ; the boats used in the
fisheries are from ten to fifteen tons, made remarkably strong

to secure them against the storms in their winter adventure. The mackarel boats are navigated by three or four men and a boy ; there are about forty-five for the mackarel fishery, and twenty-five for the trawling ; they set sail generally in the evening, go eight or ten leagues to sea, and return the next day ; the fishing is always carried on in the night. The crew are provided with tea, coffee, water, and a small quantity of spirits, for at sea they are remarkably temperate ; their indulgence is only on shore. They only take with them bread, beef, and greens, which, and sometimes fish, they often eat with their tea and coffee. They are a hardy race, and very healthy ; yet, during the summer season, they have a very small interval from labour. They get a good meal, and a very short repose by laying themselves on a bed during the few hours in the day in which they come on shore. They bring their fish in baskets to the beach, fling them in vast heaps, and instantly a ring of people is formed round, an auction is begun, and the heap is immediately disposed of : the price is uncertain, according to the success of the night. Mackarel this season (1793) were sold from 1*l.* to 7*l.* a hundred ; they have been sold as high as 15*l.* a hundred. Mackarel and soles are the great staples of the place ; nine or ten thousand have been taken at one shooting of the net. Mackarel swim deep in calms, and rise to the surface in gales, when the largest fish and the greatest quantity are taken.

" The nets consist of a number of parts, each of which are from thirty-six to fifty yards long and deep, and are kept buoyant by corks. These united form a chain of nets a mile and a half long. Before they are used in the spring they are taken from the storehouses and spread upon the Steyne ; a privilege, time immemorial, granted to the fishermen. The boats are drawn on shore at the latter end of the winter, and placed in ranges on the lower part of the Steyne, and other places near to the sea ; and I have, in the beginning of April, with a great noise heard them drag them back to the sea, in the manner described by Horace.

> ' Solviter acris hyems gratâ vice veris et Favoni
> Trahuntque siccas machinæ carinas.'

The interval from labour is very small, for numbers of the boats are in the early spring hired out to dredge for oysters, to supply the beds in the Medway and other places.

" The greater part of the fish are sent to London, packed in baskets, usually weighing about three quarters of a hundred in each; they are put into small light carts, which go post, carry from fifteen to thirty baskets each, and reach our capital in eight or ten hours.

" The mackarel are supposed to come from the Bay of Biscay. In the early spring they are taken off Dieppe; they next appear off Mount's Bay, where they are caught in seines, and sent by land to London in small baskets; the shooting of nets has not been found to answer off the Cornish shore. They arrive in the Channel off Brighthelmstone in the middle of April, and continue till the middle of July; after which they will not mesh, but are caught with hooks, and are at that season nearly unfit for eating. In June they are observed to approach nearer to the shore; they continue in the Channel till the cold season commences, when they go progressively north or east. The fry is seen of very small size in October and November.

" The herring fishery begins in October; those fish appear in great quantities along shore, and reach Hastings in November. The fishery is very considerable, and adventurers from every country engage in it. A boat has ten last of ten thousand each. The fish which are not sent to London fresh are salted or cured as red herrings. The nets resemble those used in the mackarel fishery, only the meshes are smaller; they are about twenty feet deep, and are left to sink of themselves. The congenerous pilchards are sometimes taken here in the mackarel nets, but in very small quantities.

" Soles, the other staple fish, are taken in trawls in great numbers. The fishery begins in April, and continues all the summer: in April, 1794, the weight of two tons were caught in one night. I saw in the same month a heap of soles on the market beach, none of which were less than nineteen inches long. The other congenerous fishes were turbots, generally very indifferent; brills or pearl; smear dabs; plaice, and flounders.

" Various kinds of rays are taken here; such as the skate (Br. Zool. ii. No. 30), the sharp-nosed (No. 31), the fuller ,(No. 53), the thornback, the sand-ray, which has sharp slender spines on the edges, opposite to the eyes; minute spines along the edges of the fins, and upon the fins like the fuller; the back and tail shagreened, marked with round black spots; the teeth sharp and slender. A ray, not uncommon on the Flintshire coasts, is twenty-one inches long, of which the tail is eleven; the nose is pointed, and semitransparent; two spines above each eye, and three placed in a row on the back; three rows on the tail, of which the middle runs far up the back; edges of the body from the nose to the anal fin rough, with rows of minute spines; back quite smooth, of a fine pale brown, regularly marked with circular black spots; teeth quite flat and smooth.

" Of the shark genus, the angel-fish is not uncommon. The smooth sharks, or topes, are very numerous; they grow to the length of four feet. I saw opened several of this species, and can vouch for the truth of the young entering the mouth of the parent in time of danger, and taking refuge in the stomach. I have seen from twelve to twenty taken out of a single tope, each eleven or twelve inches long. This species is split, salted, and eaten.

" I here met with the corbeagle of Mr. Jago (See Br. Zool. iii. No. 49); the length was three feet nine inches, the thickest circumference two feet and an inch. It is a rare species allied to the Beaumaris shark. The greater and lesser spotted dog-fish are very numerous.

" The common angler is frequently caught here and sometimes of an enormous size; from the vast width of the mouth it is called here the kettle-man. The launce, and two species of weevers, are very common; the greater grows to the length of sixteen inches, is two inches deep, the weight of two pounds, and is a firm well-tasted fish. The fishermen have a great dread of the spines, and cut them off as soon as taken.

" The cod-fish tribe are rather scarce, except the whitings, which are sometimes caught in mackarel nets, but chiefly with hooks. They are taken in April; but the best season is in October. I saw here the common cod, the whitingpout, the coal-fish, and the five bearded cod.

" The doree is frequently taken; I saw one of fifteen pounds weight, and the length of three quarters of a yard. I saw here the lunated gilthead and ancient wrasse, the basse, and red or striped surmullet; the last small. The red and the grey gurnards were common.

" Salmons are unknown here, which I am told is the case on all chalky coasts. The gar or needle fish are often seen here, and of great lengths. I shall not digress improperly in saying that the razor bills and guillemots, inhabitants of Beachy Head, are frequently caught in the mackarel nets, unwarily diving in pursuit of the fish. Prawns are in their season taken in vast abundance near the shores, which, wanting rocks to give shelter to the lobsters and crabs, those delicacies are brought from the more distant parts to the east.

" Variety of corallines are found on the coast of this country and that of Kent: many of them are engraven in the ingenious history of that class of natural history, so admirably managed by my friend the late Mr. Ellis, to whom Linnæus gave the title of Lynceus Ellisius; but for some years before his death, by too great an exertion of his Lyncean faculties, he was totally deprived of even the common blessing of sight."

THEATRE.

The Brighton Theatre, which fifty years ago was let for 60 guineas per annum, and some time afterwards produced 600, is now let at 1200*l.* per annum to Messrs. Vining and Bew, the former a popular actor in London, and the latter a dentist, at Brighton, attending the Pavilion, who entered upon this concern in the summer of 1831. The abilities of the former gentleman as a manager are well known, and also his correct and gentlemanly deportment. The salaries allowed to the performers are also said to be liberal. The Theatre is an externally unornamented building in the New Road, with a plain portico; but the interior is considered to be one of the most elegant out of the Metropolis. The prices have lately been reduced. The audience consists of two tier of boxes, a pit, and spacious gallery, with a wide corridor to the boxes: their fronts are white, handsomely ornamented with gold, and lined with crimson; the drop scene is green and gold. The representations are conducted in so very liberal and skilful a manner that they ought to experience a far more extensive patronage from those who are accustomed to attend dramatic performances. The scenery and other decorations are splendid, without any limit of expense. Several melo-dramas have been brought out in a very finished style: one of which, a local piece, styled the "White Hawk Lady," its scene laid at Lewes, in the times of the De Warrens, exhibited much correctness and ingenuity. Ballets have also been introduced, some of which were pretty, especially *Cinderella*. We suppose that in any situation these have more of the essence of grace and beauty, in proportion to their being without gratuitous indecorum. The former, in a style not easily to be surpassed even in fancy, and unmixed with the latter, may be seen in some of the introductory dances of "Masaniello." The orchestra is respectable; and the usual companies of performers comprise many individuals of talent*. In addition to which, many of the most popular London actors have visited the Theatre during the last two years. That clever and respectable pair, Mr. and Mrs. Keeley, are great favourites. The former's "Dandy Cock Robin" is very droll, and the latter's "Banks of the Blue Moselle," once heard, cannot easily be forgotten.

That meritorious and enterprising youth, "Jack the Giant Killer," of bean-stalk-climbing celebrity, made his appearance in a Pantomime last winter, and some equally famed fairy hero, or princess, will doubtless resort here each succeeding one.

* A daughter of Mr. Vining, of engaging and artless manners, made her first appearance this year.

The Equestrian Troop, from Astley's, was engaged here in 1832; and also performed privately before their Majesties, &c. at the Riding House.

Mr. Cook's company, which may be considered equal to the former, generally visit Brighton every year, and erect a spacious Circus in the north part of the town : these also were honoured by the King's patronage. We have been informed that the training of these wonderfully docile and intelligent animals is accomplished in this school with much less rigour than in some others.

ASSEMBLY AND CONCERT ROOMS.

The large assembly and ball-room, at the Old Ship, is 80 feet in length, by 20 in width. Meetings of various kinds, public dinners, &c. are also held at this place. The apartment is handsomely decorated with splendid lustres, and has a gallery over the entrance, and an orchestra in the centre of the south side. The card-room is an oblong apartment of convenient size; its walls are very cleverly painted in fresco, with scenes from the adventures of Telemachus.

The new royal concert and ball-room, in Cannon-place, is just completed, and belongs to Messrs. Wright, of the Colonnade. It has a frontage of 124 feet towards St. Margaret's-place, including two dwelling-houses; and the architecture is a fanciful Corinthian, but much superior to that of the Assembly-room in the Town Hall. The room itself is 60 feet long, $34\frac{1}{2}$ feet wide, and $34\frac{1}{2}$ high to the coved ceiling. The interior ornaments are modelled after the *Choragic Monument of Lysicrates*, and the fluted pilasters and entablatures bold and rich. The lighting is effected by 40 gas burners, disposed in chandeliers of unusual magnificence, manufactured at Birmingham. This room has been pronounced, by various architects and musicians, one of the best adapted to its purpose in the kingdom ; and all its details are of a very expensive character.

In addition to balls, concerts, and lectures, it is the intention of the proprietors to let this room by the night to those noblemen and gentlemen who may wish to give large parties, but either not have convenience in their own houses, or are desirous of avoiding the trouble and disarrangement thereby occurring. The architect of this splendid room was Mr. H. Wilds; builder, Mr. T. Wisden.

Harmonic meetings are held at the Old Ship, and also at the Golden Cross, near the Old Steyne.

RACES

are held on the magnificent locality of White Hawk Hill, in the month of August, which continue during three days, and in addition to much company of high rank, have all the usual excitement and accompaniments of large fairs.

HOTELS AND INNS

are too numerous to particularise; amongst the best are the Albion, the Bedford, the York, the Old Ship, the New Steyne, the New Ship, the White Horse, the Norfolk, the Sea House, the Marine, &c. &c. Inns of a very respectable character occur in every direction of the town.

Schools and Charities*.

"They asked a wise man which was preferable, fortitude or liberality? He replied, ' He who possesses liberality has no need of fortitude.' It is inscribed on the tomb of Bahram Goar, that a liberal hand is preferable to a strong arm. Hatim Tai no longer exists, but his exalted name will remain famous for virtue to eternity. Distribute the tithes of your wealth in alms; for when the husbandman lops off the exuberant branches from the vine, it produces an increase of grapes."—*Sadi.*

"Here shall soft Charity repair,
And break the bonds of Grief;
Down the harrow'd couch of Care,
Man to man thus bring relief."

Having spoken freely of the want of spirit and liberality in the inhabitants of Brighton on many occasions, we are very much gratified in being able to demonstrate unequivocally, by the following details, that they are not backward in feelings of charity towards misfortune and indigence. It is true that the donations of visitors form no small part in the aggregate of these contributions; still we sincerely believe that the proportion of the former is by no means deficient.

SCHOOLS.

NATIONAL.

Number of children receiving education in Church-street:

Boys . . .	400
Girls . . .	230

Ditto in Lavender-street:

Boys and Girls . .	300
Infants . . .	130

In Upper Gardner-street:

Infants . . .	120
Total . . .	——1180

Secretaries, the Rev. H. M. Wagner and the Rev. T. Cooke; and under the patronage of their Majesties, &c. &c. &c.   The

---

* We are compelled to derive our information on these heads from the "Brighton Directory," 1832, price 2s.; an useful little work to those whom it may concern.

annual collections at the churches in Brighton for this institution average about £200. The central school in Church-street is a lofty and handsome Gothic building, particularly as viewed from the west, and has the appearance of a collegiate hall. The praiseworthy system of *rewards* is pursued here, to which the Marquis of Bristol is a liberal annual benefactor.

SWAN DOWNER'S CHARITY-SCHOOL.

Sixty-five girls are clothed and educated, &c., with the interest of £7000, left by Swan Downer, Esq., a native of Brighton.

FEMALE ORPHAN ASYLUM,
UNDER THE PATRONAGE OF HIS MAJESTY.

17 children are boarded, clothed, and educated. Treasurer, Miss Jeffries, 62, East-street*.

UNION CHARITY-SCHOOL,
MIDDLE-STREET.

Patron, his Majesty.
For all denominations of children.

Boys	. . .	250
Girls	. . .	120

BRITISH SCHOOLS AND SCHOOLS OF INDUSTRY,
UPPER EDWARD-STREET.

300 children.
The premises are very spacious and convenient.
Originated by Montagu Burgoyne, Esq.

SOCIETY FOR PROMOTING CHRISTIAN KNOWLEDGE,
ETC. ETC.

No account:—but the distribution of books very great, and an extensive depository at the central national school. Average collections at the churches in Brighton, £160.

---

* We give the address of Secretaries, &c., for the use of those visitors who may be induced to contribute.

BRITISH AND FOREIGN BIBLE SOCIETY.

No account; but supposed to be considerable.

LADIES BIBLE SOCIETY.

Ditto   Ditto.

TEMPERANCE SOCIETY.

" Quod dat *'ginis'* in genitivo."—*Propria Quæ Maribus.*
" Eau de ' *Mort.*' "—*Suggested French reading, (as regards excess.)*
" *Burning* spirits."—*Latin,* " *ardent.*"
" Art thou a 'spirit' of *health,* or *goblin damn'd ?*"—*Shakespeare.*

Established 1832, aided by a donation of £100 from the Earl of Egremont. Earl of Chichester president.—It is not for us to venture a judgment on institutions; but whilst we admire the principle of this society, viz., the prevention of drunkenness, especially from ardent spirits*, and all its desolating consequences, we would respectfully suggest that they may be thought rather to overshoot the mark in requiring a pledge that the members will never touch spirits except as a medicine. There is reason in all things, and pledges are something like vows, which wise casuists and moralists recommend the avoidance of, as snares to the conscience. The abandonment of their " grog" by the Greenwich pensioners, which is surely not allowed them in intoxicating quantities, has a harsh and repulsive effect. Would not a pledge of avoiding all intoxication, to the utmost of their power, be better? But, on the great principle of the discouragement of excess in drinking, there cannot be two opinions amongst those who have seen the lamentably squalid state of so large a por-

---

* A very proper hit was made at Covent Garden Theatre this winter, in exhibiting a miserably emaciated and shaking figure issuing out of a barrel, with the title " *The spirit of Gin !*"—a good lesson for once ;—
" — ridentem dicere verum,
" Quid vetat?"
The judicious applauded earnestly : those in the upper regions did *not*—
" More 's the pity."
Ale as well as *wine,* "in reason," like "roasted eggs," are not discountenanced by Temperance Societies ; this milder spirit (if it may be so called) being allowed to be nourishing.—" Spiritus intus *alit.*"

tion of the population of London ; which, from being one of the neatest, is in danger (which heaven forefend) of becoming one of the dirtiest capitals in Europe ; and who learn at the same time that this sad change is produced by the slow and cheap poison of gin—" *Blue Ruin*" truly, in a ribald phrase which we are almost ashamed to mention, but is forced on the attention which is applied to the subject,—for it is nearly as bad as the *Cholera*. As for the conscious venders of this wholesale poison it is vexatious to see them making rapid fortunes, whilst thousands in at least comparatively honest employments cannot obtain a living.

COUNTY HOSPITAL

is a very neat edifice, standing on a fine elevated spot near Kemp Town, which was given by T. R. Kemp, Esq., with a donation of £1000 ; £2000 was also contributed towards the erection by the Earl of Egremont. The front is lofty and appropriate, constructed of pale brick, with stone ornaments, and has a handsome iron railing. Some astonishment is however occasioned on viewing its very moderate size, to learn that it accommodates one hundred patients : still we are assured that the internal arrangements are well conducted ; there are also separate fever wards. Their Majesties are patrons ; and there is a long list of vice-presidents, trustees, physicians, &c. &c. &c. : Treasurer, John Hall, Esq., banker. The number of in-patients admitted in 1831 was 540 ; out-patients, 211 : since the establishment in 1826, of the former 1521, and the latter 651. Total amount of receipts in 1831, 3724*l*. 13*s*. 9*d*.; average collections at the churches in Brighton, £350. We have heard it stated by a clergyman in Brighton, that the gentry of the county, though fully aware of its benefits to their parishioners, do not come forward in its support so liberally as they ought. This is a reproach, not to Brighton, but the county at large, and especially the Eastern division (as there is an infirmary at Chichester), which should no longer exist*.

---

* The confessor of a French king being asked to explain his idea of living temperately, answered, "live always as you promise to do when you have a fit of

DISPENSARY.

Patron, His Majesty.

Presidents, &c. &c.   Collector, T. D. Ruddock, printer to the king.   Number of patients in 1831, 2544.   Annual income, 681*l.* 7*s.* 5*d.*—" Accomplishing *great* good by *small* means."

PROVIDENT AND DISTRICT SOCIETY.

Patrons, their Majesties.

Vice-Patrons, Presidents, &c., &c.

President, the Vicar of Brighton.

Secretaries: the Rev. Thomas Cooke, of the new church; the Rev. J. S. M. Anderson, of St. George's Chapel; the Rev. J. N. Goulty, of Union Street Chapel.

Agent, Mr. D. King, 63, High Street.

This excellent and laudable institution was commenced in 1824, and is so well arranged in all its details, as scarcely to be susceptible of improvement, still less open to objection.   Its objects are three-fold:—direct charitable assistance; encouragement to the poor to make deposits, which are returned to them in the winter in useful articles, with the amount increased by a premium; prevention of mendicity, by having a mendicity office, where beggars may be referred, and their cases examined into: the latter provision alone is *not* fully executed.   The deposits in the first year are said to have been £600, contributed by 800 individuals; it is feared that they have since declined.   The number of the acting committee is

---

the gout." If we were always as alive to the distresses of others as whilst we are suffering illness ourselves, when we reflect that we have every comfort supplied by diligent relatives or attendants, but that others may be suffering equal pain, with the accompaniments of cold, hunger, and neglect, (for what are too generally the mercies of a parish?) we should have a vivid impression of the excellence of the golden rule "to do as we would be done by," and have "a hand open as day to melting charity."

about 100, by whom the town is divided into six districts, for the purpose of visiting and inquiring into cases of distress. The following observations, by an old but excellent writer (who was no ascetic), appear so extremely applicable to this point, that we have been induced to give them insertion:

" The giver should not lose the benefit of that personal acquaintance with sorrow, which strengthens the social ties, corrects the caprices of fastidious self-importance, and turns the narrow aims of individual gratification into gratitude to that Providence who appoints wealth as the STEWARD * and DISPENSER, rather than the CONSUMER of its accumulated bounties. I might also add, how much this benovolent intercourse between the rich and poor, the great and lowly, enlarges the mind and improves the manners of both parties. When a lady of rank surveys a healthy group of young cottagers vying with each other for skill and adroitness at their various occupations; watching with anxious glance the hour-glass, which, if early exhausted, upbraids them with having previously loitered, and reminds them of the probability of their dame's inflicting an additional task, she may form some notion of the value of the moments which she is anxious to waste; or when she sees the care-worn mother dividing the brown loaf in equal portions among her children, whose countenances brighten with the glow of pleasure, as they successively relieve the cravings of hunger, she may learn to compare the expenses of vanity and benevolence, and to estimate their specific gratifications. But the bed of sickness, especially when attended by its frightful concomitant, penury, will afford her the best lesson to check the repinings of discontent, and all the various pangs of envy, ambition, and pride, which teach the sickly daughters of spleen to quarrel with prosperity. On the side of the indigent, this social intercourse with their superiors would prove the best check to the democratical spirit that is let loose among them. They would find themselves often called upon to observe the attraction of graceful manners and the advantage of superior information. The narrow, but too general prejudice which has been excited against the apparently more favoured part of our species would be abated, and a grateful attachment to friends and benefactors would soon eradicate the idea, that Lords and Ladies are but poor creatures, were it not that they have got the upper hand in this world."—Mrs. Chapone.

In the winter of 1831-2, when the approach of the cholera was viewed as a possible contingency, an augmentation of the means of this society was strongly called for, in order to effect some temporary provisions, when, by the united charity of visitors and inhabitants, the liberal sum of £900 was contributed for that purpose.

---

* "——— Fruges consumere nati."—HOR.

JUBILEE BENEVOLENT ACCUMULATING FUND.
1809.
Patron, the King.

Stock, £931, 3 per cent. consols.

MATERNAL SOCIETY,
58, CHURCH STREET.
Patroness, the Queen.

Income in 1831, 184*l*. 19*s*. 2*d*.

LYING-IN INSTITUTION,
64, HIGH STREET.
Patron, the King.

Income in 1831, 72*l*. 18*s*.

DORCAS SOCIETY,
FOR PROVIDING CLOTHES, BLANKETS, &c., FOR THE POOR.
Treasurer, Mrs. Poole, 6, Castle Square.

Income, 1831—including sale of fancy articles, £113—319*l*. 12*s*. 6*d*.

SOCIETY FOR RELIEVING POOR WIDOWS IN THE FIRST STAGE OF WIDOWHOOD.
Secretary, Mr. Penfold, North Street.

No account.

DOLLAR SOCIETY.
1813.
So called from its annual subscriptions of five shillings each, entitling individuals to recommend one person as an object of charity. Patronised by the late Queen Charlotte.

No account.

BENEFIT SOCIETIES.

Two or three of these laudable institutions, which should always be encouraged, as conducing to the most unequivocally beneficial purposes*, exist in Brighton; but we have met with no accounts of them. One is an United Fisherman's Society, for which a sermon was preached by the Bishop of Chichester, in 1832, at the New Church, when £36 was collected for the purpose.

SWAN DOWNER'S CHARITY.

Twenty poor men and twenty-four women are annually clothed from the interest of £5000, left by this gentleman for that purpose.

PERCY ALMSHOUSES.

Mrs. Dorothy and Mrs. Anne Percy, who died about 1796, directed six almshouses to be built by their executrix, Mrs. Mary Marriott, and endowed them with the sum of £48 per annum during her life, and £96 subsequently, for the reception of six widows of the church of England who had not received parochial relief. A new gown and cloak is also given to them each second year.

FANCY FAIRS.

Considerable sums are annually raised for three or four institutions in Brighton, by means of these popular charitable contrivances. On this subject we notice a representation in *Bruce's Brighton*, 1831, adopted from the *Brighton Gazette*, which imperatively calls for attention, especially as we have heard it strongly corroborated by those who are both competent

---

* " They asked Hatim Tai if he had ever seen or heard of any person in the world more noble-minded than himself. He replied, ' One day, after having sacrificed forty camels, I went along with an Arab chief to the skirt of a desert, where I saw a labourer who had made up a bundle of thorns, whom I asked why he did not go to the feast of Hatim Tai, to whose table people repaired in crowds. He answered, ' Whosoever eateth bread from his own labour will not submit to be under obligation to Hatim Tai.' I considered this man as my superior in generosity and liberality.' "—*Sadi's " Ghulistan or Rose-Garden."*

judges and entirely disinterested.   It is this:—That however
undeniably excellent are the motives of the originators and
patrons of these modes of charity:—in a town like Brighton,
where a considerable portion of the inhabitants are occupied
in the manufacture and sale of fancy articles, an injury is
caused which is no less than a counter-balance to the good
which may be effected in other quarters.   Thus we find the statement ; and, whilst we readily give it insertion here, we desire
to add, that it is not within the compass of possibility that we
should have any interested motive for so doing.   We are fully
aware of what we are doing ; we know, that not only almost
all ladies of the highest rank in Brighton patronise or contribute to them, but that the Queen herself affords her patronage
in a high degree, and also has sent contributions of her own
work, which of course have been purchased with avidity.   But
we are *sure* her Majesty would prefer our stating that opinion,
which, for the reasons above-mentioned, we have formed, than
that we should avoid the subject with the unworthy caution
of the sycophant.

It should be remembered, that the parties so engaged, and
who may suffer injury, are by no means of the lower class, or
those who, if deprived of one mode of living, are fitted for
others of varied or onerous exertion.   Even if their prospects
in life have never been higher, in the present stage of society,
their manners and ideas are not suited for a descent to a lower
grade.   But they are too often those who have been reduced
from higher birth and expectations; a case formerly principally read in novels, but now too true in real life.   Hands as
white, and eyes as dazzling, may be exercised in such employments as those of the patrician beauties at the fancy fairs ; and
we are certain, or we should not mention it, that the latter
would never wilfully injure the former, even though the
sacrifice were required of their most cherished predilections.
They may be members of large and indigent families, for
whom such employments are especially desirable—they may be
orphans, of whom the frivolous, but not wholly corrupted
sentimentalist observes, that " God tempers the wind to the

shorn lamb"— or, lastly, they may be of that happy class (for they *should* not be *un*happy) who are thus engaged in ministering to the comfort of an aged relative or parent. These cases are not romantic or problematical; they are, at least, highly probable, if not ascertained to be true.

The romantic effect of a Fancy Fair, the theme of song and novel, is, doubtless, too pretty to be easily resigned ; but if the result be shown not to be that which its favourers would desire, let some means of transfer be adopted, both of the mode of benevolence and the popular exhibition. What that should be, it is not for us to pronounce; but it may be safely left in the hands of those whose ingenuity and spirit contrived the original expedient.

Must any of John Bull's sons, in the present day, have something very attractive to their senses to allure them to acts of beneficence and utility ? And will nothing move their dull hands and strike open the rusted clasps of their purses, but the electric flash from the eyes of rank and beauty ?

We are not entirely serious in what we are about to mention, yet we remember to have heard an enthusiast, but a benevolent one, actually recommend something very like it in spirit, though not in details, at a Chapel of Ease in Brighton. We remember to have seen, in the church of a large town in Normandy, a lady of rank and attraction walk round the immense nave, densely thronged with several thousand persons, soliciting from each an alms for the poor of the town, and acknowledging even a *sous*, and from the humblest individual, with impressive gracefulness. The appearance of an elegant figure, crowned with flowers, attended by one priest only, plainly attired, gliding through crowds composed of persons of the higher ranks, confusedly intermingled with peasants, mechanics, fishermen, and their families, in every species of costume, and files of military, had a sufficiently romantic and interesting effect. We were informed also, that the principal ladies of the place took this office in turn every Sunday. That was, doubtless, something a little sentimental and *French* in the mode, and some may seriously object to it, but if they had witnessed the apparently sincere good-feeling at the time, their objections might have been greatly disarmed, on the principle of " *Honi soit qui mal y pense*."

THE POOR HOUSE,

erected in 1821, above the old church, in a very healthy situation, is a plain, convenient edifice, of no architectural pretensions; its front is 190 feet in extent, and the average number of poor which it contains is 350. The internal arrangements are said to be very judicious. A small infirmary for the sick has lately been erected, at a short distance, a measure which confers much credit on its originators and supporters. Belonging to the Poor-house are eight acres of land.

Beyond this is the Cattle Market, erected in 1831-2; but which has proved a complete failure.

MARKET.

The new Market-house, west of the Town Hall, was erected in 1830 ; it is a spacious neat building, having some resemblance to that in Farringdon Street, London, but on a more humble scale. A market of miscellaneous character is held every day in the week, but by far the greatest occurs on Saturday. West of this building, and at the back of North Street, is a dense collection of small " lanes," as they are termed, though the diverging paths are only wide enough for pedestrians. Here may be seen the humble emporiums of industry, indicated in shops of every description, each endeavouring to attract the passenger by the promise of cheapness. Here, too, on Saturdays, may be seen the anxious wife of the artizan, diligently seeking to lay out her small pittance, which the spectator often wishes were greater, in the most advantageous manner.

THE POST OFFICE

is situated in the New Road, and is very well managed; the hour at which it closes is nine.

COACHES, &c. &c.

The number daily running between Brighton and London is not less than thirty, which start at all hours, and from five or six offices; together with others to a variety of principal towns, which the visitor will have no trouble in discovering. There are also commodious vans to London on springs.

BARRACKS.

The horse barracks are situated on the Lewes road, rather less than a mile beyond the new church, and consist of a neat regular pile of building, able to accommodate 650 men. Latterly, however, there have been only four troops quartered here; but with the title of Head-Quarters and an accompanying band. The present regiment is the 3rd Dragoon guards, which has replaced the Scotch Greys. The foot barracks are opposite the palace stables, and will contain 400 men. When his Majesty is at the Pavilion four companies are quartered here, which, in 1831 and 1832, have been those of the Coldstream guards, who have generally either the whole or part of a band.

It usually surprises visitors, on learning that there is a military band in the place, not to be gratified by hearing it oftener (on *week* days), and seeing a little more of the " pomp and circumstance of war," to break the monotony of the town, to which even a hand organ is a relief. The Scotch Greys were accustomed to parade occasionally through the town. Of course it could not be expected that abstruse concerted pieces should be got up daily for the public gratification; but even a little parade flourish, as at the Horse Guards, and a few common airs, would sound " silver sweet" to the listless stroller. We should not object to the everlasting " blue hills of the Tyrol," should be very glad to hear " the Greenwood Tree," or Mlle Sontag's Waltz, and should not even quarrel with " the March in Blue Beard."

CONSERVATORY, OR ORIENTAL GARDEN,

NEAR ADELAIDE CRESCENT.

The design of this institution is certainly novel—viz. to combine a conservatory with a promenade, and to furnish an erection competent to receive under its roof the trees of the eastern or western forest, as well as the exotic shrub and flower. An injudicious puff by some friend in a newspaper excited a slight prejudice by instituting a comparison between its dome and that of St. Peter's—for which we have, architecturally speaking, a superstitious veneration. It is certainly greater in span, though " many a mile" inferior in construction and ornament: and, with respect to mere size, if that were a criterion, Covent Garden Market would be a finer building than Whitehall or Somerset House. Besides, compared with St. Peter's, this dome may be said to lie on the ground, being not much more than one fifth of its height (400 feet); whereas it was the boast of Michael Angelo, that he would not only build a dome larger than the Pantheon, then the most considerable, but raise it in the air. But setting this aside as a point foolishly mooted; it is certainly the largest dome known to exist in the world, being 164 feet in span, which is 34 feet wider than St. Peter's, 56 than St. Paul's, and 76 than the Pavilion stables. It is constructed of iron and glass with brick abutments, and has a Moresque entrance on one side, with a covered walk surrounding the opposite semicircle, 30 feet wide : the height of the dome is 85 feet. If about half as much additional altitude had been attainable, it would doubtless have been an improvement. The interior is intended to comprise a splendid exotic garden—lofty trees, as cedars, palms, &c.,—a basin for aquatic plants and fishes,—rock scenery for parasitical plants ; and the upper part of the dome will inclose birds in net or wire work. The whole will unquestionably be a beautifully attractive place, and the temperature will be so regulated as not to be insalubrious. Subscriptions, per annum, will be £2. 2s. for admission every day ; or

£1. 1*s*. for Mondays, Wednesdays, and Fridays. On these three days it will be open to the public on payment of 1s. each; on the others, to the first description of subscribers only. The architect is Mr. H. Wilds: proprietor, Mr. H. Philips.

SCIENTIFIC, OR LITERARY INSTITUTION.

Some attempts have lately been made to establish a scientific and literary institution in Brighton, to which the inhabitants have been urged by the newspapers, whose Editors seem very uneasy under the imputation of Brighton being a mere watering-place. With submission, and without meaning offence, we think that not only *is* Brighton a mere watering-place, but that it *ought* to be. It is especially adapted for that purpose, was designed for it, and by it alone has arisen to its present eminence: had it established a scientific institution during the last century, it would probably have remained in *statu quo*. Why not be content with the honour of having the Temple of Hygeia? Why seek to force into it the attributes of the Portico? Here, if any where, the bow may be reasonably unbent. Milton himself would never have recommended science in Brighton; for he blames those who,

" When God gives a cheerful hour—refrain."

Every one has heard of the mishaps of a certain Mr. Jack (surname unknown), whose abilities and disposition were deteriorated by having " all work and no play." Most people come to Brighton to play; and to set them a task would be as ungracious as for a physician to give a problem to be solved by a patient, who required a soporific draught. They had much better, like Scipio and Lælius, wander on the shore and pick up shells and pebbles till they get an appetite for the cauliflowers and potatoes.

—— " Nugari et discincti ludere donec
Decoqueretur olus,"—

" To speak well of the bridge that carries us over," is a common proverb, implying that the contrary would be great ingratitude. The genius of Brighton should not disdain to touch with her silken feet the staircase, up which, not many years ago, she toiled, barefooted, slowly, and humbly, to her now proud elevation.

Will it be said, that such studies are every where required to raise our ideas of the power and goodness of God, the almighty and all-merciful, by whom we are fearfully and wonderfully made, and who is not far from any one of us? They may be important and requisite in their time and place; but are they indispensable here, where the magnificent conjunction of earth and sea is alone enough to elevate and soothe the mind, without telescopes, microscopes, diagrams, or lecture-rooms?

> " Awed by the scene, my soul reveres
> The great First Cause that bade the spheres
>   In tuneful order move :
> Thine is the sable mantled night,
> Unseen Almighty ! and the light
> The radiance of thy love."
>   " *The World*," 1770.

Let the visitors of Brighton, then, confine their *gee*-ology to the horses of the place, to induce them to take them an airing: instead of burrowing in the earth after " *dips*" of " *strata*," let them take dips themselves in the sea, which, in blooming effect, may be " Strata *Florida;*" and walk quietly on the cliffs to inhale the sea breeze, instead of climbing their sides with ladders, or being let down from their summits in tubs or barrels, to break the rock in pieces with hammers, in order to ascertain its consistence: and instead of poring through long cylinders at the stars, let them have licence to admire the eyes of the ladies.

A literary institution is a different question. Such a one, styled the " Athenæum," was established some years back, and failed miserably, as we have been informed by those who suffered injurious pecuniary losses from it.

PROFESSIONAL PERSONS, &c. &c.

It is not, of course, our purpose to include in this already protracted description a Directory of Brighton, especially as we have informed the reader that such an article is to be obtained there. We shall, however, put him in possession of the following brief particulars.

The number of physicians in Brighton is ten, and that of surgeons, &c. thirty-two. Both include names of great respectability; and it would be highly invidious to single out any with a view of drawing comparisons, which are " odorous *palabras*, neighbour Verges." Still, every one has a right to mention his friends, especially if he also knows them to be deserving. In this light we take leave to recommend Messrs. Badcock and Payne, St. James's-street.

The members of the legal profession are thirty-one.

There is, however, another class of persons whom we choose to specify individually, for the two following reasons. First, that we know several of them to be talented and meritorious characters, whose labours are not slight, and their gains, to a certain degree, precarious. Next, that, as by the unanimous testimony of all, their support from the resident inhabitants is of a most ineffective character, there exists the more reason for their just claims being brought before the notice of visitors. And there may be some reciprocal advantage in the latter being directed with facility to suitable quarters.

ARTISTS AND INSTRUCTORS.

(Alphabetically arranged.)

MUSIC.

HARP, PIANO, VIOLIN, FLUTE, ETC. ETC. AND SINGING.

Mr. Charles Bond, 3, Upper North-street.

Miss Chambers*.

Misses Emily and Georgiana Clements, (and singing,) 15, Marlborough-place.

Miss Corrie.

Miss Marianne De Cothi, 2, Cannon-place.

Mr. G. F. Dusart, Lower Bedford-street.

Madame Ferrari, 71, East-street.

Mr. William Gutteridge, organist to his Majesty, 16, Castle-square, (musical warehouse,) and 68, London-road.

Mr. John Kirtchner, 27, Grenville-place (Quadrille Band).

— Mencke's musical warehouse, 41, East-street.

Mrs. Joseph Nash, (and singing,) 17, East Cliff.

Mr. Edward Pettitt, 6, Cannon-place.

Miss Mary Pickering, 29, Dorset-gardens.

Signor Pozzi, (singing,) 19, Marine-street.

Madame Sala, 18, Manchester-street.

Mr. E. Seller, 36, Grenville-place.

Mrs. William Scott, 43, Regency-square.

Madame Tabois, 10, York-place.

Mr. Thomas Henry Wright, 144, North-street, and Royal Colonnade.

Mr. T. Wright, 62, King's-road, and 3, Grafton-place.

DRAWING.

LANDSCAPE, PORTRAIT, ETC. ETC.

Mr. David Barber, 17, New-road.

Mr. John Booty, 3, Royal Colonnade.

---

* This young lady's birth, her father's misfortunes, and her subsequent conduct, are, perhaps, too well known to render any observation necessary. She has been honoured with the patronage of the Queen.

Mr. John Bruce, 6, Pool-lane.

Mr. Joseph Cordwell, 4, St. James's-street.

Mr. George Crowhurst, Old Steyne.

Baroness de Fabeck.

Mr. Edward Fox, 3, Brighton-place.

Mr. James Hardy, 163, North-street.

Mr. John James Masquerier, 8, Western Cottages.

Mr. Louis Parez*, 6, Regency-square.

Mr. Francis Carter Pollard, 32, Black-lion-street.

Mr. Charles Scott, 35, West-street.

Mr. William Scott, 43, Regency-square.

Miss Emily Scott, (and portrait,) Do.

Miss Maria Scott, (and flowers,) Do.

Mr. Charles Woolcott, 30, Marlborough-place.

LANGUAGES†.

Signor Frederic Amati, 49, Montpellier-road.

Mr. J. N. Binau, French and Italian, 19, Bedford-square.

Mr. Charles de Cothi, 2, Cannon-place.

Monsieur Desquarts, 24, Regency-square.

Mr. C. Dusart, Bedford-street.

Madame Ewalt, (German, French, and piano,) 2, St. Margaret's-place.

Baron de Fabeck.

Signor Louis Straccia, Italian, 34, Western-street.

WRITING.

Mr. Prideaux Rickards, (and mathematics,) 7, Western Cottages.

Mr. William Gresley, 18, Richmond-place.

Mr. John Marchant, 49, North street.

Mr. S. T. Saunders, 5, Waterloo-place.

---

* This gentleman has published a pictorial work on "the Banks of the Loire."

† A Spanish gentleman, of the rank of Don, does or did teach the Spanish language, and also the guitar, in *Clarence Place;* we have lost the reference to his name, but think it right to mention the circumstance.

FENCING.

Mr. Claudius Michelet, 4, Grand Parade.

DANCING.

Mr. James Brown, 19, Gloucester-place.
Miss Corrie.
Mr. James Hervet D'Egville, 69, Marine Parade.
Monsieur, Mde, and Mlles Michau, 11, Cannon-place.
Mr. C. Wright, Royal Colonnade.

SCHOOLS.

The number of these of all kinds, both for young ladies and gentlemen, is about ninety. The principal for boys are, Dr. Proctor's, Kemp Town; Dr. Everards', Wick House; and Mr. Fennel's, Temple.

There are several handsome Bazaars in the town, which the visitor will easily discover. The lodging and boarding houses are by far too numerous to mention; nor can we specify their terms, which, of course, vary considerably with the locality and time of year.

PLEASURE BOATS.

"O Pescator dall' onda
Fi da lin.
O Pescator dall' onda
Fi da lin.

Vien pescar in qua,
Colla bella tua barca,
Colla bella, se ne va;
Fi da lin, lin la."

Music is never heard on the water at Brighton, except in the case of a steam-vessel taking a trip to the Isle of Wight or Hastings; but nothing could have a more beautiful effect

than either instrumental or vocal music on a calm sea, when it
is "like a silver lake." We should think, if one of the larger
description of pleasure-boats could set up a portable band, it
would add very much to the attraction. The magnificent
"Fishing Chorus" in Masaniello would sound extremely
appropriate; we should willingly hear any thing but the
Chevalier Neukomm's ridiculous (saving his merit in other
compositions) and ridiculously be-praised song, "The Sea."
"We are where we would ever be,"—just now, out of the
reach of hearing it*.

The charge for row-boats, when the whole boat is taken, is
3s. an hour, and for sailing-boats 5s.; but either take parties,
and the individual sum is then very small.

There are seven or eight large sailing-boats plying daily,
which take parties for an hour and a half's sail, usually about
nine miles, for about 1s. 6d. each. Some of these are of considerable size, 30 feet long, and 15 tons burthen, cutter-
rigged; and this description of boat in a high wind and strong
swell, is certainly safer than the lugger-rigged, from the great
ease and expedition with which the sails can be shifted. We
have been on board them in quite as rough weather as most
readers would desire, and should not easily fear for their safety.
Whilst, on the other hand, the smaller boats are equally safe
when the weather is at all calm; and can sometimes be launched,
and come on shore, with greater expedition.

The occasional parties in these boats are often highly pleasant to those who are at ease on the ocean; there is more
interest, sociability, and excitement, than in the chance meetings in a land carriage. Rencontres with very agreeable
persons are now and then thus effected, and renewed on
succeeding days; and such incidents are sometimes amongst
the greenest Oases in the chequered desert of life.

* Especially with the accent and pronunciation of the streets of London :
"Thur see—thur see—thur O! O! O! pa-a-an See!"

Small adjoining Villages.

HOVE

lies one mile to the west of Brighton, from whence it is a pleasant walk in summer, over the fields. Its harbour has been, for upwards of a century, choked up by the sand and shingles; but it has a few fishing-boats, also a small number of bathing machines and lodging-houses, including a handsome range, or terrace, now almost completed. A fishery was attempted, about twenty or thirty years ago, to be established here, including in the plan a range of dwelling and curing houses, occupying three sides of a square, facing the sea; but it entirely failed. The church is now, to all but confirmed antiquaries, a mean and unprepossessing object; but, for the sake of the former, we must give the best account of its ancient ichnography which the slight vestiges and ground marks will allow us to trace. The present fragment, which has a pigeon-house wooden steeple, appears to have been the centre aisle of a building which had three aisles, a chancel, one or two porches, or small transepts, and a large tower, of immense solidity, which fell down about forty years back, and its materials were used in erecting an object in Goodwood Park. This is a pre-bend in Chichester Cathedral. Arches four in number, on each side, out of five, which divided the building into three low aisles, are traceable on the side walls; they are of the early Gothic, with cylindrical columns, similar to those of the priory church of Boxgrave. We suppose the following, in Pope Nicholas' Taxation, refers to this place. " Vicar' de Huna, 5l. 0s. 0d. non excedit." In 1801, the population was 101 only; in 1811, 312; and the value of real property in 1815, 1839l. * : in 1831, the inhabitants had increased to 1360.

* That of Brighton, at the same period, was 71,515l.

PRESTON

is the first village on the London road, about one mile from the new church. The fine trees adjoining the road here, on both of its sides, form a very cheerful relief to the sterility of the coast, and the lively traffic and frequent parties coming from or returning to Brighton render it very pleasant. In a large house, on the right hand, it is reported that Anne of Cleves resided for some time, and a portrait of that queen is said to be still preserved in one of the rooms. The church is a humble edifice, of the 13th century, with a nave, small chancel, and slender tower, with pointed roof. Some old fresco paintings, lately discovered, are described in the Archæologia, vol. xxiii., and the " British Magazine," No. I.

Preston appears to have been a considerable demesne at the time of the Doomsday survey.

" The Bishop himself holds Preston. It always was in" (the possession of) " the monastery. In the time of King Edward, and now, it answers for 10 hides. The land is xii carucates; in domain is one-half (Qy.) in Lewes three *hagæ* of xviii pence. There is a church, and xv acres of meadow, and wood for 2 hogs' pannage. Of this manor Lovel holds two hides, and has two carucates there, and nine villains as (ceu) three bordars " *hospitibus*," eleven carucates, and one mill there. It is worth XL shillings.

" The whole manor in the time of King Edward was worth XVIII pounds, and afterwards x pounds; now XVIII pounds. Formerly it was at twenty-five pounds farm, and could render it.

" The canons of Chichester hold, in common, xvi hides, which they never gilded, as they say, and have there four carucates in domain. This is worth VIII pounds."

In 7 James, " Amongst the lands assigned for Prince Henry's maintenance is" Sussex, M. de Prestone, p. an. 39*l.*

1663. It was intended for part of Queen Katherine's jointure, and the fee farm rent was 66*l.* 3*s.* 11*d.*; but it is doubted whether this was not *another* Preston in Pevensey Rape, as is the case with some other particulars mentioned of *a* Preston in the Burrell MSS.

In Pope Nicholas' Taxation, is, "Vicar de Preston, 5*l.* 6*s.* 8*d.* non excedit," and " Bona Ep'i Cicestr'; Preston, 37*l.* 14*s.* 5*d.*" The population in 1801 was 222; 1811, 235; 1821, 319, living in 53 houses; 1831, 429; value of property in 1815, 1908*l.*

PATCHAM

is a neat and agreeable village, on the high road, two miles
beyond Preston, a distance often resorted to for one hour's
ride.   It contains about 500 inhabitants; has a decent church
on the right, and on the opposite side a pleasant seat, with a
very pretty hanging wood, or shrubbery.

*** POYNINGS.

Near this place is the celebrated " Devil's Dyke," a bold
chasm in the Downs, but whether formed by Nature or Art
has not yet been positively ascertained.   The view from hence
is one of the grandest in the county, and its easy distance from
Brighton, five miles, renders it a popular object to be visited.
A poetical version of the nonsensical tale appertaining to the
Dyke was composed by Mr. Hamper, a man of erudition, but
it is so ridiculously puerile, that it would be a waste of space
to introduce it.   The number of inhabitants at Poynings in
1831 was 268.

In Pope Nicholas is " Eccl'ia de Poninges, 8*l*. 0*s*. 0*d*."
The church is in the form of a cross, but without aisles,
having a neat square tower in the centre.   The present rector
is Dr. Holland, Precentor of Chichester, a gentleman much
esteemed in the neighbourhood.   The interior contains some remains of tracery, monuments, and painted glass.   This church
was rebuilt by direction of the will of Michael de Poynings,
one of the Barons of that noble family, in 1369.   In this
ancient and really illustrious stock, the manor of Poynings
was vested, from a period soon after the Conquest till the year
1446, when the Barony, owing to the marriage of the heiress,
merged into the Earldom of Northumberland, and became
extinct, with some other of its honours, in 1679.   Several of
this family were highly distinguished for their bravery and
worth, as recorded by Froissart, and other ancient chroniclers.
See the British Magazine, No. V., where there is a very interesting account of Poynings.

We have abridged the following particulars from the Burrell MSS. :—

Michael de Poynings, a Banneret under Ed. III., at the Battle of Cressy, summoned to Parliament from the 16th to 42nd of Edward III., on the danger of the French invasion, was appointed one of the guardians of the sea-coast of Sussex. He died in 43rd Ed. III., bequeathing his body to be buried at Poynings, near his mother's grave, southward. Left 200 marks to build a new church at Poynings * ; 10l. to make a new north aisle at Slagham, with an altar dedicated to St. " *cordcle* "† of silver, enamelled in the form of the arms of James. He left to the church of Chichester, a cup with a the Earl of Arundel ; 10l. to the Friars Carmelites at Shore-ham, in aid of the building of their new church ; to our Lady of Walsingham, 10l. ; to his wife, of plate, a pair of new basins, with ewers of silver, and two silver pots, each of half-a-gallon, and one basin of silver " *del amoigne* " †, and twelve basins and twelve salvers of silver ; to his heir, a ruby-ring, " which is the charter of my heritage of Poynings," all the armoury and breast-plates which his father left him, also a pair of basins, with ewers of silver, twelve basins, with twelve salvers of new silver ; two *Annuals* at Poynings and Slagham ; 400 marks to his daughter Margaret for her marriage ; if she died unmarried, the same to be at the disposal of his executor.

Richard Poynings, in 8 Henry VI., bequeathed his body to be buried in the churchyard at Poynings, if it do please his wife ; if not, wherever else it pleases her. He left to his beloved wife, the Lady Arundel and Maltravers (with all his heart and soul), all his goods, wheresoever present or to come ; to his venerated cousin, Wm. Arundel, son of this said wife, a piece of his piece of the holy cross.

---

* 200 marks were also left by his wife Joan, who died soon after him, for the same purpose. The ancient residence at Poynings was burnt down in the year 1727, but its vestiges are still discernible.

† Sir W. Burrell could not translate these expressions from the original Norman-French ; it is not, therefore, to be wondered at, that we have also failed.

In 31 Henry VI., Robert Poynings, of Southwark, Esq. being carver, sword-bearer, and chief actor with Jack Cade, was pardoned, but bound in recognizances in the Court of Chancery ; but having afterwards stirred up riots in Kent, an extent was issued against his estate.

The manor was estimated at ten knights' fees.

And we give a concluding extract from the British Magazine, before mentioned : —

" His ruby ring of inheritance, the charter of 'the Sires de Ponynges,' came into possession of his son Thomas, and then to his second son Richard, who made another wealthy marriage with Isabel, the heiress of Fitzpayne, and, following the military disposition of his ancestors, accompanied John of Gaunt, Duke of Lancaster, into Spain, to claim the Crown of Castile, in 9 and 10 Richard II. He died in this last expedition, when sickness through the army proved so destructive, not only to great Lords, Knights, and Squires, but 'out of 15,000 men of arms, and 4,000 archers, who went with the Duke from England, never returned,' says Froissart, 'the half part.' As if in anticipation of his fate, he appointed that, should he die in such place as that his body could not be buried at Poynings, there should be a stone of marble provided, with an escutcheon of his arms and an helmet under his head. He appointed also masses and trentals for the souls of his father, mother, grandfather, brother, sisters, and all his allies ; and also for the souls of Sir Thomas Heryngaunt, Richard Poynings, his uncle, Robert Boteler, and John de Lye, and for his own and all Christian souls. It is impossible for a thoughtful and kind heart to read this and connect it with the fact of the testator's death in a foreign land, and in the midst of so numerous an army stricken down by pestilence, without feeling pleased that the expression of some concern for the future condition of so many human creatures was not forgotten. In this legacy, his kind and noble spirit seems to have shown (in the way which the religion of the times prescribed) that affectionate solicitude for the welfare of others, which not to feel, in some form, were to be destitute of that charity which is the essence of all religion."

EASTERN COAST.

ROUTE FROM BRIGHTON TO HASTINGS.

	MILES			MILES
ROTTINGDEAN	. . . 4	PEVENSEY	. . . .	5
NEWHAVEN	 5	BEXHILL	. . . . .	8
SEAFORD	 5	ST. LEONARDS	. . .	$4\frac{1}{2}$
EASTBOURNE	. . . 7	HASTINGS	. . . . .	$1\frac{1}{2}$
SEA HOUSES	 1			—
				41

On leaving the Signal House, to the right beyond Kemp Town, the road continues in a straight direction, passing over one or two hills, with no material objects, except good sea and coast views when looking back upon Brighton, to ROTTINGDEAN, four miles distant from the former place: this road has, within a few years, been diverted to a greater space from the edge of the cliff than it formerly occupied, when it was proved to be dangerous in dark evenings by some lamentable accidents.

Rottingdean is a neat and pleasant village, with one street running up into the country, from an opening in the cliff, which affords convenient facilities for bathing. Several houses, facing the sea, are adapted for visitants, who may prefer the quiet to the bustle and publicity of Brighton, and have the advantages of the former when they choose to visit it; we believe that a few years back this was still more the case than it is at present. There are bathing machines and private baths here. The church, on the left of the road, is an old, solid looking building, with a tower, terminating in a pointed roof, between a nave and chancel; it is supposed to have been formerly larger, and is neat in the interior. One or two pleasing inscriptions may be found in the churchyard; the following is for Wm. Savage, vicar, who died Sept. 4, 1619.

> " Great Aaron's son, one of the Levite's train,
> Lies here, with comfort for to rise again ;
> A man of peace, the poorer people's friend ;
> A faithful Abraham liv'd and made an end."

The Wells at Rottingdean are currently reported to be affected by the tide; viz. to be nearly empty at high and full at low water. The causes of this phenomenon we leave for the investigation and amusement of the curious. But what will perhaps better please the generality is, that very pretty pebbles, of a bluish colour, and nearly transparent, are to be picked up on the beach, which are susceptible of a fine polish.

" Rotingeden " is mentioned, with a various reading, " Rokohingeden," in Pope Nicholas' Taxation, 1291, when the church was valued at 13*l*. 6*s*. 8*d*. per annum, and belonged to the priory at Lewes ; the vicar had also 10*l*. per annum. The valuation of real property, in 1815, was 2,895*l*., and the population, in 1831, was 880, an increase of more than 300 since the year 1801.

From Rottingdean to Newhaven no villages are met with ; the road ascends and descends several steep eminences, but has nothing interesting, except, in summer, a quiet and pastoral appearance, when the dark green of the South Downs is diversified by extensive and wide-spread flocks of fine sheep. The cliffs to the right of the passenger are in some places bold, with many inequalities of height, but continuing upon the whole on the ascent. On approaching Newhaven, an interesting view opens into the interior, following the course of the Ouse to Lewes : from the hill, about a mile west of the town, both sides of the river appear absolutely spotted with little villages, not a mile distant from each other, each consisting of a small cluster of houses, some dark shading trees, and a church. We descend a steep hill into the town, with the church on an eminence nearer to the sea on our right : its low and massive tower, with a pointed roof, or obtuse spire, contrasts not advantageously with the small and modernized body of the edifice.

NEWHAVEN.

HISTORY.

The original appellation of this place at the time of the Norman survey was *Meeching :* it seems to have attained little consequence or notoriety for several succeeding centuries.

The Chronicler Stowe asserts, that, in 1545 the French made a descent at Newhaven, "and there landed many captaines and souldiers, who, by the valiantenesse of the gentlemen and yeomen of Sussex, were slain and drowned in the haven a grete number of them, and the rest hardly recovered their ships and galleyes."

Prior to the year 1731, the harbour was in a neglected and decayed state ; in that year an act of parliament was obtained for its repair, and permanent maintenance.

The following particulars of debates and proposals on the subject brought forward in 1724 are extracted from the *Lansdowne MSS*. in the British Museum :

LANSDOWNE MS. 846.

" To the Honourable the Commons of Great Britain in Parliament assembled. The humble petition of the Mayor, Jurats, and Freemen of the ancient town and port of Rye, in Sussex, in behalf of themselves, and many hundreds of his Majestie's faithful subjects—Humbly sheweth— That the Commissioners who met at Rye on the eighteenth day of June last, (in pursuance of the act passed the last sessions of Parliament for restoring the harbour of Rye to its ancient goodness,) did not then agree on any method towards restoring the said harbour. That upon farther examination it appears very practicable to make good the said harbour, by cutting a canal from the Winchelsea river, right out to the sea, where there is immediately deep water, and will be consequently more safe and commodious, for the coming in and going out of vessels, than the present passage is. But as some doubts have arisen, whether there is sufficient authority by the said act to proceed on such scheme, your petitioners implore this Honourable House to take the premises into consideration, and to give such relief therein, as to their great wisdom shall seem proper most effectually to restore the said harbour of Rye, for the benefit of the navigation of this kingdom, and the security of the Lives and Properties of very great numbers of His Majestie's Loyal Subjects. And your petitioners shall ever pray, &c.

Here occur some letters of Mr. Warburton, inquiring into the state of the harbour, the last of which is as follows.

" Worthy Sir,

" In my last I acquainted you with my having writ to Captain Markwick, for a report of the present state of Newhaven, and the methods proper to be taken to make a harbour there.—And I have herewith sent you a copy of his answer, together with the Petition which I sent to the Honourable Mr. Pelham, one of the representatives for Sussex, with his Letter to me about it ; all which I desire you will peruse ; and give me your advice in relation to my future Proceedings, particularly as to the best ways of raising money to defray the expence of the Bill, (which I intend to get brought into the house the next sessions of Parliament,) and also making and keeping the said Harbour when the act of Parliament is obtained. I will only add that I am your most obliged and most obedient servant, Jon Warburton, Somerse.

" College of Arms, London, March, 1724."

" Sir,—I received your l^{re} last night, and have enclosed Mr. Pelhams letter, and a fair copy of the petition. The House not setting I shall be at Putney on Monday, and will do myself the Honour to wait upon you at Wimbleton. I am Sir, your humble serv^t, L. Kenn, Saturday, 4 April, 1724. To John Warburton, Esqr. at his house at Wimbleton, Surrey."

" Sir—Att my return from Brighthelmstone, ye preservation of which place is now under my care, I found yours, and have perused the paper sent to me, dated the 8th of this instant, and doe agree and am fully of your opinion, that the making or restoring the harbour at Newhaven, will to all intents and purposes answer all ye good and benefitt that can be proposed for shipping ; in the first place it will be a fine midway conveniency between Portsmouth and the Downs. 2d. It will offer well for abundance of shipping in distress of weather and violent storms, that come from South and South-west winds. 3d. In time of War, and especially one with France, as you hint, it would be a means to save many a good Merchant's Shipps from being taken by pirates, and in my Judgement will be much better and more to ye benefitt of our merchants and their shipping for a Harbour to be at Newhaven than Rye, and may be made with a quarter of the charge. In Newhaven there is harbour room enough for a great number of ships, and thus far I doe agree with you as to your sentiments about Newhaven. And now I crave leave to offer my opinion in what, and what only will be necessary to make Newhaven as good a harbour as the nature of the place will admit of, which will be a very good tide harbour, by which I mean a vessel of 800 or 1000 tun may come att Halfe fflood into the harbour, and by the way Rye can be no more than a tide harbour, and Newhaven may be made every deale as good and much safer and easier when in harbour for the shipping.—Impri. Att Newhaven, there must be a peer on the west side, but the situation of the place is on a chalke Rock, it has flints in it, it will not admit of piles to be drove without shattering and splitting the rock, that the piles will not stand fast. But that doeth not Hinder the otherwise fixing of a good strong and substantial lasting Peer*, which will be one great point towards the making and restoring of a harbour.

" 2d. On ye East there must be 3 or 4 Groynes to mentaine and keep ye beach and sand as it is ; for soe soon as a western Peer is erected it will rake to the East and lay all bare by carrying all away, beach and stones and sand, and what now defends and secures the sea from swallowing up of a fine rich parcell of land of the Duke of Newcastells, and by it spoile the intended harbour.

" 3d, Where the old peer was there must be a shutt made to direct the water all in a straight line to sea close under the peer so to be made.

" 4th. It will be proper for a light to be erected westward upon the hill at the harbours mouth which will be a good guide in ye night for shipping

---

* The reader will not mistake this for a member of the House of Lords.

either to come in or to sheere clear of the harbour, and will be nye enough to Burling and Bourne points, which is Beachy head, for all shipping to take timely notice and stand off to sea not being above two leagues and a half from Newhaven to Bourn point.

" 5thly.—To make any locks or sluses on Lewes river will not be convenient; for the river from Lewes is not rapid, is low and flat, and the marshes aboute Lewes are low, and sews butt lazely to sea; and to effect o'f makeing of locks or sluses, or any other workes of that kind with the walls and banks yt must be made is such a charge that it must not be mentioned to us this proposal, neither can it be thought soe advantageous for Lewes, since all goods of what kind soever may and have the benefit of lighterage either up or down to the harbour, the place where the shipping lyes.

" 6thly.—Neither will such locks or sluses add one jot to the better sewing or draining of the marsh lands about Lewes, but rather make it the worse.

" 7thly.—As for a small fort of 8 or 10 guns to be made neare the harbour mouth at a convenient place may be of great service in time of war, but of that when that shall be. I have several times viewed Newhaven at the request of his Grace the Duke of Newcastle, but nothing hitherto has been done. I have told his Grace that 5 or £6000 would do so much for Newhaven towards a harbour that a small tunage on vessels would not only maintain but add to the works.

" Your most humble servant, Wm Markwick—to J. Warburton, &c.

" March 14th, 1724.—Sir—I received your letters, and have considered of the proposals you make in relation to a harbour att Newhaven. I am of opinion any thing of that kind will be impracticable this year. The session drawing very near to a conclusion and we having already passed a bill in the house of commons for making one at Rye, which is in the same county. I also think that the method D. Fuller proposes for raising the money will not do; the merchants will spurn any further toll upon shipping, and that of the jews has been often rejected in parliament. However, I shall be glad to contribute any thing to the success of so useful a work, and especially for the service of a county I have the honour to represent.

" I am, Sir, your very humble servant, H. Pelham.

" Captain Markwich and I have often talked of this affair when he viewed the haven for my brother's land."

Next appears a long letter of Th. Fuller, in substance much as Capt. Markwick's, till as follows:

" This is not a new project, but was not only thought of many years ago but was attempted; and I suppose fell again, not because it was found impracticable, but for want of public spirit to advance the money, and able engineers to continue the work; for, whereas they should have run out their peer on the west side of the haven to keep off the force of the western main, they laid it on the east side, and that did a mischief by stopping vast drifts of sand, and heaping up such banks as quite choaked the channel.

" He goes on to propose defraying the expence by a tax on Jews, or toll on ships, as before in Pelham's letter.

"To the Honorable the Commons of Great Britain in Parliament assembled.

"The Humble Petition of the severall Gentlemen, Merchants, and others, living in and near Newhaven, in the county of Sussex, and the places adjacent, on behalf of themselves and several thousands of his Majesty's subjects, sheweth—That there is not between Portsmouth and the Downes (being at least twenty leagues) any Harbour safe and convenient for ships to put in at when in Distress by violent storms, occasioned by south or south-west winds, by which means great numbers of ships have been wrecked, which would, by making a harbour, and erecting a light-house in a proper place, be in a great measure, if not entirely, avoided. That Newhaven, in Sussex, (being about the midway between Portsmouth and the Downes, and lying west of Beachy-head,) is, from its situation, most fit for that purpose; and is so formed by nature that it is capable, at much less expence than any other place upon the Sussex coast, by building a Pier on the west side and three or four Groines on the east side, of being made a harbour fit to receive a large fleet of ships, drawing twenty foot water, which can go in and out at half-flood, and ride safe there both from winds and enemies. That the erecting a light-house upon the hill westward of Newhaven will be of great service to navigation, by being a certain guide to ships in dark nights, either to come into or sheer cleer of the harbour, and is near enough to Burling and Bourn points, which are commonly called Beachy-head, for all ships to take timely notice and stand off to sea. That, in case there should be a war, and more particularly with France, the making a Fort near the harbour mouth would effectually secure our ships from being taken by privateers, which was too frequently the case the last warr.

"Forasmuch as there are a great number of ports on the coast of France, over against Sussex, whereby they have an opportunity of coming out upon our merchant ships by reason they have no place to take shelter in.

"That, as the advantages to the public, and especially the trade and navigation of this kingdom, will be very considerable, by preventing of wrecks upon that coast, as well as captures by our enemies. Therefore your petitioners most humbly pray this Honorable House will be pleased to take the premises into consideration, and give them such relief therein as in your great wisdom shall seem most meet.

"And your petitioners shall ever pray, &c. &c."

NEWSPAPER EXTRACTS.
1785.

STORM.

"*Sept.* 12.—Near Newhaven the waves ran so high, that they dashed over the tops of the cliffs, and rushed into the harbour there with a degree of impetuosity that rendered the water in our river brackish within two miles of the town (Lewes), by which many of the small kinds of fish were killed, and seen floating the next day on the surface of the water.—At Bishopstone the sea ran over the fall, and forced a smuggling-boat into the mill-pond, and in an instant swept away upwards of fifty chaldron of coals that were on the mill-wharf."

1792.

EMIGRANTS.

" *Lewes Journal, Oct.* 8.—The French vessel with emigrants, which we mentioned in our last to have been wrecked near Newhaven, was entirely lost. It brought over a principal family of Normandy, a lady and her three little daughters, the eldest eight, the youngest about three years old, and a Dean, the relation of the family, with two servants; and also two Swiss officers, who had escaped from the massacre at Paris, and, after many hardships, had at length, in disguise, reached the opposite coast. They were all got on shore, bruised, wet, and fatigued, but otherwise well, and were very humanely received on their landing. Mrs. Wisdom, of the Tide-mill, attended on them with the greatest tenderness; and the Hon. Mr. Legge, who happened to be passing by, procured a carriage, and conducted them to the public-house at Newhaven.

" Lord Sheffield hearing of the misfortune the next day, immediately sent his foreign servant to act as interpreter, and to conduct them to his lordship's house at Sheffield Park, where they have been several days. We are happy in the opportunity of mentioning these instances of humanity and of attention to the distressed. The lady proves to be the sister of the Viscomtesse, whose miraculous escape and landing at East-Bourne we mentioned in a former paper."

1801.

LIFE BOAT.

" *Lewes, Dec.* 22.—The following circumstance afforded an opportunity of giving trial to a life-boat, called the *Adeline*, built upon an entire new principle, under the directions and at the expense of Mr. Langridge, of this town, and by that gentleman stationed at Newhaven, for the humane purpose of assisting shipwrecked mariners, and of rescuing them from a danger which has proved fatal to so many along that part of our coast. Between two and three o'clock, on last Friday afternoon, the flood one quarter, and the wind at south-west, blowing very hard, an object was discovered in the offing, at about five miles distance, bearing from the piers of Newhaven, W. S. W., which had the appearance of a vessel water-logged, and with only her foremast standing. This induced Mr. T. Tasker, (who is appointed master of the boat) with his assistants, to put to sea, with the view of rendering assistance to the supposed distressed vessel; and although the breakers were tremendous, and the sea running mountains high, the boat, under the management of this adventurous crew, arranged in order, as coxswain, six setters, and bowman, went out of the harbour in a lively, gallant style, and soon after came up with the object in pursuit, which proved to be a beacon, or lighthouse, of a triangular form, clinch boarded at the bottom, with a mast rigged out, and had no doubt been driven by the boisterous weather from the enemy's coast, nothing similar being in use on the coasts of this country. Finding its magnitude too vast for their strength to tow on shore, and the evening coming on, they put about, and returned safe to harbour. The boat, notwithstanding the breakers and heavy sea she had to encounter, did not ship ten gallons of water during her run out and in. The superior buoyancy and living power of this incomparable boat were witnessed by a large concourse of persons assembled on the pier; and the report of the crew is, that she pulls extremely light and easy through the water, that they are thoroughly convinced of her safety, and that no weather shall deter them from embarking in her, when the lives of their fellow-creatures are in peril, and demand their exertions to preserve them."

1803.

WRECK.

" This morning one of our fishing-boats brought in two twenty-four-pound carronades, which had been discovered and dragged up during the low tide of last night, a short distance on this side of Newhaven. The carronades, it appears, had formerly belonged to the Dragon sloop of war, which was wrecked on that part of the coast between three and four years ago. On examination, they proved to be both loaded, and to be but triflingly injured from the great length of time which they had lain in the water."

DESCRIPTION.

Newhaven is a decently built little town, without meanness as well as splendour. The traffic through it appears to be small, but the appearance of the harbour, as seen at a little distance, and particularly from the church hill, is cheerful, and indicates some employment. On the north of the churchyard is the neat monumental obelisk, erected in memory of the loss of the Brazen sloop, of eighteen guns, in 1800, off the Ave Rocks, near the town, when Captain Hanson, its commander, a distinguished seaman, who had lately made some extensive voyages, and all his crew of 105 men, with one exception only, perished. The names of the officers are recorded, and the inscriptions are irresistibly touching, indicating the strongest Christian resignation and hope under affliction. The tower of the church stands at the east end, with a small semi-circular recess for the chancel beyond it. It has two very ancient windows, which, though square-topped, have two Norman arches in each resting on a pillar. The body is modern, or modernised, with sash windows. The interior, though insignificant, is neat, with a handsome pulpit: it is divided into two aisles by small octagonal stone pillars. Galleries were erected in 1825 to accommodate 175 persons in addition, 120 of whom, by a grant from the society in London, are free. The arches of the tower appear to be early Norman. In 1831, the number of inhabitants in Newhaven was 945.

The cliffs of Newhaven are about 200 feet high, of striking and picturesque formation. A full account of their structure will be found in Mantell's Geology of Sussex, 4to., a work of erudition, prefixed to which is an ingenious elucidatory dissertation on the Mosaic history of the creation.

Newhaven harbour is esteemed one of the best tide harbours between Dover and the Isle of Wight; having several times afforded shelter to ships of 350 tons in tempestuous weather. The principal importation is coal, which is carried up the Ouse a distance of twenty miles. Coastwise, foreign timber is brought and English oak exported for the use of the dock-yards; also flour, butter, and corn. At the entrance of the harbour is a small fort: off this is also moored the *Hyperion* frigate, as the head-quarters of the coast blockade of this district, from which supplies of men are occasionally drafted to various points, and it has three cutters attached to its operations.

At the bottom of the town a small draw-bridge leads over the narrow river on the road to Seaford. Approaching this ancient port, now at a little distance from the sea, the shore is bold and wild, diversified with lofty cliffs, and an irregular strand intersected by several winding creeks: the views of the rocks of Newhaven are also striking. At the entrance of Seaford is a small fort.

SEAFORD.

HISTORY.

This was a lordship of the Earls de Warren, one of whom, in the reign of Edward I., gave to the church and monks of St. Mary de Grestinen his customs and liberties of lestage, pontage, and passage in Seaford, which was confirmed by the king; but we find that in the same reign Daniel, the king's butler, had 7*l.* rent in the same town, formerly belonging to Gilbert de Aquila. Edward II. confirmed a gift which Richerin de Aquila made to the said convent. John, Earl of Warren, having no children, made over his inheritance by a special grant to Edward, from whom he received, as a recompense, for his life, the castles of Conisburgh and Sandale and the manors of Wakefield and Halifax in Yorkshire. He died in 21 Edward III., when all his possessions fell to the crown, except a few which had been re-granted, with remainder to his natural son by Maud de Hereford. In 42 Edward III., Michael, Lord Poynings held it; at his death it was granted to Henry Fitzalan, Earl of Arundel, who having forfeited it by treason, Richard II. granted it, as a reward for distinguished services, to Thomas de Mowbray, Earl of Nottingham, and afterwards Duke of Norfolk. But in 8 Edward IV. we find it assigned to Elizabeth his queen, for life. James I. in the fourth year of his reign, assigned it to the executors of William, Lord Mounteagle, in consideration of good services done to him by that nobleman.

" 4 Jac. Rex, &c. Salutem. Sciatis quod nos in consideratione boni servicii nobis p' prædilectum et fidelem subdictum n'm Willm Dn'm Mounteagle ad nominationem ejus domus, et concedimus Geo Rivers militi et Thomæ Bridges armigero hered' et assign' suis totum ill' Burgum n'm de Seaford in Com' nr'o, Sussex, cum p'tin, p'cell possession' Ducatus n'ri Lancastr' existen', ac omnes illos redditus assis ib'm attingen's ad 58 solidos, 3 denar p' an; necnon novos redditus ib'm attingen's ad 2 solidos et 2 denarios p' an' ac perquisitiones curiæ ib'm coib's annis acciden' attingen' ad 2 solidos 6 denar'—Qui quidem Burgus de Seaford et cetera premissa p'cell dicti Burgi de Seaford p' particular' inde extenduntur ad clarum annu' valorem £2. 15s. 0d."

The nonal inquisition, in the reign of Edward III., is to the following purport:

" SEFFORD.

" Hec indentura testatur q'd in'qs' capt' est ap'd Lewes xviii die marc' an⁰ r r Edward' tert' post co'q'st xv⁰ cor' Henr' Husee et socijs suis venditor' et assess' ix' et q'ndecime garb' vell' et agn' in comitat' Sussex': Et comp't' est p' Will'm Cowes Adam Hebbe John Tanner et Rob'tm Goyer p'ochianos eccl'ie de Sefford jurat' q' dicu't p' sac'rm suu' q'd ix' garbar' p'och' p'dict' val' hoc a⁰ xlˢ. It'm dicunt q'd n'o sunt agni neq' vell' in poch' p'dict' et dicu't q'd licet ecl'ia taxat' ad vii marc' tu' n'o possu't responder' ad taxam p' eo q'd vicarius eccl'ie h't oblat'oes q' val'nt p. annu' xxxiiiˢ. It'm h't dec' navig' piscar' q' val' p' annu' xiiiˢ. iiiiᵈ. It'm h't decim' vit'lo'r et porco'r q' val't p' annu' viˢ. viijᵈ. It' dicu't p'dict' jurat' q'd su't no' mm'cator's in vill' p'dict' q' no' vivu't de ag'cultura. Un' q'ndec' val't iiij m'rc' et no' ultra, q' p'ochia p'dict' p' divers' insult' inimico'r n'ro'r de Francia sepe et multiplicit' est destructa*, ac hoi'es p'och 'p'dict' corp'alr v'lna't' et occisi. In cuj' rei testimo' sigill' p'dico'r jurat' p'sent' su't app'nsa."

---

* An evidence of several French incursions.

The town is a member of the cinque port of Hastings. It returned members to parliament, from the twenty-sixth of Edward I. to the twenty-first of Richard II, without intermission : the right was discontinued from that time to the reign of Edward VI., when it was revived, and continued to the present day. This borough had a *Customal* as well as the other cinque ports. One of the articles was, that the lord should not receive a heriot ; another, that the younger son should be his father's heir of land and other possessions *.

In this town was a hospital, dedicated to St. Leonard, for which the bailiffs and commonalty held lands in trust. Formerly there were four or five churches and chapels, and various foundations have been discovered, indicating that its size was once far more considerable. In the famous armament of 1347, it furnished five ships and eighty-one men †. Beneath the cliff is a round bastion of stone, imagined to be of the time of Henry VIII.

A little east of the town is Cuckmere Haven. The History of Eastbourne, 1787, asserts that the Dutch offered 1,000,000*l.* sterling for the possession of this harbour, or the right of anchoring here, but were from policy refused : this story does not appear very probable. There were formerly two other batteries in or near Seaford, to defend the port. In the parish is Corsica Hall, a handsome mansion, and Chinting Castle, an ancient intrenchment; and it gives the title of baron to the family of Ellis. In 1831, the number of houses was 198, and of inhabitants 1047.

NEWSPAPER EXTRACTS.
1783.
SMUGGLERS; DOWNS.

" *Extract of a letter from a gentleman, at Stafford, Sussex, Sept.* 18.— There is a most convenient port, about a mile from Seaford, for smugglers to land their goods, and so daring are they become, that a dozen or more cutters may frequently be seen laying-to in open day. On Tuesday evening, between two and three hundred smugglers on horseback came to Cookmere, and received various kinds of goods from the boats, 'till at last the whole number were laden, when, in defiance of the king's officers, they

---

* Burrell MSS: From Testa, de Nevill ; Dugdale, Mon. ; and Rowe's MSS.—Account of Eastbourne, 1787.

† Pennant.

went their way in great triumph. About a week before this, upwards of three hundred attended at the same place; and though the sea ran mountains high, the daring men in the cutters made good the landing, to the surprise of every body, and the men on horseback took all away.

" Alfreston races begin on Tuesday next. It is only three miles from Seaford. I never was in so mountainous a country in my life. Go where you will, you are still surrounded by hills and mountains, and, what seems extraordinary to me, the whole is in a state of cultivation; in some places corn, in others turnips, potatoes, and all kinds of vegetables, without even a wall or partition to be seen. The variegated colours of the earth have an amazing pleasing effect. Those who have herds, have shepherds to keep them on their own ground. I rode yesterday about seven miles over these mountains, upon the top of which, when I looked down, it made my head giddy."

1803.

LANDING OF THE FRENCH.

" The Lewes paper, received yesterday, says, that one day last week despatches from the Commander-in-Chief, his Royal Highness the Duke of York, and Major-General Lennox, were received by the Colonel commanding at Bletchington barracks, stating, that the French, should they succeed in crossing the British Channel, would certainly attempt a landing in Seaford bay, and directing a strict and vigilant watch to be kept up in consequence. The purport of these despatches were next day given out in orders at the head of the regiment stationed in the above barracks."

1804.

FARMERS.

" It would be unjust not to mention the exemplary conduct of various of the farmers in this county, on being unexpectedly called on to afford such accommodations to the troops, as, from the urgency of the case, they stood in need of; and which the following note, which was presented to Mr. Worgen, of Alfriston, will in some measure exemplify :—

" *Head-quarters, Alfriston, Friday morning.*

" Lieutenant-Colonel Frith, and the officers of his Majesty's First or North Battalion of Hampshire Militia, cannot leave Alfriston, without returning their thanks for the obliging attention which they have experienced from the inhabitants of this town and neighbourhood. They feel that they have been received as brethren engaged in one common cause, the defence of their country, and all that it contains most near and dear; and they beg leave to request, that Mr. Wargen will have the goodness to make their acknowledgments as publicly known as possible."—*Jan.* 9.

1807.

PRIVATEER.

" *Dec.* 28.—On Saturday morning last a desperate attempt was made by a French privateer to capture two loaded colliers, lying-to off Seaford, a distance of thirteen miles from this town. In capturing, and sending off one, the enemy succeeded, and was proceeding to take possession of the second; the latter, however, fortunately mounted two or three swivels, a well-directed discharge from which, it is supposed, gave an unexpected quietus to several of the assailants."

1809.

STORM.

" *Lewes, Dec.* 7.—Early this morning signal-guns of distress, rockets, &c. were fired in the bay of Seaford, a distance of twelve miles from this place. The people in the neighbourhood hastened to the beach, when a most melancholy spectacle presented itself!—as many as seven vessels being ashore, the whole within the distance of half a mile. At day-break the scene was such as almost to pass description—men on rafts, others on the shrouds, while many were discovered washing from the decks—drew tears from the beholders; but every exertion was used to preserve as many lives as possible. The following description, though only of a small part of this melancholy catastrophe, will, no doubt, prove satisfactory to the friends of those who have escaped a watery grave; the particulars of which have been collected from the crews of the different vessels:—

" On Tuesday last the Harlequin hired armed sloop of war, of 18 guns, having under convoy twenty-three sail of ships, sailed from Plymouth, at four o'clock P.M.; and on Thursday morning, about three o'clock, one of the ships was ordered to direct the fleet to keep within the convoy. About an hour after, the Harlequin, with six others, struck, and became total wrecks. The following are the names of the ships which are lost:—the Weymouth ship, four of her crew lost; Traveller brig, Albion schooner, and Unice, crews all saved; Pramsitwibow ship, 14 lost; and Methedacht ship, all lost.—Farther particulars to-morrow."

DESCRIPTION.

The church is the nave only, or part of the nave, of one of the old churches of Seaford, with a tower, and a small rebuilt chancel. It has been barbarously repaired and defaced, with several projections and additions of brick-work; but in spite of all injuries, has some vestiges of loftiness and grandeur. The tower, rather lofty, and with three slightly receding stories, which add much to its appearance, is chequered with flint and stone. The general style is the early Gothic * ; has lofty and bold arches two on each side of the nave, resting on circular columns, with foliated capitals; above these were large lancet-shaped clerestory windows, now under a roof which covers the aisles also. A strong pointed arch opens into the tower, above which, however, are the traces of a Norman one. In the tower are eight bells, re-cast by sub-scription in 1811, to the credit of the inhabitants of this small place, and an example to many others in Sussex, where the case is very different. A national school, for 100 boys and

---

* Mr. Rickman has made a decided mistake, which is a rare instance with him, in stating the church to be of the 14th century.

50 girls, is supported at the expense of the present members. The borough, from its small population, is of course dis-franchised by the Reform Bill.

From Seaford to Eastbourne the road is hilly, and the sea in general lost to sight by the rise of the lofty cliffs; to the left of the road is a long valley, in which are placed, at small distances, several inconsiderable villages, very similar in appearance, with little gray churches and dark elm foliage. West Dean is the only one passed through, to which we descend a steep hill, through a pleasantly wooded lane. The village, on the right, appears considerable; it has one large house, approached by an avenue of trees, belonging to the Willard family. The tower of the church stands, like a transept, at the middle of the north side, a variety of position not very unusual in this part of Sussex. Soon afterwards, the cliffs of Beachy-head, and the Light-house appear. We pass Friston church, belonging to a village of ten houses, and consequently of the humblest description, yet from its elevated situation, serving as a land-mark to vessels. The country opens on descending to the town of Eastbourne; the Sea-houses, &c. are seen, and the commencement of the long line of Martello towers indicates the level, which extends to Hast-ings, beyond which is seen Fairlight Down, one of the most commanding eminences on the southern coast. The hills on the right, in the form of an amphitheatre, or bay, seem to intimate that the sea formerly flowed some distance higher up. At the entrance of Eastbourne are barracks for a troop of horse, at present not occupied.

EASTBOURNE.

HISTORY.

Eastbourne contests with several other places in Sussex the title of the Roman settlement *Anderida.* Pevensey and Seaford are its most probable opponents, as the locality of all the others is too far removed from the vicinity indicated by the plans and descriptions of the best authorities. We confess our total inexperience on the subject of *Roman* antiquities in Britain;

but we have procured for the reader a far more valuable source of information than any hints we could offer, in transferring to our pages the following perspicuous and erudite document in the *Burrell MSS.* :—

OBSERVATIONS ON THE SCITE OF ANDERIDA.

" Avoiding the arguments of others, which would swell to a volume, and attending chiefly to the short authorities left us, it seems rather too difficult a task to fix with certainty the precise spot of the Sussex coast on which Anderida stood; he that can so do, and please himself on the fair ground of truth and authority, leaving his choice open to no material objection, can do more than is in my power; and, it is to be feared, the more it is weighed and compared with all that has been so ingeniously urged on the subject, the greater will the difficulty appear.

" The learned Camden placed it at Newenden, in Kent; the sagacious Somner removed it to Pevensey or Hastings, but inclines to Pevensey; our Lewes antiquary, Dr. Tabor, afterwards discovering a Roman bath and pavement, and wide-spread foundations, under ground at Eastbourn Seahouses, removed it to that spot, about four miles distance from Pevensey; which last scite meets with Mr. Horseley's consent in his Britan. Romana, and long had my entire approbation.

" But after all these were published, an old map and MS. account of Roman Britain, compiled by Richard of Cirencester, a monk of Westminster, temp. Richard the Second, which had found its way to Copenhagen, was there discovered, and is since published, containing, though not a compleat and accurate account, yet the fullest and best state of Roman Britain hitherto known to the world; great use has been made of this work by the ingenious Mr. Whitaker, author of the History of Manchester, who yet complains of its want of accuracy, and mistakes in certain parts of the work. I doubt the originals from whence Richard compiled it were faulty, as himself professes verity, and to have drawn his commentary from certain remains of a certain Roman General, by him left for the use of posterity, as well as from other authorities extant in Richard's days. Still, admitting some fault in Richard's work, we must not wantonly reject his authorities, as both his work and map united give the largest and best state of Roman Britain we ever had, or are likely to have.

" And here I take leave to dissent from Mr. Whitaker's opinion, that Richard drew up this map himself; neither the title to his map, nor what he says of it in the body of his work, p. 40, will, in my opinion, justify the assertion, but that it was copied from very ancient records. Mr. Bertram, his editor, and Dr. Stukeley, his commentator, are both of my opinion; for surely mere *Iters* through the Roman provinces, without maps to apply those iters, would have been but poor blind guides to future Roman officers; and that the Romans had maps of the then known world is evident from Claud. Ptolemy's Geographical Charts, and many others that might be mentioned.

" The late learned Mr. Clarke, in his Treatise on Coins, published since Richard's work, in a note on Hastings, p. 451, still persists Anderida must have been at Hastings, notwithstanding all that Dr. Tabor, and Richard, and his Commentators, urge to the contrary, upon good authorities; whence I think it may be inferred, Mr. Clarke had never seen either of these works, which are both well-founded contradictions of his assertion.

" From a view of Richard's map, we are led to think that the scite of Anderida was at or near Seaford, as being there placed on the east side the exit of a river flowing nearest the meridian line from London, which best suits with the Lewes river; unless we can, from the faulty smallness of its scale, rather persuade ourselves Eastbourn is meant, which would reconcile it to Dr. Tabor's scite.

" Here an objection starts, as the map has assigned but two rivers, instead of five or six, along the whole extent of the Sussex coast; the first is called *Trisantin fluvius*, supposed to be the Arundel river, as next to Regnum or Chichester, and as Little Hamton still retains half that name; and the other is called, in the Iter, *Anderida Portu*, but in the map Anderida, and is there marked as a large sea-port town. Now the second, or next, river eastward from Arundel, is the Shoreham river, having its exit near Aldrington; it may therefore be urged, this was the scite of Anderida, and not Seaford, as being the next river to Trisanton, agreeable to the map. Yet still the Shoreham river wants the peculiar mark of flowing nearest the meridian line from London, a property peculiar to the Lewes river, and at the exit of such a river stood Anderida, if we can rely on Richard's map.

" The fifteenth iter of Richard has a correspondency with his map in this particular, but will not help us out of the difficulty, for it proceeds from Regnum, or Chichester, to ' *ad Decimam* ' (lapidem), or Arundel, ten miles, and from thence to Anderida Portu, as the very next station; but a blank being left for the number of miles between these two last stations, it cannot be applied with any degree of certainty, and may as well annex this scite to Shoreham as to Seaford. This fifteenth iter grows afterwards still more defective, for a vacuity wide enough for two more stations with their distances is left between Anderida Portu and *Lemains*, or *Lime*, in Kent; which vacuity, if we fix Anderida at Shoreham, or Seaford, I would wish to fill up with Eastbourn, or Pevensey Harbour, and Hastings, as proper connecting distances from port to port.

" The small scale of Richard's map, and the defects in his iters (not his own, I would presume, but drawn from defective originals), and his omission of all but two of the Sussex rivers in his map, are too uncertain guides to fix this scite on positive unquestionable authority; yet, so far as it goes in directing us to or towards the centre of the Sussex coast to look for Anderida, it draws our attention from the remoter scites of Hastings to the east, or Shoreham to the west, and narrows the claim to some proper spot a little to the east of the meridian line, which best suits Seaford; and if the faulty smallness of its scale be duly considered, it may admit of Eastbourn as the place meant, though standing more east from the meridian.

" The want of Roman remains near Seaford is not of itself a rejection of its claim, for many of the Roman forts and ports were long since overwhelmed by the sea; but it wants some of the properties annexed to Anderida by Henry of Huntⁿ, viz. Seaford was a town standing in his time, and so was Hastings and Shoreham; but Anderida was then destroyed, and never rebuilt, he says. Seaford had no neighbouring woods, from whence the Britains made excursions, and galled the Saxons in their siege of Anderida, and whither they flew when faced about upon by the Saxons, and from whence they frequently returned to the charge, and retreated again. I believe no such woods even grew near this place, and that all behind it was open downs. Such woods grew near, and surrounded the Æstuary at Pevensey Harbour, and at Eastbourn; and from the flat shore near Aldrington, much woods might have grown there in elder times, though now the whole is mostly open arable lands: these are negatives in part to Seaford, and partly agree with Hastings, Pevensey, Eastbourn, and Shoreham.

" Again, as the Saxon conquests extended lengthways in Sussex, from west to east, and as Anderida was the last eastward fortified town which resisted and fell a victim to Ælla, so in course we must look for it more easterly than the centre of Sussex; unless we judge it a place of such strength and consequence, that all submitted to the eastward, as not able to withstand the Saxon prowess after its reduction.

" The existence of Roman remains at Eastbourn is clear evidence of a Roman settlement there of some sort, but whether as well there as at Pevensey, Hastings, Winchelsea, and Rye, to the east, as at Seaford, Shoreham, and Arundel rivers, to the west, the later Roman *Turres per intervalla*, mentioned both by Gildas and Richard, were or not placed, still remains a doubt with me, till the scite of Anderida be clearly fixed. These Turres per intervalla were, doubtless, members of the old Roman Ports, like the members of our modern Cinque Ports. Seaford is the present extreme western member of the Cinque Ports, and is the only member of the ports which sends members to Parliament; this privilege is some argument of its quondam importance; and though Hastings be its head port, which has, indeed, priority over all the Cinque Ports, yet that priority, we learn, was obtained at the Norman advent, and given it by the Conqueror for the assistance it afforded him before and after his conquest of this kingdom.

" If I might be permitted to give my opinion, after stating all this confusion of authorities, and doubts, and objections, Eastbourn sea-side will, I think, upon the whole, better answer all the properties of Anderida, mentioned in the foregoing authorities, or in any other authorities I have as yet met with on the subject, than any other place ; it was never afterwards rebuilt, and exhibited the ruins of a noble town in Huntingdon's days. It had neighbouring woods of oak, and plenty of iron thereabouts, as materials for the Roman navies; it had a good harbour near it, at Pevensey, which continued such till Henry the Third's time, and which was guarded by a strong castle, whose large remains are still in being; but, as Mr. Hay says in his poem on Mount Caburn,

> ' Whether of Roman or of later date,
> Remains a secret, which the learn'd debate ;
> Once a fair port enrich'd the fam'd abode,
> But herds now graze where royal navies rode.'

" Those who know the spot, find a place to the east of Eastbourn, and between it and Pevensey, called Langney, quasi Langaney, or Longwater ;

and here, before the sea withdrew itself, seems to have been a long gut of water, communicating from Pevensey to Eastbourn Marsh by the sea-side; this communication with Pevensey Harbour reconciles Eastbourn to the idea of a sea-port; add to this, a dock to the west of the Roman ruins under the Down, hinted at by Dr. Tabor, and the uncommon pleasant dryness of the spot, commanding a view across the bay to Hastings Cliff, adapts it of all others in this quarter as most suitable to the scite of Anderida. Here the bold headland of Beachy intercepted the view of the rest of the Sussex coast from Hastings; but here a sentry, placed on the headland not two miles from it, might (to use Dr. Tabor's expression), in a clear day, without turning his body, see the Isle of Wight, the hills in France, near Boulogne, and the Ness, in Kent; so that, from the Ness to Selsea, it must have been a small sail that could escape his eye.

" These are such striking characteristicks, such strong persuasives, of its having been the spot of all others hereabouts most useful for a Roman Fort and Port, as could not well miss the observation of a people so remarkably skilled in the choice of scites for their purpose, as the Romans were. Yet all this, and much more that might be fairly adduced as arguments in its favour, will not, ought not, to weigh against the authority of ancient evidences; nor can the scite be drawn away from Seaford, near which Richard has fixed it, but on the sole ground of the small scale of his map, where the distance of ten miles is no very great mistake, in the ground-plot of the whole kingdom; and the mistake further favoured by its leaning on the east side of the meridian, as the map places it, and as Eastbourn stands. I have but dropped this as matter of observation, not insisting on it as an authority to bias the opinion and judgment of others; as all who are competent judges will, and ought to, exercise their own opinions on the authorities before them."

The Roman vestiges alluded to, consist of a pavement of white and brown *tesseræ*, 17 feet 4 inches by 11 feet, and a bath, 16 feet long, 5 feet 9 inches broad, and 2 feet 9 inches deep; which were discovered in 1717.

At the time of the Doomsday survey, Borne was the property of the Earl of Morton or Mortain; and had belonged to King Edward, who kept it in his own hands: it contained 46 hides, had been estimated when he received it at 30 pounds, and was then worth 40. The next historical notice of the place is discoverable in that valuable record the *Saxon Chronicle*, at the date of 1114.

" A. D. 1114. In this year held the king Henry his court on the Nativity at Windsor, and held no other court afterwards during the year. And at midsummer he went with an army into Wales; and the Welsh came and made peace with the king. And he let men build castles therein. And thereafter, in September, he went over sea into Normandy. This year, in the latter end of May, was seen an uncommon star with a long train, shining many nights. In this year also was so great an ebb of the tide every where in one day, as no man remembered before ; so that men went riding and walking over the Thames eastward of London Bridge. This year were very violent winds in the month of October; but it was immoderately rough in the night of the octave of St. Martin ; and that was every where manifest both in town and country. In this year also the king gave the archbishopric of Canterbury to Ralph, who was before bishop of Rochester; and Thomas archbishop of York died; and Turstein succeeded thereto, who was before the king's chaplain. About this same time went the king toward the sea, and was desirous of going over, but the weather prevented him ; then meanwhile sent he his writ after the abbot Ernulf of Peterborough, and bade that he should come to him quickly, for that he wished to speak with him on an interesting subject. When he came to him, he appointed him to the bishopric of Rochester ; and the archbishops and bishops and all the nobility that were in England coincided with the king. And he long withstood, but it availed nothing. And the king bade the archbishop that he should lead him to Canterbury, and consecrate him bishop whether he would or not. This was done in the town called BOURNE* on the seventeenth day before the calends of October. When the monks of Peterborough heard of this, they felt greater sorrow than they had ever experienced before; because he was a very good and amiable man, and did much good within and without whilst he abode there. God almighty abide ever with him ! Soon after this gave the king the abbacy to a monk of Sieyes, whose name was John, through the intreaty of the archbishop of Canterbury. And soon after this the king and the archbishop of Canterbury sent him to Rome after the archbishop's pall, and a monk also with him, whose name was Warner, and the archdeacon John, the nephew of the archbishop. And they sped well there. This was done on the seventh day before the calends of October, in the town that is yclept Rowner. And this same day went the king on board ship at Portsmouth."—*Ingram's Translation.*

" Roger de Wolphage held a sargeantry in the hundred of Eastbourn, which was worth 10 marks by the year, and the service of carrying the standard of the foot in the army of our lord the king.

" Edward 1.—Fulk de Cantelupe holds the manor of Burne of our lord the king, as the ancestors of Alard the Fleming, for the service of one knight's fee.

" *Ibid.*—The heirs of Gilbert Frank held the third part of one knight's fee in Bourne, of the honour of Mortain. *Testa de Nevill.*

" 4 Ed. 2. Philip Brode held land and tenements in the vills of Suthre and Eastbourne, from the king as of the honour of Aquila, by sergeantry, for the service of guarding the outer gate of the castle of Pevensey. *Harleian MSS.* 708.

" In the reign of John this manor belonged to Roger de Coningsby, and was granted by Henry 3, in the 46th year of his reign, to Peter of Savoy.

---

* *i. e. East Bourne,* in Sussex ; where the king was waiting for a fair wind to carry him over sea.—*Ingram.*

Bartholomew de Baddlesmere obtained it in 7 Ed. 2. in exchange for the manor of Thundersleigh in Essex. Service, "*Unum par clavium caryophili.*"

" 3 Ed. 2. Johes le Brode Bourne & Southe, m. ibm. Pevensey castr. Tower Records, No. 19.

" Thos. de Roos, Miles, Eastbourne m. No. 48.

" The Rectory and advowson of the vicarage of Eseborne was in the possession of St. Pancras' Priory, Lewes, & granted at the Dissolution to Thos. Ld. Crumwell.

"9 Ed. 2. Barth. de Baddlesmere, son of Gunuline de Baddlesmere, m. Margaret aunt & coh. to Thos son of Richd de Clare, & obtained a charter for 2 markets every week at Bourne viz. Thursday & Monday & a fair on the feast of St. Mathew the Apostle ; as also for free warren in this Ldp. of wch he died seized 15 Edw. 2 (being hanged for rebellion,) when it passed to his son Giles de B. who m. Eliz. d. of Wm de Montacute E. of Salisbury & d. S. P. 12 Ed. 3. & his four sisters were his heirs ; Eliz. his widow surviving had this with other manors for her property, worth p. an. 78*l.* 12*s.* 6*d.* She m. Wm. Ld Roos of Hamelake by whom she had two sons, the manor descended through several generations to Edmund Lord Roos, who was forced to fly beyond sea on account of his attachment to the house of Lancaster, but yet Philippa his mother seems to have found favour from Edw. 4, if one may judge by the grant he made (pat. 19 Ed. 4, m. 16. per Inspec.) to her 2nd Husband Thos. Wingfield Esq. (of the manor of Eastbourne amongst other manors) & her part of the possessions of Thos. Ld Ross attainted.

" 23 Ed. 3. Hugo le Despencer, Eliz. Ux. ejus Relicta Egidri Baddlesmere, Borne m. Tower Rec. No. 169.—31 E 3. Agnes ux. Thomae Bardolf, Eastborne (qu. m. Do. No. 48.

" 33 Ed. 3. Eliz. ux. Hugonis le Despencer, Bourne m—Tower rec. No. 42.

" 7 R. 2. Thos. Roos de Hamelake, Bourne m. No. 68.

" 3 H. 5. Beath. ux. Thos. Roos de Hamelake, Eastborne m. No. 44.

" 9 H. 5. Johes. Dns de Roos. Eseborne, m. cum war. et wreco maris ptin. Tower Rec. No. 58.

" 7 Ed. 4. on the forfeiture of Thos. Ld. Roos for his adherence to the Lancastrians, Jn Tyrtot E. of Worcester obtained a grant from the king on the behalf of Philippa his Sister, wife of that Lord, of this Manor, inter al. 2 Dug. Bar. 41. Pat. 7 E. 4. p. 1. m. 12.

" 13 Ed. 4, June 5, the Manor of Eastborne parcell of the possessions of Thos. Ld. Roose, was granted to Anthony E. Rivers, to hold to him and his heirs male.

" 24 H. 7. Edmond de Ros d. 13 Oct. 1508, S. P. his 3 Sisters became his heirs, the eldest of whom Elenor de Ros, m. Sir Robt. Manners of Cralle Castle Northd. & had 2 sons, 1 Geo. 2 Edw. & 2 daurs. 1 Eliz. 2 Cicille, Isabel de Ros, 2d daur. m. Thos. younger son to Sir Ralphe Grey of Werke in Northd.

" 2 Ed. 6. Edw. Burton ob. 5 martii. ao. 2 Edw. 6 Joh. Burton frater et heres tertia pars maner de Eastborne.   See partis in Eastborne Burton. Bodley MSS. Vol. 186. p. 10.

" 6 Ed. 6. Robti Pashele et al. tenz. an, feod in Bourne, (Inq. capt. 6 Hen. 6.)

" 19 Eliz. Eastbourne m. cum p'ti'n ac 30 mes. 20 toft. 30 gard. 30 pomar. 450 acr. terr, 40 past', 200 Jamp'n & Bruer. 20 marisci frisci, et 23 redd' cum p'tin & 70 acr' pastur' 300 Jamp'n & Bruer.vis. franciplegii & Hundr. de Eastbourne ac Wreco maris cum p'tin in Eastbourne alibi p. Hen. Goring ar., & al et herid, II ; Goringe de Joh'i Lelwyn ar. & ux. tent. in p. l. d 21 Jan. 19 Eliz."—*All from the Burrell MSS.*

The only notice of Customs inserted is the following :

" 2 R. 2.—The Court held at Eastbourne the day after St. Lucie Jno. Rayne and William were amerced for selling of a porpoise fishe from the lord contrary to the custom of the manor."

Nonal Inquisition, temp. Edwardi III.

" Hec indent'a testat' q'd inq's' capt' apud Lewes xxvi die martii anno r. r. E. t'cij a conquestu q'ntodeci'o cor' Henr' Husee & soc' suis collector' & assessoribz ix^ne garb' veller' & agnor & xv^e in com' Sussex' d'co d'no reg' concess' virtute co'missio'is dc'i d'ni reg' eisd'm direct' p' anno ejusd'm reg' xiiij° sup' vero valor' ix^e p'd'ce in p'och' de ·Estborne p' sacr'm Joh'is de Horsye Rici' de Horsye Walt'i Bat & Joh'is Dygg p'ochianor p'och' p'dc'e jur' & exa'rator qui dic' q'd ix^a p's garb' in eadem p'och' de t'r' unde x^a p'tinet ad eccl'iam p'ochiate va'let hoc anno sc'dm veru' valore' xxvi^lj vj^a viij^d & ix^a p's veller' & agn' in ead' p'och' val't h' a° sc'dm veru' valor' iiij^lj vj^s viij^d. Et s^t est s'm ut'usq' xxx^li xiij^s iiij^d. Un' porc' Luce Scot qui est de lib'tate q'nq' portuu' h`it terr' in ead' p'och' un' nona p's garb' val' hoc anno xxi^s iiij^d. Et dic' q'd p'sonat' d'ce p'och' extendit' ad xlv^li xiij^s & iiij^d & vicar' ejusd' p'och' extendit' ad xiij^li vi^s viij^d. Et s'c est sm' ut'usq' extent' lx^li. Et dic' p'd'ci jur' q'd ix^a p'd'ca ad d'cm extent' attinger' no' potest q' dic' q'd rector d'ce p'och' h't unu' mesuag' in d'nico cu' domilz gardinis & curtilag' und' dc'a eccl'ia dotat' est & valt hoc anno xiij^s iiij^d. It dic' q'd h't lx acr' t're in d'nico ut de dote d'ce eccl'ie et valent hoc a° lxxv^s. It dic' q'd h't j molend' vento ut de dote d'ce eccl'ie & valent hoc a° xxx^s. It dic' q'd h't ix acr' p'ti in d'nico und' d'ca eccl'ia dotat' est & valent hoc anno xxvij^s. It' dic' q'd h't pastur' ad c. lib' und' d'ca eccl'ia dotat' est ac valent hoc anno iiij^s. It' dic' q'd habet pl'ita & p'q's' cur' & vis' f'nc' pl'g' cu' finilz natior & chevag' gar'conu' und' d'ca eccl'ia dotat' est & valet hoc anno xx^s. It' dic' q'd h't o'pa custumar' unde d'ca eccl'ia dotat' est & valent hoc anno xviij^s ij^d. It' dic' q'd h't de redd' ass' p' annu' und' d'ca eccl'ia dotat' est et valet hoc a° cxix^s ij^d. It' dic' q'd h't pensio'es q'lz a° und' d'ca eccl'ia dotat' est & valet hoc a° lxxij^s & viij^d. It' dic' q'd decima feni, rosett', vit'lor, lactis, piscar', & alie minut' dec'ie und' d'ca eccl'ia dotat' est va'let hoc anno x^li vj^s. It' dic' q'd h't decima' in den' mu'nat' p'cipiend apud Motecu'be de antiq° cons' und' d'ca eccl'ia dotat' est & valet hoc a° x^s. It' dic' q'a oblat'o'es und' d'ca eccl'ia dotat' est val' hoc a° lxx^s. It'm dic' q'd p'or hospit' s'ti Joh'is de Jerem' h't in d'ca p'och' xl acr. t're que soleba't seia`ii & no' sei'ant' hoc a° und' ix' garbar valer' solebat coi'bz annis xv. It' dic' q'd Rob't's de Passele h't in ead'm p'och' l acr' t're que solebant seia'ri & no' sei'ant hoc anno unde ix garbar valer' solebat xx^s x^l. It' dic' d'ci jur' q'd rector eccl'ie de Fekynton h't in ead' p'ochia q'md'a porio'em xᵉ garb' de quibusda' t'r' no' deci'and' ad eccl'iam p'd'cam unde nona p's garb' valet hoc anno xiijˢ iiijᵈ. It' dic' d'ci jure q'd p'or de Lewes h't in d'ca p'och' q'md'a porc'oem x garb' de q'busda' t'r' no' deci'and' ad d'cam eccl'iam und' ix' p's garb' valz hoc anno xlˢ. Et dic' d'ci jur' q'd no' est aliq's in ead' p'och' nisi tantu' illi qui vivu't de agricultur' & p'ficuo agn' & lane & etiam de labor' suis nec aliq's cardinal b'n'ficiat' in p'och' p'dc'a. In q'm om'i' test'm p'd'ci jur' huic' indentur' sigill' sua apposueru't.

The church belonged to the treasurer of Chichester Cathedral, and is thus valued in the 37th year of Henry VIII.

" DIGNITAS THESAURIATUS IN ECCL'IA CICESTREN: HUGO ROLFE CLICUS THESAURARIUS INDE.

" The farm of the Rectory of Estborne within the Archdeanry of Lewes appropriated to the said dignity, namely, in various tenements, lands, and glebe quit-rent, with one windmill, within the parish of Estborne aforesaid, per annum, . 66 13 4

" Out of which payments (repris') deducted according to the form of instruction.

" To two men sacrists of the aforesaid cathedral for ever annually paid by the said treasurer, from ancient foundation thence, ... 6 0 0

" Perpetual Alms:

" Given annually at three times of the year to the poor of the Vill of Estborne, aforesaid, from ancient foundation and custom, per annum, ... 60 shillings.

" Fees of the Receiver and Seneschal:

" John Alen, Receiver of the aforesaid Treasurer, per annum, 0 13 4

" John Stempe, Seneschal of the land of the aforesaid Treasurer of the church, per annum, ... 0 13 4

" Sum of the aforesaid reprisals deducted, ... 4 6 8

" And is worth clearly, ... 62 6 8

" Thence the tenth part, &c., ... 6 4 8

Printed Records.

NEWSPAPER EXTRACTS.
1784.

Extract of a letter from East Bourne, March 2.—" Yesterday evening two cutters from the continent landed their cargoes a short distance from this place, great part of which was conveyed away by men with horses, but leaving some bags of tea behind, the officers carried them away, to the amount of 200*l.* being all hyson."

1803.

East Bourne, Oct. 5.—" Every thing here is on the alert to receive the enemy : the whole of the 11th Light Dragoons have been ordered from their different out-posts, and are stationed at Hastings, Boxhill, and South Bourne. Yesterday morning the Sussex and Gloucester Militias marched into this place from Brighton, and are encamped between South Bourne and Pevensey : they immediately commenced making intrenchments, &c.

from the Sea-houses, which are to be continued along the coast to Hastings. The above regiments marched from Brighton on Monday morning with flying camp equipage—on the same evening pitched their tents near Blackington; and on Tuesday morning had their camp utensils packed, and on the line of march in seven minutes. Three regiments of regulars are hourly expected to occupy the spacious barracks erected on the Shingles. We have also a company of South Bourne Artillery, a set of fine spirited fellows. The 4th Regiment of Dragoons marched into Brighton on Tuesday morning.

" The army is in the highest spirits: the brigade I am attached to is in the best state of health, only six on the sick list; so small a number has never been known."

DEFENCES.

" *Nov.* 16.—Lieutenant-General Sir James Pulteney arrived this day, and is to take the command of the troops stationed on this part of the coast. The infantry are still busy throwing up intrenchments. Ninety-four 24 pounders are to be erected on this part of the coast. Two battalions of the 48th foot march into Pevensey barracks to-morrow."

1804.

" *October.*—Some coasting vessels are at this time ashore near Beachy Point, but great hopes are entertained of getting them afloat again, as they have hitherto received but little injury; crews all safe."

1792.

INTERESTING ESCAPE.

" *Brighthelmstone, Sept.* 23.—Among the distressed emigrants who have lately landed on our coast, there are few whose escape seems more wonderful than that of Madame la Viscomtesse de Sesmaison, who, on Tuesday last, with four children, their preceptor, and two servants, landed at East Bourne, from a very small open boat. The Comtesse (whose husband left Paris with the French Princes) remained in France as long as it was possible; but, being well assured that she and her children were marked for destruction, she got down to Dieppe, meaning to make her escape in a packet then lying off, and actually contrived to get her luggage on board it. The sailors engaged in this service told her she was noticed by the people; and, if she did not immediately put off in a small boat, they would certainly be stopped. Accordingly she embarked in the boat, supposing she should be soon put on board the packet; but was shortly informed that she had no prospect of escape, but by trusting herself and children to the hand of Providence, whose immediate interposition seemed requisite to preserve them in a dark and tempestuous night, exposed to the elements in their rudest state, and in a boat scarce big enough to contain them. Their little bark was borne in safety over a tremendous sea; and, in twenty-four hours, this interesting group arrived off East Bourne, where, hoisting a signal of distress, they were with much difficulty brought on shore. Their debarkation was rendered truly affecting, by the deportment of each individual around them. The anxious cares of the mother were strongly displayed, and could be equalled only by the tender assiduity of the elder of her children towards her, while the two youngest, insensible of the actual peril of their situation, were, with equal assiduity, endeavouring to shelter from the wind and rain their two dolls, which they had with much care rolled up in their frocks."

1804.

DEFENCES.

" Temporary barracks, to accommodate 900 infantry and 200 cavalry, were began at Hastings on Saturday. Barracks at South Bourne, for 800 infantry and 200 cavalry, were also began on Monday last. Temporary barracks are likewise to be completed as soon as possible at Pevensey, Chichester, Arundel, Battle, Box-Hill, Shoreham, and Blatchington. The barracks here are to be considerably enlarged, and several barns, &c. have been lately hired or purchased, to be converted into commodious receptacles for troops. The sluices at Pevensey are undergoing considerable improvements and repairs, that, should the enemy attempt a descent on that part of the coast, the level will be immediately inundated, and they will have to contend with the united influence of fire and water."

" The fishing-boats which were dispersed in the late gale have all returned safe to this place.—The following is an extract of a letter received here this morning from a gentleman resident at Eastbourne: 'We have now before us a distressing sight—four vessels completely wrecked, two brigs and two sloops, the disjointed fragments of which are floating on the billows in all directions. Six were on shore, but two fortunately succeeded in getting off with little damage, a brig and a sloop, and are making for the first port to refit. The crews of those which can never put to sea again were providentially all preserved.'

" We had a ball last night at the Lamb Inn here, at which many of our military friends, and others of rank, were present. Among many, whose names I cannot now recollect, were Brigadier-General Maitland, Colonel Duff, Major Vandeleur, Mr. and Miss Gilburd, Mr. and Mrs. Rogers, Mr. and Mrs. Burrough, Major and Miss Bean, the beautiful Miss F. Vidler, (who for elegance of manner, and correctness of step, is the best dancer I ever saw,) Miss Smith, &c. The graceful diversion, with all possible spirit, was continued until nearly day-break."

" The Sussex militia, encamped near the bleak summit of Beachy-head, strike their tents on Wednesday next, and commence their march for Colchester barracks."—*Oct.*

" *November.*—The Hope coasting vessel, from Liverpool, was lately run down and sunk, off Beachy-head, by one of our cutters. The unfortunate vessel was laden with pipe-clay, the crew of which were happily all preserved."

" *August.*—In spite of the menaces of the enemy, this little watering place has to boast of the fullest season ever known."

SHAM FIGHT.

" Extract of a letter from Eastbourne, dated Oct. 27:—Our camp breaks up on the 1st of next month, and the regiments go to Lewes, Worthing, Shoreham, Chelmsford, Steyning, and Pevensey. The campaign closed yesterday with a grand sham-fight, in which the following regiments divided into three brigades, under General Lennox, Brigadier-General Maitland, and Colonel Duff, took a part: the Sussex, Dorset, North Hants, Glamorgan, and South Herts Militia; the 8th, 23d, 48th, and 88th, of the Line, together with the artillery, and two squadrons of the 11th Light Dragoons. The light infantry companies of General Lennox's brigade, with the rifle corps belonging to the Sussex Militia, personated the enemy, under the command of Major Calcraft, and maintained the advantageous positions the country presented with great firmness and skill. The brigades advanced with precision, and kept up a very steady and well-directed fire. Indeed the business was well managed, and is said to have met with the complete approbation of Lieutenant-General Sir J. Pulteney, who commands in this district, and superintended the whole. The day was fine, and the concourse of spectators immense. No accident happened, or any mistake, except that two companies of Militia were, or *might have been*, completely cut to pieces, by rashly advancing up a tremendous height, under a very heavy fire, into the jaws of the enemy. A squadron of Dragoons, attached to cover their retreat, must have shared the same fate. The whole were considered as prisoners of war."

1806.

" No work has been done to the Martello towers, erecting on the Sussex coast, since November: they are, however, in a considerable state of forwardness, and we understand the workmen are to resume their operations early in the spring. The largest, which is at Eastbourne, is of a circumference and thickness that requires upwards of 50,000 bricks for the completion of a single course."

" *Brighton, Aug.* 27.—The troops stationed about the vicinity of Eastbourne, were in the field on Saturday by ten o'clock, at which time the Duke of York was expected to review them. His Royal Highness, however, did not arrive there until three in the afternoon, when some soaking showers of rain falling, the intended business of the day was postponed until yesterday morning. The troops yesterday were in the field at seven o'clock A.M. The Duke reviewed them soon after eight, and in the afternoon took his departure for Oatlands. It is here generally understood, that the Sussex Militia leave this place to encamp on the sunny summit of Beachy, on Wednesday next; and that the South Gloucester Militia march into this town from Hailsham barracks, on the same day."

DESCRIPTION.

Eastbourne is a place of resort which we feel strongly inclined to recommend to all those who require a keen and animating air, for which it is almost unrivalled ; a genteel, yet small watering-place, and the beauty of country scenes and stately trees, almost close to the sea. It consists of three townships, containing, in 1831, 2726 inhabitants. Eastbourne town is a mile and a half from the beach, the Sea-houses, and Southbourne, which lies between the two. The

walk to the sea passes by, or leads through, the grounds of
Compton-place, the seat of the earl of Burlington, a pretty
and commodious, though unpretending villa, with neat
grounds, conservatories and lodges, and some fine trees*.
Nearer the town is the seat of Davies Gilbert, Esq. M.P., which
has also some noble old trees, and sequestered park scenery.
The Sea-houses, which form the actual watering-place, are
irregularly ranged along the beach, with no great extent or
beauty, but they have a social appearance, and comprise
lodging-houses, baths, and the usual requisites. Amongst the
places of amusement are, a library, billiard-rooms, and a small
theatre, in South-street, open during the season. On the
right of the Sea-houses, part of Beachy-head is seen at the
distance of two or three miles; to view which, aquatic excursions are often made, when the tide serves : it turns a softened
face, however, towards Eastbourne; its more tremendous
heights are concealed by a winding of the shore. To the left
the sweep of the Martello towers is seen in perspective, and
when brightened by the sun, has a lively effect. Nearer the
Esplanade, but a short distance further inward, is a large
circular Fort or Redoubt, of considerable strength, bomb-proof,
and capable of containing about three hundred and fifty men,
with provisions for several weeks; it mounted about twelve
pieces of cannon. The circumference of the ditch, which is
twenty-three feet deep, and apparently forty or upwards
broad, lined with masonry, is upwards of three hundred yards.
A clerk of the Ordnance works resides here, also a Deputy
Vice-Admiral of the coast, from Newhaven to Rye, agent to
Lloyd's, and vice-consul for Sweden and Norway, Mr. R. B.
Stone, South-street.

The Lamb Inn, at Eastbourne town, is a very comfortable
one, and moderate in expense; there are also others deserving
of praise. The Assembly-room, which is a very neat one, is

---

* " The house (Lord George Cavendish's) is a very good brick building,
and a comfortable habitation in winter as well as in summer, the walls being
thick and well sheltered. Good dining, drawing, and other rooms, and
gallery, from whence are pleasing land and sea views; some remarkable fine
tapestry, being the history of Don Quixote, and some tolerably good pictures by
Sir P. Lely and Sir Godfrey Kneller."—*Description of Eastbourne, &c.* 1787.

at the Lamb : one of the cellars of this Inn has a groined roof, indicating it formerly belonged to a religious house, and another shews the commencement of a subterraneous passage leading towards the church, which has been stopped up. At the sea-houses is the Anchor Hotel, also the King's Arms; in South-street, the New Inn, a posting-house also, and the Star. Each of the townships contains lodging-houses; and, about half a mile from the Sea-houses is a chalybeate spring, called Holy-well, said to possess qualities equal to those of Bristol, which will, no doubt, be eagerly sought by those who may desire similar benefits. Eastbourne has four respectable medical practitioners, two ladies' and one gentlemen's boarding-schools, and a number of shops of general utility.

Eastbourne church is one of the best in the county, has a fine tower of pretty good height, though its elevation appears to be lessened by the ponderous buttresses; the masonry is very excellent. The church, viewed from the S. E., has really a majestic appearance, in spite of the barbarously modernised great window of the chancel, under which is a small projecting vestry. It has three aisles throughout, separated by eight arches on each side, and is, exclusive of the tower, 124 feet long by 50 broad. The principal features are early Gothic, strong pointed arches, with both circular and octagonal pillars, having flowered capitals. Most of the windows have been inserted in the fourteenth century, and are very neat; but some of the upper ones on the north side are decidedly Norman. The arch opening into the middle chancel is also of this character, but has the singularity of a high-pointed arch blocked up above it, which we cannot explain. On the south side is an arch of circular shape, over four seats or recesses; there is also much wooden screen-work. The western aisles are strengthened by two cross arches, from the side walls to the nave, with buttresses or turrets outside. On the north side of the altar is the monument of Dr. Henry Lushington, who died in 1779, and had been forty-four years vicar of Eastbourne; and of his son, Henry Lushington, of whom we learn the following particulars :—That he " went to

India at the age of sixteen, and was one of the few survivors of the unfortunate persons confined in the Black Hole at Calcutta. By a subsequent revolution, in 1763, he was, with 200 more, taken prisoner at Patna; and after a tedious imprisonment, being singled out with five other gentlemen, was, by order of the nabob, Ally Kawn, deliberately and inhumanly murdered. But, while the sepoys were performing their savage office on the first of the sufferers, fired with generous indignation at the distress of a friend, he rushed upon the assassins unarmed, and seizing one of their scimitars killed three of them and wounded two others, till at length oppressed with numbers he fell, at the early age of twenty-six years."

The north and south chancels are used as private burying-places; at the end of the northern one is a handsome painted window, erected at the expense of J. Gilbert, Esq.: it is formed of old stained glass, and contains some good figures. The interior of the church is decent. In the tower is a small organ, presented by J. Gilbert, Esq.; near it a monument for Dr. Brodie, late vicar of this parish, with a high encomium on his solid professional worth and liberality, and his great attention to the welfare of the young, which is still remembered by the inhabitants. We are informed that he offered a donation of 200l. towards refitting the interior of the church *. In the tower are eight bells, recast from six. Of the strength of these, in former times, we were told a curious anecdote. The fifth bell of the old peal, weighing eighteen or nineteen hundred weight, broke its axle whilst on the full swing, burst through two floors, providentially missing the person ringing it, struck the arch of the tower, and deriving an additional impetus sunk into the pavement about a foot, without the slightest crack or bruise from its precipitate and ponderous

* The present vicar is the Rev. T. Pittman, M. A., a gentleman not unknown in the literary world, and from whom we experienced much courtesy. The living is reckoned rather a superior one for a vicarage. It may serve as a caution against some very unfair misrepresentations occasionally met with, to state that we were assured by a respectable inhabitant of Brighton, born at, and formerly resident at, Eastbourne, that the annual value was not less than 1500l ; but thinking this improbable, we made an inquiry, the result of which was, that he had as nearly as possible *trebled* the actual amount.

descent. The great bell of St. Sepulchre's, London, weighing thirty-three hundred weight, fell down a few years back, but was sustained by the beams of the floor beneath ; yet, from this far slighter shock, the bell, which was a modern one, was broken*.

BEACHY HEAD

is about three miles distant from Eastbourne, and of course a favourite ride or walk in summer : in winter, the stormy gusts would be too repulsive. This is doubtless one of the finest marine eminences in Europe, whether seen from above or below ; in the latter course, however, some degree of fear (pronounced by Burke to be essential to the sublime), and pity at the recollected calamities it has been the scene of, will mingle in the conflicting feelings.

> " Quem mortis timuit gradum
> Qui siccis oculis monstra natantia,
> Qui vidit mare turgidum, et
> Infames scopulos, Acroceraunia ?"

Or we may borrow the application of a not less forcible and beautiful description from the pen of the elegant Fenelon : — " Le pilote expérimenté apperçoit de loin les montagnes de Leucate, dont la tête se cache dans un tourbillon de frimats glacés, et les monts Acrocérauniens, qui montrent encore un front orgueilleux au ciel, après avoir été, si souvent, écrasés par la foudre."

The perpendicular height of Beachy Head from the sea, on the best estimate, is 575 feet †. An excavation below, con-

---

* " Near the road leading down to the Chalk Cliffs are the remains of a building, called St. Gregory's Chapel (so named in letters patent establishing the corporation of Pevensey), and the fields and hill are now distinguished by that name. The bells belonging to it are said to have been carried to France, and now actually used either at Rouen or Dieppe, in Normandy."—*Eastbourne*, 1787.

† This is more than 100 feet higher than the cliff at Dover, immortalized in the tale of Lear ; fifty feet higher than the spires of Strasburgh and Antwerp, the loftiest in the world ; and 100 feet higher than the great Pyramid of Egypt. *Samphire* grows here also, but we do not hear of similar perilous means being resorted to to procure it. The name of this plant is said to be corrupted from *Saint Pierre*, its French appellation : the botanical term is *crithmum maritimum*, from the Greek Κριϑμος, its seeds having a resemblance to those of barley.

sisting of two apartments, ascended by a rude staircase, accessible only at high water, is called " *Parson Darby's*," and is said to have been the work of a clergyman of that name at East Dean, a mile and a half distant, who formed it from considerations of humanity, visiting it in heavy storms, and hanging out lights as an indication of refuge to wrecked mariners; an employment which is said ultimately to have caused his

---

This herb seems to divide its allegiance and attachment between earth and water, always growing on the sea-shore, yet on spots so far above the level of the water as not to be wholly covered by it. A curious incident, which we cannot suppose will be deemed uninteresting, depending on this peculiarity, is related in the Lewes Journal, November 19, 1832.

" During a violent storm in November, 1821, a vessel, passing through the English Channel, was driven on shore near Beachy Head, and the whole of the crew being washed overboard, four escaped from the wreck, only to be delivered, as they thought, to a more lingering and fearful, from its being a more gradual and equally inevitable, death; for, having in the darkness of the night been cast upon the breakers, they found, when they had climbed up the highest of these low rocks, that the waves were rapidly encroaching on their asylum; and they doubted not that, when the tide should be at its height, the whole range would be entirely covered with water. The darkness of the night prevented any thing being seen beyond the spot upon which they stood, and which was continually decreasing by the successive encroachments of each advancing wave. The violence of the storm left no hope that their feeble voices, even if raised to the uttermost, could be heard on shore; and they knew that amidst the howling of the blast, their cries could reach no ear but that of God. What human arm could give assistance in such a situation? even if their distresses were known, how vain were the help of man! The circle of their existence here seemed gradually lessening before their eyes; their little span of earth gradually contracting to their destruction. Already they had receded to the highest points, and already the infuriated waters followed them, flinging over their devoted heads the foremost waves, as heralds of their speedily approaching dissolution. At this moment one of these wretched men—while they were debating whether they should not, in this extremity of ill, throw themselves upon the mercy of the waves, hoping to be cast upon some higher ground, as, even if they failed to reach it, a sudden would be better than a lingering death; in this dire extremity, one of these despairing creatures—to hold himself more firmly to the rock, grasped a weed, which even, wet as it was, he well knew, as the lightning's sudden flash afforded a momentary glare, was not a fucus, but a root of samphire, and he recollected that this plant never grows under water. This then became more than an olive branch of peace, a messenger of mercy; by it they knew that He who alone can calm the raging of the seas, at whose voice alone the winds and the waves are still, had placed his landmark, had planted his standard here, and by this sign they were assured that He had said to the wild waste of waters, " hitherto shalt thou come, and no further." Trusting then to the promise of this angel of the earth, they remained stationary during the remainder of that dreadful, but then comparatively happy night; and in the morning they were seen from the cliffs above, and conveyed in safety to the shore."—*Burnett's Introductory Lecture to the Medico-Botanical Society.*

death, from damp and cold. On one occasion a Dutch vessel
was thus guided with its prow right into the cave, by which
twelve, or as some say twenty, lives were saved. Tradition
has stated, that the poor man's home was made insupportable
by a termagant wife, and some have added that she was too
fond of her cups. If so, he hit on the very wisest, as well
as most noble and generous method of alleviating his own misfortunes, by the pleasure derived from relieving the distresses
of others.

The view from the summit of Beachy Head has an air
of solitary and sublime grandeur; the keen and ethereal air
of this exalted spot would seem almost capable, with the
permission of the presiding and conservative spirit, of restoring vigour to the dying *. The height is not so much perceived by the spectator, from contemplating the straight or
waving snowy wall of cliff, as by listening to the distant and
indistinct murmur of the waves, and looking down upon the
thread-like outline of their foaming edges, as they break upon
the shore; which, to use the only illustration we can find
applicable, look like the trifling froth of a puddle, after the
most moderate shower. We need scarcely refer our readers
for an exactly suitable idea of the whole scene to the description by the immortal Shakspeare, of the precipitous cliffs of
Dover.

On one of the extreme heights is a Signal Station, with a
flag-staff, and two or three guns. Farther on, to the right, is
the Light-house, on a projecting neck of land, of lower elevation, but greater prominence, and therefore capable of being
seen at a much greater distance by mariners, when coming
within reach of the dangerous shore. It has been erected of
late years †, though seemingly called for long before; and has,

* Strange as the discrepancy of situation may appear, the nearest approach
to the purity and freshness of the atmosphere on Beachy Head, in the southern
or midland part of the kingdom, appeared to us to be the summit of the Colos-
seum in the Regent's Park.

† In the *Morning Herald*, Nov. 19, 1832, it is stated, that the erection of
this Light House was principally brought about through the instrumentality
of a John Fuller, Esq. of Rose Hill, Sussex, and formerly M. P. for that
county. If so, this beneficial act should be reckoned amongst "*Fuller's Worthies.*"

doubtless, been instrumental in preventing much destruction
of human life. Accurate charts of the coast have also been
lately executed, to a much further distance out at sea than
was formerly the case.

Off Beachy Head, on the 30th of June, 1690, the combined
English and Dutch fleets were defeated by that of France : a
not very usual tale to tell when speaking of English naval
history; but circumstances will explain the disadvantageous
position of the latter. The French fleet sailed from Brest at
the end of May, in a very strong and well-arranged armament,
consisting of seventy-eight men-of-war, several of which were
of very large size, and twenty-two fire-ships ; and carrying, in
the whole, upwards of 4700 pieces of cannon. The English
government was, at that time, in a perplexed and embarrassed
condition, owing to the opposition it experienced from the
partizans of the exiled king, James II., both abroad and at
home. The king, William III., was on the continent, and
had left only 7000 land forces for the defence of the country ;
the fleet also was lying inactively waiting for the junction of the
Dutch, without any expectation of being so hastily required
to prepare for action. Their strength when drawn out on
receiving intelligence of the French expedition was only
thirty-four sail, and when all the Dutch vessels were mustered,
and had joined them, the latter amounted only to twenty-two ;
the number also of the English and Dutch ordnance was not
more than about 3400. Lord Torrington, the English admiral,
was so convinced of the inequality of his force, that he was
desirous of avoiding an engagement ; but the Queen, who was
apprehensive of the effects of a French fleet hovering on the
coast of a divided kingdom, and with the advice of the Privy
Council, sent him orders to fight at all events. As soon as it
was light on the morning of the 30th of June, the Admiral
gave the signal for drawing into a line, and bore down upon
the enemy, then under sail by a wind with their heads to the
northward. The action began about nine, when the Dutch,
who formed the van, attacked the van of the French, with
considerable success ; about half-an-hour afterwards, the

English blue squadron engaged their rear (the French then lying by); but the red, which formed the centre, could not reach them till about ten, which caused a great opening between them and the Dutch. The French, perceiving this, weathered, and surrounded the latter, who, though defending themselves with great bravery, suffered much from the unequal contest. Lord Torrington perceiving their distress, drove, with his own ship and several others, between them and the French, and anchored when it grew calm, about five in the afternoon ; but finding they were too much impaired to renew the action, retired at night, eastward, with the tide of flood. In a council of war, held the next afternoon, the combined fleets determined to retire, and rather to destroy their disabled ships than attempt to protect them. Their retreat was very successful, owing to awkwardness on the part of the French admirals ; still they pursued them as far as Rye Bay, and having forced the Anne, an English 74, which had lost its masts, on shore at Winchelsea, sent in two fire-ships to burn her, which the captain prevented by setting fire to her himself. The body of the French fleet stood in and out of the bays of Eastbourne and Pevensey, whilst fourteen of their ships anchored near the shore. They attempted to burn a Dutch 64, which lay dry at low-water ; but strange to say, and an instance of almost unexampled courage, the captain defended her so bravely, every high-water, that they were obliged to give up their attempts, and he carried her safe into Holland.

The loss of the English, in this affair, was only two ships, two naval and two marine captains, and 350 men ; but the Dutch lost three ships, sunk in the fight, and three stranded on the coast of Sussex, and a considerable number of officers and seamen. The great energy and resources of the States' General were, however, immediately exhibited, in causing fourteen new men-of-war to be built, and put to sea. The conduct of the English admiral did not give perfect satisfaction, and he was examined before the Privy Council, when he defended his retreat on the score of prudence, and added, with some spirit, that he had rather his reputation should suffer for a time, than his country should suffer additional loss. He was, however, sent to the Tower, and some time afterwards tried by a Court Martial, and acquitted : his commission was at the same time taken away. This is an historical question which has occasioned much difference of opinion. Those who may feel any curiosity on the subject, will find ample details in *Campbell's Admirals*, from which publication we have abridged this summary account.

The Queen sent an Ambassador to Holland, with a very handsome message, expressing her sorrow at the loss they had sustained, and attaching some blame to the admiral ; whilst she promised to defray all the expense of refitting their vessels, to take the utmost care of the wounded, and to give a bounty to the widows of those who had fallen in the action.

Immediately on leaving Eastbourne commences the Pevensey level, highly interesting both to the antiquary and the patriot ; as the scene of an early conquest of England, and the chosen spot for a threatened invasion by a presumptuous despot eight centuries after, whose enterprizes and expectations were baffled by English valour and foresight long before they reached the threshold of success ;—of the Norman Conquest ; and of Buonaparte's purposed invasion from Boulogne.

As a check to the latter attempt, on a flat shore, of the easiest access, the plan of fortification by a regular chain of strong towers, each carrying a heavy piece of ordnance, was devised by the late Duke of Richmond ; and, in spite of some invidious and parsimonious observations at the time, has been proved by experience to have fully answered its most weighty and universally interesting object. Viewed singly as towers carrying only one piece of ordnance each, their power may appear to be slight : but when their proximity is considered, which enables a great number of them to bear obliquely on the same object, or even in full front to offer a strong battery at any point throughout the line, and their almost impregnable construction, on which account it would perhaps take a whole day to silence any of them ;—when the effective *chain* of communication along the coast by these means is also considered, it will be allowed that the plan realized advantages not easily to be exceeded. One proof of this is the dislike and dread which, as we have been informed, the French entertained of them. They were accustomed in popular parlance to apply to them the epithet of " Bull Dogs," or at least some synonymous French word with which we are not acquainted.

Strange retribution ! that the recklessly ambitious man, for whom the fair plains of France were not enough, who sought to lord it over the unapproachable recesses of a free island, and who sacrificed the flower of his kingdom in an attempt to occupy the inhospitable wastes of Russia, should close his career within the narrow prison of one of the smallest islands in the world ! A second Columbus in enterprize was here chained to an oar ; but with much less injustice, as from his far less worthy and generous motives of action he was not undeserving of the punishment of a galley slave *.

Had some one predicted this to him in the confidence of his power, he would have probably been as much astonished as was the Spanish king, before whose eyes, in the sealed and oracular cave of Toledo, were exhibited the coming results of his profligate rule, the loss of his kingdom, and his own untimely death.

> " By heav'n the Moors prevail, the Christians yield !
> Their coward leader gives for flight the sign !
> The scepter'd craven mounts to quit the field :—
> Is not yon steed Orelia ? yes, 'tis mine !
> But never was she turn'd from battle-line :
> Lo ! where the recreant spurs o'er stock and stone !
> Curses pursue the slave, and wrath divine !
> Rivers engulph him !"— " Hush," in shuddering tone,
> The prelate said ; "Rash prince, yon vision'd form's thine own !"
> *Scott's Vision of Don Roderic.*

As a contrast to the picture, we beg leave to apply, with a full and unflattering idea of their truth, the following lines

---

* N.B.—We have read Madame Junot's Memoirs, confessedly a partial account ; but giving them their full effect would have no objection for Napoleon's conduct to be tried by that test.

to the mild and patriot monarch who now holds the sceptre of
Britain :

" Let other monarchs
Contend to be made glorious by proud war,
And, with the blood of their poor subjects, purchase
Increase of empire, and augment their cares
In keeping that which was by wrongs extorted,
Gilding unjust invasions with the trim
Of glorious conquests; we, that would be known
The father of our people, in our study
And vigilance for their safety, must not change
Their ploughshares into swords, and force them from
The secure shade of their own vines, to be
Scorch'd with the flames of war ; or, for our sport,
Expose their lives to ruin."

                                        Massinger.

_____

Nothing requiring particular notice occurs before reaching
Pevensey : the land is flat, but rich, and not cheerless in
appearance.   At Langley Point, a mile and a half from the
Sea-houses, are two small forts, on the line of towers which
command great part of the bay towards Hastings, each
carrying eight guns, and a third battery stands on a little
eminence further inward, called Anthony-Hill.   We occasionally coast round the towers, and both here and on the
opposite side of Pevensey, the road sometimes descends to
the beach, giving us a full view of the ocean close at our feet.
By those who are accustomed to it, the return of this object is
always hailed as that of a friend, bringing with it fresh
breezes, with " healing on their wings;" distant and extended
associations ; and a soothing calm which partakes of the
vigour and liberty of immensity.——What is grander, more
noble, more anciently renowned, or more everlastingly fresh in
its interest, than the sea !   The medium of history, of arts, of
happiness, the source of all the most varied themes of
tradition, of romance, and chivalry ; of poetical aspirations,
and of heartfelt affections ; ever recent, still venerable, and
flourishing in immortal youth : the unfailing cause and support of industry and domestic welfare ; the most liberal and

universal dispenser of pleasure as well as health ; which receives all into its arms ungrudgingly, which

> " Sooths unpitied care,
> And smooths the wrinkled forehead of despair."

The village of West Ham nearly adjoins Pevensey, the outer gate of the castle opening into its precincts. On the left hand the church presents a large tower, less elevated, but having some of the characteristics of that at Eastbourne : its aisles are spacious and solid, and are said before the Reformation to have had three altars, and as many oratories. In the parish are remaining two very ancient houses, Glynleigh and Priest-hawes, the latter supposed to have been once a monastery. The extensive outer wall of Pevensey castle*, with its projecting towers, grey, and in some places mantled with ivy, flanks the road for a considerable distance ; one of the towers gives visible indications of Roman workmanship, or at least an imitation of it, the stones being laid in the cross or *chevron* style, vulgarly called " Herring-bone" masonry. The village is now inconsiderable, but has several ancient houses. The church is inadequate in its appearance to accompany the grand outlines of the castle. The eight miles from Pevensey to Bexhill are uninteresting, the views into the interior of the country limited. The first portion of Bexhill is built on each side of a long and steep hill : having ascended this, we view the spot on the right hand, where, in the late war, were very extensive barracks erected for Hanoverian troops, said to be capacious enough for the accommodation of 10,000 men. It must have been a very commanding and salubrious situation ; now laid out as a pleasure-ground or lawn, where the " German hagbert-men" paraded, " the Almayne's sullen kettle-drum" was beat, and "the banners tall of crimson sheen†," were displayed in aid of a friendly and allied land. Farther

---

* This castle will be described hereafter.

† Lay of the Last Minstrel.—Alas! poor Walter Scott! Shall we look upon his like ever more ?—Will the trumpet of Romance be blown with such ringing clearness and silvery sweetness again ?

on is another part of the populous village of Bexhill, containing upwards of two thousand inhabitants, and an old heavy
church with a low tower, on the left hand, its chancel indicating the thirteenth century. This place is occasionally used as
a marine residence, the sea being only two miles distant ; and
we are informed in the Hastings Guide, that some years ago
a circulating library and a small theatre were established ;
also that the soil was supposed to cover strata of coals, but that
this was disproved by some expensive trials. From hence to
St. Leonard's is four miles and a half, passing Bulverhythe,
another spot, besides Pevensey, which has been denoted as
that of the Conqueror's landing, but with much less reason.
There are the remains of a small chapel. The entrance of
St. Leonard's astonishes and detains the eye of the stranger
with the spectacle of a new creation, brought almost simul-
taneously to perfection, and presenting long and splendid
façades, excelling the architecture of Brighton, and nearly
equalling the most splendid suburb of London, in the Regent's
Park. The slender belfry of the new church has a tolerable
appearance in perspective, aided by a commanding situation ;
but when seen in front has a paltry and toy-like appearance.
Passing through the very elliptical Doric arch at the east
extremity, we enter upon the sheltered road, under bold cliffs
gradually increasing in grandeur, which leads into the lower
town of Hastings, and passing the Priory bridge and the
Pelham sweep of architecture, arrive at the centre beyond the
Parade, where the old and narrow streets rise to the extremity
on the London road.

HASTINGS.

THE old part of Hastings, but little altered in its predominant features since it has become a place of resort, although individually the majority of the houses have been rebuilt, consists of two long streets, called High and All Saint's Street. Between the backs of the houses a small, unnoticed brook of clear water, which is an advantage to its vicinity, flows down to the sea. Beyond the opening which brings the town down to the sea, the line of coast immediately rises into lofty cliffs; so that between the castle-hill, at the entrance under which the Pelham New Buildings and the Parade lie closely sheltered, the body of the town is completely in a hollow. The height of the two hills is not very dissimilar. The castle-hill takes a sweep inward at the end of the Parade, forming the valley up which the old streets ascend. The sea-line lies under the hill in a singularly commanded style; the houses seem almost built into the rock, in fact, in one place it has been cut away to receive them; it frowns over them, at a great elevation, with either a despotic or protecting air, as the fancy of the spectator chooses to invest it.

The ancient history of this town, as well as of several others which fall within our plan, would, if entered into with that fullness for which we could easily find materials, extend the volume to an inordinate extent, and impede its variety and discursiveness of character. The ground has also been amply explored by former travellers, and we do not undertake to conduct the reader through every historical path, plain or rugged, which has been patiently sought out by those who have made it the business of their lives. We shall marshal him at a lively and rapid course through the " highways," with brief hints of the " byways," pausing and dilating only when we find the *bonne bouche* of some very interesting retreat, or some noble prospect, which has generally escaped the notice and record of our predecessors.

ORIGIN.

Hastings is supposed to have possessed a castle in the time of the Roman dominion, either erected by them or enlarged and improved from the foundation of one erected by the natives of the island. A passage in Leland's Collectanea, taken from the chronicle of Dover Monastery, states in effect, that " when Arviragus threw off the Roman yoke, it is likely that he fortified those places which were most convenient for their invasion, viz. Richborough, Walmore, Dover, and Hastings."

ETYMOLOGY. SAXON RULE.

Its etymology is imagined to be derived from a Danish pirate named " *Hœstinga*," who is said to have landed here and built a fortress, as he also did at several other places along the southern coast. In the year 792, 31 *Offœ*, Berodaldus gave to the Monastery of St. Dionysius, Rusticus, and Eleutherius, near Paris (St. Denis), amongst other places, Hastings and Pevensey, with their marshes. And, in 924, King Athelstan established a mint here, at the same time with one at Chichester and two at Lewes.

BATTLE OF HASTINGS.

We do not think it necessary or expedient, whilst referring either to Hastings, Pevensey, or Battle, to dwell on the particulars of the Norman invasion and conquest, as they are probably familiar to most of our readers, or, at all events, may be read in detail in a variety of histories of England, some of which must doubtless be within the reach of all. They will recollect, however, that though we are not perpetually alluding to it, there is a deep and strong though latent effect of interest on this subject which involves itself in every step we take in the history and topography of this portion of the southern coast of England.

DOOMSDAY.

In the Doomsday Survey, it is supposed that Hastings is identified with a place, liberty, or district, then called *Rameslie*, which belonged to the church of Fiscamp. The arable land was thirty-five carucates, and ninety-nine villeins held forty-three carucates. There were five churches, rendering sixty-four shillings, and 100 salt-pits, 8*l.* 15*s.* The whole had been worth 34*l.*, but was then worth 50*l.*; the lordship of the abbot and the men 44*s*[*].

CASTLE AND HONOUR, COLLEGIATE CHAPEL.

The whole Rape of Hastings belonged to the Earl of Eu [†]. The seal of one of this family, a founder or benefactor of the Castle Chapel, is still in existence, bearing the figure of a knight on horseback at full speed, with a drawn sword, and the inscription, " SIGILLUM COMITIS AUGI." A castle or fort was doubtless erected by the conqueror at Hastings almost immediately after the battle, as appears by an inscription on a part of the Baieux tapestry, " ISTE[‡] JUSSIT UT FODE-RENTUR CASTELLUM AD HESTENG ;" but this is supposed not to be the principal castle which existed in considerable size from the erection of former centuries.

The men of Hastings had, in the middle of the same century, proved themselves steady friends of the banished Earl Godwin ; but after the conquest they appear to have been peaceful and unenterprising. In the year 1090, almost all the nobles and bishops of England were assembled at the Castle of Hastings to do homage to William II., then about to sail for Normandy. The monarch was detained by contrary winds for a month, during which Father Anselm consecrated in the Free Royal Chapel of the castle, dedicated to the Virgin Mary, Robert Bloet to the Bishoprick of Lincoln. The

---

[*] Moss's Hastings.
[†] For an account of Eu, see Mrs. C. Stothard's Tour in Normandy.
[‡] Robert Earl Mortain, brother to William.

history of this chapel involves many disputes, as to jurisdiction, with the Bishops of Chichester and Archbishops of Canterbury, but we have not convenient space for entering into details. At the dissolution, the value of the deanery was 20*l*. per annum, and of seven prebends, 41*l*. 13*s*. 5*d*. It was granted to Sir Anthony Browne. It was both a college and a chapel, and a place of some importance and interest. Its common seal (of 22 Edw. III.) is still extant, bearing a female figure crowned, carrying a church in her hand, with a shrine or tabernacle in the back-ground, and an inscription in Gothic capitals, " SIGIL' COMMUNE ECC'E S'TE MATRIS D'HASTINGE*."

20,000 men were assembled at Hastings, in the year 1094, by order of William Rufus, on the pretext of shipping them for Normandy; they were, however, speedily disbanded, and the money allowed by the county for each man, viz. 10*s*., taken from them by the king's agent, and sent to his master, which is, perhaps, one of the most paltry artifices that history has ever recorded.

About the year 1378 or 1380, for the date is disputed, and there are conflicting histories into which we cannot enter, Hastings was burnt by the French, having been previously deserted by almost all its inhabitants. This commences a *third* epoch in the history of the town, the *first* and original Saxon town having been destroyed by the ravages of the sea before the period of the conquest. Whether this or the second town was the one first enfranchised and incorporated with the Cinque Ports, Mr. Jeake, their able historian, professes himself unable to determine.

The castle has not attained any notoriety in the military history of England. It was held, by various persons, of the crown, together with the Honour of Hastings, amongst whom was John of Gaunt. The reversion was conveyed by Sir John Pelham to Sir Thomas Hoo, of Bedfordshire, who in the reign of Henry VI. was, for some faithful military services, created Lord Hastings, but the title became extinct at his

---

* Moss.

death.   William de Hasting, of an ancient family in the town,
one of whose ancestors at the time of the Norman survey held
the manor of Grenock, by the service of finding an oar at
Hastings when the king should cross the sea, was possessed of
the Honour of Hastings in the time of Richard III., but
beheaded by that king's orders for alleged treason.   His possessions were restored by Henry VII. to his son, and by one
of his descendants sold to Thomas Pelham, Esq., of Laughton,
ancestor of the Earls of Chichester, in whose family the Honour
of Hastings is vested at the present day.

PRIORY.

A priory, dedicated to the Holy Trinity of Black Canons
of the order of St. Austin, was founded at Hastings, in the
reign of Richard I., by Walter Bricet.   At the commencement
of the reign of Henry IV. it was devastated by an inundation
of the sea, and the canons removed it to Warbleton, on a spot
given them by Sir John Pelham.   An ichnography of the
convent, as existing before its removal, is contained in the
Burrell MSS.   The annual value at the dissolution was
130l. 2s. 9½d.   It was given by Henry to his attorney-gene-
ral, Sir John Baker.

CORPORATION—REPRESENTATIVES.

The magistrates of Hastings were termed bailiffs, from the
earliest records to the year 1588, when they were incorporated
by the title of a mayor and twelve jurats, with a chamberlain,
common clerk, and serjeant.   It has always returned two
members to parliament as one of the Cinque Ports.

MODERN ACCOUNTS.

Our collection of newspaper extracts has no articles of interest
relating to Hastings.   We extract the following account of the
jubilee in 1809, from Mr. Moss's valuable work : we have
previously alluded to its insertion when treating of Brighton.

" The dawning of the finest day that ever appeared in October, was ushered in by ringing of bells, firing of cannon, and music playing. A great many houses were decorated with flags and proper mottos for the day. Large branches of oak, boughs of laurel, and evergreens of all sorts, ornamented the fronts of several houses; others had devices suited to the occasion. Flags were hoisted upon the church-steeples. At the Custom-house was a crown in glory, surrounded by a grove of laurel, surmounted by a large St. George's Ensign, and under the crown this inscription— ' God Bless the King! Preserve him long to reign, and grant him after death, a Crown of Glory.'

" The service at church was properly attended, and an excellent sermon preached by the Rev. Webster Whistler, Rector. The Royal East Middlesex militia attended at All Saint's Church. After service they proceeded to East-Hill, where, extending their files along the irregular summit, for about a quarter of a mile, they fired a *feu de joie*, whilst the band, at intervals, played " God save the King." About the same time the sea-fencibles fired a royal salute from the battery, and the martello towers continued a distant thunder from a line of twenty miles in Pevensey Bay. The appearance of the military, with the echo of the cannon across the valley, had a grand and pleasing effect. Having repeated three loud huzzas, which were answered by the spectators on the Castle-hills, the regiment paraded the streets, with the band playing, colours flying, people huzzaing, &c. Colonel Wood then marched them to the barracks, where upwards of one thousand, men and officers, sat down to dinner in the barrack-yard, on roast beef and plum-pudding. In the meantime, the mayor, J. G. Shorter, Esq. (who had exerted himself with great loyalty and spirit in making arrangements for the day), and the principal inhabitants, assembled at dinner in the Town-hall, and spent the afternoon with the greatest joy and festivity. There was a bonfire on the hill, composed of ten waggon-loads of faggots and combustibles, and a tar-barrel, on a mast sixty feet high. Fifty rockets were discharged, and many fireworks exhibited. A ball at the Swan inn was attended by about 250 persons, and in the room was a transparency of ' *Neptune yielding the empire of the seas to Britannia, in the reign of George the Third.*' The poor in the different workhouses feasted on roast beef, plum-pudding, and strong beer. Every one had a holiday, the men and women a shilling a-piece to spend, and the children six-pence. A subscription was raised, amounting to 400*l.* 1*s.* 6*d.*, from which 1850 persons were supplied with 2880lbs. of beef, 1850 sixpenny loaves, 2880 pints of porter, 2872 gallons of potatoes, and a balance of 188*l.* left to be distributed amongst thirty of the seamen of Hastings, prisoners of war in France."

The sum of £360 was raised by subscription at Hastings and distributed to the poor on the occasion of the passing of the Reform Bill.

REMAINS OF THE CASTLE.

These are so extremely inconsiderable and indistinct, that but for their magnificent situation and its prospects, they would be hardly worth a walk to the summit of the hill. Access is obtained by a winding road and subsequently a path at the back of Wellington-square, and also by ascending the hills at the western side of the town. At the entrance is an iron gate and a lodge, with a board, informing the visitor that he must pay three-pence for a single visit, or sixpence per week, with an ascending scale. Now it is highly probable that the proceeds may be devoted to some charitable or useful purpose, for it would scarcely be charged for the repairs of the place; still there is, at the first blush, a strangeness in the idea of paying for the admittance to an Earl, which cannot be got over. The interior is so completely an indistinct outline, that very little can be made out of the ancient form: there appear to have been one or two sally-ports, and the walls are upwards of six feet thick. A neat gothic arch, supposed to have belonged to the chapel, with handsome corbels, has been lately restored. The present space enclosed was doubtless not the whole of the ancient work, as it does not appear to exceed an acre of ground. It is neatly laid out, with a grass plat and some flower-beds, and steps have been constructed on the walls with so much care, that the most delicate lady need not fear to traverse them with her slender feet. The view is beautiful at any hour of the day, and we should imagine it must be equally so on a clear night, when " the floor of heaven is thick inlaid with patines of bright gold," or the moon,

> " Sweet regent of the sky,
> Silvers the walls,"

And

> " Nightly to the listening earth
> Repeats the story of her birth,"

the spectator may dwell with admiration and soothing pleasure, like the " Tuscan Artist,"

> " At evening from the top of Fesole,
> Or in Val d'Arno, to descry new lands."

DESCRIPTION.

CLIMATE, SEA-BATHING, &c.

We can add little on this subject to what we have before observed at Brighton, and must, as there, refer the reader to competent authorities, only stating that the temperature of Hastings is much milder than at the former, consequently better suited to that class of individuals who do not wish for a keen atmosphere, which, at the same time, is of course more desirable for other constitutions. The air of Hastings is considered peculiarly advantageous in pulmonary complaints and incipient consumption.

The scenery and objects around Hastings are amongst the most beautiful in England. The commanding hills and cliffs which encompass the town, afford the alternative of an invigorating air on their summits, or a very sheltered one beneath their protecting sides. The formation of hills was thought by the judicious naturalist Ray, to be one of the most striking proofs of the goodness of God in creation ; and they soothed and encouraged the mind of the pensive monarch of Palestine.—" *Levabo oculos meos ad colles, nam ex illis venit auxilium meum.*"

BUILDINGS.

The Parade is a very confined one, though neatly kept, and extremely lively and busily attended; the ship and boat building in the vicinity, accompanied by the multitude of large and handsome pleasure-boats, with occasional small traders, gives it a very cheerful appearance. The length of the esplanade does not much exceed five hundred feet; consequently our fair or curious readers must walk along it and back *five* times, to achieve the distance of a mile.

THE TOWN HALL

is in High-street, to which we can give no praise, though a modern erection, in 1823, to supersede one erected by the liberality of John Pulteney and Peter Gott, members in

Parliament for Hastings, in the year 1700. It is a mean edifice, of inconsiderable size, standing on five low and plain arches. It has, however, a clock, which neither of the churches can boast, with a decent cupola, but so placed as not to be seen. The interior is said to contain a trophied shield, taken from the gates of Quebec in 1759, and given to the town by General Murray, one of the captors, and an inhabitant. The exterior of this building is totally destitute of ornament, with the exception of a wonderful one on the top, viz. a large round stone, brought from Pevensey Castle, which is supposed, from the accident of its shape, to have had the good fortune to be thrown out of a *Roman* catapult, (the Romans being accustomed to besiege castles in Britain,) on which it has had the further " greatness thrust upon it," of being hoisted up to the top of the Town Hall in Hastings, as a most happy municipal ornament. " Reasons" for this are, probably, " as plenty as blackberries," but " not upon compulsion." No. And so we must quote honest Mr. Burchell—" *Fudge !*"

FORT AND PIER.

At the east end of the Parade is a small but strong fort, or battery, raised to a good elevation above the sea, and well faced with masonry, forming also an able barrier against the encroachments of the waves: in the time of the late war it mounted eleven 12-pounders. A storm visited Hastings in January, 1792, very similar in its effects to the memorable one at Brighton in the year 1824.

Hastings had also a pier, which was destroyed by a storm in the reign of Elizabeth: it stood opposite the present fort. The queen granted a contribution towards making a new harbour, but the money, as Camden informs us, was embezzled, and the design frustrated: it was again mooted in the year 1826, but with similar ill success. Piles, and other remains of the pier, may be seen at low water, several of which, concealed for centuries, were exposed by a very high tide, which washed up the beach, in the year 1821.

The remains of the pier are called " The Stade," and

vessels are wound up and let down the acclivity by a strong capstan, worked by three or four horses, which is said to be an interesting sight. The shore at Hastings is remarkably bold, with a high bank of gravel : the depth close to the edge at high-water, is nearly twenty feet ; on this account, the boatmen are cautious of landing at that precise time.

PELHAM PLACE AND ARCADE.

The " New Town" of Hastings is built under the Castle-hill, which having become loose and dangerous in front, was cut in for a depth of 70 or 80 feet, where it forms a wall of the strongest solidity. The plan is a terrace or basement occupied by rooms, and a crescent receding, to which the summit of the terrace forms a promenade. The Crescent is handsomely built, and has a chapel, with a portico in the centre. In front of the basement are small shops, from which passages lead to the arcade, which occupies the bulk of the erection below the Crescent. This is a fine room, lighted in the ceiling, 180 feet long, and occupied by twenty-eight shops, in the style of a bazaar, the centre also forming a musical promenade in the evening; in another part of the basement is a coffee-room. The terrace is ascended by a handsome flight of steps. Pelham place, which was built prior to the rest, forms an eastern wing, commencing at the end of the Parade ; in this part of the building are the baths of every descrip-tion, which are both splendid and comfortable : the entrance is handsome, and two waiting-rooms, of an octagonal form, are painted in fresco, with Chinese scenery : there are also baths on the Parade. Some chalybeate springs are said to exist near the town, which have not yet been fully investigated.

CHURCHES.

Hastings now contains two parish churches and a precinct chapel. All Saint's stands on high ground, to the right of the entrance from London, and its large high tower, aided by situation, has rather an imposing appearance. The exte-riors of this church and St. Clement's have been grievously mutilated, the tracery of all the windows, with one or two exceptions only, destroyed, and supplied by wooden frames; and the whole buildings are in a ragged and defaced state; the original proportions, however, being extensive and bold, could not entirely be obscured. The architecture of All Saint's is rather puzzling, the general features appearing to be those of the fifteenth century, of which the flat, though abruptly pointing arches, are evidently examples, whilst some of the windows of the tower rather assimilate to the thirteenth. It is probable, that whilst both churches were rebuilt, about the year 1400, some remains of the older ones were incorporated or transferred. The arch, at the entrance of the tower, is lofty, enclosing both a door and window; over the former are remnants of tracery; the roof of the lower story is vaulted with stone, and has a circle with rude coloured figures of animals, &c. in the centre; a majestic arch opens into the church, resting on corbels, which spring from octagonal piers. The interiors of both churches must be confessed and regretted, to be not altogether so neat as they ought to be, and neither of them is yet possessed of an organ. The altarpiece, however, is neat, of the Ionic order, with painted tablets, and some gilding, blue drapery with a glory, I.H.S., &c. above: on the south side of the chancel are three stone stalls. Some curious old painting is to be seen on some of the pews. The pulpit cloth is part of the canopy borne over Queen Anne by the Barons of the Cinque Ports, and in surprising preservation; it is a fine and strong cloth, of a rich scarlet colour, fringed, braided, and lettered with yellow silk, which might be mistaken for gold. On the south side of the church is a small porch, containing a *benitier*, and entered by an arch said to be *Norman*, but with very little reason. It is undeniably round, like the Roman cat's ball on the Town Hall, but the recent appearance, mouldings, and workmanship are surely indicative of no higher antiquity than the fifteenth or sixteenth century, in spite of the caprice of form. The tower is seventy-three feet high, and contains five bells, but one of them is cracked: it displays a monument

for Mademoiselle Victoire (Victorine or Victoria) Ruffo, eldest
daughter of the Prince de Castelcicala, a Sicilian ambassador,
who died in 1816, aged thirty-six. "She lived like an angel,
and is now, her parents humbly hope, in Heaven." In the
churchyard, which has been liberally enlarged, are several
interesting inscriptions.

St. Clement's, which stands in a confined situation, in the
midst of the town, but has a new burying-ground near the
castle, is a lower and longer building than the other, with the
tower, which is of equal massiveness, but much less elevation,
at the east end of the south aisle. The architecture is of the
usual style in the fourteenth century; on each side of the nave
are six flat arches, with clustered columns. The pulpit
cloth here, which was the canopy held over George I., is said,
in the Gentleman's Magazine, to have been of superior materials, viz., flowered silver tissue, with gold fringe at bottom, and
silver fringe at the top: but this has disappeared, we know
not how or why, and its place been supplied by a plain red
cloth, with gold fringe. The chancel of this church is handsomely decorated, for which the town is indebted to the piety
and munificence of Archibald Hutcheson, Esq., one of the
barons in the reign of Queen Anne, who railed it in, and
wainscotted it with oak, paved it with marble, and painted the
altar and ceiling, all which then cost only £125. The two
latter were the work of Roger Mortimer, uncle to the eminent
painter of Eastbourne. The altar is of the usual appearance,
with two fine and bold figures of Moses and Aaron: the ceiling
is painted with much strength and elegance; it represents the
Celestial Empyrean, with a variety of beautiful figures, almost
all of which are female. Mr. Hutcheson also gave 300l. to
increase the vessels of the corporation, for the benefit of the
poor; and 125l. to form a perpetual fund, to be lent to poor
fishermen. He was an able financial writer, and contributed
to undeceive persons and save them from the celebrated South
Sea bubble.

The tower contains six large old bells, the tenor weighing
twenty-two cwt., but one of these also is broken. We shall

probably be ridiculed for minuteness, but we confess to being lovers of campanology, and do not like to see fractured bells, unrepaired, in the steeples of opulent towns. These two livings having been found incapable of maintaining separate clergymen, were consolidated sometime ago : service is performed three times a day between the two.

St. Mary's, in the castle, an ancient precinct, has now a chapel in the centre of Pelham Crescent, with a receding portico, having a double row of Ionic pillars, which produces a handsome effect ; but a lofty cupola, which formed part of the plan, was never erected, and the end was slightly raised, to contain a bell. On the tympanum is a clock, and under it, inlaid in brass letters, " ÆDES SANCTÆ MARIÆ IN CASTELLO, EXSTRUCTA A.D. MDCCCXXVIII." The interior is striking and elegant, and slightly reminded us both of the theatre at Oxford, and the sessions-house at Chester. It is entered by two doors, on each side of the altar, opposite to which is an elliptical sweep of gallery, with ten columns of a fanciful Corinthian order, and a handsome organ. This erection belongs to the Earl of Chichester.

MARKETS, FISHERIES, AND TRADE.

The former are held under the Town Hall, on Wednesdays and Saturdays. The trade of Hastings is now inconsiderable, but was formerly of more consequence, when its vessels sailed to the Straits. For the following particulars we are indebted to the elaborate volume of Mr. Moss. Much timber, plank, iron, and grain, is brought here, to be carried coastwise ; but the iron, which was principally cannon from the founderies at Ashburnham and Rothersbridge, has materially failed from the want of wood, which has been reserved for the hop-plantations. A lime company established here, employs some sloops in bringing lime from the neighbourhood of Beachy-head, and the average annual produce of their kilns is 120,000 bushels. The principal articles imported are coals and timber: the amount of the former, entered at the custom-house in 1823, was 8508 chaldrons, which is double the quantity of 1802.

The oak plank and timber shipped in the same year was 420 loads, which was much less than most of the preceding years, some of which exceeded 1000; in 1811 it was 15,522, an extraordinary excess, which is not accounted for *.

The Fisheries employ about sixty boats, and five hundred men, women, and children: the greater part caught is sent to London, after the town is supplied; but much of the smaller sized is dried by the poor for their winter food. The fish predominant on this part of the coast are herrings, mackerel, soles, whitings, haddocks, skates, flounders, turbots, brills, plaice, scallops, crabs, prawns, and shrimps, which is a tolerable extensive list, and, of course, from the contiguity, does not vary much from that at Brighton.

" In what is called the Trauling Season, which commences the middle of July, and continues to the end of September; and from the end of the ensuing November to the beginning of April, are caught turbot, brills, plaice, soles, gurnet, dabs, scallops, crabs, &c. Some few boats are employed in trauling the whole year round.

" Near the beginning of April, about thirty of the largest boats commence what is termed the Mackerel Season; at which time, four men and one boy, or five men, are employed in each boat, until the middle of July; each of the boats carries, on this occasion, nets called *drove-nets*. About one hundred of these are apportioned to a boat; the nets, each being forty yards long and six yards deep, being put into the sea (called *shooting the nets*) about sun-set, and are drawn out again about sun-rise (which they term *work the nets*). The boats are out one night, and return in the morning with their sivver or cargo. The reason of shooting the nets of a night is, because the mackerel will not come near them in the day time. This season is considered the most profitable of any, as the fish are generally plentiful. Two hundred and a half, at six score and twelve to the hundred, is considered a good sivver for one night, at the beginning of the season, and the fish sell at from 4*l.* to 5*l* per hundred; and about eight hundred constitute a good sivver at the latter part of the season; at which time they sell at about twelve shillings per hundred.

" About 200*l.* is considered a good season for one boat to earn; this sum, however, though considerable, is but trifling when divided between boat, men, and nets. Thus, when the length of the season is taken into consideration, it will appear that these men (many of them with large families, and who are out nearly every night) only receive about 21*s.* per week, and many do not take so large a sum.

" The Herring Season commences the latter end of September, and con-

---

* Elsewhere we find it stated, that 1500 barrels of herrings are annually dried and cured at Hastings, and sent to different markets.—The population of Hastings in the year 1831 was 8097.

tinues until the latter end of November; at which time twenty boats, upon an average, are fitted out with about forty nets each (each net being thirty, yards long and seven yards deep), carrying four men and one boy, or five men. This season is not very profitable, having, of late years, much failed occasioned by the ravages of a species of dog-fish.

"About the latter end of May the boats catch mackerel by *railing* (namely, while under sail), fishing with a line, forty or fifty yards long, with a weight attached to the bottom of it, in the shape of a sugar-loaf, weighing from ten to fourteen pounds, baited with a piece of mackerel cut into thin slips, to represent small fish; at which the mackerel bite very eagerly at this time of the season. They are met with within a very short distance from the shore, a circumstance that induces numbers of the visitors to Hastings to engage in parties for this delightful sport, which can be enjoyed at a very trifling expense, as the boatmen will provide lines and every thing that is needful.

"One method of selling the fish is by a sort of auction, called here, 'Dutch Auctions.' They are shot out on the beach, when the seller begins with his own price, and falls, until some one cries out—'I will have it.'" —*Moss.*

The scene on the beach is often lively and interesting, and will greatly amuse those who take pleasure in seeing honest industry and its reward. The variety of pretty coloured shells here is very great; and they are tastefully arranged. We would recommend all who can afford it to gratify both their families and the vendors by small purchases.

BOAT BUILDING

is the great trade, and the most skilful production of Hastings, in which it excels the whole line of coast; and, in fact, all the pleasure boats in Sussex, and perhaps other counties, are either built here, or by workmen from the place. Larger vessels also, to the extent of two hundred tons or upwards, generally cutter-rigged, are frequently launched; and some will probably be seen in progress at every visit of the stranger.

The *pleasure boats* here, at the fountain head, will of course be found very superior, and the men are celebrated for skill, caution, and civility; also for moderate charges. Mr. Thomas Hood, the celebrated (though not always unexceptionable) punster, has written a very lively address to one of them, embodying many allusions to Hastings, which appeared in an

Annual some years back. We had not time and opportunity to find out " Tom Woodgate," but we met with a brother boatman, who strongly impressed us in favour of his class, and who might be a fit representative.

PLACES OF AMUSEMENT.

The libraries are, Diplock's and another, on the Parade; Janes' and Ryall's, in Pelham-place; and one in Wellington-place; at each of which the usual facilities and privileges are obtained. The billiard-rooms are in Castle-street, on the Parade, at the library, and in the centre of the town. In the Pelham Arcade is an evening musical promenade, to which persons are admitted by a moderate subscription by the year or month, or by paying a shilling each time. Loo is occasionally introduced; but the former mode of remuneration seems preferable, and worthy of imitation in Brighton, as it is a small clear gain to the proprietors. It has also another advantage: no liberal and reflective person would willingly partake habitually of the science and expense of others, exerted for his pleasure, without giving some compensation; and if there are any of a different spirit, their meanness is justly frustrated. There is both vocal and instrumental music here, with occasional variations of the performers, both male and female, and it is a place of fashionable and popular rendezvous. The theatre, lately erected in Bourne-street, on the right of High-street, with a solid stone front, is a small but lofty building, with two rows of boxes all round, and a gallery. The interior cannot be said to be by any means tastefully fitted up, but has frequently good performers and attendance. The fair and delicate Miss M. Glover was the star when we visited Hastings. The assembly room is at the Swan Inn, where occasional or fixed balls take place in the winter. Races occur in September, on a spot about a mile west of St. Leonard's, thus belonging to both places. Regattas, both of fishing and pleasure boats, are got up in the autumn, with music, &c, principally for the benefit of the fishermen. Hare-hunting and *fresh water* fishing, a rather unusual circumstance on the coast, may be obtained at Hastings. Hastings has three *fairs*, but the only well attended one is on the 26th and 27th of July. Bathing machines are of the usual stamp; but some of the boats here are fitted out for this purpose with steps let down from the stern. There are a sufficient number of hackney-coaches, flys, horses, donkeys, &c., on hire at Hastings at moderate terms; some of the flys, particularly those drawn by ponies, appear rather superior to the generality in other places.

MISCELLANEOUS.

The principal inns are, the Albion, on the Parade; and the Marine Hotel, in Pelham-place; the Castle, a very comfortable one: there are also the Swan, the Crown, and many other respectable ones. The Post Office is in High-street, as is also the Bank. There are three respectable dissenting places of worship in Hastings, one of which has an organ. There are also various institutions—a literary and scientific one, open to strangers under certain conditions; benevolent ones also; and we have some reason to think the poor of the town are not neglectfully regarded. A singular instance of unostentatious benevolence occurs here, in the case of a person who conveyed to the corporation about fifty-six acres of land, now worth 160*l*. per annum, for the general relief of the poor,—and concealed his name!

SCENERY IN IMMEDIATE NEIGHBOURHOOD, CLIFFS, &c.

The East Hill is a fine and salubrious elevation, commanding an extensive and interesting view: it is reached without difficulty by a path with many windings and occasional steps. Near this are some traces of an ancient camp. The cliffs beneath, which commence soon after the fish-market, continue in a very lofty and bold unequal chain. Several inaccessible cavities appear near the summit, whilst paths conduct, at different elevations, nearer the shore. Ranged along one or two of these the stranger meets with a sight rather startling to him, and by no means in keeping with the grander associations, viz., a great number of the small domiciles of the *pig* class! There are situations, however, when even a pig-stye may be picturesque; they certainly remind us here a little of some of the arrangements of Robinson Crusoe, the side-walls and roof of their apartment, which serves individuals or families for " parlour and kitchen and all," being frequently a natural cavity of the rock, with an artificial fence to the play-ground in front; the situation is very sheltered, and the denizens seem perfectly contented, and are by no means shy of the passing traveller, whom they hail with zealous, though rather monotonous, strains of untaught melody. The particular reasons for the establishment of the porcine colony here we did not learn.

The cliff is very noble in parts for about a mile from the town, where there is a little break or inlet; and this is a very desirable walk : if the pedestrian should return about sunset, he will be delighted by its beautiful effect on the romantic town. The various beautiful walks or rides within three or four miles from Hastings give it a superiority over most places along the coast; in this respect it has an immeasurable advantage over Brighton, whilst as a town it is nearly as inferior. We shall not dilate on these, because we have no intention of superseding the small local guides. They comprise every desirable variety, lofty hills, splendidly wooded vales and secluded glens, brooks and fountains, a " lover's seat," with a romantic tale that may recal the " Pirate" of the lamented novelist, though this has a happier termination ; small villages, fruit-gardens, &c. &c.; in short, either to the lovers of the grand or the soft in nature, there is little left to desire.

ST. LEONARD'S

is one mile and a half due west of Hastings. An omnibus plies between them several times in the day, without, we rejoice to say, any oppression of the horses, so much to be regretted in London *. It is also, when the tide is favourable, a pleasant. boating excursion. The road passes by Wellington-square, a desirable part of the former, and over the small Priory bridge, when it approaches the sea, and soon reaches the White Rock, a small eminence, where was formerly a battery of three large guns, taken out of the San Josef, a powerful Spanish ship of 112 guns, captured by the gallant Nelson in 1794. After passing this commences a range of unfinished buildings, which exhibits a tendency to connect St. Leonard's with Hastings; in fact, this would be a desirable consummation. At present they have separate interests; and while that state continues, there must, in the course of things, be jealousies and oppositions between them †; whereas, if St. Leonard's be made to form a " new town" to Hastings, the mutual interests of both will be strengthened, whilst the feeling above mentioned, which is always to be deprecated, will be abolished. The mother and daughter will then play into each other's hands without the matronly and girlish enmity of Honoria and Flavia, in the Spectator ‡. Visitors will then select which part of the united town they prefer, whilst the public advantages and institutions of both are open to their resort. If such a junction does not take place, it seems highly probable that one or the other will suffer from mutual opposition. " Vaulting ambition" in one or both of the rivals

* What could those official persons, whose care such things should be, be thinking of, when they licensed these ponderous machines, carrying eighteen persons, to run with *two* horses? which seem to be never inspected. If they occasionally walked the streets, and witnessed the miserable and pitiable manner in which good horses are necessarily ruined by these unjust tasks, they would, perhaps, revise the enactment.

† In fact there is no more incompatibility than between Kemp Town or Brunswick-square and the old town of Brighton.

‡ For an illustration of this, see *Boswell's Johnson*, article *Plymouth Dock*.

will " overreach itself and fall on t' other side." These hints are thrown out without the slightest shadow of an interested motive; let the high contending parties look to it, and be timely wise.

CONQUEROR'S TABLE.

A piece of rock in this vicinity has been reported to have formed the table on which William the Norman dined after his landing : the only drawback to this romantic association is that it is *not true*, as it is certain he landed much nearer Pevensey. It is, however, " so like truth, 'twill serve the turn as well ;" or as Horace phrased it long before,

" Ficta voluptatis causâ sint proxima veris."

SITUATION, &c.

St. Leonard's being more open to the bay of Pevensey and Beachy Head, possesses a keener atmosphere than Hastings, between which place and Brighton it is considered to form a medium, and is therefore suited in summer to those for whom the air of the very sheltered town of Hastings would be too mild and relaxing. It follows, as a matter of course, that it will *not* be so desirable for them in winter.

ENTRANCE, OR EAST LODGE,

is a good Doric elevation, with fluted columns, in the style of an ancient triumphal arch: it is of almost the greatest possible ellipsis, but has a bold and solid effect which is not unpleasing.

"MARINA,"

the appellation given to the whole sea line of buildings, is a conceited Italian term, which we cannot abide ; but this must not blind us to the merits of the case. The architecture of the various piles is very fine indeed, variously decorated with Corinthian and Ionic columns, and with long and low piazzas in front of the basements, with occasional breaks also forming squares ; and another street of handsome architecture at the back. The style is different from either Kemp Town or

Brunswick Terrace at Brighton, and comparisons are odious; but for its especial purpose, nothing could have been conceived better.

THE ESPLANADE

is, we suppose, one of the finest in Europe. Its close contiguity to the sea renders it superior to the western one at Brighton, to which its length, however, as a whole, is not equal. It is well faced with stone, and not only varied with a grass-plat, but also with flower-beds, a most happy addition. It reminds us more of the Esplanade at Weymouth than any others which we have seen. Bathing-machines and pleasure-boats are in attendance, in sufficient numbers; and a subscription band plays on the terrace in summer. The inns, baths, &c. &c. are, we understand, executed with every modern refinement of splendour and comfort. Here, as at Hastings, there is a sufficient number of respectable medical gentlemen; also of artists and instructors. Amusements are not yet separately established to any extent in the new town; the visitors who wish to engage in them resorting to Hastings.

The Assembly-rooms, however, in which frequent balls are held, compose a grand and elegant structure of the Doric order, consisting of a centre and two wings of considerable length, with a fluted portico at the entrance, and a pediment at the other extremity. One wing is used as a Billiard, and the other as a Card-room. The portico will challenge the applause of all spectators of taste; it is light and lofty for its order. The ball-room is spacious and very handsome, with a receding gallery for music over the vestibule, a coved ceiling with medallions and a fresco border, and neat glass chandeliers. Divine service was performed here before the church was completed.

A neat Library is kept by Mr. Southall on the Esplanade, and another by Miss Powell, outside the East gate.

The resident inhabitants, a short time back, did not much exceed a thousand; but no doubt this number will be considerably increased.

THE CHURCH,

of which the first stone was laid by the Princess Sophia, in October, 1831, is now approaching completion. It is to be regretted that the style and proportions were not on a grander and more ornamental scale; it cannot be fairly said to be worthy of St. Leonard's. It is of the thirteenth century, neat in detail, but petty; on the sides are large lancet windows, not in the best style; the interior will contain 800 per_ sons without side galleries, for which the breadth would scarcely suffice : at the east end is a handsome and lofty arch, opening into a small chancel recess, and at the opposite end a lesser one opening into the steeple, which will contain a small organ. The upper parts of all the windows will be filled with stained glass. There is also, we believe, a national school.

THE SUBSCRIPTION GARDENS

occupy a small sheltered and gradually rising valley, between two hills at the back of St. Leonard's; on its sides are several villas, as in the Park at Brighton, principally Gothic, and handsome in effect, but scarcely desirable here, as they encroach on the limits of the gardens. The space is small, but appears much larger from the inequality of ground, and the various trees and shrubs. In different parts are hermitages, arbours, a fountain, and a pond for aquatic birds which is also used for skating in the winter. The concern is in its infancy, and we believe an aviary has been commenced, which will ornament the shrubbery with beautiful plumage, and lively notes, and probably music will in time be added. One of the Gothic houses on the east side, let as a boarding-house, has a small steeple and clock, which is kept up for the public benefit.

The north lodge, above the gardens, which opens on the road to Battle, is a neat specimen of a small gatehouse of the 15th century. The *environs* of St. Leonard's are of course the same as those of Hastings.

HASTINGS

TO

HURSTMONCEUX AND PEVENSEY.

	MILES		MILES
BULVERHYTHE . . .	4	HURSTMONCEUX . .	$1\frac{1}{2}$
NINFIELD	$5\frac{1}{2}$	WARTLING	2
BOREHAM	3	PEVENSEY	4
			20 *

Pass through St. Leonard's, and by Bulverhythe Sluice, formerly a harbour, but now completely choaked up. An insignificant river or brook here runs up into the country, on the banks of which are levels abounding with snipes, wild fowls, and plovers. The name of this place is Saxon. A ridiculous allusion to the old Phœnician tale of a *bull's hide* has been told of it, but without any foundation. Off Bulverhythe, the Amsterdam, a large Dutch ship, heavily laden with costly articles, was stranded, and sunk irretrievably into the sands, in the year 1743: the crew, we believe, were saved. After the sands have been washed up by a violent sea, the ribs are occasionally visible at low water. Attempts were made by adventurers, in 1827, to explore the lower part, and recover some of the cargo, when they obtained several pieces of the manufacture of Ghent, Bruges, and Antwerp, comprising China-gilt jars, in good preservation ; goblets, wine glasses, and bottles, figured with gold; knives, with broad blades and carved handles, &c. &c. which were sold to the curious at very advantageous prices†. We are here again reminded of our interesting old friend Robinson Crusoe, and should have much liked to have shared the exciting investigation.

Soon after leaving Bulverhythe, the road turns off to the right of Bexhill ‡.

* The direct road from Hastings, by which the visitor may return, is only fourteen miles.
† Jones's Hastings Guide.
‡ Bexhill was a favourite residence of St. Richard, the canonized Bishop of Chichester, who died there.

We passed through Sedley Green and Ninfield, the latter a small respectable village, noted for some ladies' schools, with a little gray church, of one aisle, and a wooden steeple. Here the view opens finely towards Beachey Head. We avoided the angle formed by Boreham, a hamlet of the parish of Wartling, seeing to the right, at Windmill Hill, another hamlet, a handsome and loftily situated house, belonging to E. J. Curteis, Esq.; and soon after entered the old and wild-looking domain, once a park, of Hurstmonceux *, and perceived the grand old quadrangle, with its various angular breaks of tower, turret, and oriel stretched nobly beneath us, within the outline of its spacious moat, and contrasted by a variety of trees of venerable and decayed appearance, dispersed singly or in groups, along the edges of the surrounding eminences.

Hurstmonceaux Castle was built in the reign of Henry VI, and is one of the oldest *brick* mansions in England.

" From the reign of Richard II., when de la Pole's house was built with brick at Kingston-upon-Hull, to that of Hen. VI., I meet with no evidence of brick being employed as a material in building, but in the first year of Henry VI. a licence was granted to Roger Fiens, Knt., &c. &c. &c.

" This noble house, which is wholly built of brick, in the castle style, is still standing complete, and is, perhaps, the largest house, belonging to a subject, in the kingdom : no doubt it was built, not merely embattled, at the time the licence was obtained, the whole being built upon one plan. It is worthy of remark, that the art of making brick was then carried to such perfection, though it should seem to be but in its infancy, that this vast structure has stood the brunt of weather for above three centuries, particularly of the salt corroding vapours arising from the sea, to which it is greatly exposed, without suffering the least injury in any part of the walls, insomuch that hardly a single brick shews the least mark of decay." —*Bp. Littleton*—*Antiquity of Brick Buildings in England since the time of the Romans,* 1757.

Our Plate must be allowed to be highly creditable both to the draughtsman and engraver. The reader must, however, bear in mind, that grand as it appears, the part of the building here represented is only two-thirds of one of its smallest sides.

* A brief history and description of Hurstmonceux Castle and its possessors, a very tastefully written pamphlet of thirty pages, price 1*s.*, was published at Windmill Hill, in 1824, and is sold by the parish clerk, at Hurstmonceux, a very honest and civil man, who is the *Cicerone.* The pamphlet, to which we are not without obligations, will be found well worth the money ; and we mention this, that we may neither injure the author nor the vendor.

Prior to the Conquest, the estate, then called Hyrst, was the property of Earl Godwin, and was then given to Earl de Warren; but, a few years after, we find it transferred by some means to a Norman family, who assumed its name, one of whom added that of *Monceux*, the name of his mother, who was born at Compton Monceux, in Hampshire. In the reign of Edward II. it passed, by marriage of the heiress of Sir John de Monceux, to Sir Richard Fiennes[*], afterwards Lord Dacre[†], in which family it continued till the year 1700, when one of them

[*] The noble family of Fiennes had been constables of Dover Castle from the Conquest to the reign of John, who gave them in exchange the manor of Wendover, Bucks. An Ingelram de Fiennes married a daughter of the Earl of Bologne, of the race of the illustrious Godfrey, and was slain at the siege of Acre.

[†] Vaux (a name which will recall the Lord Chancellor Brougham and Vaux to the reader's mind) was the primary and Norman appellation of this family, who were Barons of Gillsland, in Cumberland, and one of whom was " Ronald de Vaux, of Triermain," the legendary deliverer of King Arthur's punished daughter, Gwyneth, who had slept, by Merlin's magic art, in the evanescent castle of St. John, "five hundred years and one."—(Scott's Bridal of Triermain.)—Robert of Gillsland, temp. Henry II., founded the noble priory of Lanercost, whose Holy Rood, in ancient times, was esteemed so famous : he was also, as well as his son, Sheriff and Custodiary of Cumberland and Carlisle. The latter castle, during his presidency, sustained a siege by William, King of Scotland. Afterwards the barony passed, at different periods, by marriage of its heiresses, into two other families; first, that of Moulton, from Henry III. to Edward II. ; and, in 1307, to Ranulph de Dacre, whose ancestor had been Sheriff of Cumberland and Carlisle, temp. Henry III. We need not repeat their connexion with the wardenship of the Marches.— When Sir Richard Fiennes, by marriage with the heiress, was, in the year . . . at her grandfather's death, created Lord Dacre, Sir Humphrey Dacre, her uncle, was re-created Baron of Gillsland; hence there were two specific Barons of the ancient title respectively called Dacre "*de le North*" and "*de le South.*" Of the Fiennes Lords Dacre many individuals are recorded to have possessed noble qualities of piety, domestic affection, and general charity and humanity. —" Francis Lord Dacre, temp. Charles I., was one of those recommended by the Parliament to the King for Lords Lieutenant of Counties, and had Herefordshire assigned to him ; but, finding that the power was (by various accidents) transferred into hands who were running every thing into confusion and anarchy, he would by no means be brought to act with them, but opposed their measures ; and at length, when he found it was impossible to do any good there, he absented himself from the House of Lords (as did several others of the Peers), till the ordinance for trying the King was brought in, when he again appeared there, in order to give his public testimony against it, being one of the few peers who (as the author of the Parliamentary History expresses it) had the courage in that dangerous time to meet, and make the same resolution." —*Collins.*

having dissipated it by extravagance at the court of Charles II.*, whose natural daughter, Lady Ann Fitzroy, he had married, and who was created Earl of Sussex, sold it to G. Naylor, Esq. Subsequently it was in the possession of Dr. Francis Hare, chaplain and friend to John the great Duke of Marlborough, afterwards Bishop of Chichester. It has undergone two or thr e changes since that time, and is now the property of a gentleman named Gillon, who lets the house, built (not by him, but a *Goth* of the last century) with the materials of the castle, to G. M. Wagner, Esq. Mr. Gillon is, however, the proprietor of the castle, which may be viewed at all times.

Names of high renown are thus connected with the impression made by this interesting building. Who knows not the ancient lineage of Dacre? None but those who have not drank at the fountain-head, and viewed the dawn of the " Last Minstrel's" bright and beautiful career †. The " hot Lord Dacre"

---

* He came, however, very young to court, and was early made a Lord of the Bedchamber, when he lost much by play. The latter part of his life was passed at his estate, at Chevening, in Kent; "in which parts he always preserved a great interest and influence, and was much beloved on account of that sweetness of temper and affability for which he was ever remarkable."—*Collins*.

† Of an infinity of biographical sketches and tributary eulogiums of this lamented individual, perhaps none are superior to an early one which appeared anonymously in the Court Journal. The trait of character developed in the following paragraph may be dwelt upon with eager pleasure, as both a soothing and elevating contrast to the too generally acid and envious spirit of the *genus irritabile vatum*. There are characters who take a pleasure in depreciating all accesses to moderation with the epithet of "milk and water;" we do not like milk and water, but, in the alternative, should much prefer it to gall and vinegar.

" Were we permitted to inscribe our opinion among those who believe that the name of Scott will go down to posterity with that of Shakspeare, as a legitimate heir of Fame, we should incline rather to point out the fine moral spirit, the noble warmth of humanity breathing through every line of his works; and the untarnished virtue which, throughout all the vicissitudes of his career, elevated and strengthened the aspirations of his genius. Equally devoid of envy, guile, and arrogance, Sir Walter was, of all the readers in England, the first to sympathize with the successes of his ' better brothers,'— *(Qy.)* Byron, Moore, Campbell, or Rogers;—to applaud and encourage the competition of writers of lesser glory, such as Galt or Cunningham; and to foster and direct the indications of feeble or undeveloped talent. Although the playful coruscations of irony illuminating his works of fiction, no less than the creation of his endless gallery of butts and bores, suffices to prove how tremendous would have been his powers had he chosen, after the spirit of the times, to dip his maiden lance in the venom of satire, there is no instance on record of his having written a malicious sentence, or uttered one of those pun-

mentioned there is certainly not an amiable specimen in himself, but he sufficiently demonstrates the ancient grandeur of his race, and exhibits that heroic daring which in the others might have been tempered with milder feelings.

> " To back and guard the archer band
> Lord Dacre's bowmen were at hand ;
> A hardy race, on Irthing bred,
> With kirtles white and crosses red,
> Array'd beneath the banner tall,
> That stream'd o'er Acre's conquer'd wall ;
> And minstrels, as they march'd in order,
> Play'd ' Noble Lord Dacre, he dwells on the Border.'
> *   *   *   *   *   *   *
> ' And let them come,' fierce Dacre cried,
> ' For soon yon crest, my father's pride,
> That swept the shores of Judah's sea,
> And waved in gales of Galilee,
> From Branksome's highest towers display'd,
> Shall mock the rescue's lingering aid !
> Level each harquebuss on row ;
> Draw, merry archers, draw the bow ;
> Up, bill-men, to the walls, and cry,
> Dacre for England, win or die !' "
> *   *   *   *   *   *   *

Sir Roger de Fiennes, treasurer to Henry VI., obtained from him a licence to build a *castle* at Hurstmonceux (or otherwise to rebuild and *embattle* his house), and to enlarge his park to 600 acres. His son Richard, marrying the heiress of Lord Dacre of Gillsland, was the first Fiennes who obtained the title. The barony of Dacre was, in the year 1819, revived and restored in the person of Thomas Brand, Esq. The family-seat is now at Lilly, Herts, a parish which, prior to the year 1700, belonged to the family of *Docwra* (also originally of Cumberland and Westmoreland), of baronial rank in Ireland, ancestors (may the feeling which prompts this be forgiven) to the humble individual by whom this paragraph is written *.

Prior to giving our own observations, we must quote three

gent sallies which form the glory of a modern wit ; the noble and humane impulses of his nature were as incompatible with harshness of opinion as with a base action !"

* Vide Gent. Mag., February, 1832, and Chauncey's Hertfordshire, *passim;* also Drayton's Polyolbion, 1612, in the XVIIIth song, of the River Medway, where " Sir Henry Dokwray" is mentioned.

descriptions of the former state of this castle in the middle of
the 16th and 18th centuries; the first a MS. survey in the
time of Queen Elizabeth, never before published; the second
from the steady pen of Grose, who describes it from the letter
of a correspondent in the year 1774; and the last from the
fanciful and flippant pen of Horace Walpole.

*Extract from a curious survey, made in the time of Gregory Fynes, Lord
Dacre, of his Manors in Sussex, Aug. 23, 12 Eliz., in the possession of
the Reverend Mr. Hare, of Herstmonceux.*

" 12 *Eliz.*—The Manor House of Herstmonceux standeth on the east
side of the church of Herstmonceux, about one furlong and half from the
said church, and in the west part of the said park, entering the park-gate
towards the south-west and north parts; same house eastwards descending
towards the valley, wherein the said house standeth; the south-west and
north parts moated about; the outer part of the moat being of back wall,
and paled upon the same; and the east part thereof lyeing open to the
park and woods, sometime being a pond, and now good pasture, all the
moat being of late drained, having little or no water therein, for the more
healthful standing of the said house; the entrance of the house being
towards the north, on a bridge fifty feet long, . . feet broad, and . . feet
high, from the bottom of the moat, whereof . . feet next to the gate is a
draught-bridge, devised for strength. The house being castle-like, builded
quadrant, every way containing . . . feet in length, and as much in
bredth, builded with brick, covered with slate; the towers, gutters, and
platforms thereof covered with lead; the whole towers and other edifices
are battled. The entering into the said house is at a fair square tower,
containing . . feet, and of stories . . . My Lord's arms fairly set
forth in stone on the front, over the entering of the same, having fair lights
of the chief lodging, and second stories of the same tower emboed of stone,
the high story being a platform covered with lead, and on every side-corner
of the same gate one tower of six square embattled, being round within,
and in every of them a watch-tower, embattled, covered with lead, and
eighteen feet above the rest of the same tower. The same gate and towers
have portholes, emboed under the embattlement, for casting stones and
other defensive engines for defending the same gate; the said gate and
towers being defective, of separations of the embattlement thereof, and the
watch-towers wasted of great length, with violence of wind and weather,
needful to be seen unto. Within the entering of the gate is a fair room,
vaulted, of . . feet broad and . . feet long. Within the edifices of
the said house are four gardens, or courts, whereof the first is at the entering of the house, having a fair walk, as in a quadrant, divided from the
entering of the said garden with a wall of brick, of eight arches of every
side, bearing the inner part of the galleries, serving for lodgings. Three
parts of the same are embattled, and the fourth part, towards the north,
next the hall, hath a platform covered with lead, for a walk, and the galleries and lodging of two stories; the higher being of no force; the lights
thereof set out of the roof, of one square light, gable-wise builded, with

turrets embattled, and a fair chapel being on the east corner of the same quadrant, and the hall builded on the north, entering at the west corner of the walk and lower end. The same hall being . . feet long and . . feet over, embattled on both sides, having a square tower at every end, embattled, and covered with lead ; the hall having five lights above the said platform on every side, with galleries at both ends ; and at the upper end and lower end of the hall, entering north, on the lower story, there is one other fair walk, lyeing about another of the said gardens, having galleries on three parts of the second story thereof, embattled ; having on every side lights with turrets, as in the former galleries. And the north-east corner thereof entereth the parlour, being parcel of the east part of the quadrant of the house ; and in the north-east part of the same garden, by the parlour door, a fair half pace stairs, entering towards the galleries, which cometh to the chief lodging, called the gilded chamber, and to other chambers adjoining.

" The other two courts on the other side are for the kitchen, bakehouse, brewhouse, and other necessary houses of offices, which standeth on the west quadrant of the said house, being well served with fair water, conveyed from a spring, over the mote in troughs of timber. The same house is built castle-like in a quadrant, as before, having at every corner one fair tower, covered with lead, of six square four stories high ; and also between every of the same corner towers there is one other tower of like building, leading to the leads and embattlements ; whereas there are walks to pass round about the same house and quadrant ; and at the north side of the same house there is a draught bridge over the mote aforesaid, of . . feet broad and . . feet long, leading towards an arbour and orchard, walled about with brick, which is . . feet square, wherein standeth a fair pile of brick of four stories high, covered with slatt, having a round tower leading to the said stories, the lower part being fairly glazed ; which hath been used for a banqueting-house ; and the north-east corner of the said arbour there is one other building, sometime used for a washing-house, &c. The house having a fair prospect towards the sea, and the castle and level of Pevensey on the south, the other three parts thereof are environed about with hills and woods, parcel of the said park. The said park standeth in the east side of the Church of Herstmonceux ; the manor place being in the same park, not distant above two furlongs from the said Church of Herstmonceux ; the said park being three miles about, the third part thereof lyeing in lawns, and the residue well set with great timber trees, most of beech, and partly oak, of fair timber.

" The game of fallow deer in the same park are by estimation two hundred, whereof are sixty deer of antler, at the taking of this survey.

" The keeping of the said park is given to Thomas Cardyff, one of my lords menial servants, with the fee of sixty shillings, the gate, and feeding of ten kyne, one bull, and two geldyngs, the windfalls, and two several fields containing three acres and an half, called the keepers croft, and paying eight shillings by the year for the same crofts. Herbage, besides the charge before, will bear twelve geldings or mares in summer-time, and six in winter. The mast, or pawnage, being a mast year, is worth . . which is preserved for the deer.

" There are four fair ponds well replenished with Carp, Tenche, &c, and four stewes besides, the mote being dry.

" There is a Hernery in the same park called the Hern-wood, and they used to breed in divers parts of the park : the same hath yielded this year one hundred and fifty nests, whereof . . of showlers, and the rest of hern-shaws. There is a fair warren of Conies within the said park, which is most used, in the lawn called Howfield, being replenished by estimation with . . couple of Conies.

" The same game being of late in the keeping of the keeper, is now letten to the keeper for the yearly rent of £6. 13s. 4d., who standeth bound to serve my Lord forty dozen Conies after three shillings the dozen, yf he be thereof required, or so many as he shall be required after the rate, and the lord discharged of the ffee. There is a lodge covered with thatch, and a stable very ruinous yn timber and covering, wherein the keeper now lyeth. There are three usual gates of the said park, the one called the Church-gate, Wartlyng-gate and Cowper's-gate. There are two highways leading through the park to the church, market, and townshipps adjacent. There are besides the manor-house of Herstmonceaux, other edifices, viz. an old stable, forge, and slaughter-house, without the mote. There is a fair barn, a stable, and a mansion-house near adjoyning, lyeing together with a court and curtilage near the park pale, between the church *lyten* of the west and the park east, and the great heb-ney south, used for the lord's bayly for hay. There is also one other little house with a curtilage adjacent to the church on the west.

" The Lord Dacre hath also a Fishynge in the haven of Pemsy, amongst others for drawyng and taking eels ; viz. my said lord, the bayly of the liberty, and the heirs of . . Thitcher, Esquyer, every one of them ought to have one night's fishing yearly, and every two of the jurats of the same liberty to have likewise yearly, one night's fishing there, the como-dytye whereof worth yearly to my said Lord Dacre . . . which hath not of late years been put in execution by my lord, albeit the jurors being of the corporation of the same liberty, do acknowledge my lord's right therein, wherefore it were very requisite for my said lord to cause the same to be put yearly in execution for preserving his right and preeminens therein.

" The lord's court baron for Herstmonceux hath been always used to be kept the same days for the manor, which they call the Custome Court.

" The Lord Dacre hath the inheritance of the patronage of the rectory and church of Herstmonceux, which is in the Queen's Books £18 per An. the same being worth forty marks by the year, besides the serving of the cure at this day ; whereof one Robert Kensey, of the age of fifty-four years, is parson by the gift of the Queen Mary, in the time of my lord's minority."—*Burrell MSS.*

" The Castle encloses three courts, a long one and two smaller ones ; the entrance is on the south front, through the great gatehouse, which leads into a spacious court cloistered round. On the north side is the Hall, which is very large, and much resembling those of the Colleges at Oxford and Cambridge that have not been modernized ; the fire-place being in the middle of the room, and the butteries at the lower end. At the upper or eastern side of this hall lie three handsome rooms, one of them forty feet long, these lying one within another constitute the best apartments in the castle; beyond them is the chapel, some parlours for common use, with rooms for upper servants, composing the east front. The grand stairs which lie beyond the hall occupy an area of forty feet square; the kitchen, which is beyond the staircase, to the west, is large, and as well as the hall and the chapel, goes up to a great height, reaching to the upper story of the house. The offices belonging to it are very ample, and the oven in the bakehouse is fourteen feet in diameter. The left side of the south front beyond the great gatehouse is occupied by a long waste room like a gallery in old times, and seems as if it was intended for a stable, in case the castle was besieged, or it should be found necessary to bring the horses and other cattle into a place of security. Underneath the eastern corner tower in the same front is an octagonal room, which was formerly the prison, in the midst of which is a stone post with a large chain. Above stairs is a suite of rooms similar to those of the best apartments of the castle over which it stands. The bed chambers on this floor are sufficient to lodge a garrison, and one is bewildered in the different galleries that lead to them, in every one of the windows of which is painted on glass, the Alant, or Wolf-dog, the animal supporters of the family of Fiennes. Many winding staircases, curiously constructed in brick-work, without any timber, communicate with these galleries. The towers on each side of the gatehouse on the south front are eighty-four feet in height. The south and north fronts of the castle are two hundred and six feet and a half long, and the east and west two hundred and fourteen feet and a half.

" To Richard Bentley, Esq. Battle, August 5th, 1752.

" The only morsel of good ground which we have found (in our Tour) was what the natives assured us was totally impassable; these were eight miles to Herstmonceux *: it is seated at the end of a large vale, five miles in a direct line to the sea, with wings of blue hills covered with wood, one of which falls down to the house in a sweep of one hundred acres. The building for the convenience of water to the moat sees nothing at all, indeed it is entirely imagined on a plan of defence, with drawbridges actually in being, round towers, watch towers mounted on them, and battlements pierced for the passage of arrows from long bows. It was built in the time of Henry VI. and is as perfect as the first day; it does not seem to have been ever quite finished, or at least that age was not arrived at the luxury of white-washing, for almost all the walls, except in the principal chambers, are in their native brick-work. It is a square building, each side about two hundred feet in length, a porch and cloister very much like Eton College; and the whole is much in the same taste: the kitchen extremely so, with three vast funnels to the chimney going up on the inside. There are two or three little courts for offices, but no magnificence of apartments. It is scarcely furnished with a few necessaries, such as

---

* It is almost unnecessary to say, that at this period there was no regular road from Battle to the castle but such as was very soft. Since however the attention of the legislature has been turned to the coast of Sussex, during the late wars, military roads have been made equal to any in the kingdom.

beds and chairs. One side has been sashed, and a drawing and dining-room, and two or three other rooms wainscotted by the Earl of Sussex, who married a natural daughter of Charles II. Their arms, with delightful carvings by Gibbon, particularly two pheasants, hang over the chimney. Over the great drawing-room chimney is the coat armour of the first Lennard Lord Dacre, with all his alliances. The chapel is small and mean, the Virgin and seven long lean saints, ill done, remain in the windows; there have been four more which seem to have been removed for light, and we actually found St. Catharine and another gentlewoman with a church in her hand, exiled into the buttery. There remain two odd cavities with very small wooden screens on each side, which seem to have been confessionals The outside is of brick, and has a venerable appearance; the drawbridges are romantic to a degree; and there is a dungeon that gives one a delightful idea of living in the days of soccage, and under snch goodly tenures; they showed us a dismal chamber which they call Drummers' Hall, and suppose that Mr. Addison's comedy is descended from it. The Estate is 2,000*l.* a year, and so compact as to have but seventeen houses on it: we walked up a brave old avenue to the church, with ships sailing on our left hand the whole way. Before the altar lies a lank brass Knight William Fiennes, chevalier; who died in the year 1405. By the altar is a beautiful tomb, all in our trefoil taste, varied into a thousand little canopies, and two knights reposing on their backs: these where Thomas Lord Dacre and his son Gregory, who died without issue."

In the year 1777 this noble building, which was at that time in a complete state of preservation, and capable of lasting so for centuries, " to show," as Dr. Johnson observed, " how our ancestors lived," was unroofed, the interior removed, and all the windows, &c. dismantled, leaving only an imposing shell and outline for the gratification of posterity. The moat, which entirely surrounded the building, appears to have been about sixty feet wide and eighteen deep. It is crossed on the south side by a modern bridge of four arches (not *forty!* as a certain " Guide" observes); here is the grand principal entrance, which is highly effective. Two strong flanking turrets are octagonal in form to half their height, when they are girded by a cornice, with small corbels, from hence they take a circular shape, and are surmounted by battlements, resting on bold machicollations, and above are smaller circular turrets, rising to the height of eighty-four feet. The arch is lofty and contains a neat window above the doorway; over it is a niche deprived of a statue, probably St. George or St. Michael, and a window on each side. The recollections of the former state

C. Scott delin.

C. J. Smith sculp.

HERSTMONCEUX CASTLE.

For the History and description of the Sussex Coast.

Printed by Cad. & Harrington.

of the interior we derived from our honest guide. The entrance tower was for the warders, who had a spacious waiting room above the lower story, which has a vaulted roof, and contains arblast-windows and port-holes for cannon. The rooms to the left of this are supposed to have been stables and store-houses for provisions during a seige. In the turrets are *furnaces*, the means of preparing a terrible mode of close defence, when

> " ——— Upon tower and turret head,
> The seething pitch and molten lead,
> Reek'd like a witch's cauldron red."

The south-west and south-east corner turrets have *dove houses* in their upper stories, which may have been a wise precaution for sustenance in war-time. The west side contained the kitchen, with its large funnels; the bake-house, with its mighty oven, a brewery, and dairy. On approaching this part, the visitor should beware of a very badly covered well. From the destruction of the interior, the walls which separated the three courts, as well as the cloisters round the first, have disappeared. The two smaller courts only occupied half the breadth each. At the north-west angle is a tower called the *Floodgate* Tower, which had water-works communicating with the moat. A gallery, or corridor, eight feet wide only, runs along the north front; at the west end was a large room for servants, popularly called the " Red Room," from its floor, sides, and arched roof, exhibiting the naked brick-work: from hence to the east side the rooms are said to have been magnificently wainscotted with carved work, but their precise designation is unknown: in the centre of this front is an oriel; at the north end of the east front was the refectory, with lofty slender windows and oriels, and must have been a handsome apartment. The chapel crosses its south end, transversely, and here we trace the outline of the principal court. Its oriel at the east end was large and handsome, enclosing three long separate windows of two lights; above is a turret, supported by a strong flat arch, but, from its position, it is scarcely probable that this was a belfry. From the chapel to the south end were some large and handsome rooms, and at the corner two dungeons, or prisons, but with no particular *horrors* that we see beyond others.   On leaving Hurstmonceux, we must pronounce it to be by far the finest *domestic castellated* mansion we have ever seen; and from all we have read upon the subject, we are disposed to think it has no competitor in England.

The Church, " the brave old avenue " to which is gone, is a small early Gothic building, of three aisles, a chancel, and small north chancel, and a very low but neat tower, with triple lancet windows and an obtuse spire, at the north-west. The population is about 1400.

The objects which will strike the spectator are two only, besides the splendid monument of Lord Dacre ; a tablet in the chancel for a Mr. Luke Trevigar, a rector of this parish, 1772, and his wife, to whose united piety and virtues a striking and pleasing tribute is paid ; and a brass slab on the floor with the following inscription.

William . Fienles . Chebalier*. qp . moruit . le . XVIII . jour . de . Januer . lan . del . incarcon . nre . seignour . Jheu . Cryst . mill . CCCC . II . qpst . ici . de . sa . alme . dieu . eit mercp . et . qp . pur . sa . alme . debostement . paternoster . et . abe . priera . VI . XX . iours . de . pardon . enauera .

" William Fienles, knight, who died on the 18th day of January, the year of the incarnation of our Lord Jesus Christ, one thousand four hundred and two, lies here ; God have mercy on his soul ; and whoever will for his soul devoutly say Paternoster and Ave, shall have for it † six times twenty days pardon."

On the north side of the chancel is the monument of the first Fiennes Lord Dacre, and his son. This is a stately erection of Sussex marble, and from its colour and outlines brought to our recollection Quentin Matsy's splendid work in

---

* " ' Miles ' and ' Chevalier,' or ' Chivaler,' are both usually interpreted ' *Knight*,' but it has been conjectured that the latter was the higher title of the two."—*Gen. Mag.*, *March*, 1812.

† So we read it ; it has been elsewhere rendered " twenty-six."

the choir at Windsor.   It has a large cinquefoil ogee arch
minutely ornamented, a rich base of quatrefoils, and several
fretted niches and canopies.   The heraldic bearings and trophies have been lately restored and gilt.   The back of the
monument also, which opens into the small north chancel, now
used as a vestry, with some slight fragments of stained glass,
is similar in appearance, but has the centre boarded up, and
the rest whitewashed.

Others of the Fiennes have been here interred.   Thomas
Lord Dacre, who died in . . . ordered that a hundred wax
tapers should be kept burning over his tomb, and that " an
honest priest should sing for his soul" seven years, with a salary
of twelve marks yearly.

Of the younger Lord Dacre, to whom, in conjunction with
his father, the principal monument is erected, an unhappy fate
is recorded in the year 1541, proceeding from a rather harsh
construction of a rash and youthful frolic, but which apparently
had no reckless nor evil intention, and perhaps much less hard-
ness of heart than many ribald feats of *roués* in the present day.

Listening, as Holinshed observes, to the " lewd persuasions"
of three young associates, Mantell, Frowdes, and Rawdon, he
went with them and some others in the night to hunt deer, in
Sir Nicholas Pelham's park at Laughton, a few miles distance
from his mansion.   It is decidedly obvious, that in this proceeding he was actuated by no idea of stealing, or any motive
of paltry and dishonest gain, as he had venison enough in his
own domain ; it must have been considered in the light of a
silly jest or bravado.   Unfortunately they encountered three
of Sir Nicholas Pelham's keepers, who, faithful to their trust,
attacked the aggressors stoutly, and unhappily one of the
keepers was killed in the fray ; though very probably without
any malice prepense on the part of the intruders, who had their
liberty, if not their lives, to defend ; and as it was incontrovertibly
proved, whilst Lord Dacre was with other of the masquers in
a different part of the park, and totally unconscious of what
was going on.   The three friends, however, above-mentioned
were executed for murder, and Lord Dacre having been found

guilty by his peers, suffered the next day after them at Tyburn. He could not, as it is reported, have been convicted if he had pleaded " not guilty," as he had not been in the fray; but he was persuaded by some villanous courtiers to plead " guilty," and submit himself to the king's mercy, which these treacherous advisers took care, by means of some influence within their reach, that he should not obtain. The reader will pause, and wonder at such conduct, till he learns a fact which will turn his feelings to indignation, viz., that they expected to obtain a grant of his estate. Much exertion was however used in other quarters to obtain the king's favourable consideration, and no " small moane," as Holinshed informs us, was made for him, " being a right towardly gentleman, and such a one as many had conceived great hope of better proofe;" also only in the twenty-fourth year of his age. But he was in the hands of a brutishly obstinate monarch, which, as they had been dyed in the blood of his own wives, were not likely to be deterred from signing the death-warrant of a stranger; and the ill-fated, for we cannot call him guilty, young man was sent to seek that mercy in another world which was denied him in this.

From Hurstmonceux to Pevensey we pass the church of Wartling, a gray-looking building, with two or three aisles and a wooden steeple. On the north side appears a window, with the flowing tracery of the 14th century. From hence the road passes through a rich level, intersected with brooks, and in summer is not unpleasant: a very agreeable day may be passed between the two objects, as we can testify.

Passing through the village of Pevensey, which is now very insignificant, but has some old buildings, the traveller on his entering the castle will probably be surprised by its spaciousness. It is to the rest of the castles in this part of England, what Dr. Johnson affirmed of the castles in Wales, compared with those in Scotland—" one of the former would contain all the latter." On advancing from the outer walls he will approach the keep, with admiration of its substantial round towers, in parts excellently preserved, and the strong curtain walls between them. It reminded us of two distinct objects, perhaps

not very similar.; the castle of Falaise in Normandy, and that
of Rhyddlan in North Wales. The latter was endeared to us,
and perhaps "the wish was father to the thought." That
some *remains* of a Roman castle were here, on which the present building was engrafted, seems undeniable, the traces being
still distinguishable ; also that Roman bricks were worked into
the more recent structure : but to speak of the entire castle as
one of the principal Roman remains in Britain is careless
absurdity. The form of the outer walls is polygonal, but
tending to a circle, and they enclose a space of *seven acres.*
The principal entrance was on the side of West Ham, with a
moat and two round towers, near the top of which are several
layers of red and white Roman brick. Part of this fell three
years ago, when a lady who was viewing it, and the guide, an
old woman, narrowly escaped. Red layers also occur in the
south-east tower, in opposition to the statement of Gough,
whose account of this castle seems very incorrect. The *south*,
as we conceive, and not the *east* side of both the keep and the
outer bail was the same :—here the sea is supposed to have
flowed up at a very distant period, and before the present
town was erected. But the irregular form of the structure
rather puzzles an ordinary spectator as to the direction of the
cardinal points. Facing the south or south-west are two long
iron guns, not very old in appearance, but one of them has the
initials of Queen Elizabeth : they do not seem to be larger
than 9 pounders, and were fired at the Jubilee in 1809. The
E.S.E. wall stands on a cliff: this is the most ruinous part of
the building, and has a very picturesque appearance ; terrific
looking masses have rolled down from the walls, which are
generally ten feet thick. The keep has the most complete
features; the upper parts of several of the towers are of very
perfect and solid masonry, and exhibit their windows for
arbalists :—a kitchen, refectory, &c., or those places supposed
to be such, are in the lower stories of the round towers, with
Norman arches in the walls. Altogether, though there is not
much richness of architecture, or carved work, few ruins are
more teeming with interest than those of Pevensey castle. The

walls are occasionally beautifully covered with ivy and small hedge-shrubs, and those who have no fear of giddiness may walk round the greater part of those in the keep. On the south side was a sally-port, and on the north-east an entrance-gate to the town.

The church now appears disfigured, but was doubtless once a respectable structure. It has three aisles, with a very large and extremely low tower, with a pointed roof on the north side. The chancel, neatly covered with ivy, appears to have been larger, and has three fine lancet windows at the east end.

HISTORY.

Pevensey was termed by the Saxons *Peofnesea**. Its first authentic mention in history is in the year 792, 31 *Offæ*, when it was given by Berodaldus, with Hastings, to the abbey of St. Denis, at Paris.

One of the possible localities of *Anderida* has been assigned to this place, but with less likelihood than those we have previously alluded to. Usher also conjectures it to be the *Caer Pensavelccoid* of the Britons.

This was one of the places ravaged and partly burnt by Earl Godwin; and in the reign of Edward the Confessor, 1043,

"Earl Swayn came out of Denmark with 8 Ships and returned to England and coming to his father's House Earl Godwyns at Pevensey humbly requested of him and his Brothers Harold and Tostie to endeavour his reconciliation with the king."—*Powell's Wales. Burrell MSS.*

"Pevensey, called by the Saxons Peofensea, by the Normans Pevensell, and now commonly Pemsey; we set it in the first place, because we conceive when it gave the name of the Rape to it, it was the chief town, though no market town, so far as we can discover. It was certainly of old a famous place for shipping, for it is reckoned one of the seaports which Godwin Earl of Kent ravaged in Edward the Confessor's time, and took away many ships; but now it is only accessible by small boats, which crowd up a rill to it. What is spoke memorable of it in our historians, we shall set down in the order of time in which it happened, viz.: In 1049, Suane, Earl of Oxford, Gloucester, Hereford, Somerset, and Berks,

---

* "It may seem to take its name from the scouring of the haven by the waters of the level pent in, having vent through their sluices here into the sea."—*Jeakes' Cinque Ports.*

son of Godwin Earl of Kent, being forced to fly into Denmark, because he had enveigled Edgiva, abbess of Leominster, out of her house with an intent to marry her, contrary to the laws of those times, returned with eight ships and landed at this town, where having obtained his cousin Beorn to mediate for him to the king, upon his promise that for the future he would become a faithful subject; he took Beorn into his ship to carry him to the king, who was then at Sandwich, under pretence of making his peace; but Suane having thus got him into his power, carried him to Dort, in Holland, where he inhumanly murdered him, and cast his body into a deep ditch covering it with mud. Aldred, bishop of Winchester, obtained his pardon for alluring Edgiva; but his conscience could not pardon his treacherous cruelty in murdering Beorn his kinsman, until he underwent the penance of going to Jerusalem barefoot, in which journey he got so much cold that he died thereof at Licia, in his return home."—*Account of Eastbourne,* 1787.

" Pevensey river, though now so insignificant, was formerly, in all probability, of no mean consideration, the names of places considerably inland from Pevensey found that presumption. *Herst Haven,* about three miles inland, shows there was a station for vessels at the wood. *Herst Bridge,* north-west of Hailsham, now corruptedly called Horse Bridge, was formerly a pass of some consequence, as it combined the communication between the open country and the wild, seems to have been placed at the entrance of the great wood, as a neighbouring family seat renders probable, now vilely corrupted into *Horselungs,* but anciently denominated *Herstongue,* to show the commencement of the Silva Anderida, in that part of the country."

" About 1700, the river was navigable for small vessels to Pevensey Bridge."—*Burrell MSS.*

The town, castle, and rape of Pevensey were given by the Conqueror to Robert, Earl of Moriton, in Normandy, his half-brother.

Doomsday.

" In Burgo Pevensel T. R. E. fuer. 24 Burgenses in d'nio Regis, et reddet de gablo 14 sol et 6 den, de theoloneo xx sol, de portu 35 sol, de pastura 7 sol et 3 den, E'pus de Cicestre habet. v. burgenses. Edmer xv, Ormer v. Dodo iii."

Ibidem.

" Wills Comes Moreton dedit apud Pevensel unam vergatam terræ. Ib Monachi de Moreton et Burgenses de 66 den."

" Gislebert vicecom. 1 burgs'e de xx den. Wills de Cahainges; 2 burgenses de 2 sol. Boselin. v. de 2 sol. Wills; 4 de 2 sol. Ansfrid. 4 de 2 sol. Giroldas; 2 de 6 sol. Ansgot 3 de xii den. Bernardus 2 de 7 den. Radulfus; 2 de 12 den. Alanus; 6 de 4 sol. Radulfus; 3 de 53 den. Azelinus; 3 de 4 sol. Ipse ten' una' doma'de 32 den; et parvum'. Frae de 3 sol. Walterius; 2 burg'ses 16 den. Rogerius; 2 de 12 den. Hugo 1 de 8 denar. Un' molin' habet Comes de 20 sol. Aluredus habet de herbag 15 sol 4 denar."

N. B. The very ample documents relating to Pevensey in the Burrell MSS. are more confusedly arranged than any other part of that collection. We think it probable, however, that they may have as much interest for the reader in their original miscellaneous garb, as if we were to undertake the laborious and uncertain task of marshalling them into an abridged and regular narrative.

―――――

" Robtus Comes Moreton frater Willielmi Regis dedit Ecclesiæ et Monachis S. Mariæ de Grestein in Pevensel domum Engelerii et quicquid ad eam pertinet cum omni consuetudine, et in foresta sua de Pevensel pasnagium et herbagium et materiem ad ecclesias suas et ad proprias domos suas constituendas et ad focum suum."—*Cart. 9 Ex. n.* 21 *per Inspex.*

" Richerus de Aquila dedit Ecclesiæ et monachis S. Mariæ de Grestein omnes decimas de dominis suo de Castellaria, de Pevensell in quocunq' modo terræ lucratæ fuerint et bordarum de Buscheio liberum et quietum, et decimam piscatoriæ suæ antequam ulla pars inde exeat, quod Rieva primus confirmat."—*Ibid.*

" Stephanus Rex Angliæ Archiep'is &c., Sciatis me concessisse et dedisse Ecclesiæ S. Trinitatis Cicestriæ, Hillario Epo et Successoribus suis Episcopis, in perpetuam elemosynam, Capellariam de Pevensel cum omnibus ad eam pertinentibus, ita quod Hillarius E'pus et Successores sui inde sint Capellani Matildis Reginæ uxoris meæ, et successores ejus, et ad festa ejus invitati tanquam proprii Capellani ejus venient, et ei inde serviant."

―――――

" Joh.—Johannes Rex concessit Baronibus de Pevensel quod faciant unam villam, super Galetum quod jacet inter portum de Pevensel et Langenere."—*Vide* p. 262.

" 9 Joh.—Barones de Pevenesel debent xl. marcas, pro habenda licentia faciendi unam villam super Galetum."—*Do.*

" 6 Ric. 1.—De Scutagio militum ad redemptionem d'ni Regis, in Sussex. Gilbertus de Aquila debet xxi[l]. xvii[s]. vi[d]. de scutagio militum suorum, scilicet de quolibet milite xii[s]. vi[d].   Quia sunt de parvo feodo Moritoniæ."—*Mag. Rot. 6 R. 1.* 16. *a.*

" Ric. 1.—Ricardus primus concessit Johanni de Palerna feodum portæ de Pevensel.   Concessit etiam eidem Johanni custodiam portæ Castelli Pevensel."—See *Ayliff's Chartæ,* pp. 26, 27.

" Ricus primus confirmat Eccle'iæ et monachis S. Mariæ de Grestein ex dono Hugonis de Cahaignes in Pevensel iii acras terræ.   Ex dono Willis filii Alfwredi 4 acras terræ quas tennit Sefredus juxta Ecclesiam S. Mariæ de Pevensel ex parte occidentis."—*Cart.* 9. *E.* 2. *n.* 21 *per Inspex.*

" 4 Hen.—William, Earl of Moreton, in Normandy and Cornwall, who, 4 Hen. 1. A. D. 1104, rebelling against that king, he seized on all his possessions in England, and banished him the realm, afterwards taking him prisoner at the battle of Tenerekebray, in Normandy, he sent him prisoner to England, put out his eyes, and bestowed this manor, town, and castle, on Gislebert als Gilbert de Aquila, son of Richer de Aquila, and Judith his wife, d. of

Richd. de Abrincis, sister of Hugh, first E. of Chester, wch Richer was slain, A. D. 1685, fighting for king Wm. against his rebellious subjects of Maine, leaving issue 2 Sons, 1 Gislebert, 2 Egenulph, and 1 d. Maud, m. Robt. de Molbray, E. of Northumberland."—*Ordericus Vitalis*, 649 *A*.

" He married Juliana, d. of Geffrey, E. of Mauritane, by whom he had 4 sons, 1 Richer, 2 Eugenulf, 3 Geffrey, 4 Gislebert. Eugenulf and Geffrey were shipwrecked, with the children of Henry 1. On the grant of the afd manor, town, and castle of Pevensey to Gislebert, it was called the honor of Aquila, or the Eagle, Pevensey Castle being the head thereof. The afd. Gilbert d . . . and was succeeded by his son.

" Ricker, or Richd. de Aquila, who taking up arms against that king, to restore Wm. son of Robt. Curthose, to his father's honors, his estate became forfeited, but was restored by the intercession of his uncle Rotro ; being engaged a second time in the same rebellion, his estate again escheated to the crown, and was settled by the king on his grandson.

" Henry Fitzempress (Maud), who, after a long contest with king Stephen, to recover his right, compounded for his success, assigned the town and castle of Pevensey, and whatever Richer de Aquila had of this honor to

" Wm. son of king Stephen, who held them till Henry 2d. attained the throne, and 4 Hen. 2 surrendered them again to the king on the restitution of all the Lands which were his father's before he was king of England, upon which Henry 2 restored them again, as it seems, to

" Richer de Aquila for he, 12 Hen. 2, on collection of the aid for marrying the king's dau. certified that he held 35½ knights' fees, of wch he had been enfeoffed in the time of Hen. 1. This Richer gave the monks of Grestine, in Normandy, the lands and woods lying in the manor of Willindone, in Sussex, with the tythes of his mill there, as also herbage in his forest, and also tythes of his ldp. and castle of Pevenesel, and other lands of great value in Sussex. He d. 22 Hen. 2, 1176, and was succeeded by Gilbert de Aquila.

" Gilbert de Aquila, 6 R. 1, paid 21*l.* 7*s.* 6*d.* for his knights' fees in Sussex, on the scutage then collected for king Richard's redemption ; he m. . . . sister to Wm. E. of Warren, and d. in Normandy, 6 Joh. was succeeded by his son,

" Gilbert de Aquila m. Isabel ; his estates were forfeited for passing into Normandy without the license of king Henry 3, who, a. r. 19, granted this manor, and all the lands belonging to the said Gilbert, with the advowsons of the churches, as also of the castle of Pevensey, with the wards and service thereto belonging, to

" Gilbert Mareshall, E. of Pembroke, to hold by the service of 2 knights' fees until the same shall be restored to the right heirs thereof. On Saturday, at the eve of St. Botolph, he delivered up this castle to the king, Cart. 24 H. 3. m. 2., who, 25. H. 3. (Pat. m. 2.) bestowed it on his Queen's Uncle during pleasure, for his better support, except such lands as Gilbert Mareschall had disposed, viz. the town of Greywell, in marriage to Gilbert Basset with Isabel, d. of Wm. Ferrers.

" 20 Hen. 3, 1236. The Earldom of Warren at this time held of the king 62 knights' fees in the rape of Lewes, and 30½ in the rape of Pevenesel, of the fee of Gilbert de Aquila. Dug. Bar. 77 a.—*Testa. de Nevil.*

" 22 R. 2. Pevensey castle besieged by the men of Sussex, Surrey, and Kent, he adhering to Henry, Duke of Lancaster."

" Odo de Baieux shut himself up in Pevensey castle, where he was in hopes to hold out a siege till the Duke of Normandy should come to his relief; but the town was taken in a few days. Huntingd. p. 372. The Saxon Annals, and Simeon of Durham say, that it held out above six weeks, and Brompton, p. 595, says seven weeks. On the death of the Conqueror, A. D. 1087, Odo de Baieux was released from his imprisonment in the castle of Roan, in Normandy, by Wm. Rufus; coming to England, was confirmed in ye possession of his Earldom of Kent, as also in many of his former places of trust, amongst which was ye castle of Rochester; but when Odo found he had not ye whole sway, he raised an insurrection in Kent, in order to advance Robert, Duke of Normandy, to the throne, and having pillaged many places in that county, carried his plunder to Rochester, from whence he went to Pevensea castle, where he held out a siege for six weeks, when he was forced, for want of food, to surrender it to the king, and to bind himself to deliver up Rochester castle, where ye chief Norman Lords were shut up, under the command of Eustace, Earl of Bologne. Wm. E. of Moretagne and Boulogne, 3rd son of king Stephen, lord of the honor of the Eagle et Pevensey, and, in right of his wife, 4th Earl of Warren and Surrey, died at the siege of Tholouse, A. D. 1160, without issue.

" A. D. 1144. Stephen invested the castle of Pevensey, but finding it too strong to be taken by force, left a body of men before the place to reduce it by famine.

" In ye Treaty between Henry and Stephen it was agreed that William Stephens' son should have inter alia the Honour of the late Wm. Warrenne, whose daughter and heir he had married, and Richer de l'Aigle's share of ye Honor of Pevensey, and should do homage and give security or hostages for his fidelity to Henry."—*Burrell MSS., p.* 186, *of* 1682.

" Hen. 3. A. D. 1265. The Barons, thinking it of great consequence to their party to be entire masters of the coast of Sussex, Leicester, with this view, sent John Fitz Alan orders, in the king's name, to deliver up his son and heir, or the castle of Arundel, by way of hostage for his fidelity. The castle of Pevensey being still left very convenient for receiving supplies from France, Simon de Montfort had marched from London with a body of the City Militia, and another of the Barons' troops to invest it, but after losing a great deal of time before it, was called away by his father, who wanted his assistance, and returned to London."

" 27 Ed. 1. Baronia et Honor de Aquila is quit claim to the king by Amadeus comes Sabaudia."—*Burrell MSS.*

In 18 Edw. 1, a complaint was made by the Abbot of Battle, Prior of Lewes, and a great many others, having lands in *Pevenesel* Marsh, that one Lucas de la Gare, who was appointed by the king one of the overseers and guardians of the Marsh, instead of doing his duty had begun to raise a certain bank athwart the haven, as also a sluice, intending to finish them, so that the fresh water could not pass through the midst of the marsh to the sea, to the great peril of the neighbours, and danger of drowning their lands. The king issued a Commission of Inquiry to his justices, there-upon."—*Abridged from Burrell MSS.*

" 6 Ed. 1. Ricardus le Bod, tenet 15 librat. terrae infra libertatem Quinque Portuum per servitium essendi Janitor forinseci Porte Castri de Pevenest."—*Harl. MS. No.* 1192.

" 26 Ed. 1. Henr de Palerna, 26 Ed. 1, ten per servitia custodiendi portas de Pevenessell.

" The king, by a writ of his great seal, commanded the Barons of his Exchequer to prepare a valuation of lands appointed for a settlement of 18,000*l.* Turonois p. an. on Isabella, a daur. of France, who was to be married to Prince Edward: inter alia Honor Aquila Praeter Castrum de Pevenese cccc*l.*—*Burrell MSS.*

" By 10 Edw. 2. liberty was granted to Robert de Sassy, and Olivia his wife, to inclose as much of Pevensey Marsh as was then overflowed, and in the occupation of no man, and to hold it of the said king and his heirs, during their lives, for a pair of gilt spurs ; to be paid into the Exchequer every St. John's day, which demand was afterwards superseded by his order."—*Eastbourne,* 1787.

Pope Nicholas' taxation, 1291.

	£.	s.	d.
" Vicar' de Pevnesee	4	6	8
Eccl'ia de Westhme	8	0	0
Eccl'ia de Boxle est in usus Ep'i et taxat cum tempor'; Vicarii ejusdem .	10	13	4
Bona Ep'i Cicestre' Boxle qd. taxatur	12	17	1"

CUSTOMS OF PEVENSEY,

Abridged and spelling modernised from the Burrell MSS.

" Thes ben the usages and customs of the Towneporte and of the Leege of Pevensage of the tyme whereof no mynd is *."

All the commons of the town and leege as well as abbot, prior or knight, and other worthy men having lands were to assemble the Monday after St. Michael, in St. Nicholas Church, and to choose a bailiff, styled "receyvour," who was to take solemn oaths, and receive the "mandement" of the king, the constable of "Dovore," and the barons of the five ports. The same day he was to choose twelve jurats from the four quarters of the leege, who shall rightly assess, &c., sparing neither rich or poor according to their ability,—So help them God and all saints.

Also he shall choose to him a common clerk.

Also the men of the burgage of Pevensey have an hospital, called St. John the Baptist, in which are brethren and sisters, and one burgess shall always be overseer and supervisor of the same, to grant "corodys" to men and women, and superintend the quantity and disposition.

---

* The legal term and limitation, " De tempore quo non exstat memoria," dates at the captivity of Richard I. in the Holy Land.

And the said "recevor" may place in the same hospital any honest man or woman of the leege reduced to poverty.

Also the Lady Queen of England hath a port-reeve, who ought to pay eight marks, and levy it customarily on the inhabitants.

Also the port-reeve is the coroner, and is to proceed according to the usages of the Cinque Ports (which see): in case of condemnation, if the prisoner be of the franchise, he is to be had on the bridge to be cast into the haven, but if guildable he shall be hanged without the leege, at a place called the " *Vash-Treive.*"

The port-reeve is judge in pleas of land, &c.

The receivor and jurats may make any honest inhabitant of a year and a day a freeman, who shall take an oath and " pay to the *Light of St. Nicholas.*"

Also the men of the said franchise may " chase to" the hare or conies, hunt, fish, and fowl every where by land or water, except those places where no man " hath to do," without the leave of him to whom the close belongeth.

Also any man of the franchise may buy and sell in London or any market-town without being molested; and if hindered, the receivor and jurats of Pevensey are to interfere in his behalf.

The receivor, jurats, and commonalty claim to be a member of the port of Hastings, and to enjoy all usages, &c.

No bailiff can attach a man of the franchise, except for plea of the king or profit of the commonalty, without the king's special commandment.

———

In 1163, 9 John, license was given for building a town between " Pevenesell" and " Langele," with similar liberties to those of the Cinque Ports, a market every Sunday, and a fair, lasting seven days, on the Nativity of St. John the Baptist.

———

" 7 Hen. 2. A Donum was answered both for the counties and for the cities or burghs.

" Viz^t. Idem Vicecomes. r. c. (regi computat.) in liberatione militum de Pevenesel y marcas et q. e. (quietus est) Mag. Rot. 7 Hen. 2. Rot. 2. 6.

" 14 Hen. 2. Richerus de Aquila paid to the Scutage of Galway xvi*s.* vi*d.* per fee, for certain fees of Moreton wch he held in the C⁰. of Sussex.

" Gillebertus de Aquila r. c. de xxi*l.* xvii*s.* vi*d.* de Scutagio militum suorum; scilicet de unoquoque milite xii*s.* vi*d.* et Wᵐ. de Chahaignis the like for his knight's fees. Mag. Rot. 33 H. 2 rot. 8. C. Sudsexe. Madox Exchr. cap. 16, p. 482.

" 2 Hen. 3. De primo scutagio Regis Henrici, tertii, assiso ad 11 marcas Gillebertus de Aquila (debet) xliii marcas et x*s.* de xxxv feodis de feodis Moritoniae. Mag. Rot. 2 Hen. 3 rot. 3. a. Sudsex.

" 11 Hen. 3. Gillebertus de Aquila reddit compotum de D. Marcis pro habenda saisana de terris suis quae captae fuerunt in manum Regis reddendis ad terminos contintos in originali de Cancellaria; ita quod in ultimo termino, scilicet ad natalem domini anni xii allocentur ei, ea quae capta sunt de terris praedictis tempore quo extiterunt in manu Regis. Mag. Rot. 11 H. 3. Sudsex. Madox Exchèq. cap. 28, p. 707."

———

" On W^m. the 6th E. Warren joining Lewis the Dauphin ag^t. King John, his defection was so displeasing to the king, that he sent him a precept to deliver up his castle of Pevensey to Mathew Fitzherbert, who was commanded to demolish it.

" 2 Hen. 2." Says Madox " the honor of Gilbert de Aquila and the honor of Warenne were vested in W^m. 6th E. of Warrenne: the Record he quotes says, ' Comes de Warenna debet xliiil. et xvs. de xxxv feodis, de feodis Gilliberti de Aquila, de feodis Moretoniæ et c & xxl. de lx feodis de Baronia sua.'—Mag. Rot. 2 Hen. 3. a. m. 2. Sudsexia tit.

" I find in Testa de Nevil, under ye article of Hundred de Wodeton Com. Surry, ' Villa de Westcote que fuit Gilberti de Aquila, capta fuit in manus domini Regis, quia idem Gilbertus abiit in Normanniam contra voluntatem domini Regis, asdicitur, et Comes Warrennæ finivit pro sorore sua quae fuit uxor ipsius Gilberti pro dicta villa quam habuit in dote; i. e. in manu Comitis, et est in Baronia Gilberti de Aquila.' This fine from E. Warren was only on acc^t. of his sisters dower from those lands, to wch she became entitled 6 Joh^s. in which year her husband died in Normandy; 9 Joh^s. he paid 300 marks for y^e. custody of y^e. said lands, and it is not to be doubted, but she enjoyed her dower for life in consequence."

" Joscelin, Castellan of Pevensey, attests a charter without date from Simon s. of W^m. and grandson of Simon de Achingham, to the monks of S. Pancras, Lewes.

" 11 Hen. 3. Thereof her son Gilbert gave 11 Hen. 3, 300 marks fine for livery of his lands being probably at this time come to majority; but before 19 Hen. 3 he had forfeited the same; for at that time they were granted to Gilbert Marshall E. of Pembroke, and 25 Hen. 3 to Peter de Savoy, who, 28 Hen. 3, had custody of the above Gilbert's heir.—Watson Ped. of Warren, p. 48.

" 47 Hen. 3. John E. of Warren had ye Castle of Pevensey in Sussex, one of the royal fortifications, committed to his charge; the Earl however joined the Barons then associating ag^t ye Crown, tho he afterwards joined the King at Oxford.—Ib. p. 60. Dug. Bar. p. 780.

" 49 Hen. 3. Rex vicecomiti Sussex salutem. Summonito per quatuor legaliores Milites de Comitatu suo praedicto Petrum de Subandia apud Pevenseiam, Johannem de Warrena apud Lewes, et Hugonem de Bygod apud Boscham, quod sint coram nobis et Consilio nostro in proximo Parliamento nostro Lond. primo die Junii, Justiciam facturi et recepturi.—Rymer.

" Petrus de Sabandia (Savoy) 37 Hen. 3, Pevensey a portu Castri versus austral; usq. ad molend. Abbatis de Begham exparte occidentali de Westham et inde de libera Warrenna.

" 26 E. 1 Henricus de Palm tenet ten, suum per servie, custodiendi portas de Pevenessell—Tower Rec.

" Henricus de Palerna custodit portam, extra Turrim de Ffallium p' sergantiam illam et valet per annum mj marc et dimid.—Testa de Nevil.

" 26 E. 1. Ricus le Bod ten 15 librat terre infra libertatem v portuum p' sergantiam essendi Janitor forinsecus porte Castri de Pevensey et 100 solid terre extra praedictam libertatem in socagium et nil habet extra predictem libertatem p' quod possit attachiare.

" 7 Ed. 2 Barones de Pevensey. Pevensey Fer 7 dier.—*Tower Rec. Carta, No.* 45.

" 14 Ed. 3.—Pevense castr' de, Herbag infra muros ejusdem, cum custodia Warren de Wilington concess p' Philippam Reginam Angliæ Jo. Whitehersh. confirm, p. R. 1. p'. anno 14 E. 3. m. 10."

" Hen. IV. A. D. 1405.—Edw. Duke of York was kept a close prisoner in the castle of Pevensey."

" 7 and 8 Edw. IV.—Granted to Elizabeth queen consort for life as Willingdon."—*q. vide.*

LETTER OF LADY PELHAM, THEN DEFENDING THE CASTLE OF PEVENSEY,
25th July, 1399.

(*From Brydges' Peerage,* vol. v.)

" My dear Lord, I recommande me to yowr hie Lordeschipp wyth hert and body and all my pore mygth, and wyth all this I think zow, as my dere Lorde, derest and best yloved off all erthlyche Lordes, I say for me, and thanke y how my dere Lord, with all thys that I say before, off your comfortable lettere, that ze send me from Lownefraite, that com to me on Mary Magdaleyn day ; ffor by my trowth I was never so gladd as when I heard by your lettre, that ye warr stronge ynogh wyth the grace off God, for to kepe yow fro the malyce of your ennemys. And dere Lord iff it lyk to your hyee Lordeschipp that als son als ye mycht, that I myght her off your gracious spede, whyche God Almyghty contynue and encresse, And my dere Lord iff it lyk zow for to know off my ffare, I am here by layd in manner off a sege, with the counte of Sussex, Sudray, and a great parcyll off Kente ; so that Iue may noght out, nor none vitayles gette me, bot wth myche hard. Wharfore my dere iff it lyk zow, by the awyse off zowr wyse counsell, for to sett remedye off the salvation off yhower castell, and w^t stand the malyce off ther schires foresayde. And also that ye be fullyche enformed off there grett malyce wyrkers in these schyres, whyche y^t haffes so dispytfully wrogth to zow, and to zowr castell, to yhowr men, and to zour tenaunts ffore this cuntree, have gai wastede for a gret whyle. Fare wele my dere Lorde the Holy Trinity zow kepe fro zowr ennemys, and son send me gud tythyngs off yhow. Ywryten at Pevensey in the castell on Saynt Jacobe day last past.

" By yhowr awnn pore I. Pelham."

Thus directed.

" To my trew Lorde."

" 17 Ric. 2.—John of Gaunt, Duke of Lancaster, granted to John Pelham, Esq., the office of constable of his castle of Pevensey, during life, with the fees, wages, &c. thereto belonging, given under his seal, in the castle of Hertford, Dec. the 7th."

" 1 Hen. 4.—King Henry the 4th, by his letters-patent, dated at Westminster, 12 Feb. a. r. 1º, granted to John Pelham, and his heirs male, the office of Constable of the Castle of Pevensey, with the honour of the Eagle, and all those his manors, lands, tents, rents, services, fees, chaces, parks, warrens, mills, rivers, fisheries, as also all perquisites of Courts of the Hundred, heriots, reliefs, escheats, franchises. returns of writs, issues, fines, felons, and of and all other the profits whatsoever and franchises of the Cinque Ports, within the rape of Pevensey, which was ratified and confirmed by letters-patent, bearing date 1 July following."

" 7 Hen. 4.—The Duke of York was committed to Sir John Pelham's keeping in the castle of Pevensey till the next Parlt., being accused of conveying to Owen Glendower, the sons of Roger, E. of March."—*Stowe's Annals*, Ed. 1614, p. 332."

" 6 Hen. 5. (says Collins) the King committed to Sir John Pelham's custody Queen Joane, the last wife of Hen. IV., which Sir Jn. P. appointed nine servants to attend and bring her to his castle of Pevenseye."

" 2 Hen. 5.—Edw. Plantagenet (s. and h. of Edm. de Langley) Duke of York, by his will dated 22 Aug^t., proved 30 Nov., 1415, gives the following bequest:—

" Idem Ie devise a Thomas Pleistede xx*l*. en memoire pour la naturesse (kindness) qu'il me monstra quant je fuy a Pevensey en garde."—*Gough's Wills, published* 1780, 4*to. Lond.*

"3 H. 5.—Sir John Pelham, by his charter, dated 3 June, grants to his son, Jn. Pelham, the office of constable of Pevensey, with the fees and wages thereto belonging (granted to him and his heirs male by Hen. 4.) under the seal of Lancaster."

" 1 Ed. 4., 1461.—Sir Wm. Fiennes was appointed constable of Pevensey Castle for life; he was slain at the battle of Barnet, 1471, 11 Edw. 4."—3 *Dug. Bar.* 146, A.

" Hen. 5., 30 Sept., 1415.—Thos. West, Ld. Delawarr, died seized of the honor of Aquila."

" The manor of Pevensey, some time styled the honor of Aquila, is in the parishes of Pevensey, Helsham, Westham, and Bexhill.

" 1 Mary, 1 August.—Constable and Porter of the Castle of Pevensey, Richd. Oxenbridge. Fee 22*l*. 16*s*. 3*d*."—*MS. in Dulwich Library.—Burrell.*

BURRELL MSS. 5682—P. 639.

Parlt. Survey, taken July 1650.

" All that the manor of Pevensey als. Pemsey, sometimes styled the Honor of Aquila, with all ye rights, members, and appert^s thereof, being in ye several townships or pshes. of Pevensey, Westham, Haylsham, and Bexhill, or elsewhere in Pevensey Rape, in ye Co. of Sussex, and all those rents or yearly sums of money commonly called quit rents, free rents, old rents; seeke, portreeves, and burgage rents; copyhold, customary and all other rents whatever, to ye said manor belonging; all c^t leete, law days, c^t baron and other c^ts whatever; services, franchises, customs, custom-works, forfeitures, escheate, relief, herriots, fines upon descent or alienation, perquisites and profits of the said court, and leetes, and every of them; wayfs, estrays, deodands, good and chattels of felons and fugitives, felons of themselves, condemned persons, clerks convicted, outlawed persons, and of persons put in exigent; ways, passages, lighte, easement, streams, waters, watercourses, weares, damms, and tanks, mill-pools, wrecks of sea, tallage, tolls, suite, soken, multure, commons, grounds used for common, ways, passages, waste-grounds, woods, underwoods, timber and other trees, moores, marshes, hunting, hawking, fishing, fowling, rights, royalties, jurisdictions, liberties, privileges, immunities, profits, commodities, advantages, emoluments, possessions, heredit^s, and appart^s, whatsoever, to ye said manor, to the royalties thereof, and premises, belonging or appertaining, or therewith heretofore held, possessed, or enjoyed, reputed, taken, or known, as part, parcel, or member of yᵉ same; and also all that court, with the appurtˢ, called the inner ward of the castle of Pevensey, lyeing in Pevensey town and parish, being now a garden plot, containᵍ. 1 acre; also all that land lyeing under the sᵒ side of yᵉ castle wall, contᵍ. 1 acre; also those 11 ac. of land in the court called the Base Court, and the 3 marshes called the N. S.W. marshes in yᵉ psh. of Pevensey, now or late in yᵉ occupation of Sir Thos. Pelham, or his assigns, the same being found and returned on yᵉ survey thereof to be an overplus of measure more than granted in any original lease of yᵉ said lands and premises; and also those 60ᴀ. 0ʀ. 20ᴘ. of land lyeing in Cockmersalts in Bexhill psh. now or late in yᵉ tenure of Jn. Giles and Benj. Scarlet, Gent., or their assigns, found in measure above what has been granted in yᵉ original lease or leases thereof; also those lands lyeing in south lease in Pevensey p'sh, returned in said survey to be an overplus measure more than is mentioned in —— Ferrer's lease, now or late in yᵉ occupation of —— Ashburnham, or of his assⁿˢ, contᵍ. 1ᴀ. 1ʀ. 0ᴘ.; also 5 ac. in yᵉ tenure of Jn. Meeres, or his assⁿˢ; also 3 parcels of marsh and upland called the King's Wishes, lyeing in Moorebrook, in Kelsham p'sh, contᵍ. 10ᴀ. 2ʀ. 6ᴘ., in yᵉ tenure of Jaˢ. Fennell of Wilmington, or his assⁿˢ; als that messᵉ called the George in Westham town, near yᵉ west gate leading to Pevensey castle, with yᵉ yards and 2 gardens, contᵍ. 1 ac.; also a cottage under yᵉ W. end of Pevensey castle, adjoin. thereto, with a stable and garden cont. besides said garden, 40 feet in length and 16 feet in bredth; also all that burgage tenemᵗ garden and land, contᵍ ½ an acre in Pevensey town, in Geo. Richardson's occupation; also 0ᴀ. 1ʀ. 0ᴘ. of land under the N.E. end of the inner ward of yᵉ old castle, adjoinᵍ to yᵉ east end of yᵉ slip which lyes under yᵉ so. side of yᵉ castle wall, late in —— Nicholson's occup.: also a cottage on yᵉ waste in Thos. Lowe's occup., and another cottage lately erected on yᵉ waste in —— Perchin's occupᵗ; also a mess. barn, and garden, orchard and croft, in Westham p'sh, contᵍ 1ᴀ. 4ʀ. 0ᴘ. in Sam. Wilson's occupⁿ &c. ℣ an. 82l. 19s. 3d. ob., which arises thus—Portreeve and other rents 24l. 7s. 3d. ob., perquisites of cᵗ. and other royalties 10l. 14s. 6d., one acre in the inner ward 1l. 0s. 0d., do. under the castle wall 0l. 13s. 4d., overplus of 11 acres in the base of cᵗ and the three marshes in the same 11l. 0s. 0d., Cockmersalts 10l. 0s. 0d., one acre one rood in sᵒ leaze over measure 1l. 5s. 0d., land abutting on Hurst Haven cont. 5 acres 5l. 0s. 0d., the King's Wishes 6l. 13s. 4d., several messuages and lands 12l. 15s. 10d.

"Mem.—Certified that the portreeve elected by the homage for one year is to collect all the quit-rents and farms of the manor; to summon, make distresses and amerciaments, and to give a true account and payment to yᵉ lord; w'ch service, when it has been done by a deputy, hath cost the tenant elected for that year about 3l. There is a Cᵗ. Baron usually kept in Augᵗ. or Sepᵗ. at yᵉ west end of the castle wall, where yᵉ death of any tenant, since the last court, and the next heir is presented.

" The materials of the old castle called the castle of Pevensey, valued to be worth 40l. 0s. 0d.; all the wood and trees on the premises, val. worth 20l. 0s. 0d. The Cᵗ. called the Base Cᵗ. with the appurtˢ. cont. 7ᴀ. 2ʀ. 11ᴘ.;

also on the garden on ye so. side of the great gate of said Base C^t. cont^g. 0A. 1R. 0P. valued worth 0l. 5s. 4d. ℣ an. ; the improved value of w'ch last mentioned premises, above the present reserved rent, and the overmeasure allowed, is 5l. 2s. 3d.

" This particular is grounded on a survey taken in July, 1650. The afd. premises are contracted for and agreed to be sold to Jn. Warr, of Westmr. Gent. on behalf of divers original creditors, by whom he is authorized, 3 March, 1651. This particular is rated in fee simple for Jn. and Robt. Cobbet and Jn. Warre, at 15 years purchase, for the present yearly value of the manor of Pevensey, and several parcels of the demesnes thereof, altogether 86l. 14s. 6½d. in possession, and at 2 years' purchase, for the improved yearly value of the premises, whereon a present interest of 44 years is allowed to commence at Lady Day next, being 5l. 2s. 3d. in reversion, and at 3½ years' purchase, for the improved yearly value of other parcel of the premises, wherin a present interest is allowed for 26 years, to come at Michs. next, being 10l. 18s. 10d. in reversion, and at 4½ years' purchase, for the improved yearly value of other part of the premises; wherin a present interest is allowed of 22 years from 1649, being 27l. 15s. in reversion, and at three years' purchase, for the improved yearly value of other part of the premises ; wherin a present interest is allowed for 32 years from Michs. next, being 7l. 7s. 8d., at 40l. for the materials of Pevensey Castle, and one other gross sum of 20l. for wood or timber, deducting by way of reprize for 3l. ℣ an. for executing the portreeve's office, 15 years' value, w'ch is 45l., according to w'ch rates and values the purchase-money amounts to 1492l. 9s. 0¼d."

" 31st July, 1675.—The Ld. Treasurer orders Sir Charles Harbord, Surveyor-General, to send him valuation of the manor of Pevensey, for a lease to be made thereof for 31 years, in reversion after the Queen's Majesty, and such estates as she may make."

" 5th Aug. 1675.—T. Fisher, Deputy to the Survr. Genl. reports that the manor of Pevensey belongs to the Duchy of Lancaster, and was rated in her Majesty's jointure at 22l. 5s. 3d. in free and copyhold lands, and in profits of Cts. by a medium of seven years, 2l. p. an., and in rents of the desmesne lands demised to several tenants, 20l. 0s. 11d. p. an. wch by the Parl^t. survey seem worth, on improvement, 347l. 15s. 5d. above ye said reserved rents. These lands are mostly marsh lands, and the banks are chargeable to keep ; so that he conceives a lease of this manor for thirty-one y^{rs} after the Queen's interest not worth more than 500l., reserving said rents of 22l. 5s. 8d. and 20l. 0s. 11d. p. an. payable to the Crown. See Parl^t. Survey in my MS. A. p. 131, and the Ld. Treasurer's order to Sir C. Harbord, and his report, a length."

" King William granted this manor and castle to Bentinck, E. of Portland, whose son sold it to Spencer Compton, E. of Wilmington, to whom it gave the title of V^t Pevensey.

1620, Sept. to Sept. 1, 1628, inclusive, this manor was in the Crown—C^t Rolls.

" 1660, Oct. 1.—Henrietta Maria Queen Dowager—1660 Q. Dowager died—Jn. Raynes, steward.

" 1671, Sept. 28.—King Charles II.—1676, Nov. 20, Catherine Queen of England—Jn. Raynes, steward.

" 1705, Sept. 2.—Ditto (Thos. Medley, Esq. Dep^y to Robt Ld Ferrers, principal steward)—Thos. Medley, Esq. steward.

" 1706, Oct. 9.—The first Court of Wm. Earl of Portland.—1711, Sept. 10, Henry E. of Portland—Thos. Medley, Esq. steward.

" 1717, Oct. 7, and 1725, Oct. 26—Henry Duke of Portland—1728, Oct. 30, Wm. Duke of Portland—1729, Oct. 31, ditto—T. Medley, jun. steward.

" 1734, Jan. 23—1742, Nov. 29, Spencer Earl of Wilmington—Geo. Worge, steward.

" 1743, Oct. 3—1754, Sept. 30, James E. of Northampton—Geo.Worge, steward.

" 1755, May 22—Hon. Chas. Compton, Esq.—1756, Oct. 4, Geo. Bridges Rodney, Esq. guardian of Chas. Compton.

" 1758, Oct. 16—Chas. Compton, Esq.—1759, Oct. 25, Charles Earl of Northampton.

" 1764, Oct. 22—Eliz. Dss of Beaufort, guardian of Ly Eliz. Compton.

" 1769, Oct. 19, and 1776, Oct. 15. Ly Eliz. Compton.

" Charles 7th. E. of Northampton, on whose death, 18th Oct. 1763, it passed to his daur and sole heir, Ly Eliz. Compton, who carried it in marriage, 1782, to Ld Geo. Henry Cavendish.

" 26 G. 3. 1786, Ld Geo. Henry Cavendish—1788, ditto; 1790, ditto." (created Earl of Burlington Sept. 1831.)—*Burrell MSS.*

MISCELLANEOUS.

" 1710, Revd Jn Wright, Vicar of Pevensey, Chancellor and Reg. of Chich^r for ye benefit of his ps'hrs who laboured under the inconvenience of bad water, employed Jn Pursglove, of Herstmonceux, for his workman to convey water from the castle moat to the town: in order hereto he found it necessary to make his way under the castle wall, which is very high, and the thickness he computed to be ten feet. The foundation upon wc'h the superstructure is erected consists of piles planked over with slabs of extraordinary substance; but, notwithstanding the long tract of time since the building this weighty fabrick, there appeared no decay on the slabs, only the colour changed, from what we may suppose it when they were first laid down; the leaves of faggots found there were sound."—Transcribed 1782, (from a paper in the possession of Mr. Lambart, of Lewes), by *W. B.*—*Burrell MSS.*

W. B.'s Notes, 1783.—" The So. tower of ye inner ct. now remaining^e 1783, resembles the opposite No. tower, except y^t ye sally port is on y, right as you enter the So. tower, and on ye left as you enter the No. tower. The No. tower is most compleat. The most eastern tower of the No. face is of ye same style of architecture as the other No. tower, but has no sally port. The most W. tower on the No. face has a loop near the East re-entering angle, which nearly falls in with the main line of wall, and is constructed in a singular manner. In ye arch of the inner ct. gateway are two doors remaining open, and two stopped up, on each side; toward the great gate, in the crown of the arch, is a square hole, calculated to annoy an enemy. The towers of the inner ct. were places of habitation as well as defence. On the outside of the outer castle wall, to the South, has been a ditch. Part of the outer wall on the West angle of the South tower has been destroyed, or much damaged, as the present low wall appears of a different æra from the rest of the main wall. The bastions of the outer wall are solid masonry, on one of which in the N⁰ face has been erected a square building. The keep has been strongly fortified with round towers, one of wch in the N.E. part seems to have strengthened that part wch joined the N. E. part of the inner cᵗ; many towers of the outer cᵗ are destroyed. The lines of Roman tile in the wall of towers not equally regular. An egg found in a well several feet underground."—*Burrell MS.*

" Before we quit Pevensey, it may not be unentertaining to insert the following anecdote. At a quarter sessions (for the liberty) some years back, a man was brought to the bar, charged with stealing a pair of buckskin breeches, which charge was fully proved, he was found guilty by the Jury; but when the court were informed the offence was a capital one, and that they must proceed to pass sentence, they were so much alarmed, that they wished to reverse the verdict, and give a fresh one, in such words as to make the consequence less than death; they therefore adjourned the court; and dispatched a messenger to Thomas Willard, Esq. of East Bourne, the then town-clerk, (whose deputy was on that day attending,) to beg his opinion whether it was possible to reverse the present verdict, and receive a fresh one, together with his instructions how to proceed. It happened that Lord Wilmington, to whom this place at that time belonged, with the then Chief Baron of the Exchequer, were at dinner with Mr. Willard, when this curious application arrived, to whom Mr. W. having reported the contents, the Chief Baron jocosely said, ' instruct them to reverse the present verdict, and bring it in Manslaughter:' to which Lord Wilmington consenting, Mr. W. advised accordingly, and a new verdict to that effect was absolutely the consequence."—*Royers' Eastbourne,* 1787.

The population is returned in 1831 as only 343, but this is confined to the few houses forming the town or village in the immediate vicinity of the church and castle. In 1821, the *parish* contained 98 houses, and 752 inhabitants. The valuation of real property in 1815, was very considerable, viz. town £8320, parish £2009.

	MILES		MILES
To FAIRLIGHT DOWN . .	2	WINCHELSEA . .	1½
GUESTLING	2	RYE	3
ICKLESHAM	3½		—
			12

On leaving Hastings at the London extremity, we find no object sufficient to arrest the attention till we reach the summit of Fairlight Down, leaving the village in a picturesque hollow to the left; the church small and uninteresting in itself, is erected on a hill to the right, above the sea, hence called by Leland " the high steeple," and forming an effective landmark *. When the traveller has reached the windmill on the highest point, 599 feet above the level of the ocean, should the hour and state of the atmosphere be propitious, he will be detained by a view, which he will readily allow to be at least one of the most commanding and lovely he has ever witnessed, whether he has traversed the extent of England, Scotland, and Ireland, or even if he is not unacquainted with some of the rich prospects of the continent, short of the Alps or Mount Caucasus. We say lovely; for more abrupt and sublime views there doubtless are in abundance : but a more beautiful and variegated expanse of land and water, of rich woods and plains, villages and towns, with a diversified line of coast, and an open sea, often thickly studded with vessels of every description, he cannot easily see, or desire to see. The whole forms a complete panoramic circle; the sweep of inland scenery extending to the hills in the neighbourhood of London; and the sea view reaching from Beachy-Head to Dover cliffs, between 70 and 80 miles apart, and stretching out to the heights of Boulogne ; the entire area of the prospect both by land and water cannot be much less than 300 miles.

* " It is off Farleigh head that the northern tide, flowing from the German sea through the straights of Dover, meets, with a great rippling, the tide from the vast Atlantic, which is sensibly felt between this place and Boulogne." —*Pennant.*

C.Scott delin.

C.J. Smith fculp.

FAIRLIGHT HILL & HASTINGS.

For the History and description of the Sussex Coast.

Amongst minor objects visible are enumerated ten towns, sixty-six churches, seventy martello towers, three bays, five ancient castles, and forty windmills.

We should here in candour state, that the section of the panorama, which Mr. Scott found most available for the purposes of his art, is not an eighth part of the whole, and perhaps, especially to those to whom Hastings is a " twice told tale," the least interesting. The best time for seeing it is in the afternoon. We met with a favourable juncture when the sea was partly in shadow, and the sunshine reflected from the cliffs, at a short distance, looked like a space or carpet of molten silver stretched over the surface of the water. The sweep of Romney marsh, beyond the harbour of Rye, and the light-house of Dungeness, have a very pleasing appearance. The Castle hill at Hastings, nearly 300 feet high, appears a small eminence beneath our feet ; and the interior view of the richly wooded, and thickly peopled country, is in summer of the most captivating interest.

There is a social and cheering attraction in this prospect not to be found in the solitary though exalted grandeur of Beachy Head. We have here the distant " busy hum of men," indications of social union and amusement, and a long and various train of associations all tending to render us more in good humour with our kind, and to excite feelings of good will for their happiness and prosperity. We call to mind the various interests, tastes, hopes, and fears of countless thousands, all of whom have been gifted with various capacities of happiness ; and we reflect that in England each is blessed with the advantages and influences of a pure religion, a paternal and congenial government, equitable laws, wise institutions, suitable social customs, charitable and benevolent motives, and noble historical, and existing associations. The mind must be hard which does not admit these feelings, and it must be happy, at least for the time, when it partakes of them.

Descending from our imaginative elevation, and the hill at the same time, we reach Guestling, a beautifully situated

village, containing many pretty villas. Part of the village is
built on the steep descent of a hill, with a church of plain
appearance, and a pointed steeple, on another eminence facing
it. The country from hence to Icklesham, is of the most
ornamentally wooded and pastoral aspect imaginable, varied
by frequently recurring hill and dale. Here, if ever, the poet
might exclaim,

> "———Pallas quas condidit arces,
> "Ipsa colat, nobis placeant ante omnia Sylvæ."

At Broomham is the park of Sir William Ashburnham,
containing a neat house of stone, and a picturesque rookery,
which is much admired.

The village of Icklesham, though large and populous, has
no object of particular interest. The church appears to be a
neat building, in the decorated style, of two aisles, with the
tower in a not unusual position in this neighbourhood, *viz.* at
the middle of the north side. In Pope Nicholas' taxation, the
church of Ickelsham was worth annually 6*l*. 13*s*. 4*d*.; the Vicars of the same had 16*l*. 13*s*. 4*d*. The etymology of this
place is Eccles-ham, " the place of the church." The *new*
town of Winchelsea was built in this parish, and the vicar of
Icklesham has to this day an allowance from the Exchequer in
consideration of the tithes of that part of the parish taken into
the parish of old Winchelsea. The population in 1831 was
604: value of real property in 1815, 7062*l*.

The two miles from hence to Winchelsea are very pleasantly
wooded, and the scenery on the right is varied by hop-grounds.
On approaching the site of this town of ancient grandeur, we
readily recognize the description of a spacious level hill,
formerly entirely occupied by ranges of building, not enclosed
by walls, as the sea then overflowed the level, forming a sufficient defence. Everything indicates the locality of an old
town of great spaciousness. We pass the fragment of the *new
gate*, leave the extensive ruins of the priory on the right, and
reach the central square, exhibiting the decorated and ivy-
mantled remnant of St. Thomas's Church, and on the left the

gaol of this insignificant liberty, with an ancient wall, a Norman arch, and other indications of former extent.

HISTORY.

Winchelsea is not mentioned in the Saxon Chronicle: the name given to it in barbarous early Latin is Frigetmareventus, i. e. " wind-chills-sea ;" but its real etymology is supposed by Mr. Clark to be *Wincel*, on the authority of Somner, " angulus," and *sea*, or *ea* " mare ;"—"Angulus ad mare," a corner or projection by the sea. Few or no notices of it are discoverable before the Conquest, except that it was given by the Confessor to the Abbey of Fiscamp, which grant was afterwards confirmed by William and Henry I., with all its liberties, free customs, pleas, plaints, and causes. The old town, which stood much nearer to the Camber Point than the present, was drowned by the sea in the thirteenth century. In 1067, King William landed at Winchelsea, and, by his sudden arrival, defeated the measures agreed on by the English for shaking off the Norman yoke. Henry II. landed at Winchelsea, from Dieppe, Jan. 30, 1188. Henry III., in the thirty-first year of his reign, " for the better defence of his realm," as Mr. Jeake observes, " and it might be to conceal from foreigners the intelligence of affairs at home, and stop them of such convenient ports of passage," exchanged with the Abbey of Fiscamp, the town of Winchelsea for the manor of Chilceham, otherwise Chiltham, or Chiltenham, in Gloucestershire. We find a very unprepossessing account of the old town, whose inhabitants were not only pirates, but very cruel ones. In 1265, Simon de Montfort, intending to bring over foreign troops to cause an insurrection in England, repaired to Winchelsea at the time of Lent, intending to pass over to France, but was induced to stay and take a share in their piracies, in which they were borne out by others of the Cinque Ports, but the heir apparent, afterwards Edward I., hastened to stop this iniquitous career.

" Old Winchelsea had been a most powerful port, but, like the others, its vessels acted in most of their cruizes with savage barbarity. During

the time that Simon de Montfort, Earl of Leicester, held his iron rod over
these kingdoms, they gave full loose to their piracies, and flung overboard
the crews of every ship they met, whether it was foreign or English: Leicester had share of the booty, so winked at their enormities.   In 1266,
Prince Edward put a stop to their cruelties ; he attacked Winchelsea, took
it by storm, and put to the sword all the principal persons concerned in the
inhuman practices of the times: the rest he saved, and granted the inhabitants far better terms than they merited.   He at that time feared their
power, and the assistance they might give to the rebellious Montfort, had
he been too rigorous in his measures.   By the date of this transaction it is
evident that the destruction of old Winchelsea could not have happened
till after the accession of Prince Edward to the throne."—*Pennant.*

The period when Winchelsea and Rye were taken into the
number of the Cinque Ports was, according to Lord Coke,
between the time of the Conqueror and King John, and they
are styled " Nobiliora Membra."   Winchelsea was first incorporated by the style of the Barons, &c. &c., and afterwards of
the mayor, jurats, and commonalty.   The time of the destruction of the first town is not ascertained within a few years.   An
anonymous author quoted by Grose (his style is very like
that of Matthew Paris) tells us as follows :—

" In the month of October, in the year 1250, the moon being in its prime,
the sea passed her accustomed bounds, flying twice without ebb, and made
so horrible a noise, that it was heard a great way within land, not without
the astonishment of the oldest man that heard it.   Besides this, at dark
night, the sea seemed to be a light fire, and to burn, and the waves to beat
with one another, insomuch that it was past the mariners' skill to save
their ships ; and to omit others, at a place called Hucheburn (probably
East or Hither Bourne) three noble and famous ships were swallowed up
by the violent rising of the waves, and were drowned.   And at Winchelsea,
a certain haven, eastward, besides cottages for salt, fishermens' huts,
bridges, and mills, above 300 houses, by the violent rising of the waves,
were drowned."

This was probably not the principal inundation.

" In the eighth year of the reign of Edward I., in a writ directed to his
steward, Ralph de Sandwich, for to exchange or buy of John de Langherst,
and John Bon, if they would sell, lands that lay near Iham, and fit to the
building of the *new town of Winchelsea*.   It is mentioned that the greater
part of Winchelsea was drowned, and the sea prevailing more and more
against it that the rest was hopeless long to stand.   In the tenth year of
his reign he issued forth a commission to Stephen de Peveester, and others,

to assign places at Iham (being a hill near) for the inhabitants of old Winchelsea to plant themselves at, a copy of which follows:—

"Edwardus Dei gratia Rex Angliæ, Dominus Hiberniæ, et Dux Aquitaniæ, dilectis et fidelibus suis Stephano de Pencestr.   Hen. Engolisma, et Henrico le Waleys salutem.   Sciatis quod assignavimus vos ad assidend. placias apud Ihame, et eas per certam arrentationem, juxta legalem extentam per vos indefaciend. Baronibus et probis hominibus nostris de Wynch, edificand. et inhabitand. juxta discretiones vestras committend.   Et ideo vobis mandamus, quod vos omnes, vel duo vestrum, quos ad hoc vacare contigerit, in propriis personis vestris apud Ihame accedatis, et placeas ibidem assideatis et eas præfatis Baronibus edificand. et inhabitand. committatis in forma prædicta; salva tum Dominis immediatis placiarum prædictarum rationabili extenta cujus libet acræ per vos assessæ, et ad inhabitan. commissæ, juxta discretiones vestras prædictas sicut prædictum est.   In cujus rei testimonium has literas nostras fieri fecimus patentes. Test. me ipso apud Westm. xxvii die Novembris, anno Regni nostri decimo."—*Jeake's Cinque Ports.*

ABRIDGED CHARTERS.

"Henry, &c. greeting, We have witnessed an enrolment of letters patent of Edw. 1. in these words—i. e. ' Whereas we have provided a new town at Yham in lieu of our town of Winchelsea, which is in great part submersed by the inundations of the sea, and whose total submersion is feared, and we have resolved to commit the lands and tenements there to the Barons of the town and port of Wynchelsee, &c. and have willed that the same Barons when they shall have taken their abode their and begun to build, shall enjoy the same privileges which they had in the old town or elsewhere,' &c. &c.   Apud Acton Burnell xiii die Oct. Anno Regni nostri undecimo."

"We have also witnessed another, &c. in these terms:—Edw. &c. to John de Cobeham, appoints him with Penchester, Engolisme and Waleys to assign places at Iham ' Baronibus et probis hominibus nostris de Winchelsee,' &c.   5 March aᵒ R. xi.

"We have also witnessed ' errotulamenta quorundam brevium ejusdem quondam regis.'

"The king grants to the Barons of the port de W., Iham with the marsh except 10 acres in it which he retains, and which he got from Will. de Grandison and Isabella his wife, and grants the same privileges, &c. the same annual payment to be made as before; and he commands the sheriff to see them in possession of it.—T. Edm. Comite Cornubiæ, cons. R. apud Westm. xiii die Junii aᵒ. R. sui 16th.

"A like directed to the sheriff.   A like command, ' Salamoni de Roff. et sociis suis Justic. itinerans.'   Also a charter of Will. de Grandison and Sibilla his wife, granting to Edward the manors of Iham and Idenne, advowsons, parks, &c. (' exceptâ illâ terrâ quæ fuit H. Bertin') in escambium man. de Dymrok et 46 librarum 6 solidorum et 3 denarium et 1 quadr. redditus ann, in Dertford, 28 Apr. 15 Edw. 1st."

"These king Henry witnesses, &c. on the requisition of the now inhabitants.   15 June Aᵒ. R. Nostri quinto."—*Burrell MSS.*

" But that old Winchelsea was abandoned, and the new built so soon as 1227, as Lombard's marginal note affirms, I cannot believe; nor do I believe it to be wholly till the sixteenth year of that King Edward, for I find by a Memorandum in a book remaining with the Records of the town of Rye these words, viz.:

' ' M. D. quod anno Domini Millesimo cclxxxvii° in vigilia sanct· Agathæ virginis, submersa fuit villa de Wynchelsee et omnes terræ inter Climesden usq'; le Vochere de Hethe. Eodem anno erat tanta copia bladi per univers. Angliæ, Scotiæ, Walliæ, regiones, quod vendebatur quarterium frumenti pro duobus solidis.' Englished thus : ' Be it remembred, that in the year of our Lord 1287, in the even of St. Agath the Virgin, was the town of Winchelsea drowned and all the lands between Climesden and the Vocher of Hithe. The same year was such plenty of corn throughout all the Countries of England, Scotland, and Wales, that a Quarter of Wheat was sold for two shillings.'

" Old Winchelsea being drowned, the inhabitants, by favour of the king and authority of his charters and grants aforesaid, brought the name of Winchelsea to their new plantation at Iham, (which seems to be that which was before a member to Hasting, called Petit Iham, and the rather because Hasting yet claims that part called St. Leonard's,) and there built a town of about forty or thirty-nine squares, called quarters, after the pattern (as is believed) of the old town with spacious streets; adorned, besides the religious houses, with three churches, called St. Giles, St. Leonard's, and St. Thomas the Apostle, of which two former only some of the ruins remain to be seen, and of the latter but part of the ancient building, and that no more than some say was intended only for the chancel ; yet all three were standing, as Lambard affirms, within memory when he wrote, which was 1575. Fortified, besides the natural situation on an hill, with walls, part of which, and of three of the gates, are yet standing; that called Pipewell leading to Rye, another called Newgate leading to Hasting, and the other called Strandgate leading to the rivulet running near the foot of the hill, and so into the sea at Rye, formerly called the River of Ree, which the edifying of this new town is supposed to have run up navigable beyond Winchelsea into the country, and at the west side of the town in the place called Pewes Pond, conceived to have made the harbor where ships lay at anchor, which the sea afterwards deserting, was one cause of the decay of the place. But others attribute their decay to the fire of the French in the Reigns of King Richard II. and King Henry VI. yet was it not so much decayed in 1573, when Queen Elizabeth in her Progress gave it a visit, but that beholding the goodly situation, ancient buildings, grave bench of a Mayor, and 12 Jurats in their scarlet gowns, and city-like deportment of the people (there being then several gentry), as well as projection of the place, she gave it, as she thought deservedly, the name of " Little London." And it is yet a title of honour to the noble family of the Finches in Kent, who are Earls of Winchelsea."—*Jeake's Cinque Ports.*

" The French also played the incendiaries in this town in the reign of Richard II. and Henry VI. That it recovered its losses is evident not only from the vast vaults found in every part wheresoever the inhabitants dig, but from its supplying to the exigencies of the state twenty-one ships and five hundred and ninety-six men."—*Pennant.*

In 31 E. 1, the king was informed that the banks and ditches in the marsh of Winchelsea were so broken by the overflowing of the sea, that the land was in danger of being drowned, and that the king's tenants, by virtue of an ancient composition between them and the other landholders, that these lands should be defended by the latter, refused to aid in the repairs, which the others could not afford to do without; whereupon he ordered an equal and equitable contribution to be levied upon his own lands by his *Custos*, for which he was to receive an allowance from the Exchequer. In the following year it was represented to him that the old wall towards the east was insufficient, and that there must be a new bank there of 350 perches, which the other tenants there were unable to complete, when he ordered another contribution to be made from his own domain.—*Burrell MSS. abridged.*

Pope Nicholas' Taxation, 1291.

	£	s.	d.
Eccl'ia be' Thome de Winchelsee	10	13	4
Rector h't breve de xxxv*s*. vii*d*.			
Eccl'ia bi' Egidii . . .	6	13	4
	non excedit		
Eccl'ia de Y'h'm . . .	4	13	4

There was a third church, St. Leonard's, which probably in this valuation is identified with Yhm or Iham.

FEE FARM RENT. EDWARD I.

Translation.

" 6 Edward I.—The barons and bailiffs of Winchelsea, concerning XLII. pounds farm for the town of Winchelsea, which the king has granted them, with all its appurtenances and liberties, to be held by such farm as long as it shall please the king; so that the same barons, by the hands of the bailiffs aforesaid for that time, shall pay yearly of the said farm, to William Manfe and Johanna his wife, in the name of the king, x. pounds: the remainder of the aforesaid XLII. pounds they must pay to the Exchequer, viz. one half at the Exchequer of Easter, and another half at the Exchequer of St. Michael. And the date of the commission is the 7th of February."—*Mag. Rot. 6 Ed. I.*

Besides the three churches, Winchelsea had convents of black and gray friars, and a Preceptory of St. Anthony.

" A brass seal was found at Winchelsea, with the figures of two monks engraved thereon, and behind them a pig, the emblem of St. Anthony, with the following legend: " Sigillum Preceptorie S. Antonii Gratinen or Grestanum.' "

In St. Leonard's Church was an image of that saint with a vane in his hand; and the superstitious believed that by setting it the way they wished, they might obtain a favourable wind for their relatives or friends whilst encountering the perils of the ocean. Besides these, tradition reports that there were not less than fourteen or fifteen chapels in the town, some of which have been conjectured to belong to religious houses. What the nature of the trade was from which the town derived so much prosperity is uncertain, but circumstances appear to bear out the conjecture that it was principally in French wines. Judging from the descriptions of its ancient site, with its thirty-nine squares, we should think it probable that it contained not less than 20,000 inhabitants.

THOMAS OF WALSINGHAM.

" Situated it is upon a very high hill, very steep on that side which looks toward the sea, or overlooks the road, where the ships lie at anchor; whence it is that the way leading from that part to the haven goes not straight forward, lest it should, by a steep descent, force them that go down to fall headlong, or them that go up to creep on their hands and knees rather than walk, but, lying sideways, it winds with many crooked turnings, to one side or the other."

Truly a rather verbose and ludicrous mode of telling us that the road is not perpendicular.

Leland, about 1500.

" The olde towne of Winchelsey of six or seven years together, fell to a very sore and manifest ruin, by reason of the olde rages of the sea, and totally in the time of the aforesaid six or seven years. In the space of the aforesaid years, the people made suit to the King Edward I. for remedy, and a new plot to set them a town on, and so there was seven score and ten acres limited to the new towne, whereof part is the king's mede, without the town, and part in hanging of the hill. The King set to his help, in beginning and walling New Winchelsea; and the inhabitants of Old Winchelsea took by little, and little, and builded it. The new towne was metely well furnished, and dayly after, for a few years, increased. But before 20 years were expired, it was twice entered by enemies; first by Frenchmen; and secondly by Spaniards, who entered by night at Farely, where the high steepel is about three miles from Winchelsea, at whych invasion, the town was spoyled, and scant syns cam into the pristine state of wealth; for the common voice is, that at that tyme, were 20 aldermen in the towne, merchants of good substance. Within the walls, be two parish chirches, and there were two houses of friers, grey and black. Without the town, is a parish church longing to the liberty of Hastings."

EXTRACTS FROM THE CUSTOMAL OF THE TOWN AND PORT OF
WINCHELSEA.

" I. *Chusing of mayor.* Every year, the Monday after Easter, all the inhabitants shall assemble in a certain place, called the hundred, and there, by common consent, shall chuse a mayor.

" VI. *Acquittance of a felon.* It is ordained, in the usages of Winchelsea, that when a man ought to be acquitted by thirty-six men, that first the names of the thirty-six men ought to be called by their names; and if any of them, when called, be absent, and answer not, then the man that is appealed shall be put to death. And if they all appear and answer by name, the which being called, then of the king's grace that shall be the best twelve of the said thirty-six men, and the grace of the mayor, and of the sworn men, twelve, so that the mayor and bailiff of them all chuse twelve, the which left them, to swear what the man who is appealed shall swear on a book, that he is not guilty of that which he is appealed of, as God help him and the Holy Church, and so kiss the book. After that, the twelve men that have been chosen to swear, shall confirm the same oath that the man appealed made, and so the man appealed go quit. If any of the twelve men withdraw their hands, and will not swear, then shall he who is appealed be put to death; and if he be acquit, then shall the appellor be attached, by his body, and all his goods, to the will of the king. All men condemned in this manner shall be hanged in the Salt Marsh, on the north side of the town of Winchelsea, in the salt water of the same town.

" XI. *A fine confessed by a sick woman available.* Also they be wont to take such recognizance before the mayor and any of the jurats in the court, in case the wife be in good mind and in full health, and there personally come. But if the wife of the man be sick, or feeble, that for feebleness she may not come to the court, and she would such acknowledge by recognizance, she shall send for the mayor and some of the jurats, and they shall come for to hear her will, when they be come, the same there they shall examine, in manner aforesaid; if she consent firm and stable, be the recognizance for all to come and for ever. Also, if the wife of any man make knowledge, that in a case the conditions be, that she and her husband should be again feoffed of the aforesaid tenement, or possession, jointly to their heirs, or to the husband's term of his natural life, and to the wife, and to her heirs, or in other manner, the mayor and jurats shall behold and ratify these conditions, for the right and equity to be had and used in the said franchises at all times.

" XII. *Mortmain for masses.* Also the mayor and jurats, and commonalty, may grant and confirm the ratification of lands and tenements, rents, and other possessions, within the franchises being as much to a chauntry of masses, the sustenation of Hospitals, and to Holy Church, viz. to St. Thomas and to St. Giles, Winchelsea, without licence of the king or any other lord, any rent of the aforesaid lands and tenements, rents, and other possessions having.

" XVII. *A freeman to have summons against a freeman.* In case any freeman complaineth against another freeman, he must come into the court by summons, or by attachment, and the party defendant will account against him ; he that is impleaded may delay the same day by these words: Sir Mayor, please you to wit, that I am a freeman, and I am not bound anon to answer to the party, by the reason I have no summons, nor as a freeman, before this day, for to be against him in this court; for which, Sir, I ask my summons by the law, as freemen ought to have in this court.

" XXVI. *Escape of felony.* Also, when any man of the said liberty, or a stranger, do any felony within the liberty, and flee from the said liberty for dread of the same felony, the mayor may send for him again, within that lordship or freedom, wheresoever he be, within the realm of England, except the liberty of Holy Church, and have him delivered by the freedom of the same town, and there to be punished for his trespass: and so it hath been used of old time, unto this day.

" XXXIII. *Of the Lord of a Franchise distraining a Portsman.* Also, if any Lord distrain any merchant of Winchelsea for pickage, or standing on his ground, and if he be prayed by the mayor, by his letters, without delivering his distress, then may they take a withernam on him and all his tenants. Also the freemen of Winchelsea may be purchasers of all merchandize, where that they may be at the buying, or the selling, so that the buyer and seller either be free or stranger; but if it be so, that the buyer or seller may put on him any lawfull cause, where through that he shall claim no part thereof, and if he be convicted of forswearing, or to have no part of merchandize, for because, if he went from the town abovesaid, from the king's service, or from war, and come not in again by a certain day assigned, or if he do any forfeit against the said liberties, so that it be adjudged that he lose the said liberties; but there may be no strangers partners with a freeman as abovesaid, whatsoever he be, without his good-will.

" XXXIV. *Barons of the Ports may sell in foreign.* And as the men of the Cinque Ports were wont to be let of their liberties most on the coast of Ireland, Edward the king, uncle to Edward the third, confirmed the said liberties under his charter, which see.

" XXXV. *Brewers may make and sell Ale in foreign.* Also, if there be any brewer of the said town a freeman, who makes ale, and sells in foreign in harvest time, and the lord of the fee, or the borough, distrain for that selling, against the liberty, then the mayor, through that complaint, shall send his letter and his seal to the said lord, to deliver that distress; for barons of Winchelsea are free to buy and sell throughout England. And if he do not, after these letters, then there shall be taken a withernam on all the tenants of the above-said lord.

" XXXVI. *Holding Pleas.* Also, all manner of pleas, real and personal, of which no mention hath been made, the mayor hath competence of his fellows, sworn to natural laws ; on the which, and of the which, all manner of customs according to law, which being founded and proceeding forth from Shepway; and the coronation of the King and Queen, the said town of Winchelsea hath as the other barons of the Cinque Ports.

" XXXVII. *Alienation of Lands.* Also, in case that a stranger, or a freeman, hath lands, rents, or tenements, within the same franchise, and he bind the same lands, rents, or tenements, to any stranger or freeman, or he be bound by recognizance made in the common rolls; or else the said lands, rents, and tenements, be alienated; he shall have execution to levy the debt of the said lands, tenements, and rents, without plea of it to be found by recognizance.

" XXXVIII. *Complaints to be heard either in the Town or at Shepway.* Also, in case that any man of the said town do complain of any man of the said town, in any other place but the same town, he shall be punished for the despite to the comen, or else that it be in defence of the right of the comen, as aforesaid; and then it shall be tried before the warden at Shepway, and no where else.   *   *   *   *   *

" These writings were compiled by Thomas Hokernam, town clerk of Winchelsea, A. D. 1557."—*Lyon's History of Dover.*

" 11 Hen. VII. 1496. In the 17th article of the treaty (called Intercursus Magnus) between Henry the Seventh and the Archduke Philip, amongst other mayors and aldermen of cities and towns who bound themselves to the Archduke, under the obligation of all their goods present and future, to endeavour, to the utmost of their power, that their sovereign king, Henry the Seventh, shall faithfully keep inviolable this treaty in all its parts, I find Winchelsea mentioned."—*Fœdera, tom. xii., p. 578.—Burrell MSS.*

ROBERT DE WINCHELSEA, a celebrated native of this town, was made Archbishop of Canterbury in 1291. He was a learned man and an excellent preacher, and a lover and patron of men of learning: at one time Rector of the University of Paris, and afterwards Chancellor of Oxford. His spirit was so firm, that, confiding in the Council of Lyons, he forbade the clergy to pay taxes to the king, without the consent of the pope, and was consequently very harshly used by Edward I., but " overcame all at last by his patience." He refused a cardinal's hat from the pope, but accepted from him the pall of Archbishop of Canterbury. " That it may not be said," observes Fuller, " that his bounty was greater than my belief, I give credit thereto." At two different periods, the latter of which was a season of great scarcity, he respectively fed 4000 and 5000 persons. " His charity went home to those who could not come for it, sending to them who were absent, on account of sickness or other unavoidable hindrances. He died at Otterford, the 11th of May, 1313, and was buried in his own cathedral. Though he was not canonised by the pope, yet he was sainted by the poor, who used to repair in great numbers to his tomb and pray to him."

About the conclusion of Queen Elizabeth's reign, the sea retired from this part of the coast, and the harbour of Winchelsea became choked up with sand. The town, which once adjoined the sea, is now a mile and half distant. From this time its decrease was rapid, and during the last eighty years it has contained less than 1000 inhabitants. In the year 1831, its population was 772. It still retains its shadow of a corporation, but of course lost the right of suffrage to Parliament in the present year.

We do not know whether the manufactory still exists which is alluded to in the following extract:

" 4 Geo. III. c. 37.   An Act for better establishing a Manufactory of Cambricks and Silks, or Goods of that kind usually known under those Denominations, now carrying on at Winchelsea."

In the Burrell MSS. is a long inquiry into the rights of the townsmen of Winchelsea:

" Sworn by the deponents, Drake Hollingberry, Rd. Heleman, Jn. Easton, W. Bragg, John Beaver Bragg, Edw. Bennet, and Andrew Baker, at Winchelsea, in yᵉ Co. of Sussex, the 23d day of May, 1785, before me, Steven Swatland, a commissioner.

" Sworn by the dept., Rd. Freeman, at the City of Chichester, in the Co. of Sussex, the 24th day of May, 1785, before me, Wm. Towler, a commissioner, &c."

The SEAL OF WINCHELSEA still remains, bearing on one side the representation of a church with niches and statues, and on the other the following inscription in Gothic letters, which has never yet been attempted to be translated. We did request an interpretation of it, but no one could or would give it us; we have therefore tried one ourselves. Subsequently, however, we have received the following opinion from Mr. Cartwright, which will be respected by the inhabitants of Sussex.

" The inscription on the seal of Winchelsea is very obscure, and I question whether it was understood by him who cut it or by those who used it. Your interpretation seems to express the meaning, as nearly as it can be made out."

————

EGIDIO, THOMÆ, LAUDEM PLEBS CANTICA PROME ;
NE SIT IN ANGARIA, GREX SUUS, AMNE, VIA.

To Giles' and Thomas' praise, ye people, chaunting pray ;
Lest, in th Angarian road their flock be wash'd away.

————

DESCRIPTION.

On the right of the entrance of the town from Hastings is the Friary, an object which we regret that circumstances prevented our taking a near view of. The cloisters, which are very considerable, are formed into a handsome dwelling-house; and a chapel, or choir of a church, remains of much elegance, with a semi-octagonal east end, and an arch at the west twenty-six feet in width.

The remnant of the church of St. Thomas, in the middle of the town, occupying one of the ancient squares, is only the aisles of the chancel, the nave, tower, and transepts having disappeared, with the exception of some interesting ruins; but this forms a moderate-sized church, of rich and stately architecture, exceeded by few small specimens in England. The exterior exhibits a fine ruin of the south transept, and part of the tower, one or two flying buttresses at the east end, and some of the finest stems of ivy ever seen. A separate tower, with a ring of bells, stood in the churchyard, but has been removed, being considered dangerous, and a small wooden turret mounted on the vestry, at the west end of the north aisle. The interior, which is in the style of the fourteenth century, displays three aisles of equal and handsome elevation, separated by three lofty and elegant arches on each side, resting on well-proportioned clustered columns; walls fretted with very bold tracery of arches and columns, some of which are of Sussex marble; three monuments of Templars, with others of much curiosity, and very good windows, with a lofty and noble one in the centre of the east end, its upper tracery containing some figures in stained glass. Two of the monuments of Templars are in the south aisle, the third in the vestry; one of the former is considered to be scarcely excelled in the solid richness and grace of its semi-octagonal fretted and canopied front. It is finely engraved in Blore's Monumental Remains; he considers it to have probably belonged to Gervase Alard, one of a family much distinguished in the history of the town. In the north aisle are the tombs of a monk and abbess. The *Corporation* seat, a very neat one, on the north side of the altar, has rather a curious effect in this apparently village church. Lastly, on the floor of the centre aisle are some curious brasses, one of which has an inscription in very old Gothic characters, which we were prevented distinguishing (though, if we had, there was some chance of their being *Arabic* to us) ; for, having been accidentally benighted, the church was nearly dark when we visited it. We therefore copied a manuscript of a former rector, as given to us by our fair as well as intelligent guide (so pleasing a one is not seen every day) from the vestry.

" Alred, q'i moruit le 15 jourr d'Avril, MCCCLIIII, gist ici : Dieu de salme ait merci : Q'i pour salme, priera L jours de pardon auera."

" Alred, who died the 15th day of April, 1354, lies here : God have mercy on his soul : Whoever will pray for his soul shall have fifty days' pardon."

Leaving Winchelsea, we pass under the Land Gate, one of the most perfect remaining, and an imposing structure, and see through it a flat resembling the Isle of Ely, with the town of Rye in front looking like a considerable fortress, on the summit of a hill. One of the last Martello towers on this part of the coast is on our left; beyond which is *Camber Castle*, erected by Henry VIII. at an expense of £26,000, but soon neglected, and fallen into decay. Its walls are extensive and of irregular form, between polygonal and circular, but uninteresting in their appearance. The vaults in the interior are said to be very perfect. The view of Winchelsea, on looking back, is very pretty, with its extensive elevation surrounded by green upright banks, like ramparts, and fine trees, with occasional glimpses of ruins seen through their foliage.

RYE.

HISTORY.

RYE has been conjectured by some to be the *Portus Novus* of the geographer Ptolemy. It is termed in ancient Latin *Ripa*, and its English name is imagined to be either derived from the Norman *rive*, bank, Saxon *rhee*, or British *rhy*, a river or ford. So *St. Mary Over-rys*, Southwark, viz. over the river, with respect to London. Its authentic modern history commences in the year 893: at the latter end of that year a fleet of 250 sail brought an army of Danes from France to the coast of Kent, where, landing near Rye, they seized the fort of Apuldore. Rye was given with Winchelsea by Edward the Confessor to the church of Fiscamp, and exchanged afterwards, as previously related. In 1162 William de Ipres, Earl of Kent, died, who built the tower here, still standing, which is termed Ipres' Tower. The town was walled round by Edward III.

" Rye al's *Westrie*, wch is so called for difference sake from *Eastrie*, a town and hundred within the lath of St. Augustine in Kent."—*Lambard's Perambulation.*

Pope Nicholas' taxation, 1291.

	£	s.	d.
Eccl'ia de Rya	5	0	0
Vicar' de Rya	10	0	0

" Rye, one of the ancient towns who have long enjoyed equal privileges with the Cinque Ports, in Latin Ripa, in French Rive, stands on the edge of Sussex towards Kent; is a fair well-built town, pleasantly situated on the north side of an hill, wch affords a delightful prospect towards the sea; fortified and walled about in Edward the Third's reign; is at present governed by a mayor and jurats; is furnished with a commodious haven, and two markets on Wed^y. and Sat^y., weekly; but the former is almost quite disused, and the latter affords little but provisions. It was anciently in great reputation, being well fortified by W^m. d'Ipres, Earl of Kent; the prison of the town is a tower, wch still bears his name. This town enjoys the great privileges and immunities of the Cinque Ports. It hath sent

burgesses to Parl^t. from 42 E. 3; but in the following times was inconsiderable. When Edw. 3. walled it about, and Winchelsea decayed, it
began again to recover, and, by a lucky accident, flourished as much as
ever, for the ocean, swelled with an extr^y. tempest, broke so violently, that
it made a convenient port, whch another tempest some time after improved;
after wch the town much increased in inhab^{ts}., buildings, fishing, and
navigation, became more prosperous that it had ever been before; but the
impetuous tides have now so choaked up the haven with sands, that there is
scarce a passage left for the smallest vessels."—*Mag. Britt. p.* 500. *Ed.* 1730.

" This town (says an unknown writer, men^d. in Mag. Britt. p. 500, 501)
is encompassed by the tides about two parts in three, and on the east side is
washed by the Rother. The south side is washed by a branch of the tide,
called Fillingham water, over which was formerly a ferry, but now there
is a bridge. About 50 or 60 years ago here was a good tide harbour, while
the tide had its free course up the Rother, wch being then stopped by a
sluice about 6 miles above the town, and another about 3 miles, it is now
almost ruined by the mud and sand, brought into it by the spring tides,
and stopped from running out by those sluices.

" The fishing trade is the principal support of this town, viz. of mackarel
and herring in their proper season (the first the fishermen call spotting, the
other flewing), which are accounted the best of their kind which are caught
on these coasts : the rest of the year they catch flat-fish by trauling, which
are carried away by the *Rippiers* (fishermen of the place, so called from
Ripa, the bank it stands upon) to London market."—*Burrell MSS.*

" Rye or Rie, sometimes wrote Rhie, in Latin Ria and Rhia. I cannot
conclude to derive its name from Rie, the corn so called (as Rieton in
Warwickshire, in the opinion of Dugdale), because as the soil thereabouts
is not very proper to bear it, so the people there are generally averse to it.
Nor will I affirm that the name came from the rivulet Ree, before remembered in Winchelsea, nor from Rhe or Rey, sometime used for river;
though the river of Rother on the east, and the creek of the sea like a river
running up on the west into the country between Peasmarsh and Udimer,
called yet Fillingham water, from a farm on Peasmarsh side which it
washeth, meeting together with the said Ree, and running out into the
sea at the south east (and formerly more south) side of the town, might be
supposed to have first occasioned the name. But it seems to me rather to
take the name from the British word Rhy, signifying a ford, or as some say
a Bay; in reference to the former, importing the place where the Rivers
of Rother and Ree were yet fordable; and to the latter, the situation of
the town in the bottom or middle of the bay made by the sea; between the
Cliff at Beechy and those at Folkstone, from whence the sea over against
Rye, and near the shore, is still called Rye Bay. This ancient town is
compact as a little city, stored with buildings, and consisting of several
streets, as the lower or longer street (in which standeth the Grammar
School built by Thomas Peacock, Gent. one of the jurats of the town,
Anno 1636, and by his will, Sept. 10, 1638, devised to that use; and by
order thereof, and settlement of his executors, enjoying the yearly revenue
of thirty-five pounds), besides which are the middle street, the butchery

(where is the Market-place with the Town Hall) and the Watch-bell-street, with some cross streets running from one to the other. It is built on a little hill, now wasted, on the south west, south, south east, east, and north east sides of the town, by the flux and reflux of the sea, but especially on the two latter, where hath been washed away some streets, the Badding's Gate and wall leading therefrom to the Land Gate; yet the compass of the town may be about two hundred and seventy-one rods: beautified with a large Church, called St. Mary, the goodliest edifice of that kind in the Counties of Kent and Sussex, the Cathedrals excepted: Inclosed with walls, as Cambden says, in the time of Edw. III. There are yet standing the Land Gate, called sometimes the North Gate, leading into the Country towards Kent; the Postern Gate leading to the new Conduit; the Strand Gate or South Gate opening towards Winchelsea, where the old harbour was, though now more frequented on the east side of the town; the Gun garden gate adjoining to Ipres tower, built by William de Ipre, Earl of Kent, and from him so called, afterwards purchased by the corporation, of Mr. Newbury, about the 10th year of king Henry VII., and used to keep court in till the building of the Town Hall aforesaid, whence it got the name of the Court House, and was then converted into a prison. And besides the chapel of St. Clare, (now used for a powder-house,) the chauntry of St. Nicholas, the chancel whereof is still kept for an ammunition house, whereto it was converted, anno 17 Elizabeth, had a monastery of the Friers Heremites of St. Augustines, the chapel whereof is yet standing, erected anno 16 Henry VIII., and dissolved by him shortly after with the first dissolution, in the twenty-seventh year of his reign, because the revenues were not two hundred pounds per annum, so it had but a short standing, for that it was not elder than the sixteenth year of that king, I gather from a passage I found in the records of this town, in that year, which was thus:

" Eodem anno, silicet, quarto die Septembris, erect. fuit tegument fabricae fratrum heremitarum Sancti Augustini infra villam praedictam, ex impensis cujusdam Willielmi Marshe, Agricolæ:

" *i. e.* In the same year, that is to say, the fourth day of September, was erected the roof of the fabrick of the Friars Heremits of Saint Augustin, within the town aforesaid, at the costs of one William Marshe, Husbandman.

" The town is of beautiful prospect to look upon any way, a convenient passage into Normandy, famous for fishing, as good fish having been brought to market (before the French spoiled the fishing grounds) as any where in England, and yet the fish keep the name of the town, as Rye Herring, to sell the better in London. An ancient town it is called, and so is, and with its sister town, or twin rather, Winchelsea, hath very near shared equally in vicissitudes and misfortunes; for in the time of Edward the Confessor, they were both given to the abbot and monks of Fischamp, (as before noted in Winchelsea) and afterwards reassumed in exchange by king Henry III., as by the exemplification of another king Henry following, doth plainly appear.

" Before which reassumption of king Henry III. both towns were added to the ports, according as is before asserted; both considerable fishing

towns for so long ago as king Henry IV. anno 1400, the Rippiers of Rye
and Winchelsea, that furnished London with fresh fish, were, as Grafton
says, privileged to sell their fish there to whom they would ; and the Fish-
mongers of London prohibited to buy it to sell again by retale. Both were
burnt by the French in the time of king Richard II. as I take it, and king
Henry VI., about the twenty-sixth or twenty-seventh year of his reign ;
in which I suppose the old records and charters of the town of Rye
perished ; because none elder than his twenty-seventh year, save only some
fragments, are to be seen ; in which consumption, as conceived, the old
church was burnt, and this now standing built since, the former standing
near to Ipres tower, in the place yet called the Old Church-yard. It never
recovered its ancient shipping since the loss of the Bourdeaux fleet, as
reported in the time of king Henry VII., who in the third year of his
reign, thought it worth his visit ; as did his grandchild and successor,
Queen Elizabeth, in 1573, who, from the noble entertainment she had,
accompanied with the testimonies of love and loyalty, duty and reverence
she received from the people, was pleased to call it " Rye Royal." Populous,
to its capacity, it was in her reign, though much wasted by a pest in 1563,
so that in the months of August, September, and October, were buried 562
persons. Afterwards it was replenished by the French, who sheltered
themselves here from the Massacre in France, 1572, and other troubles of
the protestants there ; so that anno 1582, upon an account taken, were
found inhabiting here 1534 persons of that nation. By another plague it
smarted again, anno 1596. Succoured the French protestants afterward,
toward the latter end of king James, till things looking better in that
country encouraged them to return. It suffered after this by the plague,
anno 1625, by the small-pox, in the years 1634 and 1635, and 1654 and
1655. Lost many vessels in the time of the wars between the king and
parliament ; all which, with other things, have added to the decay and
depopulation thereof. One hundred years after the visit of Queen Elizabeth, the present prince, king Charles II., was pleased to see it, viz. May,
1673, when his Royal Navy, with the French fleet, lay in the bay, in sight
of the town."

MISCELLANEOUS.—ANCIENT DOCUMENTS.

" Plese a n're tres redoute S'r le Roi & a son Conseil d'avoir considera-
cion de la pouvre Ville de la Rye, coment il as este prise sovent foiz, et les
Com'unes de la d'ce Ville ount apparallez les mures de v's latr'e, et a
cause du port des dez Com'unes ils ne poont pluis reppailler des dez
Mures p' ount la d'ce Ville de p't la mer est p'nable p' Enemies ; Et a la
darrein prise de la d'ce Ville p' les dez Enemys, a lour revenue en Fraunce
si furont plusours de eux penduz et trainez a cause qu'ils ne eusent tenuz
le d'ce Ville, et si dotoms g'ndement q' la d'ce Ville vera prise autre forth
et tenuz en destruction du paiex enveron et g'nt p'il du Roialme. Par
quoi supplient au v're tres haute S'rie les dez Com'unes, pour Dieu et en
oevre de Charite, gu'nter q. les excesses et fyns faiz et levables des vitallers
et artificers et laborers devant les Justices del Pees en la Countee de Sussex, outre les gages de dez Justices, soient g'unteez alfacon et repacion des
Mures de la d'ee Ville p' trois auns prch' ensuantz, en releve de la d'ee
Ville et Salvation de tout la paix environ.—2 Richard II.—*Parl. Rolls.*

EXTRACTED FROM THE CUSTOMAL OF THE PORT AND TOWN OF RYE.

Lyon's Dover, vol. i. p. 342.

" I. That every year the Sunday next after the feast of Saint Bartholomew, all the men of the commonalty of the town, shall be assembled at the church, being within the church-yard of the parish of the same Rye, and there by the whole commonalty shall choose them a mayor.

" IV. The Mayor's Oath. Ye shall bear faith to our sovereign Lord the King of England and to the commonalty of the town of Rye, and the franchises and usages of the said town righteously shall maintain, and the common of the same keep, and right to the poor, as well as to the rich, do administer to your power. So help you ——. XIIth is of the coroner, and his office.

" XIII. And it is to be understood, that no hundred shall be holden after another, less than fifteen days asunder.   And if any man come to pursue against him that is indicted by appeal, he that is indicted shall be arraigned of the said felony ; and if he forsake the felony, he shall be charged by the mayor unto his having acquittal, under the form ensuing ; viz. he shall charge, at his own jeopardy, thirty-six men, the king's true liege men, of good fame, which shall be ready at the next hundred that unto them shall be assigned, and with thirty-six men shall put the appeal into the mayor's hands ; and the common clerk shall read the names of the thirty-six men, and make every man answer to his proper name ; and if any of the thirty-six men that shall stand before the county, or common assembly, be in default, or be present and will not answer, he that is appealed of that felony shall be adjudged unto death.   And in case every man of the thirty-six men as may be called answer to their names, as it is used and accustomed, by the king's grace the mayor there shall be left twelve of the thirty-six men aforesaid, and of the grace of the mayor and the jurats, other twelve men, so that the mayor shall choose which they will, that shall swear with him that is appealed, that he is not guilty of the felony which is to him imposed.   And he who is appealed shall first swear upon the book which is to him imposed, as God will him help, and so he kiss the book.   Afterwards must be called the twelve men, to swear with him as they are called every one severally by himself, that the oath which he who is appealed hath made is good and true ; and that he is guilty of nothing that is against him imposed ; and every man so kiss the book. And if they do so he who is appealed shall be quit.   And if any of them withdraw him from the book, he that is appealed shall be put to death. And if he be quit by the quest, then he who was appellant ought to be attached, and all his goods in the town ; and he must be hanged upon the Saltness, on the east side of the town, behind the salt water of the town.

" XVIII. And when any man taketh the decree of the church, the mayor, as coroner, shall go unto him to inquire the cause of his coming to holy church ; and if he will acknowledge his felony, let it be enrolled, and immediately he loseth all his goods and chattels, as a forfeiture, of the which the mayor shall answer to the town; and if he confesses, he may remain in the church, and church-yard, twelve days; and at the end of forty days he shall forsake the land; and sitting upon the church-yard stile, before the mayor, he shall chuse the port of his passage; and in case he will make his abjuration within the forty days, he shall be accepted. And anon, by abjuration done, he shall take the cross, and the mayor shall do to be proclaimed, in the King's name, that no man, upon pain of life and member, shall do him harm, or molestation all the while he keepeth the king's highway towards the port that he hath chosen for his passage.

" XIX. And when any man is found cutting a purse, or taking of silver out of a purse, he shall have one of his ears cut off from his head, in the market-place, at the suit of the appellant. It is accustomed, that the said cut-purse, or picker of purse, shall have one of his ears cut from his head, and then he shall be led into the town, and there swear and abjure never to come into the town, upon pain of losing his other ear; and in case he be found in any other line of life, then to lose his other ear, and to abjure the town, upon pain of losing his life; and if he be found the third time, whatsoever he swore before, he shall suffer judgment.

———

" XXV. Of true men's goods seized. Item, albeit that a true man's goods be seized among the goods of a felon, as it may fortune such goods were lent unto him; if the true man can prove the goods to be his own, and the felon do not the contrary, the said goods ought to be restored to him that so doth challenge them, for a thief cannot forfeit other men's goods.

———

" XXXIV. Attachment in trespass of blood. Item, in trespass and blood shedding, and where a man is hurt, the defendant shall be attached by his body, and put into prison, without he may find sufficient pledges to undertake that he shall be at the next king's court holden. If he appears not, he and his pledges shall be amerced, and he shall be put to better pledges, viz. two or three pledges; and so, too, in a case from court to court, two pledges. The amercements shall be the first court, sixpence; the second, twelve pence; and so every court if the mayor and jurats will. The amercements shall increase sixpence, in like sum, as it is in the increase of the pledges, until the time that he will appear to answer; and in case he fail in every of his pleas, as it is aforesaid, then his body shall remain in prison, until the time that he hath answered unto the party; and so always, provided that the increasing of the amercements be seized, and taxed, at the consideration of the mayor and jurats.

———

" XLVIII. Withernam, and of process. The mayor and jurats may, as they ought to do, take withernam of the citizens of London, as they think it convenient to be done, for any cause done against their liberties; and they may, as they ought to do, take withernam for many causes done unto the mayor and jurats, desiring them to write their letters, under their seal of office of the mayoralty, or else under the common seal, when the case it requires, to pray for him, unto the citizens of London, or unto the burgesses of Calais, or unto any other place within the realm, or without, wheresoever the King, or sovereign lord liege, hath amity, that they will do, and see to be made due payment and satisfaction of such sum of money, for covenant or trespass, which the Combaron of the Cinque Ports could justify.

" LI. Partnership in merchandize. The freemen of Rye were wont, and ought to be, partners in merchandize, of all sorts, whether they be in presence in buying or selling of it, whether they will claim any part, whether the buyer or the seller thereof be freeman of Rye, or stranger ; reserve and except, where he who so claimeth part of the said merchandize, is not worthy to have part, as he who is convicted of perjury, or else that he hath been adjudged, that he should have no part of any merchandize ; because he did come away from the franchise at the time he should pay his part for the king's service ; or else that he was come away in the time of war, and come not again within the time to him limited of his coming, for the defence of the town ; or else he hath done any thing prejudicial to the franchise, whereby he is adjudged to lose his freedom, and free custom ; or else, where before time he hath been bought in the said merchandize, hath been losing money, he hath refused to pay his part of the said loss, after his rate or proportion.

" LVIII. Orphans and their goods. In case any man or woman die within the franchise of Rye, and they be within age, then the mayor shall have the veve of the child, and of all his goods, rents, and tenements, and of all his moveable goods, and by the mayor and jurats the child shall be put to ward to the next of kinsman that the child hath of his blood, unto whom his inheritance may not descend; and all the goods and chattels shall be delivered unto the guardian, by indenture between the mayor and the said guardian, until the time the child shall be of full age ; and that one part of the said indenture shall remain in the common treasury ; and in case there be none of the child's blood, then the mayor shall take, and deliver the aforesaid goods unto some sufficient man of the franchise, in keeping until the child become of full age, at which time the child shall have them delivered to his use.

" LIX. Nomination of chaplain to Saint Bartholomew's church ; and admitting brethren and sisters there. It is the mayor of Rye, and the jurats, with the commonalty, shall have the nomination of the chaplain, who is called the custos of the hospital of Saint Bartholomew, beside Rye ; which said chaplain his name, in time of peace, shall send unto the abbot of Feram ; and, in the time of war, unto the Lord Chancellor of England, and by one of them he shall be presented unto the Bishop of Winchester, and by him shall have institution. And also the mayor of Rye shall take account of the chaplain of Saint Bartholomew's, four times in a year, if he will ; and in the said hospital be both brethren and sisters, sometimes more and sometimes less ; but nevertheless, neither the brethren nor the sisters shall be admitted into the said hospital, unless it be by the assent of the mayor and of the commons. And also the rules and statutes of the said hospital shall be read before the brethren [and ,sisters, which shall be accepted and received, before he be received.

" LXV. Burgesses to the Coronation.   The Barons of the Cinque Ports are to be summoned to the king and queen's coronation, by certain forty days before the coronation, by writing, and of all the Ports together there must be thirty-two barons, in one clothing, and they shall bear the cloth over the king and queen, with four spears, covered with silver, and four little bells gilt, hanging above the cloth, which is called the Pall, and shall come from the king's treasury; and at each of these four spears shall be attending four barons of the said Cinque Ports, and the said barons, on the said day, shall sit in the king's hall, at dinner, next to the king and queen, on the right hand."

Miscellaneous MSS.

" 2 Ed. 6.—26 Jan. 3d. vice lecta est billa" for the amending of the haven of Rye, for making of certain sluices about the towns of Rye and Win-chelsea, " quæ omnium Procerum assensu conclusa est, excepto D'no Windesor."—*Lds. Journals*, vol. i. p. 335.

" 2 Ed. 6.—6 Martii, 3d. vice lecta est billa" for the towns of Rye and Winchelsea, and for casting of ballast into the Camber, " quæ communi omnium Procerum assensu conclusa est."—*Ibid*, p. 349.

Cotton MSS. Galba C. iii. contains, p. 258, " the names of all the strangers," &c. (. . *burnt*)" Flemynges and Wallownes within her Maties Town of Rie taken before John Sharpe maior of the said T.   Edward Middleton maior of Her ma'ties town of Winchelsey and Thomas Wilford Esquier, Captn of her castle of the Camber, in the Town hall of Rie afore-said the 20th Daie of Marche in the eleventh yere of her highenes reign, Aᵒ Dⁿ 1569."

Lansd. MS. 67, p. 35.

" To Lord Burleigh.

" Our duties to your honor most humbly remembered.   So it is if it please your honor that the bearer hereof, an Italyan, now of late havenige p'used your haven and harbour of Rye, and all the indraughts sea marks and water spryngs nere to the same, he hath faithfully promysed that within fewe years he will make the saide haven and harbor of Rye (the Camber onlye excepted) more servyceable than it hath been at any tyme heretofore, w'ch worke he wolde be content, to begynne in the springe of this next yere, if it may stand with the good pleasure of your honor and of the rest of the lords of her majesty's most honorable privy councell. Wherin we most humbly desire your honorable furtherance to her matʸ to-werde such worke, as your honor shall finde the same to be profitable and commodious for the most parte of the realme useing the seas.   And also to harbor her matˢ shipps when cause requireth and to maintain the pro-vysion of fyshe, wherewith her maᵗʸ and divers of great honor have been from hence well served.   Towerde thadvancement of w'ch worke your honor shall finde us most reddye to thuttermost of our abilities.   But herin the Italyen desireth her majᵗˢ privilege that duringe his lyffe none do attempt to perform or amend any havens or creeks in England by that meanes that he shall do this worke by, the same not beinge put in use by any other heretfore. And thus referringe ourselves and the estate of this our towne and countrye adjoyning to your honorable consideration, we most humbly take our leave. At Rye, the vii[th] of December, 1591. Your honor's most bounden the maior and juratts of Rye. Robert Carpenter, maior. Robert Bett, Wyllyam Ratcliff, Wylliam Colkyn, Hen. Gaymer, William Didsbury, Thomas Colbrans, John . . . ."

In the Lansdowne MSS. is, 1586, a letter of the Mayor of Rye, acquainting Lord Cobham with the landing of Julio Marino, a suspicious person.

56 Lansdowne MS. p. 62.

" Right Honorable, we thought it our duties with that convenient speed we myght to signifie what news our passengers have brought from Deipe. Three of them came in this last midnight tyde, havinge byn longer there, w'ch gave us cause to suspect that they were there stayed. They saie that the Captainne of Deipe came unto them, beddinge them despatche and get them soone to helpe and defende their country (as they tooke it) in a mockinge looke. They reporte for truth that there is at Deipe about twelve great shippes of the burden between vii[xx] and viij[xx] tunnes a makinge ready, with all the'r speede that may be, besides divers other smaller vessels. And that there is also eighty sailes of shippes in a redynes at Newehaven (Havre de Grace), and that the en'myes is come to New-haven with twenty thowsand men.

" It may please your honor to be also advertised that our towne at this present is but weakely manned with English men, for there is called from thence three hundred and fifty four, to serve hir Majestie at the seas, and not of the worst men. And Tenterden beinge a member to our towne is able to supply our want in some reasonable measure, if they be not called from it, which if they should, they and we leike to be in great distress, for that the country adjoining uppon us is called to serve in other places. Wherefore our humble sute to your Honor is, that it wold please you to stande so good Lo' unto us as to write your lines to the bayliff and jurats of Tenterden, that they have their people in a readynes whensoever the maior and jurats of Rye shall sende for them, whereunto we know they will be very willinge if so from your they be commanded, ffor with your honorable favor toward us, we shall be bounden to pray for your good Lo. And so most humbly we leave your honor to the custody of the Almightie, from Ry this first of August, 1588. Your honor's most humble at commandment the maior and jurats of Rye.—To the right honorable our very good Lord the Lo Burleigh Lo High treasurer of England.

Lansdowne MSS. p. 27. (A damaged document of about 34 pages.)

" Articles to be mynystered unto such persons as are to be examyned touching the abuse comytted at Rye by certain fyshermen, in the month of Maye, 1582, agaynst William Haynes, Her Majesties purveyor for sea-fish, as followeth." And examinations there taken.

Queen Elizabeth's Progresses.

" Thence to Rye, where the Queen remained three days, and conferred the honour of knighthood on Thomas Guilford, Thomas Walsingham, and Alexander Culpepper, Esqs."

" Venit Riam, maritimum in Sussexia oppidum atque portum; ad quem ante illum diem nunquam Regem aut Reginam pervenisse ridicule aiunt; elapsoque ibi triduo, &c."

" Camber Castle, near Rye. Captain's fee per day, 2s; Porter's, 6d; Soldier's 9, le peece 6; Gunner's 17, le peece 6.—Thomas Wilford, captain, 1580. (MS Knight)"—*Peck's Desiderata Curiosa, 2nd book, p. 14, a. Burrell MSS.*

Jeake, p. 57.

" To the right worshipfull, our loving friends, the Maior and Aldermen of Hull.

" Right Worshipfull,—With our due and hearty commendations we salute you, Whereas of late we wrote our letters to you in the behalf of our honest neighbour and combaron, Edward Beale, touching certain duties ye required of him, which he denies to pay, being a freeman of the ports; he hath made relation unto us of your courteous usage of him, for which we thanke you, being ready to requit it to any of your people, as occasion shall serve. But yet he advertiseth us, that ye stand in doubt, that we be not free of Anchorage and Juttage, and hath prayed us to certify you therein. These are therefore to signify to you for truth, that neither we nor any of our ancestors, have ever paid any anchorage within this realme, for it is one of the chiefest things whereof we are and always have been free. And for juttage, we never heard that it hath been demanded of any of the ports untill now. For whereas, we are by our charter free of terrage; if we pay anchorage we cannot be terrage free; for groundage and anchorage is within the compass of that word terrage, for there is seldom anchor hold without ground *. And for juttage, we cannot be free of ryvage, if we be compelled to pay for juttage; for to be free of ryvage is to arrive freely and depart freely without any exaction. Besides the general words of our charter is, that we shall have all liberties and quietances throughout the realme of England, &c.; and our liberties are such, as we are free of all taxes, exactions, and demands, whatsoever, except any act of parliament bind us thereunto. Thus having briefly certified you in what sort we have ever hitherto been free from such duties paying, as you now demand of the said Edward Beale, and praying you to deal so friendly with him, as he may enjoy the liberties of a freeman of the ports, as his auncestors before him have done,

" We commit you, &c.

" Your Worship's loving friends,

" June 20, 1580.   " The Maior and Jurats of Rye."

---

* This is a gravely ironical, and, certainly, well *grounded* argument. It is something like

> " The Spanish fleet I cannot see, *because*
> It is not yet in sight!"—Ed.

Addressed " To the Rt. Honble. our singular good Lord, the Lord Zouch
St. Mawre and Cantelupe, Lord Warden of the Cinque Ports and their
Members : one of the Lords of His Majesty's most honorable Privy
Counsel of Greate Brittaine.

" Rt. Honble.—Our most humble duty remembred, the experience of
your honorable disposition, care, and desire of good, towards this our poor
decaied town, hath moved us, yet, once again, to make known to your
good lordship, our wants and miserable poor estate, as unto our only stay
and refuge, next under God and his majestie ; and whereas we have heretofore been, by reason of a harbour in some trade and commerce by sea,
enabled to bear aboute the charge and maintenance of this towne ; but now
(although we have long sewed for help in this case) is our harbour so
decaied, that all trade hath forsaken us, and besides the importable charge
in defending the rage of the sea, from eating up our waies to the towne,
and maiming the jutties and places of refuge, for our few fisher-boats yet
remaining, with the extreme poverty of our fishermen, who, by reason of
the great spoyle of fish and fishing places so decayed, that hundreds of
them are ready to begg and starve for want, and many of them, forsaking
the towne, have left their wives and children to be parish charge, and those
of trades, as, God knows, there are verie fewe, and they so burdened
and surcharged by continual sesses and taxes, we having no revenewes, nor
other means to maintain the towne, are most of them determined rather to
seek other dwellings, than here by such extraordinary impositions and
charges, to decay and impoverish themselves, whereby it is likely that in
short tyme, this towne, that hath been not long since, of good respect and
importance, is now in possibilitie (if some gracious aspect shine not upon
it) to be quite depopulate and abandoned : and whereas of late, by order
from the right honble. the Lords of his Majesties Privy Council, directed
unto us by your honorable commandment, we are appointed to that provision of powder, lead, match, with carriages and mounting of ordenance,
that formerly, in the late Queen's tyme, this towne was enjoined unto when
her majesties ordenance were here, which now are taken hence long since,
by commission ; as also then the towne was in prosperitie and abilitie ;
but now, alas ! our miserable povertie is such, though it be for that end
and purpose, wherein with willing hartes under his majesties and your
honorable commandement, we are ready to spend our lives ; yet, notwithstanding, we beseech a due consideration may be had of the present state
of this towne, and the inabilitye thereof, most humbly praying your honorable and most gracious favor, in consideration of the premises, to com-
miserate and pity this our poor towne, so far forthe as to manifest and
declare the state thereof to the right honorable Board, that thereby some
manner of relief may be extended unto us to relieve our present wants, and
especially of the said proportion ; in all which we referr ourselves to your
lordship's high wisdom, not doubting of your honorable furtherance, and
continueing alwaies good lord unto us, unto whose protection we humbly
betake ourselves, always praying for your lordship's long life, with encrease
of many honors.—From Rye, the third day of March, 1618.

" Your honor's most humbly at commandm^t,
" The Maior and Jurats of Rye."

Addressed " To the Rt. Honble. my singular good Lord, the Lord Zouch, Lord Warden of the Cinque Ports, and one of the Lords of His Majesty's most honorable Privy Counsel.

" Rt. Honble.—My humble dutie remembred unto your good lordship, may it please your honor to vouchsafe to be advertised, that the hundred pounds which, by your honor's and your lordship's commandment, was of late taxed and levied in the portes, and their members, for and towards the suppressing of the pirates of Argire * and Tunis, lately came to my hands; and I have taken order that one Mr. Fortrey, a merchant, dwelling in Gracechurch Street, London, shall pay the same when and where your lordship shall command.

" I have received advertisement from the said ports and townes, that at this present they find this charge heavy to them, especially from Dover, Rie, and Winchelsea, by reason of the little means they have to maintain that number of ships, which they must find when cause shall require, the trade of the ports being generally taken away, (for remedy wherein, their humble suit is yet depending before their and your honorable good lordships) whose present poor estate they hope that most honorable Board will so commisserate, as that they may be permitted to use that privilege of free trade, wherein they never were interrupted, until of very late years, by the special sute and means of those merchant adventurers of London that seek to enrich themselves by the decay of his majesty's ancient and defensible ports.

" They have entreated me, as well in respect of their forwardness in this service, as also in regard of the great services by them and their ancestors, heretofore done, and hereafter to be performed, to be an humble suitor to your honour by my letter, to be pleased to continue your lordship's accustomed favor towards them in their said humble suit, for their said free trading, whereby such shippes (as to their great charges they have lately builded), do not decay in harbours for want of meanes to employ them; and thus having imboldened myself to perform what I was desired to write, I humbly take leave, and ever rest, as I am bounden,

" Your honor's, at all commandment,

" Wm. Ward.

" Dover, this 27th of Dec. 1619."

Transcribed from the MS. of Sir Charles Hedges, relative to the Cinque Ports, marked 50 . . . . . No. 291 (penes Wm. Macham, LL. D. Advocate of Drs. Commons, 1771.)—*Burrell MSS.*

RYE.

Barks and vessels returned 14th Oct. 1626:—

16 barques from 14 to 40 tons burthen, amounting altogether to 295 tons. No gunners, pilots, or ordnance.

Mariners, fishermen 66.—*Burrell MSS.*

---

* This is one of the old modes of spelling that word.

" *Prosp.* Where was she born?
Ariel. Sir, in Argier."

HASTINGS.

28 barques from 18 to 40 tons, making, in the whole,   .   .   670 tons
   No ordnance.
   Mariners, sailors, and fishermen, 127.
   No gunners.
   No pilots for the English coast as masters.—*Burrell MSS.*

DESCRIPTION.

The approach to Rye is picturesque, from its being at high-
tide nearly surrounded by water : the low and massive centre
tower of the church with a pointed roof, and Ipres' tower,
are conspicuous objects. The harbour was much improved by
a new channel, cut by a Dr. Pape, vicar of Penn, in this
vicinity, who also threw a dam across the old channel, which
is considered to be a work of great ingenuity. Ships of 200
tons' burthen can come up to the north quay of the town, one
mile and a half from the sea. George I. was compelled to
put into this harbour in a tempestuous season of the year 1725,
being unable to make that of Dover, on his return from
Holland ; but had some difficulty in getting to land, and the
large ships were unable to follow him.

" The Port of Rye extends from Jewry's Gut (about two
miles to the eastward of this harbour), to Beachy Head ; and
Hastings and Eastbourne are creeks of this Port.

" The imports are principally in Dutch cheese, timber from
Norway and America, rags for manure from Hambro', eggs,
poultry, rape and linseed cake from France ; and this having
lately been made a bonding-port for wine, some has been
imported from Boulogne.

" The exports are not of any magnitude, except in wool,
large quantities of which have been exported, within the last
two years, to France and Ostend *."

The population of Rye, in 1831, was 3715, an increase of
1500 since the year 1801. It loses one member by the
Reform Bill.

* Obligingly communicated by Mr. W. Watson, Collector of Customs at Rye.

Rye is at the eastern extremity of the coast of Sussex, and more than 80 miles from Chichester. Beyond it, at the distance of a mile or two, is Kent,

" —— the civilest place in all this isle."

The ground was there pre-occupied, or our humble topographical labours might have been more successful than in the county of Sussex ; less, hitherto, were impossible.

Rye church is popularly considered to be one of the largest in England ; but if it be in the first class, it is decidedly not near the summit. It is described as having a nave one hundred feet long, and chancel sixty, with a tower between them; but the tower should have been included in the length of the nave ; the whole interior length is 161 feet. The chancels, indeed, of which there are three of equal height and length, 60 feet in the latter, and in width 28 feet in the centre, and 25 in the other two, are decidedly grand ; and if the sides were well kept, and laid open to the centre, would form one of the finest tiers of aisles in England. The transept, which is very slightly projecting, is rather more than 80 feet in length *. The architecture throughout is mixed early Gothic and Norman, or Saxon ; it must be, of course, a decided mistake to suppose that the whole of this church was destroyed in the fourteenth century. Its principal curiosity is the great Clock, which unvarying tradition asserts to have been taken from the Spanish Armada, and given to the town by Queen Elizabeth. It has a very large dial, with quarter-jacks, like those formerly at St. Dunstan's, and bells, but these are said to have been subsequently added. The church has been considerably mutilated, and disfigured with bad windows ; still it has some grand features. In the south chancel are some windows similar to those in the western aisles of Westminster Abbey ; at the east end, one very fine one, and a very elegant flying buttress. The nave is decently fitted up, and has a small organ at the west end. The north chancel is in a state of lumber, with engines &c., and has most of its windows blocked up ; still it has a

* In the north transept is a Norman arch, in the wall, with a *chain* moulding ; a very curious if not almost unique variety.

grand, though wild, appearance, and the floor is thick set with brasses; the south chancel is completely desecrated, and used as a work-room in aid of the poor-house. The centre chancel alone is well kept, and divided from the sides, but the three bold arches and pillars of each are visible. Passing under the tower, the long gilt-lead pendulum of the Spanish clock swings a few feet above the head of the spectator. Over the arch are the arms of Queen Anne, and a lofty and rather stately altar-piece appears to be of the same æra; its communion table is of old mahogany finely inlaid, with richly carved legs, and has been conjectured to be also a spoil of the Armada, an idea which is deserving of notice. In a vault in the south aisle were discovered several stone balls, but these have not the high meed assigned to them of that of Hastings; which, like " little Dicky," in Kenilworth, seems to be " all the better for its accidents ; " they are supposed to have been merely propelled by " villanous saltpetre from the bowels of the earth." We ascended to view the clock, but observed nothing remarkable in its works, which are entirely of iron ; the hour-weight is three cwt. From the top of the tower may be seen the shore of Boulogne. It contains eight bells, six of them old. We here saw an exemplification of the adage, that " necessity is the mother of invention." The ringing loft is immediately under the bell-chamber, and the sound was consequently deafening and perplexing. The expedient was adopted of covering the floor under the bells with turf a foot thick. This has been so completely successful that the sound is almost entirely lost.

Ipres' tower is now the town gaol ; it is in good preservation, but an ugly building : near it is, or was, a battery. The remains of the *Friary* are now used as a store-house.

Rye is a tolerably built town, but rather dull. The school-house is a curious old brick building, with pilasters, and other ornaments of the same, and an antique dial. The market-house, town-hall, and assembly-room, is a spacious and very neat building of brick, on pillars, much superior in appearance to that at Hastings.

CINQUE PORTS.

After considerable difficulty and delay we have obtained access to a copy of " Jeake's History of the Cinque Ports," a thin folio, which, for what reason we know not, is of the utmost possible rarity, and consequent value; and the reader has many passages from it transferred for his information into the present work. We believe that there are not six copies of the volume to be met with in the counties of Kent and Sussex, in which the Ports lie, and it is not to be found in many of the best public libraries. Its great value consists in its having been written about one hundred years back, *before* many of the documents which it contains or refers to were *lost:* and subsequent to that period, the *customals,* &c. have been kept with such jealous care that they are not seen by any one once in a quarter of a century.

Three only of the ports were incorporated before the conquest by Edward the Confessor, as Lord Coke supposes ; and from the mention of Dover, Sandwich, and Romney as privileged ports in Doomsday Book, it is supposed these were the three. Hastings and, it is supposed, Hythe were added by the Conqueror, who, from a particular regard for the former, as the seat of his victory, made it the head and chief port. Their charters were confirmed by Henry I. and Edward I.: the most important one contained privileges superior to those enjoyed by the city of London, and was anterior to theirs by nearly 100 years. They had two great courts, the lesser one, called the Court of *Guestling* or Brotherhood, which was held annually on the Tuesday after St. Margaret's day, at New Romney, and consisted of seven delegates from each of the Cinque Ports and the ancient towns of Winchelsea and Rye, with a speaker and other officers. Some resemblance of this court is, we believe, still kept up in issuing the summons annually, though, we believe, a full court has not been held for the last sixty years, though attempts were made to put in force the due formalities in 1811 and 1822. The great court for all the ports and members, called that of *Shepway*, was held by the king's summons before the lord warden at *Shepway Cross*, near Hythe; this is now only formally convened on the election of a new warden.

The principal civil prerogatives of the ports, in addition to their naval jurisdiction, are the returning members to parliament from each, and the service of carrying, by their barons, the canopies over the king and queen at the coronation, with certain privileges and honours thereto belonging.

The extent of the lord warden's jurisdiction is from Red Cliff, near Seaford, to Shoe Beacon, near the Isle of Sheppey, in Essex, and he has free warren in a considerable district in Kent.

The arms of the Cinque Ports are " per pale *gules* and *azure*, three demi-lions *or*, impaling *azure*, three semi-ships *argent*." In 5 Henry VIII. it was ordered, that " everie person who goeth into the navy of the Portis shal have a cote of white cotyn with a red crosse and the arms of the Portis underneath; that is to say, the halfe lyon and the halfe ship." And at a brotherhood held in 1603, at the time of the coronation of James I., it was ordered that the dress of the canopybearers should be " a scarlet gowne downe to the ancle, citizen's fashion, faced crymson * satten, Gascaine hose, crymson silk stockings, crymson velvett shoes, and black velvett capes."

We regret exceedingly that time and space prevent our entering into a minute account of the Cinque Ports, as we have seldom found any history so interesting. More extended particulars will be found in Hasted's Kent and Lyon's Dover, and in that very judicious work Moss's Hastings. As this gentleman confined his views to a much less ample field, he had greater opportunities of enlargement.

Several extracts from Jeake will also be found in the latter;

---

* Crimson was originally the name of a stuff, as we read of " *purple and white crimosin.*"—*Ed.*

ours, which are principally different, and therefore novel, are
as follows:

PORTS' DOOMSDAY BOOK *.

" Which I so call to distinguish it from the other, &c. &c. in imitation
of which this latter seems to have been made, containing, besides the whole
tenures and orders of the Castle of Dover, the names of the Cinque Ports,
two ancient towns and their members of old, with the services they were
to perform, and the authority and custom of the Court of Shepway, with
the articles inquirable there, which book was kept with the records of the
castle till the late times, though now, as I have heard, removed and missing.
In this book as aforesaid, the several proportions of the shipping respectively to be found by the ports and members is set down, as by the memorandum hereof among the records of the town of Rye, fol. 55 of their old
customal, and specified as an ordinance of the king, touching the service
of shipping, anno Domini, 1229."

Doomsday.

" Isti sunt portus Regis Anglie habentes libertates quas alii portus non
habent, viz. prout plenius palet in cartis inde factis."

" Hastyng.—Ad quam pertinent tanquam membra unus vicus litus
maris in Seford, Peivinse, Bulwareth, Hydonye, Iham, Bekysborn, Gre-
necha, et Northye. Servicia inde debita Domino Regi xxi naves et in
qualibet nave xxi homines cum uno *gartione* † qui dicitur *gromet.*"

" Wynchelsey et Rye, tanquam membra.—Viz\.^t. Wynchelsey x naves,
Rye quinque naves, cum hominibus et gartionibus ut supra."

*　　　*　　　*　　　*

" Sum' navium lvii naves; sum' hominum in eisdem mcxl homines, except' gartionibus; sum' gartionum lvii; sum' to^lis personarum mcxcvii
personæ."

" Servicium quod Barones Quinque Portuum recognoscunt facere Regi
ad summon' servicii per xl dies ante exit. scil. per annum si contigerit, est
per xv dies ad custum eorum proprium ita quod primus dies computetur
a die quo vela navium erexerent ad sigland, ad partes ad quas tendere
debent, et ulterius, quam diu Rex voluerit, ad custodiend, Regis ordinat.
An° Domini m.cc°.xxix°."

" These are the ports of the King of England, having liberties which
other ports have not, that is to say, as more fully appeareth in the charters
thereof made."

" Hasting.—To which pertaineth as members, one town on the sea
shore, in Seaford, Pevensea, Bulvarithe, Hydney, Iham, Beaksborne, Grench,
and Northye. The services thereof due to our Lord the King 21 ships,
and in each ship 21 men, with one boy, who is called a *gromet* ‡."

---

* That there was such a book, and so called, appears plainly. Pat. 34
Edw. III. part 1. Mem. 45 in the Tower, &c. &c.—*Jeake.*

† Query *Garçon?* French.—Ed.

‡ *Grom,* Dutch for a stripling, from whence our word *Groom.*—*Jeake.*

" Winchelsea and Rye as members.—That is to say, Winchelsea 10 ships and Rye 5 ships, with men and boys as above."

* * * *

" Sum of the ships, 57 ships; sum of the men in them, 1140 men, except boys; sum of the boys, 57 ; sum total of the persons, 1197 persons."

" The services which the Barons of the Cinque Ports acknowledge to do to the King, at the summons of the service by 40 days before the going out, viz.: yearly if it shall happen for 15 days, at their own cost, so that the first day be reckoned from the day on which they shall hoist up the sails of the ships to sail to the parts to which they ought to go, and further as long as the King will, to be kept by ordinance of the King. An° Domini 1229."

Mr. Jeake observes that the ten ships found by Winchelsea and the five by Rye, must be taken in part of the twenty-one from Hastings, otherwise there would be seventy-two in the whole.

LORD WARDEN.

The present is that distinguished military character, his Grace the Duke of Wellington, who is also Constable of Dover Castle, an office which has been for some time annexed to the former, though the warden of the Cinque Ports has a residence at Walmer Castle, near Deal.

" Warden, now commonly stiled the Lord Warden, because oftentimes the wardens have been of nobility, and sometines princes of the blood royal. It is an office none less than a knight ought to occupy. This great officer or *Limenarcha* as Cambden observes, was an imitation of the same officer, which the Romans* established for defence of our coasts, and called Littoris Saxonici, or Tractus Maritimi, Nomes, who had the charge of nine sea-ports, and it is no doubt, but these Cinque Ports and Towns were under some special government in the time of the Saxons, necessity so requiring, though guardian, from whence warden in plain English, keeper, and in Latin, custos, imports the name imposed by king William the conqueror: yet may it not thence be concluded, that the office was born with him, seeing his design was to have altered the whole language he found here, by enjoyning the teaching here of his own French tongue to children, the grammar in schools, the laws and pleadings thereof in this tongue, shortly after his settlement in the throne. These wardens therefore, being set for the defence of the ports and coasts on which they are, and as the chief commanders of their ships they were to furnish to sea, gave them as well the name of admirals, in respect of their office as to the sea, as wardens, with reference to their care in keeping and preserving the liberties of the ports at land, both as mediators between their sovereigns

---

* At least under Constantine the Great, who did, amongst others, appoint such officers, and some say the office was executed under Valentinian by Nectaridius. vid. Selden's Mareclausum.—*Jeake.*

and them, if differences should arise there; and as judges among them, and between them and others, to guard and defend them against the unjust encroachments of foreigners upon their rights and jurisdictions, and to determine such differences as might grow irreconcilable (without an interposing power) and correct the errors and irregularities in judgment as might happen among themselves; for as to the former, he is the immediate officer of the king to the ports, and hath the return of his writs that run there, they being directed to him; and as to the latter, the causes were heard, and judgment concerning them given in the old court of Shepway, and courts of chancery and admiralty, which since frequented have withdrawn to the latter most of the matters determinable in the former, and drawn too much obscurity thereon. That the warden of the ports might have a place of residence near the ports, and a seat suitable to his quality, is the castle of Dover committed to his charge and custody, of which he is also entitled the constable, as hereafter doth appear. And though I will not say, but anciently they might serve for titles of honour and office, to several persons, yet long since the constableship of Dover castle, and wardenship of the Cinque Ports, have both been conjoined in one person."

HASTINGS WITH ITS MEMBERS.

" Hastyng est capitalis Portus, cujus membra sunt, videlicet, Wynchelsee, Rie, Leucata de Pevense et Bulvarheth, in Com. Sussex, Bekesborne, et Greneche, in Com. Kanc. qui Portus cum suis membris predictis debent* invenire ad som' Regis viginti et unam naves, et in qualibet nave debentt esse viginti et unum homines, fortes, apti, bene armati, et apparati ad servicia Regis, ita tamen quod somonitio inde fiat ex parte Regis per quadraginta dies ante. Et cum predictæ naves et homines in illis existentes ad illum locum venerint, ad quem fuerunt sommoniti, morabuntur ibidem in servicio Domini Regis per quindecim dies ad custus suos proprios. Et si Rex servicio illorum post predictos quindecim dies indiguerit; seu ipsos ibidem amplius moravi voluerit, erunt naves illæ cum hominibus in illis existentibus in servicio Regis morantes ad custus Regis quamdiu Regi placuerit, videlicet, magister capiet sex denarios per diem, et quilibet aliorum capiet tres denarios per diem.

CORONATION SERVICE.

Et quoad servicia in coronatione, &c. continentur in eodem libro sic: Anno visesimo ‡ Regis Henrici filii Regis Johannis coronata Regina Alianora, filia Hugonis, Comitis Provinciæ, apud Westmonasterium dominica ante purificationem beate Marie, inter alia invenitur sic: Pannum vero de Cerico § quadratum purpureum quatuor hastis de argentatis, sustentatum cum quatuor campanellis argenteis et deauratis ultra Regem incedentem quocunque incederet, gestabant Barones Quinque Portuum, assignati ad quamlibet hastam quatuor pro diversitate Portuum ne videretur Portus Portuum præferri. Consimiliter unum pannum sericum supra Reginam post Regem incedentem. Quos quidem pannos suos esse de jure vendicant, et illos obtinuerunt in Curia, licet Marchiones de Marchia Walliæ,

---

* Debet.　　† Debet.　　‡ Vicesimo.　　§ Serico.—*Jeake.*

viz. Johannes filius Alani, Radulphus de Mortuo mari, Johannes de Monemne, et Walterus de Clyfford, nomine marchiæ jus marchiæ esse dicerent hastas inveniendas et illas deferendas. Sed quodammodo frivolum reputabatur. Asserebant autem Barones de Quinque Portubus jus suum sedendi in mensis Regiis eadem die a dextris Domini Regis, et ita sederunt. Compertum est etiam in quodam quaterno libro ad scaccarium Anno trigesimo primo dicti Regis Edwardi filii Henrici."—*Jeake.*

" Hasting is an Head-port*, whose members are, viz. Winchelsea, Rye, the Lowey of Pevensey, and Bulvarhithe, in the county of Sussex, Beaksborne and Grenche, in the county of Kent, which port, with its members aforesaid, ought to find at the summons of the king twenty and one ships, and in every ship there ought to be twenty and one men, strong, apt, well-armed, and prepared† for the services of the king; so that the summons thereof be made of the part of the king by forty days before: and when the said ships, and men in them being, shall come to that place to which they were summoned, they shall tarry there in the service of our lord the king, by fifteen daies, at their own costs; and if the king shall need their service after the aforesaid fifteen daies, or will them there longer to tarry, the ships, with the men in them, being in the service of the king, shall be abiding at the costs of the king, as long as it shall please the king, viz. the master shall take sixpence per day, and the constable‡ sixpence per day, and every one of the others shall take three-pence per day."

" And as to the service in the coronation, &c. it is contained in the same booke thus:—in the twentieth yeare of King Henry, the son of King John, queen Elianor, the daughter of Hugh, Earl of Provence, being crowned at Westminster on Sunday before the Purification of the blessed Marie, among other things it is found thus: and a cloth, foure square, of purple silke by foure staves§, silvered over, borne up with foure little bells silver and gilt, over the king, going whither he would, did the Barones of the Cinque Ports assigned beare, at every Staffe foure, according to the diversity of the ports, lest port should seeme to be preferred to port‖. Likewise the same, a silke clot hover the queene, going after the king¶; which said clothes they did claime to be theirs of right, and obtained them in court, although the Marquesses of the marches** of Wales, viz. John Fitz Alan, Ralfe de Mortimer, John de Monemne, and Walter de Clyfford,

---

* A chief port, or capital port, and so again afterward.
† Furnished, or ready.
‡ Constable of a ship in Dutch is used for a gunner.
§ Or spears, and so afterward.
‖ That is, one with another, the Barons at the staves, without respect to which of the ports they did belong.
¶ By this is to be understood, that the Barons of the ports did bear the canopy over the queen as well as over the king.
** Or Marquisate, and so afterward, viz. those lords that were governors of the marches of Wales, by the force of the Latin word, are here rendered Marquisses, and Wales a marquisate, otherwise none in England, till King Richard the Second.—*Jeake.*

in the name of the marquisate, said it to be the right of the marquisate to find and bear those staves, but it was reputed in a sort frivolous. And the Barons of the Cinque Ports did affirm their right of sitting at the king's table the same day, at the right hand of our lord the king, and so they sate. It is found also in a certaine foure square booke at the Exchequer, in the thirty-first yeare of the said King Edward, sonne of Henry."—*Ibid.*

We believe the following pamphlet to be very scarce, and think that an extract from it may not prove uninteresting.

Extracts from " A Discourse on Sea-ports, principally of the Port and Haven of Dover, by Sir Walter Rawleigh, and addressed to Queen Elizabeth, with useful Remarks on that Subject (published) by command of his late Majesty K. Charles the Second."

" Whereby it plainly appeareth, that as the excessive expence of the Low Countreys, bestowed on havens, hath not impoverished, but the clean contrary, greatly enriched them by incomparable wealth and treasure, with number of rich, fair, and populous towns; so our sparing mind, or rather greedy getting, gaining and enriching land from your Majesty's havens and navigable channels, hath utterly destroyed and spoiled many good havens by nature left us, and thereby wrought very beggary, and misery, and desolation in these your frontier towns."

" And if we search the very cause of the flourishing state of London, which almost alone in quantity, people and wealth, in this age or realm, is so increased, and contrary wise of the poverty or rather beggary and decay of Winchelsea, Rye, Romney, Hide, Dover, and many other poor towns, we shall find the decay of these havens and preservation of the Thames the only or chief occasion."

" Hereby sufficiently appeareth how incomparable jewells havens and sure harbours are, for gaining, maintaining, and encreasing people, wealth, and commodity, in any realm."

" And no lesser strength and security do they bring in time of war, as well by the multitude of mariners (a most serviceable people) and shipping which they breed, as also the inhabitation of the frontiers."

" But have in this last age consented to see many of our useful ports run to decay, and at length to ruine, and to become totally lost to the nation ; which a very little foresight and as little charge might have prevented, while the evil was growing, which at a long run becomes incurable. Among which ports I instanced Sandwich, Dover, Rye, Winchelsea, and which were reckoned heretofore as so many bulwarks against our ambitious neighbour."

HISTORICAL PARTICULARS OF THE SERVICES OF THE CINQUE PORTS.—*Jeake.*

" And it may be further noted, that since the nation hath increased the royal navy in the number of great and warlike ships, these being small (sufficient, as appeareth, to be manned with twenty men and a boy), this number of fifty-seven ships hath not been exacted, but sometimes two or three, or more, which notwithstanding to equip, hath been equivalent in the charge to the fitting out of the old total, considering their burden.

And moreover, how chargeable soever this service hath been to the ports, they, from time to time, have faithfully performed it, as several records will testify for them. For not only, upon all occasions, have the navy of the Ports been ready to guard the narrow seas from pirates infesting the coasts (by which, as some say, and firmly believe, from tradition of their ancestors, they first obtained their privileges), but employed in frequent transportations of the king's forces, if not person and family, during the long differences and wars between England and France; so as it seems to be the chief of the royal navy till the state provided a bigger and better, and that wherein the kings of old did much confide for assistance as our histories intimate. King John, in his retirement in the Isle of Wight*, was almost forsaken of all his kingdom, save the ships and mariners of the Cinque Ports, with which he secured himself till he recovered all again. In the beginning of the reigne of King Henry the Third, anno 1217, the Ports armed forty tall ships, and put them to sea under the command of Hubert de Burgo (then Warden of the Cinque Ports, and commander of Dover castle) who meeting with eighty sail of French ships coming to aid Lewis, the French king's eldest son, gave them a most courageous encounter, wherein he took some, sunk others, and discomfited the rest. And at other times† this King Henry had great benefit by the shipping of the Ports. About 1293, or 1294, in the reign of King Edward the First, an hundred sail of the Ports navy fought at sea with a great fleet of French ships, of whom (notwithstanding great odds) they slew, took, and sunk so many, that France was thereby for a long season after in a manner destitute both of seamen and shipping. Rot. Scotiæ, 10 Edward III., Memb. 16. The navy of the Ports, together with other vessels taken up for that service, under the command of Geffrey de Say, admiral of the sea, from the mouth of the Thames to the southern and western Ports, defended the seas, and hindered the bringing of succors from foreign parts to the king's enemies in Scotland. Under ‡ King Henry the Fourth, anno 1406, the navy of the Cinque Ports, conducted by Henry Paye, surprized one hundred and twenty French ships, all laden with no worse merchandize than salt, iron, and oil. In the fourteenth year of King Henry the Sixth, the Ports had summons to fit out their whole number of ships, to be ready at Winchelsea by the feast of St. George, which was anno 1436. June 25, anno 23 Henry VI., the town of Sandwich set out five ships to fetch Queen Margaret out of France. May 23, anno 27 Henry VI., the town of Sandwich, by command from the king, sent out one ship for four months service. July 18, anno 27 Henry VI., the same town, by like command, set out another ship for four months service. January 21, ab inchoatione regni Hen. VI. 49, et recaptionis regiæ potestatis primo, the navy of the Ports were set out to

---

* In the seventeenth year of his reign.

† As the eighth, tenth, and eleventh years of his reign, wherein he writes to have the Ports set out double their number of ships this time, with promise it should be no president.—13 *Febr. Pat.* 11, *Hen. III., Mem.* 8.

‡ Before this, in the tenth and eleventh years of King Richard the Second, the Ports navy both times were ordered to be ready at Sandwich, and afterwards the like in the ninth year of Henry the Fifth.—*Jeake.*

fetch Queen Margaret and the prince out of France.   March 31, anno
15 Edward IV., the king commanded the navy of the Ports to be ready
in the Downs, May 26, then next to come, for transportation of the king
and his army, and the king and his army came to Sandwich.   Anno
7 Henry VII., in May, the Ports navy transported the king's army from
Sandwich into France.   Anno 8 Henry VII., in November, the Ports navy
brought back the king's army from Calais.   Anno 10 Henry VII., in July,
the trained bands of Sandwich beat back the king's enemies landing in the
Downs.   Anno 5 Henry VIII., in May, preparation for the king's army
was made at Sandwich, and the Ports navy transported his army from
thence and Dover into France.   Anno 34 Henry VIII., in Angust, at the
king's command, the navy of the Ports was prepared, and ready, the tenth
of October, at Sandwich and Dover, to transport his horses and army into
France, and did transport them.   Anno 35 Henry VIII., in April, the
king commanded the Ports navy to be in readiness in the Downs, the
twenty-sixth of May, to do their service, which they did.   Anno 30 Elizabeth, 1588, in April, the Ports, at the queen's command, set out five
serviceable ships, and a pinace for her Majesty's service, for two months,
but they served four months at their own costs.   Anno 38 Elizabeth, 1595,
in January, the Ports, at the queen's command, set out five serviceable
ships, of one hundred and sixty tons a piece, for five months, at their own
charges.   Anno 2 Charles I., in July, 1626, at the king's command, the
Ports set out two serviceable ships for three months, which cost them
1825*l*. 8*s*. 0*d*.   One paper I have seen mentioned somewhat less."

HASTINGS

TO

BATTLE, ASHBURNHAM, LEWES, AND BRIGHTON.

	MILES.		MILES.
BATTLE	8½	ASHCOMBE T. G.	1½
ASHBURNHAM	6½	FALMER	2
GARDNER'S-STREET . . .	3	STANMER P. G.	½
HORSE-BRIDGE	4	BARRACKS	2¾
CHURCH-LAUGHTON . . .	5	BRIGHTON	1¼
RINGMER	4		
CLIFFE	2		41½
LEWES	½		

The usual route to Battle is through Ore, a small village, with a decent church, and one neat residence, belonging to a Mr. Shadwell; the next place is Beauport Park, where the road from St. Leonard's joins it, the latter of which we adopted. On passing the north gate, above the Subscription Garden, we enter the new road, and descending a hill, meet with a turn-pike-gate, built in the form of a Saxon round tower: just beyond this is a lane to Crowhurst, on the left. The church-yard at that place, we understand, contains a most picturesque yew, nearly twenty feet in circumference; and about half a mile from the church is the ruin of a private oratory, whose exact history is uncertain. In the gable is a pretty window, which, from the shape of its arch and upper tracery, appears to be of the fourteenth century. Proceeding along the turn-pike road we reach that from Hastings at Hollington: immediately before reaching it, the scenery is pretty: the thick foliage, which completely conceals the small church, lies at some distance on the left, and, more in front, is seen the hand-some domain of Sir C. M. Lamb: we turn to the left and pass this on our road to Battle; the park appears spacious, and the entrance is neat: from hence to Battle there is no particular object requiring notice; but the view of the town, abbey, and church, about half a mile before we arrive at it, is picturesque and commanding.   There is an extensive tannery at the entrance on the small brook, as its wholesome, but to some unpleasant, odour will speedily indicate.   Battle, still in a mercantile age connected with the arts of war, is well known, as containing one of the most extensive manufactories of gunpowder in England, at which accidents were formerly not unfrequent, but of late years none are on record.   There was also in the last war an extensive depôt of government stores.

The church is on the right soon after entering the town; a little further on, the wide High-street makes an angle to the righ*t*, and on the other side, facing it, is the grand old abbey gate-house.   The town is indifferently built, containing, in 1831, 2999 inhabitants.   This is a *franchise*, in right of which the inhabitants are exempted from serving on juries; and a coroner, &c. is appointed by the Lord of the Manor (Sir G. Webster), who is still or was lately termed the *Abbot*, as the incumbent is styled *Dean* of Battle.   The present Dean is Dr. Birch, and we feel bound to record an honourable trait of character; *though* he would not answer our letter of topographical inquiry:—viz., that the House of Correction for the district having no chaplain, he gratuitously performs divine service, and preaches a sermon to the prisoners there every Sunday.   The market of the town was granted by Henry I. on Sundays, but was changed to Thursday in 1606.   Here is a charity school for forty boys, and some other benefactions.

The name of the village previous to the Norman Conquest was *Epyton*, changed to *Battel*, from the circumstance of its having been the scene of the important and sanguinary conflict.   In the following year the king founded the abbey (in pursuance of a vow he had made previous to the fight) on the place where the most decisive part of the engagement had occurred, and so disposed it, that the high altar of the abbey church should be on the precise spot where the dead body of Harold was first discovered.   It was intended for the reception of 140 monks; but 60 alone were subsequently admitted, brought from the Benedictine Abbey of Marmontier in Normandy, dedicated to the same patron, Saint Martin;

one of the monks of the former had suggested the idea of the foundation to the king.

The king's motive for this foundation was, according to the feelings of the times, decidedly a good one. He intended it for the especial purpose of prayers being for ever offered for the souls of all who had fallen in the conquering engagement.

" Rob. de Glouc. MS. in Bibl. Bodleiana, fol. 98 a.

" King William bethought him alsoe of that
Folke that was forlorne,
And slayn also thoruz him
In the bataile bi forne.
And ther as the bataile was,
An Abbey he lete rere
Of Seint Martin, for the soules
That there slayn were
And the monkes well ynoug
Feffed without fayle,
That is called in Englonde
Abbey of Bataile."

William of Malmsbury.

" Sancti Martini de Bello [monasterium] quod rex Wilhelmus fundavit et provexit in loco ubi Angliam debebellaverat; multa ibi et pretiosa tum vivus tum mortuus delegans. Altare ecclesiae est, in loco, ubi Haroldi, pro patriae charitate occisi, cadaver exanime inventum est."

Matthew of Westminster.

" Fundata est igitur ibidem domus religiosorum, ubi caedes et strages crebrior fuit occisorum, pro eorundem animabus, Deum imperpetuum deprecatura, quam dux et alii devoti Deo nobiles, possessionibus ampliarunt, et religionis custodia munierunt, quae propter bellum ibidem consummatum, nomine Belli usque hodie' intitulatur."

" Abbatia de Bello construitur" *ibid.*—" Rex Gulihelmus, exultans de victoriæ, dedit laudem Deo. Eodem anno idem rex, construxit abbatiam, quam appellavit pro bello ibi commisso, *Bellum,* in qua, in perpetuum Deo gloria, et laus, et gratiarum actio pro victoria obtenta solverentur, necnonet pro ibidem mortuis exequiae à sanctis monachis ibi constitutis, cum salutarilus hostiis, Deo redderentur; ipsamque ecclesiam possessionibus et libertatibus dotatam et ditatam commisit patronatui et tutelae regum qui post eum forent in Anglia regnaturi."

Leland's Collectanea.

" Anno Mlxvij. Rex Willielmus Conquestor Angliae abbathiam de Bello construxit, et monachis instituit, ut pro occisis in bello ab ipsis in perpetuum hostiae salutis Deo redderentur."

Monasticon.

"The privileges of this monastery, detailed in the largest charter, errone-ously called ' Carta prima' in the Battle register, are great. It was not only to be exempt from episcopal jurisdiction, but was to enjoy its exemption in as ample a manner as the metropolitan church of Canterbury. It had the rights of free-warren in all its manors, treasure trove, and even sanctuary. The circuit round the abbey also, called the Leuga, was freed from every kind of tax and service. The manor of Wi*, with all its appendant royal-ties, in Kent; the manors of Alsistone in Sussex, Limensfeld in Surrey, Hov in Sussex, Craumareis in Oxfordshire, and Bristwoldinton in Berk-shire; with the churches of Radinges, Culinton, and St. Olave, in Exeter, formed the chief endowment.

"Two of the Conqueror's charters relating to the general liberties of Battle went each by the name of ' Humana Mens,' probably because it was declared in them that the church of Battle should be 'libera et quieta in perpetuum ab omni exactione et omnibus quaecunque mens humana cogitare potest.' Another liberates the church, ' ab omni thelonio.' There is one ' de Corredio Abbatis.' Three relate to the liberties of the ' Leuga;' one to the market granted to the monastery; and one reciting the gift of the meadow of Bodeham."

William did not live to see his foundation completed. An abbot had been appointed in 1076, but the church was not consecrated till 1094.

"Then went the king to Hastings at Candlemas; and whilst he there abode waiting the weather, he let hallow the minster at Battel."—*Saxon Chron.*

And by a charter at the same time added several churches to their endowments, confirmed several liberties, and the right of *treasure trove*. At the consecration were present the Bishops of Rochester (Gundulf), Winchester, Chichester, Salisbury, Durham, Bath, and Coutances, with a great number of Barons. Various subsequent charters of high endowments and privileges were given by Henry I., Stephen, Henry II., John, Henry III., Edward II. (a market and fair at *Havekerst*), Edward III. (to fortify and embattle the monastery), and Henry IV. The abbot was mitred and regularly summoned to Parliament, before the dissolution.

---

* " Together with his righ tof wreck in Denger marsh (a member thereof), as also that of any great or royal fish, called *Crassipies*†, which should be there driven on shore, except where it happened without certain limits, in which case, they were only to have two parts of the fish and the tongue, these being what the King usually had."

† Qy. *Sturgeons?—Ed.*

Disputes appear to have taken place at an early stage of its history as to its exempt jurisdiction from the bishoprick of Chichester.

"The Liber de Situ Ecclesiae Belli, 'MS. Cotton, Domit A. 11 says,' Gausberto itaque electo cum ad eum benedicendum episcopus Cicestiensis Stigandus nullatenus assentiret, nisi Cicestriam benedicendus adiret; Regem hac de causa providus abbas caute adivit, causam exposuit, quid agendum foret inquisivit. Quo cognito indignatus Rex episcopo interminatus praecepit quatinus Abbatiem in ecclesia S. Martini de Bello, omni remota calumnia, benediceret, eo etiam modo ut illic ipse vel suorum aliquis eodem die ex consuetudine, nec hospitaretur, nec sibum, quidem sumeret, in testimonium videlicet libertatis, ejusdam ecclesiae. Factum est igitur, et abbate Gausberto ante altare sancti Martini de Bello benedicto, atque in locum suum ab episcopo collocato, memoriale ad posteros transiit, Ecclesiam de Bello ab omni exactione et subjectione Episcoporum Cicestriae liberam esse, sicut, dominicam Regis capellam; nec in ea vel in omni possessione ejus quisquam aliquid calumniari possit, nisi gratis et caritative impendatur."—MSS. fol. 23 b.

Among the privileges of the Abbots was that of pardoning any sentenced criminal they might accidentally pass by. The sword and robe of William, as originally offered, were kept in the church. In the archives was also kept the celebrated "Roll of Battle Abbey," viz., of all the Norman gentry who came over with the Conqueror. It is supposed however that several names were afterwards surreptitiously inserted, in order to gratify the pride of families who wished to be thought of Norman descent.

In the year 1331 the then Abbot of Battle, Hamo, of Offington, it is supposed, signalized himself in a very courageous manner, in repulsing a body of French who had landed and attacked Rye and Winchelsea; to which latter place the abbot repaired with what force he could muster, and, fortifying it, kept the enemy at bay till such time as the country gentlemen assembled in great numbers to his aid, and enabled him to repulse the invaders. We have a luminous account of this transaction in

Thomas of Walsingham.

" Post, occupationem insulae supradictae (de Wight), Gallici galeas iterum repetentes circuerunt oram maritimam usquedum pervenerunt ad objectum villae de Winchelsea. Et cognoscentes abbatem de Bello ad illam convolasse causa custodiae, missis nuntiis petunt ut illam redimat. Abbas vero negat se empturum, quod non perdiderat, quin potius denunciat, ut ab infestatione villæ desistant sub interminatione damni quod eis poterit provenire. Gallici ejus responso exasperati petunt (si bellum velit) ut singuli ex utraque parte mittantur, vel certe plures, qui spectante utroque exercitu congrediantur; sed nec hanc petitionem abbas admisit, dicens se religiosum verum esse, et non licere sibi hujus petitiones admittere, nec illuc belli causa, sed tuitionis et conservationis pacis patriæ advenisse. His audiis, Gallici æstimantes animum abbatis suorumque defecisse; mox admotis instrumentis bellicis, scilicet missilibus, quorum copiâ fruebantur, villam acriter infestabant, pugnantes a nona usque ad vesperum. Sed abbatis et eorum qui cum ipso erant laudabili probitate minime profecerunt. Interim dum pugnant ibidem mittunt partem navium ad villam de Hastings, quæ reperientes villam pene vacuam, combusserunt eam. Gallici vero videntes se nil prævalere apud Wynchelsee, recesserunt."

MISCELLANEOUS.

EXTRACTS FROM THE CHRONICLE.

MSS. Cotton. Vitell, p. vii. fol. 168—*(translated.)*

> 4 vergates make one wist.
> 8 vergates make one hide.
> 16 feet make one perch.
> 40 perches make one *quarantein*.
> 12 quaranteins make one English *leuga*.

It is divided (the leuga) by *wists*, which, in other places, are called *vergates*. The most accustomed price of one wist is 3*s*."—*Burrell MSS.*

" This abbey (Battle) flourished greatly, not only by the royal endowments, but by those of several of the nobility; and a town of about a hundred and fifteen houses was in a short time formed under its patronage, for the Conqueror had bestowed on it all the land three miles round his foundation."—*Pennant.*

" History doth mention that there was, about that time (Nor. In.), great store of *Vines* at *Santlac* (near to Battel, in Sussex), which giveth me to think that wyne hath bene made longe sence within the realme, although in our memorie it be accounted a great deintye to heare of."— *Lambard.*

William of Newbury, quoted by Camden, says, that, " at a place called Sanguelac, in Battle, so called from a very great slaughter of the English fighting for their country, if it happens to be wetted with a smart shower sweats out real blood, and as it were fresh: as if the very evidence thereof did plainly declare, that the voice of so much Christian blood doth still cry from the earth to the Lord." This was a harmless error; but of course it was only the overflowing of a mineral stream.

" The following is the statement of the abbey property, as recorded in the Domesday Survey. The manor of Wi, in Kent, was rated at seven solins. The soc and sac of twenty-two hundreds appertained to it. In Sussex the abbey held Alistone, which paid gild for forty-four hides and a half; four hides in the hundred of Totenore; six hides and a half, including Bocheham, in the abbat's own rape; and portions of land of a much smaller kind, which were let to the Earl of Ow, the Earl of Moretaine, and other tenants in Bece, Wasingate, Nirefeld, Penehest, Hov, Pilesham, Cedesfeld, Bolington, Croherst, Witinges and Holintun. In Surrey, twenty-five hides at Limenesfeld. In Berkshire, the manor of Bristoldestone, which had been Harold's, in whose time it had been rated at ten hides; five " hagae" or houses in Wallingford; and the church of Redinges (now Reading), with an appendage of eight hides of land. In Devonshire, the church of Colitone, with a single hide; and the church of St. Olave in Exeter, with seven hides of land appended. In Oxfordshire, five hides at Cravmareis; those also had belonged to Harold. In Essex, one hide at Atahov, and one at Hersa."—*Burrell MSS.*

The abbey of Brecknock, in South Wales, was a cell to that of Battle. At the dissolution, the last abbot, John Hammond, who had been so for many years, received a pension of one hundred marks annually by patent, with a proviso that he should vacate his pension if preferred by the King. This circumstance, as implying conscientiousness on his part, and continued esteem on the part of others, is usually considered to dissipate some charges brought against him and his monks, terrible if true, but capable of being the coinage of base and vindictive malignity, or of interest; in this case most probably the latter.

In Pope Nicholas' Taxation the following was the valuation of the abbey possessions within the archdeaconry of Lewes only :—

ARCHIDIACONATUS LEWENSIS : ABBAS DE BELLO.

	£.	s.	d,
Bellum cu' p't'	48	7	$2\frac{1}{2}$
Berhorn	17	9	0
Alsiston	102	12	$10\frac{1}{4}$
Appelderh'm	29	17	$10\frac{3}{4}$
Apud Berherst	2	0	0
S'ma . .	200	7	0

APPAT, D'UI DE BELLO.

	£.	s.	d.
Eccl'ia de Bello	5	6	8
Vicar' ejusdem	13	6	8

And the Summa Clara, exclusive of out-payments at the general dissolution, was 880*l*. 14*s*. 7*d*.

NONAL INQUISITION OF BATTLE.
Temp. Edw. III.
" BELLUM.

" Hæc indentura testat° q'd inquis' capt' ap' Lewes die lune px' med' quadr'gie cor' d'no Henr' Husee et sociis suis collector' et assessor' none garbar, veller, et agn' d'no regi in com' Sussex' concessor', anno regni regis Edwardi t'cij post conq' quartodeci'o su' vero valor' none p'dce jux' tenor' d'ni reg' co'miss' d'ni reg' p'fato Henr' et socijs suis directe p' sacr'm Thome de Heslyngh Joh'is de Loxbeth Joh'is de Westbech et Thom' Avere poch' eccl'ie de Bello jur' et inquisitor' qui dic' p' sacr'm suu' q'd nona p's garb' poch' ecc'ie p'dc'e va'lt hoc anno sex marc quatuor sol' et tres den' et agn' et lan' val' ibid'm hoc anno ij^s v^d et no' plus q' nona g'rba abb'is de Bello in ead' 'poch' val' hoc anno quatuor m'rc' et xx^d. Et nona garba sacriste de Bello in d'ca 'poch' val' hoc anno vj^s viij^d. Et nona garb' elemos' de Bello in ead' poch' val't hoc a° xx^s vj lan^s et agn' d'ci elem' in ead' poch' val' hoc a° . . . Et non' garb' vicar ibid' de gleba ecc'ie val' h° a° ij^s v^d. Et in feno val' xiij^s iiij^d et in pomor' et vacheria ibid' xiij^s iiij^d in oblato'ibz ibid' x m'rc' et in minut' de'cis xl^s. Et sic val't d'ca eccl'ia de Bello ex^{tam} suam Sm' ex^{te} d'ce eccl'ie xxviij m'rc'.

" It' dic' p' sacr'm suu' de hiis q' no' viv'ut de agricultur' vid' Joh' Goryngh' q' h'et in cat' ad val' viij^s ix^d inde xv^{na} xv^d et Joh' de Joh' q' h'et in catall' ad val' xxij^s iij^d inde in xv^{na} xviij^d et Thom' de Gillingh'm qui h'et in cat' ad val' xv^s inde xv^a xij^d et Joh's More h'et in Catall' ad val' xv inde xv^{na} xij^d et Joce' Ferour h't in cat' ad val' quinq'z marc' viij^s iiij^d inde xv^a v^s et Joh's Reyas h't in cat' ad val' LX sol' inde xv^{na} iiij^s et Will'us de Helderh'm h'et in cat' ad val' xv^s inde xv^{na} xij^l et Will'us Thorndon h'et in cat' ad val' xxij^s inde xv^{na} xviij^d. S'm tocius xv^{na} xij^{li} iij^s x^d inde xv^{na} xv^s iii^d. In quor test'ta sigill' d'cus Henr' et soc' sui utunt' in hac p'te q'm sigill' d'cor Thom Joh'is et Thom' jur' sunt appensa alt'nat."
—*Printed Records* *.

At the entrance of the Abbey is the noble gatehouse (*see Vignette*), a spacious oblong erection, with a tower of considerable size flanked by bold octagonal turrets near the west end, battlemented and turreted throughout, with some good windows and doorways, and tracery of arches and niches ; the

---

* This, which is printed *verbatim*, will show the difficulty of interpreting such intricately contracted documents. We fear we have made a great mistake at the commencement of our translation of the Brighton roll, which will doubtless be soon discovered.—*Ed.*

whole indicating a late period of the decorated style, probably about the year 1400. The roof at the entrance is elegantly groined, with clustered columns in the centre. The long building on the right side, adjoining the tower, was, for a long period, used as a town-hall and court-house, but from shameful neglect, on the part of the inhabitants, the interior fell into ruin.

" Thursday se'nnight, part of the roof of Battle Abbey, Sussex, which, by permission, has been used as a town-hall, was, by the violence of the wind and rain, drove in, totally destroyed that part of the noble building, and put the inhabitants of the town in the greatest consternation ; some thinking it a dreadful clap of thunder, others that it was an earthquake." —1794.

The entire circuit of the various buildings, offices, and domestic or agricultural accompaniments of the Abbey, is said to have been upwards of a mile ; the greater part is traceable at the present day. On the left of the entrance is the present dwelling-house of Sir Godfrey Webster, formed out of the cloisters, upper chambers, and some other parts of the original buildings. In front is a terrace over a range of vaults, thus described by Pennant ; and at its S. E. extremity two ancient turrets, said to have been watch-towers. The view from hence over the park and towards the sea, is very pleasing.

" In another part are eight other vaults, parallel to one another, each of twenty-nine feet by fourteen, and a narrow window at the end. All these had been the magazines for provisions and fuel in the flourishing days of this great foundation."

Farther to the west, and behind the mansion, are the refectory and kitchen, with some other original remains. The former was a magnificent edifice, 150 feet in length, apparently of the fourteenth century ; beneath it is a fine crypt, of three low aisles. The kitchen, sufficiently capacious to include five fire-places, is older, probably soon after the year 1200 ; it has a groined roof, with well-proportioned and elegant pillars and arches, and has a stately appearance. Many other relics of great interest are to be seen in this part of the grounds.

The hall, at present in use, is about 60 feet long and 30 wide, and is a noble apartment, richly wainscotted with oak ; over which, at the north end, is a music gallery, decorated with a variety of family portraits, and others of kings, warriors, and statesmen; stained glass windows, and a fine, though small, collection of armour, very tastefully arranged. It consists of shields, lances, long and short maces, battle-axes, two-handled swords, &c. two bright suits of steel armour, and a very brilliant suit of brass, with helmets and black plumes. On comparing the latter from recollection with one exhibited at the Lord Mayor's show, which was probably one of the best in the Tower, it appeared to hold a superior rank. At the upper end is a *Dais*, separated by brass railing, with crimson cordage. Above is the great historical painting of the battle of Hastings, 30 feet by 17, executed by a distinguished modern artist, whose name we have unfortunately forgotten, at a price of, as we believe, about £1500. It is, upon the whole, the finest and boldest painting of the kind that we ever had the good fortune to see. Great attention has been bestowed on the costume, which is derived from Dr. Meyrick's researches, and from the original and incontrovertible authority of the Bayeux tapestry. The Normans are dressed in brown russelled chain armour, the Saxons in yellow surcoats, with plaid scarfs; the hair of the former is close shaven, and that of the latter long. The principal group is applied to the exact period of time when the body of Harold was discovered among the slain, and brought to the king, which put the crowning seal to his victory. Two Norman soldiers are bringing forward the body; one has a noble countenance, indicating magnanimous pity for the fallen; the other is holding up the fatal arrow with much eagerness of gesture. The countenance of Harold has decidedly a Saxon stamp, and his form is of great strength. William is mounted on a cream-coloured horse, and in the intense and surprised eagerness with which he beholds the objects before him, drops his sword on the ground. By his side, his very unpriestly brother, Odo of Baieux, looks at him with fierce delight and curious attention, to see how he receives his victory. Several groups of fighting and dying warriors are exhibited, and scenery in the back ground. A monk is pressing forward with the banner blessed by the Pope, to remind the king of his imagined obligations to the charmed

boon. Nothing could, of course, have been in better taste, than
the introduction of this picture here; it forms one of those objects which may afford the visitor some hours of pleasure and
interest at the ruins of Battle. The other parts of the house
are not shown. We obtained a glimpse of the drawing-room,
which has a groined roof, with a line of cloister arches running
up its centre. It is most richly decorated with plate and
stained glass, and gilt fret-work, and is scarcely to be exceeded
in effect at Arundel Castle, or even at the Pavilion.

The church, though much over praised, is certainly a highly
respectable edifice, and the whole of the *exterior*, as well as
interior, is in perfect preservation, a circumstance by no means
usual in Sussex. It consists of a west tower, three aisles, and
two chancels, and was probably built about the end of the
twelfth century, having pointed arches with circular columns,
also a font of mixed Norman and early English character.
It has been variously altered at different times, the tower probably rebuilt in the fifteenth century, and most of the windows
inserted in the fourteenth; those on the north side are handsome, and have slight remains of painted glass : the tower,
though not lofty, is of good proportions. The north chancel
is divided into two school-rooms. The interior is plain and
decent, well pewed throughout with old oak, and has a neat
organ, and eight bells in the tower. On the floor are several
brasses with long Latin inscriptions, which we had not time
to examine; and on the north side of the chancel, under an
arch, is a handsome. marble altar tomb, with the remains of
gilding, bearing the effigies of Sir Anthony Browne and his
lady. This knight, who purchased Battle Abbey from one
Gillim, (probably, as was too often the case in the capricious
Henry's grants, a worthless sycophant,) as a domain for his
family, had been standard bearer to Henry VIII.

From Battle to Ashburnham occurs nothing worthy of mention. The latter, like the abbey, is shown only on Mondays;
but we should warn the reader, that in this instance the house
is not to be seen by the visitor, or he might, like ourselves,
feel disappointment. A little pleasing park scenery, a mode-

rate garden, and the relics of the unfortunate Charles I., are all the attractions here afforded for a journey.

The family of Ashburnham, however, have been sufficiently noble and excellent to excite interest for the spot in which they lived and died. Fuller observes that they were of " stupendous" antiquity, having been of rank and note in England some time before the Conquest; and one of them displayed much courage and patriotism at that period, as sheriff of Sussex.

Ashburnham Park we understood to be about eight miles in circumference. The scenery at the entrance is bold, wild, and interesting, reminding us of some celebrated ones in other parts of the kingdom. On coming nearer to the house, the sides of the road take the appearance of a shrubbery, and have a pleasing effect; it here crosses a long piece of water, but of which little is seen, and winds to the left. The first object shown to strangers is the church. This is simply a neat village one, with a tower, nave, and three chancels, the latter constituting the only peculiar feature. The interior is neat, but has no particular ornament. A very small altar-piece, with Moses and Aaron, removed to the south wall, bears date 1676, and some rich old crimson damask, on the pulpit and communion-table, is probably about the same age. The family vault, in some part of the church, may be seen, and we believe even entered, by strangers, a practice of which we cannot speak with any degree of pleasure. The south chancel has a family gallery, and the north contains the monuments, and the memorials of the execution of Charles I., which were bequeathed by Bertram Ashburnham, in 1727, to the parish clerks for ever. These are kept in a glass case lined with red velvet; and have nothing in the least repulsive in their appearance. The extremely fine linen excites astonishment from being as perfectly fresh as if new. The shirt of the unhappy monarch has fine ruffles at the wrists, which have faint spots of blood : the drawers are *knit* of white silk, there is also the Holland sheet thrown over his remains after death, and his watch; this has an enamelled case and flowers worked on the dial, and is of the old turnip shape. The principal monuments are two only, one, that of Sir William Ashburnham and his lady, daughter of Lord Butler, of Herts: she in a recumbent position, he in a loose gown and periwig, kneeling and extending his arms towards her. The effect is so perfectly *outré* that a smile at first is irresistible; but when we read the inscription, which displays so much solid goodness of heart and unaffected feeling, all inclination to smile ceases, and we look at the strange figure with reverence. Another monument is for his elder brother, a fine white marble effigy with a helmet, between his two wives *. The church tower contains four bells only, and these, we understood, are seldom put in motion. The noble earl is not of our mind, or he would have a sweet and clear peal of bells so near his mansion, to send forth their lively and soothing " upland" notes over the lands of his tenants and neighbours.

The front of the mansion was then and is now a provoking riddle to us; for we actually cannot make out whether it is intended for the *Italian* or *Norman* style. The bold and handsome projecting porch, with four arches of multiplied mouldings, ought to be the latter; and we are only puzzled by some writers, who ought to be acquainted with the subject on which they are speaking, calling it Italian. But be it what

* " The church is behind the house, and in it are monuments for Sir William Ashburnham, and his lady, daughter of Lord Butler, of Herts; first married to the Earl of Marlborough, who left her a widow, young, rich, and beautiful. The inscription written by Sir William says she was a great lover of, and blessing to, his family. He acknowledges it with the greatest gratitude, and recommends her memory to be cherished by them. Both their figures are whole lengths, in white marble; hers recumbent, leaning on her hand; his, kneeling in a loose gown, and great flowing wig. There is another monument, for his elder brother and his two wives, whose figures, in white marble, are recumbent; he placed between them in armour, one of them in a winding-sheet, the other in a Baroness' robe. The inscription mentions, that his father, through good-nature to his friends, was obliged to sell this place (in his family long before the Conquest) and all the estates he had, not leaving to his wife and six children the least substance; which is not mentioned to the disadvantage of his memory, but, to give God praise, who so suddenly provided for his wife and children, that within two years after his death, there was not one but was in a condition to help others, rather than want support. His first wife made the first step toward the recovery of some part of his inheritance, selling her whole estate to lay out the money in this place. He built this church. This Mr. Ashburnham contrived the escape of Charles I. from Hampton Court."—*Pennant.*

it may, it is neat and handsome, and the view from the terrace in front, over the river-like water, which is said in its whole length to cover fifty acres, and the hanging shrubberies, is very pleasing.   There is little more than this to be seen.   A walled garden, which, when we saw it in autumn, had a splendid collection of *dahlias;* a small conservatory, with some fine orange trees; and a dairy.   The latter is hardly worth exhibiting, though remarkably neat, as well as its presiding nymph.   The walls are lined with Dutch tiles and green trellis, and have some curious old china on shelves, but with no painted glass.   In the centre is a pretty idea, a small fountain flowing from a glass vase, for the purposes of the place; but the three figures which support it should have been of alabaster, or white marble, instead of being common plaster casts.

From Ashburnham to Lewes, eighteen miles distance, is a lonely road, very barren in objects of interest, with the sole grand feature of the distant range of heights near Eastbourne, which is seen at intervals. This road is not distinguished by robberies, but seems towards the approach of night, especially, adapted to the purpose, and may recal to the mind of the imaginative traveller some of the old tales of Fielding or Smollet, in the very different state of England during the first half of the eighteenth century.   We pass through Gardner's-street, a dull village, and soon after leave to the left the tower of Hailsham* with its lofty and elegant pinnacles.   Horse-bridge, the next point, is a hamlet to the parish of Hellingly, whose mean church, with a pointed steeple, is seen on the right. Five miles from hence at Church Laughton, approaching nearer to Lewes, the road begins to get more cheerful, and is well

---

⁎ Hailsham is a small town of little or no historical interest, except that it contained the Priory of Michelham, some remains of which are still in existence: the parish is within the Duchy of Lancaster.   Barracks were built here to accommodate a regiment of infantry during the late war.

The church is tolerably large and handsome, of the date of the fifteenth century.   Hailsham has a cattle market every fortnight on Wednesday, from which the inhabitants of Brighton are principally supplied, as well as those of many other places; and, according to the old proverb, "an ill wind," &c. &c., since the cattle-market at Brighton has not succeeded, the weather-cock of prosperity will be turned back to the former.   In 1831, the number of inhabitants was 1445.

wooded. The church at Laughton, which is at some distance
on the left of the road, appears to have a tower of some pretensions, compared with others in the neighbourhood. A full
account of this parish is given in the History of Lewes. Its
church, though the burial-place of the Pelham family, of
earls, dukes, and bishops, contains no monuments. Laughton-
place, built or repaired in 1534, still remains as a farm-house,
and has a lofty brick tower : the park we have before alluded
to as the scene of the unhappy folly which led to the death of
Lord Dacre. The Pelhams afterwards removed to Halland,
another residence, lying partly in this parish, and subsequently
in the year 1724 to Stanmer.

Mr. Horsefield has given a vignette, and repeated it on the
title page, of two old oak trees on the estate of the Hon. H.
Watson in this parish. To us, however, they present little
that is striking, either in their size or the convolutions of their
branches at the top. We have seen scores of old oaks that
are of grander size and more intricate ramification*. To
specify one instance of size out of a multitude, we would refer
to the oak near Shrewsbury, which Owen Glendowr climbed
as an observatory to view the motions of his enemies; the
girth of which is twenty-seven feet, at the height of eight feet
from the ground.

Ringmer, four miles from Laughton and two and a half
from Lewes, is a handsome and cheerful village. Some have conjectured its ancient name to have been *Regni-mere*, i. e. "*pool*,"
from the ancient name of the inhabitants of the province ; but
this seems far-fetched and doubtful. Broyle, in this parish,
was one of the seats of the Archbishops of Canterbury, and
had a park of 2000 acres in extent containing deer, which
is now applied to the purposes of husbandry. Ordnance barracks were erected here during the late war, now disused,
and part applied to the purpose of a lunatic asylum. For a
full account, however, of the many interesting particulars re-

* On the subject of celebrated forest trees, the curious reader may consult
Strutt's " Sylva Britannica," and " Deliciæ Sylvarum."

lating to these two parishes, we must (as we are not wholesale plunderers) refer the reader to Mr. Horsefield's History of Lewes. The population in 1831 was, *Laughton*, 804; *Ringmer*, 1271.

Ringmer church, on the right of the traveller, is a rather capacious old edifice, of three aisles and two small chapels to the chancel, but disfigured by a modern wooden steeple in lieu of an ancient one which fell into ruin. The interior contains many curious monuments, the inscriptions on which Mr. Horsefield honestly confesses having copied from the "Family Topographer;" and we in turn will trespass on him for the following selected one on William Springett, Esq., who died May 7, 1620, aged 66 :—" a friend to virtue, a lover of learning, of prudence great, of justice a furtherer :"

> " Redress he did the wrongs of many a wight:
> Fatherless and widows by him possess their right:
> To search and try each cause, and end all strife,
> With patience great, he spent his mortal life.
> Whom blessed, we account (as Scripture saith),
> Who peace did make, and liv'd and died in faith."

There is a foundation school, dated 1695, since enlarged to a national one. A Miss Hay, of the very honourable family of that name in this county, left 2000*l*. Bank Stock, the interest to be paid quarterly to a certain number of aged and deserving poor in Glynde and Ringmer,—a noble act and worthy of imitation. A full account will be found in Mr. Horsefield's 2d vol. p. 124, of the Rev. Mr. Tutté of these two places, son-in-law of William Hay, Esq. the author, a singularly happy, beneficent, hospitable, and venerable character, who died in 1823, aged 94.

Two miles after leaving Ringmer we enter the ancient town of Cliffe, or St. Thomas à Beckett's, the eastern suburb of Lewes. The long sweep of rock, extending south-east, which shelters the street, gives it a very romantic appearance, and there is an air of pleasantness and comfort about this suburb: the view of the castle, and the back of the town of Lewes, sloping off to the west, is interesting; and the effect of the various distant lights, on a dark evening, highly picturesque. Making an angle to the right, and passing the church, we come to the small bridge (rebuilt in 1727, and since widened) over the insignificant river Ouse, which leads up a remarkably steep and hilly street into the borough of

LEWES.

HISTORY.

As the history of Lewes has been two or three times written, and lately diffusely and ably, and extensively circulated in the county of Sussex, we shall dismiss this part of the subject in the smallest possible number of lines, merely sufficient to direct the attention of visitors to points of observation.

The earliest authentic records, doubtless, commence with the Roman sway, when it is thought to have been the station *Mutuantonis.*

" Mutuantonis or Mantuantonis, was a mutation or mansion, situate by a water or river: so is Lewes situate; and a wide water it was at that time of day no doubt, except just at that point of the Down which thrusts forward towards the opposite Down, called Cliffe-hill, so as almost to meet it, leaving only a narrow pass between the river and land-floods. On this protended arm of the Downs stands the town of Lewes, the Mutuantonis or Mantuantonis of Ravenna's; and the next station is Lyme in Kent, or Lemannis. Here again lies an objection, the distance being too great without any other mutation from Lewes to Lyme. To remove this objection we find in the Notitia (tho' not in Ravenna's) the City Anderida, since found to be Eastbourn in Sussex, about eighteen miles from Lewes, as the next stage, and from thence to Lyme is one day's journey.

" In this rout of Ravenna's there is, I think, one mutation wanting; from Sylcester in Hants to Farnham in Surry is about one day's journey; from thence to Midhurst is less than another day; from Midhurst to Lewes is rather more than one day, as we must suppose the road got rid of the wild and sought the Downs soon as it conveniently could, so that this stage seems to want one mutation only; in all other respects, it agrees pretty well.

" And instead of going from Midhurst to Chichester 'tis much more reasonable to suppose the travellers or soldiers on a march, soon as they recovered the top of the Downs from Midhurst, edged away to the east and passed the Arundell river, either at Houghton Bridges or Arundell, made the streightest course thence to Shoreham river by Bramber and over Beeding-hill by Patcham, Hollingbury, Stanmer, and Falmer to Lewes, and over the river at Lewes to Glynd and Firle and up the Downs, there to Eastbourn or Anderida, from thence to Lyme in Kent, and so on to Dover."—*Burrell MSS.*

CONCERNING THE ROMAN COURTS OF JUSTICE AND ROADS.

" 'Tis improbable the inhabitants of the county should be sent to Winchester or Sandwich for any purposes of civil government: it must have been much nearer; it must have been at *Regnum* or *Chichester* for the western part; at or about *Lewes* for the midland part; and at *Anderida*, a place of strength towards the east; and, probably, at *Winchelsea, Hastings*, or *Rye*, for the easternmost parts. The province was called *Britannia Prima*. Rhutupis or Sandwich was the head colony of that province: all the settlements of the Romans, great and small, in that province were immediately subordinate to Sandwich, where the legion lay; Lewes one way and Eastborne another way, took in all the intermediate districts. Roads were as well necessary for these purposes as for the communication and march of the Roman military and convoys to relieve or reinforce their garrisons, and supply them with the necessary provisions in summer and winter. It was not possible for the Roman government to subsist without such free and safe intercourse from fort to fort, and from settlement to settlement, in a long chain throughout the kingdom. Rebellions were frequent among the oppressed natives, smarting under Roman oppression. These could not be kept under, but by chains of forts intercoursing with each other. On the first alarm the whole Roman force, thus communicating, were instantly up in arms against the divided natives, and easily quelled any insurrection. The artificial ford at Glynd can't be supposed to have led from Anderida or Eastborne to any other place than Lewes, where is the nighest pass over the broad Æstuary, that then lay below and above it; and at this place nature has formed such a fortification as can't be found again in the whole county, and where a very little art would render it a place of great strength for a Roman garrison: and that it was a Roman settlement (tho' not to be found by any known name, unless it were that of *Trisanton, Mantuantonis,* or *Mutuantonis*, amongst those handed down to us by all the Roman Itineraries) there can remain but little doubt: for the objection that their force might communicate by sea, from port to port, will not answer, as such a communication must have been too precarious and inadequate to a people in arms in their inland towns and fastnesses, and nothing but a communication by land could effectually reduce them to obedience, and keep them under from time to time:—therefore, after a march of eighteen miles from Eastborne, some fort or hold, garrisoned by Roman soldiers, was necessary at Lewes to receive and refresh their military in their marches."—Mr. Elliott.—*Burrell MSS.*

The origin of its present castle is supposed to have been a considerable time before the Conquest, and has been sometimes attributed to Alfred. King Athelstan established *two* mints in Lewes, considered to be an indication of very great consequence at that period. At the æra of Doomsday it had been made the chief seat and barony of the Earls de Warren, who possessed the whole rape. Was the scene of the great

engagement between the barons under Simon de Montfort*
and Henry III. In 1266 its lord, John de Warren, obtained
a murage grant from Henry III. to fortify the town, with
the aid of several dues and customs. It had a market established soon after the Conquest, and a merchant Guild, of great
eminence ; a Cluniac Priory, founded at the conclusion of the
thirteenth century, by the first Earl de Warren, and Gundreda his wife, whose annual revenue, at the dissolution,
amounted to the clear sum of 920*l.* It had formerly, including
its suburbs of Cliffe, Westout, and Southover, thirteen churches,
which are now reduced to six.

NEWSPAPER EXTRACTS.

" *Lewes, Aug.* 15, 1774.— On Monday evening last the spire of Berwick
Church was set on fire and consumed by lightning."

" 1782.—Last Tuesday and Wednesday the 10th regiment of dragoons
quitted their quarters in this town, and other parts of the county, and
marched on their route for Salisbury.

" Last Wednesday and Thursday, three troops of Lord Sheffield's light
dragoons marched through this town on their route from Coxheath-Camp
to winter cantonments. The men appeared remarkably healthy, and no
way affected by the severe season, or rigid field duty, to which a well dis-
ciplined regiment of light-horse must necessarily have been subject.

" The above regiment may now literally be said to be composed of gentlemen of fortune, being (as we are credibly informed) intitled to the
capital sum of 3,000*l.*, gloriously obtained in the service of their country,
by defeating a very formidable and dangerous gang of riotous smugglers,
assembled, upwards of twelve months since, at Deal, in Kent, from whom
they seized contraband goods, producing the sum above-mentioned as their
share."

" *Oct.* 15, 1792.—Very few emigrants have lately landed on our coast.—
Eight French clergymen debarked at Seaford, from an open boat, in great
distress, last Thursday ; Mr. Harben, of Corsica Hall, found them in the
hands of men not of the most liberal cast, from whose *importunities* he rescued
them ; and having humanely relieved them, he forwarded the unfortunate
men to Lord Sheffield's seat, about twenty miles from thence, where they
were, as others have been, very hospitably received and entertained. We
hear his lordship has recommended them to the committee in London.
They came from Paris about ten days ago, and we learn the history of some
of them is uncommonly affecting. Two had been confined in the same
place with the bishops and clergy who were massacred ; and they did not
effect their escape until they had been eye-witnesses to the cool and de-

---

* We never meet with this name without being reminded of the ballad of
" *Pretty Bessee,*" in Dr. Percy's collection, which is founded on it.

liberate murder of the venerable Archbishop of Arles and near 120 bishops and clergy."

" *Sep.* 24.—There was a meeting at the Star in this town last Thursday, for the purpose of concerting the best means of uniting the exertions of this country in favour of those who by unexampled barbarity are driven on our coast. Gentlemen attended from different parts of the country to give information of what had been done. The meeting entered into several resolutions, and appointed a committee to correspond with similar committees at London, and to pursue such measures as might best procure for the oppressed refugees, an hospitable reception, and a safe and unmolested conveyance to London or elsewhere. It was observed by Lord Sheffield, from the chair, that the arrival of these unfortunate persons was not a matter of choice. That we could not shut the door against the offending misery. That if we rejected or refused relief to men in their distressed situation, it would be an everlasting reproach on the national character, which had been famed for generosity and humanity. That the notion of their causing a scarcity could not seriously be believed by any man of reflection. That if ten times the number should arrive, it would be imperceptible in the consumption of provisions within this island. That the rise of meat had taken place before they had arrived in any number, and that the increased price of corn happens, of course, in consequence of the alarm of a bad harvest. It was further observed, that on the return of the three or four regiments from our foreign garrisons, or even of twenty or thirty regiments on the conclusion of a war, that no man ever pretended to be alarmed on account of a scarcity of provisions. It does not appear that more than eleven or twelve hundred have landed in Sussex, and that almost all of them go to London. To the honour of the country it should be mentioned, that they have been every where treated in their passage through it with all the attention and kindness which circumstances would admit."

" *Sept.* 10, 1792.—On Wednesday and Thursday last no less than one hundred and seventy French emigrants, mostly priests, were landed from the packets, and an open boat, at Brighton. More are daily arriving, and many of them are observed to labour under very distressed circumstances.

" On Friday and Saturday last near three hundred unfortunate Frenchmen of the above description were put on shore at East-Bourne, many of whom were very hospitably received by Lord George Cavendish, Lord Bayham, A. Piggott, Esq., and many other of the nobility and gentry of that place. They afterwards took different routes for the metropolis. Many from the above place, and Brighton, came to this town; and such as could not get places on the stage-coach hired carts for their conveyance. Five of them, seemingly of a superior order, who brought a letter of recommendation to a gentleman of this town, have fixed their abode here.

" We have just heard, that yesterday morning near one thousand more of the above unfortunate people landed at East-Bourne.

" Last night a post-chaise and waggon, heavily laden with them, arrived at the Star Inn in this town.

" Last week the ground for the erection of barracks near Lewes was con-tracted for. The quantity is four acres, lying on the south side of Hare-dean spring, as good a situation as could be chosen for the purpose. They are to be completed, we understand, in the course of six weeks, and made sufficient for the accommodation of 1,000 men."

" 1794.—Lewes fair, last week, was the best stocked of any known on the South Downs for many years past: it is supposed that there were not less than 48,000 ewes, lambs, and wethers in the several pens. The prices were higher than looked for even by the stock-masters, owing to the great increase of late grass, and the success of the Kentish farmers in their hop plantations, who were thus enabled to buy freely and largely. The Elmans, both of Glynd and Shoreham, as usual, bore away the bell beyond all com-parison. The best prices obtained were,

	£.	s.	d.	
"Sheerling Wethers, . . .	25	0	0	per score.
Draft Ewes, . . .	22	0	0	ditto.
Wether Lambs, . .	17	0	0	ditto.
Ewe ditto, . . .	14	10	0	ditto."

" 1803.—The erection of new barracks at Spital-hill, near Lewes, com-menced to-day, where, for which purpose, thirty acres of ground have been recently purchased by Government."

DESCRIPTION.
CASTLE.

This building is chiefly remarkable for having had *two* Keeps, raised on mounds within the enclosure of its walls; one at the western extremity remains in a tolerably perfect state, and has a very commanding appearance, impending over the street of the town, and picturesquely covered with ivy. The ruins of this castle are however far from interesting, very little of the primary features of architecture are discernible, and though it has been liberally repaired, this has been done in a very modernized and mediocre style. A large square tower at the entrance, probably of the 14th or 15th centuries, battle-mented and machicollated, is the most ornamental part. The view however from hence is very pleasing, and will repay the ascent.

PRIORY.

The remains of this building, which was situated on a low spot near the river at Southover, are inconsiderable. The principal are a large and smaller arch at the eastern end of the churchyard, which are neat specimens of the 13th century.

A mound near the priory has been lately conjectured to have been a Calvary, a place for exhibiting annually a representation of the crucifixion of our Saviour.

The walk from the high street by a steep descent, and a lane winding through trees and ruins, has a romantic air, and is pleasant in summer.

TOWN HALL AND COUNTY SESSIONS-HOUSE.

This edifice, which was erected in 1812 at an expense of little more than £10,000, has its front in the High-street, to which it is unquestionably a greater ornament than the huge Town Hall is to any part of Brighton. Its dimensions are 80 feet by 76. The front of stone, having pillars in the centre of the basements and rustic work in the wings, is remarkably neat, and even handsome, and has three of the boldest and most graceful allegorical groups that we have ever witnessed. The interior, in addition to convenient courts, has a very handsome ball-room, 60 feet long, 30 broad, and 27 high, decorated with paintings and statues.

CHURCHES.

ST. THOMAS A BECKETT'S, CLIFFE,

has three small aisles and a chancel, and a decent square tower. Its south side, which is open to the street, has been lately improved, and rendered neat ; the north side, as Brighton church was lately, is disfigured by the vile *shutters,* which are surely to be seen no-where else but in Sussex. Allowing the possibility of their absence causing an expenditure of 40s. per annum for broken panes, that is scarcely an object to be put in competition with perpetual disfigurement. The interior of this church is neat, has galleries of wainscot over the greater part of the aisles, and a good organ, painted white and gold, with two tall angels of gilt brass on its summit, brought from the seat of the 'magnificent' Duke of Chandos at Canons. The altar, of the Doric order, with white and gold fluted columns, is handsome, and the east end, which has no window, is further decorated. Above the north aisle is an excellent painting of the Ascension, given by B. Vander Gutcht, Esq. in 1779; and the pulpit, &c. has been recently refitted with crimson velvet and gold fringe. The tower contains four bells and a clock.

This parish, town, or suburb, contained in 1831, 1408 inhabitants. The church is considered as the head of the *Peculiars* of the Archbishop of Canterbury in Sussex, and was visited by him as such in 1832. We were truly glad to see that this mild and unobtrusive, and very benevolent and charitable man was here treated with cordiality and respect.

** ST. JOHN'S, UNDER THE CASTLE,

is a small and mean edifice, consisting of the nave only of a very ancient one, which was ruinated and disused in the time of Camden, but has been since repaired. Its architecture has been considered to indicate a Saxon æra, and it has some masonry of the herring-bone style, which is either included from some Roman original, or an imitation of it. Its principal curiosity is an antique gravestone, which has been assigned to a son of Harold, and has the following inscription, partly complete and conjecturally restored :

" Clauditur hic miles, Danaorum regia proles,
Mangnus nomen ei, Mangnæ nota progeniei :
Deponens Mangnum se moribus induit agnum
Prepete pro vitâ, fit parvulus anachorita."

For further particulars of this monument, the reader may consult the history of Lewes. The intervention of an ' *n*' has been apparently considered as no bar to the punning turns which the monks were so ready to avail themselves of on every occasion.

The interior contains a fine painting, in the style of Rembrandt, the Presentation of young Children to our Saviour. The parish contained in 1831, 2421 inhabitants.

** ALL SAINTS.

The body of this church was decently rebuilt with brick in the year 1807: the dimensions are 80 feet by 40, divided into two aisles, and it will contain 650 persons. The expense did not much exceed £2000. The old tower at the west end rises very slightly above the roof. The interior has a good painting of St. John the Baptist in prison, brought from Italy and presented by the late Earl of Chichester, and a powerful organ. Population in 1831, 2112.

ST. PETER'S, MARY'S, AND ANNE'S, WESTOUT,

Called St. Anne's,

the remaining church of three parishes, is a very ancient structure, in good preservation. It has a long nave, a south aisle, which is not indicated by its external appearance, 11 feet 3 inches wide, and a chancel. The tower at the west end has an obtuse shingled spire. The architecture is mixed Norman and early Gothic; of the three arches of the nave, two are pointed and one round; each of the capitals of the circular columns rests on four neat corbels, which has a pleasing and not very usual effect; the arch of the chancel is circular, and at its east end are three lancet windows. The church contains a very elegant monument of white marble, and a neat organ. The font is Norman, with handsome reticulated work. £100 was given for the repairing, &c., of this church by Herbert Springett, Esq., in 1620. Population in 1831, 746.

ST. MICHAEL'S, IN THE MARKET,

consists of three aisles, and was partly rebuilt in 1755 at an expense of £1366: its front, of squared flint, with stone window and door frames, is remarkably neat; at the west end is a low round tower and slender spire, a vestry, and projecting clock. The interior is very neat, but has no organ; the east window is ornamented with plain stained glass, neatly disposed, with a large red cross in the centre, given by the present Rector, Dr. Proctor. In the north aisle is the monument of Sir Nicholas Pelham, 1559, which has two short Corinthian or composite columns, and many kneeling figures.

> "His valour's proofe, his manlie vertues prayse,
> Cannot be marshalled in this narrow roome;
> His braue exploit in great King Henry's dayes
> Among the worthye hath a worthier tombe:
> What time the French sought to have sack't Sea-Foord
> This Pelham did repel 'em back aboord."

"*Pel*ham" and "*repel*'em" was, we imagine, intended as wit by the "word torturers" of a punning age. Population in 1831, 1074.

has a nave, south aisle, and chancel, and a respectable brick tower, rebuilt in the early part of the last century, at the expense of 481*l*. 15*s*. 4*d*., and containing, by gradual additions, eight bells: three small pieces of carving, brought from the Priory, are inlaid in as many of its sides. The south aisle was added after the Reformation. This church has two old indifferent paintings, and a neat organ, lately presented by a lady in the parish: but its greatest attraction is the tomb of Gundreda, daughter of William the Conqueror, and wife to the first Earl de Warren, which had been removed, at the dissolution, from the chapter-house of the priory to Isfield, and was restored to this neighbouring situation of its original one by William Burrell, Esq. in 1775. It is of black marble, sculptured with foliage, in a fine early style, and bearing around its edge the following inscription, with slight conjectural supplements, in characters which have been verified as Norman, and of the eleventh or early part of the twelfth century:—

" STIRPS GUNDREDA DUCUM, DECUS EVI, NOBILE GERMEN,
INTULIT ECCLESIIS ANGLORUM BALSAMA MORUM, *
MARTHA FUIT MISERIS, FUIT EX PIETATE MARIA ;
PARS OBIIT MARTHE, SUPEREST PARS MAGNA MARIE.
O PIE, PANCRATI TESTIS PIETATIS ET EQUI,
TE FECIT HEREDEM, TU CLEMENS SUSCIPE MATREM.
SEXTA KALENDARUM JUNII LUX OBVIA CARNIS
IFREGIT ALABASTRUM."

The author of the History of Lewes has given a neat poetical version; but we prefer offering a prose one, in which the simple tenor of the original will not be in the least rendered subservient to rhyme and metre.

" Gundred, of Ducal race, the ornament of her age, a noble bud,-Brought into the churches of England the balsam of morals-She was a Martha to the wretched; she was, for piety, a Mary: The part of Martha has died, the mighty

---

* The rhyming of the penultimate with the middle syllable of the verse was a very favourite ornament with the monks, and others, in the middle ages. Critics have noticed similar instances in Virgil and Ovid.
" —— Cornua velatarum obvertimus antennarum."—VIR.

part of Mary survives. - O, holy Pancras! witness of her piety
and righteousness,-She made thee her heir; do thou, benign, receive a mother-The hostile dawn of the sixth calend of June-
Broke the alabaster of flesh."

The parish contained, in 1831, 831 inhabitants.

There are several Dissenting chapels in Lewes; one, near
the bridge, has a neat Ionic front.

MISCELLANEOUS.

Several schools, alms-houses, and charitable associations, in
Lewes, indicate liberality on the part of its inhabitants. The
county jail *₊* is said to be decent and appropriate. There
are two or three superior libraries, a small Theatre, Horti-
cultural Society, Mechanics' Institution, &c. &c.

The bridge over the narrow river Ouse is an old one, of one
arch; its upper part has been widened, and the whole rendered
neat.

Near the town is a celebrated old mound, called *Mount Caburn*, supposed to have been originally a Roman camp. A
poem on this subject, of great merit, was written by Mr. Hay,
and includes an extensive range of local allusions.

The town has several good inns, as the Star, Crown, White
Hart, &c. &c., and several academies, and teachers. The streets
are neatly paved, and kept very clean, and the general aspect
of the town indicates much comfort: its total population is
about 9000.

Lewes has returned two members to Parliament since the
year 1298. The market-house, which, internally, forms a
small square, was rebuilt of brick in 1793; at its entrance is a
belfrey, containing a fine-toned old clock bell, called Saint
Gabriel's, brought from the ruined church of St. Nicholas,
and weighing about 18 cwt. The markets for provisions,
cattle, sheep, and corn, are considerable, as are also the fairs:
races are held at the end of July. Lewes is celebrated for
its breweries, and has one steam paper-mill, the proprietor of
which has also another at Isfield. It had formerly a considerable trade in wool; now it is principally confined to grain

and malt, and other articles of provision; it imports a considerable quantity of malt, by the Ouse, from Newhaven, for
the supply of the adjacent country.

Leaving the western extremity of Lewes, on the hill beyond
St. Ann's church, is a fine view over the Downs on the left
towards Rottingdean, and also a pleasing retrospective one of
the upper part of the town of Lewes, and the lower suburb of
Southover, with the large and rich meadows in that vicinity.
Descending into a valley we come to Ashcombe Gate; the
turnpike-houses here are of rather ambitious construction, of
a circular form, with pillars at the entrances, and will, perhaps, strike the traveller as unusually handsome. On the
left is a plain house agreeably situated, lately purchased by
Sir G. Shiffner, whose principal seat is at Coombe Place, in
this neighbourhood. The road continues nearly flat between
hills till the ascent to *Falmer*. In various parts of the road
from Lewes to Brighton we meet with spacious and venerable
looking farm-houses and buildings, affording no uncheering
idea of the agricultural state of the district. The mansion at
Falmer occupied by H. Rogers, Esq. is on the left, agreeably
situated amongst some fine old trees, and close by it is the
church, which was neatly but ordinarily rebuilt of brick, in the
present century. Interesting particulars of this parish are
contained in the " History of Lewes." The population is
about 500. In Pope Nicholas' taxation, " P'or de Lewes
apud Faleme £54. 0s. 0d¾." and " Eccl'ia de Faleme cum
Burg, (als Bercheme) £13. 6s. 8d. P'or Lewens'. " At the
bottom of the hill on which the few houses of the village stand
is *Stanmer Park*, the seat of the Earl of Chichester. Persons on foot or on horseback, are allowed to pass through
this park, but carriages are excluded, except those of privileged individuals. The park is very pleasingly wooded,
which was effected by the superintendence and assiduity
of the late Earl of Chichester. No water is however apparent, and if there are any ponds or streams, they must be
of an insignificant nature. The ride through this park

may in fine weather be strongly recommended to the visitors of Brighton : it is a favourite drive of his present Majesty. The house near the farthest end presents two stone fronts of very neat but perfectly plain architecture, and was built in 1724 : of the interior, we are unable to give any account*. The small church a little further to the right, has a very pretty appearance, with a neat spire, a restored window at the east end, which is mantled with ivy, and two curious old yew-trees in the churchyard : the village is just without the park gate. The park contains nearly the whole of the parish, and extends into those of Falmer and Ditchling.

Returning to the entrance of the park, and emerging into the high road, which, it may here be mentioned, in its course from Brighton to Lewes, is considered to be one of the very best in the kingdom, no material object occurs till we reach the horse barracks before alluded to ; and soon after the stately tower of the new church appears, to give a friendly welcome to the " Great Babylon" of water-ing-places,

> " Whose ivory throne
> Is by the side of many azure waters."

" * August 1782.—On Tuesday last, her Royal Highness Princess Amelia, attended by Lady Amelia Carr, &c. set out on a visit to Lord and Lady Pelham, at their seat at Stanmer, near Lewes ; a mark of Her Royal Highness's condescending gratitude for the invariable attachment of that family to hers. On Thursday Her Royal Highness, attended by Lord and Lady Pelham, visited Brighthelmstone, and was much delighted with the view of the sea and the Steine ; and after having subscribed to the two rooms, library, music, &c. her Royal Highness returned to Stanmer, from whence she set out on Friday for Gunnersbury."

MICHAEL DRAYTON'S ACCOUNT OF THE SUSSEX COAST,

WITH THE ORIGINAL NOTES, 1612.

Polyolbion,

SEVENTEENTH SONG OF THE RIVER THAMES, AD FINEM.

———

" Here suddenly he staid; and with his kingly song,
Whilst yet on every side the city loudly rong,
He with the eddy turn'd, a space to look about:
The tide, retiring soon, did strongly thrust him out.
And soon the pliant muse, doth her brave wing advance,
Towards those sea-bordering shores of ours, that point at France,
The harder Surrian heath, and the Sussexian down,
Which with so great increase though nature do not crown,
As many other shires, of this environ'd isle:
Yet on the weather's head, when as the sun doth smile,
Nurst by the southern winds, that soft and gently blow,
Here doth the lusty sap as soon begin to flow;
The earth as soon puts on her gaudy summer's suit;
The woods as soon in green, and orchards great with fruit.
" To sea-ward, from the seat where first our song begun,
Exhaled to the south by the ascending sun,
Four stately wood nymphs stand on the Sussexian ground,
Great Andredsweld's* sometime: who, when she did abound,
In circuit and in growth, all other quite suppress'd:
But in her wane of pride, as she in strength decreased,
Her nymphs assumed them names, each one to her delight.
As Water-down, so call'd of her depressed site:

———

* " All that maritime tract comprehending Sussex, and part of Kent (so much
as was not mountains, now called the Downs, which in British, old Gaulish,
Low Dutch, and our English, signifies but hills) being all woody, was called
Andredsweald, i. e. Andred's wood, often mentioned in our stories, and
Newenden in Kent by it Andredcester (as most learned Camden upon good
reason guesses) whence perhaps the wood had his name. To this day we call
those woody lands, by north the Downs, the Weald; and the channel of the
river that comes out of those parts, and discontinues the Downs about Bramber,
is yet known in Shoreham ferry, by the name of Weald-ditch; and, in another
Saxon word equivalent to it, are many of the parishes' terminations on this side
of the Downs, that is, Herst, or Hurst, i. e. a wood. It is called by Ethelwerd
expressly *Immanis sylva, que vulgò* Andredsuuda *nuncupatur,* and was cxx miles
long, and xxx broad. The author's conceit of these forests being nymphs of
this great Andredsuuda, and their complaint for loss of woods, in Sussex, so
decayed, is plain enough to every reader."

And Ash-down, of those trees that most in her do grow,
Set higher to the Downs, as the other standeth low.
Saint Leonard's, of the seat by which she next is placed,
And Whord that with the like deligheth to be graced.
These forests as I say, the daughters of the Weald
(That in their heavy breasts, had long their griefs conceal'd)
Foreseeing their decay each hour so fast came on,
Under the axe's stroke, fetch many a grievous groan,
When as the anvil's weight, and hammer's dreadful sound,
Even rent the hollow woods, and shook the queachy ground.
So that the trembling nymphs, oppress'd through ghastly fear,
Ran madding to the Downs, with loose dishevel'd hair.
The Sylvans that about the neighbouring woods did dwell,
Both in the tufty frith and in the mossy fell,
Forsook their gloomy bowers, and wander'd far abroad,
Expell'd their quiet seats, and place of their abode,
When labouring carts they saw to hold their daily trade,
Where they in summer wont to sport them in the shade.
Could we, say they, suppose, that any would us cherish,
Which suffer (every day) the holiest things to perish?
Or to our daily want to minister supply?
These iron times breed none, that mind posterity.
'Tis but in vain to tell what we before have been,
Or changes of the world, that we in time have seen;
When, not devising how to spend our wealth with waste,
We to the savage swine let fall our larding mast.
But now, alas! ourselves we have not to sustain,
Nor can our tops suffice to shield our roots from rain,
Jove's oak, the warlike ash, vein'd elm, the softer beech,
Short hazel, maple plain, light asp, the bending wych,
Tough holly, and smooth birch, must altogether burn:
What should the builder serve, supplies the forger's turn;
When under public good, base private gain takes hold,
And we, poor woful woods, to ruin lastly sold.
   " This utter'd they with grief: and more they would have spoke,
But that the envious Downs, into open laughter broke;
As joying in those wants, which nature them had given,
Since to as great distress the forests should be driven.
Like him that long time hath another's state envied,
And sees a following ebb, unto his former tide;
The more he is depress'd, and bruised with fortune's might,
The larger rein his foe doth give to his despite:
So did the envious Downs; but that again the floods
(Their fountains that derive, from those unpitied woods,
And so much grace thy Downs, as through their dales they creep,
Their glories to convey unto the Celtic deep)
It very hardly took, much murmuring at their pride.
Clear Levant, that doth keep the Southamptonian side
(Dividing it well near from the Sussexian lands
That Selsey doth survey, and Solent's troubled sands)

To Chichester their wrongs impatiently doth tell:
And Arun* (which doth name the beauteous Arundel)
As on her course she came, it to her forest told.
Which, nettled with the news, had not the power to hold:
But breaking into rage, wish'd tempests them might rive;
And on their barren scalps still flint and chalk might thrive,
The brave and nobler woods which basely thus upbraid.
And Adur† coming on, to Shoreham softly said,
The Downs did very ill, poor woods so to debase.
But now, the Ouse, a nymph of very scornful grace,
So touchy wax'd therewith, and was so squeamish grown,
That her old name she scorn'd should publicly be known.
Whose haven out of mind when as it almost grew,
The lately passed times denominate, the New.
So Cucmer with the rest put to her utmost might:
As Ashburne undertakes to do the forests right
(At Pemsey, where she pours her soft and gentler flood)
And Asten once distain'd with native English blood;
(Whose soil, when yet but wet with any little rain,
‡ Doth blush, as put in mind of those there sadly slain,
When Hastings' harbour gave unto the Norman powers,
Whose name and honours now are denizen'd for ours)
That boding ominous brook, it through the forests rung;
Which echoing it again the mighty Weald along,
Great stir was like to grow; but that the muse did charm
Their furies, and herself for nobler things did arm."

---

* " So it is conjectured, and is without controversy justifiable if that be the name of the river. Some fable it from Arundel, the name of Bevis' horse: it were so as tolerable as Bucephalon, from Alexander's horse, Tymenna in Lycia from a goat of that name, and such like, if time would endure it; but Bevis was about the Conquest, and this town is by name of Erundele, known in time of King Alfred, who gave it with others to his nephew Athelm. Of all men, Goropius had somewhat a violent conjecture, when he derived Harondell from a people called Charudes (in Ptolemy, towards the utmost of the now Jutland), part of whom he imagines (about the Saxon and Danish irruptions) planted themselves here, and by difference of dialect, left this as a branch sprung of their country title."

† " This river that here falls into the ocean might well be understood in that port of Adur, about this coast, the relicks whereof, learned Camden takes to be Edrington, or Adrington, a little from Shoreham. And the author here so calls it Adur."

‡ " In the plain near Hastings, where the Norman William, after his victory, found King Harold slain, he built Battle Abbey, which at last (as divers other monasteries) grew to a town enough populous. Thereabout is a place which after rain always looks red, which some have (by that authority, the muse also) attributed to a very bloody sweat of the earth, as crying to Heaven for revenge of so great a slaughter."

WESTERN COAST.

BRIGHTON TO CHICHESTER.

Setting out from the western extremity of Brighton, and entering on the road beyond Adelaide terrace, we pass through the few houses forming the village of Hove, and leave its now humble church on the right, and emerge into an open and wild country, with few objects chequering its flat and uninteresting surface. Soon afterwards, however, the road attains an elevation above the sea, and displays the inlet of the sea from Shoreham harbour, which flows up in a recursive direction for nearly two miles at high-water. The view opens a little here into the interior of the country, and exhibits the insignificant ruins of the destroyed village and church of Aldrington ; the more pleasing locality of Portslade, with its gray church on a hill, surrounded by foliage, and the villages of Kingston and Southwick.

⁎ PORTSLADE.

" North-east of Kingston, about one mile and a half, between two hills, lies the small village of Portslade, between three and four miles from Brighthelmstone ; it contains several good houses, and has an old church, that cannot boast of much beauty, though it may of antiquity ; it has a low square tower at the west end, embattled with nave and chancel, the former much altered, and the latter of the early simple pointed style."— *Gent.'s Mag.* 1814.

⁎ KINGSTON.

" The church is but part of a larger edifice, and had formerly a lofty tower, though now it rises little above the roof; it is in the centre, and supported by a very large buttress at the north-west angle; the whole of very early date, substantial and picturesque."—*Ib.*

⁎ SOUTHWICK.

" One mile and a half beyond this, in a westerly direction, is the pretty and extensive village of Southwick, finely situated and beautifully interspersed with trees. It has a highly curious and interesting church, with a tower, at the west end, of three stories, the first being plain, the second containing ten Saxon windows, and the third two early pointed arches; they are surmounted by a block coned, and a good proportioned, though not high, spire, covered with lead, and terminated by a vane. The walls of the nave and chancel are Saxon; by the arches still remaining, there was an aisle formerly on the north, but none on the south side; there are two early pointed windows on the south side of the chancel, the rest of a later date. The entrance is by a porch at the south side.' Population in 1831, 502.—*Ib.*

Pope Nicholas' Taxation :

	£.	s.	d.
Eccl'ia de Aldrinton	10	13	4
Eccl'ia de Porteslade	20	0	0
Vicar' ejusdem	6	13	4
Eccl'ia de Kingestone jux' Scorham .	16	13	4
P'or de Suthwyk *, Ag'culta' et redditus de Wisseborn als Fisseburn . .	2	1	4
Prior de Sea, in Sutewyk deci'a . .	3	6	8

" All along the sea-coast between Shoreham and Brighthelmstone is found washed up bituminous substances, exactly agreeing with the description of the kimerage coal, called by the inhabitants *strumbolo,* and which, till of late years, was the chief fuel of the poor inhabitants of Brighthelmstone, who were very careful to pick it up after it was brought up by the tide; but since that town has become more populous, by the resort of the gentry, it has grown out of use, on account of the nauseous smell it emits at burning. As no stratum of this fossil is to be found in the cliffs on the coast of Sussex, it must consequently be formed at the bottom of the sea, and by the violent agitation of the water be torn up and brought on shore by the tide."

Having neglected to mark this extract, we have forgotten whether it was derived from " Pennant's Tour," or from the History of Eastbourne, 1787, before alluded to.

Kingston displays much naval traffic, and is an auxiliary to Shoreham. On approaching this port, the scene is of a cheerful and active character, indicating no small degree of business and acquisition; there is perhaps no port on the southern coast, with the exception of the public arsenals, which displays this feature in a higher degree. The effect of the harbour is totally different at high and low water, from the circumstance of its being a tide harbour. The piers are humble in their appearance, and the entrance very narrow and difficult from the projecting shoalbank, which, to the most

* We perceive no records of a Priory at Southwick, and are entirely ignorant to what this entry alludes.

inexperienced eye, conveys the impression that great caution must always be necessary to avoid running aground. Between the town and Southwick is an observatory, overlooking the harbour, and the solid central tower of the collegiate-looking church adds its full effect to the appearance of the scattered and moderately peopled town.

Shoreham, i. e. Old Shoreham, is supposed to have been the place of Ælla the Saxon's second landing with reinforcements, a short time previous to his victory near Anderida, which led to the establishment of the kingdom of the south Saxons, comprehending Sussex and Surrey. It was given, with the whole rape, at the Conquest, to the family of Braose, who resided at the castle of Bramber, and by their extensive connexions with Normandy contributed to render this, during three centuries, the greatest port on the southern coast, especially for the importation of wines; they were accused, however, of frequent and rather harassing exactions from the merchants. In the armament of Edward III. at Calais, Shoreham furnished 20 ships and 329 men. After the connexion with Normandy ceased, the town rapidly declined: in 1432, the inhabitants are said to have decreased from 500 to 36 *; perhaps the adult males alone were here computed. Shoreham has returned members to parliament from the 23rd of Edward I.; but from its great corruption the franchise was extended, in 1770, to the whole rape of Bramber. The church was originally a chapel of ease to Old Shoreham, and was given with it by one of the family of Braose to the church of St. Florence at Salmur, or Saumur†. In Pope Nicholas's taxation occur, " Eccl'ia de Vet'i Scorham 24*l*. 0*s*. 0*d*. Eccl'ia de Nova Scorham 10*l*. 0*s*. 0*d*. hb't breve. Prior de Sela." (This was, perhaps, given after it was made a separate parish, or the possessions of St. Florence were confiscated, but, be it as it may, we cannot explain it) — " Prior de Sela in Vet'i Scorham 3*l*. 13*s*. 4*d*." Here was a Carmelite Friary and two hospitals; the seal of one is extant, bearing the inscription — " THE.SELE.OF.OVR.SAVIOR.JESVS.CHRIST.OF.THE. OSPITAL.OF.SHORAM.SUSSEX."

* Cartwright.　　　　† Ibid.

The church dedicated to St. Mary is the choir with side
aisles, transepts, and tower of the ancient building, whose nave
is demolished, except one arch walled up at the end, and supposed to be left as a support to the tower. Mr. Cartwright
describes its former length as 210 feet, but from actual mea-
surement we found it to be the following: nave, 93 feet;
tower, 24; choir, 68; total, 185 only: he also gives the
length of the transept, 92 feet, which we believe to be nearly
10 feet too much; its breadth is 22, and that of the choir
and aisles 52. The external appearance of this church is
striking and noble, exhibiting both the union and contrast of
the Norman or Saxon and early pointed style; its east end
has three fine lancet windows with clustered columns, above,
nearly equal to the window of Rievaux Abbey, in Yorkshire,
and three circular arches below: at the summit is a rude circular
window, with lozenged quatrefoils on each side, and a heavy
cross. The clerestory has five spacious early pointed windows
on each side, and two stupendous flying buttresses from the
side aisles; the windows of the aisles and transepts have been
inserted in the fifteenth century, but the latter have circular
arches above. The tower, about 80 feet high, bears a considerable resemblance to that of St. Alban's Abbey; it has two
tiers of windows, the lower circular, and the upper of the same
form within pointed arches; above are three circles on each
face. The church is not embattled, but has very bold parapets throughout, partially supported by corbels; the windows
have lately been repaired with Caen stone, and the whole is
kept in excellent order.

The interior is both graceful and magnificent, and is considered to be, in the excellent proportions and correct disposition of its mouldings, and the elegance of its arches and pillars,
inferior to few on the Continent. The western arch of the
tower is circular, and 33 feet in height; the others are circular,
but lower. Fine pointed arches, with strong clustered columns,
open from the transepts into the aisles. The roofs of the middle
and side aisles of the choir are vaulted, and the wall of each
aisle is fretted with ten circular arches. The great arches of

division are pointed, and are five in number on each side, springing, on the north side, from alternate octagonal columns with flowered capitals, and circular ones, and on the south side entirely from clustered columns, which are the most beautiful we have ever seen, each consisting of 14 pilasters with flowered capitals, combining the elegance of the Corinthian with the grandeur of the Gothic. The upper story is inferior to several others of the 12th and 13th centuries, especially that of Malmsbury Abbey. In the north clerestory is a gallery, with three plain double arches west, and two handsome trefoil ones east; the vaulting on this side ends above the pillars on handsome corbels. The east end has very rich mouldings; its small central window below has pilasters resembling the Ionic: the altar, of stone, is modern. At the west end is a high plain gallery above the arch, containing an extremely small organ, which forms a poor finish to this end; but the whole of the interior is very neatly fitted up. The tower contains six bells, but one is broken and another damaged. We cannot recommend the ascent, though often undertaken for the sake of the view; it is totally dark, requiring a lantern, and in one part, where it has been repaired, so narrow, that it reminded us of the terrifying predicament of the poor Frenchman in that redoubtable and not-to-be-surpassed-in-interest history, " The Travels of Rolando round the World ;" its summit is also dangerous, having no battlements, and a parapet about a foot high only. Adjoining the churchyard, which is very neat, is a national school.

Shoreham contains about 1500 inhabitants. It is very celebrated for the building of ships, some of which are as large as 700 tons, and sent to orders from a considerable distance. In the last year, a yacht was built here for the Corporation of Dublin.

————

" The receipt of Customs at the Port of Shoreham on foreign goods imported averages about £30,000 a-year, and the declared value of goods exported about £40,000; a great addition is about to take place, more particularly in the receipts,

Shoreham having been approved as a warehousing port for West India, Mediterranean, and other produce, for the reception of which large and commodious warehouses have been built, and others are in progress of erection.

"The number of ships which entered the port during the past year was about 1,200, exceeding 100,000 tons; consisting, principally, of vessels from Russia, Prussia, Norway, America, France, the Netherlands, Spain, and Portugal.

"Shoreham Harbour is a tide harbour, and the best on this line of coast; it was erected in the year 1816, by subscription, in shares, and has proved a very profitable undertaking to the subscribers, the £100 shares being worth £220 per share. The cause of the great prosperity of this work is to be attributed to its proximity to the large and flourishing town of Brighton, from which the seat of business is distant only three miles, Brighton being within the Port of Shoreham. The Steam Navigation Company's packets, plying between Brighton and Dieppe, also embark and disembark their passengers in Shoreham when the weather will not permit them to lie alongside the chain pier.

"An elegant and most commodious Custom-house was erected here in the year 1830 by Mr. Sydney Smirke, which, together with a noble suspension-bridge, built over the river Adur, at the expense of His Grace the Duke of Norfolk, which is intended to be opened in March next, has greatly tended to improve the town, and will shorten the distance between Brighton and Worthing at least two miles, bringing those towns to within ten miles of each other. The bridge was designed and erected under the superintendence of - —— Clark, Esq., civil engineer *."

The bridge alluded to, which forms a striking feature on approaching the town from Worthing, has piers of stone, and bears a greater resemblance to that at Hammersmith, than the Chain Pier of Brighton.

* Obligingly communicated by S. P. Edwards, Esq., Collector of Customs at Shoreham.

Three-quarters of a mile further is the church of Old Shoreham, close by the present wooden bridge, over the Adur, which was erected by annuity subscription, but with a reversion to the Duke of Norfolk, in the year 1781, and finished in ten months. It is 500 feet long, with 32 openings, and 12 feet wide, with two recesses 70 feet by 24. Here was, originally, a ferry, the tolls of which were, in the year 1387, worth 20*l.* per annum *.

Old Shoreham church is considered as the mother church of the county, and, the probability is strong on the side of its having been erected before the Conquest. It has a nave, chancel, two transepts, and centre tower, whose fine circular arches have been stopped up, and miserably disfigured. The north transept is in ruins, as is also the belfry staircase turret, though still used: this is of a square form, which was common in Saxon † or Norman buildings. The chancel has some handsome windows, inserted in the fourteenth century. The interior has four arches, low, but some of them richly ornamented, of immense solidity, and in a very perfect state; the nave end is decently kept. A low, but very rich arch, is on the outside of the south transept. The population does not much exceed 200.

A straight road leads from Shoreham to Worthing, through Lancing; but we proceed, first, five miles on the right to Bramber, the celebrated locality of the barony and castle of the Braoses, and the ancient capital of the rape; well known, also, as one of the notorious rotten boroughs, containing only twenty houses and one hundred inhabitants. The history of this family and barony is one into which our limits and the space we have devoted to the eastern part of the coast absolutely preclude our entering: there exists, also, this difference, before referred to, that the history of the western rapes of the county has been learnedly and diffusely written;

---

* Cartwright.

† The reader will see that we do not meddle with this question, though we have little doubt that many buildings still remaining are *Saxon*. If we mistake not, a Hostelry has been discovered in Southwark, belonging to the priory of Lewes, which has a *date* before the Conquest.

and we therefore refer all readers, who can procure them, to the able works of Dallaway and Cartwright.

Bramber Castle is supposed to have existed before the Conquest, and to have been a residence of the South Saxon kings. Bṛymmbuṛh signifies a "fortified hill," in Saxon. Its area comprises three acres and a rood.

At the entrance is the fragment of a Norman tower, of great solidity; in the centre, the mound of the keep is very plainly discernible. The castle was defended by strong walls, about eight feet thick. On the east side, the valley, through which the Adur now flows, was either covered with water, or was a deep morass, and afforded a still more efficacious barrier. The view from this castle is romantic and beautiful, extending to the Devil's Dyke and Chankbury Hill, a very picturesque old British encampment. The view towards the south-east and north-east is particularly interesting, where the deep and wide moat is now covered with the foliage of small trees, and exhibits, in autumn, every varied hue and colour. The church, at the entrance of the castle, is a small old Saxon one, mantled with ivy, and well kept, but bears the traces of having been formerly of much more extensive dimensions.

One mile further is Steyning, a respectably built town, now containing about 1500 inhabitants, but possessing ancient associations of some grandeur, having derived its name from the Roman via, *Stane*, which led from Arundel to Dorking, having been also the burial place of St. Cuthman, a Saxon saint, of the eighth century, who founded the church, and afterwards, as is reported, of King Ethelwulf, father of Alfred. Its Saxon appellation was Ꞅꞇenꞁnꝣham, from *staen*, a stone; and, at the Norman valuation, it was divided between William de Braose * and the abbey of Fiscamp, to which it had been granted by Edward the Confessor: the value of the former was upwards

* William de Braose possessed the town and port of Shoreham, toll and *arrinage* there with all its appurtenances, and a free market on two days in the week, viz., Friday and Sunday, and a fair of two days at the feast of the exaltation of the holy cross; also assize of bread and beer, wreck, by the sea-coast as far as his Barony extended, and chase *(chacia)* by his own mariners of Shoreham from *Benches* as far as the Isle of Wight, and to the middle of the sea.—*Bodleian MSS. Burrell.*

of 100*l.*, then an immense annual income ; had 67 hides, 123 messuages, four mills, and two churches *. In 1279, Steyning had a market twice in the week, viz. on Wednesdays and Saturdays. The former still remains, with a cattle market every fortnight, and three fairs. The possessions of Fiscamp were, on the dissolution of alien priories †, granted to the abbey of Sion, in Middlesex, by Edward IV. having been previously, on the petition of Parliament, taken into the royal hands in the year 1415. The tithes of the parish and the dues of the borough, which were in their possession, alone amounted, in 1309, to the sum of 95*l.* ‡. Steyning returned members to Parliament from the year 1278 §.

The church is the choir of the original one, with a modern tower, erected about the reign of Queen Elizabeth, at the ancient intersection, and a modern chancel, which was repaired by the late Duke of Norfolk. The tower, which is square and massy, scarcely rises above the roof, but is neatly chequered with flint, and has rather a better appearance than would be expected from the view in Mr. Cartwright's work, generally so well illustrated. The churchyard is very large and remarkably neat. Most readers will have met with some accounts of the magnificent Saxon or Norman architecture of the interior of this church, but the beauty of the detail must be seen to be appreciated. The clerestory has four handsome circular-headed windows on each side, with pilasters and a

* Cartwright.

† " It was a custom for the abbies of Normandy to have great estates in England, either granted by the Conqueror, or left by those Normans to whom the Conqueror had given the lands before. This gave rise to *alien priories,* which were no other than little cells, built upon those estates, to take care of them. These houses were governed by a *prior,* who remitted the rents to the Norman and French abbies, and were inhabited by a few poor brothers or sisters besides. Hen. 4, with his Commons, thinking it very injurious to the interest of the nation to suffer such large sums to be annually sent out of it, dissolved all these priories, which were bought up by churchmen chiefly, for a trifle ; and thus they were enabled to found colleges, and do such vast works."—EDWARD CLARKE.—*Burrell MSS.*

‡ Cartwright.

§ Pope Nicholas' Taxation.—" Abbas Fiscamp, Eccl'ia de Stenynge cu' Capella Wystalmestone 20*l.* 0*s.* 0*d.* h'et breve."—" Eccl'ia de Brambre, 6*l.* 13*s.* 4*d.*, non excedit." " Man'ia Abbis Fiscamp, Stening 51*l.* 11*s.* 1*d.*"

running moulding. Four arches are on each side of the interior, resting on circular columns, each three feet eight inches in diameter, and, as well as all the smaller ornaments, in so perfect a state of preservation, that they might be supposed to be of the most recent erection. At the east end is a very bold arch thirty-eight feet in height : these arches as well as the capitals of the pillars are remarkable for being so extensively varied, that of the former, not one is like another, and scarcely any two of the latter. The arches have each eight or ten suits or tiers of mouldings of every possible Saxon or Norman variety, some of which are exceedingly rich, exhibiting the Grecian ornaments of the lotus and the acanthus ; others are dentils, scales, reticulations, &c. &c. ; the soffits are also enriched, and the outer rims of some of the arches charged with small *paterœ ;* and the capitals of the pillars have much variety and beauty. The tower contains six bells, not very tuneable: the interior of the church has been lately refitted at considerable expense, and when painted will be extremely neat. Steyning contains a very well endowed grammar school. This place and Bramber have long been the property of the Dukes of Norfolk.

The tourist who has made this diversion from the main track to visit Bramber and Steyning will find a tolerable road from the latter to Worthing, which, at its commencement, is pretty well wooded and picturesque, but for the last three or four miles becomes flat and dreary, with the exception of the last mile from Broadwater. We return, however, now to Shoreham bridge, and pursue the direct route which leads through Lancing, a parish containing 700 inhabitants, and including two hamlets, respectively called Upper and Lower Lancing, both which are passed through in the route to Worthing. This is a respectable and well built village, containing the handsome seat of Sir J. M. Lloyd, several good houses and neat cottages ; and it has a good church of three aisles, with some Norman remains. To the left, on the South Downs, is the lately discovered Roman pavement, and which we shall speak of in our account of the vicinity of Worthing. The adjoining village of Sompting, *₊* lying between it and Broadwater, is not passed through. This demesne and manor was given at a very early period to the Abbey of Fiscamp, but the church was, in the twelfth century, granted to the Templars, free of all taxes, and is so entered in Pope Nicholas : " Eccl'ia de Suntyng est in usus Templar', et ideo, non taxat' : Vicar ejusdem 10*l*.—Man'ia Abbis Fiscamp, Suntinge 11*l*. 7*s*." At the suppression of the Templars, it was given by Sir Andrew Pevcrel, who resumed the possession, to the knights of St. John of Jerusalem. The church is a Norman building, cruciform, and has the singularity of a pilaster, or moulding, running up the centre of each face of its tower, which has excited much observation*.

The road from hence to Worthing leads over a flat shore, intersected with brooks, which bears decided marks of former inundations. In fact there is very little doubt that an æstuary formerly flowed up as far as the village of Broadwater.

---

* Mr. Cartwright enumerates the following curious and miscellaneous works of William Brownsword, vicar, 1707.—" A Divine Ode on Prophecy, as pointing out the Messiah. Dedicated to the Lord Bishop of Chichester. To which are annexed some suitable Notes, both explanatory and instructive."— " Laugh and lye down ; or a pleasant but sure remedy for the Gout, without expense or danger. Generously published and recommended from the author's own experience. In a Poem Serio-Comic. Humbly inscribed to Sir Hans Sloane."—" Laugh upon Laugh, or Laughter ridiculed. A Poem Œthico-Comico-Satyrical. Treating of the several kinds, or degrees, of Laughter."

WORTHING.

This pleasant and sociable little watering-place is now twelve miles distant from Brighton, but two of these will be curtailed by the new road over the suspension bridge across the Adur, at Shoreham. It is a hamlet to the parish of Broadwater, but exceeds the mother village in a twofold degree of population. Worthing is a place which we shall not flatter, though we have a former pleasing but melancholy brief association with it, which must for ever render it interesting to us. But we can with perfect impartiality recommend it as possessing strong inducements of comfort and pleasure not always found in larger places of resort. In fact, its very size is an auxiliary to this effect: there is more union and concentration of its visitors as well as inhabitants, and more community of its few amusements. The resident population is also united and friendly, and the lower classes decent and orderly. In fact, we scarcely know a drawback to a visit here during its season in the summer.

We should, however, specify here, as at Hastings, that, as the air is remarkably mild, it will *not* suit those who desire a bracing atmosphere, whilst for those of a different temperament it is of course highly eligible. The climate is so mild that myrtles and fig-trees grow in it to great perfection. The distance of Worthing from the metropolis is fifty-five miles. Its population, exclusive of the village of Broadwater, is now about 3000.

ORIGIN.

Worthing, under the title of *Ordings*, is mentioned in Doomsday Book, where it is valued at 117 shillings; it had also, either then or very soon afterwards, a chapel. The extent of land belonging to the hamlet is, however, only 300 acres, and it continued a small and unnoticed place until it began to attract attention as a suitable locality for a watering-place, about twenty years before the conclusion of the last century.

NEWSPAPER EXTRACTS.

We have taken several of these from our collection, some of which, as is also the case with those we have inserted in other places, are not certainly of general weight and importance, and we are not without anticipation that they may be smiled at by readers of a critical temperament. But we considered that they would prove entertaining, not merely to inhabitants, but also to visitors, as exhibiting both the former condition and the progressive increase and improvement of the places to which they refer; and as Worthing is the last of our stations for this purpose, we are the less inclined to abridge their extent.

" *Worthing, Aug.* 1, 1798.—Her Royal Highness the Princess Amelia arrived here at twenty minutes before eleven last night, attended by Lady Charlotte Bellasyse, Mrs Chaveley, Miss Goldsworthy, Gen. Goldsworthy, and Mr. Surgeon Keate. The Princess is this morning much recovered from the fatigue of travelling, and is as well as can be expected. Her Royal Highness and suite occupy two houses laid into one, near the Beach. Mr. Surgeon Keate and family reside in the next house but one.

" A party of the Derbyshire Militia, commanded by Captain Shuttleworth, consisting of 120 men, arrived here this morning from their camp on Clapham Common; they have pitched their tents in a field near her Royal Highness's residence, and are to continue while the Princess remains. Among the persons of fashion already arrived, are Lady Curzon, Mr. Tierney, M.P. and family, Mr. Ellis and family, and Miss Parker."

" *Aug.* 8, 1798.—Yesterday being the birth-day of her Royal Highness the Princess Amelia, it was observed here with much *eclât.* The morning was ushered in with ringing of bells; the Fly sloop, stationed here, displayed her colours, and at one o'clock fired a royal salute, which was answered by a *feu-de-joie* from the detachment of the Derbyshire Militia, who were marched down to the sands for that purpose. The Princess was carried on the sands in her settee chair, attended by her suite: her Royal Highness was in good spirits, and seemed highly pleased with the attention of Captain Cumberland, who kept the sloop under way, and upon different tacks, while the Princess staid, which was near two hours. After her Royal Highness had dined, she held a little Drawing-room, attended by Lady Charlotte Bellasyse and Miss Goldsworthy, when Captain Cumberland, of the Fly sloop, Captain Shuttleworth, and the officers of the Derbyshire Militia, were introduced by General Goldsworthy. The Princess gave orders that the soldiers should be regaled with a sufficient quantity of bread, cheese, and ale. In the evening a general illumination took place throughout the town and its vicinity; among the most conspicuous were the houses of Mr. Ellis, Mr. Strynger, Mr. Burke (the Circulating Library), and the two Inns, kept by Messrs. Hogsflesh and Bacon. At nine o'clock, Captain Cumberland made an elegant display of fireworks on board the sloop, which exhibited a very brilliant appearance from the shore to a vast number of spectators; at the conclusion, the vessel was illuminated from her ports to her top-gallants. Among the nobility who called to make inquiries after the health of the Princess in the course of the day were, his Grace the Duke of Norfolk, Lord (now Duke of Bedford) and Lady J. Russell, Lord Torrington, Lady Martin and daughters, Mr. and Lady Ann Ashley, Mrs. Bridgman, and Miss Byng. Mr. Strynger has, we understand, in a very polite manner, offered the use of the grass plat in the front of his house for the accommodation of the Princess, when the tide prevents her Royal Highness from going out on the sands."

This circumstance was the principal cause of the rise and prosperity of Worthing, as the visit of the Prince of Wales was of that of Brighton. The popularity of the former was afterwards increased by the residence of the beloved and lamented Princess Charlotte.

"*Aug.* 14, 1796.—Worthing, a pretty little bathing-place, about thirteen miles from Brighton, has at present to boast of many fashionable visitors. There are only two inns in the town, and a narrow road just divides them. The two landlords' names are *Hogsflesh* and *Bacon.*"

On this subject a puerile rhyme was current, something to the following effect:

> " Brighton is a pretty street,
> Worthing is much taken:
> If you can't get any other meat,
> There's Hogsflesh and Bacon."

"*Aug.* 16, 1805.—This place, which has so much increased within these few years, particularly since Princess Amelia bathed here, with elegant and first-rate houses, is now so full that families retire to Brighton for want of room. Lord Dundas's late house (who left here last week) was engaged before the family remained in it a week, notwithstanding its distance from the sea, by Miss Blake, the present occupier, who pays eight guineas a week for it. Within these three years there have been no less than six streets built here, and at present occupied by persons of the first-rate fashion and fortune in England, viz. Montague Place, Bedford-row, Copping's-row, Beach-row, Brook-street, and Hertford-street; and, from their extensive view of the sea, are generally let at any price; there are several very capital houses now building in the town and its vicinity. The beach, without a cliff, at low water extends six miles, and at ebb-tide, near three quarters, and is generally five hours' ebb, by which the ladies and gentlemen take delightful rides and walks, and in other parts it is occupied by some of the best cricket players in England, the sands being so fine and level."

"*Aug.* 28, 1805.—This place still increases in company so much, that there is not a single bed, nor even any accommodation to be got, the influx is so great. The sands yesterday afforded considerable sport by a pony race, which brought the whole of the fashionable visitors here together, for a bridle and saddle, the first two miles to be run for by four ponies. Lady W. Gordon's favourite pony, late the Duke of Queensberry's, was the favourite at starting; bets two to one against the field, the bay pony belonging to Mr. Broderick won by a whole length.

" After this race, the sporting gentlemen retired to the Admiral Nelson, where four matches were made for 500 guineas each : 1st, 300 yards; 2d, one mile ; 3d, one mile and a half; and the 4th, two miles. These matches will, it is said, be run for on Monday and Tuesday next. The Marquis of Blandford is stake-holder. Bets to a considerable amount are pending."

"*Aug.* 18, 1805.—Yesterday evening the sand was crowded with carriages of various descriptions : on inquiring the cause, we learned it was a great party of nobility, who had left Brighton, on visits here. The only places of accommodation for strangers in this town are two public-houses, opposite to each other, and kept by men of the name of Hogsflesh and Bacon; out of 153 of the above party, only 42 could get any refreshments, or even a dinner; and upwards of 100 persons were obliged to go back to Brighton, without any accommodation whatever; 27 persons dined at the house of Mr. *Hogsflesh,* and 15 at the house of Mr. *Bacon;* and some were fortunate enough to get accommodation at the Admiral Nelson, a small house up the town. This inconveniency will be removed next season, by the building of an *Hotel* on a scale suitable to the dignity of the visitors ; there is also wanted an assembly room, which, we are informed, will be built, to be attached to the hotel. About eleven o'clock last night the whole of the inhabitants of this place were greatly alarmed by a fire which happened at Broadwater, about a mile from this town; by some accident a rack of furse was set on fire, which communicated to several others of the same quality, but of greater magnitude; the dryness of the furse, which was intended for the burning of bricks, made such a blaze that most of the inhabitants actually thought the French were landed, and were burning down the town; while others, not so frightened, hastened to the spot where the supposed enemy had landed, but soon discovered their mistake, and quietly returned back to bed. Last night pony and donkey racing were frequent on the sands."

"*Aug.* 19, 1805.—From the fineness of the morning yesterday, as early as six o'clock, the sands were crowded with fashionable families. After breakfast the beach and sands were crowded with barouches, curricles, ponies, and donkeys. Last night we had the heaviest fall of rain ever remembered at this season of the year, and the whole of this day we had a tremendous thunder-storm, accompanied with heavy showers of hail and rain. On Friday a grand cricket-match was played at Broadwater, about a mile from this place, between 11 gentlemen of London, and 12 of Worthing, Shoreham, and Brighton, for five hundred guineas a side. The wickets were pitched at eleven o'clock, and decided on Saturday in favour of London by two wickets."

" A letter from Worthing, dated Sept. 23, says, ' Two vessels are now cruizing off here, the Beaumont (late the Rose) and the Lion. Yesterday a boat from the Rose was despatched to the shore for provisions, having five men on board, which was unfortunately upset about two miles from the shore. The men clung to the vessel, waiting the arrival of boats, which set off to their assistance. As she kept sinking by their weight, two of the brave fellows, that could swim, let go their hold, and told the others to stick fast by her. One of the boats came up with the swimmers, who told them not to wait for them, but to hasten to the assistance of those who could not swim, which they did. The whole were in this way saved; but the two generous tars, who were so anxious for their companions, were nearly gone before they were picked up by a second boat. However, by the care of those on shore, they were soon recovered, and had their generosity rewarded by a liberal subscription.'"

" A privateer of no common magnitude was taken by one of our gun-brigs, near this part of the Channel last night, and safely conveyed into the port of Worthing this morning."

" *Brighton, Aug.* 26.—A French privateer secreted herself last night near Worthing, and, about four in the morning, captured a sloop, laden with sugars, teas, &c. &c., to the value of 7000*l.* As some part of the inhabitants were stirring at this early hour, they gave the alarm, and Captain Remus, in a revenue cutter, recaptured the sloop about five; and, after bringing her into Shoreham harbour, went in pursuit of the privateer, which she captured in three hours after (a few shots being fired from the cutter), and brought her safe into Little Hampton."

1807.

" A most ludicrous circumstance happened lately at Worthing, which has caused much merriment. About the time of Brighton races, the bell-man of Worthing gave notice to the inhabitants and visitants in that town, that a lady had lost a wig, coming from Broadwater, and the restorer of it was to be handsomely rewarded ; but nothing was heard of it at that time. About a week ago, a bird's nest was discovered in a tree, in a meadow between Broadwater and Worthing; some young gentlemen climbed the tree for the nest, and disturbed a magpye ; when, to their great surprise, it proved to be the identical wig that was lost, with nothing in it but a few sticks, and the maker's name sewed in the inside, ' No. 68, Cryer's, Cornhill, Catalani.'"

" The Flying Artillery have left the barracks here to encamp near Worthing, which place they leave, to form flying encampments in the neighbourhood of Arundel, Chichester, &c. They do not return to this place before August."

" *July* 24.—On Tuesday last the Princess Charlotte of Wales, accompanied by Lady De Clifford, made her appearance at Worthing. The yeomanry and the volunteer corps were on duty on the occasion, and the village was brilliantly illuminated in the evening. The greater part of the nobility at present here have since paid a visit to Worthing, to congratulate her royal highness on her arrival.—Lord Craven, and a large party of ladies and gentlemen, sailed for Worthing yesterday morning, in his lordship's pleasure yacht. Off the place a royal salute was fired; the company soon after were put on shore, where they continued for several hours, and in the evening returned to this town."

" *Worthing.*—This place is as gay as in the middle of summer, and more crowded than any other watering place. The influx of diurnal visitors from Brighton, Arundel, and Little Hampton, is very great. The theatre is very well attended; the grand melo-drama of Tekeli is brought out with great splendour, and attracts very great houses."

" *Brighton, Aug.* 10.—As early as nine o'clock yesterday morning, the Prince left this place on horseback, to pay a visit to the Princess Charlotte of Wales, at Worthing. It was nearly six in the evening before his royal highness returned. During his absence, the Duke of Clarence arrived here, and afterwards dined with his royal brother at the Pavilion.

DESCRIPTION.
THE ESPLANADE

measures between half and three-quarters of a mile in length, and is twenty feet wide, forming a neat gravelled terrace, slightly yet sufficiently elevated above the level of the waves, which flow up close to its base; a barrier is also thus effected against the incursions of the sea. The bathing machines are ranged immediately below it on the beach, which is one of the finest, smoothest, and most regular expanse of firm sand on the English coast, affording the readiest facilities for bathing at all seasons, and the most extensive facilities for driving and riding that are to be met with in this part of the coast. We find it stated, that the entire level suited to this purpose is nearly twelve miles; and we have formerly visited Little Hampton, eight miles distant, in this manner, entered the harbour and town, and returned, during the time of low water. The esplanade is of course the fashionable promenade of the town; some neat pleasure-boats, though not of considerable size, are stationed off the beach, and flies, ponies, donkeys, " et id genus omne" of auxiliaries to pleasure or health are stationed in the carriage road in front of the Parade.

BUILDINGS IN GENERAL.

Worthing is not a regularly built town, but by no means suffers in appearance from this circumstance; in fact, we think it gains by it, as the visitor finds at many turns new objects which he would scarcely have expected. Like Brighton, it follows the line of the sea, but has many openings in an opposite direction, one of the principal of which is the *Steyne,* a very neat oblong space, of about four acres, surrounded on three sides by handsome dwelling houses. *Warwick House* is in this direction, which is usually let to some visitor of distinction, and has been occupied by some members of the Royal Family; it has nothing beyond neatness in its exterior, but is said to have been erected after the plan of a Roman villa. About the centre of the esplanade, a well built but very short street opens into a large space or square, forming the body of the town, with several neat shops, offices, bazaars, &c. at its right and left; at the end, is the Chapel of Ease; at the south-east extremity, the market, a theatre, library, and the back of the Steyne. At the south-west angle is the approach to Park Crescent, the most recent and the grandest pile of buildings in Worthing, which commands a fine prospect in which the spire of Tarring is a conspicuous object, and is erected in a very good style of architecture, not the least ornaments of which are the beautiful *Termini* at the entrance gate; there are several other neat piles of buildings in the place, which need not be particularized, but the tout ensemble is neat, airy, and graceful.

THE CHAPEL OF EASE

was erected in 1811-12, at an expense of 13,000*l.*, and is a neat edifice of pale brick, with a stone portico of mixed Doric and Tuscan character, and a bold though low turret. Its interior will contain about 850 persons, a portion of whom are free. Neatness almost approaching to plainness characterizes its interior; but it has a good organ, which cost 600*l.*, and is gratuitously played by a Miss Morrab, daughter of a medical gentleman in the town

THE MARKET

is a neat, quadrangular erection, between Ann and Market Streets, with a double entrance.

There are several charitable institutions in Worthing which come more properly under the head of Broadwater, but amongst them the *Dispensary* should be particularly mentioned.

BATHS.

Worthing has two of these establishments of a very superior character. The Royal Baths have a spacious boarding-house attached to them, which is a great convenience to the invalid; and the Parisian Baths have, in the ladies' department, a conservatory.

THE THEATRE,

though small, is tastefully decorated and richly painted in the interior, and considered very pretty for a country establishment. Some years back, it was still more highly patronised and extensively frequented than it is at present, and was then, under the management of Mr. Trotter, considered as a nursery for performers, especially songstresses[*]; but it is now, under different conductors, well managed, and obtains a share of approbation.

LIBRARIES.

Stafford's library, fronting the sea, is an old-established one, and well conducted:—speaking of this and the theatre, some ten years ago, we remember them in their zenith. Miss Carter's library, in Warwick-street, lately opened, is a tasteful establishment, consisting of three rooms, the two first partaking of the library and the bazaar, and the third a reading-room, opening to a lawn and flower-garden. Mr. Shearsmith speaks highly of the engaging attention of the conductresses,

---

[*] Mr. Shearsmith's (surgeon) Description of Worthing, from which we have derived several hints.

in which, from a brief opportunity of judging, we are disposed very fully to coincide.

INNS.

The Sea-House Hotel is, perhaps, the grandest establishment, but the Marine Hotel opposite affords equal comfort; of a similar character is the Steyne Hotel, and there are some other very respectable inns in the place.

MISCELLANEOUS.

Worthing has a bank; a sufficient number of physicians, surgeons, instructors, schools, &c.; coaches to London, and others to principal places along the coast, especially Brighton and Chichester.

VICINITY OF WORTHING.

The church and village of *Broadwater* lie north-east from Worthing about a mile distant, and the commencement of this walk is as pretty as one will see " on a summer's day." The church here is one of the few which are perfect " gems " in Sussex, from the extreme poverty of the generality; but this would be considered a handsome one in any part of the kingdom. It is built in the form of a cross, but without battlements to the high shingled roofs, which is rather a drawback to its external appearance. The internal length is 139 feet, viz.—nave, 61, tower, 20, and chancel, 58; length of the transept, 90; breadth of the nave and aisles, 42. The tower in the centre has Norman windows, and a round corner turret, lately erected in place of a pointed roof. A mixed style of the twelfth, thirteenth, and fourteenth centuries characterizes the interior. The nave has plain, pointed arches, with circular columns; a pointed arch, with zigzag ornaments, not dissimilar to those of Eastbourne Church, opens into the tower; whilst its opposite one is circular, and has rich capitals of palm-branches, an ornament introduced by the Crusaders. The roof of the chancel is vaulted, resting on five pilasters, each pilaster on both sides resting on a bird's beak corbel, as at Shoreham, with capitals partly foliated and partly plain. The side-windows of the chancel were altered in the fourteenth century, and a handsome one at the end is of the same date; the west window of the church is of the fifteenth century. On the north side of the chancel is the rich though heavy canopied and fretted monument of Lord De la Warr, 1526, engraved in Mr. Cartwright's work; and, in the south transept, another, to a member of the same family, 1554, when Italian ornament had been to a still farther extent combined with the Gothic, and bearing a greater affinity to some of the later ones in Arundel Church: both of these are eminently worthy of notice. On the floor of the chancel are also several interesting brasses and inscriptions. The north transept has been parted off for a school-room, as the south has for a spacious vestry. In the tower are six small, musical bells, in very good condition.

The whole of the interior of the church has been liberally and handsomely fitted-up, at an expense of upwards of 1200*l.*, more than 700*l.* of which was raised in the parish. At the end of the chancel is a solid and handsome altar-piece, with white and gold tables, and a large glory in the centre; the common altar-cloth, of blue, with yellow silk fringe and braiding, a glory, and IHS., is inscribed, " Ex dono Hen. Travers, Arm, 1723," and is in surprising preservation; but a splendid one, of similar pattern, in crimson velvet and gold, and another for the pulpit, has been given by Miss Daubuz, of Offington, who has also increased the communion-plate.

The churchyard is densely crowded with tombstones, but very neatly kept. We accidentally noticed one which, after expressing Christian hope, concluded with classic elegance— " *Filio bene merito, contra ordinem, parentes.*" This reminds one of Cicero's affecting apostrophe, not, also, without hope— " *Cujus a me corpus crematum est, quod contra decuit ab illo meum.*"

The rector of Broadwater is the Rev. P. Wood, M.A., and the curate, also of the chapel at Worthing, the Rev. W. Davison, M. A. It would be less than strict justice, on the equitable principle, " Palmam qui meruit ferat," if we were not to add, that both these gentlemen are most diligently though unobtrusively engaged in their sacred duties, and in every thing tending to promote benevolence, morality, and prosperity, within the circle of their influence.

Broadwater, including Worthing, now contains upwards of 4500 inhabitants, a population which, of course with a principal reference to the latter, has been trebled since 1801.

Much interesting information of the history of this parish will be found in Cartwright's Rape of Bramber. In the Norman survey it was held of William de Braose, but afterwards it passed into the hands of the noble family of Camois, and was the head of their Barony. One of these, in 1313, obtained a grant of a market and fair at Broadwater. In the reign of Henry VII. it was possessed by the celebrated Sir Reginald Bray ; subsequently it has been in the hands of a variety of parties, and now belongs to a Mr. Newland.

Offington, in this parish, was, in the fifteenth century, the seat of the De la Warrs, the most celebrated of whom, a statesman and ambassador, and Knight of the Garter in the reign of Henry VIII., is the nobleman who has the splendid monument in the chancel. In his will he ordered that he should be buried with honour, and that twopence should be given in alms to every person who chose to come and claim it ; towards which he left his gold garter and chain. He also bequeathed to the church his mantle of blue velvet, and his gown of crimson velvet, of the Garter, to make two altar-cloths.

In the Burrel MSS. is an inventory of the goods of the last Thomas Lord De la Warr, who died in 1 Mary, 1554: the following extracts, which we have transcribed, will show both the extent of the original mansion, and the nature and value of a number of miscellaneous articles at the time it was taken.

APARTMENTS.

" My lord's bedchamber.
The gallery chamber.
The inner gallery, with
The closet next the garden.

The gallery at my lord's chamber door.
The gentell women's chamber.
The maids' chamber.
My Lady West's chamber.
The great chamber.
The middle chamber.
The ladder chamber.
The hall.
The gallery going into the chapel.
The chapel chamber.
The black parler.
The vellet chamber.
The chamber within the vellet chamber.
Mr. West's chamber.
The chamber over.
The newe worke.   Furniture.
The tower chamber.
My Lady Shirle's chamber.
The næercerye.
The three chambers.
The chamber over the butterye.
The parler over the seller.
The new chamber within it."
Two other *parlers,* and *thirty* other chambers and offices.

VALUATIONS.

The "clocke and the bell" are valued at 26*s.* 8*d.*

The "chappell stuff" at 23*l.* 15*s.* 6*d.*; besides a "payer of organs" 3*l.*; a chalice, 14 ounces, 3*l.* 10*s.* 4*d.*; a vestment of blue velvet, with other things, 30*s.*

" ' The wardropp,' 32*l.* 5*s.*

" A ' kirtell' of crimson whyte, lined with sarcenett, and a hood to cor-respond, 5*l.*

" My lord's robes of the Garter, 18*l.*

" My lord's apparell and armour, 55*l.* 17*s.* 6*d.*

The plate is in a variety of items, about 350*l.* in the whole, and the collar, &c. &c. of the Garter, 95*l.*, and a vast quantity of linen.   Also of corn and live stock.   The best horse is worth 5*l.*, two at 4*l.*, others from 40*s.* down to 8*s.*; 8 working oxen, 11*l.* 6*s.* 8*d.*; 10 fatting oxen, 12*l.* 3*s.* 4*d.*; 181 sheep, 18*l.* 2*s.*

Property at Ewhurst, rather more than 40*l.*

" My lord's house in London" between 20*l.* and 30*l.*, besides "a gowne of blacke vellet facyd with satten," 10*l.*; " a jackett of vellet with lace," 4*l.*

200 marks for 3 years after his decease given by the king and queen out of the Exchequer, for the due performance of his will,—400*l.*

4 years' profit of certain manors in Devonshire, 134*l.* 3*s.* 4*d.*   Some small debts:—ready money, 16*l.*

" *Summa totalis* of all the inventorye is 1800*l.* 11*s.* 2*d.*"

Offington is now a plain-looking respectable mansion, not

having the appearance of great antiquity, standing in a small park, finely wooded with old trees, and belonging by purchase to J. T. Daubuz, Esq.

Pope Nicholas's Taxation:—

Eccl'ia de Bradewater cum capellâ (*var. read.*
capellis) £46 13 4
Prioriss' de Esseborn, in Bradewat' *Worthing*
de redd' assize . . . 2 1 0

In the parish also is *Cissbury*, a hill of sixty acres, surrounded by a vallum, imagined to have been originally a British encampment, and afterwards adopted by the Romans: subsequently also by the Saxons, as its name, from one of their kings, *Cissa*, evidently demonstrates.

In addition to this eminence, formerly a camp, and Chanckbury, a bolder one, crowned with a picturesque clump of firs, which faces Steyning and Bramber, there is a third, called Highdown hill; and all these formed a chain of connexion with St. Rook's, or Roche's hill, near Chichester. Highdown has also the tomb of an eccentric, though good-hearted, miller, sometimes visited by those who, in the former respect, are as silly as himself.

ROMAN PAVEMENT.
LANCING DOWN.

After the visitor has passed through Upper Lancing, he will enter on a singularly wild country, to which we hardly know what appellation to give: it is too dreary for pastoral effect; yet, having some herbage, can hardly be termed a desert. It will be a variety, at any rate. The remains are situated on an eminence of the South Downs, which, as far as space is concerned, has certainly a commanding view. We are disposed to speak well of " the show," in order to serve the honest and patient man who has discovered and preserves it: but we are not of those *dry* antiquaries, who have a pleasure in burrowing in the earth, and disturbing the bones of the defunct. We had therefore as lief not see the mouldering relics here collected, and care but little to whom they belonged. Still there are other objects of interest in the shape of curiosa, though in their material by no means handsome, pavements, some small altars, lavatories, &c. and a really valuable collection of coins. But having already stated our ignorance of and distaste to this peculiar walk of antiquity, we had better leave the reader to form his own opinion. A curious effect has the red and white flag, which the honest man has stuck up on this wild hill, with the inscription " Roman Pavement" in large characters. He has also erected a neat species of hut to receive visitors, and enclosed the ground in a neat style; and both he and his son evince a gratifying intelligence, and wish to please.

One mile to the west of Broadwater is *Tarring*, now a decayed town, but a place of much ancient importance and association. The manor was given by King Athelstan to Christchurch, Canterbury, between the years 941 and 944, and was in the possession of the archbishop of Canterbury, till it was usurped by the crown about the time of Cranmer ; but the impropriate rectory is still possessed by the Archbishop.

" There seems to have been a church or monastery at Tarring, built to the honor of St. Andrew in the time of Offa, King of the Mercians; and there were some remains of it in a free chapel, or peculiar jurisdiction, which continued here to the time of Edward III. See *Monast. Ang*. In a Cartulary of the Archbishop of Canterbury is a covenant between the Dean of South Malling and the Rector of South Malling touching jurisdiction.

" Mr. Elliot in a note says, there seems to be no reconciling the date in the Monasticon, nor ascertaining the founder from thence, who was either Earl Waldhere, or Adwlf, Duke of Sussex."—*Burrell MSS.*

In the 24th year of Henry VI. the inhabitants petitioned for a market, for these curious reasons :—that whilst the men of the town were attending neighbouring markets those remaining in the town and their wives and children had often been slain or maltreated by incursions of the French and Spaniards; which, as Mr. Cartwright observes, was very extraordinary, since there was a market not farther off than Broadwater. Their petition was, however, granted in the following charter; its original is kept in an old chest in the church tower.

Terringe villa: mercat in die Sabbati.—Tower Rec. No. 37. 21 H. 6.

" Henricus Dei gratia Rex Angliæ & Franciæ et D'us Hiberniæ, Archiepis, Epi's, Abbi'ts, Prioribus, Ducibus, Marchionibus, Comitibus, vicecomitibus, Majoribus Ballivis, Constabulariis ministris et omnibus fidelibus suis ad quos præsentes L'ræ pervenerint, salutem. Sciatis q'd cum nos p' humilem supplicationem, dilectorum Ligeor' n'ror hominum in villa de Tering in com Sussex prope mare situata habitancium intelleximus, qualiter ipsi pluribus temporibus, p' inimicos nostros Franciæ et aliarum partium ibidem, per mare transeuntes quam plurima dampna deperdita in corporibus et bonis suis indies sustinent et patiuntur, qualiter etiam præfati homines aliquod mercatum in villa prædicta minime habent, p' quod præfati homines in absentia sua in eundo ad proximum mercatum, non solum villam illam verum etiam omnia bona sua in eadem existent: indies . . . formidantur; Nos ad præmissa considerationem habentes volentesque eosdem ligeos nostros in hac parte relevare et supportare ut tenemur, de gratia nostra speciali concessimus pro nobis et heredibus n'ris, quantum in nobis est, hominibus in dicta villa de Terring habitantibus, quod ipsi imperpetuum habeant et teneant sibi et successoribus suis unum mercatum singulis septimanis, apud predictam' villam de Terring tenentur in die Sabbati, ita tamen quod mercatum illud, non sit ad ocumentum alior' vicinor' mercator.' Hiis testibus—venerabilibus patribus. J. Cantuar. totius Angliæ Primati, Cancellario nostro, W. Lincoln. Th. Bathon & Wellen. W. Car. Epi's; carissimo avunculo nostro Humfrido Duce Gloucestr';—Carissimis consanguineis nostris Humfrido Stafford, & Will'o Suff Seneshallo Hospicii nostri, comitibus, necnon dilectis et fidelibus n'ris, Radulfo Cromwell et Rudo Boteller Thesaurario ars militibus et apud Westmonasterium, undecimo die Junii, anno regni n'ri 22°.—Louthe p. breve de privato Sigillo et de data predicta, auctoritate Parliamenti."

" Transcribed from the orig. charter in yᵉ possession of Revᴶ. Mr. Penfold, minʳ. of Terring, Sussex, April 12, 1779. The seal appended represents yᵉ king on horseback in compleat armour, inscribed " Henricus Dei gratia Rex Franciæ, Angliæ, et Dⁿˢ. Hibernæ. Reverse, the king sitting on his throne, robed and crowned, holding in his right hand a sceptre, and in his left the orb with the cross, inscribed round yᵉ brim as before."— See Sandford's Geneal. Hist., plate, p. 244. Edit. of 1707.—*Burrell MSS.*

The ancient-rectory-house has been surmised to have been a manor-house or palace occasionally inhabited by Thomas à Becket. This is, of course, an interesting relic, but is not generally shown; we saw it only by sufferance. The architecture of the principal remains appears posterior to the year 1400 : one large and regularly built room is supposed to have been the chapel, now used as a Sunday-school. We were informed that about fifty years ago, the premises were far more extensive; twenty bed-rooms are even spoken of, where there are now only two.   Interest is still attached to a place of such celebrated associations, though the contrast is now both strange and cheerful; part of the building is used as a dairy, and the whole is surrounded by a good kitchen-garden interspersed with flowers, and all this where the lordly prelate walked gravely in amice and pall, incense was swung through the air, and prayers chaunted in a strange tongue— yet the most noble and musical of the ancient or modern world.

Tarring contains three hamlets, Heene, Darrington, and Salvington; the second had a chapel, and the third was the birthplace and residence of the celebrated SELDEN, termed by his antagonist Grotius " the glory of the English nation."

Sir William Jones, in a letter to Mr. Cartwright, declared " that he considered Selden so great an object of imitation, that if he could obtain a similar honour of representing the University of Oxford in Parliament, he would, like him, devote the rest of his life to the service of his constituents and his country, to the practice of an useful profession, and to the unremitted study of our English laws, history, and literature."

Selden's house still remains at Salvington, very little larger than a cottage, with some curious old wood framework at the end.   On the lintel of the door withinside are two lines, supposed to have been composed by himself, and cut by him in the wood; but they are certainly the production of one of his most trifling and least happy moments, as they have not the slightest pretensions to wit or point of any kind.

> " GRATV'S HONESTE, MIHI, NO' CLAUDAR, INITO, SEDEQUE :
> FUR ABEAS; NO' SV' FACTA SOLVTA TIBI."

Es is wanting in the first line to make out the sense. A friend of Mr. Cartwright's contributed this translation : —

> " Thou 'rt welcome, honest friend, walk in, make free;
> Thief, get thee gone, I open not to thee."

The following would be more literal : —

> " Welcome, if honest,—enter, rest thee free ;
> Thief, hence ! I was not open made for thee."

Tarring, with its hamlets, contains about 1200 inhabitants. The church is a lofty and spacious structure, and has, with the exception of Chichester Cathedral, the best spire in the county; it rises from a lofty and very well-built tower of the fourteenth century, is octagonal in form, and 137 feet from the ground; on its summit is a conductor and a vane. The body has a long and very highly pitched nave, apparently nearly fifty feet, and two side aisles, with early Gothic arches and lancet windows; the chancel is also forty feet by twenty-one, and has very good windows of the early part of the fifteenth century, the side ones of two lights, and the eastern of five, engraved in Cartwright, above which is a cross fleury. Some ancient stalls are in the chancel, but not equal to those at Broadwater. In the tower are five bells, in a still worse state than those at Shoreham, two of them being broken, and the remaining three only sounded by ropes tied to the clappers. The large old chest contains some very curious accounts of the churchwardens from 1515 to 1579, from which Mr. Cartwright has made extensive extracts. At the entrance of the church a poors' box bears the conciliating invitation, " He that giveth to the poor lendeth," &c. &c. The town appears reduced, and it is encouragement enough, in all such cases, that the interest is enormous and the security infallible.

Worthing, during the " spirit stirring" times of the anticipated French invasion, was a considerable station for military; it has now only one troop of horse, belonging to the corps in head-quarters at Brighton.

Of the various poetical effusions on the sea that have met our notice, we think some of the most fortunate have been those of Barry Cornwall, Hogg, and Cunningham; but there is a *morceau* on this subject, " The Sea-Spirit's Song," by Lord Thurlow, in the Gentleman's Magazine for 1815, which exhibits much ease and gracefulness. The following lines appeared, with initials similar to those of the author of this volume, in the Cambridge Chronicle, 1823.

MIDNIGHT SONG OF THE NEREIDS.

"Of Tethys' race
   Our birth we trace,
And we roam o'er the Ocean's most beautiful face,
   In proud and pure dominion;
   No nymph above
   Can happier rove,
Or spread to the redolent air of the grove
   The folds of her gossamer pinion.

"Sweet is our home
   'Neath the silver foam,
Through valleys of pearl and of amber we roam,
   The secrets of ocean beholding:
   The azure flowers
   That deck our bowers
Are as sweet as the wreaths of the light-footed Hours,
   When the portals of day are unfolding.

"Round every clime
   Is our track sublime;
We skim round the cold dreary mountains of rime,
   That on Thule's shores are frowning;
   'Neath Ætna's height
   Is our pathway light,
When sternly the sable abysses of night
   His beacon of glory is crowning.

"Ausonian vales
   Have heard our tales,
And we've scented the flowery perfume that exhales
   From the islands of Araby streaming;
   At Ino's name
   To her shores we came;
We have been where the Magian's altar of flame
   On Ecbatana's mountain is gleaming.

"Latona's isle
   Hath seen our smile,
And we watch'd as it sprung from the Ocean the while,
   In the pale saffron lustre of even;
   We sang its birth
   To the realms of earth,
And we raised on the winds our wild chorus of mirth,
   Till it rang on the echoes of Heaven!

" Athena's strand
    Is our dearest land,
And we joy o'er the palms of her generous band,
    When the trophies of ocean have crown'd her.
        But AN ISLE SHALL BE
        In the western sea,
The queen of the deep, and the land of the free,
    And the glories of earth shall surround her!

    " To Thetis dear
        Our vows we bear,
And we braid with fresh garlands her beautiful hair.
—— When the foaming surge was o'er thee,
        Leucothöe,
        We sang to thee,
And we laid thy fair limbs on the couch of the sea,
    And we worship now before thee.

    " To Neptune's court
        We oft resort,
Oft glad round his chrysolite axles we sport,
    As they roll o'er the surface of ocean.
        The Triton's shell
        Sounds the triumph well,
And the gorgeous sea-monsters their fealty tell,
    As they gambol in joyous commotion.

    " Around thy car,
        Our Ocean Star,
Where the bright snowy steeds and the diadem are,
    Our virgin troops are sailing.
        In frequent quire,
        Our aged Sire,
We hail, to the notes of the silvery lyre,
    When the rays on the mountain are failing.

    —" But away, away !—
    —For the fire of day
From the gates of the Orient is burning !
        To our sport, or our sleep,
        In the bowers of the deep ;
Till again in the moonlight our vigils we keep,
    When the shadows of eve are returning."

————

TO LITTLEHAMPTON AND BOGNOR.

The route through these two places to Arundel is, of course, a very devious one; we merely took it in order to have a brief survey of each. The direct road from Worthing to Arundel is about ten miles, but contains not a single object of the least interest.

The road to Littlehampton is not an unpleasant one, and passes through two or three villages, one of which, West Preston, the burying-place of Selden, has a rather curious slender tower and spire.

LITTLEHAMPTON,

although a very small village until the commencement of the present century, is a place of some ancient renown. Before the Conquest, a small portion of it belonged to the Countess Goda, daughter of Ethelred II., and afterwards the manor was principally in the hands of the foreign abbeys of Almanische and Seez, and also of the Earl of Mount Gomeri. A farm still called Baillie's Court, in a portion of the parish termed Atherington, is mentioned in Pope Nicholas: " Balli de Ateriton, in Hampton, 19*l.* 7*s.* 2*d.*" The Empress Maud is supposed to have landed here in 1139, when she proceeded to Arundel Castle, and was hospitably received by Queen Adeliza, which led to a siege by Stephen *. Philip, Earl of Arundel, designing to escape from Queen Elizabeth's severe treatment of the Catholics, was arrested here in 1586 †. In 1644, was taken here (a spoil of a Dunkirk ship) a large painting of the martyrdom of the 11,000 virgins of Cologne (or rather, as is supposed, the two, from the mistake of *Undecimilla*, the name of Ursula's companion, for Undecim Mill*i*a), and placed in the Star Chamber.

The church has lately been rebuilt in a very neat and bold style, with a large body, nearly 100 feet long, and two small entrances in the centre of each side, similar to transepts. The tower rises very slightly above the roof, but has handsome pin-

---

* Dallaway.   † *Ib.*

nacles, and three clock faces. The interior is simple, but neat, with a good altar-piece, and a very small organ. The handsome decorated east window from the old church and the font were saved by the exertions of Mr. Cartwright. In the favourite style, however, of Sussex, the tower has only one bell. This capacious and lofty erection only cost 2600*l*.

Littlehampton has trebled its population since 1801, and now contains upwards of 1600 inhabitants. This is, of course, owing to its having become a resort for sea-bathing, for which it possesses sufficient facilities, and is rather a favourite place with those who prefer quiet and retirement. The air, both here and at Bognor, is very mild. The river Arun flows from hence to Arundel; and Littlehampton is, properly speaking, the harbour, though the embouchure of the arm of the sea is in the parish of Climping. The harbour was repaired, and piers erected, in the year 1796; it has now a considerable and lively traffic, and builds large vessels for the West India trade; a small fort was erected in 1739.

There are, at Littlehampton, a library, amateur band, baths, &c., and other accommodations. A benefit society exists here on very excellent principles. The Earl of Surrey has a seat at Littlehampton. We tried more than once to obtain for this little volume the patronage of this noble family, but could obtain no answer—a circumstance which we regretted; still we shall proceed to give a *concise* account of Arundel, with that impartiality, which, as we have tried our utmost to preserve, we hope we shall be allowed to have strictly adhered to.

BOGNOR.

The river at Littlehampton, which is about 125 yards broad, is crossed by a floating ferry-bridge, of curious construction, which accomplishes the transit in about two minutes, conveying two carriages at a time. It is brought over by winding up a chain, stretched from the opposite shore, round a windlass in the side of the bridge.

From Little Hampton to Bognor the principal villages

passed through are Yapton and Felpham ; the church at the former contains this inscription :—

" Sacred to the memory of Stephen Roe, Citizen of London, born in this parish and buried at Islington, who by his will, dated Oct. 17, 1766, gave twelve hundred pounds (three per cent. South Sea annuities) to the poor of this parish, yearly for ever.

> " The parent hence shall ne'er depart,
> But love each babe with joyful heart,
> 　To view this church stone.
> Here gratitude delights to dwell,
> And young and old shall always tell
> 　The good that Roe has done.
> Soft pity now shall comfort woe,
> And ignorance have herself to know,
> 　By bounty taught and fed.
> Orphans and widows more and more,
> And children yet unborn shall pour
> 　Their blessings on his head."

Felpham, near Bognor, was the residence and burial-place of the celebrated Dr. Cyril Jackson, Dean of Christ-church, and of Hayley the poet. The epitaph for the former has simply the universally applicable sentence—" Enter not into judgment," &c. Mr. Hayley's has the following lines written by Mrs. Opie, with whom, as well as her husband, he was on intimate terms of friendship.

> " Hayley ! beloved friend ! tho' round thy head
> The muse's wreath its graceful foliage spread ;
> Tho' Fame was long thy talents' rich reward,
> And Fashion smiled upon Serena's bard ;
> Tho' thou wast form'd in polished courts to shine,
> And learning's stores and playful wit were thine ;
> Tho' Cowper's self thy tuneful strains approved,
> And praised the poet while the man he loved,—
> Cowper, who lives in thy recording page,
> To interest, charm, and teach the future age ;—
> Oh ! not on these alone thy honours rest,
> But, that thy name pale want and misery bless'd !
> That, such thy glowing zeal for all mankind,
> So vast thy charity, so unconfined,
> Thy hand had spread a scene of blessing round,
> If ample wealth thy ardent hopes had crown'd—
> That, whatsoe'er thy bounty could impart,
> Was given to teach the mind, and cheer the heart ;
> Neglected talent's drooping head to raise,
> And lead young Genius on by generous praise.

Yet, bard beloved! this higher meed be thine,
Faith in thy Saviour cheer'd thy life's decline,—
Nor by that God on whom thy hopes relied
Was the sweet recompense of faith denied.
He gave thee strength to smile 'midst torturing pain,
And even the slightest murmur still restrain ;
He cheer'd with pious hope thy dying bed ;
He, on thy soul the Christian's sunshine shed ;
And crown'd, to prove his favour's blest increase,
A life of kindness with a death of peace."

A punning epitaph by Mr. Hayley on a blacksmith at this place is recorded, but has not much point, independently of this not being a place for a jest. The best and most unexceptionable of these which we have ever seen is on an individual of the name of Strong, a carpenter, in the neighbourhood of London.

" Who many a sturdy oak had laid along,
Fell'd by death's surer hatchet, here lies Strong.
Posts oft he made, yet ne'er a *place* could get *,
And lived by *railing*, though he was no *wit* † :
Old saws he had, although no antiquarian,
And *stiles* corrected, yet was no *grammarian.*"

Bognor is situated in the parish of South Berstead, and contains about 1500 inhabitants. At the entrance, several neat villas excite rather high expectations, but the town itself is scattered

* " Between you and I and the post" (though we never made one ; they are not to be made in these times), gentle reader, we can sincerely sympathise with the worthy carpenter in this predicament.

† What a great number of editors of periodicals are exactly in the same situation with the meritorious artificer ! The misfortune is that they do not recognise this to be the case: they mistake the acerbity which they really *do* possess (and in which they are sadly encouraged by the once better-tempered public of John Bull's island, who have now a craving appetite for *bitters*,) for genuine and praiseworthy wit: whereas Mr. Strong did not conceive his humble wooden erections to be either rose-wood or cedar.

—We have encountered accidentally a certain remarkably ill-natured penny publication, styled, though it is no credit to name it, " Figaro in London," in which the editor, after blaming some dramatic error, asserts that " if it be not speedily remedied, OUR CRITICAL AVALANCHE must descend on their heads ! !" Mercy upon the shivering and to-be-shivered sufferers ! " Threatened folks live long," to be sure, but their dread of the terrific impending punishment must be truly pitiable. The whole affair calls to mind the prime minister's character of a rebellion in the Isle of Man,—" A tempest in a tea-pot."

and irregularly built. It owed its rise, about the year 1790, to a Sir John Hotham, a merchant of London, who erected the principal buildings. There are three or four good inns, and some respectable ranges of building, also baths, &c., and it may, doubtless, have its advantages to those who prefer quiet, and especially family parties. The oblong space open to the sea, somewhat ridiculously dignified with the appellation of " the Steyne," is neat and cheerful ; here is the chapel of ease, a spacious cemented structure, and a small market. Binstead's library, opposite the sea, is pleasant, and has a lawn in front: beyond, towards the east, is a small battery ; another library, farther inland, bears the title of having been patronised by the Princess Augusta. A physician and three surgeons are resident in Bognor.

A few miles to the west of Bognor is the promontory and church of Selsea, forming the opposite extremity of the spacious bay, which Beachey Head terminates to the east. This was the place where Christianity was first preached to the South Saxons by Wilfrid, an exiled bishop of Lindisfarn, to whom this peninsula was given by King Ædelwalch about the year 680, when he immediately liberated 250 persons then in a state of slavery*. He was confirmed in the possession of this tract, containing 5000 acres, by the conqueror of Ædelwalch, Ceadwalla, who afterwards, struck with remorse for his wars and bloodshed, made a pilgrimage to Rome, where he received baptism, and died, having first laid the foundation of and endowed the *Bishoprick of Selsey*. At this place the see continued uninterrupted till the year 1081, when William the Conqueror, in accordance with his plan in other places, on the advice of an Ecclesiastical Council, presided over by Lanfranc, Archbishop of Canterbury, removed it from this village to the town of Chichester.

---

* Not *so* dreadful, it is to be hoped, as that of the truly ruthless factory masters, in the north of England, compared with whose connived at, if not direct tyranny (now it is to be hoped on the eve of abolition), all West Indian tales sink into insignificance.

Bognor Rocks are only conspicuous at low-water, extending outwards two miles in length, and a quarter of a mile in width: the shore is gradually encroached upon by the sea, and is consequently protected by groins. Nine miles off this place are the *Oar* or *Ore* rocks, where, as a preventive against accidents which have before occurred, a vessel is kept moored, which in the daytime hoists a red flag, and at night hangs out large lanterns as a guide and warning to approaching mariners.

The sea promenade at Bognor is extensive, but not well kept up; it affords great facilities for fishing, and at Selsea are caught the best lobsters on this part of the coast. The view of the ocean at Bognor is singular; it is so completely shut in by projections of land a few miles to the east and west, that it might be taken for a private lake belonging solely to the inhabitants of this vicinity.

Near Bognor were discovered, in 1811, the spacious tessellated pavements of a magnificent Roman palace. A portion of these, representing the Rape of Ganymede, is finely engraved and coloured in Dallaway and Cartwright's History of the Rape of Arundel.

ARUNDEL.

GENERAL APPEARANCE.

The most commanding approach to Arundel is on the side of Worthing, though the opposite view is also richly wooded. A strong impression of ancient, feudal, and ancestral grandeur is presented by the stately front of the castle, placed on a terrace on the right, with the old central keep towering high above it, and the whole enveloped in ancient trees, and contrasted in front by the river of scanty breadth but impetuous flow, the bridge and the lower part of the town; whilst the tower, low spire, and flag-staff of the church appear on the summit of the principal and hilly street of the place.

HISTORY OF THE CASTLE AND TOWN.

The earliest conjectural accounts, in which a tendency to fabulous exaggeration may be pardoned, ascribe the name of this place to " Hirondelle," a swallow, which is still the arms of the town, though the origin of the bearing is not known. Others assert that the celebrated Bevis of Hampton (south), the conqueror of the giant Ascapart, and hero of ancient romances, who is supposed to have been keeper of the castle here, had a favourite horse, which for its swiftness he not only termed *Hirondelle*, or *Orundele*, in Norman French, but also called the demesne after its name. These are theoretical trifles, though their very existence is interesting, carrying us back, if in fancy alone, to the region of romance and enchantment. King Alfred left *Erundele* to his brother Athelm. By the Conqueror it was given to Roger de Mount-Gomeri, Earl of Alençon, who had been one of his best captains in the final engagement. Subsequently, through various mutations, it was in the hands of Adeliza, Queen of Henry I , and by her marriage, when a widow, it passed into the

family of Albini, afterwards into those of Fitzalan and
Maltravers, finally into the Mowbray's, by marriage with
an heiress. Philip de Mowbray, in the reign of Elizabeth,
was summoned as Earl of Arundel, *by tenure of the castle
only*. The family of Howard are descended from a judge of
the Common Pleas, in the reign of Edward I.; a conjectural Saxon origin has also been assigned to them at an
early epoch. The castle was certainly in existence before
the Conquest. It was besieged in 1102 by Henry I., but
capitulated on the understanding that Robert de Belesine
should retire to Normandy. In 1139, the Empress Maud
or Matilda, having landed at Littlehampton, repaired to
Arundel Castle, and was received by Queen Adeliza, who
was not unfavourable to her views. Stephen attacked the
castle, but yielding to the remonstrances of Adeliza, who
pleaded the rights of hospitality, suffered the Empress to
withdraw to Bristol. King Edward I. was entertained here
as a guest. In 1397 it was the scene of a confederation
against Richard II , but their proceedings being betrayed
to the monarch by the Earl's son-in-law, he was attainted
and beheaded. On the death of the Duke of Norfolk, in
1572, whose name is intermingled with the destiny of the
unfortunate Queen of Scots, perhaps guilty to a certain
degree, but certainly miserably ill-used by her unfeminine
and despotic sister, Elizabeth, his son continued Earl of
Arundel by patent, but he also, on suspicion of treasonable
practices, was attainted and executed in the year 1585; when
an inventory of the furniture of the castle, which included
very splendid hangings of silk and gold, was taken for
Lord Burleigh, and is copied in the diffusive account of
Mr. Dallaway, to which we must refer our readers for
minute particulars of this neighbourhood. The family were
restored by James I., and in 1644, the castle was besieged
and taken by capitulation, but plundered by the Parliamentary forces, the celebrated Chillingworth lending his skill to
the defence, which lasted for seventeen days. The strength
of the walls and outworks did not, however, answer the

general expectation. From this period till the repair by the late Duke of Norfolk, the castle remained in an imperfect state, and used only as an occasional residence.

It is entirely beyond our power and limits to enter here into an account of the celebrated family of the Mowbrays, Dukes of Norfolk, who are, to some extent, known to all who are familiar with the History of England, or the poetically attired chronicles of Shakspeare. We might dwell long on the interesting fortunes of the Earl of Surrey, one of the first improvers of the musical rythm of England; but we could say nothing which has not been often told of the almost hopeless, yet impassioned lover of the fair, though not, in comparison with his merits, worthy, Geraldine.

SONNET

IN PRAISE OF THE FAIR GERALDINE.

BY HENRY HOWARD, EARL OF SURREY.

[About 1540.]

From Tuscané came my lady's worthy race,
    Fair Florence was sometime her ancient seat;
The Western Isle, whose pleasant shore doth face
    Wild Camber's cliffs, did give her lively heat.
Fostered she was, with milk of Irish breast:
    Her sire, an earl; her dame, of prince's blood;
From tender years, in Britain she doth rest,
    With King's child, * where she tasteth costly food.
Honsdon did first present her to mine eyn;
    Bright is her hue, and Geraldine she hight.
Hampton me taught to wish her first for mine,
    And Windsor, alas! doth chase me from her sight.
Her beauty of kind, † her virtue from above;
Happy is he that can obtain her love!

We have been informed that there is still an Earl of Surrey, who is not without the gallant, chivalrous, and generous spirit of his ancestors; but who, more fortunate than his illustrious namesake, has obtained the hand of the Geraldine who was the object of his affections.

* Maid of honour to the Princess Mary.
† Of consanguinity, *i. e.* derived from her ancestors.

TOWN.

Arundel had a grant for a fair soon after the year 1200, which was extended to three by Edward I., and has returned two members to parliament since his reign, losing one in the present year. It has a market every Thursday, and a cattle market every alternate Tuesday. The charter under which the corporation of a mayor and twelve burgesses subsists bears date 1586. They are possessed of two silver gilt maces.

The town was formerly surrounded by walls: in 1339, half of it was consumed by fire, when the inhabitants were excused from taxes for that year. After the parliamentary siege, an allowance was made to some individuals who were favoured by the commissioners.

The College adjoining the church was founded by Robert, Earl of Arundel, in 1387, pursuant to the will of his father; dissolved at the Reformation, but granted by patent to the founder's family. Its present dilapidated state is partly owing to the devastations of the parliamentary soldiers.

There was also the hospital of Maison Dieu, or of the Holy Trinity, very liberally endowed for 20 poor men and a master, who was to be an ecclesiastic. This also was dissolved at the Reformation, and the possessions, which were nearly £200 per annum, then a splendid endowment, re-granted by patent (but for which it would seem probable that something had been paid to the king, who was not destitute of avarice) to the heirs of the founder; this, also, was dilapidated by Sir William Waller's soldiers, who occupied it during the siege.

The Bridge was founded by Queen Adeliza, in the twelfth century, built of wood, and a causeway *(Calcetum)* erected, of a mile in length, with a Priory, " *De Calceto,*" at the end; the monks receiving the tolls kept the bridge in good order. It was several times repaired in the sixteenth and seventeenth centuries, and, in 1742, was handsomely rebuilt of stone by the Hon. James Lumley, representative for the borough.

DESCRIPTION.

Arundel is a tolerably neat town, of no great apparent extent, enlivened by its river, which is the means of considerable traffic in coals and corn between London and the Mediterranean.   Ships of 150 tons, drawing 16 feet water, can come up as far as the bridge; and a trade is carried on still further up, by means of a canal which connects the Arun with the Thames. The name of this river instantaneously recalls the sweet and amiable poet, who sang on its banks;—

> " — Wild Arun too has heard thy strain,
> And echo on my native plain,
> Been soothed by pity's lute."

The town has several good inns, the principal of which is the Norfolk Arms, which has a good assembly-room; a small theatre, library, &c. &c.   The population in 1831 was 2803.

At the upper end of the town and nearly opposite the castle-gate is the Church, a spacious, solid, and handsome edifice, cruciform, with a low but well-built tower in the centre, whose obtuse leaden spire is painted white, and has a flagstaff on its apex as a guide to vessels at sea.   Including the large sepulchral chapel of the Norfolk family at the east end, formerly united to the college, it is the largest church in the county, measuring upwards of 190 feet in length.   Its architecture is principally that of the 14th century, with insertions of the 15th. The spacious nave is about 90 feet by 60, and has quatrefoils in circles for its clerestory windows.   The tower is about 26 feet square, and contains a gallery supporting the fine and beautiful organ, which, with its choir organ in front, is estimated to be worth £1200, and was purchased by subscription. This variety of position is seen in Ludlow church, Salop, and a few others not collegiate; it is here very effective, as it leaves the fine length of the nave unencumbered.   Irish oak is the almost indestructible material of the roof.   The whole of the body is very neatly fitted up; at the back of the corporation seat is a small painting on glass of the town arms, and at the south-east corner a rich stone tabernacled pulpit, now disused for that purpose. In the tower are six bells, and a small musical clock-bell hangs on the outside. The altar and communion-table are on the east side of the south transept; this is however *not* the fault of the Duke of Norfolk, as the altar was placed here before the Reformation. On one of its sides is a tablet for a young child of the present Rector:

> "Innocens et perbeatus, more florum decidi;
> Quid fles sepultum, viator? flente sum felicior."

Underneath is inscribed, " Suffer little children," &c. &c. *Consanguinei* or *amici*, might have been more applicable; the tears of the traveller for one so young, whom he had never seen, could not be expected.

We have now to speak of the Norfolk chapel at the east end, which forms a nave and north aisle, 75 feet in length, divided by three fine arches, and exhibiting some beautiful windows of the 14th and 15th centuries, with a grand one of seven divisions at the east end. Nothing has astonished, and must still astonish, the visitor more than to see the miserable state of neglect and decay in which this fine building and its rich monuments have long remained; it is the more incomprehensible, as there is no want of liberality in all the arrangements respecting the castle. We understood however that there was at length some expectation of repairs being undertaken, as the monument for the brother of the present Duke, which was executed at Rome, remains in packing-cases on the floor. But a great deal of the mischief is irretrievable. The fine carved and gilt oak ceiling fell down for want of repairs, and is now replaced by a common boarded one; and as the windows have been long almost destitute of glass, all the ornaments of the interior have suffered grievous injury. Some of the monuments are grand and interesting, exhibiting rich altar-tombs with minute ornaments, and lofty canopied erections with arches and pillars of the fanciful style which prevailed at the first introduction of Italian sculptures, here in one or two instances almost approaching to the airiness of the Oriental. The churchyard is walled round in a lofty and neat style. At its south-east angle are various buildings of the old college ; a school with turrets ; and a small Roman Catholic chapel.

CASTLE.

The total sum expended by the late munificent Duke of Norfolk on the new buildings was, as we understand, not less than £600,000.   A part, nearly amounting we believe to half of this sum, originated in the following curious circumstance : certain rents had been long in arrear, which were by original deed to be applied to the repairs of Arundel castle; and the tenants, rather *doggedly* certainly, refused to pay them unless they were applied to this precise purpose.   The Duke thereupon not only fulfilled the condition, but added that liberal expenditure which has produced so splendid an effect.

The Great Court is only built on three sides, the fourth rising on an ascent to the keep and the beautiful flower and fruit garden beyond it enclosed within the walls.   A terrace runs round the south and east sides ;   the former, which has a beautiful view over the river and surrounding country, is represented in our Vignette.

The entrance tower, which has bold arches and machicollations, was intended to have had elegant bartisan turrets hanging round its corner towers; unfortunately it has not been finished, but roofed in, in a very poor style.   The same remark applies, as we understand, to the interior of a Catholic chapel of the Tudor æra at the right of the entrance, which has externally much ornamental tracery.

The east and south sides are very handsome ; the former exhibits a large and bold relief in artificial stone of " Alfred instituting the Trial by Jury," with a Saxon legend explaining the purport : beneath are four rich early Norman arches.   In the upper part of this side is the handsome library, externally decorated with carved windows, an oriel, machicollations, open parapet, curiously-wrought corbels, and round turrets.   The eastern side has the principal entrance,—a deep and grand Norman arch, above which are three tiers of windows, flanked by turrets, and two statues, in niches, of Liberty and Hospitality; the latter, by the way, is not very intelligible. To enter into a description of the various ornaments of this grand front would far exceed our limits.

The lofty and commanding keep is a spacious round tower, between 60 and 70 feet in diameter, approached by an inclined plane from one of the ancient towers of the base-court. The remains of antiquity in this part of the building will please and detain the attention of the visitor; within its area are one or two subterranean excavations, not yet fully explored; and in a neighbouring tower is a well of great diameter, formerly 300 feet deep, but now partly filled up, the appearance of which is described as awful and terrific. From the keep is a beautiful view south-east and west; whilst the prospect of the very pretty garden within the walls, devoted both to flowers and fruit, was to us by no means less pleasing. We never felt the expression of the Latin term *apricus* more vividly than whilst looking at this scene; and we thought that either here or on the terrace a person must be either leaden-spirited or irretrievably unhappy, who did not, for the time at least, experience a soothing influence in the view from Arundel Castle. The curious Australian owls kept within the circuit of this tower are not the least of the novelties which will detain the visitor's attention, who could not imagine, till he had seen them, that this species of bird was found in such size and beauty. They are larger than a turkey, measuring four feet across their wings when expanded, and their size, and brilliancy of their " visual orbs," are of the most striking character. They are not remarkably tame.

An amusing anecdote is related regarding one of the finest Owl*esses*, in the time of the late Duke of Norfolk, which was called, by a great misnomer certainly, " *Lord Thurlow*." It happened that the celebrated chancellor of that name was dangerously ill, and much political anticipation was thereby occasioned. One of the attendants advanced hastily, and out of breath, to the Duke, early in the morning,—" Please your Grace, Lord Thurlow ——" " Well," said the Duke, " what's the news—is he better or worse?"—" Please your Grace "—

answered the man—"*just laid an egg!*"— quite unconscious of the amazement he should excite by his *mal à propos* reply.

INTERIOR.
VESTIBULE.

A very handsome double stone staircase, having polished brass railings with splendid mahogany architraves, leads under a vaulted and fretted roof into the

GALLERY,

which is 195 feet long and 12 feet broad, floored with oak, with doors, window cases and linings, and wainscottings, as all the other rooms, of the *finest polished mahogany* more than an inch in thickness. No decoration of this castle has a more novel and startling effect than this; to see such a costly wood used with the most lavish profusion in every part of the rooms, some of which have even carved ceilings of the same material. The late Duke purchased a large ship-load of this valuable wood, which turned out to be some of the finest ever imported into England. In this gallery are some curious old gilt chairs, lined with worked velvet emblazoned with armorial bearings.

BARONS' HALL,

115 feet in length and 35 in width, ceiled with chestnut, has never been completed, and its walls are temporarily covered with red cloth. At the end is a large and magnificent window of stained glass, representing the signing of Magna Charta, of excellent composition, and correct historical costumes and accompaniments. Fitzwalter, the principal Baron, is a likeness of the late Duke of Norfolk. In the side windows are also whole length armed figures, painted in brilliant colours, relieved by fine perspective.

This room was opened in the year 1815, with a magnificent entertainment of ancient splendour to upwards of 300 persons*.

---

* " From the sublime to the ridiculous there is but a step." Mr. C. Wright, author of a " History of Arundel," and " The Brighton Ambulator," declares that "it was a feast of which the Gods might have partaken, and been satisfied !" What a cruel pity then that they were not invited to " take their fill !" Messieurs Jupiter, Apollo, &c. Mesdames Juno and Venus, and all the rest of them. Provided always, that they should be dressed decorously, after the court fashion of the earth; and that if Bacchus was noisy, Jupiter should send him down stairs.

The chimney-piece is of fine statuary marble, bearing the head of Neptune, and various marine emblems. Some ancient pieces of armour are also kept here, one of which is said to have been the identical sword of *Bevis*.

THE DRAWING ROOM,

54 feet by 28, is hung with crimson velvet, edged with gold mouldings, has a fine white marble chimney-piece, and some handsome pier-glasses. The numerous paintings are principally family portraits, among which is a fine one of the celebrated Earl of Surrey; but at the east end is an historical painting, 10 feet, representing the Earl of the time of Henry VII. defending himself before that monarch, for having taken the part of Richard III. The countenances of both the king and the warrior are very fine, and the Princess Elizabeth, in the back ground, who holds the red rose in her hand, is a lovely and interesting figure.

DINING-ROOM,
45 feet by 24.

A very handsome painted window, 20 feet by 10, decorates the end of this apartment, representing an entertainment given by Solomon to the Queen of Sheba, with many auxiliary figures. The countenance of the former is a portrait of the late Duke of Norfolk, and that of the Queen, of Lady Frances Fitzroy, his wife; the latter figure has an elegant effect, but the precise expression which the painter has chosen to give to the Duke is by no means suited to Solomon; it is too Bacchanalian. On each side, at this end of the room, is an oblong window, of plate-glass, designed to assist the effect of the larger: in their centres are small transparencies of painted glass, the left representing the Mercy Seat in the Tabernacle; and the right, the interior of the Tabernacle. There are, also, in this room two fresco paintings, by *Le Brun*, imitating sculpture with the most astonishing success, almost inducing, at a little distance, a doubt of the real execution,—Adam and Eve, with the serpent, in Paradise, and the Four Seasons. At the opposite extremity to the painted window is a carved gallery for music.

PRINCE REGENT'S BED-ROOM

is hung with magnificent cut velvet, *i. e.* flowers of red and
green, &c. in velvet, raised on a ground of white satin ; with
gold mouldings and other ornaments : the bed has fine reeded
pillars, and a rich gothic canopy.

EARL MARSHAL'S BED-ROOM

has also splendid furniture, and a bedstead of nearly equal
beauty, with curtains of crimson damask silk ; some curiously
worked chairs ; a rich India cabinet, and a fine marble chimney-piece, said to represent *Seneca* holding the plough :—
Surely this is a mistake : we never heard of that philosopher's
agricultural talents.

THE BREAKFAST ROOM

has windows of plate-glass, commanding a fine view over the
river.　It contains some fine portraits, including one of Oliver
Cromwell, by Rubens ; and a likeness of Cardinal Howard,
almoner to Catherine, Queen of Charles II., who died at Rome
in 1694, leaving an estimable character for moderation and
benevolence.　There are also two fine paintings by Hogarth,
a view of the old castle, and a design in Covent-garden Market, exhibiting the painter's fancy and humour.

Our limits will not allow us to particularize many smaller
elegant apartments adorned with paintings and rich furniture.
In one of the rooms is a bed, said to have been used by the
Empress Maud, which, amidst modern additions and repairs,
contains a small portion of the original.

THE LIBRARY,
120 *feet by* 24.

The whole of the walls, galleries, pillars, and fan-tracery
ceiling of this noble room are composed of the richest mahogany, wrought in the most exquisite style of architectural
carving, and ornaments of fruit and flowers ; the floor alone
is of oak, and the linings of some of the closets of cedar.　The
tout ensemble is magnificent, exhibiting in costly wood, carvings
similar to the finest specimens in the cathedrals, or in Henry
VIIth's chapel.　Two or three stately white marble chimney-

pieces are decorated with noble Termini, representing heads of Homer, Sophocles, &c. We must leave this simple description to be extended by the fancy of the reader: were we to enter into details, we should only weaken its effect.

ARUNDEL MARBLES.

When briefly alluding to the general military and political renown of this family, we should have singled out one individual eminently distinguished for his taste in the fine arts and classical antiquities, through whose munificent and enterprising spirit the *Arundelian* marbles, a far more valuable collection than Lord Elgin's, were brought from Samos, and in addition to affording interesting specimens of ancient sculpture, have been of the very highest importance in settling the canons of Greek chronology. This earl was ambassador to the imperial diet for the election of an Emperor of the Romans in 1636; when, by his generous spirit, and his avidity for collecting objects of curiosity, he is said to have expended 90,000*l.*, then a much more considerable sum than at present, in the course of nine months. At the rebellion, his collection was removed to Antwerp: having been, after his death, placed at Norfolk House, in the Strand, some part was accidentally damaged by the fall of a wall, and the principal portion of the remainder coming into the possession of the Earl of Pomfret, was, by his countess, presented to the University of Oxford.

In addition to his splendid patronage of art, and enterprising travels, this earl was the friend and encourager of Sir Robert Cotton, Sir Henry Spelman, Camden, and other characters of worth and learning.

The arms of the Duke of Norfolk, hereditary Earl Marshal, Earl of Arundel, Surrey, &c. &c. &c., premier Duke, Baron, and Earl of England, are divided into four grand quarters:—Howard; Brotherton, Earl of Norfolk; Warren, Earl of Surrey; Mowbray, Duke of Norfolk. The former has an augmentation granted after the victory of Flodden.

Crests.—*Or* on a chapeau *gules*, turned-up *ermine*, a *Lion*

Statant guardant, *or*, gorged with a ducal coronet, *argent*. This was the crest of Thomas Brotherton, fifth son of Edward I. Another, that of Arundel, is, on a wreath, a Mount *vert*, surmounted by a Horse passant, *argent*, holding in his mouth a slip of oak, fructed proper.

Supporters —On the dexter side, a Lion, on the sinister, a Horse, both *argent*, the latter holding a slip of oak, as before.

Motto:—" SOLA VIRTUS INVICTA."

The superficies of the site of the castle is 950 feet by 250, enclosing five acres and a half; but it is said to have, in remote times, included upwards of a mile.

The Park *⁎* is seven miles in circuit, and contains a variety of ornamental buildings, all in the gothic or castellated style: it is also beautifully wooded, and has a herd of one thousand deer.

The road from Arundel to Chichester contains no object of interest. At least we trust the reader will not meet with the variety we did, which was near costing us a life, and depriving the world of this (valuable) book.

" Ille et nefasto te '*junxit*,' die !"

Let him beware of the cupidity and want of principle of those who let out to the traveller dilapidated horses.

By the intervention of such an occurrence, our notices of this western extremity were much abridged, especially that of Chichester. Yet the memoranda of Goodwood, though hastily written whilst suffering illness, were accompanied by a feeling of gratification, the invariable result of elegance and symmetry, which dulled the sense of pain.

CHICHESTER.

HISTORY.

Chichester is supposed, on good authority, to have been the ancient *Regnum*, founded by *Cogi*, a British chief, who, having assisted the Romans in repelling the Dobuni, added, like Caius Marcius, an adjunct to his name, and termed himself *Cogi-dubunus*. A stone tablet was discovered in the year 1723, bearing the following inscription, which was afterwards removed to Goodwood, and placed in a small temple erected to receive it, with a bust of Cogidubunus on its summit:

" NEPTUNO ET MINERVÆ
TEMPLUM
PRO SALUTE DOMUS DIVINÆ
EX AUCTORITATE IMP. TI. CLAUD.
ET COGIDUBNI REGIS LEGAL, IN BRIT.
COLLEGIUM FABROR *, ET QUI IN EO
ET SACRIS VEL HONORATI SUNT DE SUO
DEDICAVERUNT DONANTE AREAM
PUDENTE PUDENTINI FIL."

" As to the Roman settlement at Chichester, I am clear that it must be the earliest, the first or second in Britain: the inscription is undoubtedly the oldest inscription that has been discovered in Great Britain, the internal marks carry it very high. The dedication of this temple to Neptune, ' ob salutem *Domûs Divinæ*,' must be, most probably, for Claudius's safe return to Rome, for we hear of no other Emperor till long after. It agrees very well with the remarkable inscription in the Barbarini palace at

---

* " Collegium Fabrorum was as ancient at Rome as the reign of Numa Pompilius. It included all workmen concerned in any kind of building, Fabri, Ferrarii, Tignarii, Materiarii, Navales, &c."—*Dallaway*.

Rome, with the accounts given by Tacitus and Suetonius, that the *Isle of White* (sic) was subdued in Claudius's time, and consequently this part of our island. It was erected certainly in Cogidubnus's lifetime; but he lived till Tacitus was in Britain with his uncle Agricola, between anno 70 and 85. Tacitus's account implies, that Cogidubnus had been some years in that office, because he says, 'Ad nostram usque ætatem fidissimus.' From A.D. 43 to 70 is but 27 years, if so, 80, but 37, which is but reasonable allowance, and consequently fixes this marble to the age of Claudius."

" Mr. Gale's account in *Horseley*, concerning the *Pudens* of this inscription, and the *Claudia* of *Martial*, are all very probable. And my father has vindicated the use of *Domus* Divinæ, from the idle exceptions of Mr. Ward."—Willingdon, April 3, 1771.—Letter from Edw. Clarke to Sir W. B.—*Burrell MSS.*

A few of the words, or portions of words, in this inscription, as we have printed it, are conjectural, and some antiquaries have supplied them rather differently. Full discussions on this subject are contained in No. 379 of the Philosophical Transactions, and Stukely's Itinerary, at Plate XLIX.

Claudius had been honoured with a triumph at Rome, for having crossed the sea (no great naval exploit, certainly,) in a successful expedition from Gaul to Britain.

" A.D. 46. This year Claudius, the second of the Roman emperors who invaded Britain, took the greater part of the island into his power, and added the Orkneys to the dominion of the Romans. This was in the fourth year of his reign. And in the same year happened the great famine in Syria which Luke mentions in the book called The Acts of the Apostles. After Claudius, Nero succeeded to the empire, who almost lost the island, Britain, through his incapacity."—*Saxon Chronicle.*

A second tablet of the same æra was discovered about twenty years since :

" NERONI

CLAUDIO DIVI CLAUDII

AUG. F. GERMANICI

CÆS. NEPOTI TI. CÆS

AUG. PRONEPOTI DIV. AUG.

ABNEPOTI CÆSARI AUG. GERM.

R.R.P. IV. IMP. V. COS. IV.

SOLVI CVRAVIT VOTVM MERITO."

And a third in 1823, a votive altar, which is also in the possession of the Duke of Richmond :

" GENIO S. *(suo)*
LUCULLUS
AMMINI FIL.
D. P.' *(dedicavit publice.)*

Lucullus was Agricola's lieutenant, and succeeded to the chief command after his death.

The principality of the *Regni*, including Sussex and Kent, was in the family of Cogidubnus till the time of Lucius, one of the generally supposed founders of Christianity in Britain, and the last of its native princes, A. D. 165.

The modern name of Chichester is derived from Cissa, son of Ælla, who, succeeding his father, made it the place of his abode—hence called *Cissa-ceastre*. He died in 577, aged 117; and some have thought it probable that he was buried at *Cissbury*, a favourite retreat; but this idea is merely conjectural.

" A.D. 477. This year came Ella to Britain, with his three sons, Cymen, and Wlenking, and Cissa, in three ships; landing at a place that is called Cymenshore *. There they slew many of the Welsh (British); and some in flight they drove into the wood that is called Andred's-ley."

" A.D. 485. This year Ella fought with the Welsh (British) nigh Mecred's-Burnsted."

" A.D. 490. This year Ella and Cissa besieged the city of Andred, and slew all that were therein; nor was one Briton left there afterwards."—*Saxon Chronicle.*

Chichester remained unnoticed and of moderate consequence till the removal of the see from Selsea by William the Conqueror: the town was bestowed on Roger de Montgomery, Earl of Alençon and Shrewsbury and Arundel, who erected a castle joined to the ramparts of the city, and four gates, and gave the south-west quarter for the site of the cathedral and residence of the clergy. The possessions of Hugh de Belesme, one of his sons, were confiscated by Henry I., on account of his having sided with the rebellious Robert, and Chichester was given with Arundel to his queen Adeliza, and passed by her marriage to William de Albini, afterwards created, by the Empress Maud, Earl of Chichester and Arundel. The castle

* Supposed to be *West Wittering*, near Selsey and Chichester.

was ordered to be demolished by King John, but the sentence was not carried into effect till the first year of Henry III., 1216. A Franciscan convent was founded on its site, which, at the dissolution, was granted to the corporation of the city, and the property has lately been purchased by the Duke of Richmond.

Great part of the city with the cathedral was destroyed by fire in the years 1114 and 1186. Various successive charters were granted by different monarchs, commencing with Stephen and ending with James II.

Chichester was occupied by the royalists under Sir Edward Ford, sheriff of the county, in 1642; besieged by Sir William Waller, and taken after eight days' siege in the month of December. It is believed that the inhabitants made a compromise with the soldiers of the amount of one month's pay to prevent their being plundered; but the cathedral and all its adjuncts were severely devastated, and the houses of the recorder and some of the inhabitants, who were sent prisoners to London, demolished. Great injury was sustained in the city by the military operations, several houses being destroyed, with the churches of St. Bartholomew and St. Pancras; the north-west tower of the cathedral was also battered down, and has not since been rebuilt. In 1645 the city was disgarrisoned by order of the parliamentary government, and the ordnance removed to the castle of Arundel.

DESCRIPTION.

The appearance of Chichester, at a little distance, is pleasing; it is nearly embosomed in elm trees, which follow the course of the ancient walls for the space of a mile and three quarters, above which the lofty and tapering spire of the cathedral appears as if rising into the clouds. The body of the town consists of four streets, meeting at the large and handsome octagonal cross; these are decently built, well paved, and excellently lighted, and the east street, especially, has an air of ancient and solid respectability. The population in 1831 was 8270.

CATHEDRAL.

This edifice is indubitably one of the least considerable and handsome cathedrals in England. Its principal objects of curiosity are its elegant spire, the *five* aisles of its nave, and the paintings in the south transept. The original church was begun by Bishop Ralph in 1091, but nearly destroyed, whilst yet unfinished, by a fire in 1114; rebuilt by the aid of pecuniary assistance from Henry I., but a second time extensively injured by fire in 1186. It was then restored by Bishop Seffrid, who rebuilt the parts which had been consumed, and added an upper triforium or gallery to the clerestory of the nave, which remained uninjured, but, as seen at the present day, is so exceedingly clumsy, that it is to be regretted it had not been destroyed; the lower part is in better style, and the new gallery lighter and approaching to the Gothic. The parts of the church, east of the central tower, are supposed to have been erected in the thirteenth and beginning of the fourteenth century, of which era also is the spire, and the north-west bell-tower: the spire has been sometimes conjectured, from a degree of similarity in appearance, to have been erected by the same artist as that of Salisbury. The three sides of cloisters and several of the windows are of later date.

EXTERNAL APPEARANCE AND DIMENSIONS.

The actual length from east to west, exclusive of the Lady Chapel, now the library, is 325 feet, but the latter, including its vestibule, is 79, making a total of 404. The nave is 151 feet from west to east, tower, 34, choir, 100, and presbytery, 40. The transept is 129 feet by 34: width of the nave,— centre aisle, 26 feet, two original side aisles, 12 feet each, two outer ones, 14 do.; total, 78*: height of centre aisle, $61\frac{1}{2}$; of

---

* Mr. Dallaway *sums up* the width thus; nave, 97 feet; choir, 60; which has been copied in a Chichester Guide: it is scarcely necessary to add that if the items are right, the sum is in both cases decidedly wrong. We beg to add that we have the highest respect for Mr. Dallaway's work in general, but this is one of the most extraordinary errors we ever witnessed, and it was quite by accident that we thought of examining it.

the choir, 59; breadth, with its two aisles, 50; height of the
spire, to the finial under the weathercock, 271; height of
the south-west tower, 100 feet; of the campanile or bell-
tower, 120; dimensions of the cloister,—west side, 84 feet by
14½; south, 198 by 10 feet 4; east, 122 feet 4 by 10 feet 3.

A good north view of this cathedral is now opened by re-
moving several houses; still the south-west continues to be
the most picturesque, being aided both by the cloisters and
the solidly handsome Norman tower remaining at this angle,
which is well decorated with arches and strong buttresses, and
has an elegant Norman arch at the bottom of its southern face.
The transepts are without aisles, but have large and rich
windows of the Tudor æra: that in the south transept, inserted
by Bishop Sherborne, has some resemblance to the architecture
of Rouen cathedral. The windows of the outer aisles are
large and neat; those of the clerestory, Norman. Plain flying
buttresses strengthen it from the side aisles, and it has a bold
parapet with very neat corbels and some handsome spiral
pinnacles in the eastern division. The centre embattled tower
has large and handsome early Gothic windows now blank,
corner turrets, and others of a light character, rising at the
base of the spire; the latter is ribbed at the angles, has handsome canopied windows at its base, and two rich and broad
bands of fretwork at different stages of its height. The
cloisters have spacious windows of the fifteenth century filled
with mullions and tracery. About 20 feet north-west of the
end of the church is the Campanile, a very heavy structure,
which appears to much greater advantage at a small distance
than when viewed closely: it is built of friable stone, and its
lower part is in a dirty and neglected state. The upper story
rises to an octagonal turret, guarded by flying buttresses from
small turrets at the angles of the tower. It contains seven
bells, not remarkably well-toned, the tenor weighing twenty-
three cwt.; and these are seldom used except on Sundays, a
single bell in the spire steeple tolling to prayers, which has
rather a dull effect.

INTERIOR.

At the west end of the nave is a handsome porch, with a large window in a barbarously modern and incongruous style. The view of the nave at the entrance, when the outer aisles are not seen, is heavy and unprepossessing; the lower arches are not altogether unpleasing, but the double arches of the first gallery are very ugly; the upper *triforia,* which are early Gothic, and have palm-tree capitals, an ornament introduced after the first crusade as a memorial of Palestine, are much neater, and the pointed vaulting of the roof, which springs from light pilasters running up the face of the clerestory, though very plain, is well proportioned and has neat keystones. The prospect is terminated under the tower by a lofty, plain stone screen, with a large organ, the pipes of which, on this side, not being imitative of gold, but yellow marble, have a very dull effect. When we proceed laterally, however, to the outer aisles, which were erected principally to contain oratories and chantries, something better meets our view, in the fine arches and elegant clustered columns of the early Gothic, though by no means equal to those of Shoreham. The choir, which includes the great tower with its lofty but plain circular arches, is 134 feet long, and displays the stalls erected by Bishop Sherborne at the beginning of the sixteenth century, profusely gilt, but painted of an unfortunately dull chocolate colour; in front are the names of the prebendaries, and some other inscriptions in very fine old characters; a neat wainscot altar screen with panels of crimson velvet terminates the east end. The choir is paved with marble, in which respect it has a great superiority over the nave; its architecture is similar, with the exception of the omission of the outer side aisles; its ancient organ has a very full and grand tone. The presbytery, beyond the altar screen, consisting of two arches only (there are eight in the nave and three in the choir, exclusive of the tower), has rich and noble architectural features; the clustered columns below of Petworth marble, with isolated pilasters round a central shaft, and finely wrought double arches of the gallery above, which enclose a small representation of the Salvator Mundi, are entitled to unmixed praise. The want of any stained glass at this end of the church must be sensibly felt by the spectator. Below the east window commences the vestibule of the library, which has, externally, very handsome windows: a spacious vault for the Duke of Richmond's family was constructed under it in the year 1750.

The north transept is the parish church of St. Bartholomew the Great, or the Subdeanery; a similar instance occurs in the south transept of Chester cathedral; this appears internally but mediocre, and is meanly partitioned from the aisle. The south contains the two large and interesting historical paintings, and the series of portraits of the kings and bishops.

This, as we have before stated, is one of the principal of the few curiosities which this cathedral can boast, for which it is indebted to the munificence and skill of Robert Sherborne, one of its bishops, who had been ambassador from Henry VII. to the Pope, and brought back from Rome a refined taste, joined to a spirit of great liberality. He founded four prebends in this church, and greatly benefited his diocese; he recovered rights of advowson, and annexed them; endowed vicarages, and commuted pensions for tithes. His principal works in the cathedral were the new stalls, a beautiful painted ceiling to the nave, and the ornaments in this transept; but, during twenty-two years, he expended on this church, and the reparation of three manor-houses belonging to the see, the then considerable sum of 3707*l.* 4*s.* 0*d.*: he also left a perpetual fund for the marriage of poor maidens of the city. A very short time before his death, on account of infirmity, he petitioned, and obtained leave, to resign his bishoprick; and he died in 1536, at the great age of ninety-six years. He has a tomb and effigy in the south aisle of the nave, which was much defaced by the parliamentary soldiers, but still retains the armorial bearings, and the inscription—" *Non intres in judicium cum servo tuo domine, Roberto Shurborne.*"—" Enter not into judgment, O Lord, with thy servant, Robert Shurborne."

The two large paintings on the west side are respectively

12 feet 8 inches by 8 feet 8 inches, and 13 feet 4 by 8 feet 8. The first represents the foundation of the see at Selsey by Ceadwalla, on the petition of Wilfrid. The king, attended by a train of courtiers, is coming forward on the steps of a large palace, and is met by Wilfrid, with the monks of the monastery of Selsey; the church and the peninsula appear in the back-ground. Wilfrid holds a scroll, inscribed " 𝔇𝔞 𝔰𝔢𝔯𝔟𝔦𝔰 𝔇𝔢𝔦 𝔩𝔬𝔠𝔲' 𝔥𝔞𝔟𝔦𝔱𝔞𝔱𝔦𝔬𝔫𝔦𝔰 𝔭𝔯𝔬𝔭𝔱𝔢𝔯 𝔇𝔢𝔲𝔪."—" Give to the servants of God a place of habitation, for the sake of God." The king points with one hand to an open illuminated book, in which is written " 𝔉𝔦𝔞𝔱 𝔰𝔦𝔠𝔲𝔱 𝔭𝔢𝔱𝔦𝔱𝔲𝔯"—" be it as it is requested." The second painting represents Shurborne, attended by his ecclesiastics, petitioning Henry VII. for a confirmation of the charter granted by Ceadwalla, whilst, by an absurd anachronism, Henry VIII. is introduced as standing by him, and granting the petition. The bishop displays a scroll, inscribed " 𝔖𝔞𝔫𝔠𝔱𝔦𝔰𝔰𝔦𝔪𝔢 𝔯𝔢𝔵, 𝔭'𝔭𝔱𝔢𝔯 𝔡𝔢𝔲', 𝔠𝔬𝔩𝔲𝔞 𝔢𝔠𝔠𝔩𝔢𝔰𝔦𝔞' 𝔱𝔲𝔞' 𝔠𝔦𝔠𝔢𝔰𝔱𝔯𝔢𝔫 𝔦𝔞' 𝔠𝔞𝔱𝔥𝔢𝔡𝔯𝔞𝔩𝔢, 𝔰𝔦𝔠𝔲𝔱 𝔠𝔢𝔡𝔴𝔞𝔩𝔩𝔞 𝔯𝔢𝔵 𝔖𝔲𝔰𝔰𝔢𝔵 𝔢𝔠𝔠𝔩𝔢𝔰𝔦𝔞 𝔖𝔦𝔩𝔢𝔰𝔦𝔢𝔫 𝔬𝔩𝔦𝔪 𝔠𝔞𝔱𝔥𝔢𝔡𝔯𝔞𝔩𝔢 𝔠𝔬𝔩𝔲𝔞𝔟𝔦𝔱."—" Most sacred King, for the sake of God, confirm now thy church of Chichester as a cathedral, as formerly Ceadwalla, King of Sussex, confirmed the church of Selsey as a cathedral." The king points, as before, to a book inscribed " 𝔓𝔯𝔬 𝔞𝔪𝔬𝔯𝔢 𝔦𝔥𝔲 𝔵𝔯𝔦 𝔮𝔡 𝔭𝔢𝔱𝔦𝔰 𝔠𝔬𝔠𝔢𝔢𝔡𝔬." —" For the love of Jesus Christ, what you ask I grant." In both of these paintings are many curious and elaborate accompaniments. At the bottom of one is inscribed, within a border, 𝔖𝔞𝔫𝔠𝔱𝔲𝔰 𝔚𝔦𝔩𝔣𝔯𝔦𝔡𝔲𝔰; and, under the other, Bishop Shurborne's motto—" 𝔒𝔭𝔢𝔯𝔦𝔟𝔲𝔰 𝔠𝔯𝔢𝔡𝔦𝔱𝔢." These paintings were scratched and defaced by the swords of the parliamentary soldiers, and afterwards repaired by an inferior artist; but they are still justly considered as very fine early specimens of painting; the perspective of both is very good, and the colouring not only rich, but in good keeping; the figures and countenances, especially in the latter, are such as would not disgrace a superior limner of the present day.

" The historical painting in the south transept is said to be the work of one Bernardi, an Italian, who came into England with Bishop Sherborne. Painting was then brought to its highest perfection in Italy, and very probably the man might be a disciple of some of the great masters. The picture is certainly not Holbein's. I could venture to affirm this by what I have seen of Holbein's work at Cowdry. He was eminent for colouring and expression, but had no notion of perspective, and very little of composition. His landscapes are so ill-designed, that his very towers seem to be in ambush, and the horsemen who besiege them are big enough to ride over the walls. What this picture was for colouring and expression before it was so much defaced in the great rebellion, there is no knowing; but the manner is quite different from Holbein's; the perspective is not bad; the architecture excellent; and the figures are in general well disposed in the picture. I should make no question but the tradition here is the true account of it."—Rev. W. CLARKE.—*Burrell MSS.*

The small portraits, which have a rather pleasing appearance from their being surrounded by gilt oval rims on a dark ground, exhibit, on the east side, representations of various Bishops of Chichester, some with ancient legendary inscriptions; and, on the other side, a very tolerable series of the kings of England, from the Conquest, above which is inscribed—" *Confiteantur tibi omnes Reges.*" " *Recta est via quæ ducit ad vitam.*" The portraits have been regularly continued, and end with the good-humoured and benevolent countenance of George III.

On the north side of this transept is the tomb of St Richard, an altar-tomb under an arcade: the three light and elegant arches in front are, properly speaking, *neuf*-foil, each having nine cusps; above is tracery and a flowered parapet.

There are a great number of other monuments and ancient pieces of sculpture in this cathedral, which we have not space to describe. At the west end of the middle south aisle of the nave is a fine whole-length statue of Mr. Huskisson; and, in the same aisle, the monument of Collins, whose latter years were clouded by a degree of occasional insanity, with the unfortunate additional circumstance of his having, after years of comparative penury, obtained a fortune when it was too late to enjoy it. *Vide* Johnson's Biography. He is here represented in a calm interval, reading the New Testament, and expressing a sentiment similar to a declaration of the learned Selden.

The monument, of white marble, was executed by Flaxman, and erected by subscription; at its foot are two small figures of Love and Pity. The epitaph was the joint production of Hayley and of a Mr. Sargent, author of " The Mine." The description is, doubtless, exaggerated, with a similar bad taste to that which induced Mr. Hayley, and others after him, still more silly, to drag forward the sufferings of the benevolent and excellently disposed, but afflicted and hardly sane, Cowper*.

> " Ye who the merits of the dead revere,
> Who hold misfortune sacred, genius dear,
> Regard this tomb; where Collins' hapless name
> Solicits kindness with a double claim.
> Tho' nature gave him, and tho' science taught,
> The fire of fancy, and the reach of thought,
> Severely doom'd to penury's extreme,
> He pass'd in maddening pain, life's feverish dream;
> While rays of genius only served to show
> The thick'ning horror, and exalt his woe.
> Ye walls that echoed to his frantic moan!
> Guard the due record of this grateful stone.
> Strangers to him, enamour'd of his lays,
> This fond memorial to his talents raise;
> For this, the ashes of a bard require,
> Who touch'd the tenderest notes of pity's lyre;
> Who join'd pure faith to strong poetic powers,
> Who, in reviving reason's lucid hours,
> Sought on one book his troubled mind to rest,
> And rightly deem'd the book of God the best."

A similar example of a five-aisled nave occurs in the collegiate church of Manchester; but as that is in a bold and uniform style of the fifteenth century, it is to the dull nave of this cathedral as " Hyperion to a Satyr." The *burrowers* were employed in this church in the year 1829, and discovered some of the remains of the ancient bishops, which they have *engraved and published;* it is, perhaps, want of a real archæological taste, but we cannot see any pleasure in this, except for those who wish to " sup on horrors;" at least it is

---

* There is a parallel, yet with diverse features, is there not? in the conduct of those who delight to ransack all the petty stores of the soured misanthrope, Lord Byron. Why not let that poor man rest in peace? Are we never to have done with his reminiscences? Why should the kind-hearted poet Rogers—for that at least he is—be made to know that he had a false friend, who proved a bitterly scurrilous enemy? But they get money by it!

falling short of the humanity and reverence of the nations of antiquity, who respected the rights of sepulture.

Some other remains were at the same time found, as rings, chalices, crosses, to the publication of which there could exist no objection. A beautiful specimen of the ancient painted ceiling of the nave has also been published; it is added that the original was erased in 1817 — surely an act very much to be regretted. We also saw the engraving of a circular painting of the thirteenth century on the wall of the chapel of the bishop's palace (an edifice partly modernized, but neat and venerable); it measures two feet eight inches in diameter, and exhibits the Virgin and Child, delicately executed and richly coloured, and surrounded by a variegated border.

Chichester cathedral was miserably and madly ill-used by the republican soldiers. After the restoration it was assisted by the bounty of many liberal subscribers, amongst whom were a Bishop of Winchester, 200*l.*; two of Chichester, 100*l.* each; Bishop of Oxford, 100*l.*; Dr. Brideoke, 100*l.*; Earl of Northumberland, 100*l.*; William Ashburnham, Esq. cofferer to the king, 100*l.*; Hugh May, Esq. 100*l.*; T. Tryon, Esq. 100*l.*; &c. &c.,—total 1680*l.** The organ cost 300*l.* (the former one having been broken in pieces by the soldiers with their pole-axes), and is the one still in use; the wainscot of the choir 107*l.*, and the marble pavement 117*l.* 5*s.* 6*d.*

The choral body is very slender, consisting of four vicars, four singing men, and six choristers only. An addition of two has lately been made to the singing men, and the same is said to be purposed for the choristers, which ought certainly to have been done first; with this limited number, however, the service is performed in a remarkably creditable manner. The present bishop is Dr. Maltby, a gentleman of eminent learning; and the dean, Dr. Chandler, also an esteemed character.

The church and churchyard contain a variety of monuments, some of them belonging to distinguished families and characters, and not uninteresting. We accidentally noticed the follow-

* Dallaway.

ing in the churchyard, which, though simple enough, has something pleasing; it is for a Miss Gatehouse, aged 13.

> " O thou, beloved beyond what words can tell,
> Our dearest girl, a little while, farewell ! "

Besides the Cathedral, Chichester has great part of its
ancient walls remaining, St. Mary's Hospital, a picturesque
object, an ancient Town-hall, formerly a chapel, and the Cross.
This spacious and beautiful octagonal structure, of the fifteenth
century, stands near the centre of the town : on its summit
was a heavily rich finial which has been taken down and
replaced by a small cupola or lantern, neat in itself, but not
very appropriate. The Cross was thoroughly repaired by a
Duke of Richmond in 1724. A lady gave a clock to this
structure, " as an hourly memorial of her love to the city."
The worthy benefactress did not surely count on the hourly
gratitude of posterity.

EMINENT NATIVE OF CHICHESTER.

" Dr. WILLIAM JUXON, educated at London, at Merchant-Taylor's
School, and at Oxford, in St. John's College, where he became first fellow,
and then master, or president. His worth in this station recommended him
to his majesty King Charles the First to be his chaplain, in which place
he had not long continued before his majesty rewarded his gravity, learning,
and piety, with divers preferments successively, viz. the deanery of Worcester, the office of the clerk of his majesty's closet, bishoprick of Exeter,
deanry of the king's chapel, bishoprick of London, a privy counsellor,
and lastly, lord treasurer, which great office he held from 1635 to 1641,
all which places he managed with the greatest satisfaction. But when the
rebellion against his master came on, he found the same hard usage with
his brethren the bishops, for he was put out of the Lords' House with them,
and had the revenues of his bishoprick seized, as theirs was; yet had this
honour above them all, to attend his majesty King Charles the First in his
most disconsolate condition, 'till he saw him on the scaffold resign his soul
to God. From that time, with a soul full of grief for his master's sufferings, he retired to his manor of Compton, in Gloucestershire, where he
spent his time in melancholy retirement, and constant devotion, 'till the
restoration of King Charles the Second, when he was, after a few months
residence on his see of London, removed to the archbishoprick of Canterbury, to the great joy of all true churchmen. He was consecrated in King
Henry the Seventh's chapel, at Westminster; but enjoy'd not that station
long, for he died in his palace, at Lambeth, June 4, 1663, in the eighty-
first year of his age, and being carry d to Oxford, in great pomp, July 7,

was interr'd in the chapel of St. John's College, to which he was a great benefactor, though a greater to S. Paul's Church, his cathedral, and his palace at Lambeth, to which he gave 1000*l*. He was so innocent and good a man, that the enemies of the episcopal order could find nothing ill to say of him, and therefore of all the bishops was the least troubled by the contrary faction, which was a sign that he deserved the character commonly given him, viz. that he was a person of true primitive sanctity, great wisdom and foresight, signal piety and learning, admirable patience, and extensive charity, the most apostolical virtues. He hath left no writings but a Sermon on Luke xviii. 31; and as for his estate, which, after his benefactions, was considerable, he gave it to his brother's son, Sir William Juxon, Bart., who, or his posterity, now enjoy it. They have their seat at Compton aforesaid."

The parish churches, of which there are six, are universally small and mean; a free chapel has a turret in imitation of the lantern of Demosthenes, and an interior pewed with American black larch, and containing an organ; erected at an expense of 7000*l*. There are some schools and charities, and the celebrated *Mr. Hardham*, the tobacconist, left the interest of 22,282*l*. 15*s*. 9*d*., 3 per cents., to be applied in aid of the poors' rates.

The West Sussex, East Hants, and Chichester Infirmary, maintained by subscription, had in 1830 an income of 1322*l*. 3*s*. 10*d*.

The corporation consists of a High Steward (Duke of Richmond), Mayor, Recorder, Deputy Recorder, Bailiffs, &c. Here are a Literary Society, Assembly-rooms, Theatre, with splendid scenery, presented by the late Duke of Richmond, Banks, Custom-house, &c. The market days are on Wednesday and Saturday, with a cattle market every alternate Wednesday, and there are five annual fairs.

WEST DEAN,

near Chichester, is the handsome Gothic seat of Lord Selsey: this nobleman also, as well as the Duke of Richmond, is very popular in the vicinity. We have not the slightest knowledge of his lordship, but having accidentally heard a high character of his benevolence, are desirous to record it. We heard that, among other acts of charity, he orders, every Christmas, three fat oxen to be killed, which, with a great quantity of winter clothing, are distributed to the poor of his neighbourhood.

> " Swear, that Theron sure has sworn,
>   No one near him should be poor;
>   Swear, that none e'er had such a prosperous art,
>   Fortune's free gifts as freely to impart,
> With an unbounded hand and an ungrudging heart."
>
> *Pindar.*

₊ HALNAKER AND BOXGROVE.

Indisposition, as we before intimated, prevented our visiting these relics of antiquity, also, as we very much regretted, from taking a circuit of the *Park* at Goodwood; we must therefore derive a concise account from the united and carefully compared surveys of others.

Bosgrave and *Halnache* are mentioned separately in Doomsday Book, but each as a constituent of the honour of Arundel. In the reign of Henry I. it was given, with the valuation of twelve knights' fees, to Robert de Haia, who married a lady of the royal blood, and passed in dowry with his daughter to Roger de St. John, of Basing, one of the founders of the noble family of that name, who were intimately connected with the succession to the crown during two reigns (with the curious coincidence of having included a Countess of Richmond), and afterwards formed the source of several peerages. May it once more be pardoned to the humble author of this work, not from any unprofitable pride, but from reverential recollection of the departed, to state that he has the honour of ranking the highest branch of this family, St. John of Bletsoe, as intimately connected with his own immediate ancestors*.

In this family Halnaker and Boxgrove continued for about

---

* Vide *Chauncey's Hertfordshire*, quoted at page 245 of this volume, or any pedigree of the St. John's. Of the family mentioned in that page was also the last grand prior of St. John of Jerusalem in England, an earl before the reformation; who built St. John's Gate, Clerkenwell, which is still in existence. They were also barons of Culmore, Ireland, temp. James I.

250 years, it then passed by marriage into the family of Burgersh, and afterwards to that of Poynings, celebrated in Sussex; subsequently to Lord de la Warr, and afterwards to Sir John Morley, who obtained it in the reign of Elizabeth, in fee farm from the crown, which became possessed of it by an exchange with Lord de la Warr. We find in Dallaway that it passed, by marriage of Mary Morley, to James, Earl of Derby, and afterwards to Sir Thomas Dyke Ackland, of whom it was purchased, in 1765, by the Duke of Richmond, for the sum of 48,000*l*. By the following abridged extract which we had previously made from the Burrell MSS., we see that in the interim it had been in fee farm to an alien party, a variation in the chain of connexion which we have no means of explaining,

Boxgrove and Halnaker, with Eartham, West Dean, and some other places, were let in the 8th year of William and Mary to the Duke of Leeds (in consideration of his good services) for thirty-one years, from the death of Catherine, queen dowager, at the yearly rent of 3*l*. 18*s*. 4¼*d*.— *Burrell MSS.*

The Priory was founded by Robert de Haia, in the reign of Henry I., for three monks only of the Benedictine Order, as a cell to the abbey of *L'Essay*, or *de Exaquio*, in Normandy; but, by the donations of Roger St. John and his sons, William and Robert, was increased to fifteen. When other alien priories were confiscated, this obtained the indulgence of being made *Indigena* or *denizen;* and at the dissolution, when it was granted to Sir Thomas West, Lord de la Warr, its annual revenues amounted to 185*l*. 19*s*. 8*d*.

Halnaker was formerly a handsome quadrangular specimen of the Tudor era, with a turreted gateway : the great hall still remains, and has some curiously carved wainscot; over the pantries are two half figures, bearing cups, one of whom indicates, in a scroll, a courtly French invitation to the visitors, "𝕷𝖊𝖘 𝖇𝖎𝖊𝖓𝖘 𝖇𝖊𝖓𝖚𝖊"—"they are very welcome." Another salutes them with a very homely and ludicrously hearty English one— " 𝕮𝖔𝖒 𝖎𝖓 𝖆𝖓𝖉 𝖉𝖗𝖞𝖓𝖐 !"

Boxgrove Priory Church is supposed to have been built by

William and Robert St. John, in the reign of Henry the Second. It is on the same plan as New Shoreham, but on a smaller scale; a nave, three chancels, two transepts, and a central tower, and, like it, has remaining only the chancels, transepts, and tower, with a fragment of the nave; the ruins of the nave are, however, more distinct than at the former, whilst the south transept is nearly destroyed. The tower resembles that at Broadwater, and also at the cathedral at Winchester; the north-west area is the most interesting; the flying buttresses are plain and ineffective. The interior has some glazed tile pavements, a painted ceiling, stalls, and remains of chantries; but its principal ornaments are numerous and grand sepulchral erections. Although these do not include the sepulchre of Queen Adeliza, as tradition asserts, since she was certainly interred in the conventual church of Reading, founded by her first husband, Henry I., they comprise the tombs of her daughter Olivia, and her grand-daughter, of the same name, daughter of William Albini, Earl of Arundel, and amongst the other four, which are all under arcades, is that of Philippa, wife of Thomas Lord Poynings. The armorial blazonings have been principally destroyed, but one monument retains the escutcheon of St. John. But the grand decoration of this church is the sepulchral and chantry chapel of Thomas Lord de la Warr and Cantelupe, 1532, on the right of the altar, which is most profusely and elaborately carved, and ornamented with painting and gilding; a great proportion of its carvings is in a rich and solid style, indicating the junction of Italian ornaments, which has always an approach to the idea of Orientality. The dimensions are, length 14 feet, breadth 8 feet 9, and height 12 feet. Here is also the monument of Mary Morley, Countess of Derby, who died in 1752, having founded, in 1741, an hospital for 12 poor women of Boxgrove, East Lavant, and Tangmere, and a school for the education and clothing of 12 poor boys and 12 poor girls of the same parishes, a number which is likely to be augmented with the increase of the revenues. She is represented sitting under an oak, pointing to her hospital, and giving alms to travellers. The population of Boxgrove, in 1831, was 773.

The estate of Goodwood lies in the parishes of Boxgrove and West Hampnett; the latter has an ancient church with Norman remains, containing a curious monument. In a field near the spot was lately found an old massy and beautiful gold ring, bearing a signet, I.H.S., and round its edge an inscription—" Qui orat p' aliis p' se laborat"—" He who prays for others labours for himself :"—a sentiment as credible as generous on every and any principle of religion.

GOODWOOD.

Having before alluded to our disappointment in not obtaining any answers or acknowledgments from various noble families in or connected with Sussex, and our obligations for a different and courteous line of behaviour from the house of Richmond, we think it but right,

> " That thou mayst see the difference of ' his' spirit,"

simply to inform the reader of the circumstance, as, though it was not much more than we thought probable, it was yet extremely gratifying to find our expectations amply fulfilled. His Grace, in answer to our request of admission, &c. &c., informed us that the house and grounds at Goodwood might be seen at any time without an order from him—which all travellers will find to be the generous and pleasing fact—and that he only regretted that his official duties in London prevented his showing it to us himself. On visiting the house, we found in it a lady of high rank and an invalid, who voluntarily quitted, for some time, the apartments she was occupying, to allow us to take a leisurely survey of them. Had, therefore, this very pleasing mansion possessed far less considerable attractions than it did, could any reader have blamed us for feeling inclined to dilate on a spot where we experienced genuine courtesy and kindness?

GOODWOOD.

The Seat of His Grace the Duke of Richmond.

A circumstance we have twice alluded to impaired, in some degree, our means of observation; still we trust that, with tolerably copious notes, a not very bad memory, and the consultation of two or three previous works containing some particulars, we shall give a tolerable account, though not equal to what we might have wished, and that we shall avoid direct errors.

The handsome and imposing front* of Goodwood, which has a singular outline tending to the semi-octagonal or oriel form, has a centre 166 feet long, and two wings, each 106, forming a total of 378. The wings recede in an angle of 45 degrees, and at all the corners are very bold and handsome circular towers, which have the cornice extended round them, and an upper story with parapet and flat domed roof. In the centre is a light and very graceful portico and loggia, of six Doric columns below, and six Ionic above, with good entablatures and a surmounting balustrade; the wings are differently ornamented. Prior to the year 1800 the south wing was the principal front, as erected by Sir William Chambers. The extensive additions were under the direction of Wyatt: the material of the walls is squared flint, cut very small and of a light colour, which, contrasted with the Portland stone composing all the architectural ornaments, has a cheerful and pleasing effect, superior, perhaps, to the uniformity of a stone façade.

INTERIOR.

ENTRANCE HALL,

38 feet by 35 feet 3.

At its upper end is a fine colonnade of the Corinthian order; the pillars, six in number, are each composed of one piece of Guernsey granite, 12 feet 6 inches high, with a bronzed capital, two feet, and bases and plinths of white and black marble; each column was brought to Goodwood in a rough state, and cost

---

* See *Plate,* executed by a very superior artist, though not superior to the gentleman who engraved the others, with the only drawback of great haste being at the time absolutely necessary.

£100 in polishing. At the ends are imitative half columns of gray scagliola. The two chimney-pieces are Ionic, of the same granite, variegated with white and other marbles, with steel and gilt stoves; the ceiling, and all other accompaniments, tasteful. We may, at the outset, and once for all, remark, that of many noblemen's seats which we have seen in various parts of the kingdom, some of which boast of antiquity, others of magnificence, or classic and elaborate architectural decorations, we never witnessed one which universally, and in the keeping of its various parts, seemed to us so completely entitled to the distinguishing epithet of *Elegance* as the mansion of Goodwood.

The details of the extensive and valuable collection of paintings it contains are beyond our powers of accurate description, and we regret, on this and some other occasions, that we have neither the eye or skill of an artist. Still we have an ardent admiration of pictorial beauty, and perhaps this may suggest to us some ideas, in the few instances where we venture to speak, which may be in accordance with universal taste.

Beyond the colonnade of the hall is a marble table, supporting busts of the Emperor Trajan, the Apollo Belvidere, and other classical relics; some armour and trophies of Waterloo, where the present Duke, then Earl of March, distinguished himself as aide-de-camp to the Prince of Orange. And never, under any unexpected change of political feeling and position, let the solid benefit, as well as glory, of that day be forgotten. Elsewhere we meet with the portrait of the illustrious warrior Sobieski, who delivered Vienna from the Ottomans. Forget not those who saved Europe from the indomitable ambition and destructive rule of Napoleon!

> " —— Agincourt may be forgot,
> And Cressy be an unknown spot,
>   And Blenheim's name be new;
> But still in story and in song,
> For many an age remember'd long,
> Shall live the towers of Hougomont,
>   And field of Waterloo!"

Above is the large and splendid portrait, by Sir Thomas

Lawrence, of the present Duchess of Richmond, engraved in
" The Amulet " for 1833. On the table is a fine model of a
ship-of-war, executed for the Admiralty, but purchased by the
Duke for 300 guineas; and beneath, two of the curious bronze
Couvre-Feus, or fire-extinguishers, brought from Halnaker,
which were used in pursuance of the despotic orders of
William the Norman.

EGYPTIAN DINING ROOM,

45 feet 9 by 23 feet 11,

on the left of the hall at entering, was used in 1814, at the
entertainment of the Emperor of Russia and his sister the
Grand Duchess of Oldenburgh*. Its decorations were suggested by the designs of Denon from Tentyra or Dendera,
and will render it interesting from its connexion with the land
of the Pharaohs, Sesostris, and the Ptolemies. The walls are
of yellow scagliola, in imitation of Sienna, relieved by white
and gray marble : a magnificent white marble Egyptian chimney-piece with bronzes, and marble door cases, a fine pier-
glass, nine feet by five, and a variety of Egyptian symbols and
ornaments in bronze and granite. The floor is of oak curiously
parfitted or inlaid.

LIBRARY,

35 feet 7 by 25 feet 6,

is of all the apartments most highly characterized by the
quality of elegance which we have before alluded to. The
ceiling has in gilt borders fifty-nine medallions painted by
Riley, copies from the Baths of Titus, whilst beneath the surrounding book-cases are twenty-two panels containing Greek,
Etruscan, and Roman designs, after Sir William Hamilton,
from the ruins of Herculaneum. The chimney-piece has an
inlaid painting of the death of Cleopatra ; and over the doors
are Bacchus and Ariadne, also by Riley, and the latter a pro-

---

* This lady was very popular in England from her excellent disposition and
pleasing manners; the English ladies paid her the compliment of terming a
great coal-scuttle article the *Oldenburgh bonnet.*

file of the third Duchess of Richmond. The walls and draperies are of a pale pink, with gold French ornaments, and the cornice exquisitely pretty, of oak leaves, white and gold, tied with blue ribbons; between the windows are grand pierglasses: this room contains a variety of minute ornaments, some fine portraits and miniatures, and some cages with beautiful tropical birds. The number of books in it and the adjoining library is upwards of 10,000.

WAINSCOT LIBRARY,
23 feet 8 by 19 feet 10,

has a light and elegant hanging gallery copied from that at Christchurch, Oxford. It contains some valuable old books, MSS., and drawings; also ten or twelve portraits and views; two of the former, by *Romney* and *Angelica Kauffman*, are very highly esteemed.

BREAKFAST ROOM,
20 feet in diameter,

occupies the lower part of one of the circular towers, has light blue walls and drapery, and is a neat and cheerful apartment.

THE DUKE'S STUDY,

with walls, &c. of a scarlet colour, has a fine painting of the late Duke when a youth, by *Romney*; a variety of scarce engravings by *Vertue*; also all the accompaniments of a sportsman, and a pair of very rich and valuable Indian hookahs, a present to the late Duke.

DRAWING-ROOM,
35 feet by 23 feet 8,

is hung with beautiful Gobelin tapestry, presented to Charles Duke of Richmond, by Louis XV., whilst he was ambassador to his court. Besides exquisite representations of fruit and flower baskets, &c. it includes four large designs from Don Quíxote, surrounded by deep flowered borders. 1. The worthy knight at supper at the inn where he was dubbed with the chivalric order, and accompanied by the two ladies whose vocation and rank his simplicity so far mistook. 2. His nocturnal guard of the (castle) inn, when he was suspended from the window by the mischievous Maritornes. 3. Consulting the brazen head in Don Antonio de Moreno's house at Valencia. 4. The capture of Mambrino's helmet.—This room is furnished with very noble ornaments, three spacious pier-glasses, almost equalling the size of those in the Pavilion; a carpet of English manufacture, to match the tapestry, which cost 550 guineas; and an Indian screen 500. The ceiling is painted and gilt, with figures in the centre .in the French style; the curtains are of yellow silk tabinet; and the antique carved and gilt sofas, covered with splendid cut-velvet on satin, in superior preservation to that at Arundel.

The chimney-piece was executed by *Bacon,* for which he received 750 guineas, which was a liberal advance on the part of the late duke above the price required by the artist. It has figures of Venus and Adonis undrawing and sustaining a drapery; and we do not really see how they could be sur-passed by any of the works of Chantrey, Thorwaldsen, or Canova.

STATE BED-ROOM,

24 feet 5 by 23 feet 9,

is also hung with Gobelin tapestry, representing in a bril-liant and airy style the Four Seasons: the figure of Spring is very pretty, but that of Autumn the most beautiful. The furniture is of crimson damask and satin; the bed of the same, with a tester canopy of crimson velvet fringed with gold, bearing a splendid emblazoning of the royal arms and six others on the sides; the pillars are of highly carved mahogany, and the whole is raised on a dais covered with crimson silk and velvet. Over the chimney-piece is a portrait of Henrietta of

Orleans, a daughter of Charles I., a very pretty figure and innocent countenance—

> " A mouth with a smile,
> Devoid of all guile."

There are also views of Windsor and Dover Castles. The dressing-room adjoining is suitably corresponding in its style. Its ceiling is painted from the antique, and it has a rich cabinet of ebony, inlaid with ivory, silver, and precious stones.

THE SALOON,

About 70 *feet by* 19 *feet* 3 *inches,*

was the hall of the original mansion ; it is neat and pretty, but without much ornament ; at each end is a range of six fluted Ionic columns. The principal paintings are Views in London, by *Canaletti*, taken about the conclusion of the seventeenth century, displaying the gothic part of old White-hall, St. Paul's, and the river, with state barges ; also old Richmond House. There are also some family portraits, connected with the trophies of Waterloo ; some antique busts, and paintings of horses, &c. There is a neat organ in this apartment, and Divine service is performed in it by the Duke's chaplain every Sunday morning.

THE GRAND STAIRCASE,

whose area forms a handsome apartment, profusely decorated with valuable paintings, is of polished and carved wainscot, the walls of a gray colour, with crimson draperies. On a large marble stove are some fine antique heads and busts. The portraits are about twenty, some of grand size, and all in rich frames ; the noblest is that of Charles I. and his family, by *Vandyke*, 9 feet 9 by 8 feet 2, exclusive of the frame, sold at the parliamentary sale of that king's effects for 150*l.*, and purchased by the third Duke of Richmond, from the Orleans collection, in 1806, for 1100 guineas. There are several other portraits of Charles I. and II., and their families ; four of the " Beauties," including the Duchess of Portsmouth, Louisa de

Queroualle, and Nell Gwynn; Frances, the last, exquisitely beautiful and virtuous, Duchess of Richmond of the old Stuart race (*La Belle Stuart*), as Minerva or Britannia, with armour and plume *; and a very fine portrait, lately intro-·duced, of the *Marquis de Castelnau ;* two half-lengths of the Count and Countess de Queroualle, parents of the Duchess of Portsmouth. Most of these are by *Sir Peter Lely* and *Sir Godfrey Kneller*.

At the bottom of the staircase is a portrait of Cardinal Fleury. The benignant and noble countenance of this French minister, a very different character from Richelieu or Maza-rin, bears some resemblance to that of Fenelon, and is appro-priately set off by his scarlet cardinal's robe. This was the statesman who had so high an esteem for the simply and apo-stolically good Dr.Wilson, Bishop of Sodor and Man, that he solicited and obtained an order from his own government that no French cruizer, during the war, should ravage the Isle of Man, or molest the property of its inhabitants. It is really not easy to say on which of the two this confers more honour †.

THE STONE STAIRCASE

has the magnificent decoration of between fifty and sixty pictures, which our limits absolutely preclude us from speci-fying particularly. Amongst them are, the Judgment of Paris, by *Guido*—not a very happy design; a fine Charity, by *De la Hive ;* a great number of portraits, some of the finest of which are the Duke of Monmouth, by *Sir Peter Lely ;* Cromwell, said to be by Gen. Lambert, on the evening before the battle of Naseby ; Madame de Montespan, as a Magdalen,

* Vide *not* the Memoirs of the gross sensualist, Hamilton, for he pollutes every thing which he touches; but any life of this lady written with better feeling: Horace Walpole's, or Mrs. Jamieson's.

† It is truly said, that the character of a person is best ascertained by minor and every-day facts; and we like to meet with and relate such as the following: —Dr. Wilson had ordered a coat of an *insular* tailor, and told him he wished to have it fastened with a *hook and eye* (as it is termed) in front, in place of buttons. The tailor promptly replied, that if his Lordship set such a fashion, it would be followed in the island, and that both the button-makers and the tailors would be losers. " Would they ?" said the Bishop ; " then, *cover* it with buttons from top to bottom."

in blue drapery.   Amongst the paintings are some very good small Scripture pieces, and a copy of *Paul Veronese's* large painting of the Marriage in Cana; a Virgin and Child, by *Parmigiano;* a fine Head of St. Sebastian, by *Guido;* a large Vision of the Empress Helena; an Ecce Homo, by *Le Sieur;* Elijah and the Widow of Zareptha, by *Polemburg;* Alexander cutting the Gordian Knot, and drinking the Medicine of Philip, by *Solomene;* the Lady's last Stake, by *Hogarth,* in accordance with the style of Congreve, or Cibber's plays; Lions, by *Stubbs;* Sea Pieces, some by *Scott,* of Brighton; two Prize Landscapes, by the *Smiths,* of Chichester, very excellent, each 6 feet 3 by 4 feet 6.

Here are also a fine statue of a Bacchanal; a bronze Terminus, in a contemplative attitude; a Burmese Deity, lately brought over, its pedestal curiously inlaid with pieces of coloured glass, two immense horns of elks, &c. &c.

OLD DINING-ROOM,

25 feet square,

(N. B. The height of almost all the rooms is 18 feet.)

contains two very large paintings of the Festival of Bacchus and Ceres at Athens; a large portrait, unknown, in Turkish costume; Irish antiquities, battle-axes, daggers, swords, supposed to be of Carthaginian or Tyrian manufacture, from their similarity to the relics of *Hannibal's* army, found at *Cannæ,* bridle bits, and a ring of Divination (Druidical?), called, in Irish, *Ainie Druieach;* and lastly, an Egyptian mummy.

OLD BILLIARD ROOM

contains some good family portraits; and an adjoining room has a fine one by *Kneller,* representing the first Duke of Richmond being invested with the Order of the Garter at the early age of nine years. The Waiting Room also contains some good portraits.

There are two other large and handsome billiard rooms, which include collections of paintings of great extent, and the utmost beauty and value.

BILLIARD ROOM

has a noble collection of nearly fifty pictures; two fine portraits of Killigrew and Carew, by *Vandyke;* a very beautiful Marquess of Montrose, by the same; a very fine Flemish Noble, by *Rembrandt;* a Duke of Bavaria, by ditto; Francis Stuart, Duke of Richmond, a friend of Charles I., and who assisted at his interment, by *Lely;* some unknown and fancy portraits, one by *Guercino;* John Sobieski, the King of Poland, whose whole life is a romance teeming with interest, the deliverer of Vienna, with 74,000 men (not 7000, as absurdly stated in Mr. Jacques' book, and copied in another, entirely stolen from his and Mr. Dallaway, by a Mr. Dally), against 200,000 Turks and Tartars. We are possessed of an old, but excellently written, biography of this hero, which is well worthy of re-publication.

The paintings include specimens of some of the best masters. A large Sea piece, with port; a Landscape; and an Historical Figure, by *Salvator Rosa;* Saint Catherine, very beautiful, by *Guido;* St. Michael, by the same; the entombing of Christ, by one of the *Caracci;* splendid perspective of the interior of a cathedral, by *Peter Neefs;* Nativity, by *Bambocci;* Saint Agnes, by the younger *Teniers;* a Manège, by *Wouvermans;* a beautiful portrait, by *Rubens,* of Helena Forman, his second wife; " The Envied Bit," by *Piazetta,* a child refusing to part with an apple for which the longer offers a gold ring; a Frost piece, by *Ostade;* very rich Cattle piece, by *Berghem;* two Views in Venice, by *Canaletti,* &c. &c. &c.

THE NEW BILLIARD ROOM

has its walls, as well as the others, of crimson, forming a fine relief to the numerous paintings, with which they are richly ornamented. Their number here is about thirty, not quite equal, in this respect, to those of the last-mentioned, but including several of high stamp and merit, sufficient to delight and detain the lingering attention of the visitor. The principal is, the celebrated *Darnley Picture,* of eminent antiquarian and historical interest, 7 feet 4 by 4 feet 6, inscribed, " TRA-

GICA ET LAMENTABILIS INTERNECIO SERENISSIMI HENRICI SCOTORUM REGIS."

Two corresponding paintings on this subject were executed by the same artist for Matthew Earl of Lennox, the Earl's father. One passed, by marriage, into the Pomfret family, and, having been presented to Caroline, Queen of George II., is now in Kensington Palace. The other, which had been given by the Earl to his brother, the Lord of Aubigny, and, on the extinction of the ancient dukedom, had passed with that castle into the hands of the present family, was brought from thence by the third Duke of Richmond and deposited at Goodwood.

The artist's name is written in the Kensington picture alone ; his christian name is *Levinus,* but the other has been variously read *Vogelarius* and *Venetianus.*

To enter into that minute, historical, and descriptive account which this painting intrinsically merits, is beyond our opportunity in this volume. A copious and very ingenious MS. account, drawn up by *Vertue,* is in the library at Goodwood. In addition to the principal design, there are minor accompaniments, in the shape of medallions or *Rilievi,* depicting various circumstances of the tragical deed : and in one part of the painting is a compartment, 23 inches by 17, exhibiting a very elaborate and faithful representation of the battle of *Carberry Hill,* where Mary separated herself from Bothwell, and surrendered to the confederated Lords *.

The body of the painting represents a chapel, the tomb and effigies, with all the religious and heraldic accompaniments of the time, erected to the memory of the murdered Darnley, before which are kneeling the Earl and Countess of Lennox, the young king, afterwards James I., and his brother. Various Latin inscriptions are inserted, invoking Justice and Vengeance; and the picture itself was painted a very short time after the murder, as a memorial to the youthful prince, and an incitement to retribution, as if they had said

"EXORIARE ALIQUIS, NOSTRIS EX OSSIBUS, ULTOR !"

* The whole of the MS. descriptions are printed in a clever little account by a Mr. Jacques, 1822, now out of print.

The effect, though interesting, is melancholy, and it is obvious that it was executed under circumstances of recent passionate grief. Of the circumstances of the original transaction, it is unnecessary for us to speak, and it is a subject on which we should feel pain, as we are strongly inclined to compassionate the hapless Mary, the character of whose husband, Darnley, is here, doubtless with a pardonable parental feeling, egregiously flattered. We fear, however, she was not innocently ignorant of the act of Bothwell; and what can palliate premeditated murder, whether by treachery, or vested under the term of *a duel?* — bloodshed will have its vengeance, and the earth cannot hide its cry. Still, all that can be said should be said in behalf of this most unhappy queen—ill-used almost from her cradle to her grave—early thrown, with the dangerous attractions of exquisite beauty, and with the giddiness and inexperience of a child, amidst factions of savage and ambitious men, without a guide or friend; and whose crimes, if they were so, were repaid by years of persecution and bereavement, and closed, by an unjust death, from the cold and artful hypocrisy of a sister, which was nobly endured, and her chequered career terminated with virtuous and Christian hope. She has suffered enough :—*Requiescat in pace!*

Amongst other pictures in this room are a beautiful recumbent Venus, playing with a squirrel, 7 feet by 5 feet, an undoubted *Titian;* Mary de Medici, widow of Henry IV., and mother of the beautiful but wayward queen of Charles I. of England, a fine portrait; full-length portraits of George III. and his queen, by Allan Ramsey ; a fine head of Robert Bruce, the friend of Wallace and hero of Bannockburn ; Madam de Montespan ; several other fine portraits, including one of Lord Anson, whose ship, the Centurion, forms also one of three sea pieces by *Allin :* the figure-head, formerly in Goodwood Park, has been lately presented to his Majesty. Some fine small paintings, in the Flemish style ; four views on the Rhine ; portrait of *Sophonisba Anguisciola,* a female Italian artist, one of two which this young lady painted herself, and presented to Rubens and Vandyke, 3 feet 7 by 3 feet 6, playing on a spinnet, and attended by her nurse. This is, *par eminence*, the loveliest portrait in the house; the beautiful and clear-coloured face, with Madonna hair, relieved by a close-fitting dark dress, and very fine chiaro 'scuro, form one of the happiest effects that can easily be witnessed.

Either in this or an adjoining room, we forget which, is a small standard, captured at the field of Waterloo, inscribed on one side, " CHAMP DE MAI ;" and, on the other side, " DE-PARTEMENT DES BOUCHES DE RHONE."

THE BANQUETING ROOM, OR PICTURE GALLERY,

beyond the north angle of the front, is not yet completed, but its size, 86 feet by 24, will be commanding, and it will probably display to advantage some of the noble portraits and pictures with which some other parts of the house are now profusely crowded. Ascending one of the staircases, we enter the

CHINA ROOM,

33 *feet by* 13,

the furniture of which is of Indian bamboo, and the walls covered with Indian chintz. The collection of china is very valuable, especially those pieces of a green colour. This room communicates with the loggia of the portico. In one of the ante-rooms is a representation of the Duke of Argyle's seat, at Roseneath, near Aberfoyle, in " Rob Roy's country ;" and, in an adjoining passage, representations of the " Field of the Cloth of Gold."

SCARLET BED-ROOM,

32 *feet by* 18,

contains the tale of Antiochus and Stratonice, by Riley; and a copy of Corregio's Magdalen, at Dresden. In the adjoining dressing-room are portraits in crayons of several ladies and gentlemen, who formerly attended the " Goodwood Hunt."

The duke and duchess's bed-room and dressing-rooms are very neat and elegant. They contain a beautiful portrait of the present Duchess of Argyle, in crimson, by Mellichip;

three of the Duke of Richmond's children, very pleasing, by the same; a very pretty painting of the late Lady Holland, mother of C. J. Fox, by Wotton; some exquisite small miniatures, &c. &c. The duke's dressing-room commands a fine view over the park and the surrounding country, extending to the sea; and it contains several Indian curiosities, as enamelled handled swords, &c. In one of these apartments are fine portraits of the late Duke and Duchess of Gordon, father and mother of the Duchess-dowager of Richmond; all this suite of apartments is very elegant; and the circular form of those forming the area of the towers is no small addition to their general appearance.

Descending to the hall, we conclude our survey with the

NEW DRAWING-ROOM,

55 feet long by 24 wide, with an inner Drawing-room occupying the lower part of the tower, 20 feet in diameter.

The hangings of the walls, draperies, and furniture, are of yellow striped satin of English manufacture; the cornices deep and elaborate, yet light, and most richly gilded; and the ceilings tastefully clouded; the compartments also have elegant gilt borders. In these rooms are kept some memorials of Charles I., whom a Duke of Richmond attended in his last moments. The drawing-room has also, like most other rooms in the house, a variety of minor beautiful articles of furniture, which we have not attempted to particularize. Here, however, are some articles of great rarity, including a fine inlaid tortoise-shell cabinet, and some unique small paintings on silver. We must not omit the two exquisitely beautiful services of *Sèvre* china, to which our attention was particularly directed by the attentive and obliging Mrs. Hardwick, the concierge, whom we recollect with pleasure. They are amongst the most splendid of that costly manufactury; and the duke was offered, when ambassador at Paris, his choice of this present or one of silver plate, when he preferred the former. In fact, they are literally " worth their weight in *silver*." One set is blue, and the other green and gold, and they exhibit figures of animals and birds in the most excellent style of painting.

We cannot leave the house without again expressing our regret at not having in any degree done justice to the paintings. We have not even named many *chefs d'œuvre;* their number and variety perfectly astonished us, as they will do all who visit Goodwood.

. GROUNDS, PARK, &c. &c.

"Hic gelidi fontes hic mollia prata Lycori
  Hic nemus.——————
  —— Sperchius ubi et virginibus bacchata Lacœnis
  Täygeta.—O qui me gelidis in vallibus Hæmi
  Sistat, et ingenti ramorum protegat umbrâ!"

The relic of Cogidubnus we have before noticed, which is placed in a neat temple, dedicated to Minerva. Near the temple is a fine orangery, containing various aromatic plants, some of them brought from the island of Malta; and, in its immediate vicinity, a large Virginian tulip-tree, planted in 1739. There are several pretty memorials of favourite dogs, monkeys, and a tame lioness; all these, partly connected with the artificial ruin of an abbey, are within the circuit of the High Wood, a picturesquely disposed enclosure of forty acres. One of the epitaphs, on a spaniel of the Countess of Albemarle, in 1741, is sufficiently happy to merit recording.

" I once was ' *Miss,*' the mildest, best of misses,
  Nursed and brought up by Keppel's care and kisses—
  But now no more than Argus or Ulysses."

The stables near the mansion, erected by Sir William Chambers, form a very neat quadrangular structure, containing fifty-four stalls. On an eminence farther removed, and forming a handsome object, are the dog-kennels, erected by Wyatt, at an expense of 6000*l.* They are 148 feet long, by 30 broad, and are considered to be unsurpassed in all their arrangements. A hollow, formerly a chalk-pit, has been tastefully fitted up as a pheasantry, containing a number of gold and silver pheasants, which are remarkably tame.

The lion figure-head of Lord Anson's ship, the Centurion, now presented to His Majesty, who had taken a great fancy to it, formerly stood at one of the entrances to the park, and bears this inscription :—

> " Stop traveller awhile, and view
> One who has travell'd more than you.
> Quite round the globe, through each degree,
> Anson and I have plough'd the sea ;
> Torrid and frigid zones have past,
> And safe arrived ashore at last,
> In ease, with dignity appear—
> *He* in the House of Lords, *I* here."

The dairy, which we much regret not having seen, is a Gothic octagon, with carved and emblazoned buttresses, a decorated wooden ceiling, and windows of ancient stained glass. The park is nearly six miles in circuit, and contains $1214\frac{1}{2}$ acres; it includes several highly interesting spots.

Cairney Seat is an originally splendid summer erection, on a commanding eminence, and has near it a curious grotto of shell-work, executed by the second Duchess of Richmond and her daughters. In the park are upwards of a *thousand cedars of Lebanon*, planted by the Duke of Richmond, in 1761, being then of four years' growth: here are also two Spanish cork-trees in a very flourishing condition, a decided proof of the mildness of the climate in this part of the southern coast.

St. Roach's Hill, a little to the west of the park, has the remains of an encampment, supposed to have been formed by the Danes, in the year 992. The altitude of the hill above the level of the sea, as taken by trigonometrical survey for the late duke, when Master-General of the Ordnance, is 702 feet.

The celebrated Goodwood races are also held on a level in this direction; these are well-known by all to whom they are particularly objects of attraction, or they may be referred to the " Sporting Magazine," which, though totally out of our line, is, we believe, a very creditable work, and generally considered high authority in such matters.

RICHMOND FAMILY.

" —— repetens exempla priorum."

The ancient dukedom of Richmond was in the family of
Stuart, Earl of Darnley, and became extinct with the death of
Charles, sixth Duke of Richmond and Lennox, and Lord of
Aubigny, in France, in 1672. The present family are, therefore, in no respect connected with the former, except by
adoption and royal grant of the title. Consequently " La Belle
Stuart " was not an ancestress, a mistake which we were about to
make, and have known occur to several others. As there are,
however, two fine portraits of her at Goodwood, we cannot
pass over her name without a brief allusion. She was one of
those prodigies of beauty whose influence on the world has
been nearly magical, a second Cleopatra, Diana, or Ninon,
but with a more unspotted character. In her early youth,
before her charms had reached their maturity, they excited
such expectation in France, that Louis XIV. strongly desired
to retain her as an ornament to his court. It cannot be dis-
sembled that her virtue was aspersed in the dissolute court of
Charles II., but Mrs. Jamieson, who is by no means prejudiced
in her favour, concludes that the testimonies on the side of her
innocence predominated. Her intellect was, unlike that of
Cleopatra, inferior to her beauty ; but the trait of character
attributed to her by Horace Walpole argues a good heart,
though there are not wanting those who will ridicule it, viz. her
leaving her favourite dogs, &c. &c., with pensions for their
lives, to several of her female friends, with the additional
motive of affording, under this delicate veil, a degree of
pecuniary assistance. Her favour also with the queen, and
her declaration that she had rather marry a country gentleman
of small fortune, than live in a court where her virtue was
suspected, are honourable marks of disposition. She married
the last Stuart Duke of Richmond, hoping to reclaim him,
who had been not uncontaminated by the court. She did
reclaim him, and ended her life happily, and we are glad to
record it ; for the calumny of the brutal is always neither any

proof of guilt, nor should it be succumbed to: let but those aggrieved patiently and firmly take for their motto—" Post tenebras spero lucem," and they may, by the help of God, overcome the malice and cruelty of their enemies.

Charles, the first Duke of Richmond of that highly honourable family of which we are now the pleased, though very concise and humble chroniclers, was the son of Charles II. by Louise Renée de Penencourt de Queroualle, who was of a noble baronial family, in the province of Britanny, and maid of honour to Madame the king's sister. The reader will please to observe we are not extenuating any illegality, but simply stating a fact. She was afterwards created Duchess of Portsmouth, as is known to all who have read the History of England. Charles, her son, to whom the king gave the name of Lennox, was born in 1672, and was created Duke of Richmond in 1675, having been previously Earl of March, a title derived from the Marches in Wales, and Baron Settrington, Co. York. He also at the same time received a grant of the estate of Lennox, in Scotland, and was created Duke of Lennox, Earl of Darnley, and Baron Methuen of Torbolton.

By the influence of Charles II. with the French king, the territory of *Aubigny*, which had lapsed to the crown, was granted to the Duchess of Portsmouth, and erected into a duchy, with remainder to her son; in which grant respect is said to have been had to the faithful services always rendered by the ancestors of Louise de Queroualle to the kings of France. Aubigny, in Latin *Albiniacum*, is situated in the province of Berri, on the river Nere; the territory consisted of two considerable castles, two parishes and fiefs, with all seignorial rights, and the privilege of resorting to the court and parliament of Paris. The territory was confiscated in the first French revolution, and, we suppose, has not been restored, but the title is still borne.

The duke was made Knight of the Garter in 1681, and, from the accidental pleasing appearance of his wearing the blue ribbon, &c. over the left shoulder, instead of round the

neck, the style was altered from that period. He was Master
of the Horse on the removal of the Duke of Monmouth; and,
after the revolution, Aide-de-Camp to King William, in Flanders, and one of the Lords of the Bedchamber to George I.
He purchased Goodwood of the family of Compton, of East
Havant, about the year 1719, and, dying there in 1723, was
interred in Henry VIIth's Chapel, but his body was afterwards
removed to Chichester cathedral. The duke married, in 1693,
Anne, daughter of Francis Lord Brudenell, son of the Earl
of Cardigan, and widow of Henry, son of John Lord Bellasyse, and left one son and two daughters. The portrait of the
duke at Goodwood has a remarkably sweet and noble expression.

It is, much as we regret it, beyond our power here to do
more than very briefly enumerate the line of heirs to the succession. Charles, the second duke, was one of the first knights
of the revived Order of the Bath, Knight of the Bedchamber,
and Aide-de-Camp to both George I. and II., and High Constable of England at the coronation of the latter; also, at
different periods, appointed a Privy-Counsellor, one of the
Lords Justices, and placed in a variety of military posts; attended George II. at the battle of Dettingen, and the Duke of
Cumberland on the expedition against the Pretender. He was
also High Steward of Chichester, and, at the Duke of Newcastle's installation at Cambridge, was created Doctor of Laws
(according to Dallaway, which we presume is a just correction
of Collins' account, who states it as Doctor of *Physic*). He
was the first Duke of Aubigny, the Duchess of Portsmouth
dying in 1734, and visited that territory with his duchess in
1749. She was Sarah, daughter of William Earl Cadogan,
and one of the ladies of the bedchamber to Queen Caroline,
whom he married in 1719, and had twelve children, six of
whom alone survived him. The duke died in 1750, generally
lamented and esteemed. It appears to us, that the circumstance of a grandson of Charles II. being so highly esteemed
and trusted by kings of the line of Hanover, is one of the
strongest proofs of merit that could be advanced.

His eighth child, Lord George Henry Lennox, born 1737, was also a distinguished military character, and Secretary of Embassy and Chargé des Affaires at Paris to his brother, the succeeding duke. He married Lady Louisa, daughter of William Ker, Earl of Ancram (both names are immortalized by Scott), and son of the Marquess of Lothian; and his son was the late Duke of Richmond.

The ardent and romantic attachment of the excellent and virtuous George III. (we say this advisedly, in defiance of his abusers in the present day) for *Lady Sarah Lennox*, whom, but for the severe, though it may be politic, restrictions laid on English princes, he would have addressed and raised to his throne, is so well known, that it is needless for us to dwell on it, though the subject is highly interesting.

Charles, the third Duke of Richmond, born in 1735, was also of high military rank, having been elevated to that of Field Marshal, and Master-General of the Ordnance from 1782 to 1795, and during that time, receiving the unequivocal honour of being removed and restored within six months. In this post he rendered an essential service to the southern coast of England, which we alluded to at page 214, but, by mistake, attributed it to his successor. He was also K. G., Lord Lieutenant of Sussex, carried the sceptre with the dove at the coronation of George III., and was, in 1765, Ambassador to Paris. But his still higher merits were, his patronage of the arts, and of various charitable institutions. He opened, at his house at Whitehall, a kind of minor Royal Academy, placing in it fine original casts of all the best models in Italy, most of which he had collected himself at the various spots, allowing all artists above the age of twelve years free access to them, and giving annually two medals to those who executed the most perfect models. This, with other acts of munificence, is said to have been, at that time, of the very highest service to the arts. He married, 1757, Mary, daughter of Charles Bruce, Earl of Aylesbury, by his lady, daughter of the Duke of Argyle, but, dying in 1806, left no children, and was succeeded by his nephew, Charles, fourth Duke of Richmond, born 1764, a Lieutenant-General and Colonel of the 35th regiment of foot, who married Charlotte, daughter of Alexander Duke of Gordon.

The family of Gordon was of high rank in France in the reigns of Pepin and Charlemagne, and their successors, having filled some of the greatest offices, amongst which was that of High Constable. They removed to Scotland in the eleventh century, and assisted in the conquest of *Macbeth*. In that kingdom they have flourished in much esteem and honour to the present day; connected by marriage with the royal families of Scotland and France, and the *Medici*, Grand Dukes of Tuscany; always in the most cordial esteem with their sovereigns, and eminent for disinterested and devoted loyalty; which was especially proved in the reigns of the unfortunate Mary, James I, Charles I., and James II. Like Thirlestane, when their aid was needed, they were

" Ready, aye ready, for the fight."

The gallant defence of the Castle of Edinburgh for James II. (saving any error of judgment) by a Duke of Gordon, with a very small garrison, which he paid himself, is one of the bravest exploits in history. And their brave and generous qualities have continued to the present day: the present Duke of Gordon is one of the most deservedly popular noblemen in the united kingdom. We happen to know, from private authority, that this sketch is so far from being flattering, that a great deal more might have been said of this family within the bounds of the strictest justice.

The late Duke of Richmond was Lord Lieutenant of Ireland from 1807 to 1813, and in that always difficult situation (though there was then no Agitator) was, we believe, universally popular. He was also, if we mistake not, at one period Governor-General of Canada. His Grace died in 1819, and was succeeded by his son Charles, the present Duke, born 1791, who married, in 1817, Lady Caroline Paget, born 1796, the eldest and beautiful daughter of the Marquess of Anglesey, by Lady Charlotte Villiers, daughter of Earl Jersey, now

Duchess of Argyle (vide *Lodge*). The duke is a Knight of
the Garter, Privy Councillor, Post-Master-General, Vice-Admiral, or, more properly speaking, Admiral of Sussex, an office
lately revived, Colonel of Royal Sussex Militia, Militia Aide-
de-Camp to the King, High Steward of Chichester, Commissioner for Colonial Emigration, Chairman of the Committee on West Indian Slavery, &c. &c. &c. To speak of
the living is generally fulsome: the duke is well known as a
public character; but it gives us pleasure to be able to speak
with unmixed satisfaction of his conduct in these times of political excitation, although we have some lingering predilection
for principles now

" A little out of fashion ;"

and are the less inclined to abandon them because they per-
tain to the weaker party. If we could not have spoken
sincerely, we really trust that the reader who has done us the
honour of following us thus far, will believe that we should
have been silent; or we have wandered some hundreds of
leagues from our reckoning. We feel firmly persuaded, that
whilst his Grace has, and would, cheerfully comply with such
alterations as a wonderful change of time and circumstances
has rendered most desirable for the general prosperity, he
would agree only in those measures which should repair, not
subvert, the integral bulwarks of a constitution tried by ages
and cemented with blood; and that if further rash measures
were projected to destroy the justly arranged equipoise which
" bears up the pillars of it," he would be one of the first to
stand in the breach, and save the assailants from the consequences of their own imprudence. We hope that his Grace,
and other well-wishers to their country of all parties, may live
to see (though we fear at this moment we may not, and that
this may be

Extremum concede laborem)

the noon of that prosperity, alone to be founded on moderation
and conciliation, the first faint dawn of which now glimmers
on the horizon, after the dangers and perplexities of a night of
doubt, anxiety, and trouble !

PRESENT DUKE OF RICHMOND'S CHILDREN.

" Charles, Earl of March and Darnley .   *born* 1818
Lady Caroline Amelia	.	.	.	. 1819
Lord Fitzroy George Charles	.	.	.	1820
Lord Henry Charles George	.	.	.	1821
Lord Alexander Francis Charles		.	.	1825
Lady Augusta Catherine	.	.	.	. 1827
Lady Lucy Frances	.	.	.	. 1828
Lord George	.	.	.	. 1829
Lady Amelia Frederica	.	.	.	. 1830

BROTHERS AND SISTERS.

Lady Mary, born 1790; married, 1820, Lieut.-Col. Charles Augustus Grafton, nephew to the present Duke of Grafton.

Lady Sarah, born 1792; married, 1815, Lieut.-Gen. Sir Peregrine Maitland, K.C.B., &c. &c. &c.

Lieut.-Col. Lord John George, M.P., born 1793; married, 1818, Louisa Frederica, daughter of the Hon. John Rodney.

Lady Georgiana, born 1795; married, 1824, the brother and heir of the present Lord De Roos.

Lady Jane, born 1798; married, 1822, Lawrence Peel, Esq.

Lord William Pitt, born 1799.

Lord Sussex, born 1802; married, 1828, Hon. Mary Margaret, daughter of Lord Cloncurry.

Lady Louisa Madelina, born 1803; married, 1825, W. F. F. Tighe, Esq.

Lady Charlotte, born 1804; married, 1823, Capt. M. F. Fitzharding Berkeley, R.N., brother to both the present claimants of the earldom.—See *Lodge*.

Lord Arthur, M.P., born 1806.

Lady Sophia Georgiana, born 1809.

AUNTS.

Lady Mary Louisa, born 1760.

Lady Georgiana, born 1765, Countess Berkeley."—*Lodge*.

" *Creations.*—Duke of Richmond in Yorkshire, Earl of March (a title derived from the Marches in South Wales) and Baron of Settrington, in the county of York, on August 9th, 1675, 27 Car. II.; Duke of Lennox, Earl of Darnley, and Baron Methuen of Torbolton, in Scotland, on September 9th, 1675; and Duke of Aubigny in France, in January, 1683-4, 41 Louis XIV.

" *Arms.*—Quarterly, first and fourth, the arms of France and England, quarterly; the second, Scotland; and the third, Ireland (being the arms of Charles II.), the whole within a border compone, *Argent* and *gules*, the first charged with verdoy of roses of the second, and seeded proper: over all, in an escutcheon, the arms of Aubigny, viz. *gules*, three oval buckles, *Or*.

" *Crest.*—On a chapeau, *gules*, turned up *ermine*, a lion statant, guardant, *Or*, crowned with a ducal coronet, *gules*, and gorged with a collar gobone, charged as the border in the coat.

" *Supporters.*—On the dexter side, an unicorn, *Argent*, armed, crested, and hoofed, *Or*. On the sinister, an antelope, *argent*, armed, maned, and hoofed, as the dexter. Each supporter gorged, as the crest.

" *Motto.*—EN LA ROSE JE FLEURIE."—*Collins*.

TUNBRIDGE-WELLS.

"—— aquæ non ditior urna."

WE had originally undertaken to give an account of this pleasing and popular watering place, which, though not on the Coast of Sussex, forms an auxiliary to it, and is very frequently visited from Brighton and Hastings; and we had, as in the case of Worthing, a pleasing former association with it, inclining us not to omit it. Our notice must, however, now, from the great length to which we have already run, be of the briefest nature. We are now out at sea, to an extent which we had little calculated; we have, by the printer's log-book, wandered eighty miles (pages) beyond the designed end of our course. Whether we are approaching the " Cape of *Good Hope*," or may flatter ourselves, like Ariosto, with hearing, at a distance, the sound of bells and the voices of gratulation, Heaven only knows, and time alone will show. Many and various are the events which time brings in its train;—it is sometimes the repairer of disappointments, and the redresser of wrongs.

———

It is scarcely necessary to inform our readers that a clever little work, on Tunbridge-Wells and its vicinity, has been lately published by Mr. Britton, one of the patriarchs of English antiquarian and topographical lore. There is, therefore, the less need for us to enlarge on its origin, or state the accidental discovery of its mineral virtues by a nobleman in the reign of James I., its subsequent occupation by the Court when London was devastated by the plague, as may be seen in detail in the dissolute Memoirs of Grammont; the queen, however, and others of merit and interest, being present; or the gradually increasing influence which it has attained until the present day, when amongst its most beneficial patrons it ranks the Duchess of Kent and the Princess Victoria. On the subject of the celebrated Beau Nash, alone, by whom its fashionable settlement was brought to its perfection, do we digress a little, for a reason which we shall speedily communicate.

Nash's history is more immediately involved in the annals of Bath than those of Tunbridge-Wells; still he was for a series of years the *Arbiter Elegantiarum* at the latter, the despotic though useful lord of its ascendancy possessing an absolute rule, founded on opinion and policy alone, to which the highest nobility and even princes bowed without demur or murmur. His external demonstrations of consequence at Tunbridge-Wells are said to have been very splendid, as he always travelled thither from Bath in a chariot and six grays, attended by out-riders with French-horns, &c. &c. We are of course far from offering this curious individual as a correct character; still he had some redeeming qualities of ardent good feeling and humanity, which are pleasing to meet with and relate. Some also of his good institutions did not die with him; the most important of them was the Free Hospital at Bath, which is still flourishing; and at his funeral he was mourned with unaffected tears by the poor to whom he had been ever an active benefactor, and it is said that in cases when he was unable to relieve distress it was accustomed to melt him to tears!

The following anecdotes are contained in a biography of Nash in our possession, written a few months after his death; we have never seen them quoted in any work (though we cannot answer for that not having been done), and are therefore induced to give them insertion.

" When he was to give in his accompts to the masters of the Temple, among other articles, he charged, for " making one man happy," 10*l*. Being questioned about the meaning of so strange an item, he frankly declared, that, happening to over-hear a poor man declare to his wife and a large family of children, that 10*l*. would make him happy, he could not avoid trying the experiment. He added, that, if they did not choose to acquiesce in his charge, he was ready to refund the money. The Masters, struck with such an uncommon instance of good-nature, publicly thanked him for his benevolence, and desired that the sum might be doubled, as a proof of their satisfaction."

" When the late Earl of T——d was a youth, he was passionately fond of play, and never better pleased than with having Mr. Nash for his antagonist. Nash saw with concern his Lordship's foible, and undertook to cure him, though by a very disagreeable remedy. Conscious of his own superior skill, he determined to engage him in single play for a very considerable sum. His Lordship, in proportion as he lost his game, lost his temper too; and, as he approached the gulf, seemed still more eager for ruin. He lost his estate; some writings were put into the winner's possession; his very equipage was deposited as a last stake, and he lost that also. But, when our generous gamester had found his Lordship sufficiently punished for his temerity, he returned all; only stipulating, that he should be paid five thousand pounds, whenever he should think proper to make the demand. However, he never made any such demand during his Lordship's life; but some time after his decease, Mr. Nash's affairs being in the wane, he demanded the money of his lordship's heirs, who honourably paid it without any hesitation.

" A gentleman of broken fortune, one day standing behind his chair, as he was playing a game of picquet for two hundred pounds, and observing with what indifference he won the money, could not avoid whispering these words to another who stood by : ' Heavens! how happy would all that money make me!' Nash, overhearing him, clapped the money into his hand, and cried, Go and be happy!

" Nash used sometimes to visit the great Dr. Clarke. The Doctor was one day conversing with Locke, and two or three more of his learned and intimate companions, with that freedom, gaiety, and cheerfulness, which is ever the result of innocence. In the midst of their mirth and laughter, the Doctor, looking from the window, saw Nash's chariot stop at the door.— ' Boys, boys,' cried the philosopher, to his friends, ' let us now be wise, for here is a fool coming.' "

" Dr Cheney once, when Nash was ill, drew up a prescription for him, which was sent in accordingly. The next day the Doctor, coming to see his patient, found him up and well; upon which he asked, if he had followed his prescription? ' Followed your prescription!' cried Nash; ' No—Egad, if I had, I should have broke my neck; for I flung it out of the two-pair of stairs window.' "

With these brighter traits there were undoubtedly, in this whimsical character, much folly and affectation, not unmixed with vice. In his old age, his wit too much degenerated into peevishness and satire, with this alleviating excuse, that he found himself in a reduced and saddened condition, having outlived many of his patrons, and having been treated with that ingratitude so sadly common in the world, thrown by as a neglected toy by those to whose pleasure he was less able to contribute. When he was, however, on the eve of want and despair, the Corporation of Bath stepped forward, and, as some token of gratitude for his great services to that city, allowed him an annuity of ten guineas a month, a sum which, though more valuable then than that at the present day, was, to a man of his erratic and expensive habits, a bare subsistence. He died in the year 1762, and had a grand public funeral.

Tunbridge-Wells was also a favourite resort of Richardson, and was visited by Dr. Johnson and other eminent wits of the last century. One of its most distinguished settled inhabitants was Cumberland,

"the Terence of England—the mender of hearts,"

who laboured sedulously to infuse into his dramatic compositions as strong a bias to the interests of virtue and innocence as the nature of the subject would admit, in which praiseworthy course he doubtless acted a noble part in his generation. The plays he published whilst living are well known; but it is again to be lamented that even he was not in easy circumstances in the latter part of his life. His posthumous plays, published by his daughter, are not so well known, though they fully deserve it. Amongst the best, are—The False Demetrius—The Walloons—Alcanor—and Tiberius in Capreæ: the latter abounds with eloquent passages. His excellent and popular poem of Calvary, or the death of Christ, is an evidence of his sincere and genial piety. He was the intimate friend of Dr. Vincent, Dean of Westminster. Many farther particulars will be found in Mr. Britton's work.

———

Tunbridge-Wells, surrounded by beautiful and noble scenery, lies five miles from Tunbridge town, partly in that parish, and in those of Speldhurst and Frant, about 34 miles distant from London. Its site, on three hills, is almost as well known as that of Rome. One of these, however, Mount Pleasant, is inconsiderable. Mount Sion contains the principal part of the old buildings, exclusive of the Wells and Parade, whilst Mount Ephraim is ascended by one principal walk, with a variety of diverging ones up the romantic and beautiful common, covered in parts with rich furze, in others with trees, and diversified by rocks. This situation commands the most bracing air in the neighbourhood, and the view from it is beautiful. We could here favour the reader with a dozen pages of description of the general beauties and local details of Tunbridge Wells from recollection, but that prudence, for the reasons we have before stated,

Aurem
Vellit et admonuit,—

only, we would not have been supposed that we thought less highly of it than any other place we have described in this volume.

The spacious improvements* at Tunbridge Wells, in the neighbourhood of the London road, called Calverley Park Crescent, Parade, &c. we have not seen, and must refer the reader to the description of Mr. Britton.

The virtues and qualities of the waters must be sought out in medical works of authority. They are well known to contain a very powerful modicum of steel. In this respect the place resembles ancient Elba, though its gifts are suited to a more pacific and useful purpose.

" Inexhaustis chalybum generosa metallis."

The Parade, formerly called, from its pavement, the Pantiles, is a very pleasant walk, divided into an upper and lower one, the former protected by a colonnade. A very good and scientific band of music, supported by subscription, plays here three times a day. The sheltered situation under Mount Ephraim, and the fine row of elms, add much to its pleasurable appearance. Here is the handsome Assembly-room, the highly respectable Libraries, and the Theatre†, one of the best conducted out of London.

The Baths of all kinds are inclosed in a handsome building, at the end of the Parade.

---

* We avail ourselves of this word to perform an act of strict justice with reference to our statement at page 140, line 17, in the Description of Brighton. We have since been made acquainted that the dissensions there alluded to have been remedied, and that the sea wall of the Marine Parade is going on with spirit.

† When we spoke so strongly against Mr. Michael Kelly, in our account of Brighton, we did not know that Miss Kelly was his niece: that *alone* could make us regret having said it; and if there were any chance of her seeing it, we would apologise to *her* upright spirit for any thing which might cause it annoyance.

The Chapel of Ease is a fine venerable building, erected in 1684 and 1696, at an expense of 2300*l.* It is divided transversely from the entrance into two aisles, and has a massively rich ceiling, and a good though small organ. The new Church, erected by Mr. Decimus Burton, but, we believe, with much restriction as to the cost, is a heavy structure. There is a School and other charitable institutions.

The neighbourhood of Tunbridge-Wells abounds with interesting objects, including Brambletye House, the seat of one of Horace Smith's novels. Why is his pen now idle? Bayham Abbey is an extensive and interesting ruin; the High Rocks have in themselves and vicinity some of the milder features of North Wales. Rusthall has the remains of beautiful gardens in a picturesque dell, and a fine bath of clear water. Tunbridge town has the tower of a Norman castle and an old church, lately enlarged: of this place was the celebrated scholar and moral essayist, Dr. Knox: Speldhurst church has these curious epitaphs on Sir Walter and Lady Ann Waller, about 1600; the former in the quaint and piquant style of the times, the latter both acrostic and retrospectively anagrammatical:—

> I'd praise thy valour, but Mars 'gins to frown;
> He fears when Sol's aloft that Mars must down.
> I'd praise thy form, but Venus cries amain,
> Sir Walter Waller will my Adon stain.
> I'd praise thy learning, but Minerva cries,—
> Then Athens' fame must creep when Waller flies.
> Assist us, England, in our doleful song,
> When such limbs fade thy flourish lasts not long;
> Earth has his earth, which doth his corpse inroll;
> Angels sing requiems to his blessed soul.

> A ll worthy eyes read this, that hither come,
> N ever decaying virtue fills this tomb;
> N ever enough to be lamented here,
> A s long as womankind are worth a tear.

> W ithin this weeping stone lies lady Waller,
> A ll that will know her more, a saint will call her;
> L ife so directed her whilst living here,
> L evell'd so straight to God, in love and fear;
> E ven so good, that turn her name and see,
> R eady to crown that life a LAWREL tree.

Hever Castle was the residence of Sir Thomas, father of Anne Bullen; great part of it still remains in good preservation, solid but heavy, and is used as a dwelling-house. Of many other beautiful rides round Tunbridge-Wells, we have not now the opportunity to speak. We terminate our account with *Penshurst,* the ancient seat of the Sidneys, endeared by the recollections of Sir Philip Sydney and of Waller, still occupied by one of the original family, who has married a daughter of the King, and His Majesty has assisted in the reparation of the ancient seat, which contains a fine hall, beautiful tapestry, and much furniture, given by Queen Elizabeth. The appearance of the *Place,* decent and venerable church with pinnacled tower, and small town embosomed in trees, across the river Medway, is, especially when all the associations are called to mind, one of the most interesting that can be met with.—We close our devious course inland, but wish to return in recollection, and pay a final tribute of attachment to the unequalled OCEAN, with which we first began:—

" PRIMA DICTE MIHI, SUMMA DICENDE, CAMŒNA."

FINIS.